BECOMING LESBIAN

BECOMING LESBIAN

A Queer History of Modern France

TAMARA CHAPLIN

The University of Chicago Press CHICAGO AND LONDON

The University of Chicago Press, Chicago 60637
The University of Chicago Press, Ltd., London

Published 2024
Printed in the United States of America

33 32 31 30 29 28 27 26 25 24 1 2 3 4 5

ISBN-13: 978-0-226-71098-3 (cloth)
ISBN-13: 978-0-226-83655-3 (paper)
ISBN-13: 978-0-226-83654-6 (e-book)
DOI: https://doi.org/10.7208/chicago/9780226836546.001.0001

Library of Congress Cataloging-in-Publication Data

Names: Chaplin, Tamara, author.
Title: Becoming lesbian : a queer history of modern France / Tamara Chaplin.
Description: Chicago : The University of Chicago Press, 2024. | Includes bibliographical references and index.
Identifiers: LCCN 2024017624 | ISBN 9780226710983 (cloth) | ISBN 9780226836553 (paperback) | ISBN 9780226836546 (ebook)
Subjects: LCSH: Lesbianism—France—History—20th century. | Lesbians—France. | Lesbian feminism—France—History—20th century. | Lesbians in popular culture—France—History—20th century.
Classification: LCC HQ75.6.F82 P37 2024 | DDC 306.76/6309440904—dc23/eng/20240430
LC record available at https://lccn.loc.gov/2024017624

♾ This paper meets the requirements of ANSI/NISO Z39.48-1992 (Permanence of Paper).

To those who love and have loved me regardless of the gender of the object of my affections (including my mother, l. tarin chaplin, who died before this work was conceived), may you herald the world to come—a world where, as my students like to say, "love is love" and we celebrate it whenever we meet it, regardless of the form it takes.

This book is for each of you.

CONTENTS

INTRODUCTION

The Most Famous Lesbian in the World

> Between 1948 and 1961 there was in the Champs Élysées neighborhood of Paris on the rue de Ponthieu, behind the Lido, a famous and fascinating cabaret called The Carroll's Club. It was run by a lady once described as the most famous lesbian in the world, named Frede.
>
> MARILYN "MIKI" LEFF
> Hostess at Le Carroll's and Frede's life partner
> Letter to Jason Epstein, editorial director, Random House, December 13, 1996

In 1949, twenty-four-year-old Miki Leff, a Jewish "gay girl" from the Bronx who had "'come out' to the World (family included) in 1944," was so taken by articles she'd read about "the most famous lesbian in the world" that she flew (with her girlfriend Jacquie Howe in tow) to France in order to meet her.[1] After arriving in Paris the young women went straight to Le Carroll's Club only to discover that its "famous lesbian" manager, Frede, had already left for the South of France for the summer season. Undaunted, the Americans promptly followed. They found their way to Le Carroll's summer annex (known as Le Carroll's La Garoupe or Carroll's Beach) in a casino in Juan-les-Pins on the Côte d'Azur. Once there, they quickly befriended Frede's current flame, a nineteen-year-old Russian Jewish socialite known as Princess Zina Rachewski. "We spent an entire week with Zina and Frede," Miki later recalled. "They fought constantly, Frede elegant and smartly dressed, Zina a statuesque, wild, platinum goddess." Although Frede "didn't

FIGURE 0.1: Album cover: *Frede présente une soirée au Carroll's* [Frede presents an evening at Carroll's], Ducretet-Thomson, 1956. Frede is on the upper right; Miki, as the "femcee," is on the lower left. Photographer unknown. Marilyn "Miki" Leff Papers, courtesy of Roy Winnick.

or wouldn't speak English at the time" (and Miki spoke no French), Miki evidently made a lasting impression. In 1954, when Frede's affair with Zina was long over, Miki received a letter from France. It contained an all-expenses-paid invitation to move to Paris and a contract to work as hostess and interpreter at Le Carroll's.[2] Miki accepted. "Three months later," she reports, "having graduated to Mistress of Ceremonies and stage diplomat, I was in love with Paris, the Carroll's, and Frede." Frede was forty; Miki twenty-nine. Soon thereafter Frede purchased her first apartment, just outside the city at 6 rue Puvis-de-Chavannes in Neuilly. Miki moved in, noting Frede had "proposed to me before buying it." The pair were publicly known as a couple "till [Frede's] death twenty-two years later in 1976" (see figs. 0.1 and 0.2).

FIGURE 0.2: Frede (*left*) and her "wife," Miki (*right*), Paris, 1954. Note the wedding ring on Miki's left hand. On the back of the photograph is written: "Newlyweds. Property of Marilyn 'Miki' Leff." The "marriage" lasted until Frede's death in 1976. Marilyn "Miki" Leff Papers, courtesy of Roy Winnick.

Miki's description of this time, captured in handwritten notes penned toward the end of her life (she died in Philadelphia in 2006), suggests the existence of a vibrant female world that was surprisingly visible ("publicly known" in Miki's words) both within France and internationally during the decades after World War II, a period generally depicted as uniformly repressive toward homosexual behavior and nonnormative gender expression.[3] Its topography is defined by the largely uncharted queer female spaces that emerged in the late nineteenth- and early twentieth-century French public sphere. The proliferation of these spaces in the interwar years laid important groundwork for the politicization of lesbian identity in France during the 1970s and 1980s. One of the many significant developments to which this process contributed was the legalization of same-sex marriage in 2013. Yet perhaps the real significance of this achievement was *not* that it revolutionized queer practices—after all, women like Frede and Miki had considered themselves married and been publicly recognized as intimate partners over half a century earlier—but rather that it marked a critical transformation in normative attitudes toward the "proper" divisions between private and public life in modern France.

BECOMING LESBIAN, QUEERING HISTORY

The same year that the young Miki Leff flew to France in search of "the most famous lesbian in the world," the French writer and philosopher Simone de Beauvoir published *The Second Sex* (1949), in which she famously states: "One is not born, but rather becomes, a woman."[4] *Becoming Lesbian: A Queer History of Modern France* adopts and adapts this claim. The title and subtitle convey two related arguments. First, the "becoming" in *Becoming Lesbian* suggests that sexual identities are the contingent, unstable results of historical processes. Second, the subtitle (*A Queer History . . .*) argues that paying attention to the historicity of lesbian identity invites us "to look at the world askance, to see it afresh," thus providing a "queer perspective" on the history of modern France.[5] In so doing, my book "queers" the French past, revealing it to be far more sexually diverse, and far less heteronormatively gendered, than we generally recognize. Indeed, by documenting the pervasive presence of women who loved women in twentieth-century France, *Becoming Lesbian* asks us to reexamine histories past, present, and future in order to better understand the world as it is now, as it always has been, and as it always will be. My book is thus about making visible the invisible in order to see what is already there.[6]

Becoming Lesbian: A Queer History of Modern France explores the means by which women who love women became identifiable as "lesbian" in the French public sphere over the course of the twentieth century. Because modern media provides a critical interface between private and public worlds, I focus on the ways in which the media served as a powerful vector for the production and publicization of intimate life. The media rendered female same-sex desire visible as lesbian in spaces both material—cabarets, bookstores, women's centers, cafés, streets, and the press—and virtual—especially on television, radio, and, eventually, the internet. Prioritizing "lesbian visibility" inevitably raises questions about lesbian identity more broadly: What is "a lesbian"? Whose lesbianism matters, and under what circumstances? In what ways is lesbian subjectivity inflected by gender presentation, race, class, or erotic behavior? Are only women who have sex with other women lesbians, or can one identify as lesbian regardless of sexual practice? If women refuse categorization as lesbian, what does it mean when we—and do we have the right to—impose it upon them? And what are the stakes of increasing (or decreasing) lesbian visibility?

My work argues that (like the production of lesbian subjectivity itself) the answers to such questions are historically specific and politically charged. We cannot begin to answer them without first addressing the legal status of homosexuality in France since the eighteenth century.

In 1791, during the French Revolution, France became the first European country to decriminalize sodomy.[7] Since that time, sex in private between consenting adults of the same gender has been permitted by French law.[8] And yet, from the ancien régime to the present, people who engaged in same-sex activities have been the targets of persecution and prejudice in France. Into the twentieth century, French police prosecuted same-sex desire—both male and female—under the rubrics of sexual assault, incitement to debauchery, and public indecency, carefully documenting "suspect" behavior in meticulously collated files.[9] During World War II, the age of majority was raised for homosexual acts, and homosexual behavior with or between minors was criminalized.[10] In 1960, penalties for indecent exposure were doubled if homosexuality was involved. These measures were not lifted until the early 1980s.[11] Female gender transgression was likewise prohibited; under a regulation passed on November 7, 1800 (and only "implicitly abrogated" in 2013, although rarely enforced after the 1930s), women could face arrest for wearing masculine clothing—namely pants—in public unless granted special permission to do so.[12]

Throughout the history of modern France, people who identified as homosexual have been subject to harassment, discrimination, and violence. Despite this long-standing intolerance of sexual and gender variance, "sexual misfits" have nevertheless secured civil, economic, and political power in the French public sphere.[13] For example, over twenty cabarets intended for women seeking women were established in Paris in the 1930s; queer women were regularly visible on French public television in the 1950s and 1960s; numerous magazines, radio broadcasts, and early internet sites were created for lesbian audiences in the 1970s and 1980s; and—more recently—female same-sex couples acquired the right to form civil partnerships (1999), marry (2013), and procreate via in vitro fertilization (2021). This book explores this tension between persecution, presence, and public rights. It draws on theories of the public sphere, publics, counterpublics, and subcultures—all defined below—in order to explain better how dissident sexual and gender practices "become" people, how people "become" publics, and how publics shape the nation.

Simply put, the "public sphere" is the contested space of civic life.[14] The term is both descriptive—it refers to an arena where issues of public import are discussed—and normative—it is where hegemonic cultural practices are determined and dominant politics either sustained or critiqued. Like the French Republic it spawned, the French public sphere is premised on the construct of the abstract universal citizen. Civil equality and political membership hinge on the notion of the human subject as universal, "divested of all particularistic affiliations."[15] In the republican framework, individual distinctions—of race, gender, sexuality, class, religion, and ethnicity—are consigned to the private sphere, which is understood as the realm of freedom of expression.[16] The abstract universal citizen (a concept no less powerful for being fictional) is implicitly discriminatory since it is naturalized as white, male, and heterosexual.[17] Because French law does not recognize minority groups as a protected class of citizens, French queers are legally disenfranchised from claiming rights on a collective basis.[18] Consequently, when queer people demand (whether as individuals or as a group) either social recognition or political rights in France on the basis of "private" sexual or gender difference, they pose challenges both to the abstract universal individualism that undergirds French republicanism and to the public/private divide.[19]

"Publics" are dominant collectives whose opinions organize the relations between the state and civil society in the public sphere. In contrast, "counterpublics" (as defined by Nancy Fraser) are "parallel discursive arenas where members of subordinated social groups invent and circulate counterdiscourses to formulate oppositional interpretations of their identities, interests, and needs."[20] As Michael Warner has observed, *queer* counterpublics, by virtue of their nonnormative sexual practices and gender performances, are "by definition" in "conflict with the norms and contexts" of dominant publics.[21] The revolutionary potential of queer counterpublics lies, I suggest, in their desire to transform the public sphere by insisting on the social relevance and political legitimacy of dissident sexual practices and gender performances traditionally relegated to private life by the dominant culture. For my purposes, I consequently apply the term "lesbian counterpublic(s)" only to groups of women who are aware of their collective sexual subordination to a larger public (or publics), whose oppositional discourses and practices express this awareness, *and who act in the name of this shared consciousness in order to transform the public sphere.*

Becoming Lesbian describes how queer subcultures emerged in the French public sphere and evolved into lesbian counterpublics over the course of the twentieth century—a history of politicization that radically impacted both queer life and modern French history. I distinguish "subcultures" from "counterpublics"; while both are social groups that invert or transgress normative values and behaviors, subcultures are focused primarily on enhancing the lives of the individuals involved without necessarily transforming the dominant cultures in which they reside. Importantly, this distinction does not render subcultures intrinsically less public or less significant than counterpublics to their constituents. Nor does it delimit a counterpublic's aims to the political realm. Indeed, this book refuses to privilege "politics" in its traditional sense; the lesbian counterpublics examined here were sometimes utterly indifferent to high politics, and yet they still acted in the public sphere in ways that reshaped both lesbian lives and French society as a whole.

Becoming Lesbian investigates the means by which women who desire women sought to make private desires and nonnormative gender performances public in modern France, whether for personal or political ends. This process required public platforms (be they physical or virtual spaces or media), but it also required both the desire and the capacity to make that which had been considered private public. Of course, people do not act in a bell jar; these women were also subject to and affected by the dominant forces (legislative, medical, religious, political, commercial, social) that seek to regulate and profit from sex in public.[22] My book accordingly examines the interactions between these dominant forces and the public spaces (cabarets, cafés, bookstores, film festivals, streets) and media (press, journals, radio, television, Minitel, video, film) that provided public platforms for lesbian desire in twentieth-century France. I demonstrate how queer spaces, queer media, and the queer desires that shaped and were shaped by them ultimately made possible newly visible forms of what has been called "sexual citizenship"—understood as both a legal and a social status—in ways that revolutionized the public sphere writ large.[23]

I am interested in the transformative impact of lesbian counterpublics on dominant culture. However, *Becoming Lesbian* is *not* simply a celebratory genealogy of the present; it presents a counternarrative to histories that focus on "uncloseting" as the act that marches us triumphantly forward from invisibility to visibility and culminate in legal achievements like the ratification of gay and lesbian marriage. Such advances came at a cost; new political rights closed down possibilities for some women even as they enabled opportunities for others.[24]

Becoming Lesbian is also *not* a book about either trans people or gay men: it is a history of lesbianism. This focus risks eliding certain identities and sometimes minimizes important connections between groups (especially lesbians and gay men), but it also permits a number of critical historical interventions. It contradicts and problematizes powerful arguments about lesbian invisibility; reveals how queer women (and not just men) laid lasting claims to urban space; illuminates the importance of business and entertainment in shaping lesbian identities; documents the largely ignored impact of state surveillance, policing, prostitution, and criminalization on lesbian life; illustrates the presence of queer women on national television since the 1950s (two decades earlier than commonly believed); demonstrates women's sophisticated use of media technologies; explores the contested role of lesbianism in French feminism and of race in French lesbian movements; and argues for the importance of lesbianism to the acquisition of homosexual parenting and couple's rights. In making its claims, this book presents a new chronology of queer history while providing pivotal insights into the heteronormative and androcentric presumptions that have structured the French public sphere since at least the eighteenth century. Indeed, *Becoming Lesbian* illustrates that we can better comprehend the public/private divide in France and the relationship between that divide and the construction of sexual citizenship if we grasp how lesbians have negotiated these interconnected domains.

CONSTRUCTING LESBIAN IDENTITY: WHAT'S IN A NAME?

Scholarship on the history of homosexuality was initially premised on the search for a stable sexual subject—"the lesbian" or "the homosexual"—whose supposed existence gave rise to a mode of research that Laura Doan has termed "recovery history."[25] Histories of homosexuality now oscillate between projects in this vein that aim to retrieve a hidden lesbian and gay past (often in order to bolster present political agendas) and queer historicist approaches (inspired by Foucault) that call that past into question "by revealing the instability of identity categories."[26] In positing lesbian identity as an unstable process of becoming, my work is situated in this latter, queer historicist camp.[27]

Becoming Lesbian builds from a belief that "attraction between women" has always been "a force loose in the world, circulating unpredictably among us," and, further, that this force has "claims to transhistorical ubiquity" just as attraction between women and men is assumed to have.[28] However, as a historian I concurrently aim to expose how categories as seemingly self-evident as sexuality ("lesbian") and gender ("woman") and the meanings associated with them are socially constructed, historically contingent, and deeply entangled with the disciplinary politics that shape the distribution of power in modern societies. Whenever evidence permits, I attempt to convey how individuals understood their own erotic inclinations and gender performances.

This book approaches sexual identity as both an ontological construction and a hermeneutic puzzle. Such an approach inevitably struggles with questions of naming. Should I speak of Frede, "a lady once described as the most famous lesbian in the world" (a person known for "her" masculine elegance who "married" "her" girlfriend in 1954), as a "lady"? Or as a butch lesbian? Or is s/he better designated as transgender, or as a female husband? What does it mean that "her" "wife" Miki called "herself" a "gay girl" but rejected the term "lesbian"? What pronouns should I use to discuss my protagonists? Indeed, how can I write about the sexual past without also appearing to stabilize sexual subjectivity? For, clearly, in discussing these individuals and the history they were a part of, we are—I am—necessarily constrained by language. Such work requires careful attention to the etymologies of desire.

By the late nineteenth century, a French vocabulary for identifying women who "went with women" was well developed: the eroticizing *tribade*, common throughout Europe since the Renaissance (from the Greek for "to rub"), along with the less common *fricatrice* (from the Latin for the same gesture), had been joined by the pathologizing *lesbienne* (popularized by Baudelaire's 1857 *Les fleurs du mal*) and medicalized *homosexuelle* (female homosexual), *invertie* (invert), or the gender-neutral *troisième sexe* (third sex).[29] Educated women during the Belle Époque often favored *Amazone* (Amazon), the restrained *dames seules* (solitary women), or the more feminine *saphiste* (from the Greek lyric poet Sappho and also understood as a woman who had oral sex with other women).[30] A raft of ambiguously expressive slang terms addressed *femmes aux femmes* (women-for-women) or women *comme ça* (like that), especially from the working classes, while some, like *hommasses* or *jules* (meaning masculine women) and *femmellettes* or *nanas* (meaning feminine ones), paid careful mind to gender roles.[31] Others, like the derisive *castratrices* (castrators), *mal baisées* (poorly/badly fucked), *hysteriques* (hysterics), *malades* (sick ones), *vieilles filles* (spinsters), *masturbatrices* (masturbators), and *salopes* (sluts) vilified nonnormative sexual practices.

Numerous terms designating sapphic subjectivity revolved around the French word for garlic clove (*gousse*), an homage to the physical form of female genitalia. In this case, the *gousse* was presumed to be masculine and active, and the *vrille* (tendril or vine) feminine and passive.[32] One might "eat garlic" or be a "garlic seller," or, should one decide (like Frede and Miki) to set up house together, one could "get married at the garlic market" and become *accouplées* (a female couple). Other edible oral metaphors abound: a *suce-lentilles* (lentil sucker) might also be called an *éplucheuse de lentilles* (lentil shucker), who treated her female lover with the same care as a woman sorting lentils. While homophonic, the terms *gougnotte* or *gougniotte* (dialect for "girls" or "girlfriends"), *gougnette* (lesbian prostitute), *goulue* (swallower, or a woman who has oral sex with women), and *gouine* (an epithet often translated as "dyke" that, like the Anglo-American "queer," was politically reappropriated by the lesbian militant Gouines rouges [Red Dykes] in the 1970s) are etymologically distinct.[33] *Homosexuelle* was widely adopted over *lesbienne* by women in the mid-twentieth century, until *lesbienne* took on a newly politicized life in the 1970s. From the 1990s forward, however, many younger women began to drop the female-gendered *lesbienne* and to self-identify with the Anglo-American linguistic import "queer."[34] For others, *lesbienne* or *goudou* (a play on the French words for "taste" [*goût*] and "sweet" [*doux*]) remain preferable alternatives precisely because they *are* specific to women. As a vocabulary that frequently pathologizes those whom it labels, all of these terms—and others like them—were often assigned, even when not assumed.

I understand the word *lesbienne* (lesbian) as an identity category that has carried specific political valences in France from the 1970s and 1980s forward, but because it was in use since the nineteenth century, I also employ it prior to the onset of the lesbian rights movement. When addressing the pre-WWII years, I frequently adopt English translations of *saphiste* (sapphist) or *saphique* (sapphic as in "sapphic cabarets") since these terms were common at that time. Throughout I use "queer" to describe nonnormative marginalized sexual practices and gender performances, as well as the people who engaged in them and the spaces or sites where they did so ("queer worlds"). While I recognize that sometimes my female protagonists (like Miki) identified as "gay," I use "gay" mainly to refer to male homosexuals. I also use "female" and "woman" to name people identified as such according to conventional understandings of sex and gender as binary categories (female/male, woman/man), categories that nineteenth-century sexological arguments for gender inversion helped produce. My pronoun use follows from this historical practice. At the same time, I remain aware that as sexual misfits and gender outlaws who might have identified today as trans (or, to cite Jack Halberstam, "trans*"), or as individuals who rejected patriarchal ideologies and the heterosexual system, some of these people may not have seen themselves as "women" at all.[35] And I call same-sex couples composed of one masculine and one feminine woman "butch/femme" even though this English expression is a later descriptor for performative practices similar to those described here.[36] Unless contradicted by historical evidence, I presume that nonnormative forms of gender performance and sexual attraction are neither necessarily connected nor necessarily distinct.

Some of the women studied here appear to have been solely lovers of other women. Others were also sexually and romantically involved with—and some were married to—men. A few may have had emotionally intimate but not sexual connections with women. They presented as feminine or masculine with greater or lesser consistency. Some transitioned between the two or opted for androgyny. I investigate individuals assigned female at birth who were intermittently erotically attracted to women, as well as women for whom other women were the romantic and sexual foci of their lives. This variability reflects that I am interested less in writing what Daniel Boyarin and Elizabeth Castelli have called "a history of a something" than in speculating about what is at stake in assigning sexual categories at particular historical moments.[37] While I concede that to name the world is also to transform it, for pragmatic reasons I nonetheless employ (in English translation) terminology common in my sources—mainly "sapphist," "homosexual," "lesbian," and "queer"—to refer to women who desire other women, while cognizant that many of the women these sources discuss may not have thought of themselves in these terms.

FRAGMENTED HISTORIES: FEMALE SAME-SEX DESIRE IN FRANCE

The history of women in France has been a critical focus of historical scholarship for well over fifty years. Several topics are legion: French women and the French Revolution; French women and labor; French women and war; French women and religion; French women and the family; French women and (heterosexual) prostitution; French women and colonialism; French women and decolonization; French women and education; French women and feminism; French women and sexuality; and, more recently, French women, race, and the francophone world. The vast majority of this work—like work in the field of gender history more broadly—invariably presumes the heterosexuality of its normatively gendered female subjects. In contrast, by offering a reading of what it meant to "become lesbian" in twentieth-century France, this book suggests that *all* of these narratives are far queerer than we've been led to believe—and intimates that the larger consequences of this truism are as yet beyond comprehension.

Much of the scholarship to date about lesbians in France is in thrall to the world of courtesans and the demimonde, and to the community of mostly anglophone expatriate white female writers and artists active in Paris during the first half of the twentieth century. Since the 1986 publication of Shari Benstock's pathbreaking *Women of the Left Bank: Paris, 1900–1940* (about women's contributions to modernism), studies of the prolific literary and artistic creativity of interwar queer female cultural elites, both French and expatriate, have dominated the field.[38] Marie-Jo Bonnet's 1995 *Les relations amoureuses entre les femmes XVIe–XXe siècle*—a revised version of her 1981 doctoral thesis—remains the most comprehensive history yet written on female homosexuality by a French author.[39] However, Bonnet's work focuses on the West since the premodern era and treats the second half of the twentieth century in only a summary fashion. Articles in French and English by Leslie Choquette, Brigitte Lhomond, and Francesca Canadé Sautman address the social and cultural history of French lesbianism in the decades before and after World War I and concentrate mainly on Paris.[40] Nicole G. Albert's *Saphisme et décadence dans Paris fin-de-siècle* (2005) and Gretchen Schultz's *Sapphic Fathers: Discourses of Same-Sex Desire from Nineteenth-Century France* (2014) are primarily histories of the male obsession with lesbians in art, literature, and medicine in the nineteenth and very early twentieth centuries.[41] There is no work that spans the twentieth century.

In the West, narratives about women, gender, and sexuality inevitably present the period from 1918 to 1939 as a brief era of sexual freedom. In interwar France, the myth of "Paris Lesbos"—a vision of the city as an idyllic destination where women-loving women could live as they pleased—captured the spirit of the times.[42] It is typically argued that this emancipatory moment was crushed under the weight of economic crisis, the rise of fascism, and the trauma of World War II. Although it is sometimes acknowledged that the war offered gender and sexually nonconforming people new possibilities, the post-1945 decades in France (as elsewhere in the West) are invariably depicted as dominated by heteronormalizing processes (i.e., the baby boom and promotion of monogamous, reproductive marriage) that increasingly naturalized heterosexuality and privileged its associated values as foundational for social life.[43] From this perspective, it was not until the advent of the sexual liberation movements that followed the student revolutions of 1968 that homosexuality once again "came out of the closet" and lesbians and gays forged recognizable collectivities in the public domain.[44] Such accounts suggest that those engaged in same-sex practices in France went largely underground for some thirty years during the middle of the century. The collaborationist Vichy state's 1942 law raising the age of consent to twenty-one for homosexual relations (versus thirteen for heterosexual) and the ratification of the Mirguet Amendment in 1960, which increased criminal penalties for homosexuality and identified it (along with alcoholism, tuberculosis, and prostitution) as a social plague, appear to support such conclusions.

Excepting activist Claudie Lesselier's unpublished 1987 master's thesis on the years 1930–1968 and several of her later published articles, almost no histories of queer women in France address the immediate post-WWII years.[45] While more recent works by scholars like Ilana Eloit, Hannah Leffingwell, Camille Morin-Delaurière, and Blase A. Provitola discuss French lesbian activism in the 1970s, 1980s, and 1990s, none links this period to the prewar epoch.[46] Some attribute the absence of robust scholarship on twentieth-century French lesbian life to an absence of sources, arguing that since female same-sex desire was less targeted by the authorities and more socially acceptable, it left fewer traces.

In unearthing the sustained presence of French women who undermined the heterosexual imperative throughout the twentieth century, *Becoming Lesbian* tells a different story. My work reveals that the police kept copious records on suspected lesbians, that private sources are plentiful if hard to find, and that social acceptance was never widespread but largely delimited to either working-class, bohemian, or aristocratic circles in certain times and places. It is nevertheless true that locating sources for the years between the onset of World War II and the eruption of the sexual revolution in the 1970s is markedly challenging. Indeed, *Becoming Lesbian* would not exist without the voices of the over one hundred women born between 1925 and 1969 in France and its former colonies who shared their stories with me.[47]

SAPPHIC VOICES: ORAL AND OTHERWISE

Becoming Lesbian is not, strictly speaking, a work of oral history, but each chapter is deeply informed by what I learned from talking to the many women willing to engage with me.[48] Finding narrators was not simple: despite the ways in which sexuality permeates modern Western culture, even heterosexual practices are generally considered private concerns. Same-sex desire is both private and taboo; many women were happy to talk politics and culture but less comfortable speaking about intimate matters.[49] Repeated communication over time helped breach that barrier. At the same time, maintaining an empathic connection with my narrators while still engaging critically with their stories necessarily presented challenges.

My initial contacts were with women prominent in the French feminist movement, a fact that shaped my narrators' perspectives. Over fourteen years of research, however, my network expanded considerably, and the demographic profiles of the women I spoke with diversified. One-third of my narrators were born before 1945. Slightly more were born in the following ten years. With few exceptions, the remaining women were born in the late 1950s or early 1960s. The youngest, at forty-four, was the last lover of Elula Perrin, the French-Vietnamese lesbian icon and political conservative thirty years her senior who ran the Katmandou, a celebrated lesbian discothèque in Paris, from 1969 to 1989. While a quarter had been married to someone of the opposite sex, such marriages were more prevalent for women born before 1950, a statistic that reflects how the pressure to marry men eased as the century progressed.[50] A few women entered "cover" marriages with homosexual men. Most marriages produced children. Only two did *not* result in divorce. The fact that most of these marriages dissolved in the 1970s is a testament to the impact of the sexual revolution and the feminist and gay rights movements on women's choices. On the one hand, there was more support for those who wanted to leave heterosexual unions. On the other, there was more pressure to do so; in the newly politicized post-1968 world, remaining married was often interpreted either as succumbing to male oppression or as a desire to retain heterosexual privilege.

While economic status could change over time, most of my narrators—who were mainly single or divorced—were middle, lower-middle, or working class. They included teachers, pharmacists, journalists, government functionaries, shopkeepers, publishers, editors, club owners, musicians, illustrators, photographers, restaurateurs, farmers, and winemakers, as well as psychoanalysts, archivists, bar staff, computer technicians, and even the mayor of a small town in the Drôme. There were also women who lived in relative poverty, a few descendants of aristocracy, and at least one extremely wealthy heiress. One was the granddaughter of a governor general of French Indochina. Two, Catherine Lara and Marie-Paule Belle, are literal rock stars. Many came from modest backgrounds and had improved their lots through education. There were practicing or lapsed Catholics, atheists, agnostics, protestants, and Jews. Only two were Muslim. Many were leftists—socialists of many stripes—but a not inconsiderable group were centrist republicans, and a few were supporters of the Far Right.

Two-thirds of my interviews took place outside Paris in villages, towns, and cities throughout France. Fifteen of my narrators grew up outside the metropole in Algeria, Tunisia, Morocco, Chad, Guadeloupe, Senegal, Madagascar, the Antilles, and Vietnam (formerly French Indochina). Of these, one-third were *pieds-noirs*—people of French and European origin born in French North Africa under colonial rule. The others were women of color whose families had moved to France, usually after decolonization. While my narrators were predominantly white, my interview pool was nevertheless riven by difference—of class, politics, education, economics, generation, religion, civil status, sexual practice, gender performance, et cetera—just as the general French public is. I cannot claim, however, that this diversity rendered my interviewees fully "representative" of women who love women in France. The very fact that each narrator was willing to discuss aspects of private life that continue to be stigmatized made them atypical. In this, I argue for the value of that which Michael Rustin calls the "luminosity of single cases" and which microhistorians refer to as the "exceptional normal."[51] Both approaches embrace the interpretive power of particularity in ways I believe necessary when writing the nonnormative past. Finally, I was often introduced as someone researching a "history of lesbianism"; this labeling likely dissuaded some women who didn't identify publicly as lesbian from participating in my work.

The presence of so many women from outside the Paris region among my interviewees is key for at least two reasons. First, the contribution of provincial voices from smaller cities, towns, and villages in both France and its former empire permits me to push back on a Parisian narrative that has tended to stand in for, and even erase, the experiences of women living outside the capital. Second, many Parisians active in the feminist movement have already told their stories—to the media and to researchers—numerous times. Well-rehearsed stories like these are particularly susceptible to refashioning in service of the political (or personal) histories that activist women seek to promote. At the same time, it behooves us to remember that if oral sources "are not always fully reliable in point of fact," their unreliability, "rather than being a weakness," can actually be "their strength" since, as Alessandro Portelli insists in his important 1981 essay on the topic, this is "where imagination, symbolism, desire break in."[52] This is also another way that oral history illuminates the present. Indeed, oral interviews about the sexual past tell us as much about the discourses that structure sexuality today as they do about the period being addressed.

Becoming Lesbian juxtaposes the interviews I filmed against an extensive material and virtual archive. It examines private memorabilia, published memoirs, police files, municipal records, photographs, erotica, television broadcasts, mass and alternative press and radio, the Minitel (an early form of internet), and amateur and professional video and film. It also culls from more than seven hundred letters written to journals and lesbian organizations and over two dozen video interviews shot by French lesbian activists during the 1990s in order to situate female same-sex desire at the heart of twentieth-century French public life. These materials come from private homes and militant, municipal, and national archives. This book's arguments thus derive from one of the largest collections of data on French women who love women ever assembled. As such, this study provides heretofore inaccessible insights not just into French lesbian history but also into the relationship between dominant publics and the sexually marginalized individuals and groups who seek to live with, resist, and transform them.

BECOMING LESBIAN: AN OVERVIEW

This book begins with the extraordinary growth of an economically and racially diverse women's world in interwar Paris—a subculture of cabarets, dance halls, bars, restaurants, brothels, and boulevards quite distinct from that of the elite white expatriate sapphic community that has dominated much of the historiography of female homosexuality in twentieth-century France. In focusing primarily on Paris, my first three chapters build on scholarship on the history of homosexuality that places the city at its core.[53] They utilize what I call the sapphic cabaret—an entertainment venue targeting women interested in other women popularized in Western Europe in the 1920s and 1930s—as an explanatory trope through which to view the practice and publicization of female same-sex desire in modern France.[54] I argue not only that the world of the sapphic cabaret survived World War II but also that as it traversed urban and rural divides in the decades that followed, it politicized in ways that paradoxically restricted its purview for some women while extending its reach for others—even as it helped to reshape the dominant culture for all. These chapters thus introduce one of my book's central claims: rather than (as others have argued) being torn asunder by the "astonishing rupture" that was French defeat and collaboration (1940–1944), and hence sinking into "conformity and the black of night . . . for at least thirty years," the spaces and networks that these women-loving women established and developed enabled the female world created in the interwar years to outlast World War II and survive well into the decades that followed.[55]

Chapter 1, "La Vie Parisienne: Becoming Lesbian in the City," argues that the public performance of female same-sex desire in Parisian cabarets, dance halls, tearooms, and restaurants during the interwar years was critical to disseminating nineteenth-century understandings of "the lesbian" as a form of sexual subjectivity that was usually gendered masculine. At the same time, by examining the sexual self-fashioning of women like the painter Hélène Azenor, her girlfriend Flavie, and the celebrity cabaret artist Suzy Solidor and her lovers, this chapter demonstrates that even normative concepts of female sexuality and gender performance were far more fluid in the early twentieth century than is commonly believed.

In chapter 2, "Mapping the Sapphic Cabaret," I chart the surprising number of "sapphic cabarets" run by and catering to women who loved women launched in Paris and its environs in the 1930s. Chapter 2 introduces a concept that I call "sapphic genealogical geographies" in order to analyze the complicated networks that governed the transfer of knowledge, support, and power between women who loved women across time and space.[56] This chapter demonstrates how women of different classes and races who operated, performed in, and visited these spaces constituted a nascent lesbian subculture, exerting what Henri Lefebvre might term their "right to the city" and exercising considerably more influence both nationally and internationally than their numbers—or their denigrated social status—imply.[57]

I explore the relationship between sexual identity, sexual practices, and gender performance in France in chapter 3, "'A Woman Dressed Like a Man.'" This chapter argues that the commercial promotion of the *entraîneuse* (a female staff member often required to cross-dress who was hired to heat up the ambience) played a special role inside the sapphic cabaret in fostering a sexual schema—now called butch/femme—that is most often explained as a product of biological, social, or political circumstance. This chapter reveals instead how market economics in the entertainment and sex industries helped shape the binary sartorial practices and racialized frameworks that both supported and stereotyped gender-variant female performances in France from the pre- through the post-WWII years.

The next four chapters mark a shift in our story, moving from the subcultural semiprivate world of the sapphic cabaret into the French public sphere writ large. In the post-WWII decades, the growth of mass media—not just television but also cinema, radio, the recording industry, the press, literature, and, ultimately, the internet—carried discourses of queer female embodiment well beyond France's capital, enabling broad access to nonnormative models of gender and sexuality and facilitating the politicization of lesbian counterpublics. In these years, politically active women who loved women deployed alternative and mainstream media not merely to create subcultural communities but also to contest a hegemonic public sphere that divided intimacy from politics by privatizing sex while imposing heteronormativity as a primary matrix of social organization.

Chapter 4, "Sappho on the Small Screen," directs our attention to how early TV brought nonnormative female performances into living rooms throughout France and its empire in the 1950s and 1960s. Focusing on femme and what I call "failed femme" television coverage of female cabaret artists on musical variety shows, chapter 4 counters the misconception that female same-sex desire was absent from French TV until the 1970s. It further demonstrates how state media unwittingly rendered queer female sexualities and gender-variant performances visible in ways that traversed the urban/rural divide during the immediate postwar decades.

Television remains central to chapter 5, "Beautiful Whores, Good Mothers, and Feminist Activists." This chapter discusses how three archetypes (the beautiful whore, the good mother, and the feminist activist) dominated televised depictions of female same-sex desire following the French feminist and sexual revolutions of the early 1970s. The steady increase in heteronormative representations of French queer women as either erotically feminine or reassuringly maternal, coupled with the erasure of lesbianism from feminist militancy in mainstream media from the mid-1970s onward, was instrumental in liberalizing dominant attitudes toward homosexuality by the end of the century.

Chapter 6, "French Lesbian Information Activism," analyzes how mainly white French queer women began using newly accessible mass media technologies in the late 1970s and early 1980s to validate female same-sex desire, create lesbian community, and combat the compulsory heterosexuality of France's patriarchal republican state. This chapter examines three activist initiatives: a feminist telephone answering machine service called Les Répondeuses, the French lesbian magazine *Quand les femmes s'aiment* (launched in Lyon), and lesbian broadcasts on the homosexual radio station Fréquence Gaie. Drawing on over seven hundred letters and numerous interviews, this chapter argues for the importance of French lesbian information activism in constructing and politicizing lesbian counterpublics by connecting women who loved women in cities and towns throughout the French nation and beyond.

Internet technology revolutionized both public and private life in the modern era. It became, and has continued to be, vital for queer communities, facilitating contact between individuals and groups and providing access to critical resources. Chapter 7, "Virtually Yours: French Lesbians Online," studies French lesbian use of the Minitel, an early networking technology introduced commercially in France in 1982. It investigates a cooperative enterprise called Les Goudous Télématiques, the first online community and email system developed by and for lesbians in France, which operated on the Minitel between 1985 and 1989—almost ten years prior to the popularization of the World Wide Web. Whereas gay men used the Minitel mainly to facilitate sexual encounters, this chapter illustrates how French women who loved women sought to employ the Minitel to make romantic connections, form friendships, and create lesbian community across France. While their initiative ultimately failed, their efforts foreshadowed how social media technologies would transform contemporary lesbian existence around the globe in the decades that followed.

The final two chapters continue the movement from subcultures to counterpublics that this book describes. I turn first to a modern, politicized incarnation of the sapphic cabaret in Southwest France. Here, women used the tools of the modern media to take the semiprivate subculture of the interwar cabaret into the public sphere. Chapter 8, "Lesbopolis: Utopian Politics and Pleasures in Toulouse," takes a case study from Toulouse to describe the politicization of the sapphic cabaret in the last quarter of the twentieth century. It begins with France's first women-only cooperative commercial lesbian-feminist café, Bagdam Cafée, an entertainment space serving up equal helpings of food, drink, performance, and activism that was established in Toulouse in 1988. Bagdam's story politicizes the sapphic genealogical geographies first addressed in chapter 2. The women of Bagdam claimed their "right to the city" as part of a utopian manifesto premised on the politicization of pleasure that aimed not simply to stake out private space in public but to contest and reconfigure the public sphere's foundational principles.

Becoming Lesbian's last chapter raises the topic of race: very few women of color appear in this history. My last chapter asks why not and explores what happens when they do. Chapter 9, "The Difference Problem: Lesbians of Color in France," analyzes the 1999 founding of the Groupe du 6 novembre: Lesbiennes issues du colonialism, de l'esclavage et de l'immigration (Group of November 6: [French] Lesbians Begotten [Out] of Colonialism, Slavery, and Immigration) to investigate how conflicts over race divided French lesbian counterpublics at the end of the twentieth century. The group's creation reminds us that French lesbian counterpublics were historically predominantly white. It was not until the end of the twentieth century that women of color began to make their voices heard. Given France's fraught colonial past and complicated postcolonial present, the oppression experienced by French queer women of color within lesbian communities highlights the ways in which, to quote Blase A. Provitola, "dominant conceptions of [French] lesbian sexual identity"—like dominant conceptions of Frenchness—can be "imbued with liberal racism and Republican universalism."[58] This chapter also examines the Pulp nightclub, a modern Parisian sapphic cabaret, in order to describe a different vision of multiracial French lesbian community.

The book's conclusion takes us back to chapter 1's Suzy Solidor. Exploring Solidor's effect on the right-wing bastion of Haut-de-Cagnes (the tiny medieval town to which she "retired" at the end of her life), the conclusion attends to the impact of lesbian visibility on French public opinion. By demonstrating how women who desired women exerted their right to the city and became visible in the French public sphere over the course of the twentieth century, *Becoming Lesbian* thus exemplifies contemporary ideas about spatial justice while challenging the public/private divide.[59] It also rewrites histories of homosexuality that purport to be gender inclusive but are in fact about behaviors and issues—sodomy, cruising, pedophilia, and AIDS—predominantly associated with gay men. In so doing, my work resists a widespread narrative of lesbian "invisibility, insignificance, unaccountability, and impossibility" and attests to a French sapphic presence that was observable, territorial, enduring, and often utopian in its collective expression.[60] Although focused on one specific, if historically formidable, nation—France—*Becoming Lesbian* thus complicates notions of sexual normativity, dislodges men from the center of histories of homosexuality, and shows how the media emerged in the twentieth century as a—if not *the*—primary means of communication between oppressed minorities and the modern state.

1

LA VIE PARISIENNE

Becoming Lesbian in the City

The Bal de la Montagne Sainte-Geneviève was a Parisian dance hall located on a steep little street in the fifth arrondissement, close to the Panthéon and across from the École polytechnique.[1] It opened in 1908 before the Great War as a *bal-musette*—a working-class dance hall with music provided by a musette (a wind instrument resembling the bagpipe) and an accordion, and later by a small orchestra.[2] Like many dance halls of the Belle Époque (1890–1914), the Bal de la Montagne Sainte-Geneviève attracted a heterogeneous clientele of different genders, classes, races, and sexual persuasions.[3] The symbolist painter Hélène Azenor met her first girlfriend, Flavie, at the Bal in the early 1930s. Shortly thereafter, the Bal was taken over by Marie Georgette Dubois, alias Georgette Anys, a heavyset actress, cabaret performer, and director whose preference for women was well known.[4] It was Anys who hired the Bal's female orchestra to play polkas, mazurkas, waltzes, and javas in endless succession for the crowds who flocked to the venue after dark. The orchestra's members all had a masculine appeal; they sported black tuxedos known as *smokings* and kept their hair short, slicked back, and razored at the neck.[5] Legend has it that Anys joined the French Forces of the Interior during World War II and was among those who liberated her neighborhood by machine gun at the war's end. The actress continued to run the Bal (even after her career in film, radio, and television took off) until it "slid gently toward the picturesquely sordid" and closed in the early 1970s.[6]

Throughout their relationship, Azenor and Flavie were regulars at the

Bal de la Montagne Sainte-Geneviève. The couple also patronized a host of other venues that were created in the 1930s for women seeking women—venues I call "sapphic cabarets"—including Le Monocle, Le Fétiche (later known as Chez Moune), and La Vie Parisienne, a cabaret owned and operated by the French singer and celebrity Suzy Solidor that opened in 1933. As an exceedingly popular performer, Solidor played a key role in shaping public understandings not only of these venues but also of the subcultural practices prevalent among women associated with them, like Azenor and Flavie. For Azenor, the erotic connections that she made in dance halls and cabarets like the Bal de la Montagne Sainte-Geneviève and La Vie Parisienne facilitated her "coming out" into lesbian subjectivity. Not so for Flavie. After three years, Flavie abandoned her female lover for a man, never again indulging (so far as we know) in another same-sex affair.

Public leisure spaces like the Bal de la Montagne Sainte-Geneviève and sapphic cabarets—known in France as *cabarets féminins* (women's cabarets) or *cabarets pour femmes* (cabarets for women)—were commercial enterprises in which the promotion and performance of female same-sex desire was an organizing business principle. These venues proliferated across Western Europe in the interwar years. French sapphic cabarets have long had a particular cachet.[7] They provide us with understudied examples of early female participation in what is now known as "pink capitalism"—the targeting of queer publics for economic gain.[8] The history of these spaces, the women who ran them (the sapphic cabarets were all run by women), and the publics they attracted—women like Azenor as well as Flavie—raise a host of questions, from the prosaic ("How did women locate these venues?") to the personal ("What did women hope to find there?") to the societal ("What did friends, neighbors, coworkers, or strangers think of the women who patronized these spots?") to the economic ("How did these spaces function as businesses?") to the theoretical ("Did women who frequented sapphic cabarets understand themselves as 'lesbian'?"). The next three chapters explore questions like these and attempt some responses.

The women's stories that follow introduce a central argument of this book: the claim that even as nineteenth-century medical, legal, and literary discourses popularized "the lesbian" as a mannish "invert" in the French imaginary, through the interwar era female same-sex desire was not yet seen as inextricable from either homosexual subjectivity or gender inversion. Indeed, the actions of the women examined here underscore "the exceptional fluidity and interconnectedness of sexuality and gender" at this time.[9] Thus, if by the end of the Belle Époque *some* "lesbians" were already considered by many to be a "race apart," *normative* female sexuality was far less hetero, and female gender performance far less fixed, than is sometimes presumed.[10] Ironically, the publicization of female same-sex desire inside interwar dance halls and sapphic cabarets—spaces intended to provide new sexual freedoms—ultimately contributed to the rigidification of sexual scripts. In so doing, these venues paradoxically intensified the stigmatization of lesbian desire even as they contributed to the formation of lesbian subcultures.

This chapter is divided into three parts: It begins with the story of Azenor and Flavie in order to investigate what one couple's relationship can tell us about what it meant to be a woman who desired women in 1930s France. I then backtrack to an overview of the arguments about female homosexuality that proliferated in Europe during the late nineteenth and early twentieth centuries in order to clarify the discursive frameworks within which such relationships occurred. Finally, I trouble these discourses by contrasting them against evidence from the life of Suzy Solidor. Solidor's magisterial efforts to control the narrative that circulated in the media about her sexuality reveal how the commercialization and publicization of lesbian desire in France's capital both expanded same-sex opportunities for women and made it increasingly difficult to pursue them without being categorized as "lesbian." Dance halls like the Bal de la Montagne Sainte-Geneviève and sapphic cabarets like Solidor's La Vie Parisienne enabled this process. It was because these venues were initially understood as attracting *both* a newly identifiable, highly visible (if eroticized and maligned) sexual subject—"the lesbian"—*and* a broader ("heterosexual") female public sexually interested in other women that they were envisioned as especially marketable enterprises. And it was this broad appeal that made these entertainment venues such influential public spaces.

"SHE BROUGHT ME ONE NIGHT TO A DANCE HALL"

Born in Paris in 1910 into a working-class milieu, Hélène Azenor fled home at nineteen in pursuit of artistic and personal freedom and to escape her mother's bitter tirades about the young woman's homoerotic adventures.[11] Determined to become a painter, Azenor found work in the interior design industry. In the evenings she would attend classes at the art academies on the rue de la Grande Chaumière and sketch the young women hired to pose nude. In a documentary filmed in 1987 when Azenor was seventy-seven, she recalls:

FIGURE 1.1: Hélène Azenor (*standing*) and Flavie, ca. 1932 or 1933. *Instants de vie, portrait d'Hélène Azénor*, dir. Claudie Lesselier, 1987. Courtesy of Claudie Lesselier.

> Once—well, many times we had a very young model, very nice, very shapely, who posed very well, and we started to talk. . . . She brought me one night to a dance hall that I didn't know at all, called the Bal de la Montagne Sainte-Geneviève. . . . It was about 1931 . . . and truly, I asked myself where I was because I didn't think that a place like that existed. . . . And there were so many women. Of course, it was known as a homosexual ball, but there were also lots of people from the neighborhood who went there because it was a real *bal-musette*. Almost every Saturday I went to the Bal de la Montagne, and that was where I met my first girlfriend, Flavie.[12] (Fig. 1.1)

Azenor's remarks about her inaugural visit to the Bal de la Montagne Sainte-Geneviève bear unpacking: Azenor first observes that she didn't know that places "like that" where "there were so many women" existed. This initial comment might have reflected her own youthful ignorance, but it also concurs with historical fact: in 1931 there were no longer as many Parisian venues catering to women as there had been at the end of the nineteenth century. Women seeking women had previously congregated in Pigalle and Montmartre at restaurants and sidewalk cafés like La Souris, Le Rat Mort (The Dead Rat—which itself became a slang term for lesbian), and Chez Palmyre or visited the forty-odd brothels reputedly "dedicated to the cult of Lesbos" that could be found near the Madeleine and the Chaussée-d'Antin.[13] Many of these entertainment establishments had been shuttered for security reasons during World War I and failed to reopen after the war. By the 1920s a few prewar brasseries (Le Select), cafés (Chez Fysher and Chez Graff), and tea salons (Smiths, Le Thé Colombin, and Le Thé Récamier) still attracted women interested in other women, but only one women's cabaret existed in the city (Le Fétiche—later called Chez Moune—opened in 1926), and women seeking women were in the minority at the male-dominated dance halls (like the Bal de la Montagne Sainte-Geneviève) that served homosexual desires at this time. Moreover, in the early interwar years, although some (like Azenor's coworkers) "vaguely remembered hearing people speak of 'pédérastes' [male homosexuals]," many, as Azenor reports in her memoirs, were utterly "oblivious to female homosexuality," asking, "What could they do . . . together . . . two women?" and believing such practices "impossible."[14] The publicity given to the sapphic cabarets that spread throughout Paris over the ensuing decades would do much to dispel such ignorance.

Second, Azenor makes a contradictory claim: she states that the Bal "was known as a homosexual ball." In light of her previous assertion (that she didn't know that such places where "there were so many women" existed), the intimation here is both that "homosexual" refers to male (and not female) clientele and that dance halls frequented by men who desired men were sufficiently common in Paris as to be "known" even by someone as young and uninformed as she. This, again, was true: while a prefectorial decision from 1910 forbade men to dance together in public spaces, men regularly skirted this ordinance. By the late 1920s dancing between men occurred nightly at the Bal de la Montagne, Au Lapin Vengeur (near the Porte des Lilas), Le Yeddo (in Montmartre), and at bars on the rue de Lappe like the Bal des Trois Colonnes.[15] Festive drag balls held twice yearly for Mardi Gras and Lent also introduced the pleasures of mostly male cross-dressing to massive publics at the Magic-City ("a vast skating rink qua dance hall due east of the Eiffel Tower"), the Bal Bullier, and the Salle Wagram (also known as the Bal des Ternes).[16] These gatherings, which attracted literally thousands of male "homosexuals or sympathizers" and a far smaller "number of lesbians" from across France, were notorious features of French urban life.[17]

Between 1922 and 1940 (excepting in 1934 when it was temporarily closed following right-wing riots on February 6), the French season hit its apogee at the Magic-City's masked Mardi Gras carnival, which culminated in a drag competition.[18] Organized by groups like L'aide amicale aux artistes (Friendly Aid to Artists) and the Homosexuelle parisienne association, these gatherings were either excoriated in the press as "one of the vilest things about which the police close a guilty eye" or fêted for their extravagant creativity.[19] Indeed, members of the Brigade Mondaine (the vice police) were so fascinated by the goings-on that they kept tabs on the inventiveness of participants' costumes from one year to the next. Whereas in 1929 one officer remarked, "Most *travesties* brought a refined sense of taste to their disguises," according to later reports the next few years showed "a general downward trend" during which the costumes were merely "mediocre."[20] Things had evidently improved by 1931, when police described an "innovative policeman's costume worn by a young man with an electrified lightbulb on his hat. His buttocks read *sens interdit* [no entry] in red on one cheek, and *P. reservé* [reserved parking] in sky blue on the other."[21]

Finally, Azenor notes that "there were also lots of people from the neighborhood" at the Bal de la Montagne Sainte-Geneviève. Elsewhere, she elaborates: "I mingled with people of all ranks at the Montagne Sainte-Geneviève: milkmaids, employees of the Crédit Lyonnais [a French bank], and also society types."[22] Ernest Hemingway, who lived in the quarter until 1928, was among those who frequented the venue: in his 1926 novel *The Sun Also Rises* he describes the Bal thus: "Five nights a week the working people of the Pantheon quarter danced there. . . . On Monday nights it was closed. . . . There were long benches, and tables ran across the room, and at the far end a dancing-floor."[23] If unlike Azenor, Hemingway emphasizes the presence of the working classes over "people of all ranks," like her he implies that "working people" came because the dance hall was, in Azenor's words, "a real *bal-musette*." By the early 1930s, however, I suggest that not all the "people from the neighborhood" were there mainly for the dancing, and not all were immune to the pleasures of same-sex desire. Their presence points instead to the panoply of possibilities that shaped sexual practices among the French population at large, despite stereotypes and sanctions.

Azenor's brief anecdote encapsulates a historic period in which same-sex sexual behavior was not yet understood to be self-evidently demonstrative of homosexual subjectivity. Azenor insisted that as a young girl she was "neither *gousse* nor *gouine*" (neither femme nor butch), but she also claimed to have had a sharp sense of her "difference" and of the fact that many considered this difference distressing.[24] And yet, as a young adult Azenor made a name for herself as both a painter and an "out" lesbian. She socialized in what she called a "[male] homosexual coterie" and worked in a bohemian milieu; she knew the French surrealist Jean Cocteau, had met his lover the actor Jean Marais, and counted among her circle the poet Paul Éluard and his wife and muse Nusch (an acrobat, magician, hypnotist, and model to Man Ray, Picasso, and Miró who, like her husband, was known as a sexual libertine).[25] Azenor and her girlfriend Flavie traveled in spaces branded as lesbian haunts (the Bal and the sapphic cabarets as well as Smiths bookstore/tea salon on the rue de Rivoli and the brasserie Le Select). Together they read Pierre Louÿs's 1894 ode to female love *Les chansons de Bilitis* (The songs of Bilitis) and Radclyffe Hall's 1928 *The Well of Loneliness* (translated into French in 1932 and gifted by Flavie to Azenor in 1934).[26] Toward the end of her life Azenor published her two-part autobiography with the lesbian-feminist press Les Octaviennes and fittingly titled the first volume *Histoire d'UNE* (Story of ONE). Azenor's girlfriend Flavie, with whom Azenor had fallen madly in love and set up a household, was a different story. As noted above, three years after they embarked on their passionate affair, Flavie left her lover for a man. Azenor was heartbroken. Flavie may have considered herself "like that" for a time, but the label didn't stick. Or perhaps Flavie should be counted among those "people from the neighborhood" who attended the Bal de la Montagne Sainte-Geneviève out of an ultimately passing interest in the "deviant" pleasures it provided.

Azenor's story appears the less surprising of the two: here we see what might be called a "coming to consciousness" of lesbian identity in the interwar years that was nourished by social milieu and shaped by literary and artistic pursuits, which consistently embraced contemporaneous discourses regarding female same-sex desire. About women like Flavie—women whose erotic behaviors appear to have pushed back against notions of lesbian subjectivity—we know unfortunately little. This is where an exploration of historical context can prove useful. So before moving on to examine the singular impact of media coverage of Suzy Solidor and her cabaret La Vie Parisienne on public understandings of French lesbian life, let's review how the figure of "the lesbian" was already represented in French society at this time.

SAPPHIC SEXUALITY IN SEXOLOGY, LITERATURE, AND THE POPULAR PRESS

In the aftermath of the disastrous Franco-Prussian War and the Paris Commune, French attitudes toward sexual and gender deviance were inseparable from Third Republic fears about depopulation and national decline. Rocked by political and economic crises and terrified of dropping birth rates, Catholics and republicans alike emphasized the importance of marriage, family, masculinity, education, and public health.[27] Reproductive panic peaked in the 1890s when French deaths began outstripping births while the populations of England and Germany multiplied.[28] In this context lesbianism, because it was perceived as nonreproductive, became a particular source of concern. Nourished by new medical research from throughout Europe, the burgeoning field of sexology sought to explain the threat that female homosexuality posed.

Experts' theories about sapphism culled from two competing perceptions of human sexuality. On the one hand there was sexual practice. This was seen as either procreative and "normal" or nonprocreative and perverse. Sexual perversions, from homosexuality to bestiality, foot fetishism, sadism, masochism, and masturbation, were all variations on a similar theme. On the other hand there was sexual identity: Foucault's much-quoted statement that whereas "the sodomite had been a temporary aberration; the homosexual was now a species" argues for the accession of this view.[29] The Hungarian Károly Mária Kertbeny is thought to have invented the term "homosexual" in 1869 to refer to this new form of sexual subjectivity.

Normative perspectives on sex and gender shaped perceptions of sexual identity. Men were idealized as active, independent, powerful agents, fit for the public sphere of labor, commerce, politics, and war. Women were passive, dependent, vulnerable, and suited for the private sphere of domesticity, the home, and the family. Sexual practices followed from these presumptions. However, this active-male/passive-female binary "posed a conceptual problem for theorists considering desire between women," since if "women could only respond to, but not initiate, sexual encounters," then it was impossible to explain how two women could have sex with one another—unless—as Pierre de Bourdeille, seigneur de Brantôme, suggested in the sixteenth century—they "usurped the sexual vigor of males" and "betrayed their gender."[30]

The German psychiatrist Karl Westphal developed the category of "contrary sexual instinct" to explain this aberration.[31] In his conceptualization (also evident in German jurist Karl Heinrich Ulrichs's concept of a "third sex") homosexual desire was largely a product of gender inversion: a lesbian was thought to be a man trapped in a woman's body, whereas a pederast was a woman trapped in a man's.[32] The desire of the female invert for those of her own sex followed from her innately masculine disposition. Sexual inversion was thus more than sexual attraction: the female invert exhibited masculine characteristics in dress, stance, and behavioral preferences. In this "innate" biological model, "women inverts do not imitate men" but actually *are* virile.[33] Most late nineteenth-century male experts asserted, however, that biological variation explained only some instances of same-sex behavior. Other cases of "contrary sexual instinct" were considered to be either acquired or an amalgamation of nature and nurture. These divergent categories enabled clinicians and critics to distinguish between homosexuality as a naturally occurring debility and homosexuality as immoral. Not infrequently—given contemporary ideas about evolutionary and social degeneration—it was understood as both. Thus, in 1882, Jean-Martin Charcot and Valentin Magnan posited that sexual inversion was the result of both physical *and* moral deterioration; its hereditary pathology was inseparable from "the degrading consequences of a weakening of morals in a profoundly vitiated society."[34]

For sexologists, when it came to homoerotic female couples, the "mannish lesbian" garnered most of the attention, but her feminine partner was also a cause for significant concern, not least because of the ways in which she connoted varying degrees of vice. Like Westphal and Ulrichs, the German psychiatrist Richard von Krafft-Ebing and British physician and social reformer Havelock Ellis agreed that "true" female homosexuals were born with masculine physical and mental characteristics and deserved medical help, not legal condemnation.[35] These "innocent" mannish lesbians sought feminine partners (sometimes labeled "pseudo-homosexuals" by Krafft-Ebing) whose sexuality should be better understood as a function of moral failure connected to nymphomania and financial greed.[36] At issue were questions of moral responsibility: Was the female sexual invert the innocent victim of heredity and biology? Or was she responsible for her own "deviant" desires? In his 1885 doctoral dissertation (published one year prior to Krafft-Ebing's monumental *Psychopathia sexualis*), Julien Chevalier concluded that the answer depended on the case at hand. "The love of an individual for another individual of the same sex," he wrote, can be either "native" (hereditary), "secondary" (the product of an anatomical deformity like hermaphroditism), "acquired" (resulting from personal weakness or social temptation), or some combination of the three.[37] Acquired sexual inversion was the most morally suspect: it could occur via a profession—like prostitution—or from depravity born of avarice or hypersexuality or as the "consequence of a [homosocial] milieu" or from a fear of heterosexual intercourse (due to the threat of either venereal disease or pregnancy).[38] One remedy? Suppress homosocial organizations like the boarding school, "that powerful cause of shameful promiscuity during the perilous years of puberty," and the problem would diminish.[39]

New theories from sexology, medicine, and the law were popularized in literature and tabloids. Adolphe Belot's novel *Mademoiselle Giraud, ma femme* (1870), about a husband's devastating marriage to his lesbian wife, saw forty-five editions in fifteen years.[40] Writers Émile Zola and Guy de Maupassant also wrote about the lesbian in lurid terms.[41] Following the liberalization of the press in 1881, previously censored publications flooded the public sphere.[42] Pornographic pseudoscientific sex manuals like *La perversion sexuelle* (1903)—one of over 120 pamphlets authored between 1900 and 1934 by Jean Caufeynon (a medical charlatan known variously as Dr. Caufeynon, Dr. Fauconney, Dr. Eynon, Dr. X., and Dr. Jaf) in which lesbianism figured prominently—ensured that the figure of the mannish lesbian was clearly legible in France during the Belle Époque.[43] Purveyors of such materials capitalized on the French public's taste for the sensational and the depraved—and female homoeroticism sold well.

Early twentieth-century French perceptions of lesbianism and female masculinity were thus inextricable from the rabid (mainly male) interest in these topics in medicine, literature, and the press in the nineteenth century.[44] Throughout France, the growth of what Guy Debord would later term "the society of the spectacle," epitomized by the urban entertainment districts with their fancy opera houses, avant-garde cabarets, noisy brasseries, and bustling dance halls, contributed to the commodification of "deviant" desires.[45] Public and private venues soon emerged in metropolitan settings where those seeking others of the same sex could socialize and form romantic and erotic bonds. By 1900 the spectacle of two women "groping one another" in public establishments had become so common in Paris according to journalist and cabaret manager Charles Virmaître that "no one makes a fuss."[46] In 1904 the term *homosexuelle* as a designation for women who desired women entered the illustrated *Larousse* dictionary. In 1909 American heiress and writer Natalie Clifford Barney (already known for her tempestuous love affairs with the French courtesan Liane de Pougy and the British poet Renée Vivien) began holding literary salons at her home on the Left Bank's exclusive rue Jacob. Barney's gatherings attracted the cream of lesbian Paris and further enhanced the city's mythical reputation as a paradise for women with same-sex desires.[47]

But not all women involved with other women in France were sapphic-identified white members of the literati or ladies of the demimonde. Female same-sex desire also flourished in the grittier world represented in popular culture and the press, where different classes and races congregated in neighborhood brasseries, dance halls, cabarets, and brothels.[48] Like the world of artists, avant-gardists, and the aristocracy, this world was irradicably reconfigured by the Great War. World War I had destroyed a generation of French men and unexpectedly offered French women—including those interested in other women—untold career opportunities, romantic possibilities, and freedom of movement. Indeed, more women were mobilized in France on the home- and battlefronts than in any other combatant country. The war's aftermath saw massive demographic shifts: millions died from the Spanish flu; Russians, Poles, Italians, Spaniards, and Jews sought shelter in France from political and religious violence at home; Americans—especially African Americans and women—came to France seeking freedom from racism, misogyny, puritanism, and economic collapse under the impress of Prohibition, Jim Crow, and the Great Depression. The breathtaking pace of social and economic change blurred traditional boundaries, leading to impassioned debates about the proper roles for men and women in French society. The French fascination during these years with *la garçonne*—the modern woman whose androgynous sexual proclivities extended to both male and female partners and who embodied both women's emancipation and their depravity—spoke to a rejection in some circles of conservative attitudes toward female sexuality and gender performance.[49] This was especially true in the bohemian worlds of art and entertainment—of Azenor, Flavie, and Solidor—where an amused tolerance of female sexual excess prevailed.

World War I's devastating losses nevertheless exacerbated France's natalist panic, resulting in the French Parliament's passage on July 31, 1920, of some of Western Europe's most draconian laws forbidding abortion and contraception. Dominant French attitudes toward female same-sex desire cannot be uncoupled from these fears of declining fertility: here was an unruly demographic whose sexual proclivities threatened state power, since, in the words of Adolphe Willette, the architect of the Moulin Rouge, "sapphic morals damage repopulation."[50] In their rejection of male control, sapphists menaced the patriarchy. The predicament was not just that *Madame ne veut pas d'enfant* (Madame does not want a child), as the title of Clément Vautel's accusatory 1924 novel proclaimed; it was that *some* mesdames did not want a man either. And with good reason.

Although glorified between the wars as the *reine du foyer* or "queen of the household," French women were largely subordinate to French men in all arenas of their lives.[51] While many women had single-handedly supported themselves and their families by taking on male jobs in factories and businesses during four long years of conflict, in the interwar years they still could not serve as jurors (until 1938) or vote or hold political office (until 1944). Married women could not take a job or open a bank account without their husbands' permission (until 1965) and were subject to "paternal authority" (until 1970). While a life freed from men and male oppression consequently held multiple attractions, in this repressive environment those advocating for women's rights mainly distanced themselves from association with "the lesbian" to avoid weakening support for their cause.[52]

In 1931 the economic crisis initiated by the 1929 crash of the American stock market hit France. By 1933 the triumph of the Nazi Party in Germany and the rise of totalitarianism across Europe presaged mounting dangers for Jews, political dissidents, Romani, the differently abled, and homosexuals. As the noose tightened around mainly male homosexual freedoms in European metropolises (namely Berlin), "Paris essentially became the new center of homosexual life."[53] In this climate, the specter of a homosexual influx raised French fears. In 1934 the literary critic Étienne Rey asked: "Do we now have to welcome all the *pédérastes* [homosexual men] from across the Rhine, chased from their country by the moralizing furor of Hitler?"[54] In response to such outcries the Paris prefect of police, Jean Chiappe, clamped down on same-sex behavior and intensified surveillance under the guise of discouraging criminal activity. His efforts were largely unsuccessful but betrayed a growing French concern with homosexuality—both male and female.[55] In this inhospitable climate many people either suppressed same-sex desires or pursued them with difficulty. The contrast between the experiences of those who had the confidence, the motivation, or the means to frequent queer venues and those who did not could be extreme.[56] Importantly, while queer subcultures—especially women's—expanded radically during the 1920s and 1930s, when queer visibility increased, the divisions between sexual practices and sexual identities hardened under the relentless pressure of social sanction.

In 1931 investigative journalist Marise Querlin published *Femmes sans hommes: Choses vues* (Women without men: things seen).[57] Penned in an accessible salacious style, the widely read exposé, which covered "lesbianism" in history, bars, convents, boarding schools, prisons, law, and medicine, did much to disseminate negative stereotypes about "the lesbian" to French audiences.[58] Like earlier sexologists, Querlin divides lesbians by gender performance. According to a review in *Le petit parisien*, whereas Querlin urged acceptance of masculine women whose "tormented passions" were "innate" (in Querlin's words, "nature left them between two poles: neither fig nor grape"), she vehemently denounced feminine women (the "conquests of these androgynes") who abused same-sex desires as part of a "villainous race for cash."[59] Feminine women, she explained, have "exactly the same character as other [normal] women, the same appetites, the same coquetries" but are so overtly sexual that "in order not to run the risk of being possessed by a male, they choose female lovers."[60] The feminine lesbian's hyperbolic desires also manifest as a rapacious greed for worldly goods. And again like the sexologists before her, it is these women Querlin condemns most: they practice homosexual acts purely for sex and profit.

Thus, if by the early 1930s the masculine lesbian was understood in France as an active invert, the feminine lesbian was increasingly imagined as both passive *and* active: her powerlessness before a mannish tribade's advances was evidence of her unfettered appetites for either sex or money. As Carolyn J. Dean remarks, this conflicted vision in which female desire was figured as both submissive and aggressive increasingly troubled conventional ideas about gender, undermining the theory that sexual desire could be clearly divided between a binary active-male/passive-female model.[61] The sociomedical project of identifying and then condemning the figure of the feminine lesbian was a product of the drive to control an increasingly unruly and emancipated female demographic. The very existence of this pathologizing project hints at the fear that women who desired women were both alarmingly numerous and (particularly if feminine) hidden in plain sight.[62] When women like Azenor, Flavie, and Solidor pursued women romantically or—as in Solidor's case—courted them in their businesses, they subsequently did so against this ever more complicated backdrop of assumptions and arguments about the nature of female sexual desire.

SUZY SOLIDOR: "THE STRANGE DESTINY OF A WOMAN WITHOUT MEN"

The illegitimate daughter of a domestic servant and her wealthy employer, Suzy Solidor was born Suzanne Louise Marie Marion in Saint-Malo, Brittany, in 1900. Following her mother's marriage to a sailor seven years later, the young girl acquired a new last name: Rocher.[63] By 1915, the fifteen-year-old Solidor (then Suzanne Rocher) had obtained her driver's license and began volunteering for the war effort.[64] She spent the last two years of the conflict working for the ambulance corps and chauffeuring members of the military elite across northwestern France. Although Solidor later denied having any amorous adventures while enlisted—beyond the troubling thrill of combing another female driver's luxuriant tresses (a practice that invoked blushing and "an enveloping but agreeable torpor")—she recalls being "more than a little proud of [her] military allure."[65] When the war ended Solidor sought work in Paris, a choice that opened paths both to her first full-fledged same-sex relationship and to her subsequent career as a cabaret singer and proprietor.

Between the early 1930s and the late 1950s Suzy Solidor (known as the "French Dietrich" for her wartime rendition of the celebrated song "Lili Marlene") was among the most famous cabaret artists in France. Within months of launching La Vie Parisienne in Paris in 1933, the alluring Solidor, with her cropped flaxen hair, husky voice, dramatic diction, and repertoire of torch songs, salty sea shanties (her forte), erotic ballads, and poetry (she recited works by Verlaine, Rilke, Cocteau, and Francis Carco), had cemented her reputation as an icon of modernity and sexual liberation. Her success was so immediate that in 1935 she was chosen as the first singer to be broadcast on French TV, when the new technology was still in its infancy.[66] By the end of the 1930s the general public was anxious to know—and emulate—her every move: "Did Suzy Solidor tan in the summer?" "Did she want to be a nun as a child?" "Is she singing in Deauville?" "Has she been to the races?" "Does she have a pet monkey?" "What is her astrological forecast?" "What wine does she prefer?" "Is she a feminist?" "Has she traveled to Warsaw?" "Or Antibes?" "Madame, Mademoiselle, you can win 250 francs: Do you look like Suzy? Submit your photo now!"[67]

In addition to performing almost nightly for over thirty years either in her own Parisian cabarets or on stages throughout France, Europe, and—eventually—around the globe, Solidor cut records; was broadcast on radio; published novels; acted in film and theatre; graced charity benefits, art openings, ship launchings, and the extension of new metro lines; gambled at horse races; attended ballet and opera galas; and was regularly written up in the press and featured on newsreels and television, attracting the fascinated attention of French audiences.[68] Her popularity endured even during World War II, when she notoriously welcomed German officers into her cabaret. After the Liberation, Solidor was charged with collaboration and (despite her protestations of innocence) convicted of the criminal offense of national indignity.[69] Following an enforced hiatus, she returned to French stages, and her celebrity grew. By the time of her death in 1983, Solidor had become one of the most painted women in the world; a selection of over 225 portraits of the singer (many of them nudes) by artists from Pablo Picasso, Tamara de Lempicka, Georges Braque, and Marie Laurencin to Tsuguharu Foujita and Francis Bacon hangs on permanent display at the Château Grimaldi in Haut-de-Cagnes on the French Riviera. These portraits graced the walls of every cabaret she owned. Indeed, in an act of unadorned egotism, the singer never performed without them; her favorite paintings even traveled with her when she toured abroad.[70]

Solidor's first cabaret, La Vie Parisienne, was the platform that propelled her to fame. The cabaret targeted a mixed-gender audience but held special attraction for an upscale clientele of women who loved women. Hélène Azenor observed: "It was not at all the same patrons as the Bal de la Montagne Sainte-Geneviève, it was very snobbish, and Suzy Solidor was also a big snob."[71] Solidor's penchant for women was central to La Vie Parisienne's appeal.[72] She even recorded the album *Paris-Lesbien* in homage to her female fans. Songs like "Obsession," where she declares, "Chaque femme je la veux / Des talons jusqu'aux cheveux" (I want every woman / from her heels to her head), and especially "Ouvre" (Open) (which Solidor released as a 78 in 1934) left no doubt about the direction of at least *some* of her desires:

Ouvre tes bras pour m'enlacer	Open your arms to embrace me
Ouvre tes seins que je m'y pose	Open your breasts so that I can lay upon them
Ouvre aux fureurs de mon baiser	Open to the fury of my kiss
Ta lèvre rose	Your pink lip[73]

And yet, while Solidor recognized that her unconventional sexuality was a critical part of her public image, she also recognized the importance of attracting a male audience. The care with which Solidor used the media to both associate *and* disaggregate same-sex erotic practices and gender variance illustrates how fully she understood the pros and cons of lesbian identification in French society at this time.

Solidor exemplified the post-WWI figure of *la garçonne*—the liberated modern woman depicted in Victor Margueritte's 1922 novel of the same name who cropped her locks, shortened her skirts, shed her corsets, and slept indiscriminately with men and women alike—except that, unlike the novel's youthful heroine Monique, Solidor ultimately refused to relinquish her female lovers.[74] *La garçonne* (The tomboy) was a wild morality tale in which the charming protagonist leaves her philandering fiancé for an affair with a lesbian, only to return to him in the end.[75] Despite being banned by the Catholic Church and excoriated in the press, the book (which takes its title from the feminization of the French word for boy, *garçon*) became a publishing phenomenon.[76] *La garçonne* also fueled a transformation in female fashion that blurred the lines between masculine and feminine sartorial display in ways that became associated with the nascent figures of both the modern woman and the lesbian. The popularity of songs like Georgel's 1923 "La garçonne" ("La garçonne / La garçonne /

Les hommes, pour elle, ce n'est pas son lot" or "The tomboy / The tomboy / Men, for her, that's not her thing") reinforced the latter connection. The book sold over a million copies by the end of 1929, was translated into twelve languages, and made into films in 1923, 1936 (with Solidor playing the opium-smoking lesbian cabaret singer Anika who seduces the female lead, played by Marie Bell), and 1957 (with Solidor's protégé Colette Mars as the lesbian seductress, Nichette, opposite Andrée Debar's Monique).[77] In the 1936 film Edith Piaf (in her cinematic debut) sang the film's title song "Quand même." Mars sang a new theme song (titled "La garçonne," like the film) in the 1957 movie remake, performed the song on television, and released it in France on a 45-rpm record for Columbia Records in 1958.[78]

Director Jean de Limur modeled the sapphic cabaret in his 1936 film version on Solidor's cabaret La Vie Parisienne. Footage of Solidor provides a precious glimpse inside a (fictional) sapphic cabaret's walls. The key scene, at once representation and caricature in which Solidor sings and then seduces Monique (Marie Bell), depicts Solidor surrounded by her own portraits. Intermingled among heterosexual couples are the "lesbians" (discernible by their masculine dress, harsh lipstick, and severe, mannish hairstyles), who are watching as Solidor performs. Clad in a formfitting sparkly black sheath of a cocktail dress, her hips and breasts undulating, Solidor is an icon of femininity, excepting her deep, full-throated voice, which seems to "issue," as Jean Cocteau once bluntly observed, "from her cunt."[79] Like the narrative it is modeled after, the film's dialogue shames female same-sex desire while eroticizing it ("And then you see . . . we are the mistakes, the good-for-nothings, not even useful to make kids," Solidor intones solemnly as she moves in on Monique before she and the film's heroine retire together to an opium den in the cellar below), thus walking the delicate line between prohibition and provocation necessary for evading censorship while attracting audiences.

Importantly, the film highlights two different models of sexual subjectivity: on the one hand there is the lesbian (Solidor's Anika, as well as Niquette, played by the French actress Arletty, and "the singer" played by Piaf), and on the other there is the modern woman (Monique, played by Bell) who (perhaps like Flavie?) is simply sowing her wild oats. Significantly, the fact that Monique sleeps with a lesbian doesn't make her one. Although cast as an unrepentant lesbian in the film, Solidor's insistently feminine self-fashioning in the press as a sexually ambiguous modern woman and *not* as a lesbian indicates that she understood very well the public stakes of this division.

In 1936 Solidor granted an interview to her friend Joseph Kessel for the first issue of his new tabloid magazine *Confessions*, a gossip rag whose title marks the Foucauldian discursive performance so peculiar to modern sexual subjectivity: the injunction to speak of sex under the dictates of secrecy.[80] Marlene Dietrich, the writer Colette, the cabaret star Tino Rossi, the aviator Jean Mermoz, the novelist Georges Simenon, and the actor, director, and playwright Sacha Guitry were also featured in early issues of the publication. Despite being a darling of the press, Solidor's interview, which was published as "Suzy Solidor révèle son étrange destin de femme sans homme" (Suzy Solidor reveals her strange destiny of a woman without men), stands as the only printed source where the singer speaks at length in the first person. It was printed twice, first on November 26 and again on December 3, 1936.[81] Given her ambitions as a writer—Solidor published four novels between 1939 and 1944—it seems possible that if she didn't actually author the article, she played a key role in shaping it.[82] In countless later appearances on radio and television and in the press Solidor repeatedly recasts stories first told here. Despite its tabloid origins the document stands as a precious example of the public production of female same-sex sexual subjectivity in interwar France.

Three seductive photographs of the singer illustrate the November 26 version of the article: in the first, Solidor stands on tiptoe on the prow of a ship, her lace bathing suit revealing erect nipples; in the second, a close-up, she reclines nude, her back arched across the page and her hands cupping her naked breasts, lush dark lipstick defining the curve of her mouth as she gazes out at the reader (fig. 1.2); in the last, an elegant black evening dress cinched with a diamond clasp reveals her bare broad shoulders, her chin is raised defiantly, and her platinum hair glistens.[83] Her signature, "Suzy Solidor," is scrawled across the bottom of this image (an unidentified still taken from the film *La garçonne*), thus sealing her celebrity status.[84] The images from the December 3, 1936, version of the article are even more provocative; they include a two-page spread of Solidor lying in the surf fully nude, her arms crossed behind her head, smiling directly at the camera.

The opening paragraph begins with an exhausted Suzy disrobing at 3 a.m. in her tiny bedroom above her antique store on the Quai Voltaire.[85] She portrays herself as sensual, feminine, attractive to other women and in charge of her own life. "Coiffed like Joan of Arc with a cap of straight hair the color of straw" and a "long black fur coat" open at the neck to reveal "a golden throat" still "tanned from last summer's sun," Solidor claims to be "tired of standing, tired of singing . . . tired of friends known and unknown . . . tired even of the insistent admiration of the female outcasts

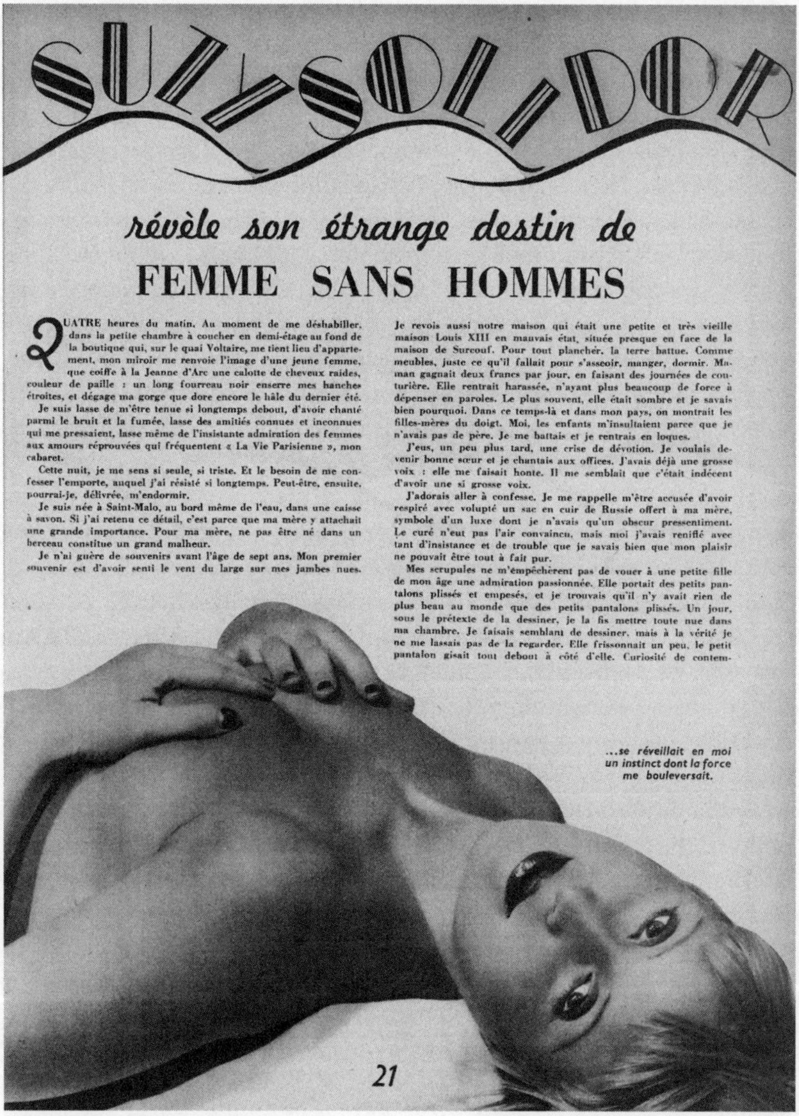

SUZY SOLIDOR

révèle son étrange destin de

FEMME SANS HOMMES

QUATRE heures du matin. Au moment de me déshabiller, dans la petite chambre à coucher en demi-étage au fond de la boutique qui, sur le quai Voltaire, me tient lieu d'appartement, mon miroir me renvoie l'image d'une jeune femme, que coiffe à la Jeanne d'Arc une calotte de cheveux raides, couleur de paille : un long fourreau noir enserre mes hanches étroites, et dégage ma gorge que dore encore le hâle du dernier été.

Je suis lasse de m'être tenue si longtemps debout, d'avoir chanté parmi le bruit et la fumée, lasse des amitiés connues et inconnues qui me pressaient, lasse même de l'insistante admiration des femmes aux amours réprouvées qui fréquentent « La Vie Parisienne », mon cabaret.

Cette nuit, je me sens si seule, si triste. Et le besoin de me confesser l'emporte, auquel j'ai résisté si longtemps. Peut-être, ensuite, pourrai-je, délivrée, m'endormir.

Je suis née à Saint-Malo, au bord même de l'eau, dans une caisse à savon. Si j'ai retenu ce détail, c'est parce que ma mère y attachait une grande importance. Pour ma mère, ne pas être né dans un berceau constitue un grand malheur.

Je n'ai guère de souvenirs avant l'âge de sept ans. Mon premier souvenir est d'avoir senti le vent du large sur mes jambes nues. Je revois aussi notre maison qui était une petite et très vieille maison Louis XIII en mauvais état, située presque en face de la maison de Surcouf. Pour tout plancher, la terre battue. Comme meubles, juste ce qu'il fallait pour s'asseoir, manger, dormir. Maman gagnait deux francs par jour, en faisant des journées de couturière. Elle rentrait harassée, n'ayant plus beaucoup de force à dépenser en paroles. Le plus souvent, elle était sombre et je savais bien pourquoi. Dans ce temps-là et dans mon pays, on montrait les filles-mères du doigt. Moi, les enfants m'insultaient parce que je n'avais pas de père. Je me battais et je rentrais en loques.

J'eus, un peu plus tard, une crise de dévotion. Je voulais devenir bonne sœur et je chantais aux offices. J'avais déjà une grosse voix : elle me faisait honte. Il me semblait que c'était indécent d'avoir une si grosse voix.

J'adorais aller à confesse. Je me rappelle m'être accusée d'avoir respiré avec volupté un sac en cuir de Russie offert à ma mère, symbole d'un luxe dont je n'avais qu'un obscur pressentiment. Le curé n'eut pas l'air convaincu, mais moi j'avais reniflé avec tant d'insistance et de trouble que je savais bien que mon plaisir ne pouvait être tout à fait pur.

Mes scrupules ne m'empêchèrent pas de vouer à une petite fille de mon âge une admiration passionnée. Elle portait des petits pantalons plissés et empesés, et je trouvais qu'il n'y avait rien de plus beau au monde que des petits pantalons plissés. Un jour, sous le prétexte de la dessiner, je la fis mettre toute nue dans ma chambre. Je faisais semblant de dessiner, mais à la vérité je ne me lassais pas de la regarder. Elle frissonnait un peu, le petit pantalon gisait tout debout à côté d'elle. Curiosité de contem-

...se réveillait en moi un instinct dont la force me bouleversait.

21

FIGURE 1.2: "Suzy Solidor Reveals Her Strange Destiny of a Woman without Men." *Confessions*, no. 1 (December 3, 1936). Courtesy of the Bibliothèque nationale de France.

who frequent 'La Vie Parisienne,' my cabaret."[86] The world-weary confessional tone ("tonight, I feel so alone, so sad") with its explicit mention of "female outcasts" is voyeuristically seductive, both stoking excitement and playing to the reader's sympathies while presuming public knowledge about the sexual deviance implied therein. Solidor's description of her childhood, from early deprivation (a home with an earthen floor) and shame ("the other children insulted me because I had no father") to her first erotic explorations with a neighbor girl ("I made her undress completely in my room") for which she was "shut up, without understanding why, in a closet," paints a picture at once savage and rebellious. Like a naughty fairytale, the narrative reaches its first climax when the statuesque Solidor (then Suzanne Rocher) meets her prince in the form of Yvonne de Bremond d'Ars, a wealthy *demoiselle antiquaire* (a lady antique dealer) whom she refers to here as "Mademoiselle."

In Solidor's version, a friend aimed to introduce her to the couture designer Jeanne Lanvin "via the intermediary" of "twenty-eight-year-old" Mademoiselle, whose antique shop on the exclusive rue du Faubourg Saint-Honoré was next door to Lanvin's famous fashion house.[87] The fact that Solidor inflates Mademoiselle's age by three years—Bremond d'Ars was only twenty-five—is not anodyne since it accentuates Solidor's relative youth and vulnerability. The Lanvin connection may have been fabricated; it has been suggested that Solidor presented herself directly to Bremond d'Ars for a position as a domestic servant or salesgirl.[88] Journalist and radio producer Hélène Hazéra, a trans activist and member of the militant 1970s drag group known as the Gazolines, provides still another alternative: she told me that Solidor and Bremond d'Ars likely met "in a brothel for women."[89] Solidor's biographer Marie-Hélène Carbonel disputes this idea, but given the girl's modest origins the story does not seem unreasonable.[90] Regardless of circumstance, Mademoiselle's solicitous attentions definitively altered Solidor's life.

In *Confessions*, Solidor depicts Mademoiselle as a classic example of the female invert: Bremond d'Ars was "dark, small, solidly planted on her flat shoes, an eternal cigarette between her fingers," with "hair shaved shorter than any man" and a "masculine-cut navy-blue suit" that revealed "an almost complete absence of breasts." Defending Bremond d'Ars's mannish sartorial choices, Solidor recounts an event from Mademoiselle's youth that took place in the fashionable beach town of Deauville on the Normandy coast. She explains how Mademoiselle's father, "who suffered a great deal from his daughter's 'particular' style," once gave the girl five thousand francs "and pleaded with her to have herself made a dress 'like everyone else wears.'" Solidor notes, "Mademoiselle did so. When she entered the baccarat lounge the next night wearing a sumptuous stylish gown, the gamblers stopped short, their jaws' dropped. A sort of pall fell over the hall." Several Englishmen were absolutely "scandalized" that "a man disguised as a woman had been permitted to enter the casino." Solidor then proposes that for "many women" wearing male attire is necessary in order to "pass unremarked and seem decent." "It would be unjust," Solidor concludes, to condemn "women of [Mademoiselle's] species" for "one might as well demand that a fish become a bird."[91] The comment bears noting: Solidor both identifies Bremond d'Ars as possessing a different form of sexual subjectivity (she is another "species") and naturalizes that difference.

While we have no proof that Solidor read sexology, her familiarity with novels like Radclyffe Hall's *The Well of Loneliness* and the sexual and gender practices it describes infuses the language she uses to narrate her life story.[92] That said, while Solidor's description of Mademoiselle as a mannish *pure* (a colloquial term for a "real" lesbian) perfectly conforms with theories of congenital gender inversion, Solidor was herself reluctant to be branded with the corresponding stereotype of the "feminine lesbian." Solidor's self-presentation thus speaks to the growing pressure that definitions linking feminine gender performance with heterosexuality exerted on women's sexual lives. Her stance is not hard to comprehend when we take the odious vision of the feminine lesbian described in literary, medical, and popular discourse into account. It also complicates contemporary perceptions that might simply label Bremond d'Ars and Solidor as a butch/femme lesbian couple, a contrast presumptively borne out in a studio portrait of the young lovers taken in the 1920s (fig. 1.3).

I want to insist on the slippery ambiguity of this self-conscious self-fashioning as well as accentuate the ways in which it sometimes escaped Solidor's control. Solidor tried to avoid social condemnation while simultaneously reserving the right to flirt with both the "female outcasts" *and* the male admirers who flocked to her cabaret. She thus provides us with a metric through which to gauge the range of socially acceptable female sexual and gender behaviors at this time, even as she becomes both entrapped in and pushes against (as we've just seen in her justification for "Mademoiselle's" choice of dress) their boundaries. By way of further example, let's look at how Solidor describes her induction into the cult of sapphic love (and her departures from it) through the remainder of the *Confessions* interview.

"One night" after a cautious six-month "courtship" during which

FIGURE 1.3: Studio portrait of Suzy Solidor (*left*) and Yvonne de Bremond d'Ars, (*right*) taken in the early 1920s. Photographer unknown. Courtesy of Alexandre Dupouy and Les Archives d'Éros.

Solidor became greatly "attached to Mademoiselle," "a terrible storm broke over Paris." "Terrified," the nineteen-year-old claims to have sought solace beneath Mademoiselle's coverlet ("I trembled like a leaf"). Seemingly aware that the story is weak (would anyone believe that this hooligan child who had chauffeured soldiers across the Western Front truly feared a thunderstorm?), Solidor concedes, "in truth, I took too much pleasure in our life together to call it scandalous" or to accuse Mademoiselle of "abduction" or "perversion." Determined to dignify her confession by "neither dissimulating nor dramatizing," Solidor nevertheless avers "each day a certain number of women are perverted by expert corruptors." Thus, if there is a frisson of guilt here, the confessional narrative nonetheless insinuates that Bremond d'Ars (who "felt a disgust for men that was congenital and absolute") corrupted her.

Solidor reveals that her relationship with Bremond d'Ars was transactional: she describes how Bremond d'Ars asked Solidor to work for her, promising, "I will make you the most elegant, and the happiest of women. You will have jewels, dresses, and furs. I am twenty-eight [*sic*] years old, and I have looked forever for a tall, thin girl with long, long legs and hair like silk." Solidor wryly notes that she hadn't realized that the job of salesgirl had such stringent physical requirements but coyly observes that she "was so naive that it all seemed very marvelous," and she accepted her patroness's offer "with joy." "One year after my arrival in Paris," she remarks, "my little hatbox in my hand, I had my car, jewels, dresses from Lanvin that I had dreamed of wearing as a model, and I could order as many as I wanted." Here, too, Solidor appears oblivious to the possibility that her public will read this admission as proof of precisely the type of avaricious greed considered characteristic of the feminine lesbian.

Seduced (Solidor was emphatically *not*, she states, "a born tribade") by Bremond d'Ars, who played Pygmalion to her Galatea, Solidor's eleven-year sapphic liaison with the antique dealer transformed the Breton peasant into a worldly Parisian sophisticate. Bremond d'Ars ensured that Solidor was given lessons in comportment, diction, music, and drama, but she was also schooled in the "cult of sapphism." Whether in her enormous bed with its heavy white satin baldachin decorated with violets (a symbol of sapphic love popularized in the poetry of Renée Vivien), through paintings ("nothing but female nudes"), or in assiduously chosen books written by a literary homosexual elite, Solidor reports, "Mademoiselle composed with patience the atmosphere propitious to my initiation."[93] Afraid that Solidor would find men tempting (a thought that suggests that Solidor might not be a "true" lesbian and could become "a traitor to the cause"), Bremond d'Ars insisted that the couple "frequent only women and male homosexuals."

Their scandalous love affair was soon popular knowledge. It was in Deauville in the early 1920s that Solidor first captured the attention of the press. Mademoiselle Bremond d'Ars "exhibited" her, Suzy recalls, "with a kind of ostentatious rage." Photographers went mad for the supple girl with the ravishing athletic figure dressed in a fishnet bathing costume sewn of mother-of-pearl and artificial roses, her naked feet bound in Greek sandals ("in the style of 'Lesbos'"), gallivanting on the beach with Bremond d'Ars, sometimes accompanied by a large dog.[94] It was also at this time that Bremond d'Ars began to commission the paintings of Solidor that later flanked the walls of every cabaret she ever owned. Solidor reports that the relationship "attained its paroxysm" when, in celebration of the tenth anniversary of their "marriage," Mademoiselle threw a lavish party and presented her with *Le livre d'amour* (The book of love), a collection of engravings by noted artists of which there was only one printing. According to Solidor, "All the lesbians, all the notorious inverts of Paris," were in attendance.

When Solidor subsequently returned to her native Brittany for a friend's wedding, "rumors reached all the way to the ears of *maman*" (Solidor's mother) after Bremond d'Ars posted her lover a telegram ("which must have cost a fortune") cautioning: "Take care of your little silken belly in that great cathedral, where it is so cold." Solidor was grateful to Bremond d'Ars but had gradually begun to chafe under the mantle of what had become an obsessive adulation. Soon thereafter a suffocated Solidor broke free, and she did it in the most dramatic way possible: this woman who had been "patiently taught" to see herself as "an impenitent, definitive, classifiable lesbian" slept with a man. She reports that to her "great surprise" she found his touch agreeable: "Despite myself, an instinct rose up in me, the power of which profoundly confused me." She says that she told him that she loved him. The damage to her relationship to Bremond d'Ars was, as she knew it would be, irreversible, even if, as she also observed, "that day I discovered that between me and a man there was a physical barrier" that no man could ever overcome.

The balance of the interview is disarmingly abstruse. By 1933 Solidor had definitively severed ties with Bremond d'Ars and begun reincarnating herself as a cabaret artist under the stage name "Suzy Solidor."[95] She describes how she first took leave "of my little room" on the rue Saint-Honoré and—with financial assistance from Maurice Barbezat (the French distributor of luxury Packard automobiles), whom she presents as her first male lover—opened her own antique store on the Quai Voltaire, mordantly called (in a backhanded stab at Bremond d'Ars?) "La Grande Mademoiselle." It was there that she began to sing and recite poetry, performing first for friends who paid a small fee for cocktails consumed during her evening gatherings. When the size of her audiences exceeded the size of her flat, Solidor "kept it as [her] private domicile" and opened La Vie Parisienne at 12 rue Sainte-Anne on the Right Bank, decking the cabaret's walls with her growing gallery of portraits. Some say Barbezat backed her new enterprise, but the person listed as co-owner on the documents of incorporation held by the City of Paris was Line Bady, a Belgian performing artist (whose real name was Jeanne Ferdinande Abel, née Pens) described by the Parisian prefect of police as Solidor's "very intimate friend" and a "member of a special world of inverts . . . who surely frequented drug addicts."[96]

By the end of *Confessions*' exposé Solidor is calling herself "a woman divided": "How can I be responsible today," she concludes, for this confused state of affairs, in which she is sometimes drawn to the "rough protective shoulders of a man" but at others yearns to press her "sterile flanks" against a "young, weak [female] creature who is clearly neither friend nor child?" If Solidor makes no secret of her desire for women (using this information to titillate her audiences, to woo her lesbian following, and to keep her cabaret and herself in the limelight), she just as adroitly manipulates the topic of her relationships with men. One crucial way she does so is via the (fabricated?) story of her torrid love affair with the married aviator Jean Mermoz, a far-right supporter of the Croix de Feu who died when his plane tragically (or conveniently for Solidor?) crashed into the sea on December 7, 1936, while enroute from Dakar, Senegal, to Natal, Brazil. Solidor's *Confessions* interview was published eleven days before his death.

In her popular 2007 biography of the singer, Marie-Hélène Carbonel plays up the significance of Solidor's passionate love affairs with men; as she explained to me, Solidor "was not a [lesbian] militant, just a woman without taboos who was prodigiously free."[97] Carbonel determinedly maintains that Mermoz was the "great love of Suzy's life."[98] Solidor certainly seemed to want the world to understand him this way; in her cabaret she read Mermoz's passionate love letters aloud before appreciative audiences and flaunted the fabulously expensive heart-shaped diamond brooch shot through with an arrow dripping blood-red rubies that she claimed the aviator had given her prior to his death.[99] This public display of normative heterosexuality was strikingly performative. Whether it was sincere is impossible to verify.

Solidor never lived with a man. After her eleven-year liaison with Bremond d'Ars, Suzy had only two enduring relationships. The first was with

Doris Lemaire, a dark-haired, dark-skinned Jew who worked as a double for the Black performer Josephine Baker (to whom she bore a striking resemblance). Lemaire made her screen debut with the actress Edwige Feuillère in *Les aventures du roi Pausole* (The adventures of King Pausole)—the sapphic significance of which is discussed in chapter 4. Packard magnate Maurice Barbezat (who remained in Solidor's orbit as either lover or admirer) apparently chose to ignore the women's passion for one another. Solidor's second and more significant relationship was with Daisy Marie-Thérèse Bartholoni, the Baroness de Vaufreland, a beauty eleven years her junior who Hélène Hazéra describes as "the last of the great Parisian courtesans."[100] Daisy's husband, the Baron de Vaufreland, was a known homosexual. For a time, this arrangement suited them all. However, within a few years (around 1938), Daisy had her marriage annulled (pleading "non-consummation") around the same time that Solidor bought a home outside Paris in Médan, which she playfully christened "The Well of Loneliness" in homage to Radclyffe Hall. The writer Colette's daughter, Colette de Jouvenel (who had left her own husband for a woman in 1935 after just two months of marriage), decorated it. Daisy was a regular guest. Ever solicitous of Daisy's welfare, when Solidor fled the country in 1946 after being convicted of national indignity, she convinced the rich industrialist Paul Elion to look after Daisy in her absence. When Solidor returned to France and moved in 1960 to Haut-de-Cagnes, a medieval bourg of some 650 inhabitants perched above the seaside seductions of Cagnes-sur-Mer on the Côte d'Azur, Daisy joined her. Doris and her then girlfriend followed. Solidor installed them in lodgings nearby. In 1973, once more concerned for Daisy's future, Solidor again turned to Elion for help; the businessman agreed to marry Daisy and buy her an apartment in Neuilly-sur-Seine outside Paris. The newlyweds spent weekends together, with Daisy splitting her time between Elion in the north and Solidor in the south for the last years of their lives. When Suzy died, she left her estate to Daisy, but her lover was obliged to pay rights of succession because the women were not considered family. They are now buried side by side in a cemetery near the beach in Cagnes-sur-Mer. Doris outlived them both.

Like Solidor, Yvonne de Bremond d'Ars arranged a subsequent female lover's heterosexual marriage for pragmatic ends; she convinced her own father to marry her girlfriend Jeanne Marguerite Borgarello, which permitted Jeanne to inherit his fortune and keep the money in the family. Jeanne, Yvonne, and Monsieur de Bremond d'Ars lived together on the rue de Picpus in Paris until his death in 1939.[101] Both Solidor and Yvonne de Bremond d'Ars thus availed themselves of the economic privileges of marriage while remaining single, obtaining greater financial security for their lovers (and by extension themselves) by shifting the burden for financial support to men. In Bremond d'Ars's case the arrangement ensured that Jeanne could profit from Yvonne's wealth after her death without paying (as Daisy had had to) rights of succession.

Some women (like Daisy) married men who were uninterested in women in order to retain mutual sexual freedoms. Women who remained single (like Solidor and Bremond d'Ars) often conducted affairs, whether lengthy or passing, with married women. For example, Frede (the "most famous lesbian in the world" discussed in this book's introduction) was involved with numerous married women before she settled down with Miki, including Marlene Dietrich, with whom she had a four-year relationship between 1936 and 1940; the Mexican film star María Félix (whose departure prompted Frede to attempt suicide); and Lana Marconi, the much younger actress wife of Sacha Guitry.[102] Married women who loved women, moreover, did not always conduct their sapphic affairs in secret. Sometimes, they arranged their liaisons openly, often with the blessings of the men involved. Indeed, during the five years that Lana and Frede spent together, Frede lived at length with both her female lover and her lover's husband, who turned a blind eye.[103] Not only does this tell us that married women were not considered off limits by women interested in other women at this time, but it also suggests that heterosexual marriage was not the bastion of heterosexual monogamy that many now believe it to be.[104]

Solidor's insistence that as the "masculine invert" Bremond d'Ars was the "true" deviant in their relationship reflects the discourses on female homosexuality that were then dominant in the public sphere. Some of these discourses introduced a new distinction: that between the mannish "real" lesbian and those who cross-dressed for profit. Journalist, psychoanalyst, and undercover reporter Maryse Choisy, who passed herself off as a lesbian to gain access to women's spaces (including Natalie Clifford Barney's private salon and the sapphic cabaret Le Fétiche) for her 1928 bestseller on prostitution in France, *Un mois chez les filles* (A month with the girls), was among those interested in the "lesbian for hire."[105] She divides Le Fétiche's female staff into masculine "authentic lesbians" (like Petit Louis, "une 'pure'" [a pure one]) and both masculine and feminine "others" who just "do it for the dough."[106] Like many, Choisy condemned the latter category but argued that since masculine inversion was congenital, women in the former category (i.e., "pure" lesbians) were innocent. In contrast, Choisy's descriptions of "heterosexual" women who cross-dressed on the job (and sometimes illegally bedded female customers for financial gain) complicated the image of the feminine lesbian and demonstrated the difficulty of definitively linking masculine gender performance to lesbian desire. Confusingly, Choisy also implies that we can somehow distinguish between "authentic" (i.e., masculine) lesbians and those who impersonate them for profit.

Eve Kosofsky Sedgwick writes that "the importance—an importance—of the category 'homosexual' comes not necessarily from its regulatory relation to a nascent or already-constituted minority of homosexual people or desires, but from its potential for giving whoever wields it a structuring definitional leverage over the whole range of male bonds that shape the social constitution." The "amorphousness of the body of 'the sexual,'" she continues (referencing Foucault), "is where its political power resides, in a sexually repressive modern context."[107] Suzy Solidor wielded power over the contested terrain of female sexual identity by leveraging the contrast between her arguably more "normative" sexual subjectivity and that embodied by Yvonne de Bremond d'Ars. Solidor's avowed bisexuality ensured that she profited from the "male bonds that shape the social constitution." In differentiating herself from the "deviant" Bremond d'Ars, she also defends herself against accusations of crossing what Sedgwick terms the "invisible, carefully blurred, always-already-crossed line" that (in our case) separates a "normal" woman from a lesbian.[108] By embracing "lesbian" identity, in contrast, Hélène Azenor rejected the notion that such a sexuality was deviant. As for Flavie, she seems to have avoided such categories entirely and simply followed her heart—or her desires.

Suzy Solidor's sexual subjectivity was insistently framed in the media throughout her life in contradictory terms: she was alternately presented (or presented herself) as an unrepentant lesbian, a bisexual *femme moderne* (modern woman), and a heterosexual romantic who preferred men but was "divided" from them thanks to her deviant upbringing.[109] Possessed of a "military allure" in her teens, she aggressively flaunted her femininity in her cabarets before adopting masculine dress and even male pronouns toward the end of her life.[110] Public perceptions remain confused. In 1945, police files identify her as "une lesbienne notoire" (a notorious lesbian); in 1947, the police argued that Suzy was "not exclusively lesbian" but only used lesbian desire "as a publicity ploy."[111] This latter argument might certainly apply to her liaison with Jean Mermoz. However, the fractious question of Solidor's "true" sexual subjectivity is, if not immaterial, at least not the point. What matters in a queer critical approach is what Solidor's life and the packaging of her desires for public consumption can tell us about what is at stake in assigning sexual categories at particular historical moments—in this case, in twentieth-century France. The women peripheral to Solidor's narrative—women like Daisy, Doris, and Yvonne de Bremond d'Ars (not to mention all of the Azenors and Flavies who frequented venues like her cabarets)—offer additional perspectives on this picture.

The presentation of Suzy Solidor as a bisexual modern woman (a framing in which she herself participated) downplays her lesbianism in favor of a more heterosexually titillating and, indeed, normalizing stance: Solidor as strong, wild, and sexually ravenous but with a heart possessed only by men. Far from rejecting this image, Solidor embraced it, only intermittently identifying herself publicly as a lesbian. Sexual and gender ambiguity proved more commercially powerful. Despite what we might call the ostentatious displays of sapphic sexual affiliation in which both she and many of her female clientele engaged, Solidor left her reputation and her repertoire open to interpretation. Her sustained appeal was due in part to the ways in which her life and work both reinforced and escaped classification. At the same time, Solidor's story changed over time, generally in response to the tenor of the times. During the conservative post-WWII years, for example, she dropped the narrative about how "Mademoiselle" had inducted her into the cult of Lesbos (which so tantalized Solidor's public between the wars) and presented her relationship with Bremond d'Ars as a purely pragmatic apprenticeship in the antique business.[112]

Whereas Hélène Azenor's memoirs speak to the ignorance surrounding and prejudice against female homosexuality in working-class milieus, Solidor's familiarity with medical explanations for female same-sex desire based on gender inversion demonstrates the popularity of these discourses in certain interwar circles. Her framing of herself as "a woman divided" speaks to the pressure that these theories exerted on women's lives. There would be no need to struggle with, to explain, to repudiate, or to lay blame for her same-sex desires if not for the fact that they were already considered perverse by sectors of the French public. The "Strange Destiny of a Woman without Men" (to quote the title of Solidor's article in *Confessions*) was only strange because French social norms increasingly determined that it was, even as French culture promoted the selfsame erotic desires that resulted in this "strangeness" for financial gain.

CONCLUSION

In the 1960s, during her first year as a student at the Sorbonne, Françoise Flamant (later a member of the first lesbian militant group, the Gouines rouges, or Red Dykes) happened upon the Bal de la Montagne

Sainte-Geneviève when returning home one evening from the Bibliothèque Sainte-Geneviève—an impressive old library located opposite the Panthéon where she frequently studied in the company of a gay male friend. By then the Bal had become "a very strange space," she told me, because it was still "a women's bar like those that existed before the Second World War." With its spiral staircase winding up to a podium on which three tuxedo-wearing women played violins, and with its aging female public practicing what Flamant retrospectively termed "an enormous heterosexual mimicry," she found it "very, very funny." Sometimes Flamant would go there to drink, and "although there were also heterosexual couples there," she underscored that "it was a lesbian club. When I saw the orchestra and the ambience, I knew. There were two such clubs in that street [another lesbian bar had since opened next door] and while that style of woman didn't attract me, it was interesting to know that it existed."[113] "I couldn't identify," she claimed elsewhere, "with these hetero-gendered roles divided between feminine femmes and masculine butches."[114] Flamant's observations testify to the fact that if by the postwar years venues like the Bal de la Montagne Sainte-Geneviève were still understood as "lesbian" (or libertine), the gendered performances practiced there were no longer viewed as modern; they were, rather, relics of a distant past.

At the dawn of the twentieth century the relationship between female same-sex desire and gender inversion fomented considerable debate. In the years that followed, gendered notions of lesbian sexual identity consolidated into two connected types: butch and femme. Suzy Solidor's story, captured in media coverage in the 1930s and 1940s, strengthened public awareness of these types in contradictory ways. On the one hand (particularly when describing her first lover, Yvonne de Bremond d'Ars), Solidor reinforced the legibility of the masculine butch. On the other hand, by refusing to adopt a stable sexual subjectivity, Solidor challenged theories about the lesbian femme. In so doing, she promoted the possibility that feminine women could choose same-sex desire without being labeled "lesbian." At the same time, Solidor sometimes flaunted her reputation as a feminine lesbian—an image the media was eager to promote—thus embodying the very model she purportedly eschewed. To confuse things further, later in life she identified as butch. Solidor's story illustrates that given the plethora of forms that human desire can and does take, neither sexual nor gender identities are givens; both must be reiteratively constructed and constantly defended. Her narrative also reminds us that public, social, and legal sanctions rarely extinguish private sexual practices; indeed, sanctions generally both produce and profit from them.

Finally, the commercialization of private sexuality in popular culture and the press seen here refutes the presumed separation between private and public life on which rights obtain in republican France.

Emergent discourses on "the lesbian" performed the important work of situating an abject sapphic sexual subjectivity within the French public sphere. While the effects of such discourses can be debilitating for the minorities described, they nevertheless fill a "representational void."[115] As such, they delivered a crucial if questionable vocabulary that demanded negotiation. Venues like the Bal de la Montagne Sainte-Geneviève and La Vie Parisienne provided the public forums where these private negotiations could take place, thus facilitating the growth of the subcultures that were essential to the politicization of counterpublics in the post-WWII era. In our conversations, Françoise Flamant hesitantly admitted that when she first visited sapphic spaces like the Bal de la Montagne as a young woman, "I was fascinated, but I was also afraid. I was looking for—What am I? I needed points of reference, and I was lucky because I was Parisian and I could go to these places."[116] If by the 1960s such "points of reference" existed in Paris (and indeed throughout France), it was in no small measure as a result of the efforts of women like Suzy Solidor three decades before.

2

MAPPING THE SAPPHIC CABARET

Women who love women have not always succeeded in carving out commercial spaces within the public sphere.[1] This is certainly true in major Western cities today, where a scant number of lesbian businesses often hug the edges of established gay male neighborhoods.[2] However, during the 1930s at least twenty new sapphic cabarets opened in Paris and its environs.[3] In addition to dramatically increasing the visibility of female same-sex desire in the French capital, their existence troubles assertions that "effort[s] to appropriate urban space for sexual activity [have] been the work of gay men in particular, whereas lesbians have tended to be more discreet and more private in the conduct of their sexual lives."[4] Since sex between adult women, while socially censured, was not illegal in France at this time, many of these venues were explicitly advertised as *cabarets féminins* (women's cabarets). They joined spaces where female couples were tolerated (like Liberty's, Le Boeuf sur le Toit, and the Bal de la Montagne Sainte-Geneviève) and served a far more economically and racially diverse female public than the Left Bank salons, which were frequented by the mostly white expatriate elite who have heretofore dominated the historiography on interwar French lesbian life. Moreover, despite the lasting impact of the Vichy regime's August 6, 1942, decree discriminating against homosexuality with and between minors and its antifeminist reinstantiation of gender norms, many of the sapphic cabarets that opened in Paris in the 1930s outlasted World War II and endured as sites of nonnormative communal and cultural continuity well into the postwar period.[5] Their survival into the 1960s reveals a previously overlooked world of sapphic sociability that remained surprisingly active during years legendary for their heteronormativity and homophobia.

The commercial world of the sapphic cabaret was sustained by complex, shifting relationships—a sapphic genealogical geography—between lovers, friends, mentors, and novices that—like most of the venues that women managed, worked in, and frequented—also outlasted the war. This female network helped shape the topography of the city of Paris and, ultimately, reconfigured the French public sphere more broadly across time and space.

Mapping the origins and spread of the sapphic cabaret and tracing the networks it nourished challenges scholarship in the history of sexuality, urban history, and historical geography that effaces lesbian visibility and relegates lesbians to spaces that are primarily private, temporary, or noncommercial, particularly within urban environments.[6] The history of the sapphic cabaret thus calls into question both the heterosexuality and the androcentricity of the modern city. However, the sapphic genealogical geography described here was not inscribed on a blank field. It emerged out of an expanding urban public sexual culture of cafés, restaurants, dance halls, brothels, boulevards, parks, and theatres, and its capacity to thrive depended on constant negotiation with other arenas of social power. The women who worked in these highly competitive businesses operated in perpetual tension, for example, with the aims of a police force charged with controlling the public sphere in the name of a moralizing state. Enmeshed in a world peopled by prostitutes and petty criminals, a sapphic cabaret's success depended largely on its capacity to sell the performance of lesbian desire to the largest possible public—meaning that some venues intentionally targeted a voyeuristic male clientele whose spending power exceeded that of their female patrons.[7] As the century progressed, sapphic cabarets, their managers, and their clients also found themselves in a losing battle with both gay male and heterosexual entrepreneurs and audiences whose business acumen and financial resources engulfed their neighborhoods and erased their histories. But by that time, in targeting—whether for pleasure, profit, or power—specific forms of female same-sex contact and specific types of gender performance, the sapphic cabarets, the mass media, and the authorities had already contributed to constituting—for better or worse—the very publics they sought either to serve or to control.

INVENTING THE SAPPHIC CABARET

The sapphic cabarets that appeared in Paris in the interwar years were a subset of the cabarets that had multiplied in urban settings across France between 1900 and 1939. The term "cabaret" initially designated a modest establishment for drinking and watching shows consisting of songs and sketches. By the fin de siècle they provided entertainment, alcohol, and food and mainly attracted a bohemian, leftist intellectual and artistic avant-garde (as epitomized by Le Chat Noir, opened by Rodolphe Salis at the foot of Montmartre in 1881 and immortalized by Théophile Steinlen's 1896 art nouveau poster). Cabarets were thus politically and socially distinct from *goguettes* (local dives where amateur singing societies sang seditious songs), *guinguettes* (open-air dance halls sometimes near rivers), *caf'concs* (concert cafés where songs and sketches were performed), and music halls, all of which served mostly working-class publics.[8] Cabarets rarely opened before 10 p.m. and usually closed between 2 a.m. and dawn.[9]

Interwar sapphic cabarets can be divided into two main categories: *cabarets féminins* and *cabarets artistiques*. The former trafficked in sex; the latter, in bourgeois entertainment. Period photographs, films, press, exposés, and memoirs reveal that audiences and staff in both categories crossed lines of race, generation, gender, and class (although admittedly more often with bourgeois women "slumming" in working-class cabarets than vice versa).[10] Racial mixing within French venues was common due to both the popularity of Black performers and the racially integrated demographics of Pigalle and Montmartre, where many sapphic cabarets were located and many immigrants and African Americans had settled.[11] Management, with few exceptions, tended white and—at least in the 1930s—young and working or lower-middle class. All of these venues were managed and directed, if not always owned, by women. A cabaret's autonomy was circumscribed by the goodwill of the (sometimes male) owners for whom it procured profits, but it was the collective talent of the female director, her orchestra, and her staff that determined success.[12]

Cabarets féminins featured female "attractions"—singers, dancers, striptease artists, and sexy revues—but functioned mainly as nightclubs where women could meet, drink, and dance together. Even the most elegant cabarets féminins were part of an underworld dependent on the commercialization of carnal desires. Unlike in Britain, "lesbian bars" in France were identified as such on the streets and in the press; both signage and advertising made their target audiences—women interested in other women (and men titillated by such women)—unambiguously clear.[13] Indeed, the cabaret féminin was above all a commercial enterprise; owners were concerned less with the gender of their clientele than with the money they spent.

Among the most famous of the cabarets féminins were Le Fétiche (opened in 1926 in Pigalle, repeatedly relocated, and later known as Chez Moune) and Le Monocle (opened in 1932 in Montparnasse).[14] Le Fétiche—also called "Au Fétiche" in police reports and styled a *maison de rendezvous pour lesbiennes* (lesbian brothel) that "made its reputation by admitting only lesbians"—was likely the model for Colette's lesbian bar in her 1932 novella about sapphic life, *The Pure and the Impure*.[15] Le Fétiche was initially operated by an enterprising twenty-two-year-old widow named Simone Mathilde Cantin née Dugardin (known as Monique Carton and later Madame Moune or, simply, Moune).[16] Le Monocle's first manager was a dashing twenty-seven-year-old Corsican former circus acrobat from Santa Réparata named Marie Lucie Franchi (first called "Lulu la Corse" and then celebrated as either "Lulu de Montmartre," "Lulu de Montparnasse," or "Frankie").[17] Described as "a masterful woman with a husky build, whose stentorian voice filled the room," Lulu ran Le Monocle for the bar's owner, René Louis Prévost.[18] Lulu got her start—as did an astonishing number of women who became prominent in the business—under Moune at Le Fétiche. Both Lulu and Moune developed long-standing business and personal relationships with cabaret staff, and each left a lasting mark on the sapphic cabaret scene, owning and managing multiple venues well into the postwar decades.[19]

Cabarets féminins boasted primarily female publics.[20] However, since sexual tourism was a fashionable and financially necessary aspect of Parisian nightlife, a certain degree of heterosexual voyeurism was inescapable; by the early 1950s even the American press reported that Parisian "lesbos joints" were "worth a curio peek."[21] While some venues staffed women who serviced male desires on the sly, peepholes and doormen were generally employed to limit male clientele. Men were likewise discouraged from interacting with female performers and patrons and escorted out if they became disruptive. That said, the fact that cabarets féminins were frequented not only by women seeking women but also by female prostitutes, mixed-gender couples, and male voyeurs shaped their public reputations as dens of iniquity.[22] This scandalous image may well have kept some women away, but it likely attracted others.

Whether seedy or elegant, the cabarets féminins were renowned for their small female orchestras and cross-dressing serving girls known as *entraîneuses*.[23] These women—whose importance to the development of lesbian subcultural style is explored in chapter 3—were hired to increase alcohol sales and heat up the ambience, tasks they undertook by chatting up and dancing or (sometimes) sleeping with the customers. Many entraîneuses were unsalaried; they were motivated to keep the alcohol flowing because their pay depended largely on the number of drinks they sold.[24] A common practice (referred to as "clipping") was to "empty part of the champagne while couples are dancing, keeping glasses constantly filled, and gliding in a new one before ordered, depending on the tourist tolerance to get away with it."[25] Good dancers made more money. Indeed, Dan Monnel, a former employee for Moune, explained, "There was no mystery to it," if one wanted to do well with women: "You had to know how to tango."[26] Not infrequently, house photographers were kept on staff. Patrons paid to be photographed with their favorite girls. Ever conscious of profits, the entraîneuse (who reaped a percentage of the take) fostered such affections, happily autographing the finished product before it disappeared into the night, tucked under the arm of a satisfied customer.

The second major category of sapphic cabarets were the cabarets artistiques. These bourgeois venues (like Suzy Solidor's La Vie Parisienne, Jane Stick's Chez Jane Stick and Le Perroquet au Nid, Sidonie Baba's À L'Heureuse Galère, and Agnès Capri's new subgenre of *cabarets théâtres*) were operated and generally owned by female performing artists with a known penchant for those of their own sex.[27] The spaces they ran align with our traditional conception of the cabaret; here it was the performers, not the audience, who were the main attractions. Cabarets artistiques sometimes lacked dance floors and featured both female and male singers, *diseuses* (literally "speakers," like Solidor, who recited poetry in addition to singing), and comedians.[28] By virtue of their elevated prices, these establishments, while similarly hedonistic, were more upscale than cabarets féminins and often slightly more conservative than the bohemian *cabarets littéraires* that came to dominate the Left Bank after World War II.

The situating of sapphic cabarets artistiques in well-heeled Parisian neighborhoods was unique in the history of lesbian bar culture.[29] Sometimes styled as *cabarets à champagne*, they attracted affluent mixed-gender audiences composed of writers, poets, artists, film celebrities, journalists, and media moguls, as well as figures from high society and the political sphere—a self-selecting crowd whose views were generally indulgent toward sexual conduct outside the heterosexual norm.[30] Originally highly subversive, the increasingly professional production of performances sometimes softened their politics.[31] On the whole, however, cabaret content remained informed by the concerns of marginalized minorities.[32]

The visceral closeness of audiences and the absence of microphones provided queer artists with a remarkable degree of interpretive freedom in these elegant nocturnal spaces. Female cabaret singers capitalized on the immediacy and intimacy of live performance to communicate their desires and seduce their audiences.[33] When their material was politically or socially contentious—in content, tone, or delivery—they used irony to evade censorship.[34]

Cabarets artistiques courted both heterosexual and queer audiences. While not explicitly advertised as sapphic spaces, some nevertheless hired entraîneuses or hosted afternoon teas "reserved for women only."[35] They all attracted sizable sapphic contingents at night; on a first date around 1933 at Solidor's popular La Vie Parisienne with the woman who would become her life partner, Rolande Aurivel recalled seeing "half of lesbian Paris."[36] If the sexual preferences of many of the women who congregated in these spaces were common knowledge—as we have seen, Solidor's sapphic liaisons were a hot topic in the tabloids—cabarets artistiques were nonetheless considered respectable, if racy, entertainment establishments with "tasteful, quality" programming.[37] Their ambiguous status reflected the relative integration of nonnormative desires within certain segments of French society, a stance that likewise rendered the pursuit of such desires less difficult. As a rule, sapphic cabarets artistiques were also safer than cabarets féminins; since the latter were linked to criminal activity, they were more heavily surveilled by both the police and local thugs, with patrons and staff facing higher risks of harassment or even arrest.[38]

MAPPING SAPPHIC PARIS

From the 1930s through the early 1970s Parisian sapphic cabarets clustered tightly in five principal locations: three on the Right Bank and two on the Left (fig. 2.1).[39] The bourgeois cabarets artistiques were all located on the Right Bank, either on or near the rue Sainte-Anne near the Palais-Royal and the Opéra or farther to the west in the chic district around the Champs-Élysées and Arc de Triomphe. In contrast, most of the cabarets féminins were either farther north on the Right Bank around the Place Blanche in Montmartre and Pigalle (nicknamed "Pig Alley" by American GIs during World War II), a historically lesbian working-class stomping ground, or farther south on the Left Bank in Montparnasse. In the early 1930s these Left Bank spots included Le Monocle and Les Claudines, which stood side by side on the boulevard Edgar Quinet (at numbers 60 and 58, respectively), southwest of the Bal de la Montagne Sainte-Geneviève. By

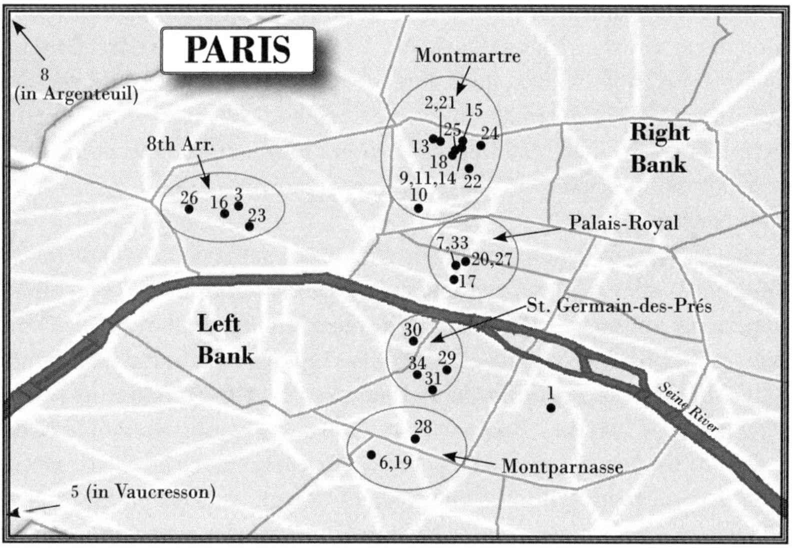

No.	Venue/Year Est./Owner or Manager	Era	No.	Venue/Year Est./Owner or Manager	Era
1	Bal de la Montagne Ste Geneviève (1920s, Paulette)	1920s-1960s	18	La Silhouette (1938, Frede)	1930s
2	Le Fétiche (1926, Lulu/Moune)	1920s-1930s	19	Les Claudines (1938, Moune)	1930s
3	Le Petit Cabaret (~1930s, Jacqueline Billat)	1930s	20	À L'Heureuse Galère (~1939, Baba)	1930s
4	Chez Nous (1930s, Montmartre, loc. unknown)	1930s	21	La Sirène (1939, Moune)	1930s
5	L'Auberge du Perroquet Gris (~1932)	1930s	22	Entre Nous (1936, reopened 1946)	1930s-1950s
6	Le Monocle (1932, Lulu)	1930s-1970s	23	Le Carroll's (1948, Frede)	1940s-1950s
7	La Vie Parisienne (1933, Solidor/1946, Mars/1961, Frede)	1930s-1960s	24	Le Fétiche (1949-1954, Moune)	1940s-1950s
8	Le Pavillon du Mystère (1933, Lulu)	1930s	25	Chez Moune (1954, Moune)	1940s-2008
9	Buenos-Aires (1933, Lulu)	1930s	26	Chez Suzy Solidor (1954, Solidor)	1940s-1950s
10	Le Joubertin (1933, Baba)	1930s	27	Aux Quatre Mules (1954, Baba)	1940s-1970s
11	Juan-les-Pins (1934, Lulu)	1930s	28	Elle et Lui (1959, M. Marcel)	1940s-1970s
12	Le Gibus (1934, Montmartre, loc. unknown)	1930s	29	Le Pousse au Crime (1960s)	1960s-1970s
13	Les Cocottes (1935, Moune)	1930s	30	Le Quod Libet (1960s)	1960s
14	La Roulotte (1935, Lulu)	1930s	31	Frida's (1960s)	1960s
15	Chez Sidonie Baba (1936, Baba)	1930s	32	Le Bacchus (1960s, 6th arr., loc. unknown)	1960s
16	Le Siroco aka Chez Jane Stick (1937, Batell/1939, Stick)	1930s-1940s	33	Le Carroll's Disco (1961, Frede)	1960s
17	Chez Agnès Capri aka Le Capricorne (1938, Capri)	1930s-1950s	34	Katmandou (1969, Elula)	1960s-1990s

FIGURE 2.1: Map and key of selected sapphic cabarets, Paris, 1930s–1960s. Note that Le Petit Cabaret was run by Jacqueline Batell, not Jacqueline Billat. Graphic courtesy of Stephen A. Sherman in consultation with the author.

the 1960s this lesbian presence had expanded north and west into the increasingly hip Saint-Germain-des-Prés neighborhood in the sixth and seventh arrondissements with the opening of Le Pousse au Crime at 15 rue Guisarde, Le Quod Libet at 3 rue du Pré-aux-Clercs, and later the Katmandou discothèque at 21 rue du Vieux-Colombier.

Each of these areas became what we might call "sapphic microterritories," in which both clientele and staff could traverse from one sapphic venue to another with relative ease.[40] Sapphic microterritories have emotional, commercial, and symbolic effects: they provide women with a sense of security in numbers, they create "economies of agglomeration" in which like enterprises profit from grouping together, and, finally, they challenge the illusion that public space is naturally heterosexual and androcentric, rather than the result of unequal, hierarchical relations of power and sexual privilege.[41] Such spaces where one can meet others like oneself are also a condition of collective visibility and offer nothing less than public proof of private existence.

Sapphic cabarets were not limited to Paris proper. In the 1930s at least two venues (and likely more) existed in small towns on the outskirts of the city, but their commercial success was hindered by their distance from the sapphic networks described above. Sapphic cabarets also existed elsewhere in the metropole, but they were fewer and farther between. As police dossiers on Marie Lucie Franchi (alias Lulu de Montmartre) illustrate, geographic isolation, even when just outside Paris, could pose insurmountable difficulties.[42] Lulu's file for 1933 contains a small business card–cum–invitation, measuring about 2.5 × 7 inches and printed in fire-engine red and dark brown on a taupe background (fig. 2.2). The front left of the card

FIGURE 2.2: "Dans le maquis chez les jeunes filles en uniforme" [In the bush with the young girls in uniform]. Invitation to the 1933 opening of Lulu de Montmartre's Pavillon du Mystère, Argenteuil, France. Dossier 1W1032-46033. Courtesy of the Archives de la préfecture de police de Paris.

features a deco-style graphic of three female faces in profile, each wearing an identical cap. On the front right, against a silhouette of trees and scrub, we read (in a clear reference to the popular 1931 German sapphic-themed film *Mädchen in Uniform*): "In the bush with the YOUNG GIRLS IN UNIFORM 5 rue du Cerisier, Argenteuil."[43] Flipping the card over reveals a hand-drawn map with directions from the Porte de Clichy on the outskirts of Paris to the venue in question. Handwritten script winds lazily across the top: "La môme tokkai [Kid Tokkai—one of Lulu's nicknames] and her girls in uniform invite you on Friday May 26, 1933, to the inauguration of the Pavillon du Mystère [Pavilion of Mysteries] (open all day)."

The accompanying two-page, single-spaced typewritten police report provides a careful description:

> Yesterday evening an establishment in the genre of a *guingette* called "The Pavilion of Mysteries" was inaugurated on the property situated at 5 rue des Cerisiers [*sic*] in Argenteuil, belonging to one FRANCHI, Marie-Lucie, alias "Lulu," born October 27, 1905, in Santa Reparata (Corsica).
>
> To give it the desired character, all the personnel from the nightclub Le Monocle, situated at 60 boulevard Edgar-Quinet, were present in their habitual [masculine] sartorial dress. The opening was nevertheless subdued, since, aside from "Billy" the proprietor of an identical establishment, "L'Auberge du Perroquet Gris," 5 place de l'Eglise in Vaucresson (Seine-et-Oise) and her guests, there were very few clients at the cocktail hour, no doubt due to the remoteness of this new place of pleasure intended for a special clientele.[44]

The presence of "Billy" and "her guests"—who had likely traveled over an hour from Vaucresson to attend the "inauguration"—suggests the importance of the initiative to women interested in this type of "identical establishment." But the report also raises red flags. Despite Lulu's efforts to populate the place with Le Monocle's "personnel . . . in their habitual [masculine] sartorial dress" and the venue's evident attractions (even the inspector concluded that "the first impression is agreeable," after describing the blue-and-gold pavilion with its bar and dance hall, the "artistically decorated walls," the cunningly converted dovecote, the "Ping-Pong" tables, and the swing at the far end of the garden), the "remoteness of this new place of pleasure" meant that even a businesswoman as savvy as Lulu was unable to make a go of it. Consequently, as noted in a police report written two years later, "when this business did not produce the expected benefits, [Lulu] abandoned it."[45] The Pavilion of Mysteries closed before the year 1933 was out. Or, at least, that is what the police were initially led to believe.[46]

In the French capital, successful sapphic cabarets were governed by geographic proximity and genealogical affiliation. Thus, after one sapphic cabaret opened, other women regularly opened their own cabarets nearby. If a sapphic cabaret closed (sometimes involuntarily after having been stripped of its license by the police or tyrannized by the Corsican mafia in Pigalle), its manager frequently attempted to open a new business in the vicinity of the original locale. Businesses were also transferred from one woman to the next across generations, a fact that established both geographic and affective genealogical continuity within the sapphic community while maintaining sapphic control over parts of the urban map. A genealogical tree illustrating the connections between sapphic cabarets and some of their managers and staff from 1926 to 2012 offers a stunning and salient visual representation of the complicated networks further described below (fig. 2.3).

Sapphic cabarets provided what we might think of as a "private-public" arena in which, because private expression was—purportedly—protected inside a public space, individual sapphic desires could become a collective public experience. By consolidating particular types of sexual desire inside of specific locations and connecting strangers via their shared sexually subordinate status, the sapphic cabaret helped transform the personal into the protopolitical. And yet, if sapphic cabarets operated under cover of darkness, were highly monitored, practiced selective admission, and were regularly subjected to police surveillance and mafia control, just how personally or politically liberating—or public—could they actually be?

Henri Lefebvre contends in his 1974 *The Production of Space* that because sexuality is only accorded a "secondary and derivative existence" in the public sphere after dark, its presence there is reduceable to a "sophisticated form of exploitation"—hardly the basis, it would seem, for personal or political emancipation.[47] Missing in such an argument, however, is the reality that the same nocturnal commodification of urban sexuality critiqued by Lefebvre nevertheless enabled many women to begin—sometimes cautiously and with much trepidation—to form intimate relationships, widen their social circles, and connect with strangers within a larger sapphic "imagined community."[48] Indeed, the nocturnal world of commercialized leisure has long supplied private persons with public spaces in which they can test the limits of the very authorities who seek to circumscribe their actions. At the same time (as Lefebvre acknowledged, and as lesbian feminists would later observe), nocturnal businesses are

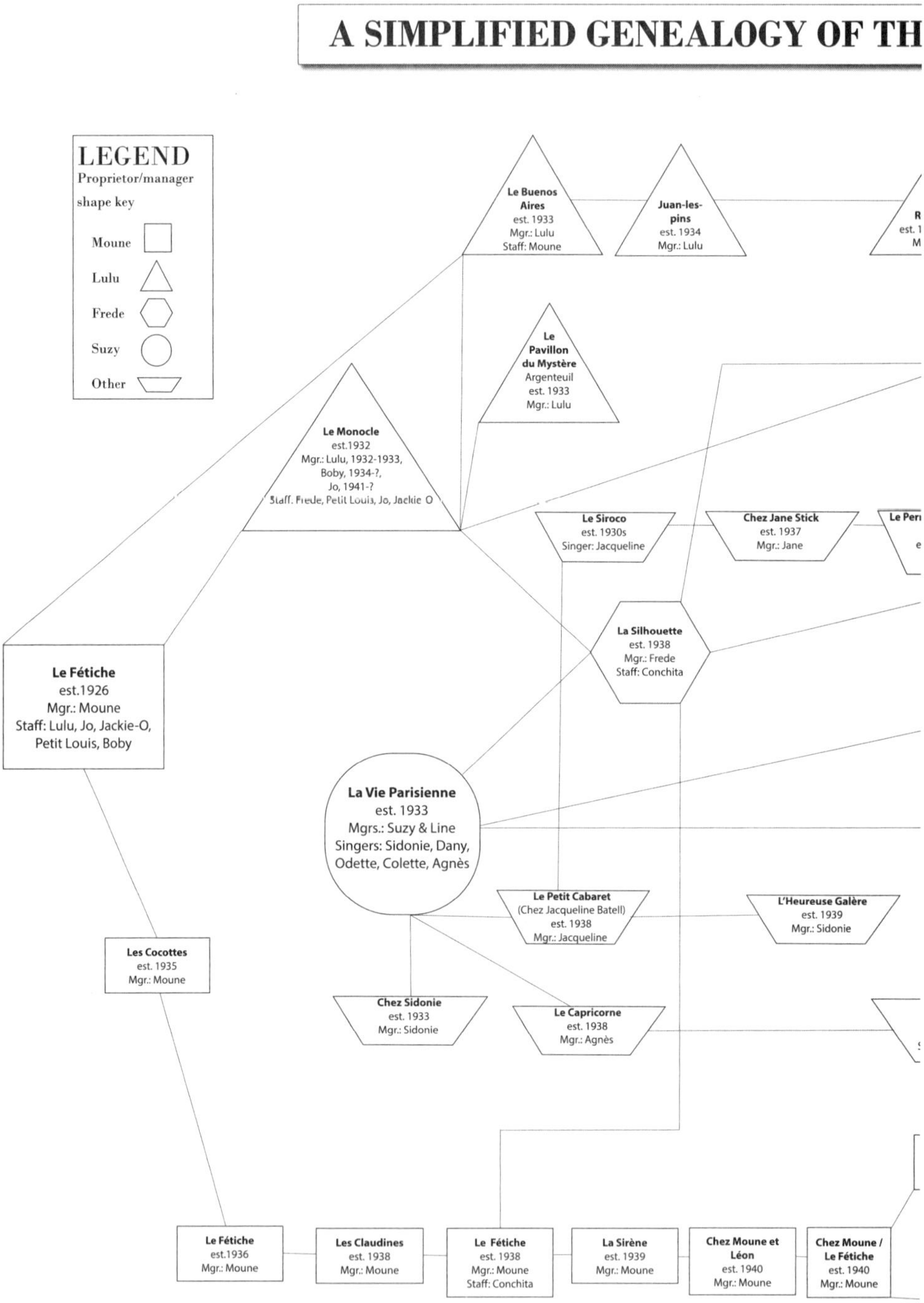

FIGURE 2.3: Simplified genealogy of the sapphic cabaret, 1926–2010s. Graphic courtesy of Stephen A. Sherman in consultation with the author.

THE SAPPHIC CABARET

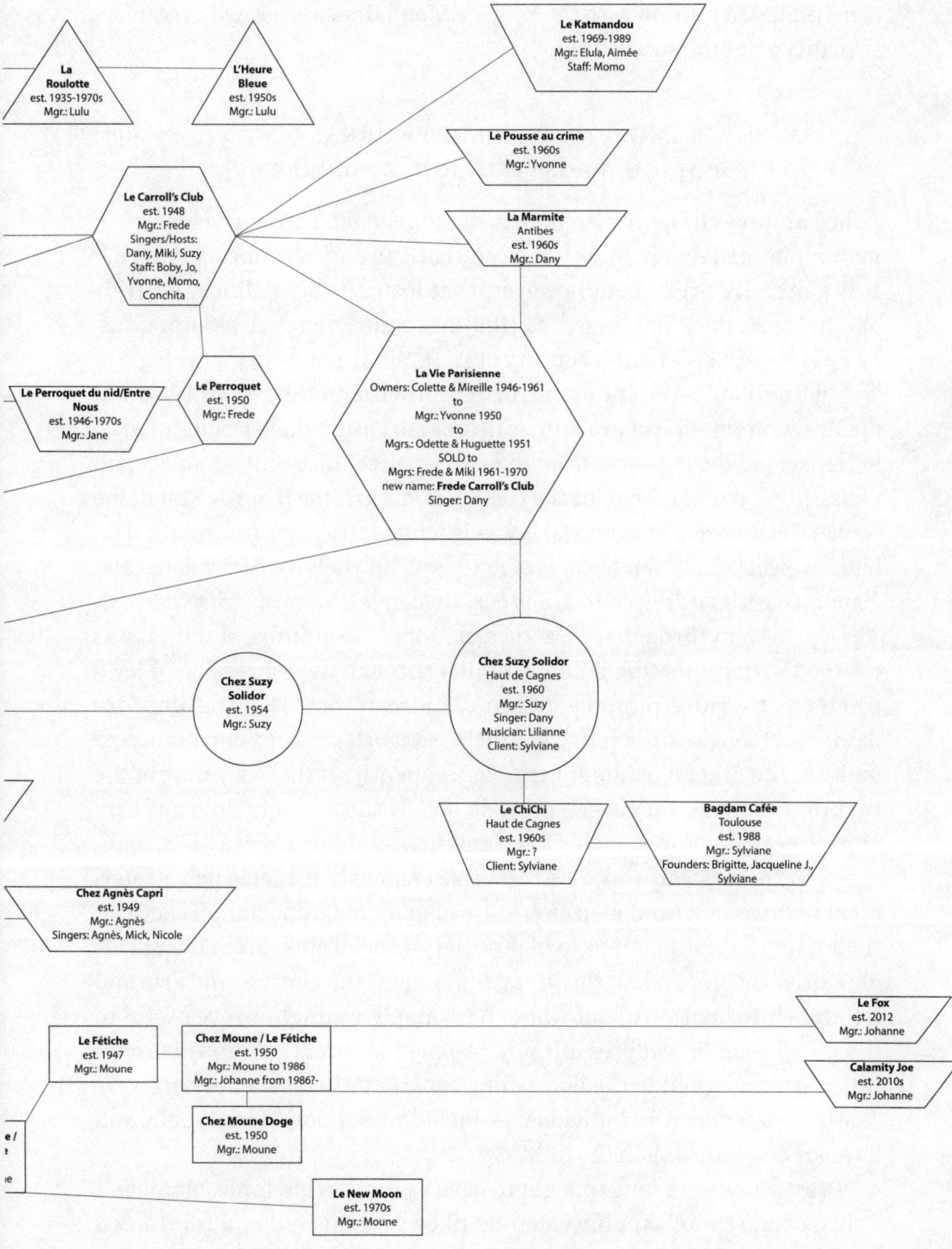

vested with distinctly different degrees of social importance and political power than those that operate during the day. They are also subject to different forms of social control. In Paris, the sapphic genealogical geographies that developed inside the interwar entertainment industry were constructed in tension with the Brigade Mondaine, who aimed to regulate sexuality after the sun had set.

NEGOTIATING NETWORKS: POLICE, PROSTITUTION, AND CRIME

Police archives have proven invaluable to reconstructing the history of male homosexuality in nineteenth- and early twentieth-century France.[49] It is generally presumed, however, that lesbians are "almost entirely absent" from these holdings.[50] My findings contradict such assumptions. From the early nineteenth century until its abolition in 1946, the logic of "regulationism"—the state control of brothels and the registration and medical examination of prostitutes in order to ensure the servicing of male heterosexual desire—was used to justify police intervention in French public life. Like its precursor the *police des moeurs*, the Brigade Mondaine (created between 1899 and 1901) was intended to gather information on both suspect persons and people of note from brothels (both regulated and clandestine), boarding houses, and certain hotels (known as *hôtels garnis*). The squad went through several incarnations.[51] Beginning in 1907, it was charged with protecting public morality through the repression of lewd conduct, obscenity, pimping, begging, and vagrancy. The Brigade Mondaine was likewise directed to use these categories to suppress homosexuality in the French public sphere. Consequently, at the beginning of the twentieth century, they began to methodically surveil nightclubs and cabarets. Due to their presumably loose morals, sapphic cabaret artists, managers, and others who worked in these spaces quickly attracted police interest. These women (and men) were also considered important because of their potential connections to high society—social elites from the worlds of politics, business, law, the press, diplomacy, the church, and arts and letters—information about whose personal lives might prove useful to those in power. Procedures initially designed for the regulation of prostitution were adapted to the flourishing cabaret milieu, and dossiers were consistently opened on individuals—including Solidor, Moune, Lulu, and later Frede—working in the industry.

Prostitutes were long thought to have a predilection for lesbianism.[52] Police oversight of sapphic cabarets likewise reflected and reinforced social presumptions that as a perversion, female homosexuality was predisposed toward prostitution and criminality. The linking of prostitution with sapphic desire was not unreasonable: women who didn't marry had fewer choices and greater economic need than those who did, and heterosexual prostitution provided a stable source of ready income. There was also evident crossover between these domains. Sapphic cabarets were located in close proximity to houses of prostitution, and even upscale cabarets artistiques were not far removed from *maisons de tolérance* (as the better brothels were known), where the clientele were wealthier, and the girls more exclusive.[53] Suzy Solidor's La Vie Parisienne at 12 rue Sainte-Anne was around the corner from the notorious maison de tolérance La Fleur Blanche at 6 rue des Moulins (est. 1860 and famously painted and frequented by Toulouse-Lautrec) and just two blocks from Le Chabanais (est. 1878 at 12 rue Chabanais), one of the most opulent houses of prostitution in Paris.[54] There was also a maison de tolérance located nearby at 29 rue Joubert, steps from Sidonie Baba's first cabaret, Le Joubertin. Agnès Capri's cabaret at 5 rue Molière was around the corner from Baba's and up the street from the brothel De Lierre, located at number 13. The opening of the cabarets féminins Le Monocle and Les Claudines in the 1930s on the Left Bank in Montparnasse, likewise maintained this connection between prostitution and "sexual deviance." Located directly across from the new luxury bordello Le Sphinx (est. 1931), the cabarets pulled a larger sapphic clientele south to the Left Bank. Some brothels provided women for female clientele, but these are harder to track.[55]

Physical proximity fostered personal and professional bonds. Police reports and press coverage indicate that more than a few of the individuals who ran and worked in sapphic cabarets were implicated in prostitution or had criminal records. Moune was described as having "barely begun to work as a [brothel] madam when she created 'Le Fétiche,'" a venue "frequented only by women who are in love with both other women and masculine attire."[56] Lulu was commonly referred to as a *souteneuse* or *mec* (pimp) in the popular press; police records identify her as a brothel manager and accuse her of extortion, assault and battery, theft, and even the endangerment of national security.[57] Le Monocle's second manager, Simone Conquet (alias Boby or Bobbie), was likewise known to the police as a *fille insoumise* (unregistered prostitute).[58]

Although not technically a prostitute, like her historical antecedent the *fille de brasserie*, or the female waitress, the sapphic entraîneuse was deemed a particularly problematic threat to public morals because of the nebulous possibilities of sexual pleasure that her flirtatious attentions to female customers could provide. Hélène Azenor's memoirs suggest, however, that such women sometimes evaded the state's control because the police failed to comprehend the complicated intersection of sexual commerce and sapphic desire. Speaking of the early 1930s, Azenor recalls: "One day I went to Le Monocle, and what did I see but all the *garçonnes* [cross-dressed entraîneuses] were pregnant! Well now! I found that hilariously amusing!" Moreover, she continues, "these *garçonnes*, they each had a girl working for them on the boulevard Montparnasse . . . thus it was really these [pregnant] girls, these *garçonnes* at Le Monocle, who were the pimps. . . . There was such a crazy atmosphere at Le Monocle, everything that could possibly be trafficked was."[59] What could the authorities possibly have made of this state of affairs? Were these pregnancies desired? Or were they the unwanted but unavoidable outcome of heterosexual prostitution at a time when contraception was illegal and hard to come by? And were these women lesbians whose pregnancies revealed that they were also working as heterosexual prostitutes? Or were all—or some—of Le Monocle's entraîneuses romantically involved with men while simultaneously secretly pimping other women (who may or may not have been their female lovers) on the side?[60] The deeper the police looked, the more muddied the picture must have become.

The police clearly knew that not all entraîneuses were prostitutes, but they also knew that female prostitutes regularly patronized cabarets féminins. It was less evident, however, whether the latter frequented these spaces in search of *female* clients. Nineteenth-century experts who equated the "hypersexuality" of the female prostitute with the "hypersexuality" of feminine lesbians suspected as much. But twentieth-century contemporaries were not so sure. In 1937 Michel Du Coglay claimed that prostitutes (women he calls *demi-lesbiennes*, or half-lesbians, a category he fails to define) headed to Le Monocle on nights that they weren't working simply because they "considered their 'Monocle evenings' as rest" and entertainment.[61] Maryse Choisy, the journalist who studied Le Fétiche as part of her moralizing 1928 investigation into life in a French brothel, would have disagreed. Choisy saw such prostitutes as "real" lesbians who came to the sapphic cabaret in search of love. In contrast, she asserted that unlike these prostitutes, most of the women hired as entraîneuses in the sapphic cabarets were simply in it for the money: "There are more real lesbians employed in any brothel" where women were paid to sleep with men, she argued, "than there are working in this bar for lesbians."[62] Azenor's observations quoted above, however, imply that the lines between these categories were not quite so clear. Not infrequently, the police turned to the women in charge in an attempt to exert some semblance of control over this otherwise chaotic scene.

Female networks generally functioned in supportive modes—assisting women in finding work, apartments, partners, and community—but they could also be used either to exert control or to gain personal advantage. By virtue of their positions, cabaret managers and owners served as conduits between the police, their employees, and their local communities. Conscious of both their vulnerability and their power, many cabaret managers cultivated symbiotic relationships with police agents and chiefs, currying favor by providing information about their staff's criminal activities, suspect behavior, or sexual preferences in return for protection or privileges. Police reports documenting these dealings form a crucial supplement to the media sources and business archives used to draw the personal and professional maps described in this chapter.

Police records reveal, for example, that Moune was in conversation with the police and had at least some influence over how her girls were treated by them. In one file Moune defends her employee (a woman known as H.B.), claiming that despite H.B.'s "doubtful morals" and history of shoplifting, she "behaves well [at Le Fétiche]." Scribbled across the bottom of the file is a note from the police asking, "Should we leave her there?" However, Moune's aims do not always appear to have been benevolent. Another dossier in the same file reads: "The director of Le Fétiche has let us know that she recently hired an entraîneuse by the name of G.L., *lesbienne notoire* [notorious lesbian]."[63] The file divulges that it was Moune herself who notified police about G.L.'s possible sapphic liaisons with a minor, information that led the police to raid the young woman's apartment in the early morning hours on July 25, 1949. Although the raid proved fruitless (G.L. was roused from a bed in which she had slept alone, with nothing amiss), Moune's role in this action is suspicious. We can only wonder about her motives and speculate about the ways in which such confidences may have been compensated.

Owners and managers were also under surveillance. Although it is unclear whether she was prosecuted, police reported that Moune had "installed a record player" at "Au Fétiche" in 1929, flagrantly disobeying an order denying her establishment the right to play music. What is more, they write, "in case of a raid," Moune had ensured that the phonograph could be promptly "stopped by the bouncer" at the door, who "with the help of an electric button placed to the left of the entry" instantly cut power to the clandestine machine.[64] According to Jane Stick's dossier, the singer and sapphic cabaret owner used her connections to avoid trouble with the authorities. Although she attracted police attention (for infractions during World War II related to illegal dancing, curfew violations, and trafficking on the black market), agents reported that "each time that she has a problem she gets her close friend Maurice Legay, a member of the Brigade Mondaine, to intervene."[65] More problematically, like Suzy Solidor, Stick nurtured "friendships" with the Germans during the Occupation.[66] Her police dossier contains letters from a person identified as "German Chief of Police 582" to the Paris prefect of police requesting that Stick's opening hours be prolonged and exempted from the general curfew. The exception was granted without delay.[67] The police further remark on Stick's "numerous relationships with men," noting how not only did they fail to deter her "from assiduously practicing the cult of Lesbos," but also that the singer "derives certain profits" from her heterosexual liaisons—thus suggesting that Stick's affairs with men may have been financially motivated.[68]

Stick's case demonstrates some of the ways in which sapphic cabaret owners and managers capitalized on their relations with the police in order to benefit their businesses. Sometimes, however, they utilized these networks for more personal ends. One particularly egregious example suggests that Lulu de Montmartre profited from her connections with the authorities to avoid serving time. In 1937 Lulu organized an elaborate ruse in which she and her twenty-one-year-old girlfriend Raymonde Lagorce bled money from a wealthy young entrepreneur (a married man and father) over a period of many months. Raymonde first duped the man into paying off her debts (she owed considerable cash—or so she said—to a bartender, a cloakroom attendant, and a doctor for medical visits) and convinced her would-be lover that if he helped her she would run off with him; she then conned the man into driving her late one evening to Argenteuil to gather her things from the home she shared with Lulu.[69] When Raymonde and her "boyfriend" entered the premises, Lulu appeared, gun in hand, firing wildly and accusing the man of breaking and entering. Threatening him with the imminent arrival of the police (and the ensuing publicity), Lulu then offered to let the whole thing drop for the tidy sum of 130,000 francs. After making the first in a series of payments, the gentleman reconsidered the deal and decided to lodge a complaint.

The trial that followed was a media circus revolving around the dangers of "lesbianism," with Lulu and Raymonde portrayed in the press as the perfect image of the brutish butch and her conniving femme.[70] The negative effects of such salacious publicity on attitudes toward female same-sex desire can only be imagined. As the mastermind behind the affair, Lulu was convicted of extortion, sentenced to a year in prison, and fined five hundred francs. Raymonde was given six months. However, although the scandal fascinated the local papers for weeks, the fines were eventually dropped, the sentences suspended, and neither Lulu nor her girlfriend did time. Given Lulu's criminal history, the lenience is particularly notable. One of my interviewees speculated that this was not the only occasion on which Lulu's value as an informant (she was deeply embedded in both the cabaret milieu and the Corsican mafia) stood her in good stead.[71]

Lulu—with her apparent zest for besting the system—was likely more the exception than the rule; for the many other women who worked in sapphic cabarets, prostitution and petty theft were responses to the poverty, hunger, and precarity that their positions as outsiders intensified. But if police records provide us with insights into how individual women attempted to negotiate their vulnerable status vis-à-vis the administrative forces that sought to control their worlds, it was the genealogical and geographic connections among and between these women that often enabled them to survive and thrive.

The extent and importance of sapphic genealogical geographies in the construction of lesbian life is evident in the neighborhood-by-neighborhood analysis that follows. In concrete terms, this analysis shifts our attention away from the Parisian district of the "gay Marais" and exposes how neighborhoods generally associated with both heterosexuality (Pigalle, Montmartre, the Champs-Élysées, the Opéra, and Montparnasse) and gay male sexuality (the Palais-Royal and the rue Sainte-Anne) were actually vibrant sites of sapphic activity over at least a thirty-year period.

PIGALLE AND MONTMARTRE: LE FÉTICHE, MOUNE, AND LULU DE MONTMARTRE

Le Fétiche, located at 32 rue Fontaine in the heart of Pigalle, is the earliest cabaret féminin that I have been able to identify.[72] The first trace of Le Fétiche in the Archives de Paris dates to 1926, when it was owned by Jean Eugène Berger.[73] In this "heart of Lesbos," which vaunted "a cubist look in pink and black with symbolic murals [of a cat, a crow, and a unicorn] by the artist Sacha Zaliouk," according to Maryse Choisy's rhapsodical waxings, "there are more pretty women per square meter than anywhere else in the world."[74] From the manager Moune, who possessed "the sweetness of an angel, the will of the devil, the tact of a woman, the authority of a man," to the staff, which included Petit Louis (described as a *pure*—or congenital invert), Jo, Jackie, and "Lulu, la Corse" (soon known as Lulu de Montmartre), many of the figures who animated Parisian sapphic nightlife for the next forty years were first employed at Le Fétiche.[75] By 1932, Petit Louis, Jo, and Jackie had decamped with Lulu to "raise the standard of Sapphism" at Le Monocle, where Jackie tended bar as "Jackie-O."[76] When Lulu left Le Monocle the following year (after, according to the police, making the venue "a success that hasn't ceased since"), she was replaced by Simone Conquet, alias Boby, a former prostitute.[77] It was Boby who offered the young Frede her first job as an entraîneuse at Le Monocle in 1934.[78] Boby remained at Le Monocle until 1939. She left to manage a café in Meudon when Le Monocle was closed briefly at the start of World War II. After the war's end, Frede returned the favor, hiring Boby at Le Carroll's Club.[79] Jo (who had followed Lulu from Le Fétiche to Le Monocle) took over as Le Monocle's manager when the venue reopened in 1941. According to the US transgender magazine *Female Mimics*, Jo became "one of the first women ever awarded the French Legion of Honor" for her work in the Resistance during the German Occupation. She remained at Le Monocle's helm for the next two decades.[80] Lulu, for her part, went on to own and manage a series of cabarets and cabarets féminins in Montmartre, including the Buenos-Aires, Juan-les-Pins, and La Roulotte, the latter through the early 1960s.[81] According to an application filed with the city in 1952, Moune also worked at the latter two establishments.[82] Edith Piaf worked at Juan-les-Pins and La Roulotte as an entraîneuse prior to her rise to fame as a chanteuse.[83]

From her first job as manager at Le Fétiche in the late 1920s, Moune likewise began to lay sapphic claims to the Paris map. When the ownership of Le Fétiche changed hands in 1931, Moune (then known as Monique) followed Lulu to her new cabaret, the Buenos-Aires (est. 1933) and briefly worked there as an entraîneuse.[84] By 1935 Moune was once again directing Le Fétiche. Soon thereafter, with Moune still in charge, the venue was renamed Les Cocottes and listed as the "ex-Fétiche" in the local papers.[85] Within a few years, Monique (now known as Moune) had moved to Montparnasse. By early 1938 she was running the cabaret féminin Les Claudines at 58 boulevard Edgar Quinet, next door to Le Monocle.[86] By April of that same year, however, she returned to Pigalle and resurrected Le Fétiche under its original name but relocated the venue around the corner to 7 rue Fromentin.[87] "Attractions. Nude Models. We laugh, we dance, we have fun until dawn with Moune!" gaily announced one advertisement.[88] Moune's growing reputation soon attracted an expanding public (sapphic and otherwise) to the neighborhood. By August 1938 Moune's photograph appeared in *Paris-soir* under the heading, "'Le Fétiche': Where to go tonight."[89]

Capitalizing on Moune's appeal, Frede opened her first cabaret, La Silhouette, at 58 rue Notre-Dame-de-Lorette in 1938, two blocks south of Moune's turf.[90] Frede named La Silhouette after a Weimar-era cabaret in Berlin that had encouraged male and female cross-dressing, swathing the walls in pleated mauve satin and advertising attractions including "Betty, les Boys and FREDE."[91] To assist in this venture, Frede "stole" several members of Moune's staff, including the entraîneuse Concepcion Marin-Lopez, known as Conchita, who followed Frede first to La Silhouette and then, much later, to Le Carroll's. Both La Silhouette and Le Fétiche were a stone's throw from the cabaret féminin Entre Nous, which first opened in 1936, closed during the war, and reopened in 1946 under the management of cabaret singer Jane Stick (another *femme aux femmes*) at 17 rue Laferrière.[92] During the Vichy regime, La Silhouette was placed under new management, and Frede departed for Biarritz, where she opened an elegant jazz bar called the Touch Wood. La Silhouette, meanwhile, was advertised in *Der Deutsche Melgleiter für Paris* and frequented by German soldiers and collaborators. Not surprisingly, it was forcibly closed during the purges after the war.

Meanwhile, Frede returned to Paris in early 1945. She opened the short-lived Le Masque (also known as Le Hasard) on the ground floor of a building in the seventeenth arrondissement; Frede occupied a tiny sixth-floor walk-up apartment in the same building at square Villaret-de-Joyeuse. Situated outside the main sapphic territories in Pigalle, Montmartre, and Montparnasse, however, the establishment failed to attract clientele and shut its doors in under two years.

World War II had a varied impact on the sapphic cabaret scene. Le Fétiche closed in 1939, but within months "Moune Carton and her boys" were again operating in the same location at 7 rue Fromentin under a new name. Now called La Sirène but "in the same ambience as the old 'Fétiche,'" Moune welcomed customers "from 10:30 p.m. until sun-up."[93] The establishment was also featured in the press: a mocking caricature of Suzy Solidor's ex, the wealthy *antiquaire* Yvonne de Bremond d'Ars, dancing cheek to cheek with another woman in masculine attire appeared in the daily *Marianne* and testified to both Moune's popularity and La Sirène's celebrated sapphic clientele (fig. 2.4).[94] After more than a decade managing cabarets féminins for others, Moune capitalized on her successes and finally launched her own business: on April 1, 1940, she was officially listed by the City of Paris as the owner of Chez Moune at 4 rue Puget in Pigalle.[95] Deftly negotiating her relationships with the changing powers that be, Moune ran the cabaret throughout the war. While it closed in 1944,

FIGURE 2.4: Illustration of Cécile Sorel (*center*) and Yvonne de Bremond d'Ars (*far right*) at La Sirène. *Marianne: Grand hebdomadaire littéraire illustré*, July 26, 1939. Courtesy of the Bibliothèque nationale de France.

Moune barely missed a beat. By 1947 she had resurrected Chez Moune as Chez Moune/Le Fétiche at 2 rue Frochot, two streets away from its former Pigalle location and just down the block from the now defunct Le Rat Mort, the famous Belle Époque lesbian haunt.[96]

Chez Moune/Le Fétiche took the place of the Cabaret Oriental, which had been owned and operated for twenty-two years by the Algerian-born Philippe M. Martzloff, who, at sixty-nine, likely retired.[97] Madame Moune's new cabaret's cross-listed name in the city register capitalized simultaneously on her own growing celebrity and on Le Fétiche's historic reputation.[98] By 1950 Moune moved Chez Moune/Le Fétiche around the corner to 54 rue Pigalle. The women who worked in these venues often lived close by. Police files from the late 1940s and early 1950s indicate that almost 80 percent of Lulu's staff lodged at either 65 or 59 rue Pigalle—each located mere doors from Chez Moune at number 54 and Lulu's La Roulotte at number 62—suggesting that these buildings were also either run by, or accepting of, women "like that."[99]

In the 1970s Moune opened yet another cabaret, Le New Moon, at 66 rue Pigalle, but although it presented "lesbian entertainment," the club was aimed primarily at heterosexual tourists. Moune operated both Chez Moune and Le New Moon until her death in 1986.[100] Chez Moune survived its namesake into the twenty-first century, when it was turned into a hipster club for heterosexuals around 2009 by a team known as La Clique. In 2012 Johanne Gabrielle, one of Chez Moune's last artistic directors during its sapphic existence, opened her own lesbian club, Le Fox, at 9 rue Frochot, steps away from Moune's former Le Fétiche. After Le Fox failed, Gabrielle crossed the road and opened Calamity Joe at number 12.[101] The fact that for three-quarters of a century all of these venues—Le Fétiche in multiple locations, La Sirène, La Silhouette, the Entre Nous, Chez Moune, Le New Moon, and much, much later Le Fox and Calamity Joe—were all within two blocks of one another was not coincidental. These establishments successively capitalized on the commercial and social benefits that accrued when urban territory became associated with sapphic space over time.

LES CHAMPS-ÉLYSÉES: RUE DE PONTHIEU AND FREDE'S LE CARROLL'S CLUB

Just as the cabarets féminins clustered together in Pigalle and Montmartre, sapphic cabarets artistiques were likewise established in close proximity in the city's more fashionable, upscale neighborhoods. Managers, staff, and talent circulated between the sapphic cabarets artistiques just as they did between the cabarets féminins. In 1948 Frede took over management of Le Carroll's Club at 36 rue de Ponthieu from Jacques Sicre, a French businessman born in Saigon.[102] She soon sought (and was granted) permission to keep the club open all night—a rare privilege that likely reflected her standing with the local police. By 1949 her police file identified the venue as attracting an "increasingly selective clientele" among which could be found "the most notorious lesbians from high society."[103] Described as a "tudor-type cellar" near the Champs-Élysées that "bursts at the seams nightly with an extremely contrasting clientele," Le Carroll's Club was located on the same street as Jane Stick's first cabaret artistique, which had opened at number 70 in 1937 over a decade earlier.[104] At that time, Stick had taken over Le Siroco, a cabaret that featured female performers like singer-songwriter Jacqueline Batell (whose music was recorded by sapphic singers such as Suzy Solidor, Dany Dauberson, and Colette Mars). Batell then opened *her* own cabaret, Le Petit Cabaret "Chez Jacqueline Batell," nearby at 27 rue d'Artois in 1938.[105] In 1950, Frede took over Jane Stick's second cabaret, Le Perroquet au Nid, which was down the street from Le Carroll's Club at 49 rue de Ponthieu. Renamed simply Le Perroquet and intended as a kind of "mini-Carroll's" and showcase for the talented Eartha Kitt, the endeavor failed after just a few months.[106] Le Carroll's Club, in contrast, was a raging success, and Frede stayed on the rue de Ponthieu for twelve years. By 1954 Frede's lover Miki had joined her there, and, as Miki later observed, the two women "were together in business and love 'til death did us part."[107]

Like Moune and Lulu de Montmartre, Frede built her business on the back of personal and professional connections in the sapphic community. Indeed, Frede could not have succeeded at Le Carroll's Club without the sapphic network that she had begun to nurture in the 1930s. Boby, the entraîneuse at Le Fétiche and then manager at Le Monocle responsible for Frede's first job ("a hardened single woman whose manners," according to the Brigade Mondaine, "left no doubt about her penchant for the cult of Lesbos"), was herself among Frede's early hires at Le Carroll's.[108] Frede also gave many women their start in the business: "Yvonne," who was hired to work at Le Carroll's as a barwoman, went on to manage Le Pousse au Crime, a popular Left Bank discothèque "frequented by female lovers of women" in the 1960s.[109] But the woman who "took on a primordial importance in the house" as Frede's first business partner was the statuesque, deep-voiced blonde singer Dany Dauberson. Dauberson (whose real name was Suzanne Gauché) had fled to Paris from her native Lyon in 1946 after her romantic dalliance with the actress Carmen Torres became a local media scandal.[110] When taunted publicly about the affair, Dauberson lashed out, striking her accuser over the head with a bottle. The woman was hospitalized, the papers had a field day, and Dauberson quickly left town for the capital.[111] In Paris, the singer found her way to Suzy Solidor's La Vie Parisienne, where Solidor took her in. Solidor mentored her and was soon referred to as Dauberson's "godmother" in the press.[112] By 1949 Dauberson was using her cachet as the "New Suzy Solidor" to attract audiences to Le Carroll's cabaret.[113] By the 1970s she was running her own venue, La Marmite, in the South of France.

THE OPÉRA: RUE SAINTE-ANNE AND SUZY SOLIDOR'S LA VIE PARISIENNE

Many of the sapphic cabarets that opened in the 1930s changed hands from one woman to the next over four decades—an important example of sapphic genealogical geographies at work. To illustrate yet again the impact of both proximity and affiliation on this process, let's take the case of Suzy Solidor and her cabaret La Vie Parisienne at 12 rue Sainte-Anne near the Opéra on the Right Bank. La Vie Parisienne provides a salient illustration of sapphic proliferation and transfer; it both attracted other

FIGURE 2.5: Three of the owners/managers of La Vie Parisienne (called Le Carroll's Club or the Frede Carroll's after 1961); *left to right*: Suzy Solidor (1933–46), Colette Mars (1946–61), and Frede (1961–70). Photo of Solidor from *La garçonne*, dir. Jean de Limur (1936). Courtesy of Alexandre Dupouy and Les Archives d'Éros. Publicity photo of Colette Mars, ca. 1956. Courtesy of the William Morris Agency. Photo of Frede from "Torrid Three from Gay Paree," *Female Mimics* 1, no. 3 (1963).

sapphic venues to the vicinity and was itself owned successively by Suzy Solidor (1933–46), the singer and actress Colette Mars (1946–61), and Frede and Miki (1961–70), who renamed the cabaret the Frede Carroll's after they took over the premises (fig. 2.5).[114]

La Vie Parisienne was not the first venue to attract homosexuals to the neighborhood around the Opéra. Since the eighteenth century, the rue Sainte-Anne had been associated with same-sex encounters as male prostitution spilled over from the galleries along the Palais-Royal. In the 1830s and 1840s there was public outcry against the throngs of female prostitutes who congregated there.[115] During the Great War, the Sainte-Anne Baths, established at number 63 rue Sainte-Anne, were popular among male soldiers; like many bathhouses throughout the city, they quickly attracted a gay male clientele, but no homosexual bars appear to have existed in the area.[116]

Little is known about the rue Sainte-Anne during the 1920s, although rumor has it that by 1930 Fred Pizella—an intimate friend of Maurice Chevalier's—had opened an American bar there. And in 1933 Suzy Solidor launched La Vie Parisienne at number 12.[117] Solidor originally co-owned the business with a performer known as Line Bady, although Solidor—wisely—soon took over control of the business.[118] (Not only did Bady belong, according to her police file, "to that very special world of sexual inverts of both sexes," but she was also identified as a drug addict and alcoholic.)[119] La Vie Parisienne provided a vital sanctuary for the two women's sapphic public.[120] The cabaret became known for its unique décor; in a narcissistic display, portraits of Solidor covered every inch of the walls and ceiling.

Solidor's cabaret played a powerful role in the sapphic entertainment community: in 1948 *Samedi soir* observed, "The charming children who sang in her cabaret were all her 'little allies.'"[121] Indeed, La Vie Parisienne provided a training ground for generations of young female entertainers who shared Solidor's interest in other women (including Colette Mars, Sidonie Baba, Dany Dauberson, and Agnès Capri, to name just a few).[122] These women often acted in solidarity in order to ensure their success. For example, when Solidor was on tour, the singer, poet, and journalist Ève Solange Terrasson-Duvernon (known by the stage name mentioned above, Sidonie Baba) ran the cabaret in Solidor's absence.[123]

In 1933 Sidonie Baba, whose musical talents had been discovered by the great chanteuse Yvette Guilbert, had opened her own "very gay cabaret" around the corner from La Vie Parisienne.[124] During the early evenings between 4 and 7 p.m., Le Joubertin (sometimes called Chez Sidonie) functioned as a *thé-dansant* (tea dance) for women. In 1936 Baba opened a new cabaret, Chez Sidonie Baba, within walking distance of her first venture.[125] In 1939 she closed Chez Sidonie Baba, inaugurating yet another cabaret, À L'Heureuse Galère ("A cabaret as big as her hand, which is petite," quipped *Le cri de Paris*), at 32 rue Sainte-Anne, right down the street from Solidor's thriving business.[126] This location also took advantage of Solidor's success. By 1943 Baba's "charming cabaret" on the rue Sainte-Anne was listed as open every night after 9 p.m. except Monday.[127] It remained open into the 1950s, although after the war—perhaps to distance the cabaret from the Occupation—Baba changed the venue's name back to Chez Sidonie Baba. By 1954 the venue (still in the same location) was listed as Aux Quatre Mules. It was later known simply as Sidonie Baba, even after programming was turned over to a heterosexual Italian man who attempted to retain a faithful but aging homosexual clientele. The venue finally closed in the 1960s. Baba meanwhile continued to operate a tiny café around the corner on the rue Sainte-Anne between 1958 and the end of the 1960s.[128]

If Baba benefited from Solidor's growing fame, she was not alone. In December 1938 the Jewish singer and actress Agnès Capri opened Chez Agnès Capri at 5 rue Molière, almost directly behind Solidor's cabaret on the rue Sainte-Anne.[129] The venture, unfortunately, didn't last long: in June 1940, France fell to the Germans. The new Vichy government began enacting ever more brutal antisemitic policies against first foreign and then French Jews. Accompanied by both her parents and her girlfriend Claude-Odette Calmon (whom the police described as "a young woman with a masculine silhouette"), Capri fled to the unoccupied zone.[130] When the Germans took over the entire country in November 1942, Capri, her parents, and Calmon left by boat for North Africa. They survived the war in Algeria, and Capri returned to Paris after the Liberation. Following a brief turn as the director of the Gaïté Montparnasse, Capri reopened her old cabaret (now known as Chez Agnès Capri) in its former location.[131] There, like Solidor, Capri made a special place for the next generation of female performers—such as Mick Micheyl, Nicole Louvier, and Colette Mars—who were also fond of the female sex.

The career of Moroccan-born Colette Mars (stage name of Nicole Félicie Emilie Huot), a divorced singer, actress, television producer, and *femme aux femmes*, also accelerated under Solidor's guidance. Mars performed regularly at La Vie Parisienne. In 1946 she took over the venue entirely after Solidor was penalized for her disreputable wartime activities.[132] Mars had (like Capri) spent the war years in North Africa. Mars left France with, as she later stated, "a [female] friend, who was adventurous, like I am."[133] The women traveled to Morocco and opened a bar together in Casablanca. Mars recalls, "I had the idea of organizing tea dances for the elegant women of 'Casa'; [Le Cintra Bar] was a huge success because women didn't usually frequent [such places] there."[134] When the bar was appropriated as an officers' club after the Americans landed, the women left for Algiers, where they ran a store selling antiques and flowers. Mars also began to sing for Radio-Alger on a weekly radio show. After the Liberation, Mars moved back to Paris. "From time to time," she recounts, "I would spend the evening at Suzy Solidor's cabaret."[135] It was Solidor who convinced Mars to start singing professionally. Shortly thereafter Mars took off with Josephine Baker to perform in Berlin. On her return, Mars picked up Solidor's reins: "We bought the place," she states, alluding here to her girlfriend Mireille Moignet, née Labrousse (presumably the same friend she lived with in Africa during the war).[136]

In 1947 Agnès Capri, while without a cabaret of her own, performed at La Vie Parisienne in what had by then become Mars's establishment. For Christmas 1948 Capri also produced a show featuring Lena Samara entitled "Violettes de Parme" (violets had long been a code for sapphic love) for Frede at Le Carroll's Club; Dany Dauberson opened the evening. Meanwhile, Mars and Moignet retained ownership of Solidor's cabaret until May 15, 1961, when they sold the business to Frede and Miki for the sum of fifty thousand francs.[137] Miki remembers going "alone to the rue Saint Anne to talk with Mireille and Colette Mars to set the price of the only real purchase of a lease that Frede ever had."[138] "The price was right," she continues, noting that "Frede sold her diamond rings and my family sent me some money and we made the 'Frede Carroll's 12 rue St. Anne' for almost ten years."[139] In keeping with the times, by 1963 Frede had disbanded her orchestra and "converted to record spinning" with "one live band night every Friday."[140]

After the war, when Solidor was forbidden to run her cabaret, sing, or record in France (for a year) and both deprived of voting rights and barred from appearing in the media (for five), the performer promptly took off on tour—first stop, New York City. Once the sanctions against her had elapsed, Solidor returned to Paris. By 1954 she had acquired a cabaret called La Boîte à Sardines. Reopened as Chez Suzy Solidor, it was situated at 4 rue Balzac on the chic Right Bank near the Champs-Élysées, close to Frede's original Le Carroll's Club on the rue de Ponthieu. When Colette Mars was not busy running Solidor's old venue, she sang at Le Carroll's, down the street from Solidor's new venture. Meanwhile, Dauberson guested at Solidor's when not singing at Le Carroll's. And when Capri lost control of her own cabaret on the rue Molière due to financial woes in the late 1950s, she also produced and performed at Solidor's new club. Unlike Capri's cabaret, Chez Suzy Solidor was a hit. When Solidor decided to retire in 1960, she relocated to Haut-de-Cagnes on the Côte d'Azur. Retirement didn't suit, and she soon opened another sapphic cabaret. Dauberson—Solidor's godchild and Frede's business partner—followed, opening a cabaret-restaurant, La Marmite, in neighboring Antibes after her companion, actress Nicole Berger, was tragically killed in a car accident.[141] Dauberson was gravely injured in the crash. She survived physically but never recovered emotionally; the loss plunged her into a lasting struggle with alcoholism.

Dauberson's choice to move south and remain close to Solidor during a time of personal trauma suggests the ways in which intimate bonds shaped sapphic geographies beyond the capital. During the 1950s and 1960s, the establishment of sapphic spaces and communities in the South of France also promoted a widening of sapphic spheres by means of travel and tourism, marking an early extension of sapphic visibility out from Paris and into *la France profonde* (provincial France). These spaces included Carroll's Beach at Cap d'Antibes (sometimes known as Le Carroll's La Garoupe, where Miki and Frede had their fateful first meeting) and the cabaret Frede opened with Miki a few years later on the Côte d'Azur's Route nationale 7 (also called the Frede Carroll's); Solidor's Chez Suzy Solidor in Haut-de-Cagnes; and Dauberson's La Marmite in Antibes. The same processes of sapphic geographic proximity and genealogical affiliation were then reproduced in other locales: Sylviane Francesconi, who later helped launch Toulouse's Bagdam Cafée in 1988, first encountered sapphic community in the 1970s in a club called Le Chi-Chi that opened within blocks of Solidor's former cabaret in Haut-de-Cagnes.

Solidor aged. After closing her last cabaret in the South of France, she lived out the rest of her life as an *antiquaire*, tippling whiskey under the table, indulging her insatiable appetite, and throwing elaborate parties. Into the 1970s Lulu de Montmartre (by then known as Lucienne Franchi or simply Frankie) was running cabarets in Pigalle, including L'Heure Bleue and La Roulotte (she had briefly lost control of the latter during the war when it was taken over by jazzman Django Reinhardt, but later managed to get it back).[142] She, too, gained weight and let herself go, losing the masculine elegance of her early days.[143] In these same years Jane Stick ran another cabaret féminin, the Entre Nous, on the rue Pigalle, where she would "sit next to the stove, knitting ceaselessly while telling hilarious stories."[144] Frede was taken ill in 1968. The diagnosis? Incurable leukemia. Nursed by Miki, she retreated to Mareil-le-Guyon, where the couple had renovated an old barn into their country home. The women nevertheless retained ownership of the Frede Carroll's on the rue Sainte-Anne until 1970. Frede succumbed to cancer in 1976 at the age of sixty-one. Miki, then fifty-one, returned to the United States and to Niki, the woman she had left behind when she flew to join Frede in Paris some twenty-two years earlier. Together they opened the Leff Bank, a French café and cabaret in Philadelphia, which they operated for sixteen years until Niki's death in 1992. Dauberson died of breast cancer in the South of France in 1979, at barely fifty-four. Madame Moune continued to manage her Parisian cabarets féminins until her death at eighty-two in 1986. By that time, all of these women and the venues they reigned over had been eclipsed by a new lesbian bar culture dominated by Paris's Katmandou discothèque (the Kat), which was run by a new queen of the sapphic night, the French-Vietnamese Elula Perrin. Even then, the sapphic genealogical networks prevailed. Monique "Momo" Dubrulle, who spent seventeen years working at the Kat, got her start as an entraîneuse under Frede at the Frede Carroll's on the rue Sainte-Anne.[145]

By the 1970s the rue Sainte-Anne had been appropriated by a growing gay male homosexual scene: entertainment maven Fabrice Emaer, who would later become the proprietor of Le Palace disco (inspired by New

York's Studio 54), opened Le Pimm's Bar at 3 rue Sainte-Anne in 1964, followed by one of France's first discothèques, Le Sept, at 7 rue Sainte-Anne in 1968. Gérald Nanty's Le Bronx, the first backroom bar, opened at number 11 soon thereafter. It was Emaer who rented the Frede Carroll's from Frede when, with her health declining, she finally relinquished control of the cabaret at 12 rue Sainte-Anne in 1970.[146] Emaer's venture, a café-théâtre, failed. In 1977 Miki finally sold the Société Frede Carroll's (which she had inherited after Frede's death) to Ysolde Chrétien, a former flight attendant who transformed the space into the ultramasculine Le Piano-Bar. Called the *rue aux hommes* (street for men) and denounced in *France soir* as one of the "centers of male prostitution in Paris," by 1977 the rue Sainte-Anne had been taken over by gay men, its lesbian past almost entirely erased from memory.[147] In autumn 2017 the building that once housed the Sainte-Anne Baths became the headquarters for French president Emmanuel Macron's then newly founded political party, La République en Marche![148] The only trace of the rue Sainte-Anne's earlier sapphic glory days resides in what is now the oldest lesbian bar in Paris, La Champmeslé, opened in 1979 and located at 4 rue Chabanais around the corner from Solidor's first cabaret. Still run today by its founder (a woman known as Josy), La Champmeslé now attracts a mixed crowd of gay, lesbian, bisexual, straight, and trans people and is no longer the bustling lesbian bar it was in decades past.[149]

Scholars often attribute the absence of queer women from the sexual map, whether urban or rural, to a lack of financial means and business savvy or to impractical political aims (lesbians, it is argued, are more likely to pursue utopian than pragmatic change).[150] This history of the sapphic cabaret demonstrates that such explanations can be patently false. Women like Solidor, Frede, Lulu de Montmartre, and Moune each managed successful, financially viable establishments over extended periods while sharing resources, experience, and expertise, thus also disproving Manuel Castells's influential claim that queer women are not "territorial."[151] This history also contradicts the idea that women either don't have what it takes to run a business or are simply too "naturally" competitive to assist one another: one of Frede's lawyers told Miki, for example, that Frede would never make her a partner because "women didn't help women." Countering such assumptions, Miki recalls, "When I became a bona-fide partner" in the first club that she and Frede created together in the South of France in 1959, "it wasn't because of my pretty eyes. It was because I knew the business."[152]

Not that there weren't conflicts or jealousies: Agnès Capri asserts that

Jane Stick (Capri's artistic director at Le Boeuf sur le Toit before Stick opened her own cabaret on the rue de Ponthieu) undermined Capri's early success. Charles Trenet, a "flamboyant homosexual" and "one of France's most beloved singers," was among those who defended Capri from Stick's "aggression."[153] Personal vendettas notwithstanding, wider conflicts among the queer female community didn't emerge until the appearance of a lesbian and gay political agenda in the 1970s and 1980s. As Rebecca Jennings has shown in the British context, in these years lesbian militants critiqued (sometimes violently) women who frequented cabaret and bar subcultures, labeling them insular "apolitical and passive victims of oppression" who were more concerned with nurturing their own love lives than with protesting against a heteronormative and patriarchal status quo.[154] Lesbian activists in these decades also denounced the commercial agenda that shaped bourgeois cabaret culture, in which entry was restricted to those fortunate few who had the financial means to consume. The political investment in lesbian visibility and the move to establish lesbian cooperatives in the 1980s (especially those like Toulouse's Bagdam Cafée, discussed in chapter 8, which occupied urban space in daylight hours) can be understood as a direct response to these critiques.

CONCLUSION

The erasure of sapphic history on the rue Sainte-Anne represents a larger erasure of queer female geographies from the history of Paris that bears emphasizing.[155] Michael Sibalis claims, for example, that "the [homosexual] heyday of the Rue Sainte-Anne coincided with the era of sexual liberation that began in France in May 1968, when strikes and riots almost toppled the conservative regime of Charles de Gaulle."[156] Stéphane Leroy agrees, stating, "The neighborhood of the rue Sainte-Anne was made desirable in the 1960s by Fabrice Emaer, the founder of the celebrated Palace."[157] Florence Tamagne discusses the existence of gay male clubs on the rue Sainte-Anne (like Le Vagabond and Le César, both established in the late 1950s) but virtually ignores Solidor, Frede, Mars, Capri, Baba, Stick, and Dauberson, as well as the multiple cabarets that these women operated.[158] In her work on the postwar years, Tamagne comments only that women "loathed cruising in places they found squalid and depressing" (she cites Le Monocle, Chez Moune, Elle et Lui, and Le New Moon, all of which "put on drag acts and sometimes lesbian SM shows, attract[ing] more tourists and voyeurs than women who loved women").[159] Her observations may accurately reflect the 1970s and after, but they misrepresent the decades examined here. The thriving history of La Vie Parisienne and its multiple transfers from one sapphist to the next over the course of almost forty years, as well as the history of the numerous sapphic cabarets established around it, not only disproves such claims but also overturns more general conclusions about the causal relationship between male and female queer urban spaces. Indeed, the larger sapphic genealogical geography I describe reveals that in the twentieth century, gay male commercial ventures did not always precede the establishment of lesbian ones, as the scholarship so frequently implies.

The history of sapphic space in modern France disrupts both heteronormative and homonormative conceptions of urban space. It demonstrates instead how women who loved women exerted—in Henri Lefebvre's terms—their "right to the city" in ways that created possibilities for building new forms of collective life.[160] It also provides contemporary readers with evidence for how earlier generations of women attempted to ensure that sapphic spaces, once occupied, would remain in the hands of other women like themselves. If this chapter creates an incomplete vision by failing to account for sites of socialization that were fleeting or not formally recognized, or by excluding establishments that were frequented but not dominated by women "like that" over these same years, it does so only in order to redress a more egregious absence and in hopes that future work will further complicate the story I am striving to tell.[161]

The sapphic cabarets opened in Paris in the late 1920s and 1930s proved vital to the development of same-sex female subcultures throughout France both before and after World War II. The dynamics nurtured in these venues helped shape queer female life more broadly in the years that followed. It is nonetheless true that the great majority of women who were affectively and erotically attracted to other women in the post-WWII decades, like those living in the interwar years, lived out their intimate predilections discreetly if they lived them at all. Many of these women married for a number of reasons: because of social, religious, or familial demands; because of the financial precarity that might accompany single life; because of a desire for children; or because they also loved men. Some found solace in homosocial religious orders. Others pursued economic independence, often as factory workers, clerks, domestics, salesgirls, teachers, or writers, either remaining celibate or cloistering quietly in the French equivalent of the "Boston marriage." Class status fettered women's choices in different ways; money could provide freedom, but social rank often carried sexual and familial obligations, and the laboring classes were not without independence. Not all women were unhappy, but some resorted to alcohol or drugs in order to cope. The widespread isolation that plagued so many women who loved women in these years makes any initiative capable of breaking that seclusion significant. It thus renders the persistent public presence of the sapphic cabarets and the female protagonists examined here all the more remarkable.

Frede, Suzy Solidor, Lulu de Montmartre, Moune, and the audacious female subcultural communities with whom they worked or for whom they performed enabled an urban geography where same-sex female desire was accepted and celebrated, countering social reprobation, religious sanction, and medical prejudice in a period that could be harshly unforgiving toward those who rejected heterosexual norms. At the same time, as commercial enterprises that sought to attract not only women seeking women but also male voyeurs and heterosexual tourists, and that were themselves implicated in police networks aimed at urban control, sapphic cabarets also contributed to the spread of sexual stereotypes and the commodification of sapphic sexuality. As we shall see, despite targeting *all* women as potential subjects of sapphic desire, by the postwar years these venues inadvertently rendered not just masculine but also *feminine* women legible as "lesbian" to both women seeking women and to the French public at large.

3

"A WOMAN DRESSED LIKE A MAN"

If you happened upon a certain doorway at 60 boulevard Edgar Quinet in Montparnasse on an autumn evening in 1932, you would have found yourself at Le Monocle, the Parisian nightclub that would soon become one of the most celebrated sapphic cabarets in France.[1] Situated opposite the swanky Le Sphinx bordello, it was easy to locate. In the early days an awning over the entry spelled out "Le Monocle" in bold script. The club was also listed in the local papers: "A cabaret of a very special kind, in which the clientele is composed exclusively of priestesses from Lesbos, has just opened in Montparnasse," announced the racy society rag *La vie parisienne* in September 1932.[2] Shortly thereafter, the French-Cuban writer Anaïs Nin visited Le Monocle, where she reported seeing "a woman dressed like a man who attracted me." "I thought a lot about her today," Nin mused in her journal, adding, "and I want to see her again."[3] The woman was none other than Frede—the same Frede who by the 1950s was running the fashionable Parisian cabaret Le Carroll's Club and who was described in the international press as "the most famous lesbian in the world."[4]

Anaïs Nin's comment, "I saw a woman dressed like a man who attracted me," expresses a vision of sapphic desire informed by the sartorial expression of female masculinity. It speaks to the historical construction of a stylized sexual subculture peopled by pairs composed of one masculine and one feminine woman. This subcultural system is now commonly referred to in English as "butch/femme."[5] Regardless of national context, explanations for how this same-sex binary came to flourish in the mid-twentieth-century West tend to fall into one of two camps: either this gendered organization of female same-sex behavior is thought to be biologically determined (the sexological perspective), or it is seen as an erotic choice.[6] By examining the gendered performances that took place in Parisian cabarets from the 1930s through the 1960s, this chapter tells a different story.

Sapphic cabarets where women "dressed like men" figure among the most popular symbols of lesbian desire.[7] By providing a new public arena for same-sex female desire, the sapphic cabaret paradoxically increased the visibility of the *femme masculine* (sometimes referred to in French as a *jules*) and her feminine counterpart (sometimes called a *nana*) at the very moment when interwar social anxieties about the erasure of sexual difference were on the rise.[8] Additionally, by rendering strangers recognizable to one another as members of a subordinate group who were united specifically (and sometimes only) by their same-sex desire, these cabarets helped expand an incipient lesbian subculture. Suzy Solidor's story, discussed earlier, nevertheless demonstrates that in the early 1930s the feminine female partner of a masculine woman was not unanimously understood as a lesbian. Over the course of the next few decades, the sapphic cabaret helped change this. Nineteenth-century cafés and brasseries had catered to women who desired women, but sapphic cabarets were unique in how they exploited butch/femme performances for profit.[9] This chapter explores that commercial staging and analyzes its effects. How did the sapphic cabaret influence how women interested in other women came to learn about, interpret, and express their "different" desires in France between 1930 and the 1960s? What role did the commercial promotion of specific forms of gender performance play in structuring these developments?

As chapter 1 demonstrates, when "the homosexual" was first described in Western science and medicine in the nineteenth century, this individual was understood primarily as a gender invert.[10] The connection between active sexuality and masculinity was so dominant in Western culture that eroticism between women was simply unthinkable: to pursue a woman one needed to "be" a man. The idea that the female homosexual was a man trapped in a woman's body was born of this belief. "True" lesbians presented as masculine and were biological anomalies. The feminine women who slept with these women were not necessarily lesbians themselves; instead, they were considered as either hypersexual, morally weak, or driven by greed. Historians have claimed, however, that during the twentieth century the argument for homosexuality as gender inversion was gradually effaced by a focus on the gender of the object of desire.[11] Here, lust for another person of the same sex trumped inversion as an explanation for homosexual behavior.[12]

This chapter contends that in France the sapphic cabaret played an important role in promoting this paradigmatic shift. If at the start of the 1930s female cabaret managers, their staff, and much of their public suspected masculine women of lesbianism, they also understood *all* women as susceptible to same-sex seduction. The performances that took place within the sapphic cabaret nonetheless came to market an influential image of "the lesbian" as *either* the masculine *or* the feminine half of a female same-sex couple, thus exemplifying both medical explanations of homosexuality that fixed on gender inversion and later explanations that tied homosexuality to object choice. (As we shall see, these paired gendered performances sometimes also reflected orientalist fantasies in which only the masculine partner figures as white.) While this binary relational construct was not hegemonic (the French police and much of the press clung to the solo "masculine gender invert" script into the 1960s), this newly twinned vision pushed the "femme" (who often plays a minor role in histories of female homosexuality) to the fore. It also challenged medical wisdom, not least because when a feminine woman—especially a bourgeois white woman—expressed desire for a masculine female partner (as Nin did in her journal), she contradicted class-based and racialized presumptions about gender inversion by taking the "active"—that is, the male—role.

In what follows, I argue that the figure of the cross-dressed *entraîneuse*—the female staff member hired to animate the *cabaret féminin* while garbed in masculine attire—played a special role in promulgating a sexual schema (butch/femme) that is usually explained as a product of either biology, moral failure, or erotic choice. My work reveals instead the important place of the commercial entertainment industry in shaping French sapphic subcultures from the interwar to the post-WWII years.[13] My goal is simple: I aim to show how sartorial practices that were both popularized *and required* by sapphic cabarets in the 1930s sustained a repertoire of paired gender performances that came to signify lesbian desire in ways that proved (not only to the French public but especially to women who loved women) remarkably enduring in the decades that followed. The outcome was threefold: First, these entertainment venues both reinforced and undermined normative gender binaries while enabling subcultural community formation. Second, they rendered the feminine woman legible *as a lesbian* to broader audiences. Third, they ensured that the already identifiable "butch" (long perceived as abnormal) was more readily subjected to surveillance, control, and persecution.

INVENTING BUTCH/FEMME AT THE SAPPHIC CABARET

Sapphic cabarets drew on traditions of cross-dressing that were already established in French theatre and popular entertainment. The theatre had long been considered "a harmless setting for the inversion of social hierarchy," and by the end of the nineteenth century, cross-dressing was a common theatrical conceit.[14] The craze for *la divine* Sarah, as the celebrated French actress Sarah Bernhardt was called by her adoring fans, was fed by the thespian's capacity to bend gender norms. The music-hall singer Polaire and the performer Ève Lavallière were equally gender ambiguous and frequently performed male roles.[15] By the late 1920s and early 1930s the "trouser role" had become a safe, nonthreatening way for the mass public to engage with masculine women in a contained theatrical environment "that only rarely challenged the dominant social order."[16]

Fascination with gender transgression also contributed to the popularization of the nineteenth-century performance art known in France as *transformisme*. Male performers like the Italian Leopoldo Fregoli and the French César Cascabel and Emile Grandsart (known as "the French Fregoli") delighted audiences across Europe by transforming in seconds from one gender to the next.[17] With his parodies of the great Yvette Guilbert (a singer whose repertoire reflected her sapphic leanings), the artist known as Monsieur Bertin inaugurated the genre of burlesque travesty in France, which quickly became a humoristic staple in Parisian cabaret line-ups. An American from Texas named Vander Clyde became a French music-hall sensation in the 1920s with his "numéro Barbette," in which the entertainer donned first female and then male dress while performing daring acrobatic feats.[18] Performances *en travesti* were also popular in the French provinces; from Normandy to the Auvergne and Brittany to Alsace, cross-dressing by both men and women was a fashionable form of theatrical entertainment.

Cabarets dedicated entirely to drag performances—venues referred to as *travestis*—opened in Paris, Marseille, and Toulon in the 1920s.[19] In Paris, Monsieur Tagada ran La Petite Chaumière on rue Berthe in Montmartre; it was the first cabaret to showcase a chorus line in drag.[20] In these venues, professional artists and eager amateurs—mostly men but also women with a taste for cross-dressing—trod the boards before rowdy and appreciative audiences. Cross-dressing in conventional theatrical or operatic productions did not necessarily indicate same-sex erotic interest; drag cabarets, conversely, reinforced this association in the public mind. The vulgarization of sexology contributed to the perception that even such theatrical practices were morally suspect—especially for women. As French journalist John Grand-Carteret (in his 1899 study *La femme en culotte* [The woman in pants]) admonished his readers, one must not forget that "cross-dressing" is "dear to the priestesses of Lesbos."[21] Along with the brasserie, the brothel, the popular press, the theatre, and the dance hall, drag cabarets contributed to cultural familiarity with and social stereotypes about nonnormative gender and sexual performances in the French public sphere. These public venues collectively provided the context from which both the sapphic cabaret and the cross-dressed entraîneuse emerged.

Sapphic cabarets were particularly renowned for the masculine women who frequented them as both employees and clients.[22] These venues hired women known as entraîneuses to beguile their female patrons into drinking and dancing, since the longer customers stayed, the more they paid. As such, sapphic cabarets promoted specific forms of fashionable display as signifiers of nonnormative desire. Le Monocle, for example, helped turn a preference in dress into a sexual symbol: its peculiar name derives from the interwar fashion (particularly popular among sapphic women) for sporting a monocle as part of a sartorial statement of sexual intent. Calling it one of "the most recognizable and readable signs of the lesbian culture of Paris," Marjorie Garber aptly associates the monocle with the Lacanian phallus, which can be "left to dangle" or "propped up imperiously as a sign of attentiveness."[23] Although risking, in Laura Doan's words, "rigidly conjoin[ing] accessory and identity," Garber makes clear that in interwar France the monocle was often evidence of not only a fashion statement but also an "erotic style."[24] A black tuxedo, white dress shirt, cravat, straight black skirt, crêpe-soled shoes, aggressive stance, cropped hairstyle slicked back with brilliantine, cigarette casually cocked between the fingers, and (sometimes, according to Colette) "a white carnation in the buttonhole" joined this trendy ocular affectation to complete the look of those manly female figures that Maryse Choisy qualified as *les actives* (the active ones) in her 1932 essay, "Dames seules" (Women alone).[25]

Through the late twentieth century, cross-dressing and female masculinity were often explained exclusively through modern categories of sexual identity: the subject was either a butch lesbian or transgender.[26] This reductive view—in which female masculinity "equals" some form of sexual or gender inversion—was in part the result of how nineteenth-century medical taxonomies gradually foreclosed on a disorderly array of other sexual and gendered possibilities.[27] The sapphic cabaret participated in this process of identity stabilization. Female masculinity in interwar France could signify a host of options, from fashionable modernity (embodied by *la garçonne*, the youthful tomboy of Victor Margueritte's 1922 novel, discussed earlier) to gender-crossing, where women "passed" as men for theatrical, financial, political, or other pragmatic reasons.[28] In contrast, inside the cabaret féminin (a location explicitly marked as sexually libertine), many masculine women attempted neither to attract the male gaze nor to "pass." They *presented*—regardless of gender identification—as *women* who desired women.[29] Their aim was same-sex sexual seduction. Their proximity to feminine women who desired them in return was the source of both their appeal and their threat.

REPRESENTING FEMALE MASCULINITY: BRASSAÏ AT LE MONOCLE

Among the few photographs that survive of French cabarets féminins from this period, the most memorable are those shot in 1932 in the dimly lit smoke-filled interior of Le Monocle by Brassaï—a man whom writer Henry Miller once described as "the eye of Paris."[30] These now iconic shots of tuxedo-clad masculine women drinking champagne and elegant female couples dancing or flirting have attracted popular and scholarly attention ever since a small selection of them first appeared in the 1934 collection *Voluptés de Paris*.[31] François Buot, Florence Tamagne, Helmut Gernsheim, and Allen Ellenzweig are among those who interpret Brassaï's photographs as "documentary statements" "not of public behavior, but of private conduct" in which "the subject of homosexuality" speaks "for itself."[32]

The photographs are fascinating and intimate. One depicts a tall feminine blonde in a fetching hat, her dress adorned with a wide collar and draping bow, her small breasts pressed tightly against those of her black-suited masculine partner (identifiable as none other than the cabaret's proprietor, Lulu de Montmartre), who inclines her head and sneaks a kiss.[33] In another, the same girl perches on a bentwood stool in front of the bar and converses with Lulu, whose hand, flashing a signet ring on the pinky finger—an established sapphic symbol—is placed possessively on her companion's thigh (fig. 3.1).[34] Behind the counter, the female bartender in white shirt and black tie pours a drink for another debonair mannish type, whose severe black skirt is rakishly set off by a satin stripe. Yet another portrait depicts an urbane young man—no, woman—smoking

FIGURE 3.1: Brassaï, "Lulu de Montparnasse habillée en smoking avec une femme au 'Monocle,'" 1932. Lulu was known to the police as Lulu de Montmartre. ArtRes 583847/RMN 00-021263. Courtesy of Art Resource / Réunion des musées nationaux Grand Palais.

and drinking, costumed in a black jacket and tuxedo collar, a thick watchband clasped around one wrist (fig. 3.2). And then there is the photograph often referred to as "Lesbian Couple at Le Monocle": here we see a heavy-set masculine woman usually identified as "Fat Claude" (but who according to the historian Xavier Demange is actually the French athlete and Nazi collaborator Violette Morris), her tie loosened and fingers grazing

FIGURE 3.2: Brassaï, "Lulu de Montparnasse buvant seule au 'Monocle,'" 1932. (The title is incorrect: This is not a photo of Lulu. She can be seen on the left in figure 3.1.) ArtRes 583848/RMN 00-021300. Courtesy of Art Resource / Réunion des musées nationaux Grand Palais.

the slender elbow of her feminine date, a woman with rouged lips, arched brows, and a fashionable marcel wave in her silken hair, whose plunging neckline reveals a waifish frame (fig. 3.3).[35]

These women appear to be mutually smitten and slightly bemused by the scenario that we are witnessing—subtle smiles are present on the lips of the bartender, the young "man," and the seated couple. This space seems

FIGURE 3.3: Brassaï, "Au 'Monocle,' un couple," 1932. ArtRes 583850/RMN 01-010190. Courtesy of Art Resource / Réunion des musées nationaux Grand Palais.

to belong to them, and they appear confident in their ownership of it. More important, it is equally possible to presume that we are witnessing photographic evidence of a community that has fully embraced a butch/femme aesthetic. And this is precisely how most viewers (and scholars) interpret these images. Jack Halberstam's conclusions are a case in point. The photographs at Le Monocle, Halberstam submits, "tell more than Brassaï can ever narrate: of inventive transgendering, the careful remodeling of the 'heterosexual matrix' by butch-femme couples reveling in the possibilities that Paris at night offered them in the 1930s."[36]

But is this reading accurate? My research suggests a more complicated picture. And clothing—what we wear, and how and why we wear it—is at its heart.

CROSS-DRESSING REQUIRED: CREATING THE (WHITE?) ENTRAÎNEUSE

When the twenty-year-old white Parisian woman later known as Frede first arrived at Le Monocle in search of employment, she was still using her given name, Suzanne Jeanne Baulé. Born out of wedlock on November 8, 1914, Frede (then Suzanne) was raised in a modest apartment on the rue Labat in Montmartre. At seventeen Suzanne abandoned her studies and landed a gig painting scenery at the Folies Bergère music hall. Tall and slim, she was soon asked to perform as a *figurante*—a silent extra—in one of the Folies Bergère's spectacular extravaganzas. Her efforts fell flat; Suzanne's allure was too masculine. Advised instead to try her luck at a new cabaret in Montmartre, Suzanne made her way to the boulevard Edgar Quinet. In a 1971 TV broadcast about her life (the first French documentary to address at length—if indirectly—female homosexuality), Frede reminisces that by the time she exited Le Monocle's doorway in 1934 with a job as an entraîneuse, her feminine garb had been replaced by a mannish black tuxedo, straight skirt, and tie (fig. 3.4).[37] Henceforth the statuesque girl with catlike eyes also had a new (and far more masculine) first name: Frede.[38]

The metamorphosis was not simple. Frede reports: "I had a little suit [that] was horrible to wear. It wasn't easy, but one didn't have a choice."[39] *One didn't have a choice*. Even given that such testimonies—like all oral histories—often tell us as much about the moment of recollection as they do about the events they describe, Frede's story reveals a rather astonishing possibility: at least some of the women who peopled the cabarets féminins cross-dressed not out of personal inclination (or, at least, not at first) but because their jobs demanded it. Cross-dressing was compulsory. Indeed, sapphic cabarets hired and required both masculine and feminine entraîneuses. According to a 1938 article in *Police magazine*, half of the twenty girls working at Le Monocle that year—designated as *les féminines*—were outfitted in evening gowns or cocktail dresses, and the rest—called *les garçonnes*—were dressed mannishly, in smoking jackets,

FIGURE 3.4: Frede shortly after being hired at Le Monocle, 1930s. Marilyn "Miki" Leff Papers, courtesy of Roy Winnick.

flats, straight skirts, and ties.[40] Staff could be asked to reverse gender roles dependent on management's needs.[41] Once obliged to adopt masculine attire, however, some entraîneuses (Frede included) consistently donned mannish garb in both public and private life.

From the outset French sapphic cabarets were thus sites of visible, vestimentary difference where the imperatives of the market supported the transgression of gender, sexual, and class norms. These economically and affectively motivated logics of social transgression were tied to racial metrics in complex ways. On the one hand (and although Brassaï's images of white women at Le Monocle suggest otherwise), nonwhite bodies were both present in and a point of attraction at the cabaret féminin. Racial diversity had increased in metropolitan France in concert with the expansion of the French empire. By the mid-1920s "negrophilia," fed by the hype over American jazz and the celebrity of African American entertainers like Ada "Bricktop" Smith and Josephine Baker (who seduced Paris at nineteen wearing little more than a skirt fashioned from bananas and who regularly appeared cross-dressed in white tie, top hat, and tails), made dark skin all the rage.[42] According to a 1928 exposé on the seamy underworld of Parisian prostitution, Baker's sexualized popularity ensured that neither a Parisian brothel nor a cabaret féminin "was complete without its Negress."[43] Other period photographs from the 1930s through the 1950s also attest to the presence of nonwhite women in French sapphic spaces.[44]

On the other hand, if French sapphic cabarets promoted racial mixing, they also reinscribed racial hierarchies in which female masculinity appears to have been—unlike in lesbian bars in the United States and notwithstanding celebrity exceptions like Josephine Baker or the cross-dressing American blues singer Gladys Bentley—largely a prerogative of whiteness.[45] The square logo sketched on Le Monocle's first business cards certainly demonstrates the commercial appropriation of a colonial fascination with race, sexuality, and gender that also shored up patriarchal white supremacy (fig. 3.5). The drawing depicts a mannish white woman with cropped hair (severely clad in a black smoking jacket and tie and sporting a monocle) watching a dark-skinned topless female attired only in a grass skirt (or are they bananas?) as she dances "savagely" while a white female orchestra plays in the background. The bare-breasted dancer photographed flirtatiously cowering on her knees beneath the masculine Lulu de Montmartre inside Le Monocle is similarly symbolically racialized by the "grass" skirt that encircles her white waist (fig. 3.6). Even spoofed, the image of the white "man" towering over the "Black" female

FIGURE 3.5: Le Monocle business card, 1933–34. "Vous trouverez au Monocle le fameux orchestra féminin Rico, Davis et Senes" [At the Monocle you will find the famous female orchestra of Rico, Davis, and Senes]. Dossier 1W 1032-46033. Courtesy of the Archives de la préfecture de police de Paris.

"heathen" reinscribes a power dynamic that is unmistakably both gendered and racialized. Such perspectives endured: two decades later photographs from Frede's Le Carroll's Club taken in the 1950s show a feminine Black woman in a turban, her colorful dress edged in ruffles, embracing a fake male lion inside a large cage (fig. 3.7). These are instances where white privilege—Le Monocle's, Frede's—traffics in stereotypes for financial profit; however, they are also illustrative of the ways that whiteness has historically been used to render certain incarnations of gender and sexual variance more socially acceptable than others.[46]

The fact that as early as the 1930s sapphic cabaret managers appear to have believed that it was commercially advantageous to provide their female customers with masculine white and feminine white *or* nonwhite women indicates the degree to which they understood female same-sex desire as a deeply gendered and racialized construct. Cabaret staff were schooled in this understanding: if a white masculine entraîneuse failed to attract immediate interest when she showed up at a patron's table to offer champagne or ask a woman to dance, she was instructed to make herself scarce so that she could quickly be replaced by one of her more feminine white or nonwhite colleagues.[47]

Management may have understood both masculine *and* feminine

FIGURE 3.6: Lulu de Montmartre and unidentified performer at Le Monocle, 1932. Courtesy of Alexandre Dupouy and Les Archives d'Éros.

gender performances as key to female same-sex desire, but they evidently thought that female masculinity possessed a particularly powerful commercial appeal. Matchbooks from Chez Moune that display a headshot of a masculine entraîneuse on one side and promotional information on the other (cabaret name, address, opening hours, phone number, etc.),

FIGURE 3.7: Performance at Le Carroll's Club, early 1950s. © Francis Bay, Series 5908, No. 57, Nice, France. Marilyn "Miki" Leff Papers, courtesy of Roy Winnick.

reinforce this argument. Such items demonstrate how sapphic cabarets publicly vaunted female masculinity as an advertising tactic, but they also suggest that the women who frequented these spaces were unafraid of being associated with nonnormative gender performances. Surely these keepsakes were used to convey coded messages; would not pulling such an item from one's purse or pocket to light a cigarette for oneself or a friend send a clear message to those "in the know"?[48]

Mainstream and tabloid press coverage of these venues was likewise obsessed with female masculinity—a clear indication of how it troubled (and titillated) social norms. For decades, journalists ensured that international audiences knew that cross-dressed female staff were a staple at the French sapphic cabaret: Evelyn Waugh, for example, reported in 1930 in the London *Fortnightly Review* that on a recent visit to Le Fétiche (the first known cabaret féminin in France), "the waitresses wore dinner jackets and asked the ladies in the party to dance."[49] In 1958 the American entertainment newspaper *Variety* asked "Who Wears the Pants?" in these venues, noting that at Le Monocle and Chez Moune (which it calls "travesty places"), "one cannot tell a man from a woman."[50] While it is possible that Waugh and others understood such cross-dressing practices as more indicative of immorality than same-sex sexual subjectivity, the repeated association in the mass media of butch/femme performance with couples known for their sapphic proclivities—women like Suzy Solidor and Yvonne de Bremond d'Ars, Lulu de Montmartre and her girlfriend Raymonde, or Frede and Miki—cemented this connection in the public imagination.

The 1963 publication of an exposé titled "Torrid Three from Gay Paree" (about three French cabarets it refers to as "switcheroos"—Le Monocle, the Frede Carroll's Club [identified as Frede's Cabaret], and Madame Moune's Chez Moune—printed in the US transgender magazine *Female Mimics*) reveals that the obsession with French female masculinity had not waned (fig. 3.8).[51] In "clubs where Women do the Man bit!" the article gushes, "all the waiters and other help are women dressed like men." These cabarets, it adds, "cater to those gals who would be guys and dress and act accordingly." At the same time, a caption above a photo of Madame Moune, who is poised to tango with a smiling long-haired young woman in a pencil skirt and high-necked blouse fastened with delicate pearl buttons, admits, "Dancing with the female customers is part of the job for Moune; this gal is one of the rare ones dressed like one" (fig. 3.9).

The admission that (even if rare) *some* women "dressed like" *women* at these venues emphasizes that there were indeed feminine women at sapphic cabarets. Moreover, while the text above the image of Moune and her feminine partner targets "gals who would be guys and dress and act accordingly," a hard look at the photograph is instructive: excepting her necktie and masculine collar, Madame Moune's attire is not all that different from what a severely dressed mature woman might wear on the street. What makes the image transgressive is not her mannish clothing; it is the feminine girl in her arms. And it was the public production of this

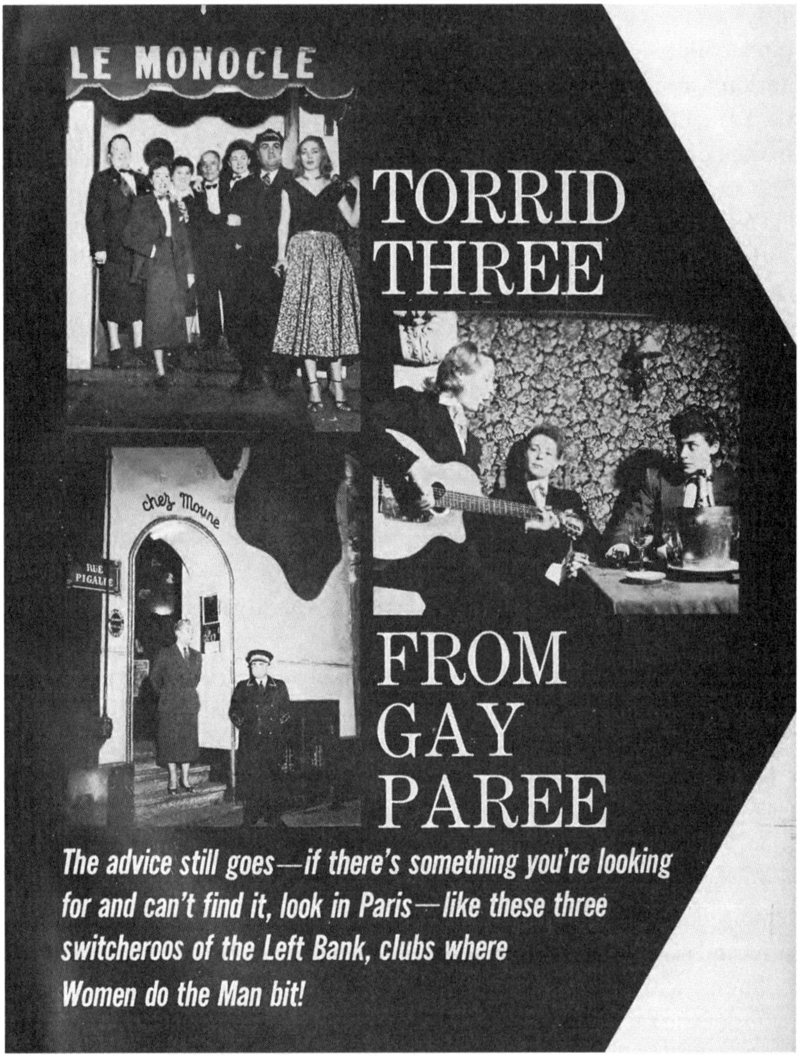

FIGURE 3.8: *Clockwise from top*: Le Monocle, the Frede Carroll's Club (identified as Frede's Cabaret; Frede on right), and Chez Moune (Moune on steps). "Torrid Three from Gay Paree," *Female Mimics* 1, no. 3 (1963).

coupled construct that made the sapphic cabarets such powerful places; importantly, their gendered practices also educated the very audiences to whom they sought to appeal.

In this way, sapphic cabarets used the entraîneuse as a vehicle to offer a particular vision of same-sex female desire to their customers. How did

FIGURE 3.9: Madame Moune and client at Chez Moune. "Torrid Three from Gay Paree," *Female Mimics* 1, no. 3 (1963).

French women seeking other women who crossed the thresholds of these venues respond?

"THEY ALL RESEMBLED ME": THE POWER OF NUMBERS

Women who visited sapphic cabarets had differing reactions to both the spectacle of butch/femme performance and the figure of the cross-dressed entraîneuse. Some had previously chanced upon female couples who performed gender and sexuality in nonnormative ways. Evelyne Rochedereux has vivid childhood memories of her gym teacher Mademoiselle F. walking through the streets with her "friend" Mademoiselle H. (the latter clad in a tie, suit, and vest and her hair styled very short) in the tiny Breton fishing village of Le Croisic in the early 1940s.[52] Others have no such memories. "Growing up," many women told me, "such women simply did not exist."[53] Nonnormative gender performance was notable because it was rare. Thus, the real revelation of the cabaret féminin lay in its numbers: it was the encounter not with just one or two cross-dressed individuals (a gym teacher, a social worker, an antiques dealer) and their feminine partners but with entire communities so paired that mattered.

For Hélène Azenor, the Bal de la Montagne Sainte-Geneviève, where in the 1930s she first met women dressed in what she later termed "lesbian fashion," was riveting precisely because she saw herself in the masculine women she discovered there: "The women, short hair, suit, and tie; I was stupefied to see that they all resembled me!"[54] Azenor was entranced by the cross-dressed entraîneuses, women whose dashing "black tuxedos with satin lapels, like a smoking jacket," she found "pleasing."[55] In contrast, Rolande Aurivel claimed to have avoided "clubs known as 'specialized,'" where "one went specifically to meet lesbians" and where "butch/femme" couples gathered.[56] Both Natalie Barney and Djuna Barnes loathed such bars, finding them garish and sleazy. Barney also disapproved of women who cross-dressed, abhorring "the need to mime the male in dress, speech, and demeanor."[57] Others adored the liberty that the cabarets' gender fluidity and sexual license allowed.

Barbara Bell and her girlfriend traveled to Paris from England in the early 1930s expressly to locate "lesbian" nightlife. They ended up at Le Monocle. Interviewed in the 1990s, Bell recalled: "I couldn't tell whether they were men or women sitting on these stools. They were really very butchy and very fem. . . . We didn't look outrageous like they were, but I suppose they dressed up for the evening, a lot of them. . . . There were so many tables, with little lamps, so many women, all lesbian, no men at all. Oh God, was I thrilled! It was out of this world. It was paradise."[58]

Like Azenor and Aurivel, Bell's use of the terms "lesbian," "butchy," and "fem[me]" may be anachronistic, yet her memories reveal both a comfort with gendered roles and the vital importance of this type of female space to the women who sought it out. Bell probably did not realize that many of the women she observed "dressed up for the evening" were entraîneuses wearing their requisite uniforms. Nevertheless (and especially given Bell's enthusiasm), the "outrageous" outfits that these women wore might well have become fashions to aspire to—reinforcing how sapphic cabarets modeled both sexual behavior and subcultural style for their publics.[59] At the same time, whereas Bell found the experience "paradise," other women considered the presence of entraîneuses deeply distressing, even repugnant. Monique Isselé, who visited sapphic cabarets in the 1950s, told me, "I was shocked by the entraîneuses dressed as men, with whom one had to dance. I didn't like it at all. Androgyny? Yes, well, I liked a masculine side but not when it was flaunted; these women were making a living; they had a percentage of what we drank. For them, it was a disguise."[60] For Isselé it was the seeming inauthenticity, even more than the entraîneuse's commercial role, that put her off. The problem resulted not from a discord between sex assigned at birth and gender performance. The problem was possible pretense: the aping of a desire for women that was not real.

Isselé's disdain toward entraîneuses who merely performed sapphic desire—although not all were "faking it"—was not uncommon. Her feelings are all the more understandable when we consider that for many women who loved other women, "normal life" was itself a form of forced impersonation. Adopting elements of masculine clothing—to the degree permitted—was one way of making same-sex female desire more visible.[61] Even Isselé acknowledges this. For a period, she wore a *lavallière* tie, and there are photos of her from the early 1950s in a jacket, tie, and plaid shirt with cropped hair (fig. 3.10) where, she notes, "I took on boyish airs, but," she adds, "I was very young." "If we looked like boys," she explains, "it was to please girls, because girls generally like boys, so we can't seduce them if we don't resemble boys, at least a little bit."[62]

Beginning in the 1930s, sapphic cabarets (and the masculine and feminine entraîneuses who worked there) modeled same-sex desire as a binary gendered behavior that could be assumed, manipulated, and transformed. Importantly, they modeled this en masse. They also commodified same-sex practices: rumor has it that *godemichés*, or dildos, were available for

FIGURE 3.10: Monique Isselé at nineteen in Clermont-Ferrand, France, 1951. On the back, Monique has written, "Disdainful, authoritarian . . . haughty allure . . . close to . . . reality!" Courtesy of Monique Isselé.

purchase in Le Monocle's WC.[63] For many women, the discovery of these venues—and the erotic freedoms they provided—was life-changing. Hegemonic perspectives nevertheless shaped expectations: girls were presumed to be attracted to "boys," and femininity attracted to masculinity. Sapphic cabarets capitalized on these beliefs. As the twentieth century progressed, however, the insistent normalization of the nuclear family (understood as reproductive, heterosexual, married, and monogamous) and the promotion of glamorous feminine fashions in France (in the form of Christian Dior's ultrawomanly "New Look") rendered female masculinity increasingly reprehensible. Consequently, archival records reveal that by the 1950s—especially from the perspective of the police—nine times out of ten only the mannish partner was targeted as lesbian. Clothing clinched the argument nearly every time.

POLICE SURVEILLANCE: "A VERY DECIDEDLY MASCULINE TYPE"

The Archives de la préfecture de police de Paris, especially its records compiled after World War II by the Brigade Mondaine, provide critical insights into the ways in which an administrative power relied on gendered conventions of dress in its attempts to identify (if not always control) female same-sex desire. While the vice police were not a monolith—individuals might be more or less prejudiced or moralizing—their officers were inevitably, as Kevin Mumford remarks for the American case, "keen observers of detail."[64] Dialogue transcribed in these documents also provides (admittedly mediated) information about how some women viewed their own behaviors.

The decision to collect *les blancs*, or white papers (a format first developed to gather information on prostitutes), about female cabaret workers was motivated by police interest in monitoring subversive sexual practices—in this case "lesbianism." At least ninety-two of the numerically coded loose-leaf reports prepared mainly between 1946 and 1951 targeted women hired as entraîneuses.[65] The sheer extent of these files (which were not arrest records and which had little judicial power) enables unprecedented examination of this milieu.[66] While sex between adult women was not illegal, with both the Mouvement Républicain Populaire and the Communist Party calling for a return to traditional values, these files betray a pointed anxiety about lesbianism in the postwar moment; almost every single dossier includes an inquiry into and a determination about the same-sex desires of the woman it concerns.[67]

Each of the reports compiled about cabaret staff reproduces a standardized set of data (name; date and place of birth; civil and parental status; type, cost, and location of current domicile) that is coupled with an individual's educational, employment, and arrest history. Most describe the appearance of the woman under consideration, specifically noting the gendered nature of her clothing. Forty of the files include photographs, which were generally taken either when a woman registered for employment or, less frequently, if she was booked for arrest.[68] The women range in age from eighteen to forty-eight. Over half were under twenty-six. Half were born in Paris. The rest hailed from all parts of France, including Corsica and the French Antilles. There were a number of foreigners: a Swiss, a Belgian, a Pole, a Bulgarian. One was American—a twenty-six-year-old singer named Mary Meade from Tulsa, Oklahoma. Those who were raised in France had all benefited from the Third Republic's educational system: most left formal schooling between the ages of thirteen and seventeen, often with a certificate.[69] A few advanced to higher education, but this was unusual—one studied medicine, another law. The majority were from the ranks of the working class and the petty bourgeoisie. Most had held stereotypically feminine jobs (shopgirls, seamstresses, secretaries, governesses, hairdressers, domestic servants), but there were also farm laborers, as well as one mechanic and one engineer. A few were aspiring actresses, models, musicians, or dancers, and one was a trapeze artist (who became an entraîneuse only after recovering from a horrifying fall in which she fractured both arms and legs and injured her spine).[70] One (a dancer later employed as Frede's business manager during the 1960s) was the daughter of the head of Heidsieck Champagne; a gold label from the vintage named in her honor appears in her police file.[71] Another woman who "issued from a very good family" wrote poetry; she was supported by her parents and "counted the writer Maurice Rostand among her mentors."[72] Although twelve were married, the vast majority were single. Six were separated. Eleven were divorced. Two were widowed. Most lived alone in furnished rooms that were rented by the day, the week, or the month. They moved frequently—often staying no more than a few weeks or months at one address.

The forty women with photographs in the files all appear to be white. Whether this was true of the remaining fifty-two women the police interviewed, we cannot know for sure. However, additional photographic evidence and testimonials suggest that while nonwhite performers and clients could both be found in sapphic cabarets after World War II, there were fewer nonwhite entraîneuses in the postwar years than in the 1930s.

Several of the white women I interviewed who frequented these venues in the 1950s expressed views—off the record—such as, "I don't think I'm a racist, but I couldn't imagine myself taking a woman of color as a lover." (One also confessed that—although she knew not why—she "was inordinately attracted to Jewish women.") Both white and nonwhite interviewees admitted to short-term liaisons that crossed race lines, but enduring interracial relationships seem to have been exceedingly rare. Postwar tensions over decolonization and immigration also diminished the commercial appeal of the *vogue nègre*. While nonwhite performers remained popular, cabarets féminins no longer appeared interested in hiring women of color as entraîneuses.[73]

Comparative analysis of police records shows that gender performance and sexual preferences influenced both how long women worked at the sapphic cabarets and how much they were paid while there. For some women, the job appears to have been a last resort; positions were held for only a few weeks or months and quickly abandoned when better opportunities presented themselves. However, at least twenty-four women in the police files constructed their lives in the sapphic cabarets, moving from one to the next over years or even decades. All save one of these women appeared masculine to their interlocutors.[74] Their persistent presence reminds us that the sapphic cabaret was one of the few places within French society where mannish women were both permitted and paid to pursue same-sex desires—a point that also suggests that some of the individuals who sought these jobs may have done so because they would today identify as trans men. Regardless of motivation, the money was relatively good. While only one-third were guaranteed a daily wage (tips made up the lion's share of a woman's salary), an entraîneuse generally earned between 1,000 and 1,500 francs for a night's work (derived from a fixed salary—if there was one—plus a percentage of alcohol sold and supplemented by flower or cigarette sales).[75] By way of comparison, in 1951 an unskilled female worker earned about 810 francs per day.[76] Those entraîneuses who slept with customers for cash—and some did, whether regularly or occasionally—certainly made more. But even the base earnings alone were evidently attractive.

The more closely we look at these files the more we can see the precarity of these women's circumstances. Class lines were often slippery. It was easy to fall and hard to rise. An illness, an injury, a divorce, a child, and suddenly there could be hardship, poverty, and sometimes the lure of alcohol, drugs, prostitution, or crime. A third of the documented women had arrest records. Several served time in women's prisons.[77] Three were charged with *proxénétisme* (procuring or pimping). Seventeen had engaged in prostitution.

Among these, half were recorded as *filles soumises* (registered prostitutes) between 1939 and 1945 (prior to the abolition of regulated prostitution in France in 1946), likely turning to prostitution in response to hardships brought on by the war. But two-thirds had no criminal records. Interestingly, despite their "suspect" places of employment, even those identified as lesbians sometimes had good reputations. Juliette Reboursière (known as Jo), a woman with over thirty years' experience in the business and the manager of Le Monocle from 1939 into the 1960s, is a prime example. Her file states: "Despite her very special [masculine] allure and doubtful morals," as well as the fact that she "frequently returned home late so drunk that she couldn't find the door to her own flat," Jo was a woman who "was much esteemed for her generosity and her good heart."[78] The nuance with which multiple reports handle the complicated connections between gender performance, sexual practices, and moral probity suggests that even for the police the link between sexual norms and social ethics was less self-evident than might be presumed.

The language—*lesbienne active*, *lesbienne notoire*, *lesbienne convaincue*, *lesbienne de nature*, or *émule de Lesbos* (active lesbian, notorious lesbian, convinced lesbian, natural lesbian, or follower of Lesbos)—and the sartorial criteria used to categorize women in these files nevertheless imply both judgment about female same-sex desire and a specific understanding of how it operated. Police almost always assumed lesbianism was present whenever women cross-dressed or otherwise transgressed gender norms. One report depicts "Gitou" (also known as "Jacky") as follows: "*Lesbienne active*, small stature, a very decidedly masculine type . . . wears only masculine clothes."[79] Of another, called "Paule," the inspector writes, "Although she denies it, there is no doubt that [she] is a lesbian. All of her exterior comportment—hair styled *à la garçonne*, masculine gestures and manners—appears to indicate this vice."[80] "Denise," described as a "convinced lesbian dressed as a man," forms "the perfect loving couple with Hélène."[81] And there is "Roby," a "*lesbienne active*, always dressed as a man, hair cut *à la garçonne* and cigarette between her lips," who apparently cannot "conceive of any other style of dress."[82] Or take "Jeannette," an entraîneuse at the Bal de la Montagne Sainte-Geneviève "always dressed as a boy," who "recently for fun put on a woman's blouse and swore never to do that again, since she found the outfit too ridiculous" (the word "imbecilic" is crossed out).[83] On the other hand, a woman's feminine clothing and manner immediately assuaged suspicions: "Nothing in her dress or speech leads one to believe that L.B. is an adept of Lesbos. She is only there [at Le

Fétiche] for the money."[84] Again and again the dossiers reveal that female masculinity "proved" lesbianism, whereas femininity "proved" heterosexuality. In this way, the police fell victim to the same fantasy that Brassaï's photographs promote: the belief that image necessarily equates to reality.

Sometimes the police were on point; clothing made the lesbian. A *France soir* article from 1951 stashed in one police file exemplifies precisely how Frede and her lover at the time, Mexican film siren María Félix, utilized clothing to emphasize sapphic sexual difference, subvert gender norms, and announce their romantic alliance. The press clipping covers the launch of designer Jacques Fath's spring collection. Parisian high society were already seated on the gold filigree chairs that lined the runway when Frede made a late entrance with María Félix on her arm. The latter was described as "sumptuously arrayed in an extremely low-cut dress of midnight blue hidden under a blue mink coat." For her part, Frede "of Carroll's cabaret, where female couples are more numerous, and more visible, than normal couples," was attired in "a Scottish smoking jacket, hair styled short, and a black skirt." When Frede reclaimed her overcoat from the cloakroom after the show, the article's author, journalist Carmen Tessier, notes that "it was lined in the same blue mink" as María's—an intimate nod to this pair's coupled status. But not all hints were so discreet: "In all the fashion salons," Tessier observes, "women sit in the first row, and men in the second. It was with complete ease that Frede seated herself behind María Félix. Throughout the entire show they smoked. María would light two cigarettes and pass one to Frede." Tessier concludes parenthetically, "*Usually it is the contrary*."[85] It is precisely this queering of gendered conventions, in which the mannishly attired Frede assumes the masculine position behind María, but María assumes the masculine role in lighting her lover's cigarette, that so troubled Tessier, her audience (among them M. Dumaine, the chief of protocol at the Élysée Palace who dropped his monocle in astonishment at the sight), and the police.[86] Indeed, the gender inversion described here was deemed so threatening that not only was it brought to police attention but the police inserted the damning article directly into the dossier they were compiling on the torrid and stormy love affair between the masculine Frede and her Mexican femme fatale.[87] Given María's femininity, it seems likely that she was understood as a rare example of the *lesbienne passive*.

While the police tracked Frede's masculine behavior, they let the nonnormative gender performances she promoted inside Le Carroll's Club slide, possibly due to the venue's celebrity clientele: along with María Félix, regulars included Marlene Dietrich (another of Frede's former lovers), Rita Hayworth, Marlon Brando, Errol Flynn, Maurice Chevalier, Simone Signoret, Yves Montand, Brigitte Bardot, Arletty, and Françoise Sagan.[88] For her part, Frede recognized that the public performance of female masculinity paid. It was Frede who, soon after she took over the management of Le Carroll's in 1948, inaugurated the practice—then considered risqué in the chic neighborhood near the Champs-Élysées—of women dancing together. Indeed, Frede reports that the first time she took on the masculine role and invited a woman to dance, her orchestra director Jerry Mengo was so shocked that he literally stopped the music. It was only after Frede curtly signaled him to continue that Mengo lifted his baton and the musicians resumed. Driven by desire (she states bluntly, "I wanted to dance with a woman"), Frede swiftly concluded that such behavior was good for publicity; she promptly "let the word circulate in the appropriate places" and hired a series of entraîneuses.[89] Soon thereafter, Frede engaged "U.S. looker Miki Leff as 'femcee'" (master of ceremonies), and Le Carroll's became known as a cabaret with a "lesbos motif."[90]

If the police, the press, and the public were interested in categorizing women's gender performances and sexual preferences, the women targeted also had a stake in this process. Scrutinizing their responses to accusations of lesbianism is informative. Most women (not surprisingly given the term's powerful stigma) denied the charge.[91] Many claimed that they worked in these venues only "for the money," often presenting their children as justification for the choice. Others argued that they were totally innocent of the "special ambience" of these places when hired.[92] Some of these women were not, had never been, and likely never would be involved with other women. Among them were women who were regularly observed keeping intimate company with men.[93] Sometimes, even without such corroborating evidence, women's denials were given credence.[94] Social status could be influential: "M.V." was the daughter of an important industrialist who worked for the government. When questioned on her choice of employment and mode of attire (she worked at Le Carroll's and was "always dressed as a boy"), M.V. claims that she was simply "preparing a report on the milieu." The agent, perhaps persuaded by M.V.'s prominent family background, appears to have accepted the tale.[95] Denials were at other times dismissed, as in this report: "Although she wears masculine clothes (for work reasons only, she claims) and has her hair cut *à l'aiglon* [a severe, mannish style], the above-named T. denies being a follower of Lesbos" (and this despite her employment at Le Monocle, Le Fétiche, and Chez Magdeleine Barry, another cabaret with a sapphic bent). Nevertheless, in dark black print another hand has written across the bottom of the file: "Nota bene: T. is indeed a lesbian." The included photo depicts an extremely masculine young woman wearing a plaid shirt with a string tie.[96]

Courageously courting scandal, not all women refuted accusations of lesbianism—some confirmed them with unexpected degrees of openness—demonstrating that even as the early postwar period became increasingly conservative, same-sex female desire was not entirely closeted. One young entraîneuse admitted that she had been "a lesbian" for many years. "Jeannette," her file tells us, "has always had boyish tastes and has preferred boy's games since childhood, which made her parents angry." Arrested for "exercising the métier of a *souteneur* [pimp], she has never had sexual relations with a man."[97] "Chouky," a chubby feminine blonde who is among the few women identified as a *lesbienne passive*, disclosed the same revelation.[98] "Bobby," a mannish young woman from Toulouse photographed in a checked suit jacket and plaid scarf, "tried to combat this vice by getting married at the age of twenty." Unfortunately, "marriage did nothing to moderate her ardor for persons of her own sex," and "Bobby" now shares the same room with "La Tour." The two women "mutually profess that they share a passion that exceeds the bonds of friendship."[99] Finally, some women were adamant about their preferences. "Conchita," a severe-looking thirty-three-year-old Spaniard who had been employed in the milieu on an immigrant's visa since 1938, pulled no punches. "As concerns her morals," her file reports, "she doesn't hide her repulsion for the stronger sex and her passion for persons of her own gender." The comment is underlined in pink. "Moreover," the agent concludes, "she makes no effort at discretion, since she is almost always dressed as a man."[100]

At issue here is *not* whether these women "actually are" lesbians. Rather, these sources highlight the importance police conferred on making this determination, as well as their reliance on clothing as a sign of sexual deviance, and also illustrate how women attempted to respond to police-imposed categories. In this way, they help us explore the conditions under which a subject identified as "a lesbian" was repathologized in France in the early to mid-twentieth century. What we are witnessing is an arena in which the varieties of erotic possibility that opened up in the interwar era were foreclosed by an analytic process bent on forcing all female sexual desire into one of two possible categories: "normal" women who dress like women and "lesbians" who dress like men. These files also reveal that while some of the women who dressed as men in sapphic cabarets desired other women and others did not, *all* of the women who worked in these spaces had an impact on the construction of an identity that came to be recognized as "lesbian."

DRESSING (AND UNDRESSING): SELLING SAPPHIC SEX

Sapphic cabarets were sometimes spaces where sex was sold, and sapphic gender performances and vestimentary codes also shaped prostitution.[101] Police files reveal that some women employed as entraîneuses—especially women who presented as feminine—engaged in heterosexual prostitution with men. Arrest records likewise indicate that others—generally described as masculine—worked as pimps, profiting from prostitution performed by their feminine female partners. A few did both. Interestingly, excepting the 1929 notation that Le Fétiche was a "brothel for lesbians" mentioned in the last chapter, the police dossiers that I reviewed were entirely silent on the subject of same-sex female prostitution.[102] Barbara Bell's memoirs give us a rare glimpse into how female clients learned of these possibilities and explain how these sexual transactions transpired. She describes her postwar experience at Le Monocle as follows:

> I was sitting on my own at the bar when a young woman came and sat next to me, very feminine. She was working there as a hostess. The bar woman introduced us. I told her I'd visited the club before the war and we got talking. Then she said, "Would you like to come upstairs with me?" She asked the madam—"that's all right,"—so she took me upstairs to a little room with a big bed. . . . We chatted for a long time and then we had a drink and then we made love. You could have your drinks brought up and when you left you paid the madam for the drinks and the girl.
>
> I'd never paid for sex before—it made the experience more thrilling. It was just an experiment, a big adventure. It wasn't sheer lust, "I must have a woman, I'm going to pay for it." Nothing of that sort. You didn't have to do anything, the girl just came to you or the madam would ask you if you wanted a partner. You could choose a butchy one or a femmy one. You could just go up with somebody you got off with at the bar as well—if you were a fast pair.[103]

Once again, Bell's emphasis on gender difference ("You could choose a butchy one or a femmy one") reinforces the fact that sartorial codes and gender performances were presumed to play a role in motivating sapphic desire. Bell's account also emphasizes that these cabarets sometimes provided access to private spaces where women could have sex with one another, whether money changed hands or not. Such spaces were especially important in an urban environment where not only was privacy hard to come by but also the agents of the Service des Garnis (another branch of the police) kept a daily record of the individuals who rented hotel rooms in Paris and the department of the Seine.[104] If two women were reported to have shared a single room, whether for one night or several, these records could be used to support accusations of lesbianism. While lesbianism was not technically criminalized between adults, such accusations, even when unproven, could lead to loss of employment or housing, social ostracism, and violence.

Regardless of the dangers, when no other options were available, women did rent rooms—by the hour, the day, or the week—to consummate their passions. Monique Isselé remembers being "solicited" once while sitting at the bar of the Entre Nous in the late 1950s and deciding to court the risk associated with this practice. She told me that the whole experience took her by surprise, since she'd never thought of herself as "fast." "I was very young," Isselé recalls:

> And she was very masculine. . . . I went with her to a hotel room. I was astonished to be there with that girl. Undressed, you know, she was all girl. And I spent a wonderful night with her. I never saw her again. I don't remember having paid her, but someone opened the door to ask whether she was available, and I was embarrassed. We were both naked, and I had thrown myself into something that was astonishing for me. She was masculine, but not too much. She was dressed, dressed for the performance you could say. And I ended up in a hotel room. I see it now.[105]

In Isselé's memory, this woman was not an entraîneuse, although Isselé admits that she may have been a prostitute. "Prostitute, that is a vague word," she demurs. Isselé remembers the interaction as shaped by seduction and desire, however, not by commerce. In this instance the conventions of butch and femme are also shown to have been a matter of degree, for if the girl was "very masculine," Isselé was not herself dressed in feminine attire. "I was masculine when I went out to the cabarets," she states, "but not like her." Both Bell's and Isselé's testimonies also present us with another important finding: they augment a long history of scholarship on gay male prostitution by reminding us that both men and women sell and pay for homosexual sex, while suggesting that the pursuit of sexual contact—not just relationships or friendships—was a key part of sapphic social life.

THE "MALE" PREROGATIVE: GENDER, VIOLENCE, AND SEXUAL POWER

The pictures painted by both Bell and Isselé of their sexual liaisons are remarkably positive, even gentle. But as we can imagine, this was not always the case. The sapphic cabaret's flourishing world of forbidden sex could also be terribly violent, and that violence was perpetrated by both men and other women. Entraîneuses often found themselves implicated in these altercations. Romantic jealousy was augmented by alcohol. And when an entraîneuse flirted with customers, she risked angering women who (often fueled by drink) felt threatened by, or jealous of, her actions. Brawls frequently broke out between masculine women who were competing for the attentions of a femme.[106] Danielle "Dan" Monnel (who started as an entraîneuse under Frede at Le Carroll's) discovered the hard way not to mess with another woman's girl. When she left the Bal de la Montagne-Sainte-Geneviève on her very first night in Paris, after an evening spent dancing "with a pretty blonde" who had propositioned her ("It was great, it was hot, it was troubling and exciting," she recalls), Dan felt a hand on her shoulder. "I turned and took a phenomenal punch" from "the blonde's [female] girlfriend," she muses, adding, "that shiner marked my debut into Paris nightlife."[107] Indeed, it was a sapphic murder (one woman shooting and killing another in the street in front of the cabaret) that precipitated the closure of the Jeu de Dames in the 1980s.[108] But in the vast majority of cases, the biggest threats in these venues did not issue from other women. They came from men.

Sapphic cabarets existed within a larger social world that, while intrigued by them, was often ill at ease with or openly hostile to the behaviors practiced there. The women who worked in and frequented these spaces were subjected to harassment, discrimination, and verbal and physical violence. For cabaret owners, this could take many forms, from outright attacks and neighbors' noise complaints to more insidious pressures from the police and local officials. Police compelled female managers to hire "in-house security" (the local mafia) and inundated them with citations for minor infractions that went unremarked in other establishments, subjecting their businesses to an interminable cycle of legal battles and fines.[109] But as difficult as such harassment was, it did not compare with the dangers posed by male violence. Women could be targeted either for succumbing to the seductions of other women who usurped masculine privilege or for usurping that privilege themselves. When entraîneuses entered sexual relationships with the women they met, they often inadvertently opened both themselves and their partners to harm. Cabaret staff learned to expect such attacks and were even trained in how to respond to them. Dan Monnel reports that when she was hired by Lulu de Montmartre to work at L'Heure Bleue at 54 rue Pigalle (the former location of Le Fétiche/Chez Moune) in the early 1960s, she received instructions from Lulu directly: "During my first evening there the boss [Lulu] taught me to use a baton, a broken bottle, or to fight with a chair, holding it by the seat and defending myself with the four legs; and then she taught me how to throw a punch, American-style. I learned all these different self-defense techniques (there were no gym classes for that sort of thing at the time), and I realized that I could have need of them."[110] Dan's experience is a reminder that women's rejection of gender and sexual norms during these years could often come at tremendous cost.

CONCLUSION

Mobilized by the impact of unprecedented and often harrowing events, during the interwar era women challenged male prerogatives, gained independence, and pursued pleasures that had previously been denied them. The French fascination with *la garçonne* and with sexual experimentation, female emancipation, and masculine travesty testified to an unprecedented period of gender fluidity and play. In a bohemian urban world of music halls, brasseries, *bals*, bars, cabarets, and restaurants, women were seen to be both capable of lust and responsive to masculine (and not just male) seduction. From the interwar years through at least the 1960s, French sapphic cabarets exploited this vision of female passion and pleasure for financial gain. At the same time, by creating a public space in which female same-sex desire was both modeled and marketed as a binary construct, the sapphic cabaret educated generations of women in a new form of sexual subjectivity—butch/femme—in which female homosexuality was expressed as much through *attraction to* the gendered performance of a same-sex partner as through the gendered performances of subjects themselves.

The role of the entraîneuse is particularly enigmatic in this story: it reveals that female masculinity could be learned and imposed while raising the possibility that some of the cross-dressed women in France's cabarets féminins may not have been erotically interested in other women at all.[111] As such, it illustrates how commercial culture played an important part in shaping French sapphic subjectivities, and especially butch/femme roles, not just in the 1930s but for decades to come. Of course, the "fact" of the entraîneuse does not negate evidence of female masculinity or butch/femme sexual systems outside the sapphic cabarets in these years. However, it does complicate our understanding of how, why, and when these practices became widespread in France. What else does it tell us?

Sapphic cabarets enabled female customers interested in same-sex intimacy to respond to three imperatives: the desire to seduce other women, the desire to evade the male gaze, and the desire—among many women—for group identification (the constitution of subcultural community). The commodification of butch/femme performance within these spaces facilitated these ends, but with contradictory results. For just as the cabaret helped produce the (binary gendered) female couple as the "self-evident" expression of female same-sex desire, the "butch/femme" and "lesbian" paradigms it promoted also hardened the parameters between normative and nonnormative sexual worlds. As French society turned increasingly repressive, it became ever more difficult for women to engage sexually with other women without the risk of stigmatization that these paradigms, and the labels applied to them, came to imply.

The Vichy regime reinforced heteronormativity and augmented homophobia. When Philippe Pétain came to power on a platform promoting "Travail, Famille, Patrie" (Work, Family, Country) after France fell to Germany in June 1940, he heralded a resurgent emphasis on family values. The French women who had built their lives running the sapphic cabarets of Paris either fled or opened their doors to the Germans. In 1942 homosexuality was for the first time in 150 years specifically targeted by the French state when, as noted previously, the collaborationist regime outlawed same-sex acts committed with a partner under the age of twenty-one, while the age of heterosexual majority remained thirteen.[112] With his gaze set firmly on the "twelve million beautiful babies" required to rebuild the nation, Charles de Gaulle retained the discriminatory language of the Vichy legislation almost verbatim at the war's end.[113] The Brigade Mondaine's decision to heighten police surveillance of the sapphic cabarets in the aftermath of the war was likely a direct response to such wide-ranging efforts to promote heterosexuality and enforce gender norms.

The police archives demonstrate that following World War II, female masculinity—readily interpreted as inextricable from perverse sexuality—was increasingly vulnerable to surveillance and persecution. This encounter with the law further accelerated the fixing of "lesbian" identities as deviant in the postwar era.[114] But the butch/femme binary promoted in the sapphic cabaret also rendered *feminine* women who desired women newly legible both inside and outside of female sexual subcultures. As female masculinity came under attack—and was targeted in the press and on the streets—"femme" sexuality found new audiences. Here, again, the sapphic cabaret played a role.

As the next chapter will show, during the 1950s and 1960s, under the guise of the musical variety show, French state television and radio inadvertently brought a whole host of female cabaret artists—many of whom capitalized on the forms of "femme" subjectivity developed in the sapphic cabarets—into living rooms across the nation. Singers like Suzy Solidor, Colette Mars, Dany Dauberson, Mick Micheyl, and the young Nicole Louvier and Gribouille used the artistic and affective license afforded by French TV's variety show genre to contravene heterosexist social norms and challenge the confines of traditional femininity and female desire. Aired during prime time on first just one and then two channels, the many TV broadcasts in which these women appeared—together with the record albums they released, the radio programs they sang on, and the press they received—had an immeasurably larger impact on the French public than they would have today. For those capable of decrypting sapphic subcultural codes, the televised cabaret venue, in particular, was rife with "lesbian" inferences in a period heretofore understood as a wasteland for homosexual representation. But if television enabled broad access to nonnormative models of female gender and sexuality long before the emergence of movements for lesbian and gay rights in the 1970s, it did so in part because the binary model that the sapphic cabaret had helped produce facilitated the legibility of "femme" sexuality. And that "femme" was now visible because she was haunted by the (absent) presence of "a woman dressed like a man."

4

SAPPHO ON THE SMALL SCREEN

From 1957 to 1959 the French singer and actress Colette Mars and her friend the journalist Micheline Sandrel produced and hosted the musical variety show *Cabaret du soir* on France's sole TV channel, RTF Télévision.[1] According to the magazine *La semaine radiophonique*, the broadcast "permitted provincials and Parisian homebodies to watch 'as if they were there' one of the most brilliant cabaret performances that existed."[2] Filmed by multiple cameras and aired live on Saturday nights, *Cabaret du soir* re-created a bourgeois *cabaret artistique* on Paris's Right Bank: elegantly dressed people cluster around tiny tables decked with ashtrays and champagne in silver ice buckets, sipping drinks, smoking, chatting, applauding each act, and sometimes dancing between sets.[3] A grand piano sits on a small stage at the back. The resident feline, a white cat frequently seen on the laps of guests, looks on. Stylishly attired in a cocktail dress and modest jewelry (including that coded sign for sapphic desire, a pinky ring), Mars usually opens the evening with a song. The broadcast continues in standard cabaret fashion, with acts by musicians, including African American jazz singers and European opera divas, dancers, drag artists, and comedians alternating in turn.[4] Informal conversations between Mars, Sandrel, and performers or members of the on-camera audience punctuate the program. First impressions notwithstanding, however, this was not your "normal" variety show.

Cabaret du soir and broadcasts like it shared key aspects of the sapphic cabaret (already a recognizable signifier for lesbianism in cinema, literature, and the press) with audiences throughout the French nation and its empire.[5] The transgressive nature of these shows was all the more remarkable given that they appeared at a time when even serious broadcasts avoided controversy (particularly once censorship intensified under Gaullist rule in the late 1950s). Frothy and fun, musical variety shows were considered politically benign options that carried broad cross-class appeal.[6] Perhaps because of the genre's innocuous status, women were disproportionately active on these shows as producers, directors, presenters, and performers.[7] And yet, while applauded by some as "essentially family television" and mocked by others as conformist conservative pabulum, many of these programs creatively undermined the supposedly apolitical normative models of heterosexuality and gender that they were widely presumed to support.[8]

This chapter pays attention to a selection of musical variety broadcasts and their female performers, as well as to related coverage in the press, on the radio, and in the diverse commodities (records, record covers, fan clubs, books, films) connected to the variety show genre, in order to challenge historical claims about lesbian invisibility in 1950s and 1960s France.[9] After briefly analyzing how identarian approaches have hampered previous research and providing background on early French TV, I sketch out the reigning narrative of the history of homosexuality on the French small screen. I then propose a set of tools that can help us "see queerly" in order to reevaluate that narrative. In the bulk of the chapter these tools are applied to a corpus of sources. I use this corpus to successively analyze (1) queer female (especially femme) representation, (2) what I call "femme failure," (3) the (queer) single woman, and (4) female androgyny on French television. I argue that the televisual traces of female same-sex desire and gender variance apparent on French musical variety shows in the 1950s and 1960s both reflected and helped produce transgressive female sexual subjectivities in an era often typified by its fierce embrace of white heterosexist sociocultural norms.[10] This material thus calls the impress of postwar heteronormativity into question and—by exposing how the sapphic genealogical geographies established in Parisian cabarets extended via television throughout the nation and beyond—reinforces my larger argument about the unexpected continuities between the sapphic subcultures that flourished in interwar Paris and the national and international politicization of French lesbian activism in the 1970s and after. It also contributes to queering the history of television—a project with broad implications that explores the media's role in counterpublic formation while unmasking the heteronormative politics that shape the public sphere.[11]

QUEERING THE HISTORY OF FRENCH TV

More than three decades ago, Nancy Fraser wrote, "Public discursive arenas are among the most important and underrecognized sites in which social identities are constructed, deconstructed and reconstructed."[12] Although arguably now outpaced by interactive digital media, since the mid-twentieth century television has provided one of the most powerful "public discursive arenas" through which the process of social identity construction transpires. Given TV's capacity to mold public perceptions of social identities, the assumptions that structure television as a narrative genre are far from anodyne. Samuel A. Chambers remarks that these assumptions include the expectation that "everyone, straight, or queer, will be judged, measured, proved, and evaluated from the perspective of the heterosexual norm." On television, he continues, heteronormativity typically "operates the same way it does in society: invisibly."[13] And yet, by challenging traditional models of female desire and gender performance, the musical variety shows discussed in this chapter paradoxically rendered this normative agenda visible—and not just to marginalized others—subtly undercutting the hegemonic hold of heterosexual domesticity over postwar France.

Most of the research on homosexuality on television has utilized an identity-based approach that seeks to recognize and analyze homosexual characters or topics.[14] The databases located at Inathèque, the research branch of the Institut national de l'audiovisuel (the French national television archive, or INA), follow this logic. Consequently, unless broadcasts are identified in the catalogue as "homosexual," "gay," or "lesbian," they largely remain lost to researchers in a vast sea of audiovisual sources.[15] This scholarly and archival paradigm—which strives mainly to pinpoint programs or individuals that have "qualified" as homosexual—produces a particular chronological narrative, which goes like this: the 1950s and 1960s were a wasteland and the 1970s a (modest) watershed for the televising of queer identities.[16] During the early 1970s French TV discussed (mainly male) homosexuality in broadcasts on England, the United States, Holland, and Spain.[17] Rare allusions to female same-sex desire in France start to surface in these same years in reports on the Mouvement de libération des femmes (Women's Liberation Movement).[18] This is followed by newsmagazines and documentaries on (again mainly male) homosexuality as a French social issue.[19] Shows often consist of conversations in which journalists bring experts—psychiatrists, medical professionals, or priests—and the general (i.e., heterosexual) public into dialogue with self-avowed

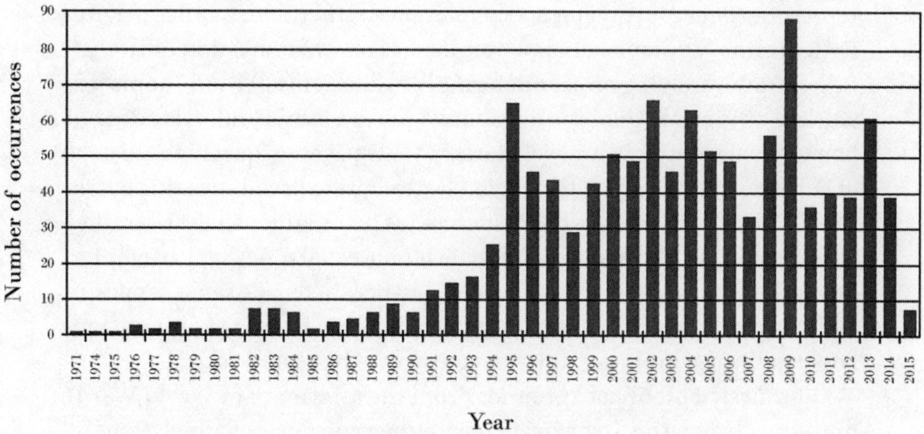

FIGURE 4.1: Graph of the results of the author's cross-listed searches conducted in June 2015 using the words "lesbien(ne)," "homosexual(le)," and "homosexualité féminine" in the databases at Inathèque de France (the French national television archives). Note the absence of broadcasts prior to 1971. Courtesy of Inathèque de France / Institut national de l'audiovisuel.

homosexuals. Thematically, most of these programs are haunted by two questions: Is homosexuality a mental perversion or a natural variation, and what are the societal and personal costs of being "closeted"? French broadcasts addressing (mostly fictional) lesbians or gays then increase gradually after 1990, correlating more or less precisely with the liberalization—some might say commercialization—of homosexuality in France. As a result, most scholars of the French media claim that it was not until the 1990s that nonnormative sexualities and gender performances became regularly, if still infrequently, visible on French TV (fig. 4.1).[20]

Given postwar social and political pressures (including the French National Assembly's censuring of homosexuality as a "social plague" in 1960 under the Mirguet Amendment, along with prostitution, alcoholism, and tuberculosis), French television's apparent reluctance to address same-sex desire during these years is unsurprising. Given the social and political advances in homosexual rights since the 1970s (including the emergence of the homosexual and feminist movements, the abrogation in 1982 of age of consent laws penalizing homosexuality, and the prohibition in 1985 of discrimination against homosexuals in employment or services on the basis of *moeurs* [moral behavior]), the increase in French TV broadcasts with queer characters or themes in the 1990s seems similarly predictable. Whether this increased visibility can be attributed to a rise in positive representations and greater social tolerance rather than to what Brigitte Rollet terms "audiovisual opportunism" is another question entirely.[21] Either way, by relying on search terms like "lesbien(ne)" and "homosexual(le)," this entire analytic arc acquiesces to a static understanding of homosexual identity. Newer scholarship that strives to "queer" the history of homosexuality—my own included—attempts to destabilize this narrative.[22] Thus, in my analysis of TV sources (as in my larger analysis), rather than looking for "lesbians" or "female homosexuals" per se, I attempt to "see queerly" in order to render visible instances of female same-sex desire and nonnormative gender performance usually considered absent from both traditional archives and the mainstream historical record.

But, first, a bit of background: From the aftermath of World War II until 1984 (when the first private, partly encrypted pay channel, Canal+, went on the air), French television was entirely public and state controlled. Produced mainly in Paris, by the late 1950s most of France was networked, with French programs also broadcast to Algeria, Morocco, and Tunisia, as well as (thanks to the establishment of the Eurovision network in 1954) to Great Britain, Luxembourg, Monte Carlo, Belgium, Italy, Austria, Denmark, Norway, Sweden, Switzerland, and Germany.[23] Nationally organized as the Radiodiffusion-télévision française (the RTF) in 1949 and reconfigured in 1964 as the Office de radiodiffusion-télévision française (the ORTF), French broadcasting was initially limited to first one and then—after 1964—just two channels. A third channel was not added until 1972. This paucity meant that in TV's early years any given program captured the lion's share of the viewing audience.

Like the BBC in the United Kingdom, French public television was committed to a tripartite agenda that aspired "to entertain, to inform, [and] to educate" the nation's citizenry.[24] Despite its democratic mission, however, the new technology didn't come cheap.[25] As a result, in 1958 fewer than 10 percent of the French public owned TV sets. The medium's influence was nonetheless far greater than ownership figures suggest since it was common for audiences to view TV communally—averaging eight spectators per receiver—in télé-clubs, schools, and cafés.[26] By 1966, 51.7 percent of French households had their own TVs. By 1972 (when a third channel was launched) that number had risen to 77.5 percent.[27] Newspapers and magazines—particularly program guides like *Télévision programme magazine*, *Télé-7-jours*, and *La semaine radiophonique* and specialized fan publications like *Music-Hall*—also reported regularly on television broadcasts, thus expanding their impact. For many cabaret performers, television, radio, film, live performance, the press, and the recording industry all worked reciprocally to heighten celebrity recognition and enhance commercial success. In this, the musical variety show format was among those TV genres that epitomized the marketing impulses of *les trentes glorieuses*—the economic miracle that transformed the French nation between 1945 and 1975.[28]

State sponsored, and state controlled, early TV broadcasts were subject to censorship, with violations penalized. Threatened by sanctions, but with moral expectations largely uncodified, early television professionals were generally timid about all things sexual.[29] Government concerns shaped administrative practice: In 1961, following Nicole Paquin's split-second nude scene in Maurice Cazeneuve's televised film *The Execution*, fears about public morality led the RTF to institute the *rectangle blanc*—a cautionary white box imposed on the lower-right corner of the screen to alert viewers to potentially "disturbing" contents, both erotic and violent.[30] *Speakerine* (female announcer) Noëlle Noblecourt was fired in 1964 ostensibly for permitting her knees to peek out from beneath a too-short skirt.[31] Popular folk singer-songwriter and radio and TV personality Nicole Louvier also disappeared from the small screen in the mid-1960s in part because her personal affections (expressed in her lyrics, poems, and semiautobiographical novels) were overtly homosexual.[32] Fearful of reproach, many TV professionals practiced self-censorship. Éliane Victor, producer/host of the popular *Les femmes aussi* (Women also), which aired from 1963 to 1974, reports avoiding controversial topics—including abortion, contraception, and homosexuality—entirely.[33]

SEEING QUEERLY: LESBIAN REPRESENTATION AND SEXUAL STYLE

One does not require the legal censorship of "sex perversion"—demonstrated by the Motion Picture Production Code that shaped Hollywood film from 1930 to 1968—in order to impose heterosexual norms on audiovisual production.[34] Early French television broadcasting is a case in point. But, as Patricia White observes, if queer representation is thought objectionable, "where do we look [for queer desire]?"[35] We might as easily ask, "How do we *know*?"[36] Building off White's work on cinema, I propose that when it comes to French TV, in order to *cherchez la femme* (find the woman) who loves women, three analytics guide our investigation: visual and linguistic coding, extratextual information, and intertextuality.[37] All three analytics are at work in the broadcasts discussed below, and each contributes in different ways to making nonnormative forms of female desire, sociability, and gender visible to both marginal and dominant publics. Because of the ways in which shared representation is critical to the development of communal consciousness, this visibility was an essential precursor to the politicization of queer female counterpublics in the 1970s and 1980s.

Visual and linguistic codes are evident in the source itself. While neither stable nor universal, such codes function as a kind of shorthand. This coding renders types of persons (masculine, feminine), modes of embodiment (posture, affect), sartorial choices (clothing, hairstyle, jewelry), composition, and performative forms of address (including language and points of view) legible as "lesbian" to publics as they become increasingly savvy about subcultural discourses and sexological theories. Linguistic codes are present in speech and song and are often grounded in gender or sexual ambiguity. With her intentional disregard for gender norms, Suzy Solidor's joking suggestion in an early 1954 TV appearance that she might name her new cabaret on the rue Balzac Chez Tonton Solidor (At Uncle Solidor's)—thus masculinizing her subjectivity—plays on the gendered contradiction between linguistic (male) and visual (female) signification to relay its coded message.[38] (For those au courant, Chez Tonton was also a name for Liberty's Bar, a celebrated Montmartre cabaret opened in the interwar years that often featured drag performers and was known for its posse of queer performers and clientele.[39]) Visual and linguistic codes can thus communicate what Judith Butler has famously called "gender trouble"—an expression for gender performances that unsettle, where something isn't quite right. Gender trouble manifests not just via sartorial or linguistic signs but also via a gaze or touch held too long, a subversive style of delivery or personification, or an uneasy or overdetermined appearance. The discordant elements "trouble" the effects of naturalness and inevitability that "keep gender in its place by posturing as the foundational illusions of [heteronormative] identity."[40]

Both visual and linguistic codes were vital to the musical performances examined below. As Martin Pénet observes in his work on interwar *chansons interlopes* (a term meaning "songs of the underworld," which refers to songs that express queer desire or "designate marginality, in particular in homosexual and lesbian milieux"), the songs sung in French cabarets and music halls (and, by extension, later on TV) could as easily derive their coded meanings from the manner in which they were performed as from their narrative content.[41] French song lyrics rarely openly mentioned homosexuality before the 1970s—instead, it was a question of decrypting messages that, if stated indirectly, were often performed overtly.[42] Given that most early lyricists were male, this interpretive freedom was particularly important for women. Sometimes lyrics fail to specify gender, leaving the sex of the song's protagonists open to interpretation: In January 1959, for example, Colette Mars sings the hit "Garde ça pour toi" (Keep it to yourself) as *Cabaret du soir*'s opening number.[43] When she croons (to the tune of "Catch a Falling Star"), "Keep it to yourself / Don't tell a soul / Love has made a fool of me / Keep it to yourself / Don't tell a soul / They'd just make fun of us," and concludes, "Those evil-hearted men / wouldn't understand a thing [about our secret love]," the gender of the object of her affections is entirely equivocal.[44] Altered intonation, double entendre and parody, and the stressing of certain syllables (especially at the end of a word, which in French can change the designated gender) could likewise communicate a desired message. Such performative ambiguity has extraordinary power, for it can be at once deniable and discreet, invisible, and available. Despite being by nature oblique, linguistic codes were thus particularly adept at establishing complicity between a queer performer and her public.

Extratextual information could be just as vital to the public's capacity to discern female same-sex desire on the small screen—all the more so if viewers were unschooled in the reading of "lesbian" subcultural codes. In France in the 1950s, 1960s, and early 1970s, audience familiarity with the biographies or erotic affinities of specific female entertainers, authors, or guests typically derived from gossip, rumor, or hearsay that circulated through and was amplified by the press. These reports then informed public perception and helped people negotiate the meanings embedded in the broadcasts they viewed. Indeed, when viewers were unable to "see queerly," extratextual information could promote queer intelligibility. Thus, while some television viewers might perceive the feminine Colette Mars as heterosexual, public buzz about her acquisition of the notorious lesbian *Amazone* Suzy Solidor's cabaret La Vie Parisienne encouraged audiences to read Mars's sexuality in nonnormative terms.[45] Solidor's sapphic reputation in the press, on the radio, and in cinema similarly preceded her own television appearances and informed her audiences. Although television never referred directly to Dany Dauberson's interest in women, press speculation about her sexual exploits—including reports of Dany's torrid affair with the Italian princess Giovanna Pignatelli, who left her husband and children for the singer—meant that some viewers were likely aware of her "tendencies."[46] Press gossip about Dauberson's "formative relationship" (at age twenty) with the actress Carmen Torres, her subsequent status as Suzy Solidor's protégée (she was dubbed "la nouvelle Suzy Solidor" [the new Suzy Solidor]), and her role performing at and managing Frede's Le Carroll's cabaret in the 1950s likely sealed the deal.[47]

Finally, producers, journalists, and performers addressed love between women intertextually by alluding to "lesbian texts"—written, oral, or audiovisual—in their broadcasts. Intertextual strategies of "indirection and inscription" provided television professionals and performers with "conventions for encoding lesbianism" and means of communicating shared cultural knowledge about female same-sex desire or gender nonconformity without necessarily naming it directly.[48] In the process, they also created further texts for subsequent citation.

Viewer familiarity with key texts known to describe love between women (whether poems, songs, books, or films) enabled the television public to interpret intertextual messages astutely. The examples are numerous: In 1954 journalist François Chalais explains—without ever mentioning same-sex desire—that director Serge de Poligny chose to add a male character to his filmed version of Colette's *Claudine à l'école* (*Claudine at School*) in order to "eliminate the [novel's] scandalous elements."[49] Familiarity with the book's "scandalous" sapphic intrigues informed audience comprehension of the substitutions and elisions to which Poligny referred. The ironic result of this erasure is that it refers us back to the unspeakable—that is, lesbianism—which is connoted via its replacement. Even fleeting intertextual associations could carry potent messages. Such is the case in Pierre-Jean Vaillard's 1956 skit on what French celebrities did on their summer vacations, where Vaillard describes Solidor reciting verses to Bilitis on the beaches of her native Brittany, a veiled reference to Pierre Louÿs's 1894 collection of sapphic love poetry, *Les chansons de Bilitis* (*The Songs of Bilitis*).[50] Thanks to its multiple cultural manifestations, televised allusions to Victor Margueritte's *La garçonne* (and to the films, songs, and women associated with it) likewise became—as we shall soon see—a powerful intertextual symbol of lesbian love and desire on French TV.[51]

During the postwar decades, visual and linguistic codes, extratextual information, and intertextuality operated hand in glove to enable audiences to decipher queer content in French programs that were broadcast at a time when neither performers nor audiences might necessarily have recognized themselves as lesbian or homosexual. The French musical variety show—a spectacular mass cultural form in which female entertainers were presented as desirable objects whose "to-be-looked-at-ness" (to quote film theorist Laura Mulvey) was both emphasized and encouraged—became a prime purveyor of a tantalizing matrix of gender nonconformity and sapphic seduction.[52] The resultant "queering" provided public models for identification and imitation, thus enabling the expansion of a sapphic subculture and laying important groundwork for the politicization of lesbian counterpublics in the decades to come.

CABARET DU SOIR: QUEER WOMEN ON FRENCH TV IN THE 1950S

Neither Colette Mars nor Micheline Sandrel were new to audiovisual media when they launched *Cabaret du soir* in the fall of 1957. With her melodious voice and infectious smile, Mars likely first attracted the attention of industry professionals in the 1940s while performing at La Vie Parisienne. She soon landed a series of small film roles.[53] Mars's earliest TV broadcasts included performances on the musical variety shows *Télé-Paris* (1954), *Bouquet de joie* (1956), *Trente-six chandelles* (1957), and *École des vedettes* (1957). Married at twenty-two and divorced the following year (she confided to one reporter that she refused to remarry since "the single life fits me like a glove"), she exuded an erotic ambiguity from the start of her career.[54] On her first television appearance, for example, Mars coyly told *Télé-Paris*'s presenter Roger Feral of a recent trip to New York, where she was delighted to have met up with the "adorable" French singer and actress Liliane Liévain (known as "Lilo" and then performing on Broadway in Cole Porter's *Can-Can* with the young Gwen Verdon) because "[Lilo] was truly a love of mine."[55] Innocent turn of phrase or coded message? It was evidently for the public to decide. Mars proceeded to sing a flirtatious rendition of Réné Rouzaud's 1951 version of "Mon petit fichu" (My little shawl) (later reprised on *Cabaret du soir* and released on vinyl), in which she croons, "With a flower in your hair / and your naked arms / and your naked arms / With a flower in your hair / where are you going / now that evening has come? / Where are you going / without your little shawl?" The gender of the object of her desire was likely to seem—at least to some members of her audience—rather obvious.

Beguiling and coquettish, Mars embodied femme performativity. In 1957, the year that *Cabaret du soir* began broadcasting, Mars also featured (as noted in chapter 1) in director Jacqueline Audry's 1957 cinematic remake of *La garçonne*.[56] Dressed in a pink satin smoking jacket and skirt and dangling pearl earrings, Mars plays Nichette, the "bona fide" lesbian who seduces the film's protagonist Monique (played by Andrée Debar).[57] As previously discussed, twenty years prior Suzy Solidor played a lesbian in the 1936 film adaptation of the book. Both Mars and Debar promoted the 1957 film repeatedly on television, each time underscoring the possibility of female same-sex desire. On February 4, 1957, for example, when Mars sings the film's title song on the musical variety show *Trente-six chandelles*, she first appears on stage in Debar's company, her arm discretely but defiantly tucked under that of her cinematic paramour, while the men present look on (fig. 4.2). The gesture reads as possessive in a way that subtly mocks the performative conventions of heterosexuality. *La garçonne* was also discussed on multiple episodes of *Cabaret du soir*, including, naturally, on the broadcast in which Debar appeared as a guest. *Cabaret du soir* thus magnified both extra- and intertextual loops between Solidor's sapphic legacy; Mars's sapphic reputation; *La garçonne* as a novel, film, and hit song (which Mars sang in the 1957 film, performed on television, and released on vinyl); and—as we shall soon see—*Cabaret du soir*'s own televisual mise-en-scène of queer female homosociality.[58]

Mars's coproducer and cohost on *Cabaret du soir*, journalist Micheline Sandrel, also presented as femme. Sandrel cut her journalistic teeth in radio after World War II.[59] A prolific reporter, she continued to work in radio throughout her career, but by the early 1950s she was also narrating and directing TV documentaries about French small towns. Elegant, articulate, and ladylike, Sandrel soon built up a formidable resumé: between 1955 and September 1957 alone she covered over six hundred subjects for television news. Sandrel rapidly established a reputation as a respected television journalist, working simultaneously on the male-dominated TV news and (after 1955) on Maïté Célérier de Sannois's acclaimed *Magazine féminin* (Women's magazine, 1950–70). From 1956 to 1964 Sandrel produced and presented the variety show *Ce soir à* (Tonight in . . .). She also produced and hosted the variety show *Rive droite*. Across multiple broadcasts Sandrel regularly and repeatedly interviewed female celebrities who shared her interest in women, conducting more than twenty interviews with Mick Micheyl, at least seven with Nicole Louvier, and three with Dany Dauberson.

Together, Mars and Sandrel exercised remarkable control over *Cabaret du soir*, selecting performers and on-camera audiences, conceptualizing the program, and managing content.[60] They regularly invited women known for breaching normative models of gender and sexuality (whether in their lives or in the characters they played) to appear on their show. These guests included singers Dany Dauberson, Mick Micheyl (twice), and Nicole Louvier (twice); actresses Andrée Debar (star of the 1957 film *La garçonne*), Marie Bell (star of the 1936 film *La garçonne*), Edwige Feuillère (star of Jacqueline Audry's 1951 sapphic-themed film *Olivia*), and Nicole

FIGURE 4.2: Colette Mars (as Nichette, *left*) and Andrée Debar (as Monique, *right*) promoting director Jacqueline Audry's 1957 film *La garçonne* on the variety show *Trente-six chandelles*. Mars is about to sing the film's title song. *Trente-six chandelles*, dir. Roger Iglesis, RTF Télévision, broadcast February 4, 1957. Courtesy of the Institut national de l'audiovisuel.

Berger (Dany Dauberson's companion, whose breakthrough role was in Claude Autant-Lara's 1954 film adaptation of Colette's *Le blé en herbe*); novelist Christiane Rochefort; and mystery writer and antiquarian Yvonne de Bremond d'Ars (Solidor's mentor and first lover). As was common in the cabaret milieu, Mars and Sandrel also included *transformistes* in their line-up; drag artists and impersonators Charpini, Jacques Dufilho, and Claude Véga (each of whom parodied femininity) were featured guests.

If *Cabaret du soir*'s formal performances pushed the boundaries of heteronormativity, the show likewise captured informal queer conversations on-screen. A prime example is the broadcast on February 15, 1958.[61] That evening, Mars and Sandrel welcomed singers Marie Souris and Paule Sabatier, actress Mademoiselle Barsacq, and ballerina Ludmilla Tchérina to the program. During the course of the show Mars and Sandrel join two women on the set—Yvonne de Bremond d'Ars and her companion, an unnamed female introduced to spectators only as "sa cousine" (her cousin)—at the table where they were seated as members of the cabaret audience. By the 1950s Bremond d'Ars (the woman Suzy Solidor once characterized as "[my] sister, mother, lover") had become a celebrity in her own right, thanks both to the success of a series of mystery novels that she authored about the antique business and to the popularity of her prize-winning Christmas displays, which decorated the windows of her elegant antique shop at 20 rue du Faubourg Saint-Honoré in Paris each December.[62]

In the broadcast, Mars, Sandrel, and Bremond d'Ars's "cousin" all perform femininity. In contrast (and despite bright lipstick), Bremond d'Ars, with her closely cropped masculine hairstyle and tailored (if bejeweled) jacket, remains discernible as a dandified image of the "mythic mannish lesbian" first popularized in the early twentieth century.[63] While some viewers could doubtless read Bremond d'Ars's sartorial codes, those who could not might nonetheless have been privy to extratextual information that rendered her character "suspect"—not just because of her notorious love affair with Solidor but also because antique dealers were famously associated with homosexuality in France.[64]

The ensuing conversation between Mars, Sandrel, Bremond d'Ars, and her cousin is ripe with innuendo: When questioned about an upcoming trip to London, Bremond d'Ars sighs, stating, "Oh my goodness, traveling, I've never liked it. . . . It tears you from the soft climate of the house. . . . We have to leave the dogs." And yet, she continues, "My cousin is happy because she adores traveling." "Yes, I have a very lovely trip in view," chimes in her doting companion. The cousin in question, Jeanne, the Comtesse Anatole

FIGURE 4.3: *Left to right*: Colette Mars, the "cousin" Jeanne de Bremond d'Ars, Yvonne de Bremond d'Ars, and Micheline Sandrel on *Cabaret du soir*. *Cabaret du soir*, dir. Jean Kerchbron, RTF Télévision, broadcast February 15, 1958. Courtesy of the Institut national de l'audiovisuel.

de Bremond d'Ars, actually *was* related to Yvonne de Bremond d'Ars by marriage—but it was merely a marriage of convenience (discussed in chapter 1) to Yvonne's father, which enabled the two women to live, work, and travel together without raising eyebrows.[65] The trope of familial connection—be that as cousins, sisters, or even mother and daughter—had long been used as a ruse by female couples seeking to keep their intimate relationships private. This ruse, as theorist Sara Ahmed also notes, enables others to "[*overlook*] *signs of difference*," thus erasing lesbian desire.[66] For audiences familiar with these women, however, the footage of Colette Mars, Micheline Sandrel, and Yvonne and Jeanne de Bremond d'Ars clustered around a table, coupled with Yvonne's fond reference to her cousin's happiness and use of the plural "we" (as in "we have to leave the dogs"), produces a recognizable tableau of queer sociability (fig. 4.3).

Catherine Gonnard and Elisabeth Lebovici contend that such queer conversations were unique to early TV; they argue that, not yet accustomed to being filmed by multiple cameras, female performers often failed to understand what was being broadcast and hence to monitor their own behavior.[67] But is this the only explanation? Or might this "lack of discretion" have been a choice, whether for personal or political reasons? After all, most of these women were professionals and, as such, were well aware of their audiences. There is, alas, no way to know. However, whether our protagonists were conscious of their actions, their informal tête-à-têtes offered French television audiences an unprecedented window into networks of nonheteronormative intimacy. The result is that *Cabaret du soir* provides us with surprisingly candid examples of televised moments "entre-femmes" (between women), where women "look at, listen to, admire, support," and flirt with one another in ways that clearly contravene heterosexual imperatives.[68]

The mise-en-scène of the (televised) cabaret, which situates these female conversations at tables on-screen, is also noteworthy.[69] Tables, Ahmed argues, are quotidian objects normatively inscribed as familial (e.g., the kitchen table) and heterosexual (man facing woman).[70] With its small tables for seating couples, the cabaret typically reproduces this heterosexual schema. But here on *Cabaret du soir*—just as in the sapphic cabarets themselves—this schema is ignored. As career women gathered together in the absence of men at a table on a public stage (rather than in a private setting), Micheline Sandrel, Colette Mars, and Yvonne and Jeanne de Bremond d'Ars invoke independence, pleasure, glamour, and female eroticism over private maternal heterosexual domesticity.[71] They congregate here not in obeyance to a patriarchal model of kinship and female servitude but by choice, interest, and common desire.[72]

Cabaret du soir was replete with such queer female moments, which were discernible—if to varying degrees—to audiences capable of reading the visual and linguistic codes and inter- and extratextual references conveyed therein. The writer Christiane Rochefort, for example, appears on the broadcast following the publication of her prize-winning first novel *Le repos du guerrier* (The warrior's rest).[73] Seated between Sandrel and Mars, Rochefort salaciously observes, "I am like King Pausole, one woman at a time [nightly] all year long!" Those familiar would pick up on the intertextual reference to Pierre Louÿs's 1901 novel *Les aventures du roi Pausole* (*The Adventures of King Pausole*), the tale of a king with 366 wives, each of whom spend one night a year with him. The king's daughter Aline runs off with Mirabelle, a harem dancer dressed as a boy. (Pierre Louÿs also authored the sapphic ode *Les chansons de Bilitis*, mentioned earlier.) In identifying with the king, Rochefort slyly critiques monogamy while linguistically queering her own gender.

On another episode, the incomparable stage and screen actress Edwige

Feuillère appears as the "guest of honor."[74] In the 1930s, Feuillère had acted in stage and cinematic versions of *Le roi Pausole* (alongside Suzy Solidor's former girlfriend Doris Lemaire). Acclaimed for her portrayal of the sapphically seductive headmistress Mademoiselle Julie in Jacqueline Audry's 1951 film *Olivia* (set in that nest of female passions, the girls' boarding school), Feuillère also starred (with Dany Dauberson's companion, Nicole Berger) in Autant-Lara's 1954 film version of Colette's *Le blé en herbe*. Conversing with Mars, Feuillère explains that she often wears jewelry made by the poet Paule Le Métayer (also present at the table), whose unmarried status is confirmed when she is publicly referred to as "Mademoiselle Le Métayer." At Mars's request, Feuillère, whose fondness for women was well known (according to one of my interviewees, the actress held court at the Parisian sapphic cabaret Jeu des Dames in the 1960s),[75] recites one of Le Métayer's poems for the audience. The poem's language is, as Gonnard and Lebovici observe, "sufficiently ambiguous that, in hearing it, it is impossible to know the nature of the love in question."[76] The power of this ambiguity for viewers desperate to find cultural representations that might reflect their own desires cannot be underestimated.

WHEN FEMININITY FAILS: FEMALE PERFORMANCE AS DRAG

For women entering the public eye in the 1950s, the trappings of femininity bore the weight of law.[77] Whether on television, stage, or film, female entertainers were universally expected to bow to the feminine imperative.[78] But even when women acquiesced, compliance did not necessarily convince. Some of the most compelling moments of queer female subjectivity on French TV during these years are thus moments when femininity takes on the troubling guise of drag. In these moments of "gender trouble," no extent of frills and furbelows suffice to prevent femininity from "failing" simply because a woman "looks like a man" despite all efforts to the contrary. We can detect such performances of "femme failure" in broadcast coverage of singers Suzy Solidor, Dany Dauberson, and Mick Micheyl.

Although she often played the femme fatale in her youth, Suzy Solidor moved fluidly between feminine and masculine gender performances throughout her lifetime. Ferociously and publicly sexual, Solidor's athletic physique and guttural singing voice infused her female curves with a virile appeal. Sexy publicity shots from the interwar period of a lipstick-clad Solidor either entirely naked or in fashionable evening gowns and fur stoles abound. Conversely, by the 1970s and 1980s, the singer increasingly chose masculine attire, especially in private life.[79] The aging Solidor referred to herself as "the Admiral," adopted male pronouns, and regularly appeared decked out in mannish double-breasted nautical jackets replete with gold braid, brass buttons, and jaunty sailor caps—a look that suited her singing repertoire (she had long specialized in songs of the sea).[80] She also developed a penchant for sporting manly cloaks worn "à l'Aristide Bruant" (an iconic nineteenth-century French cabaret singer and impresario).[81]

Interestingly, even when unabashedly performing femininity (as she frequently did throughout the 1930s, 1940s, and 1950s), it was Solidor's masculine aura—and subsequent "femme failure"—that often attracted media attention. In 1933, the daily *Marianne* commented, "All at once, during dinner, a male voice was heard. It was Suzy Solidor."[82] "Suzy Solidor has male hands. Energy dominates," wrote *Le monde illustré* in 1939.[83] The contradiction between the singer's deep voice and her voluptuous body perturbed some audiences. Journalists regularly targeted her genderqueer aspect: "Is it '*un*' interview or '*une*' interview?" an article in *La vie parisienne* inquired, adding, "We say '*un*' interview for a man, and '*une*' interview for a woman . . . but if it concerns Suzy S.?"[84] Solidor was just as apt to taunt herself about her mannish affect. Indeed, the singer had a long history of parodying gender norms. In an article published in *Samedi soir* in 1948 she states, "It's not just my voice that fools them . . . I have entirely transformed into a man." "After all," she provocatively observes, "I'm an old boy."[85] Are such comments indicative of a "trans-before-trans" persona? Perhaps, but it is impossible to know for certain. Regardless, such extratextual references inevitably helped queer public knowledge of the singer and contributed to the creation of an imagined community of sympathetic queer admirers.

Even at her most femme, Solidor's televised performances trouble normative gender codes. Instances of Solidor's "femme failure" are legion. In 1958, just two years shy of her sixtieth birthday, for example, Solidor appeared on *Les joies de la vie* on a broadcast dedicated to Odette Laure, another young entertainer whose singing career Solidor had launched.[86] On the show Laure recounts her successful audition for the grande dame, where Solidor announced, "Bébé, vous restez!" (Baby, you stay!). Dropping her voice a register, Laure repeats the line, this time growling a deep, "Bébé, vous restez!" and noting that Solidor "always spoke like that." Seconds later (to Laure's apparent surprise) the camera cuts to Solidor herself in front of a grand piano. With an enormous diamond ring on her pinky and an equally ostentatious pendant around her solid neck, the aging singer, dressed in a sober black cocktail dress, her muscular shoulders

FIGURE 4.4: Suzy Solidor sings "La voleuse et le filou" on *Les joies de la vie*. Note the pinky ring on her right hand. "Odette Laure," dir. Stellio Lorenzi, *Les joies de la vie*, RTF Télévision, broadcast October 6, 1958. Courtesy of the Institut national de l'audiovisuel.

emerging out of a satin shawl, delivers a rousing version of "La voleuse et le filou" (The thief and the trickster) (fig. 4.4). The television public could not help but perceive how the trappings of femininity—ring, necklace, dress, shawl—all clashed with the power of Solidor's masculine performance.

Dany Dauberson, a statuesque blonde from Lyon with broad shoulders and a deep, rich contralto, exhibited a similar discomfort with normative femininity. As discussed earlier, Dauberson was another Solidor protégée and a featured performer at Frede's Le Carroll's cabaret. Dauberson's fame was confirmed when the young singer represented France in the Eurovision Song Contest in 1956. That same year Dauberson was broadcast both within and outside France (notably by Télé-Luxembourg—a network then visible to over 180,000 French viewers). On this occasion she wore a gold lamé dress and pinky ring in a careful attempt to project a feminine allure.[87] As early press coverage remarks, at times this tall "viking's" "forced" attempts to "feminize" herself seemed to work well.[88] Later television coverage reveals, however, that Dauberson's efforts at gender conformity were not always successful.

On December 4, 1956, Dauberson sang the title cut "Et vous n'avez pas

FIGURE 4.5: Dany Dauberson on *Dany Dauberson, no. 4*, Pathé, 1956. Courtesy of Pathé Records.

su" (And you didn't know) of her recently released album *Dany Dauberson, no. 4* on the RTF's musical variety show *Sur un air de cabaret*.[89] The album's cover depicts Dauberson as a femme fatale, with bare shoulders emerging from a strapless low-cut gown that emphasizes her swelling breasts (fig. 4.5). At first glance, the 1956 TV broadcast seems primed to repeat this optic: Dauberson is done up in pearls and a corseted satin dress with a sweetheart neckline, its skirt festooned with a large bow. With her hair coiffed and face carefully made up (eyeliner, mascara, darkly penciled eyebrows, lush lipstick), she appears the perfect incarnation of ladylike elegance.[90] But while her voice is round and rich, her performance of femininity is clearly "off": Dauberson's strong hands—flashing a pinky ring—gesture powerfully, her stance is planted, her jaw broad, her arm movements bold. The impression is unmistakably masculine. And when

Dauberson sings phrases brimming with ambiguity like "And you didn't know, when I looked at you, everything that troubled me," adding, "And you didn't know, because I kept silent / And you didn't see the years that passed," it is easy to imagine that certain female audience members understood this song about secret love as destined especially for them.

Dauberson never speaks directly of her homoerotic inclinations on the air, but she recalls her tomboyish youth in one 1958 interview.[91] She reports that as a child her mother would take her to Lyon's Place Bellecour. Once there, her only desire was to rabble-rouse with the *galopins du quartier* (the naughty boys from the neighborhood). These exploits evidently always ended badly, with Dany's pretty dresses "covered in dust" and her mother angry.

A few years later Dauberson could be seen performing female masculinity on French television. In 1960 Dauberson belted the classic torch song "Stormy Weather" on another show produced by Micheline Sandrel, in the episode "De New York à Los Angeles" on *Ce soir à*.[92] The setting is a brick-walled bar. Dauberson is hunched over a drink, somberly dressed in a dark shirt trimmed with metal grommets, her collar flipped open and platinum hair cropped, wearing a metal dog-tag bracelet, with no earrings, dark eyebrows, and muted lips.[93] Four Black men in American army uniforms line the bar behind her. With the opening notes of the piano Dauberson wheels toward the camera and begins to sing, her glass of whiskey held close (fig. 4.6). The complex dimensions of this framing (which stereotypes both racial and gender transgression as American) deserve further exploration, but it is significant to note that Dauberson's delivery is not only sultry but also emphatically butch.[94]

Dauberson's tomboyish bearing also found expression when the singer was interviewed five years later in 1965 on *Au delà de l'écran*. Clad in pants and rubber boots, Dauberson is shown fly-fishing on her day off.[95] Remarking on her self-confident demeanor, the narrator assures us that this (traditionally male) vocation is a sport at which "Dany" (whose androgynous first name is stressed) excels, "and for which she has won numerous trophies." In the next edit Dauberson continues this reversal of gender roles, presenting a freshly caught trout to the male chefs who will prepare it for her preperformance supper. The report terminates with footage of Dany signing records at an art gallery, where her live-in companion, the actress Nicole Berger—a delicate blonde—is in attendance. As Berger appears on-screen the voice-over narration misleadingly states that Dauberson is visiting the gallery of painter Josette Guillou. Only those familiar with the actress would recognize that it was Berger and not Guillou depicted here.

FIGURE 4.6: Dany Dauberson sings "Stormy Weather" on *Ce soir à*. "De New York à Los Angeles," dir. Jean Noël Roy, *Ce soir à*, RTF Télévision, broadcast December 3, 1960. Courtesy of the Institut national de l'audiovisuel.

Although Dauberson was discreet about her private life—she certainly never discussed it on TV—extratextual and intertextual information about the singer's amorous history and nonnormative behavior circulated broadly and informed public interpretation of her transgressive on-screen presence. Knowledge of her exploits even crossed national borders: in 1960 a photograph of the twenty-six-year-old wearing a sash labeled "Miss Lesbos" appeared in the German newsmagazine *Der Spiegel* (fig. 4.7). The magazine alleged that Dauberson (crowned in Athens at the Acropolis by Guy Rinaldo, an organizer of beauty competitions) "is the reason why French actor Georges Bréhat wants to divorce his wife" because she "obviously prefers the company of Dany Dauberson."[96] When accused in the French magazine *Music-Hall* of "making all mothers tremble" after she "abducted the wife of a prince," Dauberson responded archly, "I've never abducted anyone. If anyone follows me, it is by choice."[97]

Unlike Suzy Solidor and Dany Dauberson, the cabaret singer, songwriter, and music-hall star Mick Micheyl—known as the *gamin de Paris* (the Paris street urchin) after her 1951 hit song of the same name—managed to keep all speculation about her private life out of the headlines.[98]

FIGURE 4.7: Dany Dauberson as Miss Lesbos. "French Actress Is Crowned 'Miss Lesbos' at Ceremony near Acropolis," *Der Spiegel*, no. 8 (April 4, 1960). Courtesy of Keystone Press / Alamy Stock Photo.

This did not, however, attenuate the impact of her transgressive appeal. Born Paulette Jeanne Renée Michey in Lyon in 1922, Mick Micheyl's first public persona was boyish; slight and jaunty, she regularly dressed in black, with her enormous white collar hiked up "Elvis style."[99] However, by the early 1960s, while headlining at the Casino de Paris, Micheyl had reincarnated herself as an ostrich-plumed, diamond-strewn, ultrafeminine (yet still acrobatically athletic) showgirl.[100] Subsequent TV footage reveals that feathers and spangles notwithstanding, an element of virility consistently troubles Micheyl's attempts at femininity.[101] These dual images of the young butch and aggressively (but never quite convincingly) aging femme circulated on record covers, in the press, and on the many television shows that featured Micheyl over the course of her career. In 1963 the tabloid *Noir et blanc* addressed her transformation from butch to femme with two telling photos on its cover under the headline: "Mick Micheyl: 'I've struggled for ten years to become beautiful.'"[102] Ironically, just under Mick's "butch" image, we see the tag for another article: "In this issue: 'In love, don't trust appearances!'" (fig. 4.8). At least some of her female fans must have found the juxtaposition amusing. Although she shrouded her private life in mystery ("[Please] respect the few things that I want to keep to myself alone," she implored), at least part of Micheyl's public was savvy that something was amiss.[103] Micheyl's silence suggests the degree to which fear of social censure shaped women's behavior in France in these decades; her fan club was nevertheless widely known as a "den of lesbians."[104]

Decades later, one adoring fan named Rachel recalled, "I used to read *Cinémonde*, and one day, I saw an ad for the Club Mick Micheyl, and I just adored Mick Micheyl. She had a way about her, and we could already feel the attraction. I later discovered that she was *comme ça* [like that]." Via the club Rachel began corresponding with, and then met, another young woman: "It was love at first sight," she remembers. Looking back, Rachel sees the Mick Micheyl fan club as a turning point that made it possible for her to identify and connect with other women like herself for the very first time.[105]

Brilliantly talented, Micheyl made her first television appearance in 1952 on *Télé-Paris*.[106] Age twenty-one, her short hair frizzy and wild, outfitted in a simple black sweater, black skirt, and white shirt (she told the host Jacques Angelvin that "my suitcase was stolen"—presumably with her feminine costumes inside—before the show), Micheyl sang her own composition "Je ne suis pour lui qu'un copain" (To him, I'm nothing more than a friend) on the broadcast. With the gender transposed, from its title

FIGURE 4.8: Mick Micheyl’s two looks, butch and femme. The headline? Mick Micheyl: “I’ve struggled for ten years to become beautiful.” *Noir et blanc*, March 8, 1963.

("To [her], I'm nothing more than a friend") to its lyrics ("Together, we were children / But since then, we have grown / And since then I love [her] tenderly / But [she] has never understood"), the song could speak in coded terms to queer adolescent heartbreak. Micheyl was an instant success.

By 1959 at just thirty-seven, Mick Micheyl had already written nearly one hundred songs and recorded twenty records, three of which won major prizes.[107] Like Colette Mars, Micheyl worked extensively in film and television, eventually producing and hosting several of her own musical variety shows, including *Ce sacré métier* and *Samedi et compagnie*. Micheline Sandrel featured Micheyl at least sixteen times on the TV news and collaborated on over thirty of the hundreds of French broadcasts on which Mick appeared. Micheyl was likewise interviewed on TV in many of the countries she toured, including Canada, the United States, and Japan.

Even when she attempted to appear femme, Mick Micheyl couldn't resist defying gender binaries. A brief survey of her television appearances reveals her endless engagement with tomboyish pursuits: driving a tractor at her country house (where she can also be seen building furniture); zipping around a speedway while standing (literally) on the shoulders of a motorcyclist; swinging from her ankles by a cord as she twirls thirty feet above the stage of the Casino de Paris; leading a bear on a leash while clowning on horseback; jogging, golfing, windsurfing, go-cart racing, swimming, and playing tennis before departing for a pub tour in England (where she appears in pearls and a white embroidered satin toile coat); visiting a market in Bangkok draped in a live snake; reporting from Moscow on an invitation to perform for the Soviet circus; gallivanting in drag (disguised as Robinson Crusoe, with her man Friday in blackface) on *Entente cordiale*, a musical variety show that she produced for French TV; and (repeatedly, during the second career that she took up after abandoning the stage in 1974) "painting" on steel with a drill and torch.[108] What we rarely see is Mick Micheyl in any setting that even vaguely suggests romantic attachment or reproduces familial domesticity.[109]

And yet, Micheyl lived most of her adult life with a woman known as "Kiki" (who described herself as "relatively lacking in femininity") and whom Micheyl referred to as "my angel who watches over me."[110] Kiki had briefly performed under the stage name Anne Monaco. She headlined with Mick Micheyl at the Right Bank cabaret Chez Pasdoc (L'Échanson) in 1951.[111] Kiki became Micheyl's constant companion; the two women can be seen together jointly holding a small monkey on the eight o'clock news in 1953.[112] According to the French celebrity singer Dave (whose career Micheyl launched on TV in 1969 and whom I interviewed in 2017), Kiki was wed in what the French call *un mariage blanc* (an unconsummated marriage) to Micheyl's impresario Roland Ribet (likewise—or so Dave confided to me—a closeted homosexual).[113] The exact nature of the two women's relationship, a bond that lasted to the end of Micheyl's life, was never publicly acknowledged.[114]

THE (QUEER) SINGLE WOMAN: NICOLE LOUVIER AND *A ROOM OF ONE'S OWN*

Whereas Mick Micheyl carefully hid her private life from public view, singer, songwriter, poet, author, and radio producer Nicole Louvier was adamantly open about her queer desires—ultimately to her own professional detriment.[115] Television, radio, and press coverage frequently featured Louvier at home, a space in which it was always obvious that she lived alone.[116] This persistent focus on Louvier's unmarried status emphasized her economic, social, and sexual independence. In so doing, the media situated Louvier as a female subject squarely within the wage-earning ethos of consumer capitalism that John D'Emilio argues was so essential to the development of contemporary homosexual identity.[117]

When not yet twenty, Louvier published *Qui qu'en grogne* (Whoever protests), a first-person account of lost sapphic love in which the female protagonist's female paramour forsakes her for marriage. Sapphic desires also infused Louvier's *Chansons interdites* (Forbidden songs), a slim volume of poetry where, according to a review in the journal *Arcadie* (widely known as the mouthpiece of André Baudry's homophile movement), Louvier "sings of homophile love, that of Lesbos."[118] That same year, Louvier's plaintive 1953 hit "Qui me delivrera?" (Who will deliver me?), with the lyrics, "Who will deliver me / from your body and your touch? / From your mouth, who will deliver me? / Who will deliver me / at last, from you?" won the Grand Prix de la Chanson Française at Deauville. Engagements at the Left Bank cabaret La Rose Rouge and Chez Agnès Capri (the sapphically inclined Capri exerted an important early influence on the young singer) and television appearances soon followed.[119] Between 1953 and 1968 Louvier published five novels in addition to her poetry, wrote thirty-five songs distributed across some twenty albums, and toured the globe from Belgium to Japan. Highly mediatized, her work was relayed on radio and TV broadcasts beyond France's borders.[120] The singer also appeared regularly in print: *Paris match*, *L'express*, *La vie parisienne*, *Bonnes soirées*, *Music-Hall*, and the adolescent weekly *Lisette* all featured the young singing sensation.[121]

On-screen, with her sweet, slightly nasal voice, cap of short dark hair, limpid brown eyes, and delicate physique obscured by a large guitar, Louvier favored feminine dresses in calico, gingham, or worsted wool, often with small Peter Pan collars, always with a girlish appeal. Her seemingly timid demeanor hid a fiery sensuality and sharp intellect. Born in France in 1933 to Polish-Jewish immigrants, Louvier was separated from her parents during World War II, surviving thanks to Breton peasants who hid her in the French countryside. Anguished by the experience, she began writing poetry as an adolescent as a form of self-expression. Shortly after the war's end she presented her efforts to an editor in Paris. While her talents brought recognition, her choice to make her private feelings public (whether expressing her desire for other women in poems, songs, and novels or critiquing avarice and misogyny in the entertainment industry) brought scandal and, eventually, rebuff.[122]

Each of the three times that Micheline Sandrel interviewed Louvier for *Magazine féminin*—in 1959, 1965, and 1967—Louvier's living space was as central to the sequence as her singing.[123] In the first of these broadcasts, Sandrel and Louvier are seated tête-à-tête on a small daybed in the younger woman's Paris flat. When the camera pulls back, the bottom half of a framed print of a nude woman—revealing only the portrait's hips and crotch—comes into view on the wall above. Louvier, knees pressed demurely together under the voluminous skirt of her houndstooth-checked satin dress, displays a gift that she had received during her recent tour in Japan (fig. 4.9). "It is a wedding kimono," she remarks, noting, "One marries in black in Japan." "Perhaps that reveals what they think of marriage," Sandrel ironically observes.[124] Louvier responds, "It is true that they find it sad," adding, "It is an end, it is clearly an end for them." At this point the (divorced) Sandrel breaks character, turning directly to the camera and erupting into an enormous smile. An instant later—but not before revealing, or so it seems, her personal perspective to the viewers—Sandrel is back on point, and the dialogue continues. Throughout the sequence the partial view of the painting of the nude female hangs suspended overhead.

Sandrel and Louvier's second interview, in 1965, also takes place in Louvier's flat, now crammed with the type of "things" that Georges Perec satirizes in his 1965 novel *Les choses*: a piano, a desk, heaps of books, stacks of records, a cupboard filled with clothes and costumes, and a television.[125] "This landscape," Gonnard and Lebovici argue, "organizes an adolescent and consumeristic discourse," the mediatization of which "is the exact contemporary" of Hugh Hefner's vision in *Playboy* of a masculine post-domestic urban sexual utopia.[126] But here, in this female space occupied

FIGURE 4.9: Nicole Louvier (*left*) displays a Japanese marriage kimono to journalist Micheline Sandrel. *Magazine féminin*, RTF Télévision, broadcast February 5, 1959. Courtesy of the Institut national de l'audiovisuel.

entirely by a single woman, rather than submitting to male desire, the televisual mise-en-scène of a "room of one's own" (to quote Virginia Woolf) can be read as a public index of female autonomy and sexual freedom.[127] In her work and in her life, Louvier made such fantasies of female self-sufficiency real for her public. Her tool was language—especially the language of song—because, as she states elsewhere, "At any moment song can intermingle with people's intimate lives."[128] Louvier envisioned her texts—songs, poetry, novels—as a form of *revendication sociale*, a political demand and activity whose necessary intention was provocation and change.[129] Louvier's militant agenda presaged a transformation that, by the end of the 1960s, conjoined youth rebellion with sexual liberation to challenge the sociopolitical order around the globe.

QUEER REBELLION: FEMALE ANDROGYNY ON FRENCH TV

As an increasingly unruly youth culture began flaunting French social mores in the early 1960s, French TV's variety shows amplified newly

FIGURE 4.10: Albert Raisner (*left*) introduces Jackie Seven (*right*) on *Âge tendre et tête de bois*. *Âge tendre et tête de bois*, dir. Bernard Roland, RTF Télévision, broadcast November 21, 1961. Courtesy of the Institut national de l'audiovisuel.

androgynous models of female gender performance. Take for example the November 21, 1961, appearance of seventeen-year-old Belgian-born singing sensation Jackie Seven (the stage name of Evelyne Manuel) on the teen variety show *Âge tendre et tête de bois* (Young and obstinate).[130] Words fail the show's host, Albert Raisner, when he attempts to describe Seven's queer performance. "What is the female version of 'rock 'n' roller'?" he asks. "Rock 'n' rolleuse? Rock 'n' rollette?" "Rock stars," he continues, "are boys: Elvis Presley, Johnny Hallyday. . . . Can young girls be rockers? That is what we are going to find out." As the drums snare, Seven takes the stage, hair mussed and attired in a drab jumpsuit with a hiked collar, looking for all the world like a young auto mechanic (fig. 4.10). Hips swinging and knees arcing, Seven snarls a French version of Chubby Checker's hit single "Let's Twist Again" into the mic; when the camera pans over the audience, the teenagers, female and male alike, are bopping and clapping, clearly entranced.

The androgynous attraction of the singer known as Gribouille (stage name of Marie-France Gaîte) proved even more powerful; in her brief career, the young woman appeared repeatedly on television, toured extensively, received significant radio play, and recorded numerous records. She became a lesbian icon: Sylviane Francesconi (later a cofounder of Toulouse's Bagdam Cafée, discussed in chapter 8) was so enamored of Gribouille that she named her first restaurant (opened in Vence in the South of France in the 1970s) after the singer.[131] Dan Monnel, who worked for Lulu de Montmartre and Madame Moune in the 1960s and 1970s, christened her cat after the singer.[132] Legend has it that Gribouille was discovered by Jean Cocteau. Mistaking the elfin gamine for a boy when he passed her busking on a bridge over the Seine in Paris, Cocteau sketched the young girl. He signed the portrait, "à mon ami, Gribouille" (to my friend, Gribouille), using the masculine orthography for friend (*ami*, not *amie*), a mistake Gribouille promptly corrected.[133] After hearing her sing, Cocteau arranged Gribouille's debut at Le Boeuf sur le Toit, the renowned Parisian cabaret with which he had been closely associated since before the war. Shortly thereafter she was dubbed "the new Edith Piaf" and compared to French singing sensations Jacques Brel and Barbara. Gigs at a slew of postwar cabarets and music halls—La Cabane Bambou, Le Tabou, L'Écluse, Le Petit Conservatoire de Mireille, the Bobino—both in France and abroad soon followed.

Gribouille's first televised appearance in 1962 on Aimée Mortimer's variety show *École des vedettes* led to a record deal with Pathé.[134] In the sequence's opening image, we see Gribouille, dark hair cropped short and dressed in an oversized woolen turtleneck and a pleated skirt, sketching what appears to be a self-portrait in chalk on the floor. (The shot proved iconic: in 1968 Claude Chabrol replicated the image as the first scene of his sapphic film noir *Les biches*, starring Stéphane Audran.) Invited to sing, Gribouille stands and then ambles with a slow deliberate swagger into a corner of the set, where she leans with a kind of feline masculinity against the sill of a barred window (fig. 4.11). The sounds that issue from her small frame are nothing short of astonishing. Her voice is gorgeous, the tone sonorous and mature, the delivery sober: "She was," writer Françoise Mallet-Joris states in her preface to an edited collection of Gribouille's lyrics entitled *Je vais mourir demain* (I will die tomorrow), "despair in its most seductive form."[135]

The young woman's dark affect expressed her troubled history: diagnosed as a "difficult child"—a verdict that may have issued from her evident gender and sexual variance—in the mid-1950s the adolescent Gribouille was placed in a detention center outside Lyon. It was there that she became addicted to sedatives.[136] Upon Gribouille's release she hitchhiked to Paris. Homeless, she slept in unlocked cars along the quays of the Seine

FIGURE 4.11: Gribouille sings "Le marin et la rose" on *École des vedettes*. *École des vedettes*, dir. Stellio Lorenzi, RTF Télévision, broadcast November 19, 1962. Courtesy of the Institut national de l'audiovisuel.

before—thanks to her boyish aspect (she called herself "François," raising questions about trans identification)—finding a day job as a delivery boy for a publishing house. She moonlighted as a chalk artist in order to pay for singing lessons.

Gribouille's appearance on *École des vedettes* is replete with transgressive visual and auditory codes and extratextual cues. The song that Gribouille sings on the broadcast, "Le marin et la rose" (The sailor and the rose), sets a poem by Maurice Carême to music. Both the song and the poem were standards in Suzy Solidor's repertoire; Solidor sang it in 1933 at La Vie Parisienne and can be heard reciting it on radio broadcasts from 1948 and 1961.[137] Gribouille's own compositions, particularly the songs "Ostende" and "On n'a pas le droit" ([We don't have the right] whose refrain translates as "We don't have the right / to love one another like this / We don't have the right / It is you who says so"), were hits and later became French lesbian favorites. Both songs were written for her beloved friend, cabaret singer Marie-Thérèse Orain. Her work thus both referred to and produced intertextual sapphic references. Tragically, Gribouille's meteoric career ended abruptly in 1968 when she was found dead at twenty-six from a drug overdose.

Orain ensured that Gribouille's artistry was shared with a new generation: in 1998 Orain produced an evening-length tribute to the singer, which she performed at theatres across Paris.[138] Three years later, in 2001 Orain supervised the publication of and wrote the introductory biographical essay to an edited collection of Gribouille's songs. The writer Françoise Mallet-Joris, who began an enduring love affair with (and wrote lyrics for) French singer Marie-Paule Belle in 1970, contributed the preface.[139] I interviewed Orain in November 2017. It was striking to note that—perhaps in keeping with the lyrics expressed in "On n'a pas le droit"?—she largely refrained from speaking about what was clearly one of the most important relationships of her life.

In their work, Catherine Gonnard and Elisabeth Lebovici maintain that Gribouille's performances offered "for the first time, in a way that was barely veiled on television . . . an address that is sufficiently direct to arouse the fantasies and desires of those [female] spectators who recognized her as one of their own." In other words, they maintain, "Gribouille speaks within the public space that is television media 'to lesbians.'"[140] The young Sylviane Francesconi's decision to name her first restaurant after the singer testifies to the truth of this. The lesbian community later identified Gribouille's traumatic life and untimely death as symbolic of the oppressive effects of heteronormativity on marginal lives. Thirty years after her death, an LGBT collective stepped forward to finance the renewal of the concession on her tomb in the Jewish cemetery in Bagneux.[141]

CONCLUSION

Televised coverage of women like Colette Mars, Suzy Solidor, Dany Dauberson, Mick Micheyl, Nicole Louvier, and Gribouille disrupts a French postwar narrative dominated by feminine heterosexual domesticity. It testifies to the ways in which the modern technology of television transmitted transgressive images of female sexual desire and gender performance to expanding publics in ways never before seen. While by the 1960s similar examples could be found on other French TV programs from book shows to newsmagazines, the variety show genre in particular was brimming with queer female performances, both because the move from cabaret to television was remarkably straightforward and because live performance venues were often already queer.[142]

When female performers capitalized on the liberties afforded by the musical variety show to convey passions that postwar social norms condemned, they extended the reach of the sapphic genealogical geographies first mapped in the cabarets of interwar Paris inexorably outward across the nation. The fact that so many of these women were singers is not insignificant. Song has a special capacity to communicate affect by conveying the intimate texture of emotion and desire. If we accept that affect functions, in Heather Love's formulation, as both a "motivational system" and "the grounds for forging new collectivities," then the televising of sapphic song carried similar personal and political potentialities to new lengths.[143]

Taken collectively these programs demonstrate a gradual shift in nonnormative representations of female gender and sexuality on French television, from early broadcasts in which a mature femme or failed femme sensibility reigned, toward later shows in which young, emancipated and androgynous women figured more prominently. Given that during these same years it was generally the butch who—as we saw in the last chapter—carried the stigma of sexual and gender transgression, the pervasiveness of femme and failed femme performances on early French television is especially intriguing. While such performances were sometimes misconstrued (since femme women often passed as heterosexual), the circulation of extra- and intertextual discourses about lesbianism in the media during the 1950s and 1960s increased the public's capacity to read these performances in nonnormative ways.

An argument regarding the absence of "the lesbian" from French culture and literature between the late 1930s and the late 1960s has been used to justify claims that lesbianism was invisible in midcentury France.[144] The women broadcast on the French variety shows examined in this chapter permit us both to contest the utility of the term "the lesbian" at this time and to nuance this thesis. Performances of female same-sex desire and gender transgression were regularly discernible on early French television. Let me be clear, however, that whether such performances read as femme or butch, *none* of the coded indices visible on TV at midcentury—from the pinky ring and flirtatious, reciprocal feminine gaze to the suggestive lyrics, hiked collar, deep voice, or boyishly planted stance—*necessarily* equated to evidence of lesbian (or trans) identity as it is understood today. Instead they might better be characterized as its vatic prefiguration, something akin to what David Halperin designates as a queer cultural style or practice.[145] Indeed, while these women may have shared an interest in other women, many if not most of the artists who engaged in performances of variant gender and sexual desire on French TV in these years appear to have resisted lexical categorization as nonnormative sexual subjects in their public lives. By neglecting to name the difference it showed, early French television, a medium that enabled "the means to make the fiction of a [lesbian] public real," followed suit.[146] It was not until after the homosexual rights movement produced modern homosexual identity in the very act of politicizing it that French TV turned its cameras on social entities explicitly labeled as lesbian or gay.

In *Lesbian Rule: Cultural Criticism and the Value of Desire*, Amy Villarejo observes that "the majority of scholarly projects undertaken under the sign of the lesbian assume an emancipatory or liberatory effect, regardless of the extent to which they are able to specify in what particular way or definite mode they contribute to an emancipatory itinerary, however designated."[147] To a certain extent, this chapter participates in this agenda. Despite being unable to calculate the exact nature or range of their impact, in offering French audiences these myriad televised instances of sapphic desire and gender variance, I suggest that postwar French television—and by extension midcentury French society—was less normatively rigid and heterosexual, and thus more queer, than we have generally believed. And television was not alone: instantiations of (especially youthful) female sexuality tout court were straining conservative social mores at this time. The 1950s saw the riotous success of, for example, nineteen-year-old Françoise Sagan's scandalous coming-of-age novel *Bonjour tristesse* (1954), Françoise Mallet-Joris's lesbian-themed *Le rempart des béguines* (1951), and Roger Vadim's film *And God Created Woman* (1956), starring the sexually ravenous Brigitte Bardot. All three works shattered traditional patriarchal expectations that a woman should be a virgin at marriage, renounce same-sex passions, remain faithful for life, and ultimately suppress her desires in favor of a man's.

By enabling the circulation among strangers of a specific set of nonnormative discourses about female sexuality and gender performance, early French TV supported the production of what Michel Warner calls the "context of publicness" requisite for the politicization of "deviant" sexual identities.[148] In this, it contributed to the emergence of activist movements for feminist and homosexual rights in the following decades. And yet, when homosexual activists began demanding political rights and public recognition in the early 1970s, state television fell back on a series of well-worn stereotypes in its efforts to contain and codify female same-sex desire.

Thus, if on the one hand, via its emancipatory participation in a kind of "poetic worldmaking," the televising of the sapphic cabaret in the 1950s and 1960s helped lay the groundwork for the formation of a specifically *lesbian* counterpublic, on the other hand, some of the hard-won victories of this newly formed counterpublic would only be gained during the decades that followed at the expense of some of its historically elusive freedoms.[149]

5

BEAUTIFUL WHORES, GOOD MOTHERS, AND FEMINIST ACTIVISTS

On February 21, 1971, French TV aired a thirty-minute interview on the final broadcast of Daisy de Galard's innovative TV magazine *Dim Dam Dom*.[1] Bright, modern, and fun, the show featured sequences on fashion, entertainment, culture, and biography.[2] Launched in 1965 and aired monthly on Sunday nights, *Dim Dam Dom* rapidly acquired cult status. After a six-year run, de Galard demanded a winning line-up for the show's swan song. Curiously, she chose a woman from the world of the sapphic cabaret for the closing clip.[3] The broadcast recounts Frede's cross-dressing debut as an entraîneuse at Le Monocle; her "liaison" with Marlene Dietrich; the "special" ambience of the swanky Le Carroll's Club and the women who danced with one another there; Frede's attachment to the married actress Lana Marconi ("which," as Frede remarks under her breath, "was more than a friendship"); and Frede's meeting with Miki, after which the two "started to construct things, together." Photographs of singers from the sapphic cabarets, including Colette Mars and Dany Dauberson, flash across the screen. Their songs augment the soundtrack. In closing, when Frede observes that Miki (seated on the floor opposite, looking pretty and perpetually amused) "saved my life . . . mentally and physically," concluding, "il faut être deux" (one needs to be coupled) to be healthy and happy, Frede removes all doubts about the intimate nature of their relationship. However, if lesbianism was evoked at length for the first time on French TV on this broadcast, it was never explicitly named.[4]

Dim Dam Dom's "Frede" aired less than two weeks before women from the newly established Mouvement de libération des femmes (Women's Liberation Movement, or MLF) joined members of André Baudry's homophile organization Arcadie on March 10, 1971, and violently disrupted journalist Ménie Grégoire's radio show titled "L'homosexualité, ce douloureux problème" (Homosexuality, that painful problem).[5] Grégoire had chosen to include the theme on her popular talk show *Allô Ménie* (1967–81), a broadcast produced by Radio-télévision Luxembourg. Celebrated for its confessional style, *Allô Ménie* popularized psychoanalysis and brought the private lives of its studio audience and phone-in auditors to the airwaves. Hosted on this occasion at the Salle Pleyel in Paris, which, according to Grégoire, was "full to bursting" thanks to the "passionate and impassioned" nature of this "hot topic," the program included as interlocutors Baudry, a priest, a psychoanalyst, a lawyer, the queer journalist Pierre Hahn (speaking from the audience), and—for some reason—the singing group Les frères Jacques.[6] Storming the stage and attacking the speakers (in the melee one woman reportedly "took hold of the priest's head and pounded it repeatedly against the table"), some thirty mostly female activists brought the broadcast to a chaotic close as they yelled "We're not suffering" and "Down with the hetero-cops!"[7] The riot that ensued—sometimes referred to as the "French Stonewall"—is considered the founding act of the Front homosexuel d'action révolutionnaire (Homosexual Revolutionary Action Front, or FHAR, 1971–76), the activist homosexual rights group that helped create modern French sexual identity politics.[8] The fact that this riot was organized and enacted mainly by women and directed at the media is not anodyne.

As we have seen, queer representations were not absent from French television in the 1950s and 1960s. However, mainstream television and radio only began to provide platforms for the open discussion of homosexuality once the feminist and homosexual rights movements had erupted into the public sphere in the aftermath of the French student revolutions of May 1968.[9] The French media's willingness to address this subject head on was a direct response to the demands of activists whose appeals for political rights and social tolerance made front-page news in the early 1970s out of a topic long shrouded in secrecy and shame. Television became a key vector for these discussions, at once catalyzing and summarizing other media coverage and emerging as a powerful public arena for the production and dissemination of discourses about same-sex desire. In 1975, for example, a prime-time debate show on homosexuality drew some nineteen million French viewers.[10] Although women were less visible in early broadcasts, by the 1980s (at which point homosexuals were becoming "more and more in evidence" on French TV) mainstream media professionals had begun promoting a particularly restricted—and I argue particularly French—vision of lesbian identity to the French public.[11] Three stereotypical archetypes reigned in French nonfiction TV coverage of female same-sex desire: the "beautiful whore," the "good mother," and the "feminist activist." I am interested in the production of these archetypes as well as in their symbolic and practical import. Intriguingly, as lesbian identity politicized in these same years, women who loved women both rejected *and* co-opted this imagery.

Before addressing these archetypes in turn, this chapter opens with a description of the early history of nonfiction coverage of "out" homosexuality on French TV. I then examine the archetype of the beautiful whore by looking at how women utilized feminine coquetry, beauty, and so-called situational lesbianism (in which female same-sex desire is explained as a response to an individual and not a gender) on French TV either to cloak radical messages in reassuring tones or, conversely, to undermine the nascent construction of lesbian politics. Next, I turn to the archetype of the good mother to address the vexed connections between motherhood and lesbianism in France and study how women in same-sex relationships argued as mothers for social standing and legal rights on French television. Finally, I examine the archetype of the (lesbian?) feminist activist to interrogate debates regarding the invisibility of lesbianism in the early French feminist movement by analyzing television coverage of activists from the MLF. This last focus investigates the forces that contributed to the erasure of lesbianism within the French feminist movement while revealing the persistent power of traditional attitudes toward women, gender, sexuality, and the family in French society.

This chapter contends that French TV's insistent focus on female homosexuality as either erotic, maternal, or apolitical played a small but significant role in shifting public opinion toward greater acceptance of homosexuality and homosexual rights at a time when male homosexuality was increasingly represented—due to the emergent AIDS crisis after 1983—as dominated by sexual promiscuity, disease, contagion, and death.[12] As Patrice Corriveau observes, after the media became obsessed with the "gay cancer epidemic" (the phrase is from the March 19, 1983, edition of the daily newspaper *Libération*), "the image of homosexuals quickly began to suffer."[13] Heteronormative depictions of lesbianism countered such negative publicity, providing important traction for the controversial arguments in favor of homosexual partnership and parenting rights that were just beginning to gain political purchase.[14] Indeed, French TV's nonthreatening depictions of female same-sex desire during the 1980s and 1990s ultimately helped soften the public image of homosexuality in ways that first augmented support for the inclusion of same-sex partners in the PACS (French civil partnership, legalized in 1999) and later bolstered the fight for gay and lesbian marriage (legalized in France in 2013). The mainstream media's promotion of eroticized, maternal, and apolitical models of lesbian identity in the last decades of the twentieth century served as a lynchpin in the battle for homosexual rights in postwar France. In so doing, it also provided grist for the politicization of queer female counterpublics.

FEMALE HOMOSEXUALITY ON FRENCH TV IN THE 1970S AND AFTER

With French TV ownership rising from 70.4 percent in 1970 to 90.1 percent in 1980 and French households watching an average of over two hours of broadcasting per day, in the post-1968 landscape television was fast becoming a major conduit through which French citizens experienced their world.[15] Dubbed the "voice of France" by President Georges Pompidou in 1970, TV in France was, as noted previously, completely state controlled and delimited to just three channels until 1985.[16] Consequently, through the mid-1980s French TV was subject to political censure and reflective of dominant social mores. In this very particular audiovisual climate, French broadcasts on homosexuality delivered more consistent messaging, garnered larger audiences, and exerted greater influence over viewing publics than they would today (when privatization and the multiplication of terrestrial, satellite, cable, and internet channels has fractured audiences into ever smaller and more specialized groups). Between 1970 and 2000 French public television aired well over 1,750 broadcasts that dealt with homosexuality in some form.[17] At least 380 of these—and likely more, since cataloguing strategies are inconsistent—directly address lesbianism.[18]

French television began to discuss homosexuality as a social issue in 1970. However, same-sex desire was first framed as a "foreign" concern (that year alone featured sequences on homosexuality in England, the United States, Spain, and Holland).[19] Early coverage of homosexuality in France identified same-sex desire as the predilection of bohemian performers, artists, and writers before acquiescing that it might also be a topic of broader social concern. In almost all cases, homosexuality was condescendingly portrayed as either a painful (if titillating) problem to be cured or as an object of compassion to be pitied. For example, the first nonfiction television broadcast to report on (male) homosexuality in France (on the tellingly titled "Portrait d'un psychiatre" from the series *Émission médicale* in 1970) depicts its protagonist from the back, hiding his identity and referring to him as "le malade" (the sick person).[20] In "L'homosexualité," the first full-length TV documentary on (male) homosexuality, produced in 1973 also for *Émission médicale*, the mother of a homosexual is shown in silhouette.[21] Here we experience shame by association: she shares her profound sadness with the viewing audience, telling us that at night she dreams of her son's homosexuality and wakes up sobbing. Her distress reflects the intense effects of French social stigma—a stigma that remained remarkably harsh and widespread in the 1970s despite purported liberalization.

In this climate, French women were understandably reluctant to come out on the air. When André Baudry's homophile organization Arcadie was profiled on *Tribune libre* in 1977, a woman shown only in silhouette testified: "I cannot show my face because that would cause problems in my professional life. I would risk losing my job and would be ridiculed by my male and female colleagues."[22] A sequence in a later show ("Les homosexuels" on *Les mercredis de l'information*, aired in 1983), filmed at the Katmandou discothèque, features all of the women save two wearing masks to protect their anonymity.[23] Only the Kat's manager, Elula Perrin, and one client, a lovely brunette who identifies herself as a stripper, speak unmasked to the cameras. Both work in professions in which homosexuality is far from a hindrance. Indeed, for Elula, it was key to her success. In other broadcasts women simply remain closeted. This was the case in the 1975 program "La sexualité racontée par les femmes" (Sexuality as told by women) on Bernard Pivot's celebrated book show *Apostrophes*.[24] The show featured writers Kate Millett and Hélène Cixous, with the American Millett, looking characteristically disheveled, defending—in personal terms—female same-sex desire against Arianna Stassinopoulos's lesbophobic attacks. Millett states, "*We* [emphasis mine] who are lesbians or homos, we consider ourselves human beings. [The problem] isn't just that you don't 'tolerate' us, it is that you refuse us our humanity." The feminine Cixous—who divorced in 1964 and later became the life partner of writer and director Ariane Mnouchkine—refrains from comment. Cixous's discretion suggests that the threat of social judgment may have kept her silent. This is not surprising when we consider that a 1980 survey in the weekly newsmagazine *Le nouvel observateur* reported that 49 percent of the French population still viewed homosexuality as a social evil.[25]

The dangers of "coming out" on television were grave. Éliane Morissens, a fifty-two-year-old high-school teacher, appeared on a Belgian program titled “Fragments de bonheur” (Fragments of happiness) on *T.V.F. Magazine* on October 28, 1980. The show’s discussion focused on French author Geneviève Pastre’s recently published monograph *De l’amour lesbien*. Following the broadcast Morissens was dismissed from the post she had held for twenty-three years on the grounds that she had undermined the reputation of her educational institution (although never identified) and slandered her superiors (also unnamed). When she fought back—ultimately going on a hunger strike that lasted thirty-eight days and challenging her firing before the European Commission of Human Rights—French lesbian activists rallied, raising money for her defense and petitioning judicial authorities on her behalf.[26] In 1988 (a full eight years later) the commission ruled against her, arguing that Morissens’s professional responsibility necessarily delimited her personal freedom of expression.[27]

With cases like Morissens’s attracting popular attention, it is unsurprising that people were rarely willing to speak openly about their same-sex desires on French TV, a medium that compromised secrecy with both images and sound. As one 1979 news broadcast reported, “There are almost 4 million homosexuals in France, but we’ve had a terrible time finding even twelve who would agree to talk about this on television.”[28] This temerity becomes more understandable, however, when we note that on the same show, every “normal” individual approached on the street and interviewed about the topic refers to homosexuality as a monstrosity. Indeed, into the 1990s (even after French laws doubling penalties for homosexuals convicted of indecent exposure were dropped in 1980 and discriminatory age of consent laws were removed in 1982) French homosexuals of both sexes continued to wear masks and/or have their voices distorted when they appeared on television in order to protect their anonymity.[29]

When women did unabashedly claim lesbian identities on French television—whether argued from nature (“I was born this way”) or nurture (“I developed these feelings”)—their lesbian “difference” was often attenuated. This could be done via feminine coquetry (e.g., by flirting with male interviewers), attestations of romantic fidelity, claims of maternal responsibility, or attempts to depoliticize the topic, all framings that were appealing to heterosexual French audiences. When French media professionals discussed lesbianism, their coverage generally reflected deeply held patriarchal convictions about the proper nature of female gender performance and the sexual availability of women to men in French society. As a result, French TV hosts and journalists either eroticized or domesticated female homosexuality, regularly choosing attractive interlocutors who cleaved to traditional gender norms. The eroticization of love between women was captured in the archetype of the beautiful whore.

THE BEAUTIFUL WHORE, OR THE LESBIANISM EROTICS OF FEMININITY

The archetype of the beautiful whore was epitomized on French TV by the French-Vietnamese Elula Perrin who, with her business partner and then lover Aimée Mori, ran the glitzy Katmandou discothèque (known as the Kat) in Paris from 1969 to 1989.[30] The Kat was located at 21 rue du Vieux-Colombier in the fashionable sixth arrondissement. It opened one year after the student revolutions of May '68, attracting a clientele of smartly dressed women along with celebrity entertainers and their entourages. Men were not forbidden entry, but their presence was discouraged (house rules barred them from inviting women to dance, buying them drinks, and pursuing or—god forbid—touching them unbidden).[31] Despite its elevated prices, as the Kat's reputation spread, it began drawing a more varied demographic from both inside and outside the capital.[32] Over and above the pull of its pounding music, crowded dance floor, female patrons, and flashy décor (featuring gilded mirrors, red velvet banquettes, and a black lacquered bar), the Kat's appeal derived from the allure of its exotic manager; Elula's power over the lesbian club scene from 1969 until her death in 2003 was undisputed.

Dubbed "the New Queen of Lesbos" by the press for her role in the Kat's success, Elula became an object of widespread media interest after the publication in 1977 of the forty-eight-year-old's salacious autobiographical memoir *Les femmes préfèrent les femmes* (*Women Prefer Women*), which sold over 150,000 copies in two years and was translated into multiple languages.[33] Her eleven subsequent books (two of which were coauthored), all touching on lesbian themes and including autobiography, nonfiction, fiction, and detective novels, further enhanced her reputation.[34] For the next few decades, Perrin was everywhere: in international, national, and provincial newspapers; in newsmagazines and fashion magazines; in the feminist, gay, and libertine press; on the French precursor to the internet known as the Minitel (she had her own Minitel site); on the radio; and on every major French TV channel.[35] Elula owed her appeal to her coquettish, seductive style. When the media wanted a lesbian, her name rose to the top of the list. While not a great beauty, she was feminine, pretty, quick witted, and knew how to flirt with both women and men. She employed her charms to publicize a series of positions on female same-sex desire that were at once conservative and titillating, comforting and revolutionary—and the media loved her.

On July 11, 1977, Elula appeared on Philippe Bouvard's *L'huile sur le feu* (Oil on the fire) in the broadcast "Female Homosexuality," which was intended—like all of Bouvard's shows—to inflame public opinion.[36] It marked the first open discussion of female homosexuality on French TV and stands as the most influential early example of a self-identified lesbian appearing *à visage découvert*—unmasked—to French TV audiences.[37] This iconic broadcast became a signal reference for a generation of women who loved women; many of my interviewees recalled how meaningful it was for them to see this show, and almost all who had not personally viewed it had heard of its importance.

When the broadcast begins, Bouvard cautions us that this discussion about "the dangers and inconveniences of female homosexuality" is "not suitable for everyone." He then suggests that to distinguish this form of female "perversion" from "l'homosexualité masculine," we must examine how "medicine and psychiatry deal with what some don't hesitate to refer to as a *fleau sociale*" (social plague—referencing the term used in the 1960 Mirguet Amendment), as well as inquire whether "men have some responsibility for female homosexuality" because they fail to satisfy their women. This introduction both depicts female same-sex desire as lapsed heterosexuality and ensures that this discussion remains in the medical register of deviance and perversion. The camera then cuts to Perrin (fig. 5.1). Her short auburn hair curls in a soft bouffant, and her blue eyeshadow matches the blue flowers on her silky dress. Her wrists are adorned with gold bracelets. There are rings on her fingers, and her fingernails are painted red. She is the picture of propriety: bourgeois, middle aged, feminine—in sum, "normal." Yet, as Bouvard informs us, her biography is unusual: Elula, we are told, is a childless divorcée with a degree in law, an ex-ballet dancer, ex-professor of history and geography, *animatrice* (host) of the Katmandou ("a very specialized cabaret"), and the author of a book "very explicitly entitled" *Women Prefer Women*.

While Elula's mixed-race origins and colonial upbringing are left unmentioned, they clearly shaped her character.[38] She was born in Hanoi (then Tonkin, French Indochina) in 1929 and schooled by British and French nuns. Elula's mother was a French-Vietnamese dressmaker; her father, a freemason who owned Boylandry, an import-export company, was Maltese and Italian and raised in Tunisia. In 1945, when the Japanese attempted to take over Indochina (which had been under Vichy control since 1940), Elula's family was interned. Her father was among those

FIGURE 5.1: Elula Perrin, the first woman to "come out" as a lesbian on French TV, on Philippe Bouvard's *L'huile sur le feu*. "L'homosexualité féminine," dir. Alexandre Tarta, *L'huile sur le feu*, Antenne 2, broadcast July 11, 1977. Courtesy of Alexandre Tarta / Passport Songs Music and the Institut national de l'audiovisuel.

massacred in the camps by the Imperial Japanese Army toward the end of the war. Friends speculate that Elula may have been raped at this time.[39] Shortly after the bombing of Hiroshima—an event she gratefully remembers as having saved what remained of her family—Elula, her mother, and younger brother were evacuated to Marseille. She moved to Paris at seventeen in 1946 and began studies in law at the Sorbonne. She soon met and married Guy, a jazz aficionado with a penchant for dance and the son of a moderately wealthy family of soap-makers from Marseille. Together they started a *ballets nègres* with a group of Senegalese, Dahomean, Guinean, and Cameroonian students: Elula was featured as a "danseuse africaine." Armed with their hit show "Black Incantation," the troupe cobbled together a tour to Spain, but audiences and finances quickly dwindled, and so did company morale. The troupe disbanded in Casablanca. Stranded and broke, Elula took a job as a "Cuban" singer in a Russian nightclub. Within three months she and Guy had scraped together enough to lease a club of their own. Called The Shango and decorated in Afro-Cuban style, the club may have succeeded had Elula not taken up with her first lesbian lover and abandoned the barroom for the bedroom. The experience changed her life.

Convinced by a heartbroken Guy to remain married, the couple returned to France in 1950. But Elula soon fled, following her lover to Paris and auditioning unsuccessfully for Suzy Solidor. When her love story ended, Elula returned to Marseille and to Guy in 1951. She then began to lead a double life, remaining married in name only. For thirteen years she taught history at religious schools for girls and was twice fired for homosexual misconduct (charges she denied). Her lesbian love affairs multiplied. In the summer of 1966, she decided to shed her heterosexual facade. She ventured into the club scene and by 1968 had decamped with Aimée Mori to Paris. The Katmandou (soon hailed as "Paris' most exclusive female gay bar" with a nightly capacity of nearly five hundred guests) opened its doors December 2, 1969.[40] "I was extremely lucky," she later recalled. "I was finally launched in the only profession where my sexuality couldn't hurt me—indeed, quite the contrary."[41] By the time the Kat closed some twenty years later it had become "a mythical space for thousands of women."[42] Elula went on to manage several more clubs, including the Privilège—an enormous venue that welcomed 1,500 women each Saturday evening—before retiring shortly before her death from cancer at seventy-four in 2003.

When Elula appeared on Bouvard's 1977 broadcast she was already recognized as a rising star in the world of sapphic nightlife. Her interlocutor was Dr. Henri Amoroso, introduced as a "neuropsychiatrist with degrees in occupational and forensic medicine, a member of the French society of sexology, a member of the French society of criminology, and the author of five books, including *La condition sexuelle des français* [The sexual condition of the French]." This formidable list of qualifications frames Amoroso as the expert and sets the terms of debate, which render female homosexuality both malady and vice. Amoroso puffs up like a pigeon at the recitation of his credentials; Elula smiles and looks mildly amused. The live TV audience (including—as insiders might recognize—Elula's closest friends, most of whom, like Elula, presented as hyperfeminine) either laughs derisively at his homophobia or is visibly disgusted by it. Bouvard functions as his wingman.

The program's tone is flirtatious:

BOUVARD: Do we agree that you hate men?
PERRIN: No, I do not agree.

BOUVARD: But you wrote it in black and white, Madame!

PERRIN: Okay, I'll admit a hatred of men in general, that's to say, of the gun-bearers. Thank god, you don't always carry them.

BOUVARD (baiting): And what do you call a gun, Madame?

PERRIN (coquettishly batting her eyes): Monsieur Bouvard, despite the late hour, must I dot the i's for you?

When Dr. Amoroso suggests that having slept with only one man in her life (her husband), Perrin might be mistaken about her lesbianism, she ripostes, "How many men must I sleep with? Three? Four? Five? Give me a number Monsieur Amoroso!" adding later, "You are dying to be the second, but I can promise you that you won't be!" to which he replies, "Madame Perrin . . . you seem as if you'd be an agreeable partner . . . but I have a charming woman of my own, who is worth ten of you." Ignoring his comment and assuring the audience that she is "on a terrain completely unknown to most TV viewers," Perrin attacks Amoroso's expertise, stating, "I know far more [lesbians] than you ever will," and crushing point for point his baldly sexist and homophobic rhetoric. When Amoroso suggests that lesbians need psychotherapy, she sniffs, "Monsieur Amoroso, do you have the impression that I am not at ease in my own skin?" The camera closes in, following Elula's legs from her sandals up her calves to where her knees disappear under the drape of her dress, tenaciously objectifying her body. Finally, Perrin insists that she is there not to speak about herself but rather to advocate on behalf of those women who desire women who may not have the self-assurance, the freedom, or the means to do so.

Radical claims notwithstanding, it was Perrin's femininity, her conservatism, her charisma, and her willingness to play to and with a male public that were key to her media appeal. On the one hand, her views—perceptible across media platforms—were staunchly traditional: she defended gender norms ("Social integration [for homosexuals] is currently possible only to the degree that we each keep the qualities that are appropriate to our sex"[43]), disdained butch dykes ("I can't stand the image of the virile lesbian. It is ridiculous"[44]), and rejected both gay marriage (desiring only that "we be left free to choose whom we love in the privacy of our bedrooms and the secrecy of our hearts"[45]) and gay parenting ("Children should be brought up by a man and a woman—although, if I had had a baby, I would have wanted a daughter who was a lesbian"[46]). She also rejected feminist activism ("Militancy? I'm Asian . . . I prefer a less aggressive route"[47]) and saw homosexuality as innate, not acquired (both countering and appropriating Beauvoir with the statement, "One does not become, but rather is born, a lesbian"[48]). On the other hand, Elula often contradicted herself: She was a founding member of the lesbian-feminist journal *Désormais* (1979–80, eight editions) and slammed men (with their "fifteen centimeters—and I'm being generous" of patriarchal privilege[49]). She defended lesbian beauty despite her dislike of butch style ("Men always say lesbians are too ugly to get laid, but that isn't true"), arguing, "I'll take the fattest, most masculine lesbian over a man any day."[50] And she tempered her supposed qualms about feminists, commenting, "In my opinion, you can't be a feminist without being a lesbian."[51]

Elula was attractive, entertaining, and titillating, and the media lapped her up. However, while heterosexual audiences may have found her fascinating, she remained controversial among the women she championed. Perrin's sapphic public was divided on her impact: Perrin's conservative politics (despite her métisse origins, she was a right-wing supporter of French colonization and, by some accounts, a racist), her hyperfeminine personal style (a return to the "femme" femininity that reigned on French television during the 1950s and early 1960s), and her reputation for sexual libertinism (she was accused of being a Don Juan) all came under attack. "There never has been a good TV show on homosexuality," claimed one self-identified lesbian viewer in 1984, adding, "The shows with Elula Perrin are rubbish."[52] And yet, the majority of her queer female audience forgave her political and personal peccadilloes in favor of what they saw as her work on behalf of a larger cause: "If Elula Perrin manages to prove to a wide audience that a small minority should be able to freely express their sexual difference openly," wrote one viewer in the late 1970s, "then she has my backing."[53] Forty-five years later, my interviewees largely agreed. True, Elula was not interested in (emphasis hers) "*changing society*"; she only wished "that *society would change*" its attitudes toward homosexuals and cease to regard them as "pariahs" or "sexual cripples."[54] Nevertheless, Elula's refusal to hide her sexuality and her steadfast insistence that lesbians had "the right to survive out in the daylight" altered the terms of debate while establishing her as one of the most important public faces of lesbianism in post-'68 France.[55]

As the "Queen of the Sapphic Night," Perrin single-handedly modeled what it meant to "be" lesbian while giving numerous women the courage to come out; she also made it safer for a heterosexual public to "think" lesbianism. Perrin flirtatiously promoted what is now understood as a politics of public indifference even as she advocated for the right to do as she pleased—and not just in private. She deliberately played the beautiful whore with the heart of gold. An opinionated, right-wing, outspoken, flirtatiously attractive woman who might now be termed a "lipstick lesbian" with conservative opinions about topics from lesbian parenting to butch masculinity, her repeated appearances in the French media between 1969 and the mid-1990s both legitimized *and delimited* a very specific incarnation of lesbianism, providing a crucial, heterosexually palatable but still progressive model for thinking about and existing as a woman who loved women in contemporary France.

The media loves both glamour and sex because they sell: Elula may have incarnated the beautiful whore, but she was only one example of this pervasive type. In 1980, three years after Elula first appeared on French TV, François Mitterrand won the presidency, and the Socialist Party took power. Mitterrand's platform included a promise to abrogate the prejudicial homosexual age of consent laws. On May 28, 1982, after the repeal was announced but before it was voted through on August 4, the TV newsmagazine *Aujourd'hui la vie* aired a special broadcast titled "L'homosexualité."[56] The show's goal was to bring together gay and straight members of the general public in order to explore how attitudes toward homosexuality had shifted in French society since the mid-1970s. Interestingly, although presenters and guests fervently declared that things had changed for the better, the conversation reiterated the same themes and approaches that had characterized the topic in years previous. To begin, the "expert" was once again a medical man: Dr. Gilbert Tjordman, whose role was to insist that while homosexuality causes suffering, it must not be considered an illness. A middle-aged mother testified to the normalcy of her homosexual neighbors. A schoolgirl equated the homophobia she saw in her entourage with racism. As in the *Émission médicale* broadcast from 1973, one young man—a self-avowed homosexual—is shown only in silhouette. However, two homosexuals appear unmasked, a young male educator and an exceptionally pretty female, a strawberry-blonde with a lush mouth and steely blue eyes named Anne Lambert. Mademoiselle Lambert reveals that she wrote to the producers asking to be on the show because she wanted to demonstrate that one *can* find enduring love as a lesbian. The unstated implication is that most people still believe this impossible. The camera lingers repeatedly on her lovely face, the elongated drop earrings that glint against her sloping neck, the soft cream silk bow of the blouse tied loosely at her throat. Anne objects to the homoerotic works of art—in classical paintings and close-ups of Greek vases—chosen to augment the broadcast, stating: "Heterosexuals are not defined by their sexuality, and neither are we." Dr. Tjordman half concurs, noting that "homosexual promiscuity is much more a male issue than a female one"; in response, the twenty-eight-year-old Anne emphasizes that she and her girlfriend (with whom she is "very, very happy") have been together nine years.

The sexualization that Anne objects to is a regular refrain in twentieth-century French mainstream media coverage of female same-sex-desire. Thus, we see a tension between the attempts to eroticize the topic and the efforts of the women interviewed either to deny or to embrace this same perspective—often to disparate ends. At times, the contrast is jarring. In 1993 the newsmagazine *52 sur la une*, for example, featured a special broadcast on lesbian love entitled "Amour de femmes" (Love of women).[57] The show opens with footage of a young blonde and a dark-haired girl, both in white bodysuits, caressing one another's faces while wearing white gloves. It reads as a futuristic soft-porn fantasy. When the male narrator finally appears, he tells us that while male homosexuality has been "known since antiquity," female homosexuality is often treated "as if it didn't exist." He notes that for this evening's broadcast, they "filmed female couples who express themselves freely but with modesty, tenderness, and discretion." "Here," he continues, "are portraits of women who live their homosexuality as if it were a natural state." The descriptors "modesty," "tenderness," and "discretion" conveniently mitigate the threats of impropriety and masculine appropriation that female same-sex sexual desire is often presumed to contain. The qualifier "*as if* it were a natural state" is likewise key. Unstated is the presumption that female same-sex desire could not possibly be natural. The underscoring of "female couples" immediately removes the threat of promiscuity. And yet, this program also indicates significant liberalization. For example, Muriel, the youngest of the five women profiled, states bluntly: "How does one fall in love with a woman? Just like with a man: Shit, it just hits you!" "Love is love," she adds later. "Your partner cheats on you. Don't you think that I would feel the same rage [as a heterosexual] if Sandrine [her girlfriend] cheated on me? The same, 'I'm suffering, I hurt, help me'?" In this broadcast the interviewees counter the stereotypes embedded in the production. Elsewhere, they reinforce it.

Sometimes, women's love affairs with one another are "reassuringly" framed as situational tales of individual desire. Here, erotic attraction is explained as independent of, rather than resulting from, a partner's gender identity; this was the case for Chantal, who claims in a 1983 broadcast bluntly titled "Les homosexuels," "I don't feel at all like a homosexual. . . . I fell in love with a person, and my beloved just happens to be a woman."[58] Situational attraction opened the possibility that the woman in question might return to heterosexual practices, easily augmenting male fantasies about female same-sex desire while disarming the danger that lesbian love necessarily comprised a rejection of men. Individually "aberrant" female same-sex behaviors—particularly when women were feminine—also fit French social norms more readily than those ascribed to "committed" (mostly male) homosexuals. After the show aired, however, Chantal Labat, the director of the broadcast (who identifies as lesbian), was excoriated by the lesbian community. When pressed by *Lesbia* magazine, she defended her choices, stating: "My number one concern was just to get the show on the air." The broadcast was made, in her words, "to enter a maximum of French living rooms, and to try to get [heterosexuals] to understand, in nonaggressive terms, the daily lives of homosexuals."[59]

In contrast, the 1994 program "Je suis une femme qui aime les femmes" (I am a woman who loves women), featuring two girl-band members (Karine and Gaëlle), seems designed primarily to inflame the lust of male viewers.[60] Despite the broadcast's presumed focus on female homosexuality, both women speak at length about their older boyfriends and identify as bisexual while arguing for lesbianism as a form of enlightened eroticism. A third guest on the program (Marie-Françoise, aged twenty-six and the manager of the lesbian nightclub L'Entr'acte) accuses Gaëlle of being closeted, but the comment is quickly passed over, and the cameras linger instead on close-ups of the two singers crooning provocatively to one another onstage. The broadcast also features Léa, a thirty-year-old self-proclaimed lesbian Don Juan, as well as a woman identified as Anne Marie, whose female partner died of cancer and who speaks about how the social imperative to keep the relationship secret eradicated forms of emotional support generally accorded grieving widows. The final guests are Dominique and Catherine, two women in their fifties who met twenty years prior when both were married mothers. As elsewhere, the overall message of this broadcast vacillates between eroticized objectification (lesbians are beautiful and sexy, but their desire for one another is a product for heterosexual consumption) and de-eroticized normalization (lesbians are also widows, married, and/or mothers, just like heterosexual women).

GOOD MOTHERS: "THEY LIVED HAPPILY EVER AFTER AND HAD MANY CHILDREN"

Since at least Marie-Antoinette (derided as both a tribade and bad mother in eighteenth-century *libelles* [political pornography]), French media coverage of female sexuality and maternal behavior has helped shape public attitudes toward women and contributed to either the restriction or the expansion of their social, civil, and political power.[61] Good mothers serve the nation and are worthy of support. Bad mothers are dangerous to the body politic: their offspring require removal and protection. The popularization of the "mannish" lesbian in the interwar years, with her predilection for male attire and assumption of masculine privilege, reinforced perceptions that female homosexuals were both unfit for and disinterested in maternity.[62] Suzy Solidor's lesbian character in the 1936 film *La garçonne* (discussed in chapter 1) captured this perspective when she observes, "We are failures, good-for-nothings, not even useful for making babies." In 1948 Simone de Beauvoir posited (in the controversial chapter on "the Lesbian" in her epic study *The Second Sex*) that bad mothering actually produced lesbianism.[63] As sexual deviants, lesbians were either antimaternal, bad mothers themselves, or the products of bad mothering. Female homosexuality was thus a threat to republican motherhood, the pronatalist logic whereby women are believed to have both a natural talent for and a public obligation to bear and rear children for the state.[64] When in their quest for equality French lesbians were pressed to invoke the site of discrimination (i.e., homosexuality, traditionally understood as a private choice) when battling for rights to motherhood and marriage (traditionally understood as public duties), the ensuing debates revealed as much about heteronormative attitudes toward gender and sexuality in France as they did about prejudices against female same-sex desire.

With divorce rates spiking in response to feminist and homosexual activism, by the 1980s the fear that lesbians posed a danger to children—who require the stabilizing influence of both a mother and a father and whose vulnerable psyches are easily damaged—had begun to haunt custody battles. This is not surprising when we consider that the lesbian mother was thought to contradict the "natural" course of parenting from conception forward. What *is* surprising is that when television covered the plight of "good mothers" who, as lesbians, were at risk of losing their children, negative associations twinning "deviant erotics" and "deviant maternity" were increasingly called into question. It seems that the media—and the public—simply could not square obvious examples of domestic, maternal love with the negative stereotypes about female homosexuality that had reigned for so long.

French feminists generally sought either freedom from maternity ("Libère-toi maman, tu es d'abord une femme" [Liberate yourself, mama; first you are a woman!]) or the right to control when and how maternity occurred ("C'est tout de même plus chouette de vivre quand on est désiré" [Life is much better when one is wanted (as a baby)!]).[65] Campaigns to legalize contraception and abortion (culminating respectively in the passage of the Neuwirth Law in 1967 and the Veil Law in 1975) were evidence of these concerns. Male homosexual activism initially ignored parenthood, arguing mainly for the right to love who and how they pleased. The concerns of French women who loved women and who either already were or wanted to be mothers fell between the cracks. By the late 1970s, however, such women began to demand recognition and rights.[66] In 1979, women from the Groupe de lesbiennes du Centre des femmes de Lyon organized the first group focused on the defense of the legal rights of lesbian mothers.[67] In the early 1980s, mixed-gender activist groups like David et Jonathan (established in 1980) and the Association des parents gays (founded in 1986; "et lesbiens" was added to the title in 1996) also began drawing attention to discrimination against homosexual parenting. Supported by the women's and homosexual rights movements, more and more women came out—often leaving heterosexual marriages to do so. In the process, more and more conflicts over the relationship between homosexuality, parenting, and adult/child relations erupted into the public sphere.

A series of ferocious legal challenges connected to lesbian child custody, lesbian "concubinage," child welfare, and lesbian access to domestic support and social services began to catch the attention of journalists, producers, and writers in the early 1980s. Importantly, the compassionate tone of this coverage—which aired right before the onset of the AIDS crisis—soon tempered the negative press given to homosexuality, disease, and "perversion" (especially sex with children or adolescents, which was then being promoted by associations like the Groupe de recherche pour une enfance différente [GRED]).[68] Although most female plaintiffs lost their cases, TV coverage of lesbian mothers (all of whom were presented in nonthreatening, heteronormative terms) was largely sympathetic. Lesbian mothers also negotiated TV coverage with care, learning to emphasize their status as citizens like all others rather than arguing for rights on the basis of their inclusion in a maligned group—homosexuals—a strategy that would have opened them to accusations of *communautarisme*. By the end of the 1990s a gradual but radical transformation in mainstream media depictions of female homosexuality had occurred; lesbians morphed from avatars of sexual perversion into potentially "good" mothers whose sexual difference was effaced by their feminine commitment to babies, nappies, and maternal love.

The first lesbian custody case to attract significant media attention in France erupted into the public eye in 1981. It concerned a divorced lesbian from Lyon desperate to retain custody of her four-and-a-half-year-old son.[69] Local television news noted that the case was breaking alongside escalating debates over whether to remove homosexuality from the French Penal Code. Journalists argued over the circumstances under which civil courts could interfere in people's private lives.[70] Despite the support of feminist, homosexual, and leftist political organizations, the woman (later identified as Evelyne Anselmo) initially lost her case and, with it, access to her child. News coverage either portrays Anselmo sympathetically or depicts activists marching under banners proclaiming "Fags and lesbians protest" and "Make love when I want, with whom I want."[71] Here, the media intentionally focuses on the most radical banners, despite the far more conservative claims of women in groups like the Femmes accusées d'homosexualité et maternité (Women Accused of Homosexuality and Maternity), who were simply arguing for the right to retain custody of their own children. Significantly, this is the last time that we'll see this type of deprecating media coverage of lesbian mothers. A year later, Anselmo's case was appealed by none other than the celebrated feminist lawyer Gisèle Halimi. The TV cameras were once again present, but the tone had changed.[72] This time Anselmo's appeal was successful; Halimi's reputation as a champion of feminist and homosexual causes attracted the respectful attention of TV news and underscored both the injustice of the earlier ruling and the important fact that lesbians' rights were citizens' rights.[73]

The next lesbian legal battle to capture media interest was waged between early 1982 and late 1984 by a young couple from Brittany known only as Nadia (aged thirty-four when the coverage began) and Annie (aged twenty-three). Its importance was evident: despite having left her husband to live (as the judge ruled) in a "state of 'concubinage' with a homosexual woman," Nadia had nonetheless been granted custody of her three children.[74] Moreover, she and her new partner Annie had managed to obtain a "certificate of concubinage" from the mayor of Saint-Lumine-de-Clisson, their tiny town in the Loire-Atlantique. Mayor Pluchon's initial refusal (he argued that concubinage "is [between] a man and a woman") was overcome when Nadia brandished her divorce papers under his nose, arguing that the same term (concubinage) had been used to describe her romantic relationship with Annie at the time of her divorce. Both decisions were historically significant: this appears to have been the first time that a known homosexual was granted custody in a divorce case and the first time that a homosexual couple was granted some form of legal recognition in France. Interest in the case further escalated after the French Social Security Administration nevertheless refused to recognize the women's certificate and denied their three children the same family allocations that heterosexual couples living "in a state of concubinage" received. The women sued, and the media had a field day.

Articles with titles like "Lesbos in the Village" and "The Concubines of Saint-Lumine" were splashed across the front pages of the local and national press (including *Libération*, *Le matin*, *France soir*, and *Ouest-France*). Developments were featured on state television. Sociologist Evelyne Le Garrec even discussed them in her best-selling book on lesbian life, *Des femmes qui s'aiment*, which was also featured on Bernard Pivot's TV book show *Apostrophes*.[75] Both the fact of this widespread attention and the way in which the reporting unrolled bear noting.

In the first televised coverage of the pair in 1982, Nadia and Annie's lawyer Maître Le Pellerin speaks on their behalf. When asked why his clients (then still unnamed) refused to appear on TV, Le Pellerin replies that despite hoping their case's publicity might help other homosexuals, the couple desired to preserve their privacy.[76] In this, they were part of "that calm and tranquil" "provincial invisibility" that, as one lesbian journalist remarked in the lesbian press, "only became visible when it ran up against homophobic prejudice."[77] And indeed, one year later, faced with the recalcitrance of the state administration (and perhaps encouraged by their lawyer's likely desire to stimulate public sympathy), the women shifted course and "came out" on the small screen.[78] They appear soft-spoken, articulate, feminine, attractive, gentle. Nadia has a halo of dark curly hair; Annie's is long, parted on the side. They sit side by side, glancing attentively at one another when their eyes are not focused on the camera (fig. 5.2). A month later, in May 1983, they appear on television again, this time discussing their relationship and insisting that they are accepted by the people in their village and that, like any other couple, if they "live their love serenely," it cannot be bad for their children who also, we are assured, were not denied the presence of their father.[79] While the women emphasize their maternal bona fides, here they also acknowledge their common cause with other same-sex couples. As the months passed and opposition mounted, however, their tactics changed. By October 1983 they were underscoring their similarity to heterosexuals. The about-face is stark. Thus, on the local news for *Télé pays de la Loire*, Nadia explains: "I don't think that it is interesting to be recognized as homosexual, since that simply encloses one in a ghetto. It is the recognition of our rights as individuals that we are demanding, not a recognition of our homosexuality." Annie pipes in: "We seek recognition as individuals. Each individual has rights, and we seek to have those rights recognized and actualized, which is not an easy thing."[80]

In December 1983 their lawyer downplayed the significance of a

FIGURE 5.2: Nadia (*left*) and Annie (*right*) defend their family's right to government support. "Jugement du procès intenté par les homosexuelles Nadia et Annie," interviewed by journalist Julie Poirier, *Télé pays de la Loire*, FR3, broadcast December 1, 1983. Courtesy of the Institut national de l'audiovisuel.

potential victory, submitting that while winning the case would be trailblazing, "relatively few homosexuals would take advantage of it" either because they wouldn't want to be publicly known as homosexual or because few homosexual parents relied on social services (a stance that also countered negative stereotypes of homosexuals as needy freeloaders).[81] Unfortunately for Nadia and Annie, the local court tribunal in Nantes nevertheless feared setting a precedent, and their case was denied. "The judgment," as journalist Chantal Brets reported, "certainly won't help to liberalize morals in France," but it will "have the merits of helping the Social Security Administration avoid spending a bit more money, if it isn't contradicted by the higher court in Rennes, where Nadia is mounting an appeal."[82] Over the course of the case, the argumentative tactics transformed from those based on sexual identity to those based on abstract individualism. This shift speaks to the necessity of abstaining from any hint of *communautarisme*, which was deemed a political red herring to be avoided at all costs. Importantly, this strategy also used lesbian women's domestic and maternal status to make claims on social support in ways that challenged the private/public divide.

Motherhood is similarly depicted as a social bond that eradicates the divide between lesbians and dominant heterosexual publics in the local news broadcast "Different Couples," which aired in 1982. The show, produced for *Antenne 2 midi*, featured three couples, each vaunted for their "difference." But whereas the first two (heterosexual) couples had differences of social class or age, the final "couple" (whose situation, we are told, is "more delicate") was not technically a couple at all; it consisted, rather, of nine-year-old Armelle and her "homosexual mother," Nicole.[83]

Armelle's girlish, sweet soprano voice leads us in. She states: "My name is Armelle. I am nine years old. I live in Neuilly with my mother and her female friend." In the sequence's opening shot, we see Armelle in a puffy jacket and knee-length skirt, with her hair styled in a pageboy, running to meet her mother after school. Her mother ("the lesbian") wears makeup but is similarly coiffed and dressed in a slightly longer skirt fashioned from an Indian print fabric. The camera cuts to an image of Nicole supervising Armelle as she does her homework. Armelle reads her report card to her mother: she is a model child. Her mother reads, "Excellent student, very studious," and Armelle continues: "'A' in arithmetic. 'A' in composition. 'A' in grammar," etc. The message, reinforced by her mother's evident care, is not only that Armelle is adorable and intelligent but also that Nicole, as her "good mother," is at least partially responsible for her success.

In the next sequence (which oddly hearkens to the famous "potato scene" in Chantal Akerman's 1975 feminist film, *Jeanne Dielman, 23 quai du Commerce, 1080 Bruxelles*), Nicole is shown chopping potatoes and carrots in her kitchen. Here, Nicole admits that she had great difficulty accepting her own homosexuality (observing that this is not a "difference" she has chosen but rather one that was "thrust upon her"). Nicole remarks that having a child was in part her way of being recognized as a woman in society. The statement, especially when situated in this domestic setting—in a kitchen, chopping vegetables—further validates feminine gender norms. At the same time, Nicole emphasizes that she has always been very frank and natural with her daughter about her homosexuality, noting that the difficulties come from "the gaze of others." Indeed, Nicole admits that her female partner refused to appear on the broadcast for that very reason—because she fears social judgment. The unstated message is that such judgment is unjust.

Moving forward, we cut to an "evening among friends," where we see a male friend of Nicole's with his children and Armelle. The directorial choice emphasizes that there *is* a male presence in Armelle's life, a fact that becomes especially significant after Armelle later admits that she has never met her own father. Armelle avows that although she sometimes wishes she "had" a father, her mother has friends whom she refers to as "Papa" because she likes them a lot—inferring that she simultaneously desires and yet does not lack father figures. In the final sequence, the camera cuts to a shot of a bride and groom exiting a church. We hear Armelle's voice: "Homosexuality," she observes, "is two men or two women who love each other. That doesn't bother me at all, but I don't want to be homosexual. I would prefer to have a husband and children. But it doesn't bother me at all. I think it is normal. They are different, but they are normal." The sequence closes with Armelle watching the bride and groom. The message is clear: all is well so long as the "good" lesbian mother has not imposed her "unwanted" sexual deviance (is it *really* normal?) on her child. With its emphasis on the lesbian "good mother"—whose good child gets good grades, is fed good food, and attended to by a good (if not real) papa—and promotion of heterosexual marriage, the broadcast at once normalizes and objectifies the very difference it addresses.

THE (LESBIAN?) FEMINIST ACTIVIST

The third lesbian archetype in French media coverage of female same-sex desire in the post-'68 years was characterized not by presence but by absence: an archetype I've named the "feminist activist." While women who loved women presented themselves as feminist activists in the French media in the early 1970s, it was not until the late 1970s that we see *some* women who loved women "come out" on French TV as *lesbian* activists per se. This shift in public representation, with the politics of gender first trumping and then becoming subordinate to the politics of sexuality, mirrored the radicalization of lesbian identity in late twentieth-century France. The media played a key role in this process.

Lesbian identity was politicized in the feminist and homosexual rights movements. In France, both the Mouvement de libération des femmes (MLF) and the Front homosexuel d'action révolutionnaire (FHAR) emerged in the early 1970s in the aftermath of the May 1968 French student revolutions. The student revolutions escalated after police brutality toward young people (who were protesting against the war in Vietnam, imperialism, capitalism, consumerism, institutional bureaucracy, antiquated educational practices, and sexual repression) catalyzed French workers to join them and engage in a series of decentralized anti-authoritarian strikes. Ten million people ended up in the streets in a violent public expression of anger and disillusionment in which pleasure and autonomy were articulated as political demands and human rights. The resultant chaos almost took down the French government. State suppression of media coverage of the events, followed by the retaliatory firings of scores of striking audiovisual professionals, exemplified long-standing recognition of the media's capacity to foment social and political change.

While their results are contested, the May events are generally understood as having initiated a moral revolution that liberalized significant sectors of French society and undermined traditional attitudes toward gender and sexuality.[84] But the May '68 movement was also heterosexist and misogynistic. Indeed, it was likewise in 1968 that France adopted the international standards of the World Health Organization and classified homosexuality as a mental illness—a diagnosis that reinforced homophobia (whether social, familial, or interiorized).[85] If the May '68 students demanded sexual freedoms, for most these did not include the right to same-sex desire.[86] Moreover, as Evelyne Rochedereux, a founding member of one of the first lesbian-feminist groups, the Gouines rouges (Red Dykes), told me, May '68 was "a 'guy's movement.'"[87] The movement's hypermasculine stance was epitomized, in Antoinette Fouque's words, by posters claiming "Power comes from the barrel of the phallus" and by "the graffiti of erect penises that joyously covered the walls of the Sorbonne, the Latin Quarter, and then Vincennes."[88] Hence, despite women's participation in the May '68 events in "massive and unprecedented numbers," their relegation to "second-class ground troops" and treatment as "mother figures, secretaries, or sex-objects" served as a forum for feminist consciousness-raising.[89]

In this context women were quick to recognize that if they wanted greater social and political power they had to organize. They also required greater access to and control over the media. Small feminist circles coalesced, principal among them Féminin, Masculin, Avenir (Feminine, Masculine, Future, or FMA), which formed around Anne Zelensky, Jacqueline Feldman, Christine Delphy, and Emmanuèle de Lesseps, and the Vincennes group, around Monique Wittig, Antoinette Fouque, Françoise Ducrocq, and the American Margaret Stephenson (later known as Namascar Shaktini).[90] Most of these women already identified—or soon would identify—as homosexual. Together they formed the kernel of the loose coalition that the media baptized the Mouvement de libération de la femme.[91] The groups frequently learned of one another's initiatives through the press.[92]

Armed with a heightened political and mediatic consciousness, the MLF's first militant action—the August 26, 1970, placing of a wreath on the Tomb of the Unknown Soldier under the Arc de Triomphe in Paris (intended, as the women's banners proclaimed, for "one even more unknown than the soldier—his wife")—was planned to attract maximal media attention. "We wanted," according to Christine Delphy, "to create a dramatic event in solidarity with American feminists" who were protesting on that same day in the Women's Strike for Equality (held on the fiftieth anniversary of US women's suffrage in the first major protest of the American women's liberation movement).[93] To that end, the French women alerted the press and the state-run television and radio administration, the ORTF, in advance. Television footage of the police arresting nine women including Delphy and the writer and lesbian theorist Monique Wittig was broadcast on the evening news, and photographs of the disturbance were featured on the front pages of the national papers.[94] The protest was also discussed on the radio.[95]

Neither the women themselves nor the journalists reporting on the event addressed the fact that the majority of the women present identified as homosexual—these were feminist activists, not lesbians.[96] But female same-sex desire was pervasive in the MLF: one feminist claimed that 90 percent of women in the movement were either experimenting with lesbianism or avowedly homosexual—even if they refused (at least initially) "to talk about their homosexuality, even among themselves."[97] While it wouldn't be long before some of these same women started to form lesbian groups like the Gouines rouges in order to bond over (homo)sexual difference, when speaking to the media *as feminists*, almost all discussion of this intimate dimension of their lives was absent. What we see here is both women's reticence to discuss same-sex desire and television's reticence to cover it, even as they both began to do so. What precisely were homosexual feminists talking about, and what was the media featuring? Work, patriarchy, power, and—paradoxically—the abolition of that division (so sacrosanct in France) between the personal and the political, the private sphere and the public one.

Evening news footage, for example, shows Christine Delphy discussing women and work as part of a feminist intervention at a conference of over two thousand women held in Versailles between November 20 and 22, 1970.[98] Known as the États généraux de la femme (the Estates General on

Women, a play on the French Revolution's own Estates General), the conference was organized by *Elle* magazine following a survey of over nineteen thousand French women conducted by the Institut français d'opinion publique (French Institute of Public Opinion). Featuring a range of male and female panelists from the worlds of government, education, law, medicine, politics, and industry, the conference aimed to debate the reforms required to improve the feminine condition. Determined to co-opt the media event and expose the sexism that undergirded the proceedings, the MLF prepared their own survey in response and demanded access to the rostrum. In TV coverage of the conference, Minister of Labor Joseph Fontanet argues that if women make less than men, it is because they deserve less since they are, on average, less qualified.[99] Angrily seizing the microphone, Delphy retorts that such arguments are patently false and merely benefit (male) employers and the government, all of whom profit to the tune of "millions and millions of new francs," both from this dire injustice and from women's unpaid household labor. "Why doesn't the government pay for the work that women do at home?" she demands. "THAT is a question that numerous attendees have posed, but no one on these panels has answered. Housework is free. Yes! Women work [at home]. Yes, they work for free and are not paid!" The intervention captures Delphy's incipient materialist feminism, which asserts that women's "principal enemy" is patriarchy, not just capitalism, and that it is gender difference, and not just class, that is the source of women's oppression.[100]

Almost a year later on July 20, 1971, another set of MLF activists including Anne Zelensky, Claude Hennequin, and Emmanuèle de Lesseps were interviewed as part of a broadcast dedicated to feminism following the French translation of Kate Millett's *Sexual Politics*.[101] During the program, the cameras penetrate into the sanctity of an MLF meeting. We see Zelensky, Hennequin, Lesseps, and others explain the movement's aims and agenda. One woman, off camera, discusses a recent debate over whether the MLF should forbid the FHAR to march with them in an upcoming Mother's Day rally "because they [the FHAR] create slogans that are not . . ." She trails off, but the insinuation is evident: the outrageous queer flamboyance of the FHAR's more vocal members (epitomized by a group of trans activists known as the Gazolines) threatened the respectability of the MLF's cause. These women, many of whom were themselves homosexual, were hesitant to link feminist struggles to homosexual desire in anything but the most oblique terms. When the camera returns to Zelensky, she insists: "Contrary to all other political groups [in the feminist movement], there is no separation between private and public life. We live in the movement, we laugh, we love, we amuse ourselves, we change, we try to evolve as human beings. It sounds banal, perhaps, but we are trying to change life." If the "we love" ("nous aimons") in Zelensky's description invoked love between women, the reference barely registers.

Media professionals were similarly disinterested in identifying connections between feminism and lesbianism. In TV news coverage of the "Days of Denunciation of Crimes Committed against Women" (the MLF's first congress held at the Mutualité in Paris on May 13 and 14, 1972), a journalist reports that the women are meeting to discuss legal free abortion, contraception, rape, childbirth, and homosexuality. But the latter comment accompanies footage of men who are presumably the women's partners cuddling and caring for babies at a nursery while the women meet. The choice emphasizes heterosexuality, even as the presence of male caregivers inverts gender norms. Journalists entirely ignored the fact that the congress was famously disrupted by lesbians from the Gouines rouges (including Delphy, Wittig, Cathy Bernheim, Catherine Deudon, and Marie-Jo Bonnet, who mounted the stage to call for an end to patriarchy while singing, "We are dykes, lesbians, depraved and foul").[102] When the writer and activist Françoise d'Eaubonne, a woman instrumental to the founding of the FHAR, appears in May 1972 on the TV newsmagazine *Aujourd'hui madame* in a broadcast dedicated to "Le féminisme" (their second program on the subject), the topic of homosexuality is likewise absent.[103]

Lesbianism, as a satirical sketch aired in June 1972 about the mythical MPLPF ("Mouvement pour le pouvoir féminin," or Movement for Feminine Power) hammers home, threatened the feminist cause.[104] On this program a timid male journalist is shown interviewing the MPLPF's fictional leader. The exchange takes place at a shooting range with gun-toting feminists attired in military dress. "Le" Secretary General (the feminist leader, who insists that the frightened man refer to her with male-gendered language) and her cohort are painted as butch female viragoes, barking directions and striding around with manly bluster as they intimidate the man who has stumbled into their lair (fig. 5.3). It is precisely this kind of man-hating (homo)sexual subtext that the MLF sought to avoid.

In 1974 the national TV news covered the MLF's call for French women to collectively strike and withhold their unpaid domestic and sexual labor in order to demonstrate their essentiality to society's functioning. Interviewees included Evelyne Rochedereux and Dominique Poggi, both lesbian feminists and founding members of the Gouines rouges. Despite female homosexuality's obvious utility as a choice that withholds sexual labor from the patriarchy, neither woman mentions it.[105] Likewise, when the regional news in Nancy featured the publishing house Des Femmes,

FIGURE 5.3: The female leader of the fictional Movement for Feminine Power subdues a male journalist. The banner on the left proclaims "Man descended from apes. Not [so] women." "Le MPLPF," dir. Henry Polage, *Sérieux s'abstenir*, Channel 1, ORTF, broadcast June 8, 1972. Courtesy of the Institut national de l'audiovisuel.

a venture established by Antoinette Fouque's group Psychanalyse et politique (known as Psychépo), whose essentialist feminism was cultivated in a climate of female same-sex desire, the subject of homosexuality was absent from the program.[106]

The examples continue. In 1975 Anne Zelensky was again interviewed about her feminism on the program *L'equilibre*. When the journalist comments that he is afraid that the MLF is launching a war between the sexes, Zelensky smiles and replies: "No. We cannot launch it because it already exists." The MLF's goal, she continues, "is to create a world where human beings are not denied the capacity, whether as a result of their gender, their color, or their age . . . to blossom in whatever manner they wish." Even after admitting, "I'm good with [women]. I communicate better with them. I militate with them," Zelensky (who according to her memoir was by now erotically involved uniquely with women) makes no mention of sexuality. Instead, she cautions that she'd rather not live in a world without men, stating that she is battling not to reverse gender oppression but to create a world in which all human beings have the right to live freely.[107] Thérèse Clerc, later famous for her lesbian militancy, discusses feminism on the national TV news on November 9, 1975. She speaks of her divorce and her support for abortion but says nothing of her "conversion" to lesbian sexuality during these same years (which she describes at length in Sébastien Lifshitz's 2012 documentary on elderly homosexuals in France, *Les invisibles*).[108] And when Zelensky appears yet again on TV in an interview about her 1977 book *Histoires du MLF* (cowritten with Annie de Pisan), which does make reference to Zelensky's homosexuality, the televised discussion is silent on the topic.[109] Similarly, there is no mention of female homosexuality in a televised sequence on Les Répondeuses (the lesbian-feminist information service discussed in the next chapter), although two of the announcements featured lesbian initiatives (one for a carpentry workshop run by women under the name 3G, the other for the communal lesbian-feminist café/bookstore Carabosses).[110]

Notwithstanding Elula Perrin, who embraced lesbianism even as she distanced herself from activism, it was only after a series of crises fractured the French feminist movement in 1979 and 1980 that *some* women begin to appear regularly as *lesbian* activists rather than as feminists on French TV.[111] In this, they mirrored the chronology of radical lesbian activism. Ilana Eloit convincingly describes how, when the MLF first emerged in France, all women, regardless of sexual preference, were encouraged to recognize themselves inside the unified political category "woman."[112] Here, the troubling particularity of homosexual difference (often understood as ghettoized) was, as Christine Bard submits, comfortingly abandoned in favor of a liberating assimilation into the abstract homogeneity of female experience.[113] At this time, with lesbianism "considered to be a revolutionary form of sexuality in service of feminism," and any "repression experienced by [female] homosexuals formulated as an experience among others generated by patriarchal domination . . . lesbianism [was] not claimed as a separate identity."[114] But women who loved women as an affective erotic choice and not just a politically motivated experiment quickly learned that their concerns were not always welcome in (heterosexual) feminist circles.[115] It was in part this dissonance between lesbianism as a sociopolitical experiment and lesbianism as an enduring desire that led to lesbian militancy and drove the formation of a unified lesbian movement—a lesbian counterpublic—in France in the 1980s.

Eloit argues that because French feminism claimed its legitimacy on the basis of women's inclusion in a universalist social contract that was inherently (but unavowedly) heterosexist, radical lesbianism required a rupture with the feminist movement. The history of French lesbian activism, she states, can be described as the movement from "nous, les femmes" (we women) to "nous, les lesbiennes" (we lesbians).[116] She further argues that French lesbianism was so completely disavowed by the French feminist movement that it could only be understood as an American import. Adapting a theory of racial domination, Eloit's French lesbian is thus configured as a racialized other banished (to America) from the homeland (France) who later returns from afar to haunt her white French feminist forebear. While this description may apply to Monique Wittig, who moved to America after being effectively exiled from the French feminist movement and whose subsequent influence over French lesbians supports Eloit's claims, the bigger picture is more complicated. For as French TV representations of female homosexual activists reveal, the move from feminism to lesbianism was less consistent than Eloit's argument suggests. Indeed, while it is true that *some* women-loving women, like Wittig, separated from the MLF and embraced radical lesbianism as a personal *and* political choice, others continued (and continue) to navigate the tension between French feminism's universalizing claims and their own "private" desires in more complicated ways.

In recent years, multiple lesbian activists and scholars have argued that French feminism would never have existed without the efforts and the energy of women who love women and that modern French lesbian subjectivity was first politicized inside the feminist movement.[117] There is a great deal of truth in these claims. At the same time, French feminists are often accused of erasing lesbians from French feminist history—Eloit's arguments lead the charge. But early media coverage of the feminist movement, which consistently privileged discussions of gender over those addressing same-sex desire, demonstrates that women who loved women were sometimes complicit in this process. The absence of public discussions of female homosexuality in mainstream media coverage of the MLF suggests why: French social norms weighed heavily on women's lives—including the lives of women who loved women. Consequently, if the archetypes of the beautiful whore and the good mother reveal that the French mainstream media played a key role in disseminating "normalized" discourses about female homosexuality to the wider public in post-'68 France, the archetype of the feminist activist reveals that at least some French lesbian feminists played a part in that normalizing process.

CONCLUSION

Femininity is of critical important in France, where the concept of gender complementarity and performances of heterosexuality and submission to masculinity are integral to dominant perceptions of Frenchness. For French women, maternity is a corollary to this national ideal. Even the very symbol of France, Marianne, is depicted with breasts bared, at once the beautiful whore, good mother, and feminist activist, poised to nourish the nation and vanquish its enemies. The rigidity of this heterosexual paradigm has posed particular challenges for women with same-sex desires. By championing the feminine status quo, French mainstream media coverage in the late 1970s and 1980s of both femme lesbians like Elula and lesbian mothers like Nadia, Annie, and Nicole made lesbianism more palatable to the French public. In this they inadvertently addressed what had long been a major dilemma for lesbians in the feminist movement; they argued for privilege and power for women without discrediting the feminist cause by "tainting" it with the stain of a deviant sexuality that could not be recuperated within a heterosexual model.

Some lesbians saw "assimilationist" approaches as strategic. After the TV newsmagazine *Les dossiers de l'écran* aired a 1984 broadcast on homosexuality, one female viewer wrote: "It is true that for [male and female] homosexuals this show is of no interest . . . but . . . for heteros it is a good 'lesson.' Maybe they'll be a little less frightened each time, because that line-up of homos is pretty reassuring, no?" She acknowledged that some activists critiqued the show for not being representative of the gay community but insisted, "At this time I think it is better to 'bias' [heterosexual] people in this way . . . they already have a hard time dealing with [homosexuality]. . . . Whatever would happen if we revealed our real problems! That would overwhelm their little minds, don't you think?"[118]

The republican construct of abstract individualism has long supported the hard division between public and private, thus erasing sexual orientation from political life and encouraging certain forms of closeting. The effects of this are visible in the media coverage examined here, most notably in queer women's refusal to appear unmasked on French TV and in the relative absence of discussions of female same-sex desire in coverage of the French feminist movement—even by women who self-identified as lesbians. But we should be cautious about how we interpret such evidence. Indeed, my narrators frequently asserted that they were completely "out" and had always been at ease with their erotic choices. It was fascinating, however, to see how frequently such assertions could be undercut by an unacknowledged accommodation to dominant norms. When pressed, countless women revealed that they chose not to divulge their romantic or erotic relationships with other women to some combination of family, friends, coworkers, or strangers—often defending avoidance, ambiguity, or outright deception through recourse to a republican discourse that privileges private discretion even as it promotes and permits heterosexuality in the public sphere. These contradictions emphasize both the power of the French republican model and the risks associated with contravening what Adrienne Rich called "compulsory heterosexuality," a compulsion that is arguably even more severe in France, where traditionalist arguments for heterosexual gender complementarity continue to carry more force than they do in North America.[119] Indeed, in 2018 when some French women (including iconic actress Catherine Deneuve) chastised other women for calling out male sexual harassment, abuse, and assault during the #BalanceTonPorc (Denounce Your Pig) campaign—the French equivalent of the #MeToo movement—they revealed precisely how powerful French imperatives regarding gender complementarity and heterosexuality remain today.[120] The fact that some key (lesbian) feminists have long advocated for the politicization of the personal in all arenas except homosexuality and have not seen the contradictory logic of this lacunae is yet more evidence of the continuing sway of French gender and sexual norms.

In the era of Twitter and Facebook, it has become overwhelmingly evident that marginalized groups depend on access to and coverage in the media if they want to levy political power. Lesbian counterpublics coalesced around this consciousness in the post-'68 moment. Moreover, unlike some of the women described above, not all women who loved women acquiesced to the pressure of the patriarchy. Some were adamant in their refusal of both heterosexuality and heteronormativity. These women created their own forms of media in order to contact others who shared these desires. To them, and the women that they were in dialogue with, the public avowal of same-sex desire via the development and use of new media technologies was critical not only to living an authentic life but also to exerting political influence in the public sphere. The lesbian counterpublics that emerged out of the feminist and homosexual movements in France in the 1970s were mindful of these facts from the start.

6

FRENCH LESBIAN INFORMATION ACTIVISM

I am with Danièle Cottereau in her small house in Aulney-sous-Bois in June 2013. She's tall and animated, with a ready laugh that issues hoarsely from the back of her throat. She chain-smokes cigarettes in rapid succession. We've been speaking for over an hour. I've just asked about her work for the homosexual radio station Fréquence Gaie (FG, or Gay Frequency), which began broadcasting in Paris in 1981, right after Mitterrand's Socialist government took power and began easing state control over public radio. Danièle excuses herself and disappears into the back of the house. When she returns, she's carrying several boxes and a pile of binders. She flips one open and presents me with an image. In pen and ink on white paper is an illustrated cartoon.

A grinning young woman in black pants and polka-dot bedroom slippers lounges on a pile of pillows on the floor under an open window. A pair of bare feet, toes wiggling, jut into the left side of the frame. Scribbled beneath are the words, "ideal woman." The girl is focused, however, not on the barely visible feet of the romantic ideal on the left but on the hi-fi against the opposite wall. A telephone handset, its coil connected to a rotary phone on the floor, is suspended "off the hook" above the hi-fi by a fishing line, its pole emerging improbably from a stereo speaker on an upper shelf. So placed, the dangling handset renders the hi-fi audible to another person via the phone line. This young woman is not listening to the radio alone; she is sharing the experience by phone with a friend. A framed picture is hung on the wall. It depicts a smiling portrait of someone

FIGURE 6.1: "Bravo girls for 'Go Fish.'" Fan mail cartoon by Kiki sent to Danièle Cottereau in 1984 to acknowledge lesbian broadcasting on the radio station Fréquence Gaie. Courtesy of Danièle Cottereau.

wearing a hat tipped low over their eyes. The image is autographed: "Avec mes amities [Fondly], D. Cottereau"—the same Danièle Cottereau then standing at my side. In block letters on the lower right we see: "BRAVO LES FILLES POUR LA PÊCHE A LA LIGNE!" (BRAVO GIRLS FOR "GO FISH"!). Danièle informs me that *Pêche à la ligne (au féminin)* (Go fish [for girls]) was a radio show on FG dedicated to airing lesbian personal ads.[1] The cartoon is signed "Kiki" and was sent to Danièle in the early 1980s, during the years that she produced and hosted the broadcast in question (fig. 6.1).

I start with this cartoon because its symbolic melding of broadcasting (the radio, the radio announcer), reception (the hi-fi, the girl), and retransmission (the phone, the friend) provides a vivid example of how women used media technologies to facilitate the creation of lesbian counterpublics in post-'68 France. French lesbian counterpublics differed from the subcultural communities that had preceded them because of the ways in which they politicized private life in order not merely to create social connection but also to argue for social, cultural, and legal change. These counterpublics were not (as Danièle's possession of Kiki's cartoon makes evident) fashioned from the top down; rather they were horizontally coconstituted. Indeed, this drawing demonstrates how one listener communicated back to a radio broadcast via a graphic cartoon. Others expressed their views via letters or phone calls to the station. Such communications influenced programming, and announcers regularly responded to viewer feedback on the air. This type of interactive lesbian communication network in which knowledge is circulated, commented on, adapted, and retransmitted represents what Cait McKinney in the American context has called lesbian "information activism."[2] Defined as "the collective, often unspectacular labor that sustains social movements," information activism "brings together people, their visions of justice, and the media that they use to organize, store, and provide access to information."[3] This has been particularly important for women who desire other women because, as McKinney states, "access to good lesbian information is so *precarious*: unavailable, inconsistent, temporary, or even impossible."[4] French women who desired women turned to information activism in an attempt to address this multifaceted dilemma.

This chapter focuses on three examples of lesbian information activism in France in the 1970s and 1980s: a feminist phone service known as Les Répondeuses (The Responders), which functioned in Paris and Grenoble from 1977 through 1984; one of the first French lesbian magazines, *Quand les femmes s'aiment* (*QLFSA*, or When women love one another), which was published alternately in Lyon and Paris from 1978 through 1980; and the lesbian radio shows produced by Danièle Cottereau and her female collaborators for Fréquence Gaie in Paris between 1982 and 1985. Each example is explored through the close analysis of a cache of largely untapped sources. This diverse body of materials—including cartoons, cassette tapes, programming schedules, posters, newsletters, index cards, radio broadcasts, documentary video, phone logs, my filmed interviews, and over seven hundred privately held letters—offers insights into how French women used new media technologies to politicize lesbian subjectivity, connect lesbian communities, and produce lesbian counterpublics in France, its empire, and beyond in the last quarter of the twentieth century.

"LEAVE A MESSAGE AFTER THE BEEP": LES RÉPONDEUSES

Les Répondeuses were a Parisian telephone call service developed and staffed by a group of about a dozen dedicated feminist and lesbian volunteers. Notwithstanding one brief hiatus, the group operated twenty-four hours a day, seven days a week, from May 1977 to January 1984. Created by Mimi Bastille, Danielle Prévôt, and feminist videographer and documentary filmmaker Carole Roussopoulos, by the spring of 1979, Les Répondeuses had quadrupled in size.[5] While most members were white, at least one, Djamila, was a woman of color. By 1980 there were seventeen women in Les Répondeuses, Djamila among them.[6]

Les Répondeuses utilized the telephone network, two tape recorders, an answering machine, an editing board, and a microphone to provide a women's news and information service. Perpetually underfunded, the group often scrambled for workspace. They initially set up shop in the corner of a member's bedroom but soon managed to rent a tiny office dedicated to their mission.

On July 1, 1978, a little over a year after launching their service, Les Répondeuses temporarily suspended operations while they sought new space, better technology, and more money. To help cover costs, Les Répondeuses requested that callers pay a nominal monthly fee. In return, they offered their newly produced journal, *La gazette*, which provided information in print form. *La gazette*'s first issue recounts their origin story like a fairy tale: "A long time ago," it begins, "before the era of Les Répondeuses, information circulated by word of mouth," frequently via calls made to or by the same few women. "One of us," they explained, who was feeling "crushed by the incessant ringing" of the nefarious object after "having repeated for the fiftieth time the same news yet again," said to herself "'But what do they take me for? An answering machine?' And EUREKA!!! The idea was found!" Then, "with a wave of her magic wand," the beleaguered feminist "conjured up an answering machine." Calling a friend, she said, "Voilà! This is how to satisfy those endless callers." And thus, they proudly announce, "We were born." But the women quickly realized that "making that machine function all week was really a ton of work!" "Who among you would have done it?" they ask, "And with what resources?"[7] To fill their empty coffers, Les Répondeuses held fundraising parties for women, like the one they hosted "live from 8 p.m. to dawn" at the Salle Wagram on March 23, 1979.[8] These became annual traditions. They also dropped flyers in appropriate venues and both advertised and plied their callers for donations in the feminist, lesbian, and women's press (fig. 6.2). Convinced despite challenges of the value of their service, Les Répondeuses hoped that their unique model of feminist information activism would be replicated throughout France. At least one spin-off operating independently out of Grenoble is known to have existed during these same years.

FIGURE 6.2: Flyer: “Les Répondeuses of the Women’s Liberation Movement. Twenty-four hours a day, women inform women.” Courtesy of Brigitte Boucheron.

Remarkably, given the ephemeral nature of early audio sources, Les Répondeuses left copious traces—recorded and written—of their activist endeavors. French TV coverage shot to mark International Women's Day in 1982 shows the group at work: it is among the rare filmed sources that capture them in action.[9] On a scrap of paper that survives in the archives, Les Répondeuses clarify explicit directives.[10] Callers were instructed to dial in to a central line and leave messages concerning current events, questions, or announcements of interest to women on an answering machine. The oral format required brevity (the closing salutation instructed: "And now, *you* have forty-five seconds to leave us a message!"), so women were also invited to contact Les Répondeuses by mail. Working alone or in groups of two or three, the women logged incoming oral and written messages nightly in small notebooks. Responses to questions were researched, and messages prioritized. Les Répondeuses then recorded a new three-minute outgoing message for the answering machine. Sometimes there was musical accompaniment. By calling in and listening to the updated outgoing message, callers could hear a curated selection of new announcements and responses to inquiries received the day prior.

Each member of the group dedicated one or two nights per week to running the service—a fact that likely contributed to their initial success since the commitment was not too onerous. However, within weeks of launching their project, Les Répondeuses were receiving over two hundred calls per day. In two years, that number more than doubled—a fact that testified to their success but also increased their workload and created difficulties for callers. As one woman avowed: "Bonjour. One has to get up mighty early to reach you! If not, the line is always busy. But I'm happy to hear you nonetheless!"[11] To handle additional traffic, by March 1981 they were operating three telephone lines instead of one. Unfortunately, the technology did not always function smoothly: "Can you rerecord today's message?" one woman asked. "We can't hear it. There is an echo and too much noise."[12] Glitches notwithstanding, their process was simple, their ingenuity striking, and their impact immense.

Les Répondeuses publicly identified as a feminist, not lesbian, organization, but like so many early feminist initiatives, women who loved women were both critical to their operations and prominent among the public they served. On their cassettes and call logs are details about meetings, marches, film festivals, photo exhibitions, and magazines; requests for guidance on sexual health, depression, abortion, and rape; queries seeking women's groups; information on current events (Elula Perrin's 1977 appearance on TV, Annie and Nadia's child support case, a senate vote on a proposed law against sexism); recommendations for female plumbers, electricians, auto mechanics, and childcare; listings for lessons taught by women on finance, law, physics, self-defense, video, singing, and piano. There was an announcement from the Mouvement des femmes noires (Black Women's Movement) about a meeting of their Committee for the Abolition of Sexual Mutilation, one publicizing the formation of a group "conscious of their oppression as women, immigrants, and Algerians," and another advertising a meeting on feminism and Marxism hosted by the women's section of the French Communist Party, Elles voient rouge (They See Red).[13] While most messages referred to happenings in Paris, others were for ventures as far away as Toulouse, Marseille, Brussels, Amsterdam, and Rome. The expectation was both that women from outside Paris would call in and that those in the city might travel elsewhere to attend events. In May 1977, for example, two women from Saint-Ay (near Orléans in the Loire Valley) announced that they were hosting a national meeting of lesbian feminists. They publicized their gathering via Les Répondeuses, reminding women to "bring your blanket[s]"—an indication that there would be rudimentary lodging on site.[14]

The Saint-Ay gathering was among the first attempts to develop a national lesbian movement. Organized under the joint aegis of women from the Parisian and Orléanist factions of the Groupe de libération homosexuelle, over forty women from all parts of France attended. A not insignificant number had learned of the meeting thanks to Les Répondeuses. Those in attendance included women from the Groupe de lesbiennes du Centre des femmes de Lyon who later launched the journal *Quand les femmes s'aiment* (discussed in the next section). While the Saint-Ay meeting was "rich and dynamic," it was also fraught; "a dozen women from the Paris region," some of whom were reportedly "a bit clueless," ransacked communal living quarters, got high, and kissed in public—to the great embarrassment of both villagers and other attendees.[15] But the experience was generative, in part because it enabled women from disparate regions to connect. Significantly, it was after Saint-Ay that the Lyonnais group began to emerge as a national leader in lesbian organizing, shifting the focus away from Paris for the first time. Women in Poitiers also hosted a follow-up gathering in Exoudun later that summer. Les Répondeuses' capacity to foster contacts on a national level was vital to such developments.

While their focus was on feminism, Les Répondeuses addressed a range of overtly lesbian initiatives that ran the gamut from deeply personal to staunchly political. Some mixed the two. One anonymous caller declared: "I am a lesbian."[16] She then inquired, "I want to know if there is a center for us, [for] women who love other women," and added, "If yes, I would like you to please call me back. . . . When I pick up, you must say 'Hello lesbian.' If you don't, I won't answer, because I'm ashamed." Shame or no, she continued, "Mesdames lesbians, I love all of you, all women!" and signed off with multiple kisses. The transition from pride to shame to pleasure is striking. Other women publicized lesbian social events (like tea dances "with the Amazons!" or a party thrown by "the Movement for Liberation from Lesbian Shame"), sought lesbian roommates, announced meetings on lesbian sexuality, or promoted magazines aimed at lesbians, such as *Quand les femmes s'aiment*.[17] One woman was looking for "two or three other female homosexuals to start a commune."[18] Another wanted to meet lesbians "in my region of Saône-et-Loire."[19] Some wanted partners: "Can you provide the addresses of places like Helzapoppin' or the Jeu des Dames [both lesbian bars]?" one woman asked, noting that she wanted to know "where those who arrive in Paris and don't know anything" could meet women one-on-one "and not in groups."[20] The fact that this woman was not interested "in groups" suggests a desire for romance, or for sex. Someone (possibly Elula Perrin herself) recommended, "If you would like to spend an agreeable evening among women," you must try the Katmandou discothèque. "But take care," the caller specified, "proper dress required!"[21] The day after, someone else called trying to reach a woman she'd met at the nightclub the night before.[22] Not all callers were cheerful. Sometimes women who identified as lesbian (or thought they might) were driven to phone Les Répondeuses out of despair. One caller confided, "I am alone. I am homosexual. I would like to contact a woman who would like to live with me for a moment. I have a young girl of eight and a half."[23] Women who loved women sought validation, connection, intimacy, and community. But they also called because they wanted nothing less than to change the world.

Suzette Robichon told me that when she and Nelly Martin were inspired to create the Groupe des lesbiennes de Paris in November 1977, they advertised via Les Répondeuses.[24] Between thirty and a hundred women were soon attending their meetings. Both women were political, and Robichon became an important figure in the lesbian movement. But privileging politics could be tricky. In 1981 two consecutive letters to the phone service share that "a certain number of lesbians" who had become "aware of the pleasure and necessity of meeting in order to affirm our identity" had been gathering on Mondays at the Maison des Femmes. The authors note that they sought new members, "activist or not," since "we wish our group to be as open as possible, to be both a place [to meet new women] and a political force."[25] Their inclusivity speaks to the challenges of bringing women who loved women from outside the political realm into contact. As demonstrated by a third letter (signed Corine B. and sent on October 12, 1981), this is where Les Répondeuses proved especially useful. Corine states: "It has been some time since the [Groupe des lesbiennes de Paris] (now renamed 'MIEL') has been intending to express our gratitude [to Les Répondeuses]," since "the majority of the girls who come to our meetings have found out about them thanks to you."[26]

Founded in 1981 and not dissolved until 1995, MIEL (an acronym spelling the French word for "honey," which stood for the Mouvement d'information et d'expression des lesbiennes, or Movement for Lesbian Information and Expression) sought to defend lesbianism, foster lesbian community, fight for lesbian rights, and combat lesbophobia. It was among the first French LGBT organizations to identify the latter as a specific social problem. The women of MIEL organized conferences, produced publications, and created festivals throughout France. They opened their own telephone support line, Canal MIEL, in 1982, as well as a lesbian café, L'Hydromiel, in 1983. Catherine Gonnard and Aline Tashjian, two of MIEL's principal actors, were also behind the development of the first lesbian website (called Les Goudous Télématiques), discussed in the next chapter. Gonnard likewise became editor in chief (from 1989 to 1995) of *Lesbia magazine*. First published in 1982 as simply *Lesbia* and renamed *Lesbia magazine* under Gonnard's tenure, the magazine (which ceased publication in 2012) provided the French lesbian community with enduring representation in the French mediascape. The publicity that Les Répondeuses granted MIEL in its early days was critical to all of these future developments.

Les Répondeuses were likewise closely linked to and supportive of the feminist bookstore Carabosses (1978–85), opened at 70 rue Jean-Pierre Timbaud in Paris's eleventh arrondissement and later relocated to 58 rue de la Roquette. Under the management of Éliane Viennot, Carabosses carried a wide range of books, magazines, and journals of interest to women who loved women.[27] Viennot also helped launch an associated café for women, called Barcarrosse. Both the bookstore and the café were significant spaces for lesbian socializing and political activism. Les Répondeuses supported both businesses, joining Carabosses in cosponsoring a conference on International Women's Day at the Salle Wagram in 1981, at which they co-organized four debates (on feminist projects, women and politics, women and love, and women and rape) and a series of musical, theatrical, and cinematic performances. The entire event was adamantly women-only since, as publicity on Agence France-Presse declared, "it is when we are among women that we feel truly free."[28]

While solidarity seems to have reigned among Les Répondeuses' feminist public, there remained important divisions concerning both sexuality and gender. In 1977 (presaging political rifts to come) one angry caller targeted a portion of her "sisters" when she announced, "Down with heteros!" and abruptly hung up.[29] "Why all this *musique de mec* [guy's music]?" another complained, referring to one of the soundtracks chosen to accompany the daily message.[30] And yet if some callers abhorred men, others protested with them—a practice that did not preclude combating male (often heterosexual) power. Thus, for example, when one of Les Répondeuses' callers invited her sisters to protest with mixed-gender gay rights groups against the repression of homosexuals in the United States at the first officially authorized French Pride March in Paris on June 25, 1977, she argued that it was "essential that French women . . . appear in the first row of this antipatriarchal struggle."[31] Another woman called for women to join the Groupe de libération homosexuelle and Socialist Party in a mixed-gender demonstration against fascist attacks on homosexuals.[32] And yet another triumphantly reported on the success of the 1978 May Day Parade, where over "one thousand people marched behind the homosexual banner." The latter proudly signed off: "We'll keep Les Répondeuses posted about our future activities."[33] Occasionally, men phoned in too, as when a man who identified himself as a homosexual activist "desirous of helping his *copines* [female friends] in the movement" asked women possessing incriminating documents about the police to share them with him.[34] Precisely what the man intended to do with these papers was unclear.

The women's organization known as the 3F—established in Paris in March 1977 and run and heavily patronized by women who identified as lesbian—regularly advertised its courses via Les Répondeuses' answering machines. The 3F charged a nominal fee for classes "given by women for women" "in domains that until now have been exclusively masculine," from carpentry, plumbing, and auto repair to karate and self-defense.[35] Aimed at providing women with "greater autonomy in their daily lives," by 1982 (when the 3F was operated by six female volunteers) workshops on legal topics regarding work, family, and renters' rights had been added to their roster of offerings.[36] Les Répondeuses likewise publicized the activities of the Groupe lesbienne banlieue nord (a lesbian group from the housing projects in Paris's economically disadvantaged north suburbs). Known as Les Baragouineuses, the group formed in 1978 and was composed of about a dozen women, "some of whom," one caller confessed, "still have a bitter taste in their mouths from their time in [heterosexual] women's groups." In addition to meeting socially, Les Baragouineuses staffed a telephone support line for lesbians on the first and third Wednesdays of each month and participated in "collective actions" (such as when they "savagely plastered their lesbianism on the walls of Saint-Denis" [their neighborhood] to celebrate the Fête des Murs [Festival of the Walls] on February 2, 1980).[37] Three years earlier, on May 16, 1977, lesbian feminists from Paris's seventeenth arrondissement had organized a similar "bombing" event to deface sexist advertisements in their quarter. They, too, had used Les Répondeuses' service to publicize their plan and round up supporters. Les Répondeuses also inspired other lesbian call services, but these were primarily in keeping with the homosexual support lines that had been springing up in the United States and Great Britain at that time.[38]

Les Répondeuses' vital contributions to women's networking were covered in both mainstream and activist media: In addition to the 1982 TV footage mentioned above, Les Répondeuses had a cameo on national TV in a 1980 interview with actress and feminist Delphine Seyrig (herself a videographer and founding member of the Centre audiovisuel Simone de Beauvoir, or CASdeB).[39] The documentary film *Mais qu'est-ce qu'elles font*, produced in 1981 by the feminist association La Griffonne (and reissued in 2014 by the CASdeB), has rare footage of the organization at work.[40] The film also features sequences on the 3F and the bookstore Carabosses. Les Répondeuses advertised their service in the feminist, lesbian, and women's press (from *Questions féministes* and *Lesbia* to *Elle*), but they were also listed in the "Business" section of the Paris telephone directory.[41] The mainstream national press likewise covered their efforts, though not always with positive results. As Les Répondeuses reported, "Each time *Libé* [the national left-leaning newspaper *Libération*] speaks of [us]," the women received "lots of messages on their machine from guys who poured out their filth, their insults, and their obscenities."[42] Sometimes violent language escalated to action: a group identified as FANE left a menacing message on the service warning the Collectif contre le viol et les violences sexistes (Collective against Rape and Sexist Violence) that they would be attacked before the end of the year. The same voice had previously left messages threatening the women at Carabosses. The bookstore was subsequently attacked, the culprit caught, and the women filed charges.[43] Les Répondeuses later declared that they "refused to be intimidated" by "sexist ruffians," commenting, "Happily, women leave heartwarming messages for us: these are balm to our wounds."[44]

Les Répondeuses were instrumental in transforming feminist and lesbian life in France, but their technology had limits. Indeed, the telephone system itself was far from dependable: "Try to phone ahead," Les Répondeuses cautioned, "before attempting to go to any of the events we advertise," but "if you don't get an answer, go anyway, because sometimes the phone has been cut off, but the group is still meeting."[45] Moreover, while valuable to Parisians, despite their good intentions the information Les Répondeuses provided was frequently irrelevant beyond the immediate calling area. In addition, listening to recordings was time consuming, and calling costs could be prohibitive, especially for those accessing the service from afar. The technology's potential for anonymity also had pros and cons: it made it harder to connect with women outside the movement (many of whom listened to, but did not leave, messages) while holding out hope to those women—especially with same-sex desires—who felt isolated and alone. Shortcomings aside, Les Répondeuses exemplifies the type of grassroots information infrastructure that French women who loved women invested in and depended on in their efforts to create a more habitable public world for lesbian desire. The lesbian press was likewise central to this process.

QUAND LES FEMMES S'AIMENT: LESBIAN PRESS, LESBIAN PUBLIC

During the late 1970s the lesbian press emerged in France as one of the most powerful forces in the production and politicization of French lesbian identity. Indeed, Ilana Eloit claims that because it became a "point of convergence" between individuals who had previously been isolated, "the lesbian press *made* the lesbian movement."[46] In this section I analyze the history of a French lesbian journal published every three months between April 1978 and July 1980 called *Quand les femmes s'aiment* (*QLFSA*, or When women love one another). I then turn to a series of letters written to the journal by its readers in order to chart precisely how this mode of lesbian information activism worked.[47]

Created by women from the Groupe de lesbiennes du Centre des femmes de Lyon and vaunted by its original editorial staff as "the first openly lesbian journal" in France (a claim subject to dispute), *Quand les femmes s'aiment* had a significant impact on the politicization of contemporary lesbian identity both inside and beyond French borders.[48] The journal's title was a riff on the French feminist slogan "Quand les femmes s'aiment, les hommes ne recoltent pas" (When women love one another, men don't reap [the rewards]). The Lyonnais team alternated production responsibilities with women from the Groupe des lesbiennes de Paris (who produced issues three/four—a controversially more costly double issue—and six, while issues one, two, five, and seven were produced in Lyon). Editorial teams consisted of groups of about ten women each. All told, thirty-two women from Lyon and twenty-six from Paris participated in the production process. The first Lyonnais issue was financed through personal contributions from the group itself. Each subsequent issue was funded by previous sales. Successive editorial teams were not stable; women left, and new women joined from one issue to the next. This turnover sometimes generated conflicts over content, style, and approach, especially after lesbians from Paris were suspected by those in Lyon of trying to take over operations. The Lyonnais group's insistence on holding the reins and its status as the journal's headquarters raised its national profile and helped decenter Paris as a locus of French lesbian life.

QLFSA's origin story echoes the same frustrations that had led to the creation of Les Répondeuses. In their first editorial, the group explains that they had been trying to figure out how to contact and connect isolated lesbians, to "organize meetings and places to talk," and to spread information about lesbian life to those who wanted it. Like Les Répondeuses, they had been overwhelmed by demands for information and assistance. Their response? "What if we try a journal?" Acknowledging that they had "neither the pretention, nor the means to produce a national journal, much less a journal for all lesbians," their aspirations were nevertheless ambitious. First, they were adamant that the journal should provide a platform for multiple voices. A significant portion of the journal's contents consequently consisted of submissions from readers. To that end, the group implored, "WE EAGERLY AWAIT YOUR LETTERS, ARTICLES, IDEAS, CRITICISM, TESTIMONIES, ADDRESSES, INFORMATION, THEORETICAL TEXTS, STATES OF MIND, DEEP THOUGHTS, AND SHORT STORIES." This approach provided their audience (most of whom had never imagined sharing private desires) with a means to make public the most intimate (and often troubled) aspects of their lives. Second, by encouraging activism and empowering their readers to assume "lesbianism" as an erotic and political identity, the group aimed to establish "a lesbian movement."[49]

On the last page of their inaugural issue, they printed a call to arms. They argued that despite a first attempt at Saint-Ay, lesbians across France had not managed to organize at a national level. One reason, they submitted, was that individuals and groups were still far too disconnected, with activists divided among women who identified as lesbian (in Paris and Aix-en-Provence), feminist (in Bordeaux, Lyon, Bourges, Orléans,

Marseille, and Paris), or homosexual (associated with the Groupes de libération homosexuelles in Paris, Orléans, Rouen, and Tours). Intent on merging these disparate forces, the Groupe de lesbiennes du Centre des femmes de Lyon announced their plan to resuscitate the projects formulated at Saint-Ay and invited all lesbians, "whether isolated or organized in groups," to a new national meeting.[50] *Quand les femmes s'aiment* publicized this plan and reported on its outcome. The Lyon meeting (held in November 1978) helped ignite the slow burn that—almost two decades later in 1996—led over twenty lesbian associations to federate as the Coordination lesbienne nationale. Renamed the Coordination lesbienne en France in 2002, the organization endured until 2017.

Only 750 copies of the first issue of *Quand les femmes s'aiment* were printed. When they sold out, the editorial team printed 250 more. These, too, were quickly snatched up, "proving" the women wrote, "that [the journal's] existence corresponds to a demand," even if that precise demand was unclear given the "hard criticism" they also received from both individuals and groups about their inaugural effort.[51] Advertisements in the homosexual, feminist, women's, and mainstream press—including in the mixed-gender homosexual journal *Masques: Revue des homosexualités*, the gay men's magazine *Gai pied*, the feminist review *Les cahiers du féminisme*, and the leftist national newspaper *Libération*—ensured that a broad audience was alerted to the journal's existence. *Quand les femmes s'aiment* could be purchased in feminist bookstores throughout France and abroad, including in London, Lausanne, Geneva, Zurich, Rome, and Montreal. Individual subscriptions were also available (an avenue ardently promoted once it became clear that the journal cost more to produce than it recouped in sales).

Despite all efforts, publication numbers stabilized at barely 1,500.[52] And yet, its restrained print run notwithstanding, *Quand les femmes s'aiment* reached far more readers than anyone ever anticipated.[53] Personal copies circulated widely; women shared the journal with their romantic partners and friends, discussed it at local meetings, and forwarded it to activist organizations both within and outside of France. Feminist and homosexual archives and associations as far away as Denmark and Quebec added the journal to their collections and circulated it among members. Articles from *QLFSA*'s pages were also translated and reprinted elsewhere, notably in the pages of *Sappho*, an anglophone lesbian journal out of London.

The first issue of *QLFSA* poses a key question: "Why a lesbian journal?"[54] In bold letters, the query appears under a large question mark and above a comic of a group of women seated on the floor in a loose circle. (The illustration is signed by the same Kiki who created the comic for Danièle at the radio station Fréquence Gaie that opens this chapter.)[55] The cartoon women provide their own answers: "To organize and fight against the diverse forms of oppression that we suffer from / To meet lovers / To create a history / To stop hiding and help others who feel stuck / To create a space, a lesbian space! / So that existing as such is simply a fact, and not a demand / To treat ourselves to a wave of culture that, if we dared, we would call lesbian / To resist the cultural suffocation of hetero society." With any luck, they reflect, the journal might just become even "more than the need we have for it, and the pleasure we find in it." The responses speak to an emergent double desire both to produce "lesbian culture" and to fight lesbophobia, one that will drive French lesbian activism through the end of the century.

Despite differences between editorial teams in Lyon and Paris, *Quand les femmes s'aiment* retained a remarkably consistent structure: reports on events and gatherings, lesbian news, lesbian oppression (legal and social), and especially letters and poems aimed at breaking isolation were endorsed and published without difficulty. Certain topical issues, however—particularly those with political import—provoked argument.[56] Articles were consequently collectively vetted, authored individually or in small teams, and then resubmitted for discussion and approval. As one woman explains, "We didn't want just anyone to do just anything."[57] Specific themes emerged: love, sexuality, gender performance, coming out, relationships, maternity, repression, marginality, the creation of lesbian culture and space, and the relationship between lesbianism and feminism. Editors were careful to offer platforms for opposing viewpoints, and articles were often written more in a spirit of investigation and exploration than as position pieces promoting one stance over another. Both the opinions expressed and the topics avoided offer insight into issues at stake among French lesbians at this time.

Unlike equivalent male publications, *QLFSA* was at odds over whether to address female same-sex sexuality and desire explicitly.[58] Lesbian love is often idealized as a healthy, natural, tender practice between equals that is devoid of power dynamics. The journal's title—*Quand les femmes s'aiment*—is telling in this regard; after all, it is *love* between women and not desire that is emphasized. Perhaps this is also, as one article observes, because an acknowledgment of the "desire [that] smolders" between women at political gatherings might wreak havoc on solidarity, for "what would happen if we were to let ourselves go?"[59] While erotic metaphors abound in the printed poetry and fiction submissions (water imagery runs rampant), explicit descriptions of sexual desire are scarce. One-night stands, seduction, pickups (*drague* in French), and butch/femme roles are discouraged. A drawing of a couple, one woman with short hair and the other long, the latter holding a baby in her arms, attracted pointed criticism for its normative heterosexual mimicry.[60] As one reader notes: "We are lesbians, we are in groups, but [unfortunately] that doesn't stop us from reproducing the schemas that we find in bourgeois [straight] couples."[61] Female masculinity is acceptable, but only within limits: one can be a masculine woman, but one should not want to be—and certainly not exercise power like—a man. When sexuality does appear it often has an implicit ethical stance in which equality, love, monogamy, respect, and mutuality are privileged. Romance wins. But not always.

Some women reproached the journal for not confronting lesbian sexuality directly: "Me, I want to see erotic illustrations, yes madame!" writes one reader.[62] In response, the last issue (no. 7) published a series of "audacious" submissions: "Your sex under my fingers, which moves . . . the adorable sex of a woman, fine, racy, clear, bitter . . . heavy and troubling . . . the madness of our mouths . . . [I shall] moisten your whole body with my dripping sex, my mouth drinks you . . . noisily, I lick and suck you and still never drink you whole."[63] But articles of this sort were strikingly rare. While the editorial committee claimed to censor only materials it judged "too violent," in retrospect some wondered whether "violence" might have been a ruse for avoiding the pornographic.[64] Given the long-standing eroticization of lesbian desire for heterosexual ends and the fact that the journal could be purchased by those "outside" the community, this hypothesis is not unreasonable. However, it may also betray efforts to frame lesbian sexual expression as devoid of the patriarchal power dynamics that often plague heterosexual relations.

Lesbian motherhood was of particular interest to the Lyonnais editorial teams. Issues 2 and 6, both published under their watch, reflect this. Issue 2 opens with "a dossier on 'mothers and lesbians.'"[65] While acknowledging that this subject was not germane to all, the Lyon group believed the topic vital to many, particularly, they argued, given the rising numbers of lesbian custody cases in France. Lesbian motherhood, they report, reveals a contradiction inherent to "pseudo-Christian" and capitalist society: on the one hand, lesbianism is represented as a danger to population growth; on the other, the law denies custody to lesbian mothers on the pretext that lesbian sexuality poses a moral danger to children. The dossier reports on lesbian legal battles abroad and on French family law.

Lesbian motherhood reappears at length in issue 6. By then a group of lesbian mothers in Lyon who identified themselves as the FAHM (Femmes accusées d'homosexualité et maternité, or Women Accused of Homosexuality and Maternity) were meeting regularly. They publicize their mission in the journal. Their principal preoccupations? "Fighting repression, activism, and [defending lesbian] custody in divorce cases."[66] Issue 6 also covers a meeting of lesbians from the mixed-gender Comité d'urgence anti-répression homosexuelle (CUARH, or Emergency Committee against Homosexual Repression, 1979–87), an organization fighting for political and legal change that emerged out of the first Université d'été homosexuelle (Homosexual Summer University) in 1979.[67] Writer and activist Geneviève Pastre (soon named president of Fréquence Gaie, the homosexual radio station discussed in the next section) helped found the CUARH, which quickly became a critical force in gay and lesbian activism.[68] As *QLFSA* reports, CUARH lesbians from Lyon, Besançon, Nancy, Strasbourg, Dijon, and Paris had come together to denounce both the oppression of lesbian mothers and the "quasi-impossibility of adoption" for homosexual couples. CUARH lesbians also used *QLFSA*'s pages to announce that they were launching a national campaign on behalf of homosexual parents and to invite concerned lesbian mothers to contact them.[69]

Finally, articles in *QLFSA* regularly ruminated on the relationship between lesbianism and feminism. That link was evident, for example, in issue 2 of the journal, whose cover features a photomontage of the defiant gesture—the two-handed triangle symbolizing both female power and the female sex—first popularized by women in the Mouvement de libération des femmes (MLF) in the early 1970s (fig. 6.3). But the relationship between feminism and lesbianism became increasingly strained following two scandals that fractured the MLF by the end of the decade. Their twinned significance merits a detour to contextualize the reconfiguration of the lesbian political landscape during the years that *QLFSA* was published. The first scandal took place in 1979 after Antoinette Fouque's group Psychanalyse et politique (or Psychépo) declared themselves the sole legal representative of the French feminist movement, aggressively claiming the name "Mouvement de libération des femmes" and registering the MLF's symbol—a raised fist inside the glyph signifying women—as a *marque déposée* (an official and exclusive trademark).[70] The second involved a schism in the editorial board of what had been considered the French feminist movement's major theoretical journal *Questions féministes*.[71] This schism largely concerned a debate over writer and lesbian theorist Monique Wittig's controversial assertion that "lesbians

FIGURE 6.3: Cover of *Quand les femmes s'aiment*, no. 2 (November 1978). Groupe de Lesbiennes / Centre des Femmes de Lyon. The two-handed triangle symbolizing both female power and the female sex was popularized by feminists in the early 1970s. Produced by the Collectif du numéro 2. Courtesy of Patricia Mercader.

are not women" in her 1978 article "The Straight Mind," which *Questions féministes* published in French translation in 1980.[72] In this piece, Wittig identifies heterosexuality as a political regime, calls the categories "man" and "woman" into question, and identifies lesbianism as both an act of resistance and the only viable response against patriarchal oppression and the appropriation of women.[73]

Women from the Parisian Groupe lesbiennes de Jussieu (known after

June 1980 as the Front des lesbiennes radicales [FLR], or Radical Lesbian Front) took up Wittig's charge and mobilized against the French feminist movement. "Lesbianism," one of the group's members claimed, "is the future of feminism."[74] Appropriating Marxist theory and championing the destruction of the phallocentric capitalist social order, the FLR insisted—following Wittig—that all men (and hence heterosexuality) be forsaken.[75] Radical lesbians first vetoed contact with both heterosexual feminists and mixed-gender movements for homosexual rights. They then denounced female heterosexuals as "collabos"—a reference to the "horizontal collaborators" who had shamed France by sleeping with the occupying German enemy during World War II. Lesbians who remained loyal to heterosexuals of either gender were condemned as "kapos"—a vitriolic invective associating them with concentration camp prisoners who had cooperated with their German captors in the extermination of their fellow inmates during the Holocaust. FLR posters announced "Hetero-feminism is class collaboration" and called on lesbians to "Break the Silence: Recover Our Violence."[76]

The intensity with which the FLR demanded a world without "women" (through the eradication of heterosexuality) provoked tremendous anxiety within certain lesbian communities.[77] The resultant political confrontations between radical lesbians and lesbian feminists (who maintained solidarity with their heterosexual sisters) were frequently nasty.[78] Political positions were transformed into personal attacks. In response, many women, including lesbian feminists from the Groupe de lesbiennes du Centre des femmes de Lyon, denounced what they saw as a death blow to feminist solidarity.

Lesbians from Lyon shared space at the Lyon Women's Center with the feminist movement. The Lyon group's historical relation to feminism led most lesbians there to reject the FLR's stance. Many lesbians in Lyon felt indebted to the women's movement and attributed their own activism to their early experiences in it. We can see their positions reflected in the pages of *Quand les femmes s'aiment*: "I battle on two fronts," one woman wrote, "as a lesbian, and as a woman, [and] the bond between lesbianism and feminism interests me." "It is thanks to the [feminist] movement that I've come to understand that loving women doesn't have to mean behaving like a man," said another. Others reported that the feminist movement "gives us a certain force and protection because feminism is now socially acceptable."[79] Thus, while they acknowledged the benefits of meeting among themselves, most lesbians from the Lyon group perceived themselves as lesbian feminists committed to fighting in concert with heterosexual feminists for a better future inside a mixed-gender world.

In what was to become the journal's final issue (no. 7), the Lyonnais collective from *Quand les femmes s'aiment* clarified this position as they called for a "third way." Identifying themselves as "des radicales dans la nuance" (nuanced radicals), lesbians from Lyon specified that it was not by chance that "the universe we have chosen and in which we live (except at work) is largely a women's world." However, they added, "thinking of feminism in terms of the hatred of men does not necessarily remove us from heterosexual society. If there is a lesbian conception of feminism, it is that it proceeds from the love of women." Lesbian feminists therefore must not reject women simply because they interact with, or love, men. In sum, they conclude, "We are in the MLF and not [solely] in a lesbian movement."[80] In the same issue, lesbians from the CUARH argued that radical lesbians were akin to "religious fanatics" because their politics were not "inscribed in historical reality, however unbearable that might be."[81] And, indeed, the FLR's extremism ultimately proved a form of political suicide. Thus, despite making crucial contributions to the theorization of lesbian subjectivity and producing a series of important initiatives—including founding the Archives recherches cultures lesbiennes (Archives of Lesbian Research and Culture) in Paris in 1983—radical lesbianism gradually lost credibility as a viable political stance.[82] In the end, as I argue elsewhere, unmitigated rage against the system—regardless of the utopic vision it served—proved unsustainable: one woman told me, "Ultimately it took too much energy to be that angry all the time, so I left."[83]

QUAND LES FEMMES S'AIMENT: THE LETTERS

Over the three years that *Quand les femmes s'aiment* was published, the Groupe de lesbiennes du Centre des femmes de Lyon received a veritable avalanche of letters from female readers located both within the metropole and throughout the world.[84] In 2013 over five hundred and twenty of these letters were still held privately in Lyon by Patricia Mercader, who had worked with the Lyonnais group and who generously shared them with me.[85] Most were sent between June 1978 and September 1979, a period that correlates with the Lyon group's intensive involvement in national organizing, including its participation in French lesbian gatherings in Lyon (November 1978) and Paussac (July 1979) and at the first Université d'été homosexuelle held in Marseille (July 1979). Mapping the locations from whence these letters were sent provides a visual representation of just how widely the journal circulated (fig. 6.4). Whereas the vast majority of readers were French women living in provincial towns and cities, there

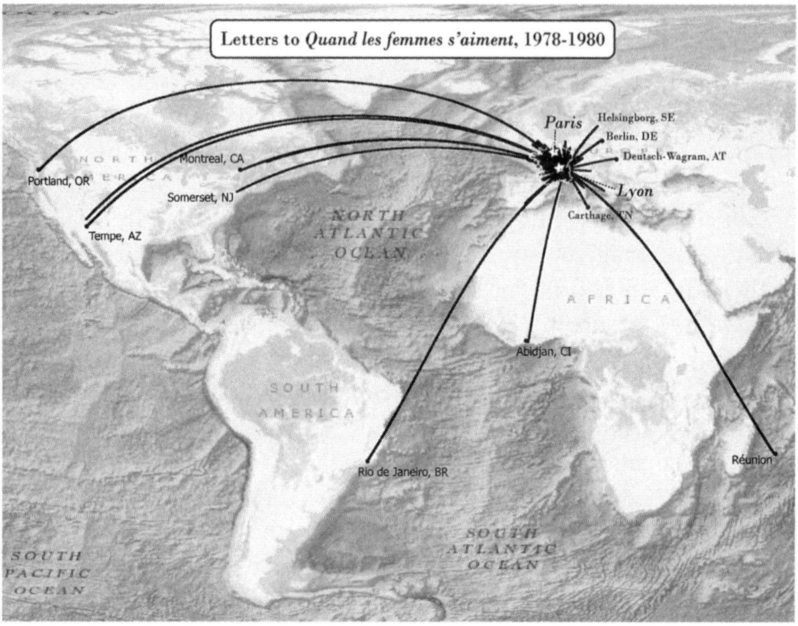

FIGURE 6.4: A global map of letters sent to *Quand les femmes s'aiment*, 1978–1980. Map courtesy of Stephen A. Sherman in consultation with the author

are also letters from Paris as well as from Switzerland, the United States, Germany, Belgium, Holland, Canada, Wales, England, Italy, Brazil, Tunisia, and South Africa. The astonishing global reach of this tiny publication suggests the importance of its contents to the women who sought it out.

Few of the letter writers indicate their ages: when they do, they tend to be either very young (under twenty) or over forty-five. Most write about isolation, depression, and romantic or familial rejection; almost all report being overjoyed to have come across a journal of this type and describe a desperate desire to connect with other women like themselves. A significant percentage are intrigued by (and a few already active in) political organizing. Many letters warranted responses. The group handled this unsolicited mountain of extra work with admirable dedication. Letters were frequently discussed as a group, but replies were penned by individuals. This personalized strategy was deliberate: intimate exchanges encouraged bonding. And, indeed, at least thirty readers entered into extended dialogues with their interlocutors, writing repeatedly to specific women with whom they established epistolary relationships. By turns heartrending, angry, inspiring, funny, or frustrated, these letters (and the *QLFSA* articles they often discuss) communicate the personal and political desires that brought women who loved women together. They also tell us something about the stakes of being "out" in France at this time.

For many women, the first contact they had with *QLFSA*'s editorial team occurred when they wrote to request a subscription. Over three hundred women had the journal sent to their homes. Direct mail had the distinct advantage of permitting readers to avoid purchasing the magazine in public—an action many found virtually impossible to take. One of the most common requests was that the journal be sent *sous pli fermé*—in a sealed envelope. This request was not made unprovoked; a subscription form provided in the pages of the journal permitted readers to check this preference, if desired. The availability of the "sealed" option can be read as a sign of respect (it acknowledged the very real dangers of "coming out"). It was also a pragmatic tactic: the journal's creators understood that one cannot grow a lesbian community unless one can reach one's potential audience, including individuals not yet comfortable identifying as such.

Letters reveal that not all the women who requested sealed mailings justified their desire for discretion, but when they did, their explanations suggest that the choice was fraught. Unsurprisingly, many feared negative sanctions, whether personal or public. Some express their fears obliquely: a woman from Villard-de-Lans, for example, simply requests the journal be "sealed *parce que*, *parce que*" (because, because) (letter 15). The implication of this verbal ellipses is that the reasons for such a request should be self-evident. Other women voluntarily elaborate. For a student from Drancy the problem was parents (letter 86). Another similarly writes, "[Sending it sealed] is indispensable for familial reasons" (letter 294). Some dreaded repercussions at work: "I asked for *pli fermé*," writes a woman from Lillers, "because I am a teacher." "If I was ten years younger maybe I would brave the taboos and general idiocy," she continues, "because in the end, I ask myself, what could I be reproached for? I live alone and cause no scandals." "But at my age," she avers, "I'd have no hope of finding work [again] if I were to have troubles like those that have arrived for some" (letter 492). Others were frightened of idle talk among neighbors: A woman from Annecy notes, "My postman isn't very evolved and has a loose tongue" (letter 218). In Clermont-Ferrand, the problem was similar: "The packages are deposited with my building's concierge," who, the writer implies, is given to gossip (letter 166). Another writes, "If you answer my letter again, please send it in a sealed envelope because people are curious" (letter 213). Of course, the threat was less curiosity than judgment. "On my hallway," another reports, "there are some people whose spirits are ten centuries' behind" (letter 256). Importantly, the fact that so many women felt the need to explain their choices to the group suggests that coming out was beginning to be widely understood as both an expectation and a political imperative. Why else defend themselves to the very women who had offered the choice in the first place?

Women wanted privacy, but they also wanted connection. Despite repeated requests, *QLFSA* editorial teams were unwilling to print personal ads—a rubric important to subsequent lesbian magazines from *Lesbia* to *Lettres à Sappho* (which consisted of nothing but).[86] Perhaps they considered the practice unsafe? After all, the journal was widely available, and personal ads could expose women to harassment, including from husbands (current and ex), parents, neighbors, or coworkers. *QLFSA* was nevertheless eager to facilitate contact between readers in a more protected way. Subscription forms asked, "Are you willing to let us share your address with others?" and women could indicate "Yes" or "No." As the Lyon group well knew, it was one thing for women to request contact information for lesbian groups or other women in their regions, but quite another to provide one's own address for public distribution. Sharing such information necessitated a willingness to be "out" to other women (even if not to "the world") and to identify oneself as lesbian in ways beyond one's control.[87] Some women could not convince themselves to take this step, even if they seemed to want to. A married ("unhappily, what a heavy handicap!") forty-five-year-old teacher writes, "I need to meet women in the same situation," but nevertheless concludes, "it is impossible to give you my address (my husband . . . is always jealous). Maybe one day?" (letter 341). For others, confidentiality was a nonissue. While one woman admits that "in Nantes, sapphism is taboo," she quickly adds, "Send new addresses if you've got them and send mine out" (letter 35). Sometimes, it was the interaction with the journal and the women who published it that enabled the move into lesbian subjectivity and community. In these cases, self-naming served as the gateway to politicization. A series of letters from Gisèle A. provides one example of this process.

In her first letter, dated January 1, 1978, Gisèle struggles to name her "difference." She states: "I thought that writing would be easier than speaking. . . . But I am coming to understand that the difficulty lies in the contents, and not the form." "In short," she continues, "what goes awry, and is lodged between my mouth and my pen are the words 'lesbian,' 'homosexuality,' and above all the phrase, 'I am a lesbian.' OK. Writing does not have the same effect. It is said, and I stay safe. But the problem remains unresolved." Compelled, nevertheless, to contact women like herself,

Gisèle recounts how that very night she had traveled by bus to the Women's Center in Lyon in order to confirm the group's address so that she could send this letter, noting, "I'm done with thinking and rethinking and turning in circles, my arms nailed to my sides, my mouth filled with mud, my brain a swamp." "I can no longer support this contradiction," she writes, "between the desire to speak and the inability to do so. Because the day that I loved a woman I wanted to shout my joy in the streets and to share it with everyone close to me [but instead] I kept my mouth shut and lied" (letter 17). Almost a year later, Gisèle's tone had utterly changed. By then, she had moved from Lyon to Mainvilliers, near Chartres. Thanks to the journal, she had managed to contact lesbians in her new region. Gisèle writes, "It is so good to know that you exist / that we exist and to say so. To say, and also to do, create a journal, a network, a community, an ensemble. To break the solitude, the isolation, the walls, to rip off the gags and the blinders. And finally, to live in harmony" (letter 15). This later letter is euphoric, even utopic; validation has enabled acceptance and connection, and for Gisèle the result was transformative. In naming her own difference and recognizing herself in others, Gisèle's evolution exemplifies what Natacha Chetcuti calls "déshétérosexualisation" (de-heterosexualization), the means by which women who desire women undo (or overcome) the normative effects of compulsory heterosexuality, thus freeing themselves to "become lesbian."[88]

The unprecedented success of *Quand les femmes s'aiment* as both emotional support and activist organizational tool was a direct effect of its appeal to women who felt excruciatingly isolated, whether in the provinces or in Paris. "I am terribly lonely, and I feel like I'm starting to disintegrate," writes Noële from Nantes, continuing, "I hope you'll be kind enough to help me. I'm counting on you" (letter 66). "Alone in my little provincial city," writes another woman in Chartres, "your journal is the only link, the only opening to another world" (letter 176). Twenty-two-year-old Kamila O. contacted the group from the psychiatric service at a hospital in Antibes where she had been sent "for social and sentimental reasons." "Write to me," she implores, adding, "Sometimes it takes more courage to live than to die" (letter 21). "I am alone in Amiens," communicates Marie C., adding that while she doesn't want to "speak at length of [her] story," she has nevertheless "known the alienation that is specific to homosexuals." Life in public, Marie C. continues, is an endless assault: "The [heterosexual] norm slaps us everywhere: the posters, the cinema." ("Does there exist," she asks, parenthetically, "a film by lesbians for lesbians that is not exhibitionist?") She describes the pain of being endlessly subjected to heterosexuality ("the [hetero] couples entwined in the streets") and the violence of erasure ("the friends who speak of my girlfriend as if she means nothing") and finishes, "I can no longer bear this alone" (letter 146). Another woman similarly writes, "I've had it with hearing my girlfriend invent a guy in front of her work colleagues so as not to be suspected of anything. It is a massacre of our personalities, and it must stop" (letter 16).

The magazine not only validated desires that others deemed shameful; it also extolled the power of lesbian community. Here, too, it responded to a need, for even when women succeeded in creating intimate relationships, they spoke of suffering as couples from a lack of social contact. "If you know of any girls in the region, let us know," writes Nadine from Thueyts (near Puy), because "we are rather isolated: 2 girls, 1 cat, 1 tortoise" (letter 93). The creation of community also offered an on-ramp to lesbian politics. Many letter writers wanted to find or found activist groups, to report instances of prejudice or generate activist responses. Two women in Ardèche sought to write a book about lesbianism but note that "writing it together doesn't interest us, we want to meet other women with whom we can work on it" (letter 91). Mireille C. from Paris writes, "I'm astonished that no demonstration of feminists and homosexuals has been planned given the recent executions of homosexuals and acts of aggression against women in Iran. This seems to be an extremely serious precedent" (letter 128). *Quand les femmes s'aiment* strove to respond to such calls and to motivate political activism internationally. Its readers were integral to this mission. Thus, Mia A., a student from Tempe, Arizona, observes, "It is stimulating to speak 'feminism' with women in France because we (lesbians in particular) are so isolated, fragmented, 'torn away' from other women (even in our own country)" (letter 2). In another letter Mia regrets that she won't make it to the Université d'été in Marseille ("too costly") but notes that she'll soon be visiting "lesbian feminists in Montreal" and would be happy to transmit news from France to them. She signs off "En lutte lesbienne" (in lesbian struggle) (letter 1). Even when women's initiatives were unsuccessful, the mere existence of the journal mattered. Women from the Danish Lesbian International Group confide that despite having themselves failed to organize "an international lesbian seminar" in March 1979, it was "good to know that you are out there somewhere."[89]

While *Quand les femmes s'aiment* purported to provide a platform for diverse views, conflicting perspectives (especially when considered "politically incorrect") were not always provided equal space in the publication's pages. Take, for example, letters concerning the journal's coverage of Elula Perrin. A review by the editorial team slams Perrin's book *Les femmes préfèrent les femmes*. Elula's descriptions of her lovers—"belle et bête" (beautiful and stupid), "charmante et bête" (charming and stupid), and "très belle, mais trop bête" (very beautiful but too stupid) (a list that we are told "is not exhaustive")—draw ire for their misogyny and classist snobbery. The reviewer, Dominique, concludes, "I confess that I didn't have the strength to persevere past page 158."[90] While one letter writer agrees, stating, "I appreciate your remarks. They were on the money" (letter 117), another observes sharply: "We know that E.P. is . . . politically reactionary, bourgeois, on the right, but give her some respect: she was the first [to come out in the media]." "Don't you think that we need solidarity and compassion between women, and above all, between lesbians?" she asks (letter 209). Another woman, from Granville, similarly states, "You tell me that you can't publish my letter because you don't agree with anyone who supports Elula Perrin." "Well," she continues, "I think it is sordid to dirty the reputation . . . of the first contemporary woman to defend female homosexuality." She confesses that she's read Elula's book "three times," adding, "*I* had the strength to read all the way to the end" and asking, "Does that make me an idiot?" (letter 224).

Quand les femmes s'aiment folded after the publication of its seventh issue in June 1980. Looking back almost a decade later, women from the editorial team expressed surprise over the journal's demise, especially given "the consistent coverage it provided, the high degree of reader satisfaction, the journal's success, and the smoothness with which the publishing process functioned."[91] "The only reproach that we've heard from your readers," wrote women from a bookstore in Strasbourg, "is that you are too optimistic."[92] Although the Lyon Women's Center lost its lease in the summer of 1980, the next issue of *QLFSA* was scheduled to be published in Paris, which should have provided a buffer. Nothing indicated that the journal wouldn't continue to thrive. The last issue had even announced that an article on lesbian couples' desires for children was forthcoming. But with the feminist movement in crisis nationally, the Women's Center in Lyon failed to relocate and closed. Committed as it was to feminist solidarity, the Lyonnais lesbian group—and *Quand les femmes s'aiment* with it—lost energy and dissolved.

Its short shelf life notwithstanding, *Quand les femmes s'aiment* stands as an important early example of the global impact of text-based lesbian information activism. One of its biggest contributions was that it helped make lesbianism viable and visible as a personal choice and political strategy in the French public sphere. The journal also motivated similar efforts:

a flurry of new lesbian journals was published in France after 1979, with most appearing in the 1980s. These included *Désormais* (eight issues, 1979–80), *Paroles de lesbiennes féministes* (two issues, 1980–81), the radical lesbian reviews *Espaces* (twenty-one issues, 1982–83) and *Chroniques aiguës et graves* (four issues, 1982–83), *Vlasta, fictions/utopies amazoniennes* (four issues, 1983–85), the *Bulletin des Archives recherches cultures lesbiennes* (eleven issues, 1984–92), *Saphonies* (two? issues, 1986), *Lettres à Sappho* (thirteen? issues consisting mostly of personal ads, 1985–88), and *La grimoire: Journale lesbienne internationale* (fifteen issues, 1987–97). None of these lasted more than a decade. *Lesbia* (later called *Lesbia magazine*), founded in 1982, was the sole exception; despite being produced entirely by volunteers, the journal was available (after 1985) in newsstands, circulated over ten thousand copies monthly by 1988, and remained in publication until 2012.[93] *Lesbia*'s success was due in part to the fact that it eschewed strict political allegiances and could thus appeal broadly to the panoply of lesbian counterpublics that initiatives like *Quand les femmes s'aiment* had helped bring into existence. But as material objects circulating in a pre-internet age, even successful lesbian journals were not easily accessible. Their very physicality inevitably proved an impediment to the expansion of the lesbian community they sought to promote. Lesbian radio offered a new way to circumvent this barrier.

AMAZONES DU SOIR, BONSOIR!: LESBIANS ON THE RADIO

The group of women who disrupted Ménie Grégoire's radio show "L'homosexualité, ce douloureux problème" on March 10, 1971, signaled their understanding of the power of radio to shape public opinion regarding queer identities. Knowing that radio, like television, had privileged access to the private sphere, queer activists further recognized the medium's capacity to speak to those who might be fearful of pursuing homosexual desires. In order to advance their emancipatory agenda and combat disparaging depictions of queer sexuality in mainstream media, homosexuals throughout France in the late 1970s began to dream of producing radio content of their own.[94] However, at this time, homosexuality was still penalized under French law, with doubled sanctions for indecent exposure (under the Mirguet Amendment passed in 1960) and a higher age of consent (since 1942) for homosexual acts. Moreover, despite the dismantling of the state-run ORTF in 1974, French radio remained under state monopoly. Four stations dominated the airwaves: France Inter, France Musique, France Culture, and France Inter Paris. Use of the FM band was reserved for these stations as well as for the army and police. The AM band was not used in France after World War II. Peripheral stations like Radio-télévision Luxembourg, Radio Monte-Carlo, and Europe 1 were audible inside France but were broadcast from beyond French borders. French pirate radio stations, including queer ones, developed illegally in this oppressive climate.

It was only after François Mitterrand fulfilled a campaign promise following his 1981 election and liberalized the airwaves that the French radio station Fréquence Gaie (Gay Frequency, or FG), which had first aired on September 10, 1981, could broadcast as a state-sanctioned *radio libre* (free radio). Transmitting from a garret apartment in Belleville in Paris's twentieth arrondissement loaned by the gay activist Guy Hocquenghem, Fréquence Gaie followed in the footsteps of at least one pirate radio station run clandestinely by and for gay men: Radio Mauve—later called Radio Fil Rose—created in 1978.[95] Patrick Oger, an anonymous participant in this earlier initiative, founded Fréquence Gaie and was the station's first president and early financial benefactor. FG quickly became "the first homosexual radio ever officially authorized by a government" and the only queer radio station in the world to broadcast twenty-four hours a day, seven days a week—a status that, although no longer on the air, it retains to date.[96] As Danièle Cottereau remarked to me, "Even San Francisco never managed a comparable achievement."[97]

The station's success was immediate. Launched with only the most rudimentary technology, repeatedly forced to relocate, and completely run by volunteers (90 percent of whom identified as homosexual), FG responded to a burgeoning demand for queer expression. By November 1981, the technology was upgraded, transmission power increased, and the station became audible within a fifteen-mile radius of Paris.[98] FG's programs ranged from humorous and playfully flippant to highbrow and hard-hitting to outrageously provocative. On one popular program featuring gay male personal ads, journalists on motorbikes made house calls to confirm with their own eyes their callers' specious claims about physical attributes like penis size. But not all coverage was brash. Cultural broadcasts, music shows, political debates, programs on health and sexuality, radio romances, and interviews with everyone from Jean-Marie Le Pen (the homophobic leader of the far-right National Front) to Catherine Lara (the rock star who had declared herself "libre d'aimer une femme ou un homme" [free to love a woman or a man] in her 1983 hit song "Autonome") followed in rapid succession. Despite the wide-ranging appeal of their programming, FG was nonetheless continuously plagued by conflict, with internal factions jockeying for power while the external political context likewise threatened the station's survival. Fréquence Gaie was refused a license when the French government's Holleaux Commission stepped in to regulate the newly liberated airwaves. Spirited protests by the homosexual community on July 20, 1982, succeeded in reversing the decision. However, Michèle Cotta, then president of the Haute autorité de la communication (High Authority on Communication), ordered the station to share its frequency with three other broadcasts—Radio Libértaire (an anarchist station), Radio Verte (an environmentalist station), and Radio Ark-en-Ciel (an art and performance station)—allocating six hours daily to each channel. Another wave of queer protests ensued.[99] By the end of the year, thousands of telegrams and six thousand supporters in the streets successfully pressured the government to restore Fréquence Gaie's autonomy, this time on a new channel (97.2 MHz) shared only with Radio Ark-en-Ciel.[100]

Fréquence Gaie was primarily operated by and directed at gay men; when the station first launched, out of 120 volunteers, only 26 were female.[101] For women, this ratio did not improve with time: within two years, while total personnel had risen to 180, the number of women involved had dropped to 14.[102] On average, about 12 percent of FG's radio announcers were female. Because of their comparatively small numerical presence, at the height of its success a very small group of women—like Danièle Cottereau—were handling almost all of the heavy lifting on lesbian programming. Unlike its personnel, FG's audience (whose numbers soon averaged between 100,000 and 150,000 daily) was equally divided between genders, with some 40 percent claiming to be heterosexual.[103] In a decision some critiqued as tokenism, on June 21, 1982, FG elected a woman—writer and lesbian activist Geneviève Pastre—to serve as the station's new president and figurehead. Under Pastre's tenure the roster of programs produced by and for French lesbians on FG grew. Danièle Cottereau, then thirty-two and "a child of 1968" who identified as an "out" lesbian but was by her own account neither intellectually inclined nor particularly politically active, was already part of FG's small team of female volunteers.[104] (She had begun participating at the station in April 1982 and was quickly hooked.) By early 1983 Fréquence Gaie hit its zenith and was ranked fourth in an Institut français d'opinion publique survey of Parisian radio stations. While always dominated by gay male programming, for a few brief years Fréquence Gaie broadcast some of the most creative—and most sexually explicit—lesbian radio ever produced.

Fréquence Gaie was not the first radio station to produce broadcasts by and for queer women in France. In fact, lesbians and feminists had been broadcasting clandestinely on French radio since 1978, when a group known as Les Radioteuses was shut down by the police after their first broadcast. They resurfaced first as Radio Nanas and then, in 1981, legally relaunched as Les Nanas Radioteuses. In the new free climate of the early 1980s, lesbian broadcasts included *Coup de foudre* (Love at first sight) on Radio Atlantic out of Nantes, a lesbian program called *Maille à l'envers* (Knitting in reverse) out of Angers, and the lesbian shows produced by Femmes Entre Elles (FEE, or Women among Themselves) on Canal Gay Radio Savane out of Rennes.[105] FEE also promoted lesbian use of the medium by coordinating conferences with other lesbian radio broadcasters from Marseille, Amiens (*Les Jardins de Sélène*), and Paris. By 1983 free radio stations aimed at lesbians and gays (dubbed "Antennes roses" or pink stations) were broadcasting from over twenty-seven different towns and cities across France.[106] In 1984 the French queer community convened its first International Meeting of Male and Female Hosts of Homosexual Broadcasts in France. By then France counted at least thirty-six (some claim as many as fifty) queer radio stations. Insofar as lesbian broadcasting was concerned, Fréquence Gaie led the pack.

In the 1980s, Danièle Cottereau played a critical role in creating, producing, and hosting many of these shows. From August 1983 these included *Coeur de femmes* (Hearts of women, with discussions of female love and desire) on Saturday nights; *Pêche à la ligne (au féminin)* (Go fish [for girls], which focused on audience testimonies) on Wednesday nights; *La vie en rose* (Life in pink) on Fridays; *À tout coeur* (With all my heart, a serial romance) on Wednesday nights; *Pour ou contre* (For or against, a call-in debate show hosted by lesbians and gays on topics ranging from terrorism to "the male, objectified," film festivals, "love at first sight," work, nude publicity, fortune-tellers, domestic pets, riot police, graffiti, hitchhiking, gay camping, and "having kids when we are homos") on Mondays from 2:00 to 3:00 p.m.; *Dix questions, dix réponses* (Ten questions, ten answers, with announcers responding to callers' questions—such as "Will there be a women-only space at the next fundraiser for FG?") on Thursdays from 1:30 to 2:00 p.m.; *Cinéma de traverse* (Cinema sideways) on Wednesday and Friday afternoons; *Sapho Nights* on Tuesday nights; and *Amazones du soir, bonsoir!* (Amazons of the night, goodnight!), which aired thirty-one shows from May 8 to December 9, 1984, on Tuesday and Sunday nights from 9:30 p.m. to midnight.[107] Danièle's life was so marked by the experience that when she published her memoir in 2011, she took *Amazones du soir, bonsoir!* as its title.

To celebrate the twentieth broadcast of *Amazones du soir, bonsoir!*, Danièle created a bespoke comic book. In it she explains that the show was intended "to explore women's perspectives—lesbian women, naturally—on different aspects of 'culture' . . . in sum, cinema, literature, theatre, jazz, poetry, music, all that interests us, and that, we hope, interests you." "Let yourself be guided into the night," the publicity for the show announced, "cradled by Danièle's voice," as she discusses lesbian "slices of life," and she and her troupe tell fantastic "tales sprinkled with witches, ogresses, and games" to make you "tremble a little before falling asleep."[108] Not counting Danièle as presenter, the show was produced by a team of six: Marilyn and Dominique, the station managers "(*bonsoir commandants*!)"; Catherine, the audio engineer; Mijane, "who will enchant you with her poems"; and Denise "to jazz things up." Danièle's good friend Cathy Bernheim, a writer and lesbian activist well-known among French feminists after the 1983 publication of her pseudo-memoir *Perturbation, ma soeur: Naissance d'un mouvement de femmes, 1970–1972*, covered cinema. Danièle likewise collaborated on other broadcasts with female teams of varied sizes drawn from a half dozen other women.[109] The work commitment was considerable. Indeed, Danièle later told me that had she not been "fortunately unemployed" during many of those years, she could never have dedicated so much time to the station.[110]

Our only audio access to these programs survives thanks to a select few of Danièle's committed fans, who recorded her broadcasts on cassette tapes. For some, these recordings were like "Proust's madeleines," enabling them to relisten to broadcasts first heard "live" and share them with friends.[111] "I prolong my pleasure by listening again to recordings of the shows that I've made since the beginning," writes Martine, adding, "That makes a dozen cassettes so far."[112] For others (as we know from letters in Danièle's personal collection), such recordings enabled them to listen to programs that, often for familial reasons, were otherwise impossible to access. This was clearly the case for Monique, who still lived at home with her parents and who treasured the cassettes that her male cousin taped and clandestinely passed on to her ("I listen to them attentively," she reports).[113] During the years that Danièle was on the air, several women gifted her with copies of the cassettes they had recorded. To my knowledge, none of these exist in archives. In 2013 Danièle let me copy the only tape she still had in her possession.[114] The cassette was a Christmas gift from a fan, an edited mixtape compiled of excerpts, the woman notes, "from all these cassettes recorded since I first began listening to Fréquence Gaie." It is above all an homage to Danièle's interventions on the air; today, it provides us with precious audio traces from a panoply of FG's lesbian programs.

I press play. Click: Danièle's voice, deep, velvety, and warm, reveals that we are suddenly in a newly explicit sexual universe. She croons:

> Yes . . . and we are also going to talk about . . . well, whether you are into one-night stands, or encounters in bars, or if your sexuality is part of a shared life with a woman . . . above all else you can tell me about the frequency of your sexual intercourse, you can tell us if you make love in the morning, at noon, in the afternoon, from five to seven, or at night. You can tell us if you have fantasies, sadomasochistic fantasies, if you are *corréphiles* (that is to say, if you like little girls), if you have other fantasies, you can tell us if sex, in your opinion, has to go with feelings, you can tell us if you use vibrators, or dildos [laughter], and then you can tell us if you use poppers.

Danièle's appeal for listener feedback reminds us that these broadcasts were intensely interactive. And women responded. "I think you should have a show on young girls between the ages of twelve and twenty," writes one fan.[115] Others ask for broadcasts on fantasies. Many share opinions, information, or experiences. Some seek companionship. Often, Danièle told me, calls would begin, "I'm seeking a woman with whom to go to the cinema," but end with, "and more if we hit it off." Women were reassured that any phone numbers they provided were destroyed at the end of each broadcast. Danièle believes female listeners were even more communicative on the radio than gay men because women lacked both physical spaces to meet and the resources required to access these spaces: as she comments, "You didn't know where to go, and you couldn't afford to go if you did."[116]

While not all discussions of sexuality on these broadcasts were lighthearted (one listener wrote to express her appreciation for a show on rape), most—as the tapes and radio scripts from Danièle's personal collection reveal—unrolled in a spirit of titillation and desire, but also good humor and gaiety.[117] In another recorded excerpt from the cassette that Danièle lent me, the female announcers howl with laughter over the French translation of Emily Sisley and Bertha Harris's bestseller *The Joy of Lesbian Sex*. "So," Danièle remarks, "this book is really comical, it's really American style . . . hmm, you know, I'm going to read you a little chapter called 'The Anatomy of Sex.'" She continues, "The first thing is the genital apparatus," then adds as an aside, "Don't make me laugh!" "The female genitalia," she notes, tongue in cheek, "exists in a great variety of forms, of sizes, of positionings and general configurations." She goes on, her tone serious: "At the level of the pubic bone, is the clitoral area." "You won't learn a thing tonight, Danièle!" cuts in a woman's voice, laughing. Danièle giggles but continues determinedly: "At the crest of the clitoris" there is a "mass of erectile tissue, relatively small but powerful." ("Where are you getting this from?" asks another female voice.) Danièle laughs again and remarks, "In the Joys of Lesbos!" before resuming, "So, as I was saying, relatively small but powerful, which gives you the greatest pleasure [now she can barely speak for laughing]." Her cohosts erupt in giggles. Danièle roars in amusement, concluding, "Oh yeah, we are absolutely cooking now! Yeah, the little folds of skin that surround, that you surr--, that surround more or less . . ." and again Danièle bursts into laughter, which spreads so infectiously among the women present on the platform that it drowns out all speech.

Over the course of her work for Fréquence Gaie, Danièle also did investigative reporting for the station. One early assignment concerned the newly popular phenomenon of the "backroom."[118] After visiting a backroom aimed (unsuccessfully) at female clientele, Danièle discussed the new rage for "backrooms" in gay male bars with her listeners. First, she explains the concept to the uninformed: "A backroom," she states, "is supposed to be a space where you go without knowing anyone, where you fuck [adding parenthetically]—I mean you might as well use that word because it is more appropriate to the thing—uh, where you fuck the first person you meet." "Or with everyone," cuts in another female voice. "Yes," Danièle replies. A third woman chimes in: "Me, I'd love that!" "Why then," her coconspirators ask, "aren't backrooms more popular among lesbians?" "Well," Danièle observes, "because it is more difficult to get a rise out of a clitoris than out of a cock."

This turn to explicit discussions of sexuality marks an important sea change in the public face of French lesbian life. Not because it heralds the emergence of lesbian erotica (or porn) in the French public sphere (that had long existed), but rather because lesbians themselves were finally both producing and controlling what had become, thanks to the liberalizing social and legal context, a very public narrative. Free radios like Fréquence Gaie were perfectly poised to capitalize on these changes. Given audience demographics, heterosexual men were undoubtedly also listening to broadcasts targeting lesbian audiences. For Danièle, however, male access to lesbian radio fantasies was completely irrelevant. She treated this inevitability merely as an unavoidable (if distasteful) consequence of radio's public accessibility, an accessibility that she understood as absolutely vital to queer women's emancipation.[119]

Danièle's mission was to make the kinds of broadcasts that she herself had always wanted to hear and hadn't found forthcoming; in the early 1980s, she recalls, French lesbian public life—be that in activist gatherings or via magazines and journals—was "oh so very, very serious!"[120] In contrast, Danièle sought to create programs that celebrated female same-sex desire while providing lesbians with concrete resources for living their lives as they pleased. To this end she often rebroadcast information gleaned from Les Répondeuses on her radio shows in order to increase the accessibility of their contributions.

Among Danièle's unique gifts as a radio announcer, producer, and writer was her capacity to embody and discuss lesbian desire frankly, without shame and with tremendous humor, pleasure, and passion. But if sex was on the menu, it was not uniquely so—lesbian romance also figured prominently. For the broadcast *À tout coeur*, Danièle wrote and delivered lesbian love stories told in the first person in weekly installments. A character named "Magda" figured as her love interest on the show. A few typed transcripts still exist in Danièle's records. From April 27, 1983: "I fell in love with her, immediately. With her body, shimmering in the February sun, with the way that she carried her head, so proudly." And then, a week later, on May 4: "I wanted to invent words for [her] that would have meaning only for us, words that would travel from mouth to mouth, from heart to heart, graceful words that would bend under the tongue, round words coated in chocolate that would melt with pleasure under [her] palate." Fans loved it: "I wait with impatience for the next installment of Magda's story," writes Hélène, who described herself as "*une jeunette* [a young girl] who takes great pleasure in listening to you!"[121] Some of Danièle's female fans were so convinced these stories were autobiographical that during episodes where the romance went badly they bombarded the radio switchboard with concerned calls, warning: "Danièle, leave her! This woman is not for you!!"[122]

By the 1980s, most French households owned one television, usually ensconced in the most communal room in the home. Radios were more plentiful because they were both more portable (particularly after the invention of the transistor in 1947) and more affordable (they were not subject to the *redevance audiovisuelle*—a tax imposed on television sets used to fund the French audiovisual sector). Radios were hence far more amenable to private use. In this the medium was clearly as important as the message. In hundreds of letters, Danièle's female fans testify to radio's special capacity to cross the public/private divide and create intimate bonds. In the privacy of their bedrooms, women could listen without fear, awash in the unaccustomed pleasure of having their most secret desires voiced aloud, sometimes for the very first time: "You have no idea how important this radio [station] is to me," confides Jocelyne. "How many nights have I waited for sleep to come while listening to you?"[123] "Just a few words to welcome you within my walls," notes Laurence, "where your voices murmur, there, next to me, posing questions to me as I lie here in my bed."[124] Many of the letters are clearly from women who had not yet either come out as lesbian or acted on their same-sex desires. "My heart beats at the sound of your voice," writes Valérie, adding, "I'm not yet a lesbian, at least in acts . . . you are my only link to that community of women who love one another and whom I am learning to love."[125] "Lots of women don't dare affirm themselves as homosexuals," writes Dani. "*Sapho Nights*," she continues, "permits an opening at that level."[126] "Fréquence Gaie," writes Anne, "is a link for me [as a woman] who is still living my love for women clandestinely. I am not alone, thanks to you, and that does me good."[127] Danièle recognized that for some of these women she served as "a kind of ersatz"—a substitute—someone on whom they could safely project same-sex desires without publicly assuming a lesbian identity.[128] But for many, she also facilitated lesbian subject formation, especially for her youngest listeners.

Young people have always been among radio's most avid users, particularly after the commercialization of transistor radios in the 1950s made the newly portable technology cheaper to buy. When Fréquence Gaie went on the air in 1981, it provided a special solace to young women and men whose erotic desires were "out-of-step" with those of their peers and who, consequently, were at higher risk for depression, self-harm, addiction, and suicide. And as her letters confirm, many in Danièle's audience were young women under twenty-five.[129] In 2023 Barbara Osorovitz, who at seventeen had been one of Danièle's youngest fans, told me, "Danièle had such a unique gift. Her voice was so warm and so tender. She had this remarkable capacity to lift your spirits in twenty minutes." Indeed, Barbara observed, "listening to Danièle on nights when one felt particularly dark and troubled likely saved more than one woman from suicide."[130] Certainly, when twenty-three-year-old Valérie writes, "I love you [Danièle] . . . for what you are, and because you have been able to assume what you are, whereas I cannot yet do so," and adds, "It is because people like you exist that life remains worth living," it is easy to surmise the gravity of the feelings expressed.[131]

It was not unusual, Danièle reported, for young female fans to develop passionate crushes on their lesbian radio role models. Valérie felt so compelled to contact her idol that she tracked down Danièle's private address by deducing its connection to the theme song from *Amazones du soir*. The song's title, "Rue Thermopyles (à Danièle)," did indeed reveal the street in the fourteenth arrondissement on which Danièle lived. "Excuse me," Valérie apologizes, "for having discovered your secret," but "I prefer to send my letters to your home since I don't wish to write to a postal box but rather to one woman in particular."[132] Interestingly, "Rue Thermopyles" was written by the young Barbara Osorovitz, mentioned above. Danièle and Barbara had met after the seventeen-year-old phoned the switchboard one evening to express her admiration for a broadcast. Danièle invited Barbara to come on the show, only to discover upon her arrival that the boyish young girl was underage. Fearful of legal sanctions for corrupting a minor, Danièle quickly rescinded the offer, but the two women struck up a friendship. On August 2, 1982, just two months after they met, the Mitterrand government decriminalized homosexuality and equalized age of consent laws. Two years later, in 1984, at Danièle's urging Barbara submitted "Rue Thermopyles" to the first Concours de la Chanson Gay. Barbara walked away with the first prize. The winning submissions were released as a vinyl 45-rpm and packaged in a hot pink paper sleeve with "Concours de la chanson gay" scrawled across its cover. Motivated buyers can still find the record available for purchase on the internet.

Like all free radio stations, Fréquence Gaie was forbidden from airing commercial advertising. As a result, throughout its history the station struggled financially. Fréquence Gaie offered perks to those auditors who would support the station with donations: a membership card and free entry at FG's fundraising parties were among the advantages vaunted. These huge gatherings at the Bataclan or the Cirque d'Hiver featured French celebrities (like Juliette Gréco, Frank Noël, and Gérard Berliner) as well as FG's radio announcers—a draw to a starry-eyed public eager to catch sight of their idols (there are photographs of Danièle performing in front of adoring female fans). While audiences flocked to these events, the radio was always in crisis, with no members of staff on salary and never enough money to go around.

On May 3, 1984, just two years after her nomination as FG's president, Geneviève Pastre resigned following an internal coup begun by the right-wing civil servant Julien Blanchet, which involved the cancellation of Pastre's own show, *Voyage en grande lesbianie* (a broadcast on lesbian expression in the arts, literature, and music). Despite her concerns over the mounting misogyny, Danièle stayed, even taking on administrative roles as vice president and then director of financing and launching *Amazones du soir, bonsoir!*[133] When the station continued to spiral into debt, the financiers at *Gai pied* offered to take FG under their wing. The station lost much of its independence after the acquisition. The association was dissolved, a select group of announcers salaried, and the rest let go. Shortly thereafter, Pastre's broadcast was reinstated, and she briefly returned, but for Danièle the experiment was over. In a letter of explanation to Pastre, she states: "After hearing Didier Varrod say on three occasions that there would be no more shows by lesbians for lesbians on FG, I had no more reason to stay. And I was right, because they use your name to justify the presence of lesbians [at the station] but have allotted you, in the last fifteen days, virtually no time and only when the airwaves are deserted."[134] Danièle's fans were aghast. "You cannot leave us," writes Valérie, "because legends are irreplaceable, they make history." She continues, "Fréquence Gaie ceased to exist for me the day that you ceased to exist on the airwaves, and I know that I speak for numerous other women." Pleading, she signs off, "My little Amazon heart bleeds, but you can still save it."[135]

However, Danièle did not return. Cathy Bernheim left with her. With the station increasingly controlled by *Gai pied*, gay male interests crowded out what remained of lesbian broadcasts. Only a handful of women had stayed. By 1985 lesbian journalists writing for *Lesbia* decried the absence of lesbian programming on the station by rebaptizing the station "Fréquence Pédé" (Gay boy frequency). They bewailed the fact that in the four years since the station's inception, it had consistently failed to produce programs for women on par with those produced for men. The situation, they argued, was unlikely to improve. "I wonder," *Lesbia magazine*'s then editor in chief Christiane Jouve acerbically remarked, "how many lesbians will listen with joy to 'The Game of 1,000 Cocks' [as one popular broadcast was crudely titled]. If something is needed for all tastes," she continued heatedly, "ours should be as valuable as theirs."[136] But women's complaints went unheeded.

As Fréquence Gaie professionalized, lesbian broadcasts disappeared. Lack of funding continued to pose problems. In a last attempt to generate new revenue, the station launched a complementary presence on the nascent networking technology known as the Minitel, but after 1985 FG never succeeded in resuscitating its homosexual audiences, lesbian or gay. By the end of 1986 only Fréquence Gaie's Minitel site remained. Although the station continued to broadcast, first as Futur Génération (while under the financial control of *Gai pied*) and then simply as FG, audiences kept shrinking. From 1993 to 1998 the station nevertheless mobilized in the battle against AIDS, with Éric Lamien producing programming on the epidemic with financial support from the minister of health.[137] When that funding was pulled, FG's glory days as a bastion of homosexual radio definitively ended. In 2001 the station, now called Radio FG or FG DJ Radio, commercialized. It remains known mostly for its contributions to the electronic, house, and underground music scene. Its homosexual roots, both lesbian and gay, are long forgotten.

In the 1980s mainstream media journalists argued that whereas the 1981 depenalization of homosexuality was to be celebrated for restoring equal rights to all French citizens, Fréquence Gaie actively discriminated against heterosexuals by addressing only a small—queer—portion of the French public.[138] Danièle pushed back against such claims, asserting that the restoration of legal equality for homosexual practices was not sufficient to emancipate French minds. Fréquence Gaie, she claimed, did some of this work. And yet, when interviewed on France Culture in 2021 about her radio days, Danièle insisted that during her years at the station she had no awareness of FG's larger historical impact. Fréquence Gaie sought, she maintained, neither to proselytize nor to "liberate" its listeners.[139] "My goal," she states, "was simply to go toward women and to get them to join us, in one fashion or another, whether that was physically [by listening], or by telephone, or by letter. To get them to come into that space, because that space was not a bell jar, it was defined, from the start, as an open space. I tried to respond to that imperative."[140] And in this, she succeeded roundly. As Jocelyne, one of Danièle's most dedicated fans explains, "Fréquence Gaie [was] proof that we exist." It pushed back "against narrow-mindedness and intolerance" by showing "that we are an integral part of society" and forced "[heterosexuals] to realize that we are here, rowing like them, in the same boat." Consequently, she concludes (addressing Danièle directly), "You are a miracle come true."[141]

CONCLUSION

Lesbians politicized across France within the newly formed feminist and homosexual rights movements that emerged out of the student revolutions of 1968. Although women who loved women were at the fore of both of these activist projects, their role in this new universe was far from self-evident.

When the Socialist Party came to power in France in 1981, the creation of a Ministre déléguée aux droits de la femme (Minister of Women's Rights) under Yvette Roudy was expected to energize the feminist movement. But the government neglected to deliver on many of its promises, failing, for example, to pass an antisexism bill that would have made discrimination against women on the basis of gender illegal. Moreover, with many of the feminist movement's key battles won—abortion was legalized in 1975 and rape elevated from a misdemeanor to a crime in 1978—and with the internal fracturing of feminist solidarity by the disparate actions of both Psychépo and radical lesbians, French feminism lost momentum. According to Frédéric Martel, in the 1980s the homosexual movement likewise collapsed. In *The Pink and the Black: Homosexuals in France since 1968*, Martel declares that the 1980s were a period of "oddly universal" "demobilization" in the homosexual movement in which the "end to militancy" was "abrupt," "collective," and "lasting."[142] But if the feminist movement foundered, similar conclusions can only be drawn about homosexual militancy if we completely ignore the lesbian activism that fomented across France during these years.

Throughout the 1970s, lesbian activists had struggled to define their relationship to both heterosexual women and homosexual men. But in the early 1980s, lesbianism emerged as a political force. And it did so in no small part thanks to the ways in which women appropriated various forms of media. Lesbians used a range of media technologies, from answering machines to journals to radio to (as we will see in the next chapter) new forms of online networking, to create "actionable information that could *do* something."[143] They also encouraged their audiences to talk back to them—in letters, in phone calls, and in person. By discussing, debating, and celebrating female same-sex desire as both a personal given and a political choice, lesbian information activism produced French lesbian subjects and facilitated the growth of French lesbian community. Both emboldened and frustrated by a decade of feminist and homosexual activism, women who desired women began to name their desire as a common source of oppression and connection. While they sometimes disagreed about ways and means (from styles of gender performance to the gender politics of radical separatism), in the 1980s French women who desired women increasingly rejected French heterosexual norms and demanded change. Young women came out to their friends and families. Women left marriages to pursue same-sex relationships. Lesbian mothers fought for the right to retain custody of their children. Hundreds of lesbians began gathering in groups in towns and cities throughout France.[144] Lesbianism was theorized as a political stance, defended as a legal status, explored as a form of cultural creation, and publicized as both an affective and sexual practice. Lesbian information activism enabled these developments.

The lesbian networks that Les Répondeuses, *Quand les femmes s'aiment*, and Fréquence Gaie produced were particularly nourished by the exchange of letters. I am hardly the first to suggest that epistolary practices were central to the creation of modern subjectivity. Scholars have long argued that in the modern period, people discursively produced themselves as gendered and sexual subjects through the letters they wrote.[145] Supported by increased access to French secondary schooling (extended to girls in 1880), epistolary practices democratized during World War I when France became "a nation of letter-writers" in response to the traumatic separation of loved ones.[146] After World War II, *la presse féminine* further encouraged a female public to partake in what the RTF's director of programming Jean d'Arcy dubbed "the right to communicate" by encouraging women to write letters to the media—be that magazines, radio, or television—in order to express their opinions about topics of the day.[147] By voicing their ideas to editors, journalists, and programming directors, French women came to see the mediascape as a space in which even the most modest of citizens could utilize pen and paper to engage in public contest and debate. Their letters thus created what Lauren Berlant calls "*public* intimacy," in which individuals feel "that their emotional lives are already shared and have been raised to a degree of general significance while remaining true to what's personal."[148] Drawing on Berlant, Judith Coffin, in her study of readers' letters to Simone de Beauvoir, describes how such intimacy "encourages a hopeful and reassuring fantasy of belonging" despite "enormous social and economic inequalities" and thus shapes our "affective public political world[s]."[149]

Part of the power of the epistolary forms of lesbian information activism examined here, then, issues not just from their utility as vehicles for self-exploration and revelation or civic expression but also from their imbrication in public webs of dialogic exchange. For as Natacha Chetcuti argues, one does not name oneself as lesbian in isolation. It is, rather, a social experience that is often accomplished through interaction with other women who have already emancipated themselves from the heterosexual system.[150] While Coffin cautions us—citing Joan Wallach Scott—that "the passage from the personal to the political . . . [is] far from self-evident," the historical context in which these epistolary exchanges emerged enabled women to see specific forms of sexual desire not only as individual predilections but as connections to a collective, communal identity deserving of both public recognition and legal rights.[151] That community was formed thanks to the media.

If Les Répondeuses was an experiment in feminist affiliation that worked relatively well for lesbians and *Quand les femmes s'aiment* was a short-lived lesbian-feminist success, Fréquence Gaie proved a mixed-gender project that ended poorly, with gay male voices perpetually drowning out and overshadowing those of their lesbian sisters. Unfortunately, this latter experience was not unique. Eight infuriated female founders of the mixed-gender homosexual review *Masques: Revue des homosexualités* quit in 1982, protesting their exclusion from positions of power, their marginalization on the pages of the publication, and the dismissal of their contributions to the common discourse. In their letter of resignation they report that they were repeatedly admonished with statements like "You are acting like a woman and not like an individual." They angrily retort that while it was "classic to be confronted in the dominant culture with the idea that objectivity is the property of men [who are] the 'subject' of all discourse," it was "nevertheless more than regrettable" to be confronted with that stance in the very heart of a homosexual initiative.[152] Not surprisingly, the lesbian projects that followed from such experiences were increasingly separatist in nature.

In 2010 at a lesbian colloquium organized in Paris on the occasion of the fortieth anniversary of the French feminist movement, lesbian journalist and activist Suzette Robichon, who participated in the Paris editorial teams of both *Quand les femmes s'aiment* and *Masques* and later founded the Franco-Quebecoise lesbian journal *Vlasta, fictions/utopies amazoniennes* (1983–85), declared: "Lesbian media permit, among other things, for us to break the silence, to speak, to claim ourselves as lesbian. They transmit the elementary need for connection and exchange." In this, she continued, lesbian media "makes it possible . . . to move from the register of intimate confession to claim collective existence, to say 'we,' to put an *s* to lesbians."[153] As the 1980s progressed, French lesbians turned to new media technologies in their quest to achieve these ends.

7

VIRTUALLY YOURS

French Lesbians Online

More than forty years after its appearance in 1982, few remember the Minitel—a now defunct French prototype for the internet based on a closed-network videotex system that connected a computer to telephone lines via a modem—or the interest it generated among gay and lesbian communities in France.[1] There is nevertheless no doubt that the French Minitel and the internet, which superseded it, revolutionized queer life around the globe. Despite the vital import of the internet for queer communities today, very little research on the early history of this phenomenon has been published.[2] That which exists often risks distorting our understanding of the past by glossing over marked differences between gay (mostly understood as male) and lesbian engagement with new technology.[3]

As we have seen, since the 1970s lesbian activists in France have used the modern mass media to forge identities, create communities, and fight for recognition from a republican nation that refuses to acknowledge the rights of groups. The Minitel—and later the internet—became indispensable instruments in this work. This chapter is about the first online website and email service for lesbians ever created. It examines the intersection in the 1980s between a group of self-avowed lesbian activists, Les Goudous Télématiques (or the GTs), and an innovative networking technology, the Minitel, which promised a new way to form lesbian communities that stretched beyond Paris into provincial towns and villages. With its capacity for email, chat, press reviews, news forums, and online listings, the Minitel enabled instant communication, group dialogue, and information access. Lesbian activists sought to utilize the Minitel as a feminist technology that could advance their shared vision of collectivist, noncapitalist community based on solidarity and affective ties. They laid the groundwork in France for a shift in social and sexual relations, the wide-ranging effects of which have transformed the nature of contemporary human existence.

The Minitel made possible new forms of French lesbian identity untethered to specific locations, organizations, embodiments, or proximities. It also made possible unique ways of being "out of the closet" in a virtual space that was at once private (experienced in the intimacy of a home or office) and public (accessible to others and premised on representation and communication). The result was dialectical; the Minitel not only put a self-identified group of lesbian individuals into contact but also helped construct and politicize a specific incarnation of the social category—"lesbian"—that it was deployed to support. In so doing, it contributed to the emergence of a French lesbian imagined community—a lesbian counterpublic—characterized not by geographic proximity but by a level of social cohesion born of personal intimacy, common understanding, shared political vision, and mutual experiences of social exclusion. Examining sexual history thus offers insights into the ways that novel communication technologies have reshaped how we understand both modern subjectivity and community not just for French lesbians, nor even just for French people, but for all individuals with access to these systems. While the internet has arguably atomized contemporary life, isolating us in front of our computers and our phones even as it promises virtual connection, the early history of the Minitel also demonstrates the potential of such technologies to bring people together in the physical world. Utopian in conceptualization, Les Goudous Télématiques' website was ultimately unsuccessful in practice. Given the centrality of the internet to queer life by the twenty-first century, however, both the GTs' achievements and their failures contribute to the evolving history of the relationship between lesbian identity, community formation, sexuality, and technology in modern France and beyond.

CYBERQUEER HISTORY AND LESBIAN IDENTITY

Gay newsgroups and bulletin board systems, in which users post plain-text messages to a publicly accessible online space, appeared in tandem with mainstream internet services in the 1980s. The first French gay and lesbian

Minitel sites were also launched at that time. As the technology improved and became commercialized, queer ventures kept pace, developing first web content and then commercial gay-oriented chat spaces and graphical 3D worlds like the short-lived Pride!Universe. Many of the first queer sites were created by individuals involved in telecommunications and the computer industry. One of the first globally accessible queer online spaces to attract lesbian participation was the American Usenet newsgroup net.motss. In 1983 gay users established net.motss despite initial resistance from homophobic Usenet authorities. The acronym "motss" (which stood for "members of the same sex") was deliberately obscure.[4]

Conservative opposition to early cyberqueer activity was all too common. In France the Confédération nationale des associations familiales catholiques (National Confederation of Catholic Family Associations) not only argued that "homosexuals' . . . natural tendency toward sexual vagrancy" was "given free rein thanks to the Minitel" but also warned that gay use of the Minitel would cause France to be "the country most affected" by the AIDS virus.[5] In 1988 the German service provider Prodigy attempted to obtain a court ban against gay forums.[6] In the United States, America Online (AOL) was found to have outed a client, passing on personal data about the homosexual orientation of a member of the US military.[7] Such reactions give the lie to the utopian rhetoric that often dominated early discussions of queer cyberspace, which idealized the liberating possibilities of virtual technology. They also justified the fears of French women who resisted this new technology on the grounds that it could not adequately protect the privacy of those it served.

But not everyone was worried. In 1983, the same year that net.motss went online, the French gay male community enthusiastically recognized the Minitel as a new way to hook up expediently and anonymously. Within the next year, the popular gay male magazine *Gai pied* set up its Minitel site, GP-Rézo. In record time the site was logging about a thousand use hours per day, and the magazine was raking in profits.[8] In fact, *Gai pied* cofounder and gay rights activist Jean Le Bitoux remarked that the technology provided the magazine with "an inexhaustible source of revenue."[9] Email discussion lists—in which messages were sent via email to members rather than publicly posted to electronic bulletin boards—soon heightened queer interest in computer-mediated communication because they offered an additional degree of privacy and security. Although queer internet and Minitel sites in North America and Europe quickly provided multiple services (job postings, travel ads, medical information, etc.), gay men adopted the new technology first and foremost as a means of sexual communication. For the most part, early lesbian agendas for the technology—in France and elsewhere—could not have been more different.

Much of the early history of lesbian engagement with computer-mediated communication relies on chronologies written by queer internet activists Amy Goodloe and Eva Isaksson, both of whom appear unaware of the existence of French lesbian initiatives on the Minitel.[10] (Of course, scholarship on the cyberqueer world is hindered by the lack of data that thwarts cyberstudies in general.)[11] Goodloe, the founder of the American website Lesbian.org (established in the mid-1990s), reports that the first American lesbian email discussion list, SAPPHO, was launched in May 1987 (almost two years after the GTs went live in France). Most subscribers were American, frequently with links to educational institutions, where email was becoming a regular feature of academic life. Lesbian lists like LIS (Lesbians in Science, established in 1991) and OWLS (Older and Wiser Lesbians, established in late spring of 1994) appeared shortly thereafter.[12]

Eva Isaksson began to set up European lists in the early 1990s, creating the first Finnish list, sapfo, in 1993. Sociologist Nina Wakeford claims that this was the same year that lesbian "chat" spaces first appeared; however, she neglects to take into account the presence of chat forums on the French Minitel almost a decade earlier.[13] (Goodloe commits the same oversight, dating the first invitation-only chat room—called "clitchat," on AOL—to the early 1990s.)[14] The site Euro-Sappho launched in 1994, and the first European World Wide Web page, A Dyke's World, appeared in 1995. In North America niche lists with names like GrrlTalk, SacredSisters, Biker-Dykes, LezCouplesWithKids, and NiceJewishGirls multiplied. In 1997 Isaksson, again omitting mention of France, counted over sixty lesbian lists, fifty running on US servers and nine on European ones, including LLI in Italy and Sapfo-Norden, a Norwegian list running on a Swedish server. According to Isaksson, more than 90 percent of the lesbian online population hailed from North America, where the largest body of resources (hardware, software, networking services, and facilities) was located.[15] As in the sapphic cabarets founded in the 1930s, by the end of the 1990s, commercially oriented sites proliferated as both sympathetic and opportunistic entrepreneurs cued into the financial potential of the lesbian and gay market.

Queer online spaces help produce specific incarnations of sexual subjectivity. The early history of lesbian online sites is illustrative in this regard. When Isaksson reveals, for example, that SAPPHO's founder (known online as "Ambar") was a heterosexual woman who ostensibly wanted to provide lesbians with an online meeting place, she unintentionally raises questions about the relationship between identity and the presentation of online personas that are pertinent to the narrative discussed here.[16] How many of the women who logged on to the GTs did not self-identify as lesbian? How many used the site as a place for exploration, education, or titillation? What did the appellation "lesbian" mean to each of them? Given that, like all identities, lesbian identity is situationally and historically contingent, such questions remind us of the disciplinary effects shaping the category. As we shall see, the GTs ultimately encouraged both the politicization and the de-eroticization of the lesbian identity that they aspired to serve.

LESBIANS ON THE MAINFRAME: LAUNCHING LES GOUDOUS TÉLÉMATIQUES

The handful of white French women who came together to create Les Goudous Télématiques, the first lesbian Minitel site, were part of that visible minority of politically out lesbians whose identities had been forged through participation in the French women's movement and the fights for gay and lesbian liberation that followed May 1968. Some of this energy dissipated once the Socialists swept to political power in France in 1981. With the catastrophe of AIDS a bit beyond the horizon and lulled by a recent series of political gains—including the 1982 repeal of the discriminatory 1942 law on sexual majority for homosexual acts, the declassification of homosexuality as a mental illness, and the dissolution of the "homosexual brigade" within the French police force (a taskforce charged with cracking down on homosexual activity)—many in the gay and lesbian community turned away from politics to pursue more personal pleasures. Others, including over twenty groups of lesbians from throughout France who were buoyed by recent victories but anxious about the battles that remained, generated an unprecedented level of social, cultural, and political activity into the 1990s. Interaction with the media played a key role. Lesbian engagement with the Minitel is part of this story.

Developed in 1977 as a virtual replacement for paper telephone directories, the Minitel went public in France in 1982. By the end of the century, the Minitel had fifteen million French users and hosted twenty-five thousand services. In contrast, as late as 1997, only 0.7 percent of the French were connected to the internet.[17] Although it could initially transmit only text, not images, the Minitel could be used—much as the internet later was—to make purchases, send emails, and participate in online chats. Minitel users could also access an array of services and information; online banking, stock market quotes, news and weather reports, travel reservations, and insurance were all available through the new technology. Unlike the internet, which is accessed through the open system of the World Wide Web, the Minitel functioned through a closed system run by the French Télétel network that rendered it impermeable to hackers and safe from viruses—features that contributed to its enduring popularity.[18]

The Minitel had both nonprofit and more costly for-profit servers, and enterprises could choose to subscribe to one or the other.[19] The speedy multiplication of erotic bulletin boards and sex-chat lines (collectively known in France as the Minitel Rose) on the Minitel's for-profit servers quickly became the subject of heated debate. This was in part because during the period in which the GTs existed (from 1985 to 1988), calls to the erotic bulletin boards of the Minitel Rose accounted for fully half of the time spent online by French consumers.[20] Indeed, these sites were the primary factor behind both the popularity and the condemnation of the new technology. Early critics like the minister of telecommunications Gérard Longuet and the minister of the interior Charles Pasqua (who also attempted to have the magazine *Gai pied* banned on moral grounds in 1987) often linked sexual services on the Minitel Rose to homosexual promiscuity—not without reason, given that, as discussed above, many gay male businesses enthusiastically embraced both the sexual possibilities and the revenue that these sites provided.[21] As we shall see, the GTs' decisions to function as a nonprofit and to reject the pornographic foci of the Minitel Rose reveals how profoundly lesbian and gay male agendas, politics, and social self-conceptions could differ.[22]

The initial idea for a lesbian Minitel site was the fruit of discussions among three young activists: Catherine Gonnard; her partner, Annie Cariou; and their friend Aline Tashjian. Gonnard and Cariou had moved to Paris in 1979 from Quimper in Brittany, where they had experienced firsthand the oppression and isolation associated with identifying as lesbian in a small town. Once relocated to Paris they became involved in the gay rights movement, participating in the founding of the mixed-gender activist group the Comité d'urgence anti-répression homosexuelle (Emergency Committee against Homosexual Repression, or CUARH) and its lesbian spin-off, the Mouvement d'information et d'expression des lesbiennes (Movement for Lesbian Information and Expression, or MIEL). It was at MIEL in Paris that Gonnard met Tashjian. While writing for the CUARH's monthly magazine, *Homophonies*, both Gonnard and Tashjian observed the frenzy that had erupted over the Minitel Rose in the gay press. "It was crazy," Gonnard reports. "Suddenly there was a way to make money in the movement. *Homophonies* had a Minitel site, and Aline and I understood very quickly what the stakes were. . . . [But] while the guys were much more gifted than we were at making money . . . they only went after the sex. Only that. And we felt like this wasn't the way we should be doing it."[23] The Minitel, they agreed, was an opportunity to build community. In the spring of 1985, they brought their agenda for a lesbian Minitel site to a series of national meetings organized by MIEL known as the Forum lesbien (Lesbian Forum).[24]

The first meeting of the Lesbian Forum, held on April 27–28, 1985, at the Maison des Femmes (Women's Center) in Paris, attracted an audience of mostly lesbians from throughout France who were active in the lesbian press and radio and in feminist and gay politics.[25] The Lesbian Forum produced a range of special interest committees, each addressing different aspects of lesbian existence. The project for the GTs was developed during the meetings of the committee Information et coordination par et pour les lesbiennes (Information and Coordination by and for Lesbians, or ICPPL).[26] The ICPPL sought to inform French lesbians about women-centered activities, services, and spaces; to valorize their initiatives (activist or not); and to organize projects on a national level. They identified two vectors of concern. The first dealt with access and reflected their desire to reach all women who were attracted to and loved women, whether closeted or out, alone or in groups, old or young. The second stemmed from their belief that "those who use the media should participate in it."[27] They were particularly interested in helping women who lived in rural locations and smaller cities make contact with one another and with the larger lesbian community in Paris, and vice versa.

This was hardly the first time that French lesbian activists had attempted to address problems associated with community formation, communication, and connection. In May 1985 Parisian lesbians had tried and failed to create a public news forum for lesbians by replicating the example of Les Répondeuses. While Les Répondeuses had proven viable for a restricted locale, the ICPPL concluded that its purview was too Parisian to meet their current goals. Consequently, at a second gathering of the Lesbian Forum on June 23, 1985 (also held in Paris), the ICPPL debated the merits of a national lesbian telecommunications network on the Minitel. Over thirty women from Rennes, Strasbourg, Rouen, Besançon, and Paris attended the meeting. Those in favor of launching a lesbian Minitel site realized that the project's success depended in part on their ability to convince a female public of the merits of the new technology. To this end, Gonnard, Cariou, and Tashjian drafted a mission statement explaining that a dedicated lesbian Minitel site would accomplish five important goals: first, break lesbian isolation; second, favor regional and national exchange; third, support social, cultural, artistic, and other initiatives; fourth, create a fast news and information service in real time produced by and for lesbians; and fifth, permit communication between two or more lesbians through a private message system that functioned via email and chat rooms.[28] Not only would such a Minitel service, through its "rapidity, interactivity, and conviviality," counter the "double oppression" that lesbians experienced as both women and homosexuals, but also, Gonnard, Cariou, and Tashjian argued, "in the case of a tightening of social values or of repression, it [would] be a rapid and discreet means to spread information."[29] The sociopolitical agenda was clear. And unlike most gay male Minitel sites, sex was not—at least not explicitly—on the program.

The gathering closed with the announcement of a third meeting to be held the following September in Rennes. The choice of location underscores the ICPPL's desire to decenter Paris as the locus of lesbian existence and illustrates a deliberate attempt to fight back against the social and moral constraints characteristic of smaller French cities and towns. The group volunteered to organize lodging for participants to alleviate any financial concerns that might hinder attendance. The Rennes meeting proved pivotal, for it was there that the lesbian Minitel project took on its structure and received its distinctive name.

Legally established as a nonprofit association, the GTs were composed of a governing board of five members, who were assisted by six other women. None were paid. The GTs' bylaws required that three of the group's five acting board members reside outside of Paris. The choice to seat their legal address in Rennes rather than the capital likewise reflected their resolutely anticentrist politics and commitment to geographic diversity. Most of the GTs lacked any training in information technology or telecommunications. All were between the ages of twenty and forty-one. The women chose their moniker—Les Goudous Télématiques—by combining the technologically descriptive adjective *télématique* (telematic) with the plural of the noun *goudou*. The latter, as noted in this book's introduction, is an affectionate French word for "lesbian" that co-opts the negative epithet *gouine* (dyke) and plays on the French words for "taste" (*goût*) and "sweet" (*doux*).

Even if the GTs had been technologically savvy, getting a Minitel site up and running in France required the paid assistance of two entities: a telecommunications company to build it and a company entrusted to oversee the daily functioning of the service, handle repairs, provide statistical feedback on monthly traffic, and analyze fiscal status. The French firm SERTEL (Services Télématiques) was hired to perform the first service; the Association pour l'autogestion par des systèmes informatiques éclatés (Association for the Extension of Self-Managed Computer Systems, or ASPASIE) was employed to cover the latter. One of ASPASIE's employees, a lesbian who regularly attended soirées thrown by MIEL, had pledged her support for the project—a detail that buttresses Wakeford's claims that early lesbian online activity "tended to be facilitated by women working in the computer industry."[30]

Together, the GTs were determined to make their site—and the access it provided to lesbian businesses, organizations, news, events, and services—available to any woman in France with access to a Minitel terminal. Importantly (and in contrast to the internet, which often entailed the purchase of a computer and hence disenfranchised economically disadvantaged populations who are, as is common knowledge, disproportionately female), this meant that every French woman with a home phone could participate, because the French national phone company provided Minitel terminals (each consisting of a text-based screen, a keyboard, and a modem) free of charge to its clients.

Only those women interested in using the GTs' email and chat room features were required to purchase an annual subscription, which entitled them to a password and private mailbox.[31] (In 1985 this cost 35 French francs, or just over US$11.00, per year.) This decision was ultimately unwise, however, because it meant that although large numbers of women might freely browse the site to access information, read news articles, or peruse current events, members alone generated income. Unless users wanted email privileges and purchased subscriptions, all charges for time spent online bypassed the association and were billed directly by the phone company; the GTs didn't see a penny.

The GTs' nonprofit business plan (which eschewed advertising) reinforced their dependence on private and public funding sources. Although members of the governing board gave generously of their personal savings and held regular fundraising events, private donors were hard to come by—those companies they did approach, like IBM and Apple Computer France, declined. To lure public funding, the GTs sent out business dossiers to Danielle Mitterrand (wife of the French president), Françoise Fabius (wife of the French prime minister), and Yvette Roudy (then minister for the rights of women—and purportedly a closeted lesbian), as well as to the minister of culture, the national phone company, and regional and departmental councils across France.[32] Despite their best efforts, support for the project was almost nonexistent. In the absence of both private and public monies, the association was heavily dependent on attracting members who would avail themselves of the paid services that generated income for the GTs directly. For reasons outlined below, this turned out to be difficult.

To gauge interest in this new networking possibility among the lesbian community, the GTs formulated a questionnaire for distribution in the lesbian and gay press. Thirty completed questionnaires exist in the archives.[33] Slightly more than one-third of the respondents lived outside Paris. Although they ranged in age from twenty-one to fifty and practiced diverse professions (including teacher, dancer, nurse, student, typesetter, office worker, researcher, and administrator), only four (a professor, a student, a technician, and a social worker) had access to the Minitel in a work environment. This latter finding proved significant; as subsequent studies show, workplace use was a frequent prerequisite to home adoption of the new technology.[34] It also reveals the pertinence of gender difference to the GTs' story. None of the women fit the gender-specific socioeconomic profile—that of a "youngish (thirty- to fifty-year-old) educated male working in senior or middle management"—most often associated with Minitel use.[35]

It was far from remarkable, consequently, that though the majority of the questionnaire's respondents were aware that the Minitel could be procured for free from the phone company, only two women actually had a Minitel at home. Despite almost unanimous agreement among questionnaire respondents that the exchange of "communication and information between lesbians" was "very important," a series of prejudices against the technology remained. Respondents protested that the terminal was "horrifyingly ugly!" and considered the Minitel "too complicated," untrustworthy ("we don't know who is on the other end"), "too impersonal," or "too expensive" (because, as noted above, time spent online cost money). Only one of the thirty women had heard of the GTs' Minitel service, and now that each had read about it, just one woman in five intended to take advantage of it. The survey boded ill, accurately predicting the GTs' areas of vulnerability. All misgivings aside, the service went live on October 24, 1985, a fact that, the GTs quipped, "filled us with satisfaction."[36]

Organized on-screen under four rubrics—directory, current events, press reviews, and message board (which included email and access to chat rooms)—the GTs' service was primed to become *the* Minitel service by and for lesbians. The site provided the first-ever comprehensive online national directory of businesses, associations, organizations, and services—from bars, restaurants, bookstores, nightclubs, and activist groups to facilities, vacation spots, clubs, medical doctors, lawyers, and psychological support services—either run by or catering to a lesbian clientele in France.[37] With approximately three million Minitel terminals in use throughout France by the end of 1986, it seemed probable that thousands of women would find the site compelling. "Accessible, simple, speedy, cheap, and convivial," it appeared sure to succeed.[38] Certainly, over the next three years the eleven core members would volunteer a herculean amount of unpaid time and energy in order to keep the lesbian Minitel project alive.

Collating the materials for the online directory—a prerequisite to launching the site—proved a massive undertaking. Regional volunteers from throughout France helped locate contacts. All groups, individuals, and businesses wanting to be listed were required to fill out a form authorizing the GTs to publish their contact information and "calendar of activities." To ensure national coverage, the form included a space to provide information about others "in your region or sector of activities about whom we might be unaware." Respondents were likewise asked to specify whether their organization or service was "lesbian," "[male] homo[sexual]," "mixed," or "other," as well as whether they were "associative" or "commercial" and whether their activities were national, regional, or local.[39] Although most listings were adamantly women-only—including *Lesbia*, a sports and leisure activities club called Mytilène, and MIEL (all in Paris), as well as the Strasbourg group La Lune Noire (Dark Moon)—a considerable number were from mixed-gender or male groups that hoped to reach a larger lesbian audience. Thus, the Association des médecins gais (Association of Gay Doctors) admitted that it was 95 percent male but nevertheless requested a spot on the site. Likewise, the national helpline SOS Gaie described itself as mixed and noted, "Sadly, we only have men staffing our phone." It nonetheless assured the GTs that "we've had about fifty-two calls from lesbians, and two out of three times the conversations are mutually enriching."[40]

Ideologically nonpartisan, the GTs listed religiously based groups like the SOS permanence lesbienne of the Centre du Christ libérateur (the lesbian helpline for the Center of Christ the Liberator) and David et Jonathan (a mixed-gender homosexual Christian alliance) alongside such controversial organizations as the pedophilic GRED, discussed in chapter 5. Special interest groups, from a committee dedicated to sending French athletes to the 1990 Gay Games in Vancouver, Canada, to a pair of lesbians offering workshops on auto maintenance, to the Mouvement adolescence guaie [*sic*] (Gay Adolescent Movement, a club for gay teenagers), all requested inclusion. The GTs' geographic range was also impressive: they posted information from regions including Alsace, Aquitaine, Burgundy, the Côte d'Azur, the Franche-Comté, the Pays de la Loire, Lorraine, Occitanie, Picardy, Provence, and Tourraine. Organizations and publications from beyond France were also represented. The Quebec journal *Amazones d'hier, lesbiennes d'aujourd'hui* (Amazons of yesterday, lesbians of today) and the Swiss lesbian magazine *Clit 007* both sought to expand their circulation by appealing to French lesbians online. Lesbians from Mexico also posted a request for "much-needed reviews, posters, and books . . . in French, English, or Spanish" and cordially invited their French counterparts to attend the first meeting of Latin American lesbians, scheduled for 1987.[41] Oddly, for reasons he fails to explain, only Daniel Defert, partner of the late Michel Foucault and president of AIDES (the first AIDS awareness association in France), rejected the GTs' invitation to have his organization listed on their site.[42] Correspondence between the GTs and their "listees" nevertheless reveals that by the time the site went live, virtually every known lesbian or lesbian-friendly contact in France was accounted for.

Once these original contacts were made, the listings for current events and press reviews fell into place with relative ease. For the latter, the GTs simply scanned the pages of the lesbian and national presses and posted online summaries of books and articles pertinent to the lesbian community. But it was the rubric of current events that provided one of the strongest justifications for the site's existence. As the ICPPL had unanimously agreed (and most of the questionnaire respondents had concurred), extant lesbian reviews, journals, and radio services—although proliferating rapidly—were unable to keep the French lesbian community informed about breaking news and events. There were two reasons for this failure. On the one hand, although select magazines were available in newsstands throughout France, it was evident that some women did not feel comfortable either subscribing to or purchasing products clearly aimed at homosexuals. The fact that these magazines were often shelved (regardless of content) in sections reserved for pornography further complicated this issue. On the other hand, monthly (e.g., *Lesbia* and *Homophonies*), biannual, and quarterly publications (including *Vlasta* and *Masques*) and even weekly radio shows were by their very nature unable to provide up-to-date information. Private, accessible, and virtually immediate, the Minitel offered a discreet, timely solution. Moreover, the GTs argued that the current events rubric was politically efficacious. The Minitel could be used to garner support for political campaigns and human rights issues from battles over employment, housing, and immigration discrimination to questions of child custody and sexual harassment. The GTs thus made almost instantaneous mobilization on a national scale possible for the very first time.

The message board rubric was also deemed particularly important to the GTs' site because the email and chat functions allowed women who were socially or geographically isolated to connect. Unfortunately, because of the disappearance of data so characteristic of cyber networks, few traces remain of what transpired when women accessed these services. From the message board printouts that do survive, it appears that the posted communications were often relatively banal, like many email and text messages sent today. Not surprisingly, the GTs themselves appear to have been among the site's most active users. They sent personal messages ("We tried to reach you tonight at 10:30 p.m. Isabelle is taking the train, she doubtless arrives Saturday. . . . Dress warmly, because the heating here is only decorative!") and reported on business ("It's 11:15 p.m. here; didn't have time to get the latest news posted, but the mail for Chalon is sent and the badges are good"). Other users organized rendezvous, both political and festive ("Party on February 1; disguises required under pain of being undressed by the raging Goudous of Lille!"). A scant number attempted to establish new contacts ("I'm from Morbihan and want to have more contact with lesbians from Paris. Here nothing happens"), suggesting that the GTs' instincts that the Minitel could foster community were right. No extant messages are sexually explicit, although there is reason to believe that intimate—or salacious—exchanges would have been neither preserved nor donated to archives for public view.[43]

Although few, these messages are notable in that most lack pseudonyms—a key feature of the heavily eroticized world of gay male Minitel use at that time. Although it can be argued that the pseudonyms employed by French gay men were intended more as erotic shorthand than as cryptic code, they nevertheless helped to hide a user's identity.[44] In contrast, as illustrated by the text the GTs generated for publicity flyers ("the gatherings of all our friends on the Minitel—a great banquet of lesbians where all the masks and pseudonyms fall"), the GTs adamantly identified the Minitel as a safe space to be "out."[45] The fact that women both posted to the GTs' site using their own first names and employed the technology for quotidian rather than purely pornographic purposes further indicates that the GTs' users understood the Minitel as serving a wider range of needs. The GTs' nominative transparency also contradicts claims that online anonymity was crucial to the technology's role in promoting gay and lesbian connections beyond the confines of the city.[46] Moreover, if the French gay male community saw the Minitel primarily as a means for contacting transitory sexual partners, for the GTs, the ultimate goal of virtual technology was the enduring extension of an out lesbian community.

Community formation took place in the message board's forum: the ten chat rooms where from two to five women could communicate in real time. Although the chat rooms were labeled with evocative names like "Sappho's Rocks," "Martina's Court" (a reference to lesbian tennis icon Martina Navratilova), "Sarah's Loge" (a tribute to the legendary bisexual fin de siècle actress Sarah Bernhardt), and "Amazon's Breast," none of the interviewees with whom I spoke made any reference to these "spaces" as collectively imagined geographies.[47] In another context it has been suggested that the successful collective construction of a virtual space within the Lesbian Café (an online site for women in the American Midwest furnished with a "fireplace," "pool table," and "bean bag" and "rocking" chairs) may have helped bind virtual community together.[48] Perhaps the GTs' failure to fashion the forum into a sufficiently welcoming virtual environment—with fewer chat rooms or more ambient features—contributed to their difficulty in attracting online activity.

Given how quickly the Minitel seduced both the broader public and the gay male community, it seems surprising that drawing users to the GTs' site appears to have been so difficult. And yet, as the earlier questionnaire had foreseen, the barriers that persistently blocked women from adopting the new technology were multiple. These included unfamiliarity with the lesbian Minitel project; fears about its impersonal nature, security, complexity, or expense; and a combination of ignorance about and uninterest in the possibilities that the Minitel's bulletin boards, email, and chat functions provided. In a series of articles published in the lesbian and gay press, the GTs took up each of these obstacles in turn.[49] They also distributed buttons displaying their newly copyrighted logo, developed publicity slogans, organized parties to advertise their venture (fig. 7.1), and produced a publicity video, as well as giving computer workshops at the lesbian-run Mytilène club in Paris, at which email use was a central focus.[50]

Such initiatives reveal that one of the GTs' principal challenges was simply getting users online. In an article published in *Lesbia* in February 1986, the GTs try to coax women to cross this Rubicon. Its lighthearted tone is evocative of the unabashedly utopian spirit that often animated early discussions of the new technology:

> "Tell me, Annie, specialist of the Minitel," sighs Charlotte, our imaginary user, "what key should I hit?"

FIGURE 7.1: Flyer: "Party to Support the Goudous Télématiques, November 30, 9:00 p.m.," 1986? Produced by Les Goudous Télématiques. Courtesy of Catherine Gonnard.

"It is very simple," Annie explains. "You fold down the keyboard, you turn on the screen, you pick up the telephone, and you dial 36 14 91 66. Suddenly, you'll hear a dial tone. Okay? Now press on the key 'Connect' and then hang up the phone."

Amazed, Charlotte gasps: "It worked! Wow! I'm on the Minitel!"

Once Charlotte has reached the GTs' home page, Annie explains how

> to access the email and chat functions by typing in the code and password ("GOUDOU, of course, that sweet little word") and chides, "Don't forget to hit SEND. . . . You see how easy it is to use the Minitel? It's child's play!" she observes.
>
> "Yes," Charlotte concludes, "but can I find a 'tribade' out there who wants to climb the Himalayas with me?"
>
> "More than one, likely," Annie replies.
>
> "This Minitel is soooo much easier to use than most women think," Charlotte concludes, "and it opens so many possibilities. I'm amazed!"[51]

The GTs repeatedly reassured their public that "membership gives you total security," that the service was affordable, and that they had "nothing to do with the [porn] services that [were] overrun by heteros and gay guys."[52] And yet, in the eyes of potential members, the issue of privacy remained a problem. Although the GTs believed that requiring users to subscribe discouraged intruders (notably men) from prowling the site, control was patently unenforceable, a fact that was especially worrisome in the site's chat rooms. Such concerns aside, because the chat rooms were understood as venues for community contact and interaction, the GTs made extra efforts to encourage their use. Although they did not follow the practice common on commercial sites of hiring "animators" to keep users engaged in online conversation, the GTs were not above using their own unpaid online presence to stimulate participation. Annie Cariou, for example, admits that board members routinely logged on to the chat rooms, sometimes under cover of multiple pseudonyms. In this case, however, pseudonyms were used not to maintain anonymity but, rather, to convey the illusion of activity. "When a girl would show up in our chat room and see multiple conversations taking place, well, it stimulates interest, you know? It gives her the sense that something is happening and makes her want to be involved."[53] They justified any subterfuge by understanding it as central to their site's communitarian mission. My interviewees were eager to prove that these tactics "worked" by reporting at length about the long-standing friendships and romantic relationships that formed subsequent to meeting online. Comments like "One girl from Marseille and one girl from Rennes met this way, and they were together for years!" were common.[54]

Despite their enthusiasm, the GTs never managed to convince their audiences that the Minitel offered women a vital service. Indeed, only seventy-five to ninety lesbians actually subscribed to the service from 1985 to 1988.[55] Although subscription numbers and online activity do not necessarily correlate (given that, as stated above, not all those who browsed the site were paying members), the former was particularly fiscally imperative. While a lack of online traffic warned that the project was in trouble, the GTs were reluctant to raise subscription rates because they were committed to keeping the service affordable. Their anticommercialism was further bolstered by their political antipathy toward the profit-oriented projects developed for the gay male market. "We were suspicious of those who had money," Cariou recalls. "The guys had bars, discos, all that, and for lesbians there was always one café, one bookstore . . . and we bewailed our poverty, but we were really kind of proud of it."[56] She continues, "In the milieu of activists it wasn't proper to speak of money. . . . It wasn't supposed to be part of our values."

Fundraising efforts aside (and although the GTs eventually tripled their yearly subscription rate), it was the GTs' ongoing inability to attract paying users to email, bulletin board, and chat use that ultimately led to the failure of the entire enterprise.

CONCLUSION

The history of the GTs contributes to the history of sexuality in France while nuancing our understanding of how queer communities and individuals originally used cyberspace. First, debates among French lesbian activists during the 1970s and 1980s over the moral politics of pornography, along with their tendency to privilege committed relationships over casual sexual encounters, meant that they conceived of the Minitel's potential differently—more politically and romantically—than did the majority of gay French men. Second, while the lesbian public targeted by the GTs exhibited a slower uptake of the new technology than did gay men, in part this was because, as women, lesbians were largely outside the male-dominated domains of business, banking, and administration in which the Minitel was first introduced. They were thus excluded from the circuits that most encouraged—and provided instruction in—its use. This point reminds us that an exclusive focus on sexual orientation can obscure the effects of gender difference, which in this case were also instrumental in undermining the GTs' chances for success.[57] Third, the problematic relationship between lesbian politics and finance—seen by many as a competitive domain of patriarchal, capitalist oppression—further undermined the stability of the GTs' project and thus the achievement of their social and political aims.

The story of the GTs reveals precisely how a matrix of ideological positions (about sex and money) and systemic oppressions (regarding technology, gender, and patriarchy) collectively prevented this specifically feminist project from succeeding. Yet despite the premature death of the first lesbian Minitel site, which was "torn from our loving arms," as its board members solemnly announced, "by the cruelty of the World of Money" (and whose memorial service was celebrated "at the foot of the Tour Saint Jacques—metro Châtelet—on 18 June 1988 at 4:00 p.m."), the GTs' historical trajectory demonstrates their project's potential.[58] Letters mailed to the organization from Belgium, the United Kingdom, California, and Mexico also indicate that the ultimate failure of the GTs' site did not attenuate the extent of its actual influence.[59] For the three years of the site's existence, the GTs both called forth an expressly national lesbian community and provided an unprecedented tool for the construction of a politically and socially activist form of contemporary lesbian identity: in this, their story is pivotal to the contemporary creation and extension of lesbian counterpublics.

As should by now be apparent, however, the lesbian identity promoted by the GTs was also exclusionary: although not explicitly antierotic, its very structure downplayed lesbian sexuality and implicitly criticized the commodification of lesbian sexual practices.[60] By the end of the 1980s, a plethora of commercial lesbian Minitel sites premised on sexual entertainment, from 3615 ELSEM to 3615 LESB, would jump in to fill this void. The GTs nevertheless served as a vital precursor to the activist lesbian cybernetworks that now dominate queer political life in France. Within a decade of the GTs' demise, for example, the Coordination lesbienne nationale (established in France in 1997 and renamed the Coordination lesbienne en France in 2002) launched its presence on the World Wide Web at www.coordinationlesbienne.org. Through at least 2017 it acted as a national and international clearinghouse for lesbian news and politics, conducting regular online video meetings with more than twenty regional lesbian associations and numerous individual members from throughout France, many of whom host (or hosted) their own web presences.[61] Like the GTs before it, the Coordination lesbienne nationale was committed to utilizing computer-mediated communication to support the creation of national lesbian community, mobilize all regions of France by decentering Paris, break lesbian isolation, fight lesbophobia, and celebrate lesbian existence. Like the GTs' site, the Coordination lesbienne nationale's site had a structure that implicitly displaced the sexual in favor of political, social, and cultural agendas.

The GTs' passion for the project—evidenced by the many hours they devoted to site development, community education, chat room animation, and subsequent archiving of materials—speaks to the French site's significance as one of the earliest incarnations of the modern relationship between technology, information systems, community, and identity. The story of the lesbian Minitel also sheds crucial light on a series of broader issues in the history of France and beyond. For historians of the media, it underscores the critical role played by communication networks in consolidating the connections through which subcultural communities and counterpublics are formed. For historians of technology, it is an example of an important yet distinctive precursor to the adoption of the internet, especially by marginalized individuals. For historians of sexuality, it adds much-needed complexity to the story of the Minitel, usually understood purely through the Minitel Rose as connecting female prostitutes and straight male clients or as part of a gay male culture of cruising and pornography. For historians of feminism, it captures a hitherto unknown form of lesbian activism, one that was simultaneously antimetropolitan, anticapitalist, and technologically savvy. For historians of political culture in postwar France, the story of the lesbian Minitel stands as a critical example of how French lesbian activists engaged in the utopian projects that animated the Socialist Left during the sweeping sociocultural changes of the late 1970s and 1980s. For historians of the public sphere, this "failed" early history portends the ways in which queer use of internet technology has challenged republican divisions between public and private in the decades since. Finally, as the explosion of virtual lesbian sites on the internet in the twenty-first century suggests, this history of the first lesbian Minitel inevitably also reveals that, in the end, the GTs' project was simply a revolutionary idea whose time had not yet come.

8

LESBOPOLIS

Utopian Politics and Pleasures in Toulouse

In 2009 Mayor Pierre Cohen received an audience of over three hundred lesbians in the elegant baroque ballroom of Toulouse City Hall's Salle des Illustres (Hall of the Illustrious), a room traditionally reserved for registering marriages.[1] The occasion marked the twentieth anniversary of a lesbian organization initially called Bagdam Cafée (*sic*) and later known as Bagdam Espace Lesbien. It also celebrated the annual festival that Bagdam sponsors, Printemps lesbien (Lesbian Spring), which occupies the city of Toulouse each April.[2] In 2009 the festival theme was "Laughter as a Weapon." Flanked by both deputy mayor of tourism Sonia Ruiz and Saliha Mimar, Toulouse's city councillor for the promotion of diversity, Mayor Cohen officially sanctioned lesbian sexuality in the French public sphere by declaring Toulouse (known as the "Pink City" thanks to the rosy hue of its brick facades) to be first (mistakenly) "Lesbofolle" (Lesbian-crazy) and then, after correcting himself, "a Lesbopolis"—the "largest, busiest, and most important city [for lesbians] in the country or region."[3] In 2013, four years after this remarkable performance of political solidarity (and despite the violent efforts of tens of thousands of homophobic protestors), France legalized same-sex marriage.

Lesbian activism has had a particularly vibrant history in Toulouse, and Bagdam Cafée is at the heart of that story. Focusing on Bagdam—which has its lesbian roots in another provincial city, Poitiers—builds on our analysis of the contributions of lesbians in Lyon discussed in chapter 6 to further illustrate the importance of provincial activism to the history of "becoming lesbian" in modern France. Bagdam's history challenges

French histories of homosexuality and feminism that take Paris as their de facto measure. Indeed, in 2004 the regional newspaper *La dépêche* (formerly *La dépêche du midi*) dubbed Toulouse "the promised land for lesbians in France."[4]

In addition to decentering Paris, Bagdam brings together two interests that have shaped this book: sapphic cabaret subcultures and lesbian information activism. Bagdam's history also underscores two themes central to the politicization of French lesbian subjectivity: first, a commitment to *non-mixité*, or the creation of women-only spaces; and second, an insistence on *visibilité*—visibility—and the use of public space and the mass media to create community and attain legitimacy in the French public sphere. Both of these themes invoke the political and personal importance of the very group identities—the counterpublics—that the French Republic works so hard to ignore. Lesbian Toulouse reveals how pleasure, humor, and performance have shaped late twentieth-century lesbian politics while demonstrating how these politics have challenged the boundaries dividing private from public in modern France.

Bagdam Cafée and the projects that developed out of it (including the Festival du Printemps lesbien) are the unruly children of the sapphic cabarets first established in Paris in the interwar years. It is a complex legacy. On the one hand, the lesbianism that Bagdam passionately promotes is sometimes defined in ways that exclude—or can seem to exclude—women whose self-identifications don't conform to Bagdam's vision. It is not so much, "If you are not with us, you are against us," but rather "If you are not with us, you are not awake." Ironically, the result risks hardening sexual identity categories and instantiating new sexual norms. On the other hand, Bagdam's vigilant political commitment to visibility and defense of lesbian subjectivity demonstrates that it really is possible to remake the world.

TOULOUSE: LESBIANS IN THE PINK CITY

When Bagdam Cafée, France's first completely *non-mixte* (women-only) associative commercial café opened its doors in Toulouse in 1988, the center of gravity in the French lesbian world shifted south. Some would argue that it has never really moved back—or at least, that there are now two poles of lesbian life in France, one of which is most definitely not Paris. From day one, lesbians in the Pink City were distinctive for their relative disinterest in feminist battles in Paris and their simultaneous commitments to lesbian visibility and non-mixité. If Toulouse proved amenable—at first grudgingly, then with increasing warmth—to a growing community of women who loved women, the reasons for that acceptance (or so these women claim) are deeply historical. Rebellious, sociable, and independent-minded, by the Middle Ages the entire region (then the capital of Languedoc and, unofficially, of Occitanie, or southern France) was known for its "Latinity, a penchant for heresy, and peripheral marginality."[5] The reputation stuck. "Toulouse," Brigitte Boucheron (one of Bagdam's founders) reflects, "is an entity that is relatively independent from the rest of France."[6]

A trading center between the Pyrenees, the Mediterranean, and the Atlantic since the Iron Age, by the twelfth century the city of Toulouse vied with Paris for control over the birth of France. Its wealth and independence were thwarted by its "religious proclivities"—Toulouse was the target of the Albigensian Crusade that sought to crush the heresy of Catharism in the thirteenth century and later became a Huguenot stronghold.[7] A robust fifteenth-century market in dyer's woad (a blue pastel) collapsed in the face of indigo imports from South Asia and gave way in the seventeenth century to the wheat trade, until nineteenth-century crop failures and industrial depression devastated the region.[8] These later developments also conspired to push city politics left. Working-class artisanal neighborhoods sustained a local commerce in hosiery, sausages, sugar-coated violet confections, wine, guns, produce, and leather. Anticlerical and stridently republican, worker's associations and trade unions thrived; the French Socialist leader and antimilitarist Jean Jaurès was one of Toulouse's city councillors in the early twentieth century.[9] The Popular Front's Socialist Party won its greatest victory in Toulouse in 1936, and the city's relative isolation and radical politics attracted refugees throughout the twentieth century. Spaniards fleeing Franco, Italians fleeing Mussolini, and Jews fleeing Hitler all settled within the city limits, further diversifying an already rich demographic.[10] Despite the fact that this historically left-leaning city tilted center-right between 1971 (when on the cusp of economic crisis and inundated by an influx of Algerian immigrants) and 2008 (when the Socialists swept back into power), it was at least in part because of Toulouse's history as a magnet for radical thought that a small cadre of lesbians, including Brigitte Boucheron and Jacqueline Julien (both of whom became critical to Bagdam's creation and continued success), succumbed to its allure.

A PRELUDE TO TOULOUSE: "QUEEN PERGAME" OF POITIERS

Brigitte Boucheron and Jacqueline Julien met as university students in Poitiers—a small city in west-central France strategically situated on a promontory between the Boivre and the Clain rivers, known for its Romanesque architecture and its university, founded in 1431. Jacqueline remembers seeing Brigitte "sitting next to a young girl with spectacular red hair" in a course on Italian language and literature. "I imagined," Jacqueline muses, "that they were together. They weren't. They were just classmates, but I *saw* Brigitte *lesbienne*, although I knew nothing of her then." "It was only later," Jacqueline continues, "that I *really* knew, only after she'd come to know 'my' Thérèse—when [Thérèse] was with Éliane, with whom she ran the bookstore."[11] The bookstore was the Librairie Pergame, "a mélange of reading room and curiosity shop; a beautiful place, with its mezzanine, its second room [upstairs] as a living space, its fireplace and banquettes to sit and banter with the leftists and the intellos," and its endless supply of "kirs, espressos, and *petits crèmes*" brought back "from the minuscule bar on the other side of the rue Carnot."[12] The year was 1968, and France was about to erupt in revolution. The Librairie Pergame became the lynchpin in a series of events and encounters that, within a few years, would lead to both Jacqueline Julien and Brigitte Boucheron relocating to Toulouse, where they became the driving force behind lesbian activism—a position that, more than fifty years on, they still hold today (fig. 8.1).

The Librairie Pergame was a radical enterprise. In addition to serving

FIGURE 8.1: Brigitte Boucheron (*left*) and Jacqueline Julien (*right*), in Lausanne, Switzerland, en route from Toulouse to Geneva, 1980? Courtesy of Brigitte Boucheron.

FIGURE 8.2: The Librairie Pergame, Poitiers, France, early 1970s. Drawing by Éliane Laubus. Courtesy of Éliane Laubus.

as a gathering place for student activists, neosituationists, and surrealists, it sold new books at reduced prices (unusual at the time) and was a distributor for the controversial publishing house of Jean-Jacques Pauvert (famous for editing works by the Marquis de Sade and for publishing the sadomasochistic 1954 novel *Histoire d'O*).[13] The Pergame also stocked rare books and reeditions of revolutionary out-of-print classics and had a superb collection of books on art (fig. 8.2). It was there, drawn first by the gatherings of young "anarcho-situationists" in the light-filled front room and then enticed by the charms of Thérèse Yakovenko and Éliane Laubus (the bookstore's dark-eyed, fine-boned manager and Yakovenko's paramour) into the tangled bedclothes of the sleeping alcove in the apartment above, that Brigitte Boucheron came into her own.

Small, dark, and spirited, by the time Boucheron moved to Poitiers in 1966 to begin a degree in art history, she was also increasingly aware that men held no interest for her. Born in 1947 in the tiny town of Chevanceaux in Southwest France (but more attached to the region of Berry, where she spent summers), Brigitte describes herself as "a typical profiteer of *les trentes glorieuses* [the thirty so-called glorious years of French economic expansion between 1945 and 1975]: peasant grandparents, shopkeeper parents, children at university." She received a Catholic upbringing—mass, confession, communion—but "without the faith." Brigitte understood that she was "different" at thirteen ("and that pleased me immensely," she recalls). Fleeing heterosexual dating in favor of collective outings with female classmates, she changed schools twice as a teenager (moving from La Rochelle to boarding school in Poitiers), each time kicked out when unreciprocated crushes became too obvious. And yet, she sighs, "what delicious trouble when the skin of our arms touched during a movie outing!" The second time, "one of the—unstated—reasons" for her expulsion, she explains, "was that my 'Dulcinea' was the daughter of a prof, who, if I remember correctly, was a [fervent] Catholic."[14] Disgraced yet again, Brigitte was sent home to La Rochelle to complete high school. She reports that at each dismissal it was the school and not her parents who made the fuss: "In my family," Brigitte observes, "happiness had the force of law."[15]

After starting university in Nantes, Brigitte transferred to Poitiers, where she was swiftly "reunited" with her "platonic" high-school sweetheart "Mirabelle" ("hetero forever," Brigitte laments, although she notes Mirabelle once remarked, "I am not that which I do"). ("Ah, the times when we would glut ourselves on mirabelle jam and nuts!" Brigitte grins. "Orgasms are nothing in comparison.") But the "romance" ended in 1968, with "the marriage of my Mirabelle." The result? She fumes, "The Catholic religion and hetero ideology are my personal enemies!"[16] But in her words, it was not until 1969 "that things became interesting." "Up to that point," she recalls, "I was just a little tomboy, who was starting to be a feminist, and who had put her homosexuality 'on hold.' I didn't know any other *goudous* [an affectionate term for lesbians]," she continues, and then "along came the Librairie Pergame and 'the couple Éliane-Thérèse.'" It was also the Librairie Pergame that brought Brigitte Boucheron and Jacqueline Julien into one another's orbit.

Jacqueline Julien was born in Rabat, Morocco, in 1945. With "the post-colonial wars on the horizon," she explains, her father, "ever the opportunist," had resettled the family to France in 1950, "before things got messy."[17] Jacqueline was raised from the age of five in conservative Châteauneuf-en-Thymerais, a tiny town equidistant between Chartres and Dreux. Her father became the town's deputy mayor. Jacqueline describes the members of her bourgeois family as, "like so many French people," right-wing, racist, and antisemitic. Jacqueline's brother (eleven years her senior) fought in the Algerian War, participating in torture sessions "that he described during evening meals." Jacqueline attributes her growing sense of revolt and early political engagement to the repressive, reactionary nature of her home environment. Now an elegant, self-possessed woman, it took time for her to overcome punitive responses to her early lesbian experiences and definitively buck the constraints of "compulsory heterosexuality."[18]

Early on Jacqueline recognized that she was drawn to girls, and she acted on it. There were consequences; like Brigitte, Jacqueline was twice expelled from lycée for "unacceptable morals." First, she was kicked out of the Collège de Dreux after being discovered in bed with her girlfriend. Jacqueline's parents transferred their errant daughter to a girl's boarding school in Chartres but to no avail. It was there that Jacquline met her "second great love," Thérèse Yakovenko, the daughter of a Ukrainian father whose anti-communist parents had fled to Paris after the revolution.[19] High-school sweethearts for a time, Jacqueline and Thérèse were likewise "found out." As punishment, the school refused to board them, but the administration took pity on their bourgeois parents. Both girls were permitted to finish their final year of studies while under strict orders to refrain from communication under threat of institutionalization. It was after this that Jacqueline determined to leave the country. Following graduation, her diploma firmly in hand, Jacqueline fled France (and familial turmoil) for Italy. Disowned and disinherited by her maternal grandmother and emancipated at eighteen by her furious father (at a time when the age of majority in France was still twenty-one—"You want to go? Fine, go!!"), Jacqueline sought refuge in Bologna and then Florence and Rome. She wanted to be an artist, a writer. Instead she began to teach French—and discovered the first stirrings of the nascent women's movement. Jacqueline's self-imposed Italian exile lasted more than two years.[20]

Although no longer regularly involved with one another, it was Jacqueline who, between absences, helped get Thérèse hired in Poitiers by the Pergame's first owner, a certain Wladimir without a head for business. Perhaps out of sympathy for their common dispossessed ancestry

(Wladimir was also an immigrant), or perhaps convinced by Jacqueline's powers of persuasion, Wladimir charged the inexperienced Thérèse with restoring the Pergame's fortunes and invited her to run the shop. Eventually Thérèse Yakovenko inherited the Librairie Pergame ("God knows she deserved it," Éliane later observed).[21] She became its sole proprietress until her hospitalization in 1995, one year before her death from multiple sclerosis at age fifty. "Queen Pergame," as Jacqueline dubbed her, "shared her new kingdom" with her lover Éliane Laubus, "an enlightened chamberlain [Éliane was well read, well educated, and an adjunct lycée professor of French literature when the two women first met] who instructed her on books and publishers."[22] The relationship was "not at all clandestine—they were notorious. We didn't yet speak [openly] of feminism, and even less of lesbian visibility or pride," Jacqueline remarks, "but they were *beautiful* and very 'visible' and proud, those two" (figs. 8.3 and 8.4).[23]

The couple "Éliane-Thérèse" was a revelation for the young Brigitte Boucheron, then being pursued by a male Spanish anarchist who, Éliane later avowed, "Brigitte—despite her claims otherwise—didn't know how to say no to."[24] While Brigitte became increasingly aware that men were not for her, she nevertheless could not yet conceptualize a "lesbian" future. It was "Éliane-Thérèse" that changed all that. In 1997 Brigitte wrote (in an homage to Thérèse, published on the anniversary of her death):

> Oh how I jumped for joy and clapped my hands when I realized that these two women [Thérèse and Éliane] lived together! Finally, finally, I was a reality, I entered into reality, into my reality, I had found "my own," they were there, in that bookstore, with its fireplace, its wooden beams, its staircase and its window filled with precious little books. I would never depart . . . the Pergame was the place of so many firsts: [a place to] seduce, to be seduced, to make love (in the studio above the bookstore) . . . in a few months, in 1969, the Pergame became the magical décor that gave birth to the two principal axes of my life, feminism and lesbianism.[25] (Fig. 8.5)

The intensity of Brigitte's response underscores what we might call visibility's visceral charge: the "Éliane-Thérèse" encounter represented the realization of a utopian possibility that had been otherwise inconceivable to her because it had been previously absent from the visible world. Quoting the lesbian Quebecoise poet Nicole Brossard, Brigitte later marveled that the Librairie Pergame "incarnated 'the intuition of my certitudes.'"[26] But it was not until the birth of Toulouse's Bagdam Cafée in 1988 that these two "principal axes"—feminism and lesbianism—were finally united.[27]

FIGURE 8.3: The couple "Éliane-Thérèse." Thérèse Yakovenko (*left*) and Éliane Laubus (*right*), lovers and managers of the Librairie Pergame, Poitiers, France, 1968. Courtesy of Éliane Laubus.

The Librairie Pergame was unique in Poitiers as a commercial space of urban sociability and leftist political activism during the late 1960s and early 1970s.[28] Its visibility was self-evident: "There were teachers, feminists, lesbians . . . everyone passed through there, everyone," Éliane recalls, continuing, it was "the place to be—you had to go there, if you wanted to know what was going on."[29] The Pergame carried all the radical

FIGURE 8.4: Éliane (*left*) and Thérèse (*right*) in the flat above the Librairie Pergame, Poitiers, France, 1974. Courtesy of Éliane Laubus.

papers (including *Le torchon brûle* [1970–73], the first journal edited by the MLF), and its queen Thérèse and her consort Éliane served as both resource and inspiration for a generation of young women. The testimonies I collected were steeped in a kind of nostalgic idealism that betrays the intense pleasure associated with this *lieu de mémoire*: the Pergame was at once a kind of "desiring machine"—to draw on Gilles Deleuze and Félix Guattari's formulation—through which new forms of social reality were produced and a site where, as Pierre Nora might suggest, "memory crystallizes and secretes itself."[30] As such, the Pergame and its female managers provided an incipient model for the expression of both a radical feminist and lesbian consciousness and a utopian politics of pleasure.

By its very architecture as both civic venue and associated domestic

FIGURE 8.5: Brigitte Boucheron (*left*) and Éliane Laubus (*right*) camping in the Cévennes, France, summer 1977. Courtesy of Brigitte Boucheron and Éliane Laubus.

living space, the Pergame was also inscribed within an emergent feminist dialectic that fused the public and private spheres. It was not, however, homosocial—a factor later deemed essential by the women of Toulouse for the construction of a lesbian-feminist counterpublic—although after 1970 Thérèse and Éliane held women's meetings in the upstairs studio on a weekly basis. And, beyond the normal venues used to publicize the store's location (small ads run in the local papers, a listing in the Poitiers telephone book), they did not self-consciously utilize the media to promote the Pergame's commercial or political interests. Indeed, Éliane insists that since they only aimed to attract clientele already sympathetic to their politics, advertisements—often in the form of posters created by a friend—were placed extremely judiciously.[31] Nevertheless it was a vital training ground for later lesbian activism. And it made a not-inconsequential impression upon its young devotees regarding the importance of both pleasure and visibility in making manifest personal, social, and political power.

FEMINIST TOULOUSE

Brigitte Boucheron moved to Toulouse in 1970. She was twenty-three, and both the women's movement and the homosexual rights movement were about to erupt across France. Brigitte quickly became active in the Toulouse division of the Front homosexuel d'action révolutionnaire (FHAR). It was at a FHAR meeting in 1972 that she met and fell in love with twenty-year-old Sonia Ruiz—the same Sonia who, as deputy mayor of the City of Toulouse, would stand at Mayor Pierre Cohen's side during the celebration of Toulouse Lesbopole at City Hall in 2009. Sonia was born in 1950 in Oran, Algeria. Her father, a Spanish Republican, had been exiled there in 1939. Her mother was a Franco-Spanish Jew. Sonia arrived in France in 1964, shortly after the end of the Algerian War, when her father resettled his wife and four children in Tarbes, in the Hautes-Pyrénées, not far from the pilgrimage town of Lourdes and the Spanish border. Life at home was chaotic—her parents did not get along ("there was much psychic violence"), and her mother was "dictatorial, possessive, and jealous," deploying Sonia as a pawn in a verbal war against her father.[32] It was, Sonia remembers, a childhood "not without a lot of love, but interwoven with suffering and sadness." Bookish and introverted, Sonia recognized that she was drawn to other girls as an adolescent, but these early stirrings remained largely platonic: "I had surrounded myself, as a form of self-protection, with a carapace of fat. I ate. And I became *une jeune fille obèse* [an obese young girl]," a description, she comments, that remained accurate "for decades." Photos from the time reveal Sonia as more plump than fat, but her self-conception told her otherwise. As a result, she asserts, "My sexuality was extremely perturbed." The comment is interesting given that Sonia also claims that when she realized at seventeen that she was physically attracted to girls, she "wasn't at all bothered" by the idea, since it released her from having to seduce men—something she apparently neither felt capable of nor desired. Sonia observes that it was not until she fell in love and became lovers with Brigitte Boucheron (Sonia's first sexual relationship), that she came to appreciate her own body and "to love [herself], as a 'large' woman." This discovery, Sonia marvels, was absolutely "prodigious . . . it was beautiful, it was tender, it was explosive, it was magnificent, truly magnificent." The relationship lasted three years; a deep friendship remained after. If Brigitte awakened Sonia's sexuality, she also radicalized her politics. As a frequent visitor from Poitiers, Élaine Laubus contributed to this process (fig. 8.6).

FIGURE 8.6: Éliane Laubus (*left*), Brigitte Boucheron (*center*), and Sonia Ruiz (future deputy mayor of tourism for Toulouse, *right*), Toulouse, France, 1973. Courtesy of Brigitte Boucheron.

Sonia had moved to Toulouse to pursue university studies in history and the history of art. Attracted to the political fervent flaring up around her, she began hanging out with a student group of Trotskyists in 1972 but remembers "it was always the men who did the analysis, and the women who listened."[33] Curiosity about her own desires drew her to FHAR, where she met Brigitte. However, "Brigitte was very political, but also didn't want to be around men much, which is why," Sonia recollects, "in very little time we turned toward the women who were distributing the MLF's journals at the University Restaurant of the Arsenal, two steps from City Hall." And it was "with them," she continues, "that we succeeded in organizing a group composed exclusively of women in a locale at 30 rue des Blanchers, two steps from the Place du Capitol." Initially these gatherings constituted, Sonia recalls, "a feminist and not a homosexual 'coming out.'" The homosociality that feminism fostered was nevertheless a game changer; it soon motivated the women to pursue a more permanent "room of their own."[34]

Brigitte and Sonia participated in cofounding the Maison des Femmes de Toulouse (Toulouse Women's Center, or MDF) at 19 rue des Couteliers in 1976. By then, Jacqueline Julien, now married to a man and a mother, had also arrived in Toulouse (baby son in tow) after three years abroad. Newly separated—her soon-to-be ex-husband followed later in order to facilitate coparenting—and politicized by the Italian feminist movement, she was eager to return to a life among women. Brigitte, Jacqueline, and Sonia ran the Maison des Femmes with a small but radical activist core of about a dozen homosexual and heterosexual women (the former did not yet identify as lesbians—"we were women, my dear, women-who-loved-women," Jacqueline specifies).[35] A second circle of another dozen women "regulars" attended the MDF, and a third circle—an additional thirty or so—joined for special events. The women produced a journal (*La lune rousse*, thirteen editions between January 1977 and March 1982), created a "ciné-club" (among the first such non-mixte projects in France, developed by Irène Corradin and her partner, the historian Marie-France Brive), organized political actions, hung out, partied, and cooked together ("hellish concoctions," Jacqueline remembers).[36] From the start (though not yet all identifying as such), lesbians played a major role. In this the association distinguished itself from most other women's groups throughout France, where lesbians were invariably in the minority. In Toulouse they were so present and so overt in their interests, passions, and concerns, that certain women viewed the Maison des Femmes as a "nest of lesbians" and refused to integrate into the new structure because "it made 'a destination of homosexuality.'"[37] Both Brigitte and Jacqueline nevertheless identify this period as emphatically feminist—and dominated by the political concerns of the women's movement, concerns that had little in common with the radical lesbianism beginning to percolate farther north in Paris.[38]

For the core group—mostly white, educated, petit-bourgeois and bourgeois women in their twenties and thirties—the Maison des Femmes quickly became the focus of their lives. Around the world during these years, second-wave feminism provided women with an opportunity to experience, often for the first time, what it might mean to live inside a different social order that prioritized women. Small wonder that women who loved women found non-mixité intoxicating. Notwithstanding their newfound sorority, in Paris the battles over the fraught relationship between feminists and lesbians were heating up. Bitter arguments about the complicit role of heterosexuality in buttressing patriarchal society ended with the schism between heterosexual feminists, lesbian feminists, and radical lesbians discussed in chapter 5. While these battles are considered constitutive of the history of feminism in France, Toulouse remained primarily peripheral to them—a fact that proved consequential. As Jacqueline explains, "We were Toulousaines . . . spoiled by the opulence (or so we believed) of our [lesbian] numerical majority." For better or worse, "we didn't want to be caught up in a fracas that we judged to be a 'Parisianisme.'" "We wanted to be, we saw ourselves as, 'outside all that,'" Jacqueline remarks.[39] While all was not rosy—there were still bitter conflicts between various feminist factions—unlike in Paris, in Toulouse the female homosexual community held the upper hand.

Nevertheless, when feminism entered mainstream politics in 1981 (following the triumphant accession of the Socialists to power under François Mitterrand and the appointment of Yvette Roudy as minister for the rights of women in the same year), reform, not revolution, was the order of the day. The Toulouse Maison des Femmes, like the French feminist movement at large, collapsed. Literally. The building that housed the women's center was declared uninhabitable, and the women evicted. But just as the feminist movement was losing momentum, the French lesbian movement began to come into its own—just not, or not yet—in Toulouse.

Drained by the infighting that she observed tearing lesbian and feminist communities apart in the early 1980s, Brigitte Boucheron retreated from political activism for almost a decade. It was then that she became convinced that unless pleasure became a major component of lesbian political strategies, all efforts to gain lesbian civil and political rights would eventually fail. Jacqueline Julien agreed. She states, "After the closing of the Maison des Femmes de Toulouse, the fact was that Brigitte and I and the others were exhausted, but do you know why? By the lack of *pleasure*. We found ourselves in a dead end that we couldn't see a way out of."[40] This was so clearly *not* the anarchist world of Thérèse and Éliane and the Librairie Pergame in Poitiers, where politics and pleasure had been fused. Consequently, when Brigitte and her new partner, Sylviane Francesconi (an out-of-work restaurateur from Saint-Paul de Vence, a small town on the Côte d'Azur), dreamed up the launch of Bagdam Cafée at the end of the 1980s, pleasure figured prominently on the political agenda. "Lesbian fury is legitimate," cofounder Jacqueline Julien likewise argues, "but we must never forget the joy that is at the center of the deconstructive politics of lesbianism." Thus, she continues, "in producing laughter, in spite of my rage, I choose pleasure over suffering," and in this way, "I share my delight at being a lesbian, not just as a 'sexual preference,' but as a way of thinking, of constructing and deconstructing, and of hoping from morning to night for a different order for the world."[41]

UTOPIAN GAIETY AT BAGDAM CAFÉE

Since 1988 Bagdam (first as Bagdam Cafée and later as Bagdam Espace Lesbien) has been at the center of lesbian life in southwestern France and has played a critical role in French lesbian activism nationally. Established by Brigitte Boucheron, Jacqueline Julien, Sylviane Francesconi, and Sonia Ruiz, along with ten others, the café adopted and adapted its name from the 1987 hit film *Bagdad Café*, about the unlikely friendship between two women from vastly different worlds. Brigitte often explains how they transformed the film's "Bagdad" to "Bag*dam*," where "dam" stood for *les dames* (the women), and added an *e* to "Café(e)" in order to feminize the word and play on the French term for "fairy"—*fée*.[42] Bagdam's logo—two women, one white, one Black, locked in an embrace—was also adapted from the film; it figured prominently on their calling cards and promotional materials (fig. 8.7). Although the biracial image signals their openness to women of all races and ethnicities, the women involved in Bagdam's initiatives were nevertheless (for reasons discussed in the next chapter) predominantly white.

FIGURE 8.7: Promotional advertisement with Bagdam Cafée's logo, early 1990s. Courtesy of Brigitte Boucheron.

As a space dedicated solely to lesbian politics, pleasure, and culture, Bagdam's agenda was broad. In 1995 alone Bagdam hosted thirteen literary evenings, nine seminars with major lesbian activists from throughout Europe and North America, twenty-seven concerts, eleven film showings, eleven art exhibitions, four lectures, and multiple parties and fundraisers for the panoply of legal battles regarding lesbian rights that the Bagdamiennes regularly supported. By the end of the same year, the café had expanded sufficiently to put three employees on salary (only one of whom—Sylviane—was full-time) to handle accounting, the restaurant, the bar, and bookings. It also counted over twenty volunteers (including its president, Jacqueline, and secretary, Brigitte), all of whose work was essential to Bagdam's success. Although the café was open to the street, as a limited-access association it could be frequented only by either card-carrying female members (who paid a yearly fee) or female visitors who paid a nominal sum for each entry. And while full members were relatively few in number (154 in 1995), during its decade of existence the café logged approximately eight thousand entries annually—more than fifty-seven thousand in its first seven years.[43] Now, eight thousand entries is not equivalent to eight thousand *new* customers, but the numbers are still impressive, since they suggest that Bagdam welcomed an average of twenty-five women each night.

"Coming out" as a lesbian café was nevertheless not self-evident in late 1980s France. When Bagdam opened its doors in 1988, the word "lesbian" was absent from both its official documents of incorporation and the café's physical environment. While clearly run by and intended as a space for women who loved women, the association asserted that given social prejudices against female homosexuality, publicly appending the word "lesbian" to the café might inhibit some women from visiting. Or at least, that was their justification for the elision.[44] Nevertheless, within five years Bagdam's founders became politically emboldened. By 1994 they began to argue that whereas pleasure and non-mixité were imperative to lesbian community, visibility was a precondition for civil and political legitimacy. Thus, if on the one hand, they wanted to break the isolation that haunted the lives of many women who loved women, on the other, they aimed to force the dominant culture to acknowledge, respect, and welcome lesbianism as a legitimate choice. Adopting the new motto *Sans visibilité, pas de légitimité* (Without visibility, no legitimacy!), the Bagdamiennes set out to impose lesbian existence on the French public sphere.[45] To this end, they sought out the mainstream media.

Reaching beyond gay and lesbian publications and guidebooks, by the mid-1990s Bagdam began aggressively advertising in the local and national press and attracted the interest of journalists at regional, national, and international levels. This action alone was unprecedented. Nowhere else in France had a lesbian business, association, or organization extended themselves so energetically toward the broader media. Of course, the Bagdamiennes were not entirely in control of the coverage they received. Thus, despite Bagdam's willingness to "come out," some media outlets continued to soft-pedal the café's "lesbian dimension," even as it was mentioned. For example, while the magazine *InfoSud* observed that "a woman who doesn't like women won't feel at ease at Bagdam," they later (confusingly) commented that "there are also lots of lesbians who don't like women"—leaving readers to draw their own conclusions about the exact nature of the space.[46] Agendas and guidebooks to the city of Toulouse continued to list the association under "Feminist Movement" well into the 1990s (which, in Bagdam's eyes, was just as well, given the pornographic focus of some of the region's gay male establishments, all listed under "Homosexual").[47]

Bagdam's reputation as a lesbian refuge was soon bolstered by coverage on regional and national TV. One year after Bagdam opened, on November 6, 1990, the cable channel Canal+ aired a special program on lesbians as part of its series *La grande famille* (The big family).[48] Publicized in *Télérama* (France's equivalent of the American *TV Guide*), the broadcast, which had a talk-show format that gathered guests around a large central table, featured five lesbians, including Jacqueline Julien in her capacity as cofounder of Bagdam Cafée.[49] In her intervention, Jacqueline "outs" Bagdam as a lesbian space and insists on the importance of lesbian visibility.[50] For Toulouse this was a historical shift worth emphasizing. While the broadcast aired late (after midnight—provoking questions about just how influential it could have been), *Lesbia magazine* (by then France's best-established homosexual monthly and a tough critic) judged the show to be balanced, "intelligent[,] and worth viewing."[51] Of course, women who loved women didn't always assess Bagdam's media coverage so kindly. When Brigitte Boucheron appeared on national TV on a special called "Y a-t'il une culture lesbienne?" (Is there a lesbian culture?), the show's host Jean-Luc Delarue had the audacity to invite a man as the specialist.[52] The lesbian guests were—to put it mildly—unimpressed. And yet Brigitte asserts that despite the difficulties that engaging with mainstream media invariably presented, the Bagdamiennes categorically accepted all interview invitations in order to make certain that the broadest possible public would be brought into contact with positive images of lesbians and learn about Bagdam's existence.[53]

FIGURE 8.8: Jacqueline Julien explains to viewers that "we live in a world made by men, for men." "Vent 1901," dir. Philippe Courtemanche, *Vent Sud*, France 3 Sud Midi Atlantique, broadcast March 20, 1996. Courtesy of the Institute national de l'audiovisuel.

Experience proved them right. The most extensive television coverage of Bagdam Cafée ever produced—a thirty-minute program dedicated entirely to the Bagdamiennes—aired in 1996 on *Vent Sud*, a newsmagazine that broadcast on the regional channel France 3 Sud Midi Atlantique, which served the region now known as Occitanie.[54] After opening with a black-and-white clip of Jacqueline Julien sporting a man's tie and sitting cross-legged on the floor while reading an erotic text about lesbian love that she had written, the show cuts to interviews with Brigitte Boucheron and the (lesbian) historian of lesbianism Marie-Jo Bonnet. The broadcast offers Brigitte ample time to publicize Bagdam Cafée and explain its mission, while Bonnet historicizes the notion of same-sex female sociability within the long tradition of French café society and salon culture. The program then cuts to Jacqueline behind the bar, who explains to viewers that we live in a world "made by men, for men" (fig. 8.8), before concluding with rousing footage of a Quebecois girl band bringing down the house inside the women's world of Bagdam Cafée.

Bagdam's television spots challenged heteronormative expectations while promoting lesbian visibility—and each broadcast invariably also brought a rush of new faces to the café. Media coverage for both general and gay and lesbian audiences likewise produced an avalanche of correspondence from women throughout France and, indeed, the world. Women wrote to Bagdam for many reasons—to express appreciation, to get information about lesbian-friendly services (hotels, restaurants, bookstores, lawyers, doctors), to request employment, and—not infrequently—to convey their loneliness and ask for guidance or romantic advice. The women of Bagdam—principally Brigitte Boucheron—responded assiduously to these missives, answering literally hundreds of letters each year. Like the lesbians of Lyon from *Quand les femmes s'aiment* before them, Bagdam's epistolary mission supported the extension of lesbian community while its media presence worked to liberalize public attitudes toward homosexuality not just in one city but throughout France and beyond.

Bagdam's utopian gaiety deployed humor and pleasure to bolster radicalism. This was part of a larger shift in French lesbian activism throughout the 1980s that privileged convivial visibility as a new form of protest. The performances that regularly graced the café's small stage effectively and explicitly politicized the tradition of the sapphic cabaret. By way of explanation, let's consider *Longitude femme, latitude lesbienne*, an evening-length slideshow with musical accompaniment and audio narration created as a Bagdam Cafée performance piece by Jacqueline Julien and her then lover Caroline Godon-Gauthier in 1992.[55] *Longitude femme, latitude lesbienne*'s comic plot functions as a radical manifesto that recounts the history of lesbian life from Eve to Sappho to Natalie Clifford Barney, then propels us into a utopian lesbian future in the mythical here and now of "Bagdamorum." "For women like us," the droll narration begins after a carillon of bells, "history began very badly. A man's history—and what a man, because he consisted [advance to a slide with an image from Michelangelo's Sistine Chapel ceiling] of God the father himself." The creation story (which describes Eve as "a clearly superior being" since she was formed "on the second try") gallops forward by centuries, turning hetero history on its hubristic head and leading us to an analysis of lesbian existence—and sexuality—in all its varied glories.

A section mischievously entitled "La lesbienne triste" (The sad lesbian) captures the sardonic tone. It starts with a sepia-tinted close-up of a woman's face, her chin cupped somberly in her hands as she gazes disconsolately at the camera. Against a thrumming tango score, the narrator mournfully declares, "The sad lesbian is sad because she has reasons to be sad. And because," the narrator (clearly amused) adds, "we find her annoying, she ends up even more lonely, distrustful, and sad!" "Sometimes," the narrator states as the slide advances to another sepia image, this time of a scowling young woman in dark clothing sitting alone in front of a stand of trees, "the sad lesbian is a former angry activist!" (a jab, perhaps, at the Radical Lesbian Front?). "Disappointed," our narrator grieves, "and, therefore, exhibiting little solidarity, she is unlikely to take pleasure in the simple joys of our gatherings." Here the music accelerates, and the narration brightens. The slide now advances to a group photo taken behind the bar at Bagdam Cafée in which women are grinning madly, their teeth flashing and heads tilted back, emanating such joie de vivre that they look like they will burst. "The sad lesbian's prolonged isolation," the narrator continues, "only increases her bitterness, and her pride keeps her from flirting with the same ease [advance to a slide of bartender Sylviane Francesconi and her barmaid singing karaoke with arms akimbo and goofy smiles] that seems to be the rule [two women, shot from behind, sharing the same barstool, locked in a tight embrace] all around her." "PS," our guide concludes, now singing gaily, "we're calling on all joyful lesbians to do everything they can to help the sad lesbian smile again!"

Over the course of an hour, the lively presentation reinterprets heteronormative history in its "true" light as a misstep on the way to lesbian fulfillment. Here, we are in a world of linguistic playfulness and gender mockery: women's oppression since "la nuit du temps" (the beginning of time) gives rise to the homonym "l'ennui du temps" (endless boredom); the winner of the "Prix Mabel" (a feminization of the Prix Nobel or Nobel Prize) discovers the "error of XX and XY chromosomes," revealing lesbians as "the most evolved of all creatures" (the Y is exposed as actually being a degenerate X that has "lost a lower limb"—"when we think that *they* [men]—and not we—are the ones who lack!" [a dig to Freud and Lacan]). Heterosexuality is merely a "stagnant stage" where some unfortunate females get stuck. ("But no excessive pessimism! Even after marriage some women manage to escape the hetero world to discover their true—lesbian—destiny!" we are assured.) In utopian Bagdamorum, our happy narrator concludes, where lesbians represent the absolute height of human evolution, "lesbian life is always golden." And is there an end? It seems not. Because after the final "Fin" (The end), we get yet another screen: "Non!, à suivre . . ." (No! To be continued . . .), as the musical accompaniment escalates to Tina Turner's raucous voice singing "The Best." The affirmative message couldn't be clearer.

"La lesbienne triste," like the longer diorama it is culled from, delivers a discursively constructed utopia in which a joyful and relaxed lesbian existence is figured as a kind of self-evident status quo. Spectacles like these used arch humor and collective creativity to combat stigmatism and personal grief, transforming negative feelings into an emancipatory political practice by spoofing the stereotypes endemic to straight culture. *Longitude femme, latitude lesbienne* delivered an audiovisual utopia in which a joyful and relaxed lesbian existence was indisputable and lesbian sexual pleasure normalized. The theatrical event was such a smash hit that after touring lesbian France (from Toulouse to Amiens, Marseille, and Paris) during the 1990s, Julien and Godon-Gauthier turned the slideshow into a DVD in the 2000s for distribution at film festivals and lesbian events. The Bagdamiennes (as the women of Bagdam continue to call themselves) maintain that it was precisely because they put a premium on pleasure that social, cultural, and political initiatives like this one blossomed and endured.[56]

As captured in their motto "Reaffirming, over and over, that separatism born of PLEASURE stays pleasurable," the Bagdamiennes came to understand pleasure as inextricable from female spaces that were *deliberately* homosocial and hence fundamentally utopian.[57] It remains worth reiterating, however, that the lesbians of Toulouse, as radical as they were, were not separatists. Unlike lesbian separatist intentional communities in America, Italy, Austria, Switzerland, Germany, and elsewhere, while the café was not open to men, as lesbian *feminists* (and not radical lesbians), the Bagdamiennes did not completely reject contact with men or with heterosexual women and heterosocial society. Interestingly, intentional separatist utopias—the kind evident in the hundreds of "wimmin's lands" established throughout North America in the 1970s and 1980s—are mostly absent in France.[58] Instead, we see the infusion of utopianism and what I call (riffing off of Sara Warner) a "gay utopian politics" into the more enduring histories of French lesbian radicalism more generally.[59]

For the most part (and the Radical Lesbian Front was an important exception) French lesbian non-mixité implies a political practice based on an argument about the importance of the interaction of *all* women—hetero and homo—among themselves. That said, non-mixité does not necessarily exclude specific alliances with mixed-gender groups of other political persuasions (antiracist, antinuclear, antifascist, antiliberal, etc.). The Bagdamiennes nevertheless believed that intentionally homosocial female spaces in which pleasure was prized offered a critical antidote to France's patriarchal republican state. In Toulouse, Bagdam Cafée provided this vital utopian respite from heterosexist reality.

For the women of Bagdam, non-mixité had, and has, both political utility and affective value, but their stance on the question of heterosociality was not uniform. Boucheron's own convictions lay closest to lesbian separatism, although for pragmatic reasons she has remained willing to collaborate with mixed-gender groups when political circumstances require. She writes, however:

> In their immense majority, men have *absolutely no interest* in the radical transformation of the rapports between men and women. This is an objective fact: only the dominated are interested in change, dominants have no interest in losing their dominant status. That would make no sense. . . . Since the appearance of the MLF, just consider the hundreds of thousands of women who have *dedicated, and continue to dedicate their lives* to the transformation of the rapports between men and women. How many men have dedicated, and dedicate, their lives to this? . . . Those [men] who don't accept [non-mixité] indicate ipso facto their machismo and their negationism . . . the same [men] don't contest the right to reunion and expression of Blacks, Armenians, Jews, Arabs, Latinos, and all the rest, because they cannot conceive of denying that these human groups have been subjected to injury. Visibly, for them, women have not been subjected to equivalent harm. I call this negationism.[60]

In Boucheron's view (a position shared by many but not all the women at Bagdam and by many but not all lesbians), "As women, our first reflex, must be *to work first, and above all for us*. . . . Working with men always comes back to working *for* them. . . . Mixité absolutely distances us from ourselves."[61] Sonia Ruiz, in contrast, who went on to enter civic government and thus engage with the heterosocial system, later wondered whether Boucheron's inability to collaborate well with men would ultimately undermine Bagdam's political reach.[62] Ruiz acknowledged and approved, however, non-mixité's second, more utopian dimension, one that was both pleasurable and political: the belief that lesbians should create women-only spaces because it was women's company that they most enjoyed, and because it is only in such spaces that women can truly be free.

Despite its relative success (for many years its books were in the black, and the organization actually made a small profit), the café's heavy reliance on volunteer labor rendered it vulnerable, and after ten years of operation Bagdam Cafée closed its doors on January 1, 1999. Since that time, reincarnated as the Bagdamobile, the newly mobile Association Bagdam Espace Lesbien has continued to host international colloquia; hold workshops on lesbian history, theory, culture, and life; maintain a web presence; participate in legal actions, marches, and political demonstrations; and sponsor the annual Festival du Printemps lesbien that Mayor Cohen endorsed in his 2009 declaration. The women of Bagdam Espace Lesbien have also published six edited volumes, each one a collection of articles derived from a yearly conference.[63] Bagdam's president Jacqueline Julien insists on the importance of the word "Espace" (Space) in the association's new name, because, as she states, "we left the four walls [of the café] in order to occupy the city."[64] The Printemps lesbien is also part of this mission. Barring the spring of 2021 (when it was shut down due to the COVID-19 pandemic), since 1998 this festival has taken possession of the city's public sphere every spring via film festivals, readings, performances, theatre, parties, and exhibitions. The result is that despite not having a large lesbian commercial presence or geographic footprint in the city (and although recent political developments increasingly threaten their hard-won achievements), lesbians have had unprecedented political and cultural importance in Toulouse. For decades their public reach regularly matched (and sometimes superseded) that of Toulouse's gay male community—a situation virtually unheard of in other major cities around the globe.

In 2016, the theme for the Festival du Printemps lesbien, "Building Utopia," was inspired by the 2015 publication of Françoise Flamant's *Women's Lands*, a history of the experiments in feminist lesbian separatist utopias that mushroomed across the American Pacific Northwest in the 1970s.[65] Reiterating the importance of lesbian utopics in the festival program, the Bagdamiennes state, "We grow strong from the certainty that a utopia is first and foremost the COURAGE to never relinquish personal desire, even when it involves a radical break with those who would deny our claim, forever granting it second-place status." "Needless to say," they continue, "the end of our battle to render visible and hence legitimate that desire cannot wait another day." "Utopia," they proclaim, is "alive and well, here and now!"[66]

The enduring presence of Bagdam Espace Lesbien in the city of Toulouse and on the internet (where Boucheron, now in her seventies, still maintains a website and regularly publishes an e-newsletter) attests to the vibrant survival in France of a kind of pragmatic lesbian utopian gaiety based in identity politics that might seem, to many, passé. All of the organization's offerings ferociously indict the systems—heterosexist, religious, misogynist, racist, and capitalist—central to the functioning of Western patriarchy. Bagdam's utopic commitment to visibility and to the creation of non-mixed, women-only spaces as opportunities for political activism, conviviality, and erotic encounter remains central to its mission. Bagdam has endured, I would argue, because it incarnates both the outrage *and* the jubilation that have long been central to lesbian activism in France, making utopian gaiety an intrinsic part of its political agenda. To this end it embodies a politics that is both revolutionary and utopian at its very roots, one that calls contemporary society into question and is aimed at its fundamental reconstitution, rather than political or social reform. In its celebration of love between women, and its presumption that the culture of women who love women is both always already part of global culture and necessary to it, Bagdam functions as a constant critique of a world that denies respect and dignity (not to mention basic human rights) to broad contingents of its population. Do we need to be reminded that in 2024 in Afghanistan, Brunei, Iran, Pakistan, Qatar, Saudi Arabia, the United Arab Emirates, Yemen, Mauritania, Nigeria, Somalia, and Uganda, the death penalty is still a legal "solution" to the "problem" of homosexuality?[67]

CONCLUSION

By way of a conclusion, let us return to the 2009 mayoral celebration of Toulouse Lesbopole in the City Hall's Salle des Illustres that opened this chapter in order to circle back to my larger argument: the claim that a lesbian politics of utopian gaiety has reconfigured the practices, performances, and parameters that divide public from private in contemporary France. On this occasion, Deputy Mayor Sonia Ruiz remarked that this was a historic moment not only because she was there as a lesbian in the midst of hundreds of "nanas" (girls) but more importantly because they were all there in Toulouse's City Hall—a quintessentially public space—and claiming it as their own. What struck me in particular about her declaration was the emphasis that Ruiz places on the lesbian occupation of a common public municipal space and the way in which this visible occupation legitimized the lesbian community, thus allowing what the French consider a "private" choice (lesbian desire) to receive public recognition. This striving for public recognition of private difference was both central to Bagdam's agenda throughout its history and largely antithetical to a French republicanism that consistently relegates difference to the private sphere.

The intervention of Marian Lens on this occasion (a lesbian activist from Belgium who attended the ceremony) further accentuates this critical disjuncture. Lens observes that the mayor's speech was groundbreaking: "He officially invited Bagdam Cafée, but also recognized our specific [lesbian] history, our economic, social, cultural, but also political difference and reality. Lesbians," she continues, "are not consubstantial with the [male] homosexual community. And what is more, the City of Toulouse is going to dedicate funds to a group of *lesbians*—and that makes this a historically important moment."[68] Lens's remarks bring our attention to the ways in which both the mayor and the City of Toulouse officially recognized and fiscally supported a gathering of individuals whose rights derive not from their abstract equality (i.e., irrespective of differences of gender, sexual orientation, race, or religion) but rather *because* of a common specificity, that is, their lesbianism. Such recognition and support troubles the privatization of identity that is generally considered foundational to French universalism. It could not and would not have been achieved without the pleasurable and playful modes of social activism that sustained French lesbians who were battling for revolutionary change at the end of the twentieth century.

One of the things that I'm arguing for throughout this chapter is the value of utopian gaiety in the practice of contemporary lesbian politics. Importantly, in advocating for a world free from patriarchal and heterosexist oppression, lesbian "modelling or scenario-building" (what Ruth Levitas calls the "imaginary reconstitution of society") is "not simply a thought experiment in the conventional sense, for it necessarily operates at the level of affect as well as intellect."[69] Both negative and positive affect can of course manifest in praxis, and my intention is neither to denigrate the politically productive function of negative affect nor to argue that positive affect alone can create social change. But utopian battles are exhausting ones. By both embracing utopia as method and incorporating a politics of pleasure, lesbian utopian gaiety—as this chapter has demonstrated—nourishes our capacity "to live in this world as citizens of another."[70]

The "negative turn" in queer studies, focused as it is on damage and loss, resists the ludic emphasis proposed above, arguing instead that the "utopian desires . . . integral to the history of gay and lesbian identity" risk effacing the "dark side" of queer experience.[71] Such erasure, Heather Love claims, is dangerous, since it "makes it harder to see the persistence of the past in the present."[72] But whereas Love reminds us of the importance of "feeling backward," in part because "antihomophobic inquiry depends on sustained attention to the intimate effects of homophobia," many of the women examined here emphasize the importance of what we might call a ludic form of "feeling forward" as a critical element of political survival.[73] Surely humor and pleasure recharge lesbian revolutionary vigilance, especially in the face of ongoing or resurgent opposition? Indeed, the utopian gaiety evident in organizations like Bagdam Cafée was effective precisely because the radical vision that they presented was a playful response to violent forms of personal and social repression, thus carefully wrapping the iron fist of political argument in a disarming—if sometimes outrageous—velvet glove.

And yet, although this chapter illustrates some of the ways in which utopian gaiety has enabled lesbians to combat the patriarchal heterosexism of postwar French republican society and thus reframe the parameters of French citizenship, two historical developments within queer communities nevertheless menace the continuation of this agenda. The first is the emergence of what Sara Warner dubs "homoliberalism," which she defines as the "economic, political, and social enfranchisement of certain normative-leaning, straight-acting homosexuals at the expense of other, inassimilable sexual minorities."[74] Tethered as they are to a nascent politics of homonormativity, homoliberals eschew all "acts of gaiety" that "involve a flamboyant and flagrant flaunting" of nonconforming sexual behaviors and pleasures.[75] Indeed, there is little doubt that a kind of solemn commitment to *invisibilité* has taken center stage in France since the debates on civil unions and same-sex marriage came to the fore in the late 1990s. The results are distressing, since they privilege white, conservative, straight-acting minorities (represented, ironically given her métisse origins, by women like Elula Perrin) to the detriment of those with less conformist (or more flamboyant) identities. The second menace to the continuance of French lesbian utopian gaiety is in some ways more insidious: it comes, paradoxically, from that outgrowth of radical lesbian and gay politics known as queer theory. José Esteban Muñoz asks us in his final monograph, *Cruising Utopia*, to "look beyond a narrow version of the here and now on which so many around us who are bent on the normative count," because, he maintains, a queer utopia is "about an insistence on something else, something better, something dawning."[76] "Queerness is not yet here," he claims, but rather, "it approaches like a crashing wave of potentiality."[77] In this way, Muñoz is also inviting us to invest in precisely the kind of utopian gaiety that I have described here. And yet, while queer theory can espouse its own pleasurable utopian projects, despite its antinormative agenda it also risks eliding the misogyny and masculine privilege that have stood at the heart of lesbian oppression in France for over a century.

9

THE DIFFERENCE PROBLEM

Lesbians of Color in France

> Everywhere and forever, white heterosexual society has always planned the expulsion of that which does not conform to its worldview. Strategy number one—and this goes for any majority: the erasure of the minority.
>
> JACQUELINE JULIEN, "L'insoutenable visibilité de l'être"[1]

In secular republican France, French citizens are considered "one nation, indivisible," only by virtue of their (invisible) abstract equality; they are accorded rights in spite of, rather than due to, their differences, which are allocated to the private sphere. The French 2000 law on *parité* (parity) requiring equal gender representation on electoral lists was one official exception to this politics of abstraction.[2] In this case, it was argued that sexual difference (the fact that people are intentionally designated male or female at birth) was an acceptable form of public difference because it is "natural" and hence foundational to all civilized cultures. But whether considered natural or not, many forms of (purportedly private) difference—sexual, gender, economic, religious, ethnic, racial—have crucial impacts on the public realms of political and civil rights and social experience. Small wonder that the public sphere is contested terrain.

What we might call the "difference problem" continues to haunt both women who desire women and the French nation as a whole. Some of the most recent radical critiques of difference in the French public sphere have been produced by French lesbians of color. Their voices have been largely absent from this narrative. In this chapter I explore why, and I attempt to begin to share their stories. But first, we must address the roles of race and religion in contemporary French society. Analyzing how French lesbians have studied the relationship between visibility and lesbophobia can help us do so.

LESBIAN VISIBILITY AND LESBOPHOBIA IN CONTEMPORARY FRANCE

In 2015, two years after France legalized same-sex marriage, a study of French lesbians sponsored by SOS Homophobie revealed that lesbophobia remains disturbingly prevalent in France: of 7,126 women surveyed, 59 percent reported that they had been the targets of lesbophobia in the preceding two years.[3] Most often, lesbophobic acts were perpetrated in public by men. The study, which set out to determine the relationship between visibility and lesbophobia in contemporary France, predictably deduced that lesbians who were "less visible, experienced less lesbophobia."[4] The study nevertheless continues, "In no case are we counseling lesbians and [bisexuals] to be less visible," and concludes, "This observation rather encourages us to become aware of the lack of societal acceptance in the face of certain types of couples, but also in the face of certain types of women [who are] still too little recognized and accepted in France."[5]

The visible performance of female masculinity is implicitly identified here (with the phrase "certain types of women") as a specific trigger for male lesbophobic rage. However, despite obvious attention to visibility, in keeping with French policy, the survey reads as "color-blind": it included no questions about racial or ethnic difference. Nor did it query religious affiliation or belief.[6] And yet, as we know, sexual and gender prejudice cannot be considered in isolation from race, ethnicity, or religion. This is particularly true in secular France, a country where racism is inextricable from its colonial past, where culture and religion shape gender expression, and where sartorial practices that render religion visible (especially in the form of the hijab, the burka, or the niqab, collectively referred to in anglophone media as "the headscarf") have become objects of heated debate.[7] Lesbophobia is implicated in this calculus; take, for example, the ways in which queerphobia and sexism inside Islamic Maghrebi communities have been used to divert attention from queerphobia and sexism in French society as a whole, all while justifying racist political platforms purportedly developed in defense of secular republican ideals.

The profound links between visibility, lesbophobia, gender expression, race, and religion in France remind us that any history of female same-sex desire that seeks to understand the French public sphere needs to take into account not just sexual orientation and gender expression but also factors like these. Intersectional approaches (theorized in the United States by Kimberlé Crenshaw to describe how different aspects of identity "intersect" in ways that shape unequal experiences of discrimination, oppression, or privilege) facilitate such work.[8] The fact that French lesbians of color have been developing this analytic since the 1990s but have received little recognition for it—even from inside the French lesbian movement—is a surprising and troubling problem to which I'll return. Broader French disinterest in the approach is unfortunately more predictable.

Official French stances on race, religion, sexuality, and gender are ripe with paradox.[9] The impact of their interconnections is frequently disavowed. As Congolese French queer journalist Douce Dibondo observes, intersectionality is "rarely acknowledged in French academic and mediatic spaces" in part because French society refuses to name race or understand racism despite its presence "in every stratum of French-speaking society."[10] Freedom of religion has been enshrined in the French Constitution since 1789. The state also provides funding for both secular and religious education. But the 2004 French law on secularity that bans conspicuous displays of religious affiliation in schools has been used to suppress forms of religious expression that are specific to certain racialized religious minorities—namely, nonwhite Muslims. France gathers no census or other data on race or religion and only indirectly uses geographic or economic data to target policy toward ethnic groups (as, for example, in the Zones d'éducation prioritaire [Educational Priority Zones] that funnel extra money to schools in impoverished districts inhabited mainly by people of color). In 2018 when the French National Assembly removed the word "race" from the French Constitution, Emilia Roig, founder of the Berlin-based Center for Intersectional Justice and herself a queer French woman of color, responded, "Race may not exist, but racism still does, and it kills."[11] The collecting of racial and religious data both violates secular French republican principles and raises the specter of Vichy, with its antisemitic identity documents. France has passed antiracist laws and policies (criminalizing hate speech and provocations to racial violence) and outlaws racial discrimination at work, in housing, and in the provision of goods and services. But the laws are insufficiently applied and fail dramatically to address the extent of the problems both in white society and within communities of color.

WHERE IN THE WORLD ARE THE LESBIANS . . . OF COLOR?

The history of French lesbians of color—a category that includes migrants, refugees, exiles, and citizens—is hard to write in France. But not just because race is refused as a category of analysis, and certainly not because women of color who desired other women didn't exist. It is difficult because such women were often either in hiding (especially in certain ethnic or religious communities where lesbianism is condemned) or fetishized, ignored, threatened, or silenced by white French society.[12] Large populations of people of color first arrived in France between World War I and World War II. Most were men entering a working-class labor market. Women were in the minority. Women of color who desired women are nevertheless discernible in the interwar years, mainly in cabarets, clubs, music halls, brothels, and prisons. But material evidence of their presence seems to disappear as we enter the postwar era.

Todd Shepard argues that "the Arab man" became a staple of white male fantasy in the postcolonial period, playing "a substantial role" in 1970s discussions of politics, sex, and national identity.[13] Arab women's (hetero)sexuality figures strongly both in nineteenth-century French orientalist dreams (we have only to think of the odalisque in paintings by Ingres or Gauguin's Tahitian women) and in twentieth-century arguments over decolonization (in which unveiling, as scholars from Frantz Fanon to Joan Wallach Scott have suggested, symbolizes a patriarchal struggle for white French hegemony).[14] In the last quarter of the twentieth century, Elula Perrin appropriated and eroticized such racialized tropes in her books in order to titillate lesbian desire. And she was not, as Blase A. Provitola remarks, "an outlier." Provitola demonstrates that eroticized racism was "omnipresent in [lesbian] novels diffused by lesbian publishing houses such as Éditions Double Interligne, KTM Éditions, and Éditions Gaies et Lesbiennes" well into the twenty-first century.[15] But according to my interviewees, fantasy and reality rarely collided in part because women of color were not easily integrated into white French society.

It was not until the 1970s, as Paola Bacchetta (a queer scholar at UC Berkeley who is among the few academics to have written on French lesbians of color) observes, "that the French state's patriarchal and heterosexist 'family regrouping' laws" first permitted women of color to enter France in large numbers.[16] As Bacchetta writes elsewhere, "By presum[ing] and reify[ing] a particular formation of the heterosexual family," these laws "made women's legal status dependent on the status of male counterparts: fathers, husbands, brothers."[17] The result, she notes, was that women of color entered France in conditions that imposed sexism and lesbophobia. I might add that this was particularly true in Muslim communities, where religious precedent and patriarchal tradition reinforced French policy. As a woman of color, daring to "become lesbian" in public and political terms meant exposing oneself to the threat of emotional abuse, physical violence, and exile. Contravening gender norms via masculine gender performance exacerbated such reactions. In this oppressive context, opting for invisibility makes sense.

Most of the white women I interviewed remembered few women of color in the entertainment venues they frequented from the 1950s through the 1980s. Women of color certainly performed in these spaces (the seductive African American–Cherokee singer Eartha Kitt headlined at Frede's clubs in the 1950s, and Josephine Baker remained popular into the 1970s). They also sometimes patronized such spaces as clients, but not in large numbers. In the private sphere, notwithstanding the infrequent mention of the occasional lover of color or knowledge of a "friend of a friend," interracial socializing also appears to have been remarkably rare. Annie Astier, a white woman from Saint-Véran, argued that the problem wasn't one of skin color, but that one literally "didn't know how or where to meet 'them.'"[18] Sylvie P., a white woman from Strasbourg, remembers no lesbians of color "in [her] entourage."[19] "I was young, stupid, and blind," confessed Catherine Vautier-Péanne, a white woman from Paris who likewise remembers seeing only white women in the venues she frequented—venues where we know from photographs that women of color were present.[20] Aresky, a white woman from Marseille, didn't know any lesbians of color because (despite the facts that her mother "had only lived with Black men and that her brothers are *métis* [mixed race]") she claimed not to have had "a talent for identifying them."[21] "Maybe, through the 1970s and '80s," Nicole Bonnin (also white) from Poitiers speculates, "we were still too close to decolonization for women of color to have felt comfortable joining us in social spaces."[22] Perhaps. Or maybe some white lesbians overlooked, ignored, or rejected lesbians of color even when they were there.

Lesbians, both white and of color, who did "mix" were often able to do so because education, economic privilege, political beliefs, or erotic desire ultimately trumped factors—religion, familial sanction, racism—that might otherwise have inhibited it. This was the case for Bernadette S., a white woman from Grenoble who argued that she "never gave a damn about skin color" and who had lasting relationships with two women of color, one an Egyptian Jew and the other an African.[23] White lesbian activist Jacqueline Julien, born in Morocco but raised near Dreux, remarks that women of color frequented Toulouse's Bagdam Cafée but also notes that these women were "not from the banlieue or racialized working-class neighborhoods," emphasizing the impact of economic privilege on racial integration.[24] Anita F., a white woman from Marseille, remembers a few women of color at local gay and lesbian bars like the Boulangerie Gaie and the Douce Amère but argues that since these women "didn't make an issue" of their race, they just "blended in."[25] Nicole Miquel, a white woman originally from the Vosges who operated several lesbian bars including the Scandalo in Paris in the 1980s and 1990s, observed that "we had to wait until the late 1990s before a clientele of color felt comfortable enough to show up."[26] Once they did, certain commonalities—of education and class—could sometimes erase racial boundaries. But all did not necessarily go well.

Kachina, a lesbian of color from Guadeloupe who emigrated to France in 1969 to work in a factory as a specialized laborer, assured me that there had always been many lesbians of color in Marseille but remarked that very few were "out" since they were afraid "of what would be done to them" both in their own communities and in white ones.[27] Under her breath she added, "Pour vivre heureux, vivons cachés" (To live happily, live hidden). Kachina also remembered experiencing racism from white lesbians. At the beginning of the 1980s, her girlfriend was white, and others in (white) French lesbian circles "didn't like that." Each time that she and her partner tried to participate at meetings, Kachina related, they were rejected. When she added, "I don't know if that was really racism toward me or if it was a form of intellectual racism," she hinted that there were also class issues at play.

Danielle R., a French woman of color, emigrated from Madagascar to France with her family in 1971 when she was seventeen.[28] Danielle's story involves young love in Paris (with a female classmate of color from Cameroon), familial rejection, verbal insults, arrests (for homosexual sex both as and with a minor), repatriation (to Madagascar), a suicide attempt, forced institutionalization, and conversion therapy (in Geneva).[29] For her parents, she stated, "my homosexuality was an illness that needed to be cured." When the treatment failed, Danielle fled to Montpellier to rejoin her—now single and pregnant—high-school sweetheart. It didn't last. By 1975, however, Danielle was living life as an "out" lesbian in Paris, frequenting both lesbian activist organizations (she joined the Radical Lesbian Front in 1980) and lesbian bars and discothèques like La Champmeslé and the Katmandou. Despite her "out" status, after having agreed to appear on a televised discussion of homosexuality on *Les dossiers de l'écran* in 1984, she "chickened out" at the last minute for fear of being recognized by heterosexual colleagues and neighbors.[30] She laughs about it today (remarking that she was "sure that everyone, even at work," knew she was a lesbian) but notes that at the time, her fear was very real. Questioned on whether her race or ethnicity mattered within the lesbian milieu, Danielle responded that in her case, due to educational and financial privilege she had been "assimilated as white." Lesbophobia, for her, came from outside lesbian spaces: family, school, medical institutions, or urban neighborhoods. Lesbophobic sexual violence, or the threat of it, came primarily from Arab men. As a student in the late 1970s, Danielle and her girlfriend were obliged to avoid certain streets near their university in Nanterre (northwest of Paris) for fear of being attacked by young Arab men who wanted "to teach us a lesson." She likewise recounted how one of her lesbian friends, a woman of color from Montreuil (east of Paris), "really knows how to fight, because she's obliged to defend herself with her fists" against young men of color from the projects.

While Danielle was born into a moderate degree of privilege, like many lesbians, as a single woman of modest means she was downwardly mobile. She has lived most of her adult life in France inside or close to what the French state terms Zones prioritaires (Priority Zones) or Zones urbaines sensibles (Sensitive Urban Zones). These are neighborhoods like the Goutte d'Or district in northern Paris where there is a high percentage of public housing and where unemployment levels regularly double or even triple those elsewhere in France. Such zones are typically neighborhoods with large numbers of North African, sub-Saharan African, and sometimes Asian residents living below the poverty line that have been stigmatized in French public discourse as "no-go zones," "lawless zones," or (even more problematically) "mini-Islamic states" due to their high levels of crime, violence, prostitution, and drug trafficking.[31] Danielle confides that she has never felt safe in the neighborhoods where she lives, has often been subjected to harassment, and doesn't think that the situation has improved with time. Since this harassment occurs even when she is in public alone, she sees her masculine presentation as the root of the problem. My conversations with Filo, a lesbian of color from Cameroon living in Marseille, support this argument in reverse: Filo told me that she'd had far more problems in French society as a result of her race than her sexuality, and she attributed the lack of the latter to her feminine gender presentation.[32]

Danielle R. was one of the last women I spoke to during my second round of interviews for this book in 2013. By the time that we talked, I had already heard many narratives like hers. But while the lesbophobic persecution to which Danielle was subjected in both white communities and communities of color was regrettably commonplace, Danielle's presence as a woman of color in a predominantly white French lesbian world during the 1970s and 1980s was unusual. It is worth noting that her stories, both negative and positive, risk reinforcing two stereotypes that have been successfully mobilized for political ends, particularly (as I explore further below) by France's far-right National Front, now called the National Rally. The first stereotype intensifies fears that all Arab men are sexually violent and/or queerphobic, thereby distracting us from the fact that both sexual violence and queerphobia are also perpetrated by white men and women. This framing of men of color as sexist monsters further supports a vision that both women of color and queer people are victims who require saving by—mostly male—white people. Not only is the stance flagrantly imperialistic, but it also eviscerates the agency so essential to the formation of activist movements.[33] The second stereotype suggests that white French lesbians were not (or are not) racist, thereby obscuring a history of racism and racial conflict inside the French lesbian movement. That is not to say that some French white lesbians have not been dedicated to fighting racial injustice. But many of these efforts were fraught.

In 1988 the mainly white lesbian activist group MIEL conducted a survey on "being lesbian today" in France.[34] Unlike the 2015 lesbophobia survey sponsored by SOS Homophobie discussed above, the MIEL survey did include a question—one—addressing race and ethnicity. But when asked, "Do [French] lesbian groups make space for lesbian minorities (Black, Jewish, Arab, handicapped, elderly, minors . . .)?" more than a quarter of those surveyed failed to respond.[35] Of those who bothered to answer, 70 percent said no. Observing that "we must consider this topic more seriously," the women of MIEL attributed "weak investment" in the issue to the fact that even those who valued "in-depth reflection on lesbian minorities" were still "not ready to contribute to it."[36]

In fact, some white French lesbians had nonetheless been "making space" for race since the early 1970s. For example, the white lesbian-feminist sociologist Colette Guillaumin has written at length about how racism, like sexism, is a social construct that maintains dominant relations of power. Her first work on the topic appeared in 1972.[37] From March 28 to 31, 1986, French lesbians were involved in the eighth annual gathering organized by ILIS (the predominantly white International Lesbian Information Service) in Geneva, Switzerland. The conference sponsored a march to support lesbians of color seeking political asylum. A flyer for the event features a cartoon of a Black Wonder Woman, her hair styled in an afro, bursting through text that reads, "Lesbienne je suis, lesbiennes suivez-moi!" (I am a lesbian, lesbians follow me!).[38] Claudie Lesselier, a white French member of the Radical Lesbian Front and founder in 1983 of the Archives recherches cultures lesbiennes (ARCL) in Paris, has been a supporter of women of color in France since the 1980s. Indeed, the November 1987 issue of the ARCL journal that she published includes one of the earliest testimonials that we have from a Maghrebi lesbian of color.[39] Lesselier has also worked tirelessly in organizations like RAJFIRE (the Réseau pour l'autonomie des femmes immigrées et réfugiées, or Network for the Autonomy of Female Immigrants and Refugees, founded in 1997) to aid undocumented female immigrants to France, especially those who are particularly vulnerable because they are separated, divorced, or single. However, if the efforts of women like Guillaumin and Lesselier both support and "prefigure contemporary debates on intersectionality and sexual citizenship in France" (as Provitola observes more broadly), their work and the work of women like them has largely "failed to garner substantive attention" due to the strength of "the very dynamics that they sought to denounce."[40] Consequently, by the end of the century, lesbians of color took the narrative into their own hands.

LESBIANS OF COLOR AND THE GROUPE DU 6 NOVEMBRE

In 1999 the Groupe du 6 novembre: Lesbiennes issues du colonialism, de l'esclavage et de l'immigration (Group of November 6: Lesbians Begotten [Out] of Colonialism, Slavery, and Immigration) was founded in Paris in response to racism within the white French lesbian movement.[41] The group's title "references," as Paola Bacchetta explains, "a critical relationship to histories, bodies, and political geographies of the postcolonial world." "The notion 'begotten of' [issues du]," she continues, "evokes not only respect for ancestral lands but also the necessity and desire to 're-compose' our own herstory.'" The Groupe du 6 novembre became the "first heterogeneous autonomous self-declared lesbian of color group in contemporary France."[42]

The Groupe du 6 novembre insisted on separatist organizing for women of color in order to foster spaces for analysis, reflection, and dialogue regarding the multiple forms of oppression (heteropatriarchal, racist, lesbophobic, capitalist, classist, sexist) to which women of color are subjected. By 2001 this racially mixed group of women from the Maghreb, the Caribbean, Latin America, and sub-Saharan Africa self-published the bilingual anthology *Warriors/Guérrières*, in which the group contests dominant white conceptions of lesbian identity with intersectional analysis.

Lesbians of color had organized in France prior to the emergence of the Groupe du 6 novembre, but they had done so mainly as feminists. In keeping with historical precedent that had isolated women within immigrant communities, these groups came together primarily along national lines, for example, in associations made up of only Algerian or only Moroccan women.[43] There were a few exceptions to this practice, such as the Coordination des femmes noires (Black Women's Network) formed in Paris in 1976 for women of color throughout the francophone world and the Association des femmes arabes immigrées (Association of Arab Women Immigrants) formed in Gennevilliers in 1982. During the 1970s and 1980s, feminists of color were active in groups like these on behalf of immigrant women's rights. They protested long-standing practices like female genital mutilation and polygamy and against topical issues like the Debré laws that sought to reduce the number of foreign students in France. They also produced their own publications.

In the 1980s young women of color—some of whom identified as lesbian—formed their own groups to fight against parental restrictions, sexual harassment, and domestic violence and for education and the rights to divorce and to work. These groups included the Nanas beurs (banlieue slang for "Arab chicks"), Les meufs rebeux (slang for "Arab women"), and later the Voix d'elles rebelles (Their Rebellious Voices). Lesbians of color were among those who worked to open the Maison des Femmes (Women's Center) in Paris at cité Prost in 1982. And lesbians of color also joined white women in founding the Collectif féministe contre le racism et l'antisémitisme (Lesbian Collective against Racism and Antisemitism) in 1984. According to Bacchetta, this latter group engaged in "spectacular street theater" including "demobiliz[ing] the entire Paris subway system to protest public indifference about rape on a subway."[44] The Groupe du 6 novembre adopted some of these theatrical strategies but rejected interracial approaches, insisting instead on the political necessity of separatism. Creation of and control over their own media was critical to their work.

The Groupe du 6 novembre produced *Warriors/Guérrières* in 2001. The name echoes the title of Monique Wittig's 1969 Amazonian novel about a sex war against men, *Les guérillères* (The guerrillas). To publish their work, the Groupe du 6 novembre established their own press, Nomades'Langues Éditions, whose name reads as a French homophone for the English "no man's land." The largely bilingual French-English volume had a print run of one thousand copies and includes manifestos, poems, a short story, interviews, paintings (reproduced in color), and songs. It was sold primarily to lesbians in France via associative spaces or alternative bookstores. In an introductory essay, the group asserts that this "special publication is *exceptional* in a French context, because historically this is the first time that we, lesbians from migration, colonization, descendants of slavery, have possessed a space of our own."[45] While the anthology opens with contributions specific to French lesbian experience, it also features works by American lesbians "not," as the group explains, "to serve as models" but rather "to show that lesbian migrants exist in all countries and encounter the same difficulties" wherein they have "the same need to express themselves and to be visible in their (in our) difference."[46]

Warriors/Guérrières is a manifesto for lesbians of color. By providing forums for political and creative expression, it aims "to mark a turning point, a transformation in a 'lesbian world' that is far too narrow." "The barriers" between lesbians of color "and other lesbians are historical and political barriers," they write, and these don't simply "disappear just because the 'Waspiennes' of France claim to love women." Indeed, "that they love women, bees, or poppies," the Groupe du 6 novembre angrily remarks, "will in no way bring them closer to migrant lesbians from the dominated classes."[47] Despite their common struggles, they argue "the lesbian, white feminist project does not transcend racism, ethnocentrism, [or] the privileges that imperialist societies, globally dominant, assure to whites."[48] A website, art exhibits, film festivals, demonstrations, and appearances at global conferences (including the UN World Conference against Racism, Racial Discrimination, Xenophobia and Related Intolerance in Durban, South Africa, in 2001) followed. The Groupe du 6 novembre networked with lesbians of color in other French cities and former colonies, as well as with lesbians of color from around the world. In so doing they utilized the mediatic tools of lesbian information activism to create a new type of counterpublic, one with a radically different anticolonial, anticapitalist, and antiracist message and a revolutionary critique of power.

The Groupe du 6 novembre coalesced after triggering actions occurred in two separate settings. The first took place at the fourth meeting of the Coordination lesbienne nationale (CLN), held in May 1999 at Die in the Drôme, during the so-called year of political visibility associated with the passage of the PACS (civil solidarity pact) that granted same-sex couples (among others) the right to form civil partnerships. The Die meeting included both racially mixed and racially segregated workshops on race and racism among its plethora of offerings.[49] Reports suggest that the sessions were volatile. Jennifer Gay, a white American attendee living in France, was unsurprised by the rage that the topic provoked, since, as she observed, "it was the first time that we had addressed . . . the problem of racism in the lesbian community in France."[50] White French women appear to have been more perturbed. Discussion veered from confused—"Should one say 'lesbians of color'? 'Lesbians begotten from immigration'? 'Black, Arab, [or] Asian lesbians'?"—to defensive and hostile. Needless to mention, comments like "It's not my fault that I was born white" or "At one point or another in history, all peoples have been dominators" did not land well when the groups reconvened. One attendee, Marie-Hélène Lefebvre from Caen, noted that "as 'a Franco-French woman'" (by which she presumably meant white) who had previously supported "positive discrimination," she found the "criticisms of universalism" being made by lesbians of color deeply troubling.[51]

In return, women like lesbian filmmaker Dalila Kadri Cheriet (known as Dalila Kadri), a French woman of color of Algerian descent, called out the racism of the "lesbos francofrançaises" (white French lesbians) who directed the Centre Évolutif Lilith (CEL), a large lesbian-feminist organization in Marseille. Kadri denounced those "white middle-class lesbians of a certain age," almost all "profs or former profs," for organizing huge fundraising parties "attended almost entirely by young lesbians from the banlieue, almost all Arabs and Blacks, who pay dearly to get in." "With the money that they make," she scoffed, the CEL hypocritically planned "leisure activities that essentially benefit only themselves." That, too, she insisted, "is racism."[52] Such comments quickly set the terms of what became an increasingly divisive debate.

Conversations around race exploded in French lesbian circles later in 1999 at the eleventh annual French-organized international lesbian-feminist film festival Cineffable: Quand les lesbiennes se font du cinéma (Cineffable: When Lesbians Make Movies), held in Paris that October. Over four days, seven thousand women attended, and eighty films—both feature-length and shorts—were screened.[53] Control over visibility was at the center of conflict. The annual women-only festival (in its thirty-fifth year in 2023) is run by volunteers and entirely self-funded in order to maintain its independence. Cineffable advertises itself as "the great theater where lesbians can situate themselves at the center of the world." Its entire mission lies in making female same-sex desire visible by supporting the production and circulation of lesbian film. "*Être visible* [Being visible]," its website declares, "is showing ourselves to others, but also learning to see ourselves, becoming conscious of our power, gathering in order to construct and legitimize ourselves such that we need not demand the right to exist. Lesbians resist all definitions, they are what they want to show, singly, or in couples, in bed, or elsewhere, to thousands."[54]

A convivial festive affair that provides food and drink between screenings and workshops, Cineffable regularly includes debates on topics of interest to the community. In 1999 a discussion of "cultural diversity" in lesbian cinema aimed to critique the representations of race, Judaism, and "different minorities" in films on the program.[55] One of the films included was the first feature-length fiction film by a lesbian of color to treat lesbians of color in France. *Ombres Solaires: 1ère partie: La rencontre* (1999) is a lesbian love story that takes place in Marseille between two women of color, one an "out" lesbian raised in France and the other a "phantom (or is it [a] fantasy?)" from Algeria who is trying to establish contact with feminist resistance networks during the Algerian War.[56] The film was directed and produced by the same Dalila Kadri who had denounced the CEL at the CLN meeting in Die.[57] Along with a group of about five or six others, Kadri would make similar (and stronger) arguments at Cineffable.

A written report on the Cineffable debate on "cultural diversity" (moderated by Kadri and the African American lesbian director Aishah Shahidah Simmons) is still accessible online.[58] The debate focused on six key points. First, cinema represents society and reflects it. Women of color are invisible in French society. Lesbian cinema is no different. Second, making movies is a luxury. Making movies when Black, in a country where you generally have to be a white man to do so, is a political act. Third, most women "born out of immigration, colonialism, or slavery" are restricted to making short films because feature-length films cost too much to produce. Access to the means of production is crucial. The system claims equality of access, but in reality there is "a real system of apartheid" at work. Fourth, Western racialized stereotypes about lesbian sexuality get reinforced in films made by whites. Racial stereotyping is also endemic to white lesbian cinema. Fifth, acting in lesbian films is a political act. And sixth, in order to combat the pervasive invisibility of lesbians of color in film, white programming committees need "to be sensitive about choosing films that may not concern them, but that may touch others," to "invite more women of color to the rostrum," and to "construct networks of women of color." In sum, the moderators demanded not only that lesbian cinema render the heterogeneity of lesbian experience visible but also that white lesbians serve as allies in stopping racist violence while supporting lesbians of color in resisting their own objectification by inventing—and publicizing—their own cultural forms, "so that [we] can say something other than that which white women would say in [our] place."

The claims sounded reasonable to many, but the debate on "cultural diversity" was just the beginning. Jacqueline Pasquier, a white woman who was then editor in chief of *Lesbia magazine*, describes what happened next in her review of the festival proceedings. Her perspective attests to the divisive nature of racial politics not just in the French lesbian community but also in France at large. Pasquier's grandfather Pierre Pasquier was a French colonial administrator who served twice as governor general of Indochina (1926–27 and 1928–34). Jacqueline was born in Chad in French Equatorial Africa and resided there until she was relocated to France as an adolescent. In a childhood photograph that she showed me when we spoke, she can be seen smiling at the camera at about age ten, clad in a sleeveless floral dress, a safari helmet on her head and a lion cub tucked under each arm.[59] With her personal history deeply implicated in the history of French empire, Jacqueline had a vested interest in the topic of race. The image she chose to illustrate her article, a black-and-white photo of Cineffable jury members from the editorial team at *Lesbia magazine*, shows two white women flanked by two women of color at work. This "integrationist" image can be read as a rebuttal to the accusations of racism made against white women like herself during the festival. The text itself is incendiary.

Pasquier writes: "If the festival is a space for dialogue, it should in no way be a space of aggression." And yet, she reports that at the end of the afternoon, a sort of "commando" of five or six women "from the *Grand sud* [Global South, an obvious reference to race] surged onto the podium in the cafeteria." The group—whose banners carried sarcastic slogans reading "I'm not racist. The proof? I've slept with a Black woman," "You're lucky, a beautiful Arab woman like you—you're every woman's exotic fantasy. Can I have your number?" and "Would you rather be fat, unemployed, Jewish, or Black?"—disrupted "the amicable ambience" that reigned among the women gathered there. Pasquier describes how "after posing for what was probably the photo of the century" and "impos[ing] silence" on the room, the "commando" launched a "violent invective" against an unnamed person present at Pasquier's table, who, the attackers declared, "should be skinned alive" for "racial profiling" at her prestigious Parisian nightclub.[60] As might be presumed (and as Pasquier later confirmed to me), the woman in question was Elula Perrin, whose métisse heritage and paradoxically right-wing politics were common fodder for popular critique. The fact that Pasquier's partner, the white writer Hélène de Monferrand, had just coauthored two detective novels with Perrin (*L'habit ne fait pas la nonne* and *Ne tirez pas sur la violoniste*, both published by Éditions Double Interligne in 1998) and that the three women shared political persuasions would not have been lost on some of *Lesbia magazine*'s readers.

Prior to concluding, Pasquier paints the incident as "scandalous" and denounces the intruders as poorly educated (they mispronounce "Elula" and cannot identify the name of her club), cowardly (they flee the scene), and paranoid ("they see racism everywhere!"). Conveniently erasing French racism, Pasquier then chastises the group for daring to see their own experience as comparable to that of "our sisters who are subjected daily" to racial violence "in certain corners of the world." Flipping racial victimization on its head, Pasquier archly concludes that this disruption has posed "a real security problem" for future Cineffable festivals, both in terms of who should be permitted to attend and also—in a direct rebuke to Kadri—in terms of whose films should be shown.

The *Lesbia magazine* article on the intervention of women of color at Cineffable encapsulates the defensive self-righteousness endemic to white privilege within certain French lesbian circles. No wonder that lesbians of color were outraged. The activists submitted a response protesting the magazine's defamatory depiction of their actions, but *Lesbia magazine*—perhaps influenced by Pasquier, who, as noted, was then editor in chief—failed to publish it. The Groupe du 6 novembre was founded in the weeks that followed. The women of the group rapidly recognized that they needed their own media outlets. One of the first sources they found was a journal published by a network of lesbians from Lyon called *Madivine* (sometimes written *Ma Divine*, an expression that means "lesbian" in Haitian Creole). The title of the group and its journal reprised that of an earlier lesbian journal, also called *Madivine*, launched by lesbians in Lyon in 1983 following the collapse of *Quand les femmes s'aiment*. The 1983 iteration had seen only one issue, and the second iteration was no different. The contents however, diverged widely, for this one was consecrated entirely to lesbians of color.

On the journal's cover is a 1967 photograph of three Black American lesbian-feminist members of the Black Panthers, all in black leather, fists raised in the Black Power salute. Above them is a quote (in French translation) from Audre Lorde: "I continue to combat all forms of oppression. Racism. Sexism. Homophobia. No one is free so long as others are oppressed. Break the silence."[61] The table of contents lists essays by French lesbians of color, poetry, translations of key texts by American lesbians of color (including Lorde and bell hooks), an article by Colette Guillaumin, and a statement from the Groupe du 6 novembre apropos of the Cineffable affair and *Lesbia magazine*'s coverage of it. In their rebuttal, the Groupe du 6 novembre defend their actions as "spontaneous" and further claim that, far from having "fled the scene," they had been vigorously applauded for their efforts by many white women in the space. They also denounce Pasquier for utilizing her influence and "mediatic privilege" to offer a "deformed version" of their intervention and then refusing them the right to respond. "How," they ask, "could such an article [as Pasquier's] have been accepted and published . . . with the support of the entire editorial team"? Identifying this behavior as "ideologically alarming," they call on "all lesbians from forced migration, from colonization (past, present), and/or descended from slavery to participate in their actions to fight all forms of oppression, racism, discrimination, sexism, lesbophobia, situations of social, economic, or political exclusion, and precarity."[62] In proffering an intersectional, anticolonial analysis of lesbian-feminist oppression, the Groupe du 6 novembre attempted to radicalize the entirety of the French lesbian movement. Other groups and publications followed in their wake.

Two years later, in 2001, Arab lesbians in France and Algeria collaborated as Les N'Déeses, a lesbian collective nourished by cultural and linguistic exchange. By 2002 Les N'Déeses had mounted a multilingual website, called Sehakia (Arabic for "lesbian"), which posted practical and legal information for lesbians in Arabic, French, and English and served as a space for Maghrebi lesbian intellectual and cultural production both in France and abroad. Three years after that, in 2005, the Groupe LDR (Lesbiennes contre les discriminations et le racisme, or Lesbians against Discrimination and Racism) was founded by an African lesbian feminist with an aim to combating racism and discrimination against the lesbian community in France and globally. Committed to maintaining solidarity in diversity, the Groupe LDR fervently rejected the whitewashing that often occurred in French lesbian milieu. Finally, in 2009 a group of women formed the association Lesbiennes of Color (LOCs), a still extant federative organization for lesbians of color from Africa, the Americas, the Antilles, the Caribbean, the Middle East, and Asia. The LOCs maintain a Facebook page and created the website Espace LOCs out of a need for a "political 'safe' space" where they could "make [themselves] visible to each other, but also to take public positions together without waiting for others to accord [them] the privilege of speaking."[63]

Dalila Kadri died by suicide in 2017 at age sixty-seven. Upon her death, lesbians from the Collectif des racinées (Unrooted Collective), a Lyonnais group dedicated to political antiracism and decolonial feminism, many of whom had first congregated around Kadri in the 1990s, posted a fanzine to the filmmaker in tribute to her political and personal impact on the lesbian community. This was not, as they said, an "homage" but rather a "*femmage*" (riffing on the French word for women, "femme") to the filmmaker.[64] Just eight years earlier, Kadri had joined lesbian sociologists Salima Amari, Jules Falquet, Claudie Lesselier, and others in organizing the colloquium Lesbiennes, migrations, exil, et racisme: Quand les "minoritaires s'en mêlent" (Lesbians, migrations, exile, and racism: When minorities intermingle) at the University of Paris 8 (also known as the University of Vincennes), bringing a conversation long relegated to the margins into the educational sanctum of French society. Salima Amari, then Falquet's student, went on to finish a dissertation in 2015, which was published in book form in 2018, on immigrant and second-generation lesbians of color from North Africa.

In *Lesbiennes de l'immigration: Construction de soi et relations familiales* (Lesbians from immigration: Self-construction and familial relations), Amari draws on fifty-two interviews conducted in Paris, Lille, Lyon, and Toulouse to convince us to set aside the Western notion that modern French lesbianism is necessarily a public experience.[65] She argues that even as Maghrebi migrant women (and women of Maghrebi descent) who desire women seek to distance themselves from the "threefold constraint[s] (virginity, marriage, and motherhood)," they often continue to privilege filial and familial loyalties anchored in a working-class ethos premised on the sexual division of labor.[66] Amari further maintains that due to their powerful ties to communal and familial social structures, living a lesbian life as a woman of color in France requires not "coming out" but rather finding creative alternatives for expressing same-sex desire, often through subterfuge or selective truth-telling. "Tacit understanding" with family and loved ones, Amari insists, is frequently the strategy of choice, since it circumvents conflict and permits the maintenance of familial and community bonds.[67] In this, Amari essentially suggests that for North African women of color who live in France, "becoming lesbian" has little to do with the kinds of public practices and performances that this book has argued were critical to the production of French lesbian subjectivity. And yet, as the Groupe du 6 novembre and the multiple groups organized by lesbians of color that followed demonstrate, when women of color *did* come out in France, they actually became visible in many of the same ways as white lesbians before them: via access to and use of public spaces and media.

DYKES IN BLACK AND WHITE: LA VIE PARISIENNE UPSIDE DOWN

While cruising the internet as I completed research for this book, I came across a YouTube video from the 1998 Paris Pride March that took place barely a year before the emergence of the Groupe du 6 novembre.[68] Its thrumming beat drives us through three minutes and twenty-four seconds of hot dykes, some topless, dancing on and around the float for the Pulp, a popular lesbian nightclub that took the French underground scene by storm when it opened in 1997 at 25 boulevard Poissonnière on the Grands Boulevards (an intoxicating stretch of shops, arcades, brasseries, and entertainment venues that has been attracting a heterogeneous mix of Parisians since the late eighteenth century). The short video offers an entirely different view of the French lesbian landscape at the end of the twentieth century. It cuts in quick succession through joyful images of white women and women of color dancing together on the float and in the streets in a powerful multiethnic public expression of unadulterated glee and erotic abandon. Among its cheekiest images are shots of young women on top of the Pulp Pride parade float, playfully gyrating against naked, life-sized, plastic and impossibly sexist female blow-up dolls (both white and Black), kitted out with erect nipples and oral and genital holes for sucking and fucking. If we pay careful attention, we can catch a glimpse of fifty-nine-year-old Elula Perrin on the street below, clapping and smiling as she marches in their midst. Clearly "becoming lesbian" in France has been, and remains, a complex, multilayered process.

Like Toulouse's Bagdam Cafée but less overtly political, the Pulp was a late twentieth-century incarnation of the interwar sapphic cabaret. The Pulp opened, as queer art historian and journalist Elisabeth Lebovici explains, "exactly at the moment when five [queer] Parisian clubs were required [by the French administration] to close" on charges of drug trafficking.[69] Its name referenced the "lesbian pulp novels" produced between the 1930s and late 1950s that (despite their sordid plotlines) offered queer readers "a space that made their existence identifiable, or at least plausible."[70] Dark and musty, with a tiny dance floor and red double doors opening onto the street, on packed evenings the Pulp welcomed as many as five hundred patrons. On such nights the line at the entrance of (mostly female) pierced and tattooed hipsters, chic Parisians, wannabe provincials, students, and underground celebrities could snake all the way to the end of the street. In Lebovici's words, the Pulp was "the centrifugal force, the somber and pulsating echo chamber that turned 'la vie Parisienne' and the image of lesbians as we had known it, upside down."[71] In the context of my work, Lebovici's comments cannot help but raise the specter of Suzy Solidor and quite another La Vie Parisienne, one that had first turned "the image of lesbians, as we had known it, upside down" in France some six decades earlier.

Run by Michelle (Mimi) Cassaro and DJ Sophie Lesné and featuring a cutting-edge soundtrack of electronica, rock, and punk, the Pulp was also home to resident DJs Chloé and Jennifer Cardini, as well as to a rotating cast that included DJ Sextoy (Delphine Palatsi) and DJ Tampax (Axelle Le Dauphin), both goddesses of the French lesbian club scene. The fact that Scratch Massive (a mixed-gender DJ duo composed of Maud Geffray and Sébastien Chenut) and gay radio DJ Ivan Smagghe were also pillars of the Pulp's DJ roster speaks to the club's mixed-gender policy: The club's slogan "The girls' club where boys like to come too" appeared on promotional matchboxes and print publicity. But while men were admitted, the club's feminist politics demanded that they were also monitored and removed if they misbehaved with the female clientele. According to Fany Corral, who programmed the Pulp's music, "It was a space to educate heterosexuals." She laughs, adding, "I remember explaining to one guy who we'd kicked out: 'Listen up buddy, the whole world belongs to you. We [lesbians] have one hundred square meters. So here, if we tell you no, it means no.'"[72] Queer journalist Didier Lestrade notes, "Everything at Le Pulp had a political grounding because it harbored modern, arty, messy, drunk feminists."[73] Perhaps in a rebuff to the elitism that reigned at Perrin's clubs (the Katmandou had closed in 1990, but her subsequent clubs Privilège and the Rive Gauche were equally expensive), entry was free. According to Mimi Cassaro, the Pulp "was a club managed by dykes with dyke energy. Some high, some very organized, some very political, with very different forms of activism. It was a girl thing—it had never existed before. It was also a place where we succeeded in breaking down barriers between gays, straight people, and different social classes."[74]

For three years, the Pulp published a monthly magazine, which was distributed for free as a form of publicity. *Housewife: Le magazine du Pulp* was originally associated with L'Entr'acte (a dance hall that hosted afternoon tea dances opened by Laurence, a lesbian who presented one of Fréquence Gaie's only interactive broadcasts aimed specifically at young lesbians).[75] The Pulp took over publication after *Housewife*'s fourth issue. *Housewife* was lesbian, campy, hard-core, queer guerrilla activism, a fanzine that, like the profusion of lesbian media that preceded it, collapsed the distinction between those who control media and those who consume it. The bilingual French-English mini-magazine ran to sixteen glossy pages printed in color and had a distribution of 2,500 copies. At least twenty-seven issues were produced over the course of three years. It was edited by Axelle Le Dauphin and the Canadian artist and writer Dana Wyse.[76]

Racial diversity was a given in *Housewife*. Lesbians of color figure in every issue; racial difference is celebrated, and racism mocked. On opposing pages, for example, the authors reprint a "shameful product" they've found elsewhere promising skin-whitening ("extra-fast") against an advertisement—and "product"—of their own devising. Theirs (which is facetiously hawked by Wyse's fabricated "Jesus Had a Sister Productions") promises that if you take "just one pill" you can "Be Black Immediately! No surgery required."[77] Alternately scathing, hilarious, irreverent, and tender, *Housewife*'s cover pages testify to the magazine's disparate interests and raunchy humor; issue 9 declares in English, "Black Is Beautiful," and issue 13 exclaims in English, "Cow-Girls Are Back!" Issue 22 announces in French, below the smiling image of a gun-toting Black woman, "Become Friends with Your Ex: The Best without the Worst," and in bold black letters below that (in English): "How to Find Your Clitoris" (fig. 9.1). Issue 23, in French, next to a photo of the smiling man in question: "Meet Heinz Schwarz: The man that Germany claims can convert any lesbian into a heterosexual. Just by the sound of his voice." Or, finally, issue 24, which angrily announces in blue ballpoint pen scrawled on a white background: "I've had it! I hate my computer! I've gone to Canada to see my mother. Create your own *Housewifes* and mail them to me. The winner takes 3,000 francs!" Inside? Nothing but blank pages.

The coverage in *Housewife: Le magazine du Pulp* attests to the club's multiracial clientele: Lestrade, who was a great fan of the venue (although he didn't go often because of his HIV positive status and deep involvement with AIDS activism during those years), writes:

> In a country as divided as France, where the basic concept of community is fought against by the entire political class and where lesbians have always been less acknowledged, these lesbians were breaking the unspoken clubbing diktat by mixing up ethnic and sexual groups. Their club was for every kind of freak who did not feel comfortable in other Parisian clubs. With its dirty feel and low ceiling, it didn't exactly look great, but it embodied the modern punk spirit—and its trashier aspects are what gave its DJs and organizers a cultural status.[78]

FIGURE 9.1: Cover of *Housewife: Le magazine du Pulp*, no. 22 (June 1999). The headline reads "Become Friends with Your Ex: The Best without the Worst." Produced, conceived, and written by Axelle Le Dauphin and Dana Wyse.

Clémentine Goldszal, in her title for the third of a four-part retrospective on French lesbian life published in *Le Monde* in 2022, names the Pulp "the lost paradise of Parisian lesbian culture." In the same article, Axelle Le Dauphin refers to it as a "laboratory of experiments" and a "temple for all those girls who had no cash, came from the banlieue, and weren't welcome in the *clubs de gouines* [lesbian clubs] because too Black, too Arab, or too poor." "You lined up and you entered," recalls director Rebecca Zlotowski; "The crazy pleasure of the place [derived from the fact that] it was democratic, and very much associated with music."[79] While the Pulp was adamantly intended as *un club des filles* (a girl's club), by enthusiastically mixing genders, races, and classes, the Pulp moved French lesbian culture into a new era—a period when lesbians would be, for better or worse, encompassed within a new queer politics of nonnormativity.

The Pulp was forced to close in 2007, when the City of Paris took over its building to transform it—perhaps appropriately given its egalitarian ethics—into low-income housing and a parking lot. A Pulp website established in the late 1990s trailed on for a few more years as a virtual meeting place, but eventually it too shut down. For a younger generation of lesbians who didn't know the Pulp during its heyday, the club and its DJs, particularly Sextoy, one of the first female French techno DJs to develop an international reputation, have taken on the status of myth.

DJ Sextoy, a tiny, tattooed force of nature and epic international figure of the lesbian night, who owed much of her celebrity to the Pulp and who first came to public attention on the airwaves of Radio FG—the heir to Fréquence Gaie—died of unknown causes at age thirty-three in 2002. By then she had DJed in London, Tokyo, New York, and Moscow, spinning for jet-setting clientele at shows by Jean Paul Gaultier, Louis Vuitton, Baccarat, and L'Oréal and at the Cannes Film Festival. One year prior to her death, she wore Gucci while hosting the 2001 Fête de la Musique for Bertrand Delanoë, mayor of the City of Paris, on the grand square in front of the Hôtel de Ville. On hearing of her passing, Delanoë paid public tribute to the queer icon in an official press release, an act we might see as prefiguring Mayor Cohen's public celebration of Toulouse Lesbopole in 2009. Mayor Delanoë eulogized Sextoy as an "amazing artist" who, "through her talent and her audacity," had become "one of the emblematic figures of the electronic music scene in Paris and internationally."[80] At his request Sextoy was buried in Paris's Père Lachaise Cemetery, one of the most visited cemeteries in the world and the final resting place of a panoply of French and foreign celebrities. Delanoë's own status as one of the first openly gay politicians to hold a major office in France (he came out on French TV in

1998) paired with DJ Sextoy's burial at Père Lachaise are both testimonies to the changing face of the French public sphere.

Such achievements aside, conflicts over race, religion, and politics were nonetheless splintering French lesbian counterpublics by the start of the twenty-first century. In the wave of queerphobia that erupted across France in 2012 during the push to legalize gay and lesbian marriage—just a few short years after the Pulp closed its doors for good in 2007—the principle of "France for the French" (code for white nationalism) convinced a segment of the lesbian and gay community to get in bed with the far-right National Front. How did this happen, and what does it mean for the future of French lesbianism?

CONCLUSION

In the 2018 article "Queer Fascism and the End of Gay History," historian Laurie Marhoefer takes up "the very old, erroneous claim that fascism was queer."[81] Notwithstanding mainstream media's periodic obsession with "queer fascism" however, popular opinion generally situates queer politics on the liberal left. And yet, racist right-wing sympathies among some individuals in the (mainly white) French lesbian community demonstrate that this too is not always so. Indeed, as Marhoefer observes, "There is no natural political position for people who feel same-sex desires."

In France, race has been a decisive factor in dividing lesbian and gay allegiances across the political spectrum. In supporting homosexuals of color and women of color, books like Franck Chaumont's *Homo-Ghetto: Gays et lesbiennes dans les cités* and purportedly antiracist feminist organizations like Ni putes, ni soumises (Neither Whores, Nor Virgins; Chaumont serves as the group's director of communications) have paradoxically contributed to the vilification of Arab culture, which is uniformly depicted as both misogynist and queerphobic.[82] The situation is complicated, not least because Arab culture often *is* misogynist and queerphobic.[83] The persistence of these problems can shroud important efforts to eradicate sexism, racism, and queerphobia that emerge from inside these same communities—pulling attention away, for example, from strategies developed by lesbians of color in organizations like those explored above. Meanwhile the Far Right, as incarnated by Marine Le Pen, the leader of the National Rally (the former National Front) who has thrice been a candidate for president (and who advanced twice—in 2017 and 2022—to the second round of the French presidential elections), profits from such negative stereotypes. Le Pen uses them to court the homosexual (and Jewish) vote while demonizing people of color, particularly inside Islamic communities in France whose religion and culture, she argues, are incompatible with French republican values.

Since 2011, when Marine Le Pen took leadership of the National Front, she has rebranded herself as the defender of homosexual vulnerability while studiously distancing herself from the politics of her homophobic father, Jean-Marie Le Pen, who, as former party head, famously stated that homosexuality was a "biological anomaly" and that AIDS victims should be sent to "AIDS-atoriums."[84] In contrast, Marine Le Pen focuses on the "de-Islamization" of French society in order to situate herself as the bulwark that will protect lesbians and gays from racialized homophobia. (Oddly, any such appeal is premised on the presumption that one cannot simultaneously be both a person of color and queer.) Marine Le Pen has surrounded herself with queer politicians, including the openly gay Sébastian Chenu (not to be confused with Sébastien Chenut, of DJ Scratch Massive and the Pulp fame). A founding member of the gay rights organization GayLib, Chenu was named vice president of the French National Assembly in 2022. By pitting a vilified *communautarisme* (understood as tribalism/factionalism and not to be confused with the English "communitarianism") against the abstract individualism of the French Republic, Marine Le Pen has successfully wooed mainly white lesbians and gays who are fed up with terrorist attacks, economic crises, and religious conflict and who want to retreat into the safe invisibility of the (white) republican world. Several such women were among those whom I interviewed for this book.

In essence, Marine Le Pen uses white privilege and the "Islamic threat" to gain homosexual support, a strategy that distracts from her party's own disinterest in (if not outright contempt for) homosexual rights and permits her to attract both homosexuals *and* homophobes. And unfortunately, when white French lesbians like journalist Caroline Fourest (who opposes Le Pen and her politics) defend *laïcité* (secularism), protest against public veiling, or condemn sexism and violence against women and queer people in Arab communities, they risk inadvertently furthering the right-wing alliances on which what is now called "homonationalism" is based.[85] Thus, as Sam Bourcier observed in 2005, in France, "*Déblancher* [unwhitening] and *dé-straightiser* [unstraightening] both the media and education has to be a priority."[86] Such actions would go a long way toward recognizing and—if not rectifying—at least pushing back on forms of racism and homophobia that remain all too entrenched in certain sectors of French society.

Part of the problem that the abstract principles of French republicanism pose to marginalized minorities like the lesbians discussed here is that when they inhibit groups from making claims on the public sphere *as groups*, they negate the very processes of collective identification and politicization that enabled women who desired women to come together in France as a social force—a counterpublic—in the first place. Moreover, if women who love women adopt a private politics of indifference anchored in republican universalism (thereby gaining assimilationist privileges as abstract citizens), they undermine those on the fringes who are either excluded from or choose to reject the republican imperatives—whiteness, marriage, parenthood, *laïcité*, adherence to sexual and gender norms—to which the French nation broadly aspires. At the same time, when lesbians gather together in "difference," the process of politicization that *Becoming Lesbian* describes has paradoxically narrowed possibilities for female sexual expression, hewing instead toward a binary definition of sexual identity that pits female same-sex desire against heterosexuality while eschewing other incarnations of erotic attraction and gender performance. Until recently, "becoming lesbian" in France has also largely meant ignoring the myriad ways in which sexual subjectivity is traversed by multiple forms of identification—particularly racial and religious. Arguments for intersectionality, whether theorized by lesbians of color in organizations like the Groupe du 6 novembre or embodied by dykes like those from the Pulp, offer a path forward.

CONCLUSION

In March 2016 I visited Haut-de-Cagnes on the French Riviera, a medieval village of some 650 people to which the celebrated singer Suzy Solidor "retired" when she relocated from Paris to the South of France in 1960. Shortly after she arrived, Solidor opened a cabaret in the vaulted cellar beside her new house on the town's main square. Haut-de-Cagnes is perched above the city of Cagnes-sur-Mer in the commune of the same name, which has been governed by the center-right since 1962. Almost one-third of its population voted for Marine Le Pen in the first round of the 2017 presidential elections, a percentage almost ten times higher than that in the Paris region of Île-de-France. In the immediate postwar years the townspeople were known for their conservatism and their homophobia.

When I arrived in Haut-de-Cagnes it was raining and already dark. I wasn't tired, however, nor cowed by the weather, so I decided to stroll through the tiny town's steep cobbled streets before turning in. I came across two old men smoking on a porch under a neon sign that read "Cercle des Amis" (Circle of friends). They looked like locals. I approached, introduced myself as a historian from America, and asked if they had ever heard of a woman named Suzy Solidor. To my surprise, their faces lit up, and they summoned me inside. The place appeared to be some sort of neighborhood club; it was noisy, crowded, and filled with old men drinking cheap wine out of short stout glasses around long wooden tables. My "hosts" introduced me to the crowd. And thirty-three years after her death, Suzy Solidor emerged, like an apparition in their midst.

Over the next four days, I met Solidor's former gardener, her cook, and the artists living in what had been her home. I read letters that she had written on thin blue stationery and looked at photographs of the singer posing with neighbors. I spoke to those who adored her and those who despised her, from the admiring former guardian of the Château Grimaldi (an impressive fortress that dominates the town square and now serves as a museum where forty of Solidor's celebrated portraits hang) to the grudging restaurateurs whose establishments had competed with hers. In a retirement home in the neighboring city of Cannes I interviewed Solidor's last accordionist, a ninety-two-year-old lesbian musician named Liliane Robert. Sometimes Liliane napped while I worked, her frail frame tucked into a narrow bed surrounded by stuffed animals. On the wall over her head were paintings by her mother, Émilienne Delacroix, a seamstress turned artist who was mentored by Picasso and Jacques Prévert. A signed photograph of Picasso hung beside them.

Liliane performed with Suzy Solidor for over twenty years. When we met, she was still leading Haut-de-Cagnes's May Day Parade, slowly marching in front of the revelers, her gnarled fingers playing the heavy black-and-white accordion fastened by a wide leather strap to her stooped back. One of the most magical moments I had while filming interviews for this book occurred before I left Liliane's room that evening. She took out her accordion and sang for me.[1] Liliane claimed that the song, titled "Fallait-il?" (Did we have to?), had been sung by Edith Piaf but never recorded. She was wrong. Piaf released the song in 1961, shortly before Liliane began performing in Solidor's cabaret. "It was my 'fetish-song,'" she told me. "It always brought down the house." "Fallait-il?" tells the story of the end of a troubled romance. The lyrics are gender neutral. But from Liliane's perspective there was no doubt; this, she assured me, was a tale of lesbian love: "One girl leaves," Liliane explained, "and the other is heartbroken."

I also met Jean-Marc Nicolaï, who had grown up in his great-grandmother's house next door to Solidor's on the Place du Château. He now serves as a guide for Haut-de-Cagnes's Department of Tourism. Jean-Marc described his great-grandmother's outrage at the "bad [lesbian] behavior" that Solidor attracted to their town.[2] As a small boy Jean-Marc used to play on the Place du Château. His great-grandmother would keep watch from a nearby bench. He remembered "very well" the day that she sprang to her feet and cried out in panic: "Jean-Marc, come quick, come quick! Come back to the house, quickly, quickly! I don't want you to see that. . . . Come inside! Come inside!" The cause of old Madame Nicolaï's distress? Two women, passionately embracing on the threshold of Solidor's home.

The sight was not unique: many townspeople spoke to me of how the lesbians who descended on the town shortly after Solidor arrived shocked locals by flaunting their private desires in public. Others were intrigued. Gregarious, extravagant, and opinionated, Solidor revivified Haut-de-Cagnes's declining economy and brought glamour and excitement to the townspeople's lives. She employed locals but also included them; every year on her birthday she threw an enormous costume party that became a celebrated annual event. Solidor became a member of the community. Despite local resistance and her own disregard for feminist activism, both Solidor's sapphic cabaret and her very existence incarnated a form of lesbian politics. Her impact on Haut-de-Cagnes makes this clear. In transforming—in queering—the public sphere, she transformed public opinion. Indeed, Jean-Marc Nicolaï confided in me that he believes that his willingness to accept that people have the right to love who they want regardless of gender is a direct result of his childhood exposure to lesbian visibility in the community where he lived.

Throughout this book I have argued that becoming visible was integral to "becoming lesbian" in modern France. The creation of modern lesbian subjectivity required the affirmation of group identity—the creation of lesbian counterpublics—whose "private" difference was rendered publicly visible in order to challenge political and social discrimination in the French public sphere. Access to and control of public spaces and media were necessary to that history. But the results were (and are) never stable; as the effects of race, religion, and gender performance on lesbian oppression illustrate, difference is riven by structural inequalities, stereotypes born of difference are constructed and contested, and representations change. Moreover, whereas visibility can empower and connect, if we cannot control its meaning it can also endanger. And whereas invisibility can disempower and isolate, it can also protect. Thus, both when we are denied the capacity to represent ourselves to the world and when the world fails accurately to reflect that representation back—or intentionally distorts it—we lack power.[3]

Becoming Lesbian analyzes the historical appropriation of spaces and media that connected the queer female subcultures that emerged in sapphic cabarets in early twentieth-century France with the lesbian counterpublics forged in material spaces and mediascapes following the student revolutions of 1968. In France this spatial and mediatic appropriation—evident in the efforts of groups to exert rights in the public sphere *as groups*—is particularly fraught because, as Marianne Blidon observes, it "comes up against the problematic status of 'difference'" and the difficulty of "adopting a strategy based on a notion of collective identity" in a nation where collectivities are disavowed.[4] By demonstrating how women who desire women confronted the French republican ideal, this book exposes the ways in which marginalized groups help shape the divisions between public and private that structure sexual citizenship and social geography in France today. Control of and access to the media is a critical part of this process.

In utilizing the lives of women who love women to explore the ways in which being seen, in its most profound sense, is central to human dignity, this book also makes three additional claims: First, it argues that lesbian histories *matter*, not simply for what they tell us about other things but because the experiences of women who desire other women—women like Frede and Miki; Lulu de Montmartre and Madame Moune; Colette Mars and Gribouille; Danièle Cottereau and Catherine Gonnard; Éliane Laubus, Brigitte Boucheron, and Jacqueline Julien; Dalila Kadri and DJ Sextoy—matter. Second, *Becoming Lesbian* insists that due to the double domination that *all* lesbians experience as both women and sexual minorities, lesbian history cannot be subsumed within histories of feminism, histories of homosexuality, or queer histories more broadly. And finally, third, by revealing lesbian identity as a process of "becoming," this book demonstrates that sexual desire is a living construct that waxes and wanes across time and place, even over the lifetime of a single individual; Suzy Solidor, a woman who alternately presented herself as hyperfeminine, masculine, lesbian, bisexual, and heterosexual is a perfect example. Given these convictions, *Becoming Lesbian* is thus a plea for seeing and celebrating how the world that we live in already is, always has been, and always will be far queerer, that is, far less normal and far more diverse, than we generally recognize. Rendering that queerness more public renders our world both more real and—potentially—more equitable.

Around the globe we remain at once fascinated and troubled by the boundaries that divide public from private. Whether addressing if homosexuals should be allowed to marry, the rights of Muslim women to veil or unveil, the presence of transgender soldiers in the military, support for gender affirmation surgery, or medical assistance to either begin or end life, in our everyday world we are regularly assailed by issues that invite us to determine if, and how, individuals should be permitted to express their private lives in public. *Becoming Lesbian* reminds us that we are not alone in these concerns and demonstrates that they have a complex past. Indeed, the international salience of these matters, visible in the recent resurgence of far-right politics and religious extremism—two arenas that have long sought control over the public/private divide—make histories like the French one told here more important than ever.

> To those who are privileged to speak, we will not offer the luxury of our silence.
>
> GROUPE DU 6 NOVEMBRE

ACKNOWLEDGMENTS

This book was written across almost fifteen years and a global pandemic. The list of those I am privileged to thank is very long. *Becoming Lesbian* would not exist without the testimonies of the many women who courageously spoke with me about their lives. My first debt is to them. A few among them became exceedingly dear to me, especially Jacqueline Julien, Éliane Laubus, Brigitte Boucheron, Caroline Godon-Gauthier, and Monique Isselé. Jacqueline and Brigitte introduced me to the history of lesbian activism in France—their commitment to bettering the lives of women who love women is inspiring. The same can be said of Catherine Gonnard, who was especially generous with her knowledge and resources in the early years of my research. I learned so much from Catherine, and from her work with Elisabeth Lebovici. The late Danielle Charest convinced the Archives recherches cultures lesbiennes to let me photograph documents outside regular opening hours. I am grateful to Danielle, and sorry that she did not live to see this book. My first contacts with many women came via a 2010 conference at the University of Angers on the French feminist movement. I thank Christine Bard for organizing that event and for her scholarship. In post-lockdown France, I met Barbara Osorovitz and her wife, Natacha Chetcuti-Osorovitz. Barbara, your enthusiasm for my project buoyed me. Natacha's work on lesbians has influenced my own.

I often tell my students that while writing is a solitary enterprise, no work of scholarship is produced in isolation. This one is no different.

Becoming Lesbian has benefited from the insights of a far-flung group of scholars whom I'm blessed to count as colleagues and friends. At the University of Illinois Urbana-Champaign, Antoinette Burton is a remarkable mentor; she has read and responded to more versions of this work than I (or she, I imagine!) care to count; I am especially thankful to her for organizing a manuscript workshop in 2021 with Regina Kunzel, Camille Robcis, and Andrew Israel Ross. My thanks to each of them. Andrew and I met when we served on the American Historical Association's Committee on LGBT History. Since then, he has provided me with the type of smart, detailed feedback that is every scholar's dream. My dear friend Mark Steinberg (a.k.a. "Papa Velour") likewise read the entire manuscript and gave me vital input. I will not forget a ride through Chicago where we reworked the introduction, or a conversation with Mark and the unparalleled Daniela Steila in a château in Burgundy where we debated the book's title. I love you both. Here at the U of I, I also thank Peter Fritzsche for hiring me and for his insights and unstinting support, Clare Crowston (now in Vancouver), Mark Micale, John Randolph, Ikuko Asaka, Teri Chettiar, Dana Rabin (my current chair), and all of those who attended the history workshops for their time and suggestions. And then there is the magnificent Anke Pinkert. Anke, what can I say? You are so terrifically wise, insightful, hilariously funny, and have a huge heart. I adore you.

Beyond the Midwest, Judith Coffin—who makes the most daunting tasks seem easy—and Whitney Walton both provided steady encouragement. I was trained as a historian by Bonnie G. Smith, Joan Wallach Scott, Matt K. Matsuda, and the late John Gillis. I thank them all. The lovely Dagmar Herzog brainstormed the structure of this book with me in a conference hotel room in Baltimore. I remain grateful and am awed by her brilliance. Jérôme Bourdon's work ethic inspires me; his brain stimulates mine. Dancing "together" during lockdown via Zoom, with me in Urbana and him in Tel Aviv, was pure joy. Jadwiga Pieper Mooney's indomitable spirit ignites my own. My writing group, Lidia Radi, Lisa Maruca, and Catherine Wearing, have kept me grounded and setting that daily writing timer for over three years. I would not be done now if not for them. I thank Amy Villarejo for inviting me to present at Cornell and Carolyn Dean for bringing me to Yale. Laura Doan, Todd Shepard, and Laurie Marhoefer have challenged, helped, and inspired me. The late Michael Sibalis's pioneering work on the history of homosexuality in France paved the way for many of us. Michael introduced me to Régis Revenin, whose guidance, especially in the police archives, proved vital. Conversations with Julian

Jackson and his beautiful book on gay men in postwar France inspired me to write this one.

I am grateful to executive editor Alan Thomas and to my editor Dylan Montanari at the University of Chicago Press for their work and for answering my many emails! Doug Mitchell, editor of the history of sexuality par excellence, shepherded my work into their care; he is deeply missed. Thanks are due, too, to Elizabeth Ellingboe for her meticulous copyediting, Fabiola Enríquez for help with the book's images, Lisa DeBoer for thoughtful indexing, Kristen Raddatz for promoting the book, and Lucina Schell for working toward a French translation. To my readers at the press, your questions, challenges, and attention to my errors have made this book better. Sections of this book were republished with the generous consent of the *Journal of the History of Sexuality*, *French Historical Studies*, the Liverpool University Press, and the University of Nebraska Press. I am beholden to the editors and readers who worked on these publications.

I thank my students, undergraduate and graduate, for bringing me fresh perspectives. My former advisee Ryan Allen, PhD (History), offered vital feedback. Steve Sherman, PhD (Urban Planning), made magic with the maps and genealogical chart. My research assistants Thierry Ramais, Robin Sudanan Turner, Charlotte Prieu, and Jesse Keruskin and undergrads Zain Al-Khalil, Octavio Cuesta de la Rosa, and Julia and Gigi Mulvaney handled countless tasks essential to advancing my work. Wenjing Yu reached out to me from Paris when I was completing this book. I am so glad we became friends. Her wonderful master's thesis on the cabarets féminins opens new avenues for research.

Multiple institutions and organizations supported the writing of this book. At the University of Illinois Urbana-Champaign I am grateful to the Campus Research Board, the Illinois Program for Research in the Humanities (now the Humanities Research Institute), the Center for Advanced Study, and the European Union Center for their generous assistance. Special thanks are due to the College of LAS for appointing me as the Lynn M. Martin Professorial Scholar from 2023 to 2026. The National Endowment for the Humanities, Cornell University's Zwickler Memorial Research Grant, and the Camargo Foundation in Cassis, France, also provided me with the precious funding, time, and space that intellectual work requires. I have presented excerpts of this project at conferences around the world. I thank all of my colleagues, especially at the Society for French Historical Studies and the Western Society for French History, for their feedback.

Historians require archives and archivists, and this book has benefited from many. I thank the women who shared their personal papers, especially Brigitte Boucheron, Jacqueline Julien, Éliane Laubus, Danièle Cottereau, Patricia Mercader, Claire Guillaud, Mireille Vigne, Odile Debloos, and Valérie Léonard. Roy Winnick provided the treasure trove that is Miki and Frede. I am grateful for his patient confidence and for his introduction to Denis Cosnard. The mischievous Alexandre Dupouy at Les Archives d'Éros provided stunning photographs. I thank Nicole Fernández Ferrer and the Centre audiovisuel Simone de Beauvoir; Michèle Larrouy and the Archives recherches cultures lesbiennes; Christine Bard and the Centre des archives du féminisme; Annie Metz and the Bibliothèque Marguerite Durand; the Archives de la préfecture de police de Paris, especially Bernard Bassett; Gladys Pilastrini at the Réunion des musées nationaux Grand Palais for exceptional help with the Brassaï photographs; the Bibliothèque nationale de France; Rachel Denoeud, Claude Mussou, and Sophie Le Goff at the Institut national de l'audiovisuel; the Fonds Suzy Solidor at the Musée Renoir in Cagnes-sur-Mer; the Archives de la ville de Paris; the Centre Louise Labé at the Université Lumière Lyon 2; Brenda J. Marston at the Human Sexuality Collection, Rare and Manuscript Collections, Cornell University Library, Ithaca, New York; and countless librarians at the research library at the University of Illinois Urbana-Champaign.

Dear friends in France and elsewhere enrich my life. Rachel Denoeud—your generosity, intellect, resourcefulness, and kindness know no bounds. Luli Halpern, thank you for the "happiness kit" when I sorely needed one. I thank Adam Sutcliffe, Dietrich Lawrence, Andrew Shallcross, Masumi Iriye, Lucia Pasini, Bibia Pavard, Richard Ivan Jobs, Pelin Tığlay, and Jane Kuntz for their friendship (and Jane for ideas about French translations!) and Linda Gardiner for the use of her Paris apartment. Katherine Panter Roland, Trees-ah Moretti Elder, and Ellen Hoffman, I am sorry that this work has kept me farther from each of you than I would like for so long. To Hope Dye, Lisa Colpoys, Cathy Schneider, Janet Kafkas, and Suzanne Kaufman, thank you for making Chicago begin to feel even more like home.

The women I claim as my real and adopted family, my cousin Neesa, my aunt Georganne, my niece Flora-Sae, and my former students the wonderful Anqi Pan (now pursuing a PhD in the history of sexuality) and the luminous Emily Pinheiro (now a PhD and soon to be an MD and whom I love and cherish as my own), have also been an audience for this book's ideas. I spent more than ten years in partnership with the brilliant, compassionate Angie Estes. This book was born of our profound collaboration and would not exist without her. Thank you for helping me to think so deeply about what it means to be a woman who loves women in this world.

To the men in my life (including my father, Anton S. Chaplin, and my brothers Scott and Daniel) who now know far more about French lesbians than they ever imagined they would, thank you for engaging so respectfully in this work and for supporting the ways in which it has absorbed my time and energies. My book is the better for my conversations with you, and my world far better.

The pandemic brought me the unexpected, astonishing gift of Marcelo Halpern. Since then, you have become my staunchest ally, my best friend, my beloved, and my betrothed. NYIP indeed. I thank you for your boundless generosity, for your deep commitment to social justice, for feeding me in oh-so-many ways, and for cocreating the beautiful world that we share. You are my miracle. I love you.

NOTES

INTRODUCTION

1 Marilyn "Miki" Leff Papers, collection of Roy Winnick of Princeton, NJ (Roy is Miki Leff's nephew) (hereafter cited as Miki Leff Papers). Quotes are from Miki's handwritten notes (in English, dated November 2000) and from an undated cassette recording of Miki speaking with a male interviewer found in her documents. Miki was born Marilyn Leff in the Bronx, New York City, on either May 16, 1925 (according to the date on her US Social Security Summary Statement of Earnings), or May 16, 1927 (according to the French translation of her birth certificate and the date on her gravestone). I suspect the earlier US date is correct.

2 Miki was a quick study: a later contract specified that Miki's "knowledge of two languages, French and English, and her friendly relations with personalities in the foreign press, will make her a useful auxiliary for our house." Contract signed by Le Carroll's manager C. Rivollier, dated November 29, 1957, Miki Leff Papers.

3 Sarah Fishman's monograph *From Vichy to the Sexual Revolution: Gender and Family Life in Postwar France* (New York: Oxford University Press, 2017) argues that proscription did not always equal practice, particularly amongst the working classes. However, her book virtually ignores homosexuality, thus reinforcing arguments about the repression and invisibility of homosexuality at this time. On post-WWII repression in other national contexts, see David K. Johnston, *The Lavender Scare: The Cold War Persecution of Gays and Lesbians in the Federal Government* (Chicago: University of Chicago Press, 2004), and Brian Lewis, *Wolfenden's Witnesses: Homosexuality in Postwar Britain* (New York: Palgrave Macmillan, 2016). Julie A. Podmore and Line Chamberland are among the many scholars who take postwar lesbian invisibility as a "societal, historical, and spatial" given. See Podmore and Chamberland, "Entering the Urban Frame: Early Lesbian Activism and Public Space in Montréal," *Journal of Lesbian Studies* 19 (2015): 192.

4 Simone de Beauvoir, *The Second Sex*, trans. and ed. H. M. Parshley (New York: Vintage Books, 1989).

5 This definition of "to queer" comes from Mark Gevisser, *The Pink Line: The World's Queer Frontiers* (London: Profile Books, 2020), xi.

6 For early work on the politics of lesbian visibility, see Terry Castle, *The Apparitional Lesbian: Female Homosexuality and Modern Culture* (New York: Columbia University Press, 1993).

7 On French law and homosexuality since the Revolution, see Scott Gunther, *The Elastic Closet: A History of Homosexuality in France, 1942–Present* (London: Palgrave Macmillan, 2009), esp. 6–38. Véronique Blanchard summarizes the history of French laws on sexuality more broadly in *Vagabondes, voleuses, vicieuses: Adolescentes sous contrôle de la Libération à la libération sexuelle* (Paris: Éditions François Bourin, 2019).

8 This was true even after laws protecting public morals and prosecuting sexual crimes were enshrined in 1810 in the Code Napoleon.

9 "Outrage aux bonnes moeurs" (gross public indecency) was the charge used to censor the Moulin Rouge pantomime *Rêve d'Égypte* in 1907 after Colette and her lover Mathilde de Morny kissed onstage. On the scandal that ensued, see Claude Francis and Fernande Gontier, *Colette* (Paris: Perrin, 1997), 205–6. After 1920, laws against "antinatalist propaganda" were also used to prosecute same-sex practices. For example, the homosexual review *Inversions* (1924)—the second of its kind in France and the first to appear since *Akademos* had ceased publication in 1909—was charged with public indecency on the grounds that it promoted an "infertile" form of sexuality. *Inversions* was forced to cancel publication after its fifth issue. Gross public indecency was not abolished from the French Penal Code until 1994.

10 The Vichy measure against pederasty and lesbianism concerned sexual acts with or between minors under twenty-one. Such acts were subject to a prison sentence and/or fine. The law was retained by de Gaulle's post-Liberation administration after the war as Article 331. In contrast, the age of consent for heterosexual acts was thirteen in 1942. See Antony R. H. Copley, *Sexual Moralities in France, 1780–1980: New Ideas on the Family, Divorce, and Homosexuality* (London: Routledge, 1989), 203–4. The passage on July 18, 1960, of the Mirguet Amendment, which named homosexuality as a "social plague" and increased penalties for public indecency when related to same-sex behavior, further supported these measures. On Vichy gender policies as a response to the post-WWI emergence of what Mary-Louise Roberts has called a "civilization without sexes," see Francine Muel-Dreyfus, *Vichy and the Eternal Feminine: A Contribution to a Sociology of Gender* (Durham, NC: Duke University Press, 2001), and Miranda Pollard, *Reign of Virtue: Mobilizing Gender in Vichy France* (Chicago: University of Chicago Press, 1998). See also Mary-Louise Roberts, *Civilization without Sexes: Reconstructing Gender in Postwar France, 1917–1927* (Chicago: University of Chicago Press, 1994).

11 On the decriminalization of homosexuality in France, see Antoine Idier, *Les Alinéas du Placard: L'abrogation du délit d'homosexualité (1977–1982)* (Paris: Éditions Cartouche/TMR, 2013).

12 After 1805, if a woman wanted to wear trousers, she required a permit from the

police. The interdiction was partially raised in 1882 and 1909 if she was either on horseback or engaged in the "sport of bicycling." Female deputies were not permitted to enter the National Assembly in pants until 1980. To date, employers are still permitted to impose the wearing of skirts if they so desire. See Florence Tamagne, *A History of Homosexuality in Europe: Berlin, London, Paris, 1919–1939*, 2 vols. (New York: Algora Publishing, 2004), 1:47. See also Christine Bard, *Une histoire politique du pantalon* (Paris: Éditions du Seuil, 2010), 12; and Christine Bard, *Les garçonnes: Modes et fantasmes des années folles* (Paris: Flammarion, 1998), 13. For debates over the abrogation of the ordinance, see Christine Bard, "Le droit au pantalon: Du pittoresque au symbolique," *La vie des idées*, March 1, 2013, https://laviedesidees.fr/Le-droit-au-pantalon.html.

13 I take the term "sexual misfits" from Michael Lucey, *Someone: The Pragmatics of Misfit Sexualities, from Colette to Hervé Guibert* (Chicago: University of Chicago Press, 2019).

14 Scholarship on the public sphere is vast. Jürgen Habermas initiated contemporary debate with his field-changing *The Structural Transformation of the Public Sphere: An Inquiry into a Category of Bourgeois Society* (1962; Cambridge, MA: MIT Press, 1991). Joan B. Landes was among the first to critique the androcentrism of the Habermasian public sphere: "The bourgeois public," she claims, "is essentially, not just contingently, masculinist." Joan B. Landes, *Women and the Public Sphere in the Age of the French Revolution* (Ithaca, NY: Cornell University Press, 1988), 7. On the historicization of Habermas's conception of the public sphere, see Benjamin Nathans, "Habermas's 'Public Sphere' in the Era of the French Revolution," *French Historical Studies* 16, no. 3 (Spring 1990): 620–24.

15 Jeremy Jennings, "Citizenship, Republicanism and Multiculturalism in Contemporary France," *British Journal of Political Science* 30, no. 4 (October 2000): 577.

16 On the French Republic and republicanism, see Edward Berenson, Vincent Duclert, and Christophe Prochasson, eds., *The French Republic: History, Values, Debates* (Ithaca, NY: Cornell University Press, 2011).

17 The concept of the public sphere as a "unified fiction which, because it can appear real, exerts real political force" is from Harold Mah, "Phantasies of the Public Sphere: Rethinking the Habermas of the Historians," *Journal of Modern History* 72 (March 2000): 168. Simon Watney's work on AIDS in the media exemplifies the fictional nature of this concept: when Watney notes that the media almost uniformly imagines the public sphere as white and heterosexual his point is not that the public *is* uniformly white and heterosexual, but rather that this fantasy of the public sphere powerfully disenfranchises all those individuals who are not. Simon Watney, *Policing Desire: Pornography, AIDS, and the Media* (Minneapolis: University of Minnesota Press, 1996).

18 Consequently, the French path to homosexual rights contrasts sharply with that taken in countries like the United States, where minority groups have legal status and thus greater political power.

19 Enda McCaffrey explores this dilemma in *The Gay Republic: Sexuality, Citizenship and Subversion in France* (Burlington, VT: Ashgate, 2005).

20 See Nancy Fraser, "Rethinking the Public Sphere: A Contribution to the Critique of Actually Existing Democracy," *Social Text*, no. 25/26 (1990): 67.

21 Michael Warner, *Publics and Counterpublics* (New York: Zone Books, 2005), 56–57, 63.

22 On the theorization of sex in public and public sex in France, see Andrew Israel Ross, *Public City, Public Sex: Homosexuality, Prostitution, and Urban Culture in Nineteenth-Century Paris* (Philadelphia: Temple University Press, 2019).

23 Gert Hekma clarifies that despite the ways in which classical liberal theory defines citizens "in abstraction," the fact is that "citizens have genders, sexualities, and bodies that matter in politics." The concept of "sexual citizenship" (first articulated by David Evans in *Sexual Citizenship: The Material Construction of Sexualities* [London: Routledge, 1993]) takes this truism into account. Sexual citizenship, as Hekma further explains, "bridges the private and public and stresses the cultural and political sides of sexual expression." See Gert Hekma, "Sexual Citizenship," GLBTQ Archives, accessed June 11,2022, http://www.glbtqarchive.com/ssh/sexual_citizenship_S.pdf. For the French case, see also McCaffrey, *The Gay Republic*, and Daniel Borrillo and Éric Fassin, eds., *Au-delà du PaCS: L'expertise familiale à l'épreuve de l'homosexualité* (Paris: Presses Universitaires de France, 2001).

24 Others before me have made this claim about gay men. See especially, for example, George Chauncey, *Gay New York: Gender, Urban Culture and the Making of the Gay Male World, 1890–1940* (New York: Basic Books, 1995).

25 Laura Doan, *Disturbing Practices: History, Sexuality, and Women's Experience of Modern War* (Chicago: University of Chicago Press, 2013), esp. chapter 2, "Genealogy Inside and Out" (58–93).

26 Laura Doan, personal communication with the author, January 2019. Volume 1 of Michel Foucault's *The History of Sexuality* is the key reference. Michel Foucault, *The History of Sexuality*, vol. 1, *An Introduction*, trans. Robert Hurley (1976; New York: Viking, 1988). Foucault's work is all too often used, however, to justify the advent of homosexual identity as a historical truth, rather than to encourage inquiry into the conditions that produced sexual subjectivity and gave it importance at a specific moment in time. See David Halperin, "Forgetting Foucault: Acts, Identities, and the History of Sexuality," *Representations* 63 (1998): 93–120. George Chauncey charts changing medical perceptions of female same-sex desire in "From Sexual Inversion to Homosexuality: Medicine and the Changing Conceptualization of Female Deviance," *Salmagundi*, no. 58/59 (Fall 1982–Winter 1983): 114–46.

27 Embracing queer historicism does not mean that I am uninterested in the historical precursors to queer political agendas today. But following Colin R. Johnson, I track transformations in gender and sexual alterity over time in order "to expand . . . the insufferably cramped logic of modern sexual identitarianism by demonstrating not only that the current state of affairs has not always been what it is today but also that it need not be what it is today and actually in some respects is not, even today, what we imagine it to be." Colin R. Johnson, *Just Queer Folks: Gender and Sexuality in Rural America* (Philadelphia: Temple University Press, 2013), 18.

28 Elaine Blaire, "Designing Women: Making Space for Women to Behave Badly in 'Portrait of a Lady on Fire' and 'The Favorite,'" *New York Review of Books*, December 17, 2020, 41.

29 All translations from the French are my own, unless otherwise stated. Other names for female same-sex desire include *uranienne*, *gomorrhéene*, *anandryne*, *femme aux femmes*, and *femme-homme*. Christine Bard discusses terminology in *Les garçonnes*, 96. Victoria Thompson notes that by the 1830s and 1840s we already see references in France to a "protohomosexual 'type,' labeled alternatively pederast or *antiphysique* (for men), tribade or lesbian (for women)." "This early homosexual," she continues, "not yet the medically defined and criminalized 'invert' of the late nineteenth century, was increasingly used to symbolize a 'reversal of the regular order.'" See Victoria Thompson, "Creating Boundaries: Homosexuality and the Changing Social Order in France, 1830–1870," in *Homosexuality in Modern France*, ed. Jeffrey Merrick and Bryant T. Ragan Jr. (New York: Oxford University Press, 1996), 104.

30 The Amazons were a mythological Greek tribe of matriarchal warrior women who lived without and fought men. The term is often used to refer to a woman who desires other women.

31 While *jules* was used exclusively for lesbians, *nana* also applied to women more generally. *Jules* were sometimes associated with pimps. By the late 1960s the term *jules* was contested as aping a patriarchal masculinity that many women found objectionable. See Florence Tamagne, "Paris: 'Resting on Its Laurels'?," in *Queer Cities, Queer Cultures: Europe Since 1945*, ed. Matt Cook and Jennifer Evans (London: Bloomsbury, 2014), 244. See also Francesca Canadé Sautman, "Invisible Women: Lesbian Working-Class Culture in France, 1880–1930," in *Homosexuality in Modern France*, ed. Jeffrey Merrick and Bryant T. Ragan Jr. (New York: Oxford University Press, 1996), 179; and Nicole Albert, *Lesbian Decadence: Representations in Art and Literature of Fin-de-Siècle France*, trans. Nancy Erber and William A. Peniston (2005; New York: Columbia University Press, 2016), especially chapter 4, "The Birth of the Female Invert" (85–93), for a lexicon of these expressions. Line Chamberland claims that whereas the term *femmes aux femmes* was commonly used in Quebec, where it "left no doubt as to the exact nature of the relationship between the two women, including the sexual component," it was not used in France "where [feminine] lesbians were frequently called *gouines* and butches were called *Jules*." My interviewees used the term *femmes aux femmes* sufficiently to suggest that she is mistaken. Line Chamberland, "Remembering Lesbian Bars: Montreal, 1955–1975," in *Gay Studies from the French Cultures: Voices from France, Belgium, Brazil, Canada, and the Netherlands*, ed. Rommel Mendès-Leite and Pierre-Olivier de Busscher (New York: Haworth, 1993), 234.

32 The term brings to mind the title of Colette's collection of twenty novellas, *Les vrilles de la vigne* (*The Tendrils of the Vine*). The first novella, from which the collection takes its name, was first published in 1905.

33 Laure Murat quotes Alfred Delvau's observation (from his 1864 *Dictionnaire érotique moderne par un professeur de langue verte* [Freetown: Imprimerie de la Bibliomania Society, 1864]) that "the Third Sex: is that to which the *pédérastes* [gay men] and *gougnottes* belong." See Murat, *La loi du genre: Une histoire culturelle du "troisième sexe"* (Paris: Fayard, 2006), 67. The insult *sale gouine*—meaning "dirty dyke"—is still heard all too frequently today.

34 On the use of the term "queer" in France, see Denis M. Provencher, *Queer French: Globalization, Language, and Sexual Citizenship in France* (Hampshire: Ashgate,

2007). See also Bruno Perreau, *Queer Theory: The French Response* (Stanford: Stanford University Press, 2016).

35 Whereas "trans" generally refers to transgender or transsexual people, the asterisk in Halberstam's "trans*" signifies not an identity but a "politics of transitivity" that "holds off the certainty of diagnosis." Jack Halberstam, *Trans*: A Quick and Quirky Account of Gender Variability* (Oakland: University of California Press, 2018), xiii, 4. On the pitfalls of necessarily equating female masculinity with lesbianism, see also Jack Halberstam, *Female Masculinity* (1998; Durham, NC: Duke University Press, 2019), esp. 46.

36 The English "butch/femme" is sometimes rendered in French as *butch/fem* in order to distinguish the queer identity of the feminine partner (*fem*) from the French *femme* meaning both "wife" and "woman."

37 The phrase is from Daniel Boyarin and Elizabeth Castelli, "Introduction: Foucault's *The History of Sexuality*," 363, as quoted in Afsaneh Najmabadi, "Beyond the Americas: Are Gender and Sexuality Useful Categories of Analysis?," *Journal of Women's History* 18, no. 1 (Spring 2006): 17.

38 Shari Benstock, *Women of the Left Bank: Paris, 1900–1940* (Austin: University of Texas Press, 1986). Much of this scholarship is biographical or autobiographical. See, for example, Natalie Clifford Barney's *Women Lovers, or the Third Woman*, ed. and trans. Chelsea Ray (Madison: University of Wisconsin Press, 2016), xi; Andrea Weiss, *Paris Was a Woman: Portraits from the Left Bank* (San Francisco: Harper San Francisco, 1995); Tirza True Latimer, *Women Together, Women Apart: Portraits of Lesbian Paris* (New Brunswick, NJ: Rutgers University Press, 2005); Jennifer Shaw, *Exist Otherwise: The Life and Works of Claude Cahun* (London: Reaktion Books, 2017); and Jeffrey H. Jackson's trade paperback *Paper Bullets: Two Artists Who Risked Their Lives to Defy the Nazis* (Chapel Hill, NC: Algonquin Books, 2020), which is also about the gender nonconforming Claude Cahun and Cahun's lover Marcel Moore.

39 Marie-Jo Bonnet, *Les relations amoureuses entre les femmes XVIe–XXe siècle* (1995; Paris: Éditions Odile Jacob, 2001), first published as *Un choix sans equivoque* (Paris: Denoël-Gonthier, 1981).

40 Leslie Choquette, "Gay Paree: The Origins of Lesbian and Gay Commercial Culture in the French Third Republic," *Contemporary French Civilization* 41, no.1 (2016): 1–24; Brigitte Lhomond, "Between Man and Woman: The Character of the Lesbian," *Journal of the History of Homosexuality* 25, no.1/2 (1993): 66; Sautman, "Invisible Women."

41 Albert, *Lesbian Decadence*; Gretchen Schultz, *Sapphic Fathers: Discourses of Same-Sex Desire from Nineteenth-Century France* (Toronto: University of Toronto Press, 2014).

42 David C. Rose, "Paris Lesbos," *Journal of Lesbian Studies* 13 (2009): 362–72.

43 Sarah Fishman's 2017 *From Vichy to the Sexual Revolution* is one of the more recent incarnations of this work.

44 Julian Jackson's *Living in Arcadia: Homosexuality, Politics and Morality in France from the Liberation to AIDS* (Chicago: University of Chicago Press, 2009) is one of the few books to argue for bolder connections between the 1950s and the 1970s.

45 Claudie Lesselier, "Aspects de l'expérience lesbienne en France, 1930–1968" (DEA thesis, Université Paris 8, 1987); Lesselier, "'Pourquoi une femme avec une

femme?' Écrire l'amour lesbien, 1945–1968," *Amazones d'hier, lesbiennes d'aujourd'hui* 18 (March 1987): 14–32; Lesselier, "Silenced Resistances and Conflictual Identities: Lesbians in France, 1930–1968," *Journal of Homosexuality* 25, no.1/2 (1993): 106; and Lesselier, "Formes de résistances et d'expression lesbiennes dans les années 1950 et 1960 en France," in *Homosexualités: Expression/répression*, ed. Louis-Georges Tin and Geneviève Pastre (Paris: Éditions Stock, 2000), 105–16.

46 See Ilana Eloit, "Lesbian Trouble: Feminism, Heterosexuality, and the French Nation (1970–1981)" (PhD diss., London School of Economics, August 2018); Hannah Leffingwell, "'Our Point of Departure Is Feminist': *Féminin Masculin Avenir* and the Intersectional Origins of Women's Liberation in France, 1967–1980," *Gender & History* 34, no. 1 (2022): 263–81; Camille Morin-Delaurière, "Étude comparée de Rennes et de Paris: Une autre histoire des relations entre les mouvements féministes et lesbien en France (1970–1980)," *Féminismes et lesbianismes* 33, no. 2 (2020); and Blase A. Provitola, "In Visibilities: The *Groupe du 6 novembre* and the Production of Liberal Lesbian Identity in Contemporary France," *Modern and Contemporary France* 27, no. 2 (2019): 223–41. See also Hugo Bouvard, Ilana Eloit, and Mathias Quéré, eds., *Lesbiennes, Pédés, arrêtons de raser les murs: Luttes et debats des mouvements lesbiens et homosexuels (1970–1990)* (Paris: La Dispute/SNÉDIT, 2023). The introduction to this collection (cowritten by the editors) offers an excellent guide to the most recent scholarship on French lesbianism in the post-1968 decades (11–35).

47 For a list of interviewees, see the bibliography. While many women wanted to be identified by their own names, some requested that I use pseudonyms. My references respect these requests.

48 It is now well settled that oral history can provide important empirical information that simply does not exist in traditional sources. On writing oral history, see Lynn Abrams, *Oral History Theory* (London: Routledge, 2016). On the methodological challenges of using oral history to reconstruct the sexual past, see the brief overview in Rebecca Jennings, *Unnamed Desires: A Sydney Lesbian History* (Melbourne: Monash University Publishing, 2015), esp. xviii–xxii.

49 That said, taboos shifted dependent on context. For instance, among certain women who identified as lesbians, desiring men was inadmissible. Pregnancy was often presented as the only justifiable motivation for engaging in heterosexual sex. In keeping with the political correctness that followed the North American feminist and lesbian sex wars of the 1970s and 1980s, sexual practices that involved sadomasochism, pornography, role-play, and the use of dildos (called *godemichés*) and phallic substitutes beyond fingers and tongues were contentious and primarily—but not always—avoided. Those women who did speak positively of such practices often requested to do so "off the record," a fact that reminds us that, like heteronormativity, homonormativity has power to constrain the historical narrative.

50 On female same-sex desire within marriage in the United States, see Lauren Jae Gutterman, *Her Neighbor's Wife: A History of Lesbian Desire within Marriage* (Philadelphia: University of Pennsylvania Press, 2020).

51 Michael Rustin, "Reflections on the Biographical Turn in the Social Sciences," in *The Turn to Biographical Methods in the Social Sciences*, ed. Prue Chamberlayne,

Joanna Bornat, and Tom Wengraf (London: Routledge, 2000), 49, 45. For a classic example of the "exceptional normal" in Italian microhistory, see Carlo Ginzberg, *The Cheese and the Worms: The Cosmos of a Sixteenth-Century Miller* (Baltimore: Johns Hopkins University Press, 1992).

52 Alessandro Portelli, "The Peculiarities of Oral History," *History Workshop Journal* 12, no. 1 (Autumn 1981): 100.

53 Much work on the history of homosexuality has zeroed in on cities, since urbanization has been considered a key condition for the emergence of nonnormative sexual and gender behaviors. George Chauncey's *Gay New York* set the standard. See also Nan Alamilla Boyd, *Wide-Open Town: A History of Queer San Francisco to 1965* (Berkeley: University of California Press, 2003); Lillian Faderman and Stuart Timmons, *Gay L.A.: A History of Sexual Outlaws, Power Politics and Lipstick Lesbians* (New York: Basic Books, 2006); and Marc Stein, *City of Sisterly and Brotherly Loves: Lesbian and Gay Philadelphia, 1945–1972* (Chicago: University of Chicago Press, 2000). On Europe, see Tamagne, *History of Homosexuality*, which focuses on London, Paris, and Berlin. On France, for an early example, see Gilles Barbedette and Michel Carassou, *Paris Gay 1925* (Paris: Presses de la Renaissance, 1981).

54 Lesbian cabarets and bars have been critical to the development of lesbian subcultures in various national contexts. Most research on this history focuses on the 1950s through the 1970s. On the United States, see Lillian Faderman, *Odd Girls and Twilight Lovers: A History of Lesbian Life in Twentieth-Century America* (New York: Columbia University Press, 1991); and Janet Kahn and Patricia Gozemba, "In and around the Lighthouse: Working-Class Lesbian Bar Culture in the 1950s and 1960s," in *Gendered Domains: Rethinking Public and Private in Women's History*, ed. Dorothy Helly and Susan Reverby (Ithaca, NY: Cornell University Press, 1992), 90–106. On Canada, see Chamberland, "Remembering Lesbian Bars," and Liz Millward's more recent *Making a Scene: Lesbians and Community across Canada, 1964–1984* (Vancouver: University of British Columbia Press, 2015), especially chapter 1, "The Lesbian, Drinking, Is Never at Her Best," 43–75. On the lesbian bar in film, see Kelly Hankin, *The Girls in the Back Room: Looking at the Lesbian Bar* (Minneapolis: University of Minnesota Press, 2002). On the United States, see Elizabeth Lapovsky Kennedy and Madeleine D. Davis, *Boots of Leather, Slippers of Gold: The History of a Lesbian Community* (New York: Routledge, 1993). On the European context, see, for example, Tamagne, *History of Homosexuality*.

55 This work illuminates continuities between the pre- and the post-WWII period that dispute the current scholarship on the topic. Marie-Jo Bonnet, Claudie Lesselier, Anne-Marie Sohn, and Florence Tamagne all maintain that World War II destroyed what had been a vibrant lesbian community in France. Bonnet makes the case for an "astonishing rupture" between the pre- and post-WWII periods. Bonnet, *Les relations amoureuses*, 339. Lesselier likewise emphasizes that female homosexuality went underground in France after World War II. Lesselier, "Aspects de l'expérience lesbienne," and Lesselier, "Silenced Resistances," 106. Sohn insists that after "a first golden age" in the interwar period, "homosexuality plunges into clandestinity." Anne-Marie Sohn cited in Michael Sibalis, "La vie homosexuelle en France pendant la Seconde Guerre mondiale," in *Homosexuel.le.s en Europe pendant la Seconde Guerre mondiale*, ed. Régis Schlagdenhauffen, Julie

Le Gac, and Farbice Virgili (Paris: Nouveau Monde, 2017), 149. Tamagne closes her two-volume history of homosexuality in Europe with the claim that with the rise of fascism in Europe "the black of night" was back for homosexuals "for at least thirty years." Tamagne, *History of Homosexuality*, 2:271. Elsewhere Tamagne claims continuities in pre- and postwar (male) homosexual bar culture but still insists that lesbians "rarely visited bars" ("Paris," 243). My research reveals that while a few sapphic cabarets (like La Silhouette) closed in 1939, many others (including La Vie Parisienne and Chez Jane Stick) remained open throughout the war, and still others (like Le Monocle) reopened after a brief closure.

56 Florence Tamagne insists that a comparative analysis of homosexuality in Europe between the wars reveals three tendencies: communal in Berlin, "societal" (i.e., acceptable among the British elite) in London, and individualist in Paris. Tamagne, *Histoire de l'homosexualité en Europe: Berlin, Londres, Paris, 1919–1939* (Paris: Éditions du Seuil, 2000), 53–75. In contrast, I argue that if we look solely at *female* milieu in France, we see instead a profoundly interconnected picture that aligns more closely with the arguments proposed about the collective nature of sapphic subcultures in both interwar Germany and midcentury England and the United States. On Germany, see Laurie Marhoefer, *Sex and the Weimar Republic: German Homosexual Emancipation and the Rise of the Nazis* (Toronto: University of Toronto Press, 2015), especially chapter 2, "Lesbianism, Reading and Law," 52–79; and Marti M. Lybeck, *Desiring Emancipation: New Women and Homosexuality in Germany, 1890–1933* (Albany: State University of New York Press, 2015), especially chapter 5, "Emancipation and Desire in Weimar Berlin's Female Homosexual Public Sphere," 151–88. On Britain, see Rebecca Jennings, *Tomboys and Bachelor Girls: A Lesbian History of Post-war Britain 1945–1971* (Manchester: Manchester University Press, 2013), 107–33. On the United States, see Kennedy and Davis, *Boots of Leather*.

57 Henri Lefebvre, *Le droit à la ville* (Paris: Éditions Anthropos, 1968). The "right to the city" derives from Lefebvre's argument that hegemonic groups enact their dominance through the ways in which they inhabit and produce particular spaces via embodied practices. See also Lefebvre, *The Production of Space*, trans. Donald Nicholson Smith (Oxford: Blackwell, 1991).

58 Provitola, "In Visibilities," 223.

59 See Lefebvre, *Le droit à la ville*, as well as David Harvey, *Social Justice and the City* (London: Edward Arnold, 1973), and Edward Soja, *Seeking Spatial Justice* (Minneapolis: University of Minnesota Press, 2010).

60 The quote is from Valerie Traub, *Thinking Sex with the Early Moderns* (Philadelphia: University of Pennsylvania Press, 2016), 283.

CHAPTER ONE

1 The Bal de la Montagne Sainte-Geneviève was located at 46 rue de la Montagne Sainte-Geneviève.

2 On the Bal's early years, see Mondomix's interview with Emile Vacher, son of the first owner, on January 1, 2009, http://blogs.mondomix.com/accordeon.php/2009/01/23/emile-vacher. See also Ange Bastiani, *Les bals secrets de Paris* (Paris: Solar, 1973), 82–83. According to a police report from March 17, 1939, the Bal was

previously known as the Pradal. File 103119, JC/CAB1, Archives de la préfecture de police de Paris (hereafter cited as APP).

3 Press coverage reveals that Arabs also attended the Bal in the 1930s. "Yéyette-aux-yeux-doux" (Sweet-eyed Yéyette, a.k.a. Paulette Robert), for example, was murdered by Adoub Cherif after she met him at the Bal. See "'Yéyette-aux-yeux-doux' préféra Raoul à Chérif," *L'humanité*, May 25, 1939.

4 Martin Pénet identifies the Bal's directress as La Grande Paulette. See Pénet, "IV - 1919/1939: Des années vraiment folles par Martin Pénet," in *Contribution subjective à une mémoire gaie: Littérature, cinéma, arts, histoire . . .* (blog), published February 7, 2018, by Jean-Yves Alt, http://culture-et-debats.over-blog.com/article-341637.html. Whether this is a mistake or a reference to another woman is unclear. Gilles Schlesser states that the Bal reopened in 1951 with Anys as director in *Le cabaret "rive gauche": De la Rose Rouge au Bateau ivre: 1946–1974* (Paris: Éditions de l'Archipel, 2006), 234.

5 Police reports note that between 11:00 p.m. and 1:30 a.m. on March 17, 1939, the Bal held about two hundred clients and was so packed that the dance hall overflowed. File 103119, JC/CAB1, report dated March 17, 1939 (APP).

6 Bastiani, *Les bals secrets*, 82–83.

7 The bar scene in Radclyffe Hall's *The Well of Loneliness* is set in Paris. French literary representations of lesbian bars can be found in Guy de Maupassant's "Paul's Mistress" (1881), Émile Zola's *Nana* (1880), Colette's *The Pure and the Impure* (first published as *Ces plaisirs . . .* in 1932), and Françoise Mallet-Joris's *Le rempart des béguines* (1951). French cinematic depictions of sapphic cabarets appear in all three versions of *La garçonne* (1923, 1936, 1957), as well as in *Simone Barbès ou la vertu* (1979) and *Gigola* (2010). That said, with fifty clubs and cabarets for women in the interwar years, Berlin surpassed Paris in the size of its sapphic scene. On Berlin, see Ruth Margarete Roellig, *Berlins lesbische Frauen* (Leipzig: Gebauer, 1928). In other Western European countries, this happened later. For example, the first lesbian bar did not appear in Amsterdam until 1955. See Gert Hekma, "Amsterdam Gay Bar Culture 1930–1970," accessed June 23, 2022, https://www.academia.edu/14426607/Amsterdam_Gay_Bar_Culture_1930_1970?email_work_card=title; originally published in Hungarian in *Budapesti Negyed* 55 (2007): 215–26.

8 "Pink capitalism" is a term for the LGBTQ market and the industries and technologies that target it. It often privileges gay men while ignoring women and trans people.

9 Laura Doan, *Disturbing Practices: History, Sexuality, and Women's Experience of Modern War* (Chicago: University of Chicago Press, 2013), 20. Elizabeth Wilson contradicts this argument, claiming "'gay identities' were well established" in "Parisian lesbian and gay circles during the *belle époque*." See Elizabeth Wilson, *The Sphinx in the City: Urban Life, the Control of Disorder, and Women* (Berkeley: University of California Press, 1991), 61.

10 Laura Doan and Jane Garrity, introduction to *Sapphic Modernities: Sexuality, Women and National Culture*, ed. Laura Doan and Jane Garrity (New York: Palgrave Macmillan, 2006), 8.

11 Interestingly, Azenor's mother "always dressed [Azenor] as a boy." Azenor in Claude Lesselier's documentary, *Instants de vie, portrait d'Hélène Azénor* (France,

1987) (DVD of original video recording courtesy of the Centre audiovisuel Simone de Beauvoir, Paris).

12 Lesselier, *Instants de vie*.

13 The comment is from Charles Virmaître's *Trottoirs et lupanars* (Paris: Librairie Jouffroy, 1893), 158, quoted and translated in Leslie Choquette, "Gay Paree: The Origins of Lesbian and Gay Commercial Culture in the French Third Republic," *Contemporary French Civilization* 41, no. 1 (2016): 3, 5. See also Leslie Choquette, "Paris-Lesbos: Lesbian Social Space in the Modern City, 1870–1940," *Proceedings of the Annual Meeting of the Western Society for French History* 26 (1999): 122–32. On the use of the term *rat mort*, see Adolphe Willette, *Feu Pierrot* (Paris: Floury, 1919), 107. On Chez Palmyre, see also Leslie Choquette, "Beyond the Myth of Lesbian Montmartre: The Case of Chez Palmyre," *Historical Reflections / Réflexions historiques* 42, no. 2 (Summer 2016): 75–96. Following the war in 1919, Chez Palmyre became Liberty's Bar and was frequented more by male than female homosexuals. See Martin Pénet, "L'expression homosexuelle dans les chansons françaises de l'entre-deux guerres: Entre dérision et ambiguïté," *Revue d'histoire moderne et contemporaine*, no. 53–54, (October–December 2006): 117. On lesbian brothels, see Pierre Delcourt, *Le vol à Paris* (Paris: A. Piaget, 1888), 22, cited in Nicole Albert, *Lesbian Decadence: Representations in Art and Literature of Fin-de-Siècle France*, trans. Nancy Erber and William A. Peniston (2005; New York: Columbia University Press, 2016), 65–66. Andrew Israel Ross cautions against taking Delcourt's numbers at face-value (email with the author, June 9, 2022).

14 Hélène Azenor, *Histoire d'UNE* (Paris: Les Octaviennes, 1988), 221.

15 Between 1927 and 1934 the Parisian prefect of police Jean Chiappe sought to crack down on the practice. See "Les années 30," Hexagone Gay, accessed December 16, 2017, http://www.hexagonegay.com/30.html. Dance halls that permitted same-sex dancing set up lookouts to signal the arrival of the vice squad. If police showed up, male couples quickly reorganized themselves with female partners in order to avoid arrest. Brassaï, "The Bal de la Montagne Sainte-Geneviève," in *The Secret Paris of the 30s*, trans. Richard Miller (London: Thames & Hudson, 1976), n.p.

16 Brassaï, *The Secret Paris*, n.p. See also Gilles Barbedette and Michel Carassou, *Paris Gay 1925* (Paris: Presses de la Renaissance, 1981), 16–19; Willy, *The Third Sex*, trans., intro., and notes, Lawrence R. Schehr (Urbana: University of Illinois Press, 2007), 57–59; and Charles-Étienne's fictionalized depiction *Le bal des folles* (Paris: Curio, 1930). The Bal at the Salle Wagram is not to be confused with Le Wagram, a teahouse at 208 rue de Rivoli where women danced together, especially before World War I. See Charles-Étienne, *Notre-Dame-de-Lesbos* (Paris: Librairie des Lettres, 1919).

17 File 103119, JC/CAB1, report dated March 1, 1933 (APP). In 1933, the police noted that "the notorious lesbian Suzy SURCOUF" (cabaret singer Suzy Solidor) and "the personnel of Le Monocle" (a sapphic cabaret) figured among the crowd; Josephine Baker and Damia were in the jury. See also Barbedette and Carassou, *Paris Gay 1925*, 66–67. Julian Jackson claims that "not all homosexuals recognized themselves in this event" and "many barely knew of its existence." Jackson, *Living in Arcadia: Homosexuality, Politics and Morality in France from the Liberation to AIDS* (Chicago: University of Chicago Press, 2009), 32. However, the extensive

publicity surrounding the Bals increased the visibility of same-sex desire in ways both negative (attracting public curiosity and outrage) and positive (creating community and offering alternate models for gender and sexual expression).

18 The Magic-City first opened in June 1911. In August 1914 it was requisitioned by the military and transformed into a leather factory. It reopened as a dance hall in 1919 and "became one of the great travesty balls for Mardi Gras and Lent." See file 103119, JC/CAB1, undated notes (APP). It closed at the onset of World War II. See Michel du Coglay, *Chez les mauvais garçons: Choses vues* (Paris: Éditions Raoul Saillard, 1937), 149; and Farid Chenoune, "Leur Bal: Notes sur des photos de Magic-City, bal des tantes de l'entre-deux guerres," *Modes pratiques*, no. 1 (November 2015), https://devisu.inha.fr/modespratiques/117.

19 Jean Bastia, *Le quotidien de Montmartre*, no. 29 (March 23, 1930), 1.

20 File 103119, JC/CAB1 (APP), reports dated March 8, 1929, and February 18, 1931; see also report dated March 3, 1932.

21 File 103119, JC/CAB1 (APP), report dated March 13, 1931.

22 Azenor, interviewed in Barbedette and Carassou, *Paris Gay 1925*, 72–73.

23 Ernest Hemingway, *The Sun Also Rises* (New York: Charles Scribner's Sons, 1926), 19.

24 Azenor, *Histoire d'UNE*, 174.

25 Azenor, *Histoire d'UNE*, 210.

26 Azenor, *Histoire d'UNE*, 216–17. Louÿs's claimed his poems were translations of Bilitis, a fictional female contemporary of the Ancient Greek poet Sappho. Although now known as Louÿs's own fabulations, they are considered to have literary importance.

27 See Judith Surkis, *Sexing the Citizen: Morality and Masculinity in France, 1870–1920* (Ithaca, NY: Cornell University Press, 2006), 1.

28 Michael Finn, "Female Sterilization and Artificial Insemination at the French Fin de Siècle: Facts and Fictions," *Journal of the History of Sexuality* 18, no. 1 (January 2009): 26.

29 Michel Foucault, *The History of Sexuality*, vol. 1, *An Introduction*, trans. Robert Hurley (1976; New York: Viking, 1988), 43.

30 Rebecca Jennings, *A Lesbian History of Britain: Love and Sex between Women since 1500* (Oxford: Greenwood World Publishing, 2007), 76–77; Daniel Maira, "Des tribades et des godemichés: Mollesses viriles dans le *Recueil des dames* de Brantôme," *French Studies* 70, no. 4 (2016); 503. This view also rendered it impossible for a man to take the passive role in sex.

31 See Karl Friedrich Otto Westphal, "Die conträre Sexualemfindung: Sympton eines neuropathischen (psychopathischen) Zustandes," *Archiv für Psychiatrie und Nervenkrankheiten*, no. 2 (1869–70): 73–108.

32 This "third sex" uniting homosexuality, cross-dressing, and gender inversion was described in 1864–65 in German activist Karl Heinrich Ulrichs's concepts of *Urning* (a congenitally assigned male with a female psyche, attracted to men) and *Urningin* (a congenitally assigned female with a male psyche, attracted to women). On the history of sexology, see Sylvie Chaperon, *Les origines de la sexologie (1850–1900)* (Paris: Éditions Audibert, 2007). See also Arnold I. Davidson, *The Emergence of Sexuality: Historical Epistemology and the Formation of Concepts* (Cambridge, MA: Harvard University Press, 2004), 16. While influential,

the theory of "contrary sexual instinct" was not without critics. The French poet and writer Marc-André Raffalovich coined the term "unisexual" to express his belief that congenital homosexuals were not gender dysphoric and were attracted to those like and not unlike themselves. Marc-André Raffalovich, *Uranisme et unisexualité: Étude sur différentes manifestations de l'instinct sexuel* (Lyon: A. Storck; Paris: Masson & Cie, 1896). See also Patrick Cardon, "A Homosexual Militant at the Beginning of the Century: Marc André Raffalovich," in *Gay Studies from the French Cultures: Voices from France, Belgium, Brazil, Canada, and the Netherlands*, ed. Rommel Mendès-Leite and Pierre-Olivier de Busscher (New York: Haworth, 1993), 183–91. In its extravagant adoration of the feminine, much sapphic literature produced by women like Renée Vivien, Natalie Clifford Barney, and Liane de Pougy in early twentieth-century Paris also runs in this vein.

33 Brigitte Lhomond, "Between Man and Woman: The Character of the Lesbian," *Journal of the History of Homosexuality* 25, no. 1/2 (1993): 66.

34 Charcot and Magnan, quoted in Robert Nye, *Masculinity and Male Codes of Honor in Modern France* (New York: Oxford University Press, 1993), 21–22. The influence of biologist Jean-Baptiste de Lamarck, psychiatrist Bénédict Augustin Morel, and naturalist Charles Darwin on nineteenth-century theories of sexuality is evident here. See also Gretchen Schultz, *Sapphic Fathers: Discourses of Same-Sex Desire from Nineteenth-Century France* (Toronto: University of Toronto Press, 2014), 156–57.

35 Havelock Ellis, *Studies in the Psychology of Sex*, vol. 2, *Sexual Inversion*, 2nd ed. (Philadelphia: F.A. Davis, 1908), 133.

36 On this, see also Carolyn J. Dean, *The Frail Social Body: Pornography, Homosexuality, and Other Fantasies in Interwar France* (Berkeley: University of California Press, 2000), 177–87.

37 Julien Chevalier, *De l'inversion de l'instinct sexuel au point de vue médico-légal* (Lyon: Imprimerie Nouvelle, 1885), 90, 96, 100.

38 Chevalier, *De l'inversion*, 90, 97, 167–68.

39 Chevalier, *De l'inversion*, 74.

40 On how Belot and his novel "inaugurate[d] a wave of novels representing female homosexuals and anticipated the psychiatric discussions soon to follow," see Schultz, *Sapphic Fathers*, 65–85.

41 See, for example, Guy de Maupassant's "Paul's Mistress" (1881) and Emile Zola's *Nana* (1880).

42 On the impact of the change, see Vanessa Schwartz, *Spectacular Realities: Early Mass Culture in Fin-de-Siècle Paris* (Berkeley: University of California Press, 1998), 29.

43 On Caufeynon, see Peter Cryle, "Foretelling Pathology: The Poetics of Prognosis," *French Cultural Studies* 17, no. 1 (2006): 107–22; Michael L. Wilson, "Suspect Physiognomy: The Male Prostitute in Belle Époque Print Culture," *Proceedings of the Western Society for French History* 34 (2006): 195–96; and Brigitte Lhomond, preface to the republication of *Histoire de la Femme* by Dr. Caufeynon (Paris: Côté-Femmes, 1989), 7n1. Caufeynon's prolific publication record (while likely exaggerated, he claimed to have sold eight hundred thousand copies of a book on "safety" in lovemaking) indicates that an average French person seeking information about sapphic sexuality could likely have located his texts with ease. See

Angus McLaren, *The Trials of Masculinity: Policing Sexual Boundaries, 1870–1930* (Chicago: University of Chicago Press, 1997), 148.

44 Gretchen Schultz observes that "the sheer quantity of French [male] writing about female homosexuality" in the nineteenth century "eclipses any comparable corpus in English, evincing France's profound fascination with the subject." Schultz, *Sapphic Fathers*, 4, 16–26.

45 Guy Debord, *La société du spectacle* (Paris: Buchet/Chastel, 1967).

46 Virmaître made this observation more than a decade prior. See Charles Virmaître, *Paris-Impur*, 2nd ed. (Paris: A. Charles Librairie, 1889), 219–20.

47 See Shari Benstock, *Women of the Left Bank: Paris, 1900–1940* (Austin: University of Texas Press, 1986), 7.

48 Despite attention to the sapphic "secret Paris" of the 1930s in the work of photographer Brassaï, popular French biographies on cabaret singer Suzy Solidor and club-owner Frede, and a 2015 best-selling novel on the topic (*Lovers at the Chameleon Club*), this other "queer female world"—of cabarets, bars, cafés, and restaurants—has received scant scholarly attention. For popular coverage of the *cabarets féminins*, see Brassaï, *The Secret Paris*; Marie-Hélène Carbonel, *Suzy Solidor, une vie d'amours* (Gémenos: Éditions Autre Temps, 2007); Denis Cosnard, *Frede* (Paris: Éditions des Équateurs, 2017); in fiction, see Francine Prose, *Lovers at the Chameleon Club, Paris 1932* (New York: Harper Perennial, 2015). François Buot gives slightly more space to women in *Gay Paris: Une histoire du Paris interlope entre 1900 et 1940* (Paris: Fayard, 2013).

49 See Christine Bard, *Les garçonnes: Modes et fantasmes des années folles* (Paris: Flammarion, 1998), and Mary-Louise Roberts, *Civilization without Sexes: Reconstructing Gender in Postwar France, 1917–1927* (Chicago: University of Chicago Press, 1994).

50 Willette, *Feu Pierrot*, 107.

51 On the *reine du foyer*, see Christine Bard, *Les femmes dans la société française au 20e siècle* (Paris: HER/Armand Colin, 2001), 34–58.

52 Francesca Canadé Sautman notes that Arria Ly, "a militant suffragist who usually dressed in mannish style, challenged a male journalist to a duel in 1911 for calling her a lesbian." Sautman, "Invisible Women: Lesbian Working-Class Culture in France, 1880–1930," in *Homosexuality in Modern France*, ed. Jeffrey Merrick and Bryant T. Ragan Jr. (New York: Oxford University Press, 1996), 180–81.

53 Florence Tamagne, *A History of Homosexuality in Europe: Berlin, London, Paris, 1919–1939* (New York: Algora Publishing, 2004), 1:68.

54 Étienne Rey, "Propos parisiens," *La vie parisienne*, July 7, 1934–December 29, 1934, 981.

55 See "Un gros débat," *Bec et ongles: Satirique hebdomadaire*, December 9, 1933. Michael Sibalis insists that it was because the Third Republic refused to take stronger legal action against the "homosexual debauchery" that was believed to be "on a constant increase" throughout the 1930s that the Vichy government raised the age of sexual majority for homosexual acts with and between minors. Michael Sibalis, "Homophobia, Vichy France, and the 'Crime of Homosexuality': The Origins of the Ordinance of 6 August 1942," *GLQ: A Journal of Lesbian and Gay Studies* 8, no. 3 (2002): 306–8.

56 Tamagne argues that "for the majority of homosexuals who were not part of high

society and who lived in the obscurity of the provinces, homosexuality remained a stain that had to be kept carefully hidden." Tamagne, *History of Homosexuality*, 1:21.

57 Marise Querlin's *Femmes sans hommes: Choses vues* (Paris: Éditions de France, 1931). See also Henri Drouin, *Femmes damnées* (Paris: NRF/Gallimard, 1929).

58 Like Dr. Caufeynon's pamphlets, Querlin's *Femmes sans hommes* proved commercially successful: it was reissued in 1953 and again in 1964 before being published in English in 1965 as *Women without Men*.

59 Review of Querlin's *Femmes sans hommes* by Jean Vignaud, "Les lettres sur les femmes," *Le petit parisien*, March 31, 1931.

60 Querlin, *Femmes sans hommes*, 110–11.

61 Dean, *The Frail Social Body*, 188.

62 I build on Dean's argument that "a vast array of interwar novelists and cultural critics imagined that lesbians" were both "omnipresent and yet impossible to detect" in French society at this time. This omnipresent invisibility expressed both the threat that female sexuality posed and a fantasy that determined "the parameters within which some self-described lesbians"—particularly feminine ones—"forged an alternative language for their own sexuality" in the interwar years. Dean, *The Frail Social Body*, 176–77. Querlin's informant Lulu (likely Lulu de Montmartre, addressed in chapter 2) tells her there are "an incalculable number" of women who love women "not only in Paris, but also in the provinces"—as well as in England, Germany, America, and Holland. Querlin, *Femmes sans hommes*, 43.

63 Her mother married Eugène Prudent Rocher in 1907.

64 Solidor discusses her wartime experience in a 1978 radio interview directed by Marie-France Nussbaum. "La mémoire de Suzy," France Culture, aired August 15, 1978. Except when otherwise noted, all radio and television broadcasts cited hereafter are from the Institut national de l'audiovisuel (Fonds INA).

65 "Suzy Solidor révèle son étrange destin de femme sans homme," *Confessions*, no. 1 (November 26, 1936). See the discussion of the two versions of this article below.

66 M. H. Berger, "Première chanteuse de music-hall 'télévisionée par les PTT,'" *Excelsior*, June 29, 1935.

67 Unreferenced newspaper clippings, 8MUS01, 8MUS02, Solidor Pressbooks 1937–1938, Fonds Suzy Solidor, Musée-Renoir (Château-musée archives), Cagnes-sur-Mer, France (hereafter cited as Fonds Solidor).

68 According to the databases at Inathèque de France, by 2015 Solidor had either performed on or was mentioned in 49 TV broadcasts and 138 radio shows, most prior to her death in 1983.

69 Limore Yagil argues on her behalf, claiming Solidor "played an important role in the Resistance" and providing undocumented evidence to support his view. The purge courts obviously disagreed. Yagil, *Au nom de l'art, 1933–1945: Exils, solidarités et engagements* (Paris: Fayard, 2015), 399. On Solidor's war years, the charges against her, and her response to them, see Karine Jay, "Suzy Solidor (1900–1983): Portrait d'une artiste à la frange d'orée d'art" (master's thesis, Université de Jean Moulin Lyon III, 1994–96), esp. chapter 4, 114–51, and Carbonel, *Suzy Solidor*, 173–243.

70 Tirza True Latimer contends that Solidor's portraits "stretched the parameters

of her erotic appeal, reified the gender, class, and sexual mobility to which she aspired, and substantiated her status as a celebrity." Latimer, *Women Together, Women Apart: Portraits of Lesbian Paris* (New Brunswick, NJ: Rutgers University Press, 2005), 123.

71 Azenor in Lesselier, *Instants de vie*.

72 References to her fondness for "the weaker sex" permeate press coverage during the 1930s and the early 1940s. See Le Pointeur, "Cibles: Suzy Solidor," *La vie parisienne*, February 26, 1938. 8MUS02, Solidor Pressbook 1938, Fonds Solidor.

73 "Ouvre" was written by a man (Edouard Haraucourt) but is now considered a lesbian anthem. The Odeon record produced in 1934 censored the last two couplets. The complete version was not released until 1992 on the album *Suzy Solidor: Succès et raretès 1933–1939* (Chansophone, 1992).

74 Victor Margueritte, *La garçonne* (Paris: Flammarion, 1922).

75 Mary-Louise Roberts suggests that Margueritte's protagonist "functions as a symbol of postwar cultural crisis" whose heterosexual redemption at the novel's end "appeases both cultural and gender anxieties." Roberts, *Civilization without Sexes*, 46–62 (quote from 47).

76 Victor Margueritte, however, was charged with "outrage aux bonnes moeurs," and his name was expunged from the Legion of Honour.

77 Figures from Bard, *Les garçonnes*, 65. The first cinematic adaptation of the novel (a silent film directed by Armand du Plessy in 1923) was censured for its portrayal of female homosexuality. Subsequent versions (including Albert Dieudonné and Jean de Limur's 1936 version and the 1957 version discussed further in chapter 4) were more restrained.

78 Mars sings "La garçonne" (lyrics by Jean Wiener and Albert Willemetz) on *Trente-six chandelles*, RTF Télévision, broadcast February 4, 1957. She recorded it for Columbia Records with the orchestra of Jo Moutet. "La garçonne," *Colette Mars* (Columbia Records, 1957).

79 Jean Cocteau, "Suzy Solidor," *Music-Hall*, no. 3 (1955): 13. Cocteau quoted in *Suzy Solidor: Un étrange destin*, dir. Alain Gallet, France 3 Ouest, broadcast February 28, 2006.

80 Foucault, *The History of Sexuality*, 1:20–35.

81 Barring the first sentence (addressed below), the two texts are identical. Many of the photographs are not. See "Suzy Solidor révèle son étrange destin de femme sans homme," *Confessions*, no. 1 (November 26, 1936), and "Suzy Solidor révèle son étrange destin de femme sans homme," *Confessions*, no. 1 (December 3, 1936). Both articles appear to be from issue no. 1, the first issue of the magazine. The Bibliothèque nationale de France (hereafter cited as BNF) lists only the November 26, 1936, publication in its online catalogue. I downloaded a copy from their website in 2012. However, when I requested image rights for a photograph from the article for use in this book, they were unable to locate it. The BNF eventually provided me with a version of the same photograph from the December 3, 1936, article instead. At the time of publication, their catalogue has not yet been corrected to include the December 3, 1936, article.

82 The *Confession* exposé's melodramatic prose style resembles Solidor's own work. Her novels are *Térésine* (Paris: Éditions de France, 1939), *Fil d'or* (Paris: Éditions

de France, 1940), *Le fortuné de l'Amphitrite* (Paris: Éditions de France, 1941), and *La vie commence au large* (Brussels: Éditions du Sablon, 1944).

83 The second image is also featured in the December 3, 1936, version of the article.

84 A different publicity shot from *La garçonne* appears in the version published on December 3, 1936. It is captioned, "It was, in essence, the beginning of la 'Vie Parisienne,' my cabaret." There is no mention of the film from which the image derives in either article.

85 For some unknown reason, the December 3 version of the article begins "Four o'clock in the morning" rather than "Three." This is the only difference between the two texts. Quotations in my discussion in this chapter are all from "Solidor révèle son étrange destin," *Confessions*, no. 1 (November 26, 1936).

86 As noted above, Solidor's golden tan had already attracted media interest. Indeed, in 1933 Solidor's penchant for nude sunbathing was reported on from as far away as Hanoi. See "Le bain de Suzy," *Chantecler* (Hanoi), November 5, 1933.

87 In a 1978 radio interview Solidor claimed to have met the celebrated designer but avowed that she never pursued a post: "I stayed with the antiques' dealer instead," she recalls. "La mémoire de Suzy."

88 Jay, "Suzy Solidor," 25.

89 Hazéra, cited in Carbonel, *Suzy Solidor*, 30n5. Carbonel comments that "this seems highly unlikely." I am not so sure. Hazéra repeated this story in our interview, June 13, 2018, Paris, France.

90 Marie-Hélène Carbonel, interview by author, March 10, 2016, Nice, France.

91 Interestingly Foucault also uses the term "species" in volume 1 of *The History of Sexuality*, which Solidor applied to women like Bremond d'Ars.

92 There is evidence that other women read sexology in France in the early twentieth century. Claude Cahun translated Havelock Ellis into French and was open about the impact of sexology on her self-understanding of her own sexuality. Writer and artist Djuna Barnes mocked sexology in her *Ladies Almanack*. See Latimer, *Women Together, Women Apart*, 17. Freud's *Three Essays on the Theory of Sexuality* (1905), which posited the bisexual nature of human sexual response, was translated into French in 1923. Magnus Hirschfeld's work on homosexuality was just beginning to circulate in France at this time. See Dognan in Barbedette and Carassou, *Paris Gay 1925*, 60.

93 "Solidor révèle son étrange destin," and Latimer, *Women Together, Women Apart*, 108.

94 Images and quotes from the television documentary *Suzy Solidor: Un étrange destin*.

95 After Solidor broke with Bremond d'Ars, she abandoned her mother's married name, Rocher, in favor of Surcouf, after Robert Henri de Surcouf, the man she claimed as her biological father, a descendent of Saint-Malo's famed corsair and privateer Robert Surcouf (1773–1827). Although Robert Henri later had episodic contact with Suzy (there are photos of them together, and they bear a striking resemblance), the patronymic was disputed by his scandalized family. Suzy then replaced Surcouf with "de Solidor" and then "Solidor" in 1931, this time taking her name from the Tour Solidor, a fortress that rises up between her native Saint-Malo in Brittany and the sea. See Latimer, *Women Together, Women Apart*, 110.

The name gave rise to an oft-repeated anecdote: "Do you know why they call her 'Suzy Solidor'?" one wag asks another. "Why, because of the Tour Solidor, in Saint-Malo," answers the second. But no, replies the first, it is because even though she has a bed, "Suzy seule y dort" (Suzy sleeps there alone). Interestingly, the presumption here is not that Suzy actually sleeps alone, but rather that no man shares her bed. Le Pointeur, "Cibles: Suzy Solidor."

96 D33U3 617/ 571456, Archives de la ville de Paris (hereafter cited as AP). Report dated January 1943, Dossier Rocher and Abel 1W 1762-102-821 (APP).

97 Carbonel, interview. Despite her popularity in inter- and postwar France (and among French lesbians "of a certain age" today), there is scant scholarship on Solidor's life. This consists mostly of a handful of websites (one can listen to gorgeous audio files of her voice online and see clips from film and TV); an excellent chapter by Tirza True Latimer in *Women Together, Women Apart*, her book on lesbian representation in interwar Paris; and popular material, namely the 2006 TV documentary, *Suzy Solidor: Un étrange destin*, and Carbonel's biography. In 2021 Charlotte Duthoo published a fictional diary about Solidor entitled *Les nuits Solidor. Mémoires imaginaires d'une égérie* (Paris: Le Cherche Midi, 2021). Like Carbonel, Duthoo insists on the importance of Jean Mermoz in Suzy's life, thus underscoring a preference for men that Solidor's life choices fail to support.

98 Carbonel, interview.

99 Carbonel, *Suzy Solidor*, 147–48, and Duthoo, *Les nuits Solidor*, 13–16.

100 Hazéra, quoted in Carbonel, *Suzy Solidor*, 77.

101 On this rather complicated arrangement, see Carbonel, *Suzy Solidor*, 164–65.

102 Miki Leff Papers. On Marconi and Frede, see Cosnard, *Frede*, 101–3. On Deitrich and Frede, see Diana McLellan, *The Girls: Sappho Goes to Hollywood* (New York: Griffin, 2000), 244–45, 328. McLellan mistakenly claims, however, that Errol Flynn was describing Frede in his memoirs where he speaks of the two women together. He was not; the woman in question ("Frankie") was Lulu de Montmartre. Like Solidor, Frede was also courted by men and capitalized on this to enhance her celebrity: indeed, she had planned to publish a memoir entitled *Les hommes dans ma vie* (The men in my life) recounting the numerous marriage proposals "from fashion designer[s] to Maharajah[s]" that she had received from men over the course of her life. Jany Casanova, "Frède [*sic*] Carroll [*sic*] écrit des mémoires fracassants," *La vie parisienne* 103, no. 201 (September 1967). Television journalist Micheline Sandrel likewise focused audiences away from her interest in women with the publication of *Le guide de l'amant parfait et du mari passable* [The guide to the perfect male lover and the acceptable husband] (Paris: Éditions de la Pensée Moderne, 1966).

103 Miki Leff Papers.

104 Lauren Jae Gutterman, *Her Neighbor's Wife: A History of Lesbian Desire within Marriage* (Philadelphia: University of Pennsylvania Press, 2020).

105 Maryse Choisy's *Un mois chez les filles: Reportage* (Paris: Éditions Montaigne, 1928; repr., Paris: Éditions Stock, 2015) is mainly about female heterosexual prostitution but also addresses the *cabarets féminins*. Choisy also wrote about lesbians in "Dames seules" in a special edition of *Le rire* on May 12, 1932; *Un mois chez les hommes* (Paris: Éditions de France, 1929); and *L'amour dans les prisons* (Paris: Éditions Montaigne, 1930).

106 Choisy, *Un mois chez les filles*, 61–62.

107 Eve Kosofsky Sedgwick, *Between Men: English Literature and Male Homosexual Desire* (New York: Columbia University Press, 1985), 86.

108 Sedgwick, *Between Men*, 89.

109 “Solidor révèle son étrange destin.”

110 See the undated captioned photographs from Haut-de-Cagnes in Solidor’s photograph album 13MUS03, Fonds Solidor.

111 August 3, 1945, and December 3, 1947, in file 77 W 1834-266677 (APP).

112 Suzy Solidor radio interview on *Un quart d’heure avec . . .* [Suzy Solidor], RDF/RTF, aired April 7, 1948.

113 Françoise Flamant, interview by author, December 5, 2010, Paris.

114 Flamant, quoted in Anne Pauly, “Chez Moune: Chic lesbien et lutte des classes,” Red Mull Music Academy Daily, September 29, 2016, http://fr.redbullmusicacademy.com/daily/2016/09/chez-moune-chic-lesbien-et-lutte-des-classes. Pauly’s article unfortunately reproduces errors about Moune’s business, among them the claim that Moune opened “the first cabaret féminin in Paris” in 1936 on rue Fromentin. Moune began managing Le Fétiche in the late 1920s and did not own her own cabaret, first called “Le Fétiche” / Chez Moune, until 1940.

115 Schultz, *Sapphic Fathers*, 188.

116 Flamant, interview.

CHAPTER TWO

1 The argument that gay men have historically established more businesses than lesbians is well documented. See, for example, George Chauncey, *Gay New York: Gender, Urban Culture and the Making of the Gay Male World, 1890–1940* (New York: Basic Books, 1995), 27.

2 Stéphane Leroy claims that in 2005 “almost 97 percent of homosexual establishments in Paris [were] destined for men only.” Leroy, “Le Paris gay: Éléments pour une géographie de l’homosexualité,” *Annales de Géographie* 114, no. 646 (2005): 582. And yet, restaurants operated and patronized by women who loved women proliferated in France in the late nineteenth century well before their male equivalents. See Leslie Choquette, “Gay Paree: The Origins of Lesbian and Gay Commercial Culture in the French Third Republic,” *Contemporary French Civilization* 41, no. 1 (2016): 2. By the early twentieth century, however, French commercial venues aimed at men seeking men surpassed those run by and for women. Choquette, “Gay Paree,” 2, 9–10. The opening of sapphic cabarets in interwar Paris transformed this landscape once again.

3 I count as French sapphic cabarets both cabarets féminins explicitly courting female clientele and cabarets artistiques run by and welcoming women who desired women that also appealed to mixed-gender audiences. The cabaret féminin Le Fétiche opened in 1926. The sapphic cabarets opened in the 1930s include Le Monocle (1932), L’Auberge du Perroquet Gris (1932, in Vaucresson), La Vie Parisienne (1933), Le Pavillon du Mystère (1933, in Argenteuil), the Buenos-Aires (1933), Le Joubertin (also known as Chez Sidonie, 1933), Juan-les-Pins (1934), Le Gibus (1934), Les Cocottes (1935), La Roulotte (1935), Chez Sidonie Baba (1936), Entre Nous (1936), Le Siroco (1937), Le Capricorne (established as Chez Agnès Capri

and also known as Le Molière and Le Petit Théâtre de la Nuit, 1938), La Silhouette (1938), Les Claudines (1938), Club Liegois Chez Rylls (1938), Le Fétiche/La Sirène (1938), Chez Moune et Léon (1939), Chez Jane Stick (1939), and À L'Heureuse Galère (opened by Sidonie Baba in 1939); Caprice Viennois, El Garrou, Le Lido, Chez Nous, Elle et Lui, Chez Magdeleine Barry, and Le Petit Cabaret "Chez Jacqueline Batell" all opened in the 1930s as well. Seven of these lasted through at least the 1950s. Excepting Le Monocle, Chez Moune, and La Vie Parisienne, most of these have never been identified let alone analyzed by historians. I do not consider the Bal de la Montagne Sainte-Geneviève a sapphic cabaret during the 1930s because it did not target a specifically female audience until after the war.

4 Michael Sibalis, "Paris," in *Queer Sites: Gay Urban Histories since 1660*, ed. David Higgs (London: Routledge, 1999), 11. David Higgs (the editor of the volume in which Sibalis's article appears) justifies excluding women from a collection on queer urbanism by arguing that evidence of lesbian urban existence is too hard to find (*Queer Sites*, 2). Such assertions contribute to the effacement of the histories examined here in part by discouraging research.

5 Marie-Jo Bonnet, Claudie Lesselier, and Florence Tamagne all maintain that World War II destroyed what had been a vibrant lesbian community in France. See Bonnet, *Les relations amoureuses entre les femmes XVIe–XXe siècle* (1995; Paris: Éditions Odile Jacob, 2001), 339; Lesselier, "Aspects de l'expérience lesbienne en France, 1930–1968" (DEA thesis, Université Paris 8, 1987); Lesselier, "Silenced Resistances and Conflictual Identities: Lesbians in France, 1930–1968," *Journal of Homosexuality* 25, no.1/2 (1993): 106; and Tamagne, *A History of Homosexuality in Europe: Berlin, London, Paris, 1919–1939* (New York: Algora Publishing, 2004), 2:271. Elsewhere, Tamagne claims continuities in pre- and postwar (male) homosexual bar culture, but she still insists that lesbians "rarely visited bars." Tamagne, "Paris: 'Resting on Its Laurels'?," in *Queer Cities, Queer Cultures: Europe since 1945*, ed. Matt Cook and Jennifer Evans (London: Bloomsbury, 2014), 243. My research reveals instead a lively bar culture from the pre- to the post-WWII eras. Thus, if a few sapphic cabarets closed in 1939, many remained open throughout the war, and others reopened after brief closures.

6 Most work mapping lesbian lifeworlds issues from gender studies or social geography and focuses on the recent past, thus revealing how perceptions of lesbian visibility are often linked to contemporary feminist consciousness. Sy Adler and Johanna Brenner, for example, maintain that whereas "gay communities and culture preceded the political organization of gay men," lesbian communities are a product of political organizing and have always been contiguous with feminism. Adler and Brenner, "Gender and Space: Lesbians and Gay Men in the City," *International Journal of Urban and Regional Research* 16, no. 1 (1992): 33.

7 I discussed these issues at length in the summer of 2023 with Wenjing Yu while she was preparing an excellent master's thesis on the commercial aspects of the cabaret féminin. See Wenjing Yu, "Cabarets féminins: Histoires d'une visibilité exceptionelle d'espaces lesbiens (1920–1960)" (master's thesis, L'École des hautes études en science sociales, 2022–23).

8 By 1870, there were more than one hundred *caf'concs* in the capital. Gilles Schlesser, *Le cabaret "rive gauche": De la Rose Rouge au Bateau ivre: 1946–1974* (Paris: Éditions de l'Archipel, 2006), 52. These venues soon doubled in number

but were dethroned as mass entertainment in the interwar years by the music hall, a large concert hall with an orchestra in which the audience is separated from the stage. Music halls charged entrance fees, forbid smoking, and didn't provide drinks (unlike both the *caf'conc'* and the cabaret, where entrance was free, smoking was permitted, and one paid for drinks). The cabarets that survived this transformation targeted bourgeois bohemians and sexual outlaws.

9 A few sapphic cabarets kept afternoon hours for tea dances between women and opened later to mixed publics. Chez Jane Stick (est. 1937) offered a "Thé-Cocktail" (Tea-Cocktail) for women only from 5 p.m. to 9 p.m. Suzy Solidor's La Vie Parisienne likewise had afternoon teas but officially opened at 11 p.m.

10 Hélène Azenor observed that unlike contemporary clubs, these interwar spaces had cross-generational appeal "in an ambiance far more intimate" than is true today. Azenor quoted in Gilles Barbedette and Michel Carassou, *Paris Gay 1925* (Paris: Presses de la Renaissance, 1981), 71. There is copious photographic and cinematic evidence that sapphic cabarets were racially mixed spaces. Maryse Choisy also remarks on black women in the cabarets féminins in *Un mois chez les filles: Reportage* (Paris: Éditions Montaigne, 1928; repr., Paris: Éditions Stock, 2015), 38. Jean de Limur's 1936 film version of *La garçonne* (described in chapter 1) features a Vietnamese character, "Mademoiselle Fou-Sen, charged with giving the cabaret a bit of exotic color," who knits at the bar above the opium den. The cabaret scene in which Suzy Solidor sings opens with a scantily dressed black woman shimmying "wildly" à la Josephine Baker before distracted patrons. Y. F., "Les débuts à l'écran de Suzy Solidor," *Mon ciné*, January 23, 1936.

In contrast to French sapphic cabarets, which crossed class lines, the North American and British lesbian bar culture that emerged later (in the 1940s and more commonly the 1950s) was anchored almost entirely in working-class neighborhoods. See Elizabeth Lapovsky Kennedy and Madeleine D. Davis, *Boots of Leather, Slippers of Gold: The History of a Lesbian Community* (New York: Routledge, 1993). In Montreal lesbian bars were founded in the 1950s and only gradually transitioned from red-light districts to more "respectable, sex-segregated" but nevertheless primarily underground bars in the 1970s. Julie A. Podmore, "Gone 'Underground'? Lesbian Visibility and the Consolidation of Queer Space in Montréal," *Social and Cultural Geography* 7, no. 4 (2006): 606. On these shifts in North American cities, see also Kennedy and Davis, *Boots of Leather*; Lillian Faderman, *Odd Girls and Twilight Lovers: A History of Lesbian Life in Twentieth-Century America* (New York: Columbia University Press, 1991); Joan Nestle, *A Restricted Country: Documents of Desire and Resistance* (New York: Firebrand Books, 1987); Roey Thorpe, "The Changing Face of Lesbian Bars in Detroit, 1938–1965," in *Creating a Place for Ourselves: Lesbian, Gay, and Bisexual Community Histories*, ed. Brett Beemyn (New York: Routledge, 1997), 165–82. On class segregation in lesbian cabarets in Germany, see Clayton J. Whisnant, *Queer Identities and Politics in Germany, A History 1880–1945* (New York: Harrington Park Press, 2016), 96–97; and Marti M. Lybeck, *Desiring Emancipation: New Women and Homosexuality in Germany, 1890–1933* (Albany: State University of New York Press, 2015), 164.

11 See, for example, Pierre de Régnier, "Noirs et blanches," Paris, ma grand'ville, *Gringoire*, January 12, 1939. Notwithstanding disputed references to bisexuality

in studies of Josephine Baker and Ada "Bricktop" Smith, there is a paucity of work on race and female same-sex desire in France both in this period and after. On Baker, see Jean-Claude Baker and Chris Chase, *Josephine: The Hungry Heart* (New York: Random House, 1993), 132–40. On Bricktop, see T. Denean Sharpley-Whiting, *Bricktop's Paris: African-American Women in Paris between the Two World Wars* (Albany: State University of New York Press, 2015), 44–47. Bricktop denies her own desire for or involvement with other women but agrees that "everybody was fooling around with everybody else." Ada Smith Ducongé and James Haskins, *Bricktop* (New York: Atheneum, 1983), 106.

12 Monsieur Martini tried to transform Le Sphinx, a venue under his direction, into a cabaret féminin in 1955. According to police coverage of the initiative, despite raising salaries by a third in order to attract Moune's staff, the project failed at least in part because "the orchestra (composed of women) is mediocre." See 77W 4696-509723 (APP).

13 La Sirène, for example, was advertised as "Le cabaret féminin le plus chic de Paris" (The most fashionable cabaret féminin in Paris) in the April 16, 1939, edition of *Paris-soir*, and Maryse Choisy refers to Le Fétiche as a "bar à lesbiennes" in *Un mois chez les filles*, 84. In contrast, according to Rebecca Jennings, in Britain such spaces "were not listed in any public forum until the late 1960s, partly through a fear of drawing hostile attention to themselves, but also due to the reluctance of most major newspapers to carry advertisements which alluded to homosexual women." Rebecca Jennings, *Tomboys and Bachelor Girls: A Lesbian History of Post-war Britain 1945–71* (Manchester: Manchester University Press, 2007), 117.

14 Le Fétiche is often referred to as Chez Moune and reputed to have opened in 1936, but files at the Archives de la ville de Paris date it (only under the name Le Fétiche) to 1926. See D34U3/ 62428/ 3Ju906 (AP). Lulu began working at Le Monocle in 1932 when it was restyled as a sapphic cabaret, but, as noted below, the cabaret first opened in 1931 as L'Ange Bleu. The fact that the venue was rebranded as lesbian less than a year after opening suggests the financial appeal of sapphic clientele at this time. See 30565/ 1931 /507369 /60496.32 (AP). The website Hexagone Gay states that there was another lesbian bar in the 1920s, called Le Sphinx, but they seem to have mistaken it with the luxury bordello of the same name built in the same location at 31 boulevard Edgar Quinet in 1931. See "Les années 20," Hexagone Gay, accessed November 18, 2017, http://www.hexagonegay.com/region/paris20.html.

15 File 103119, JC/CAB1, report dated February 18, 1931 (APP). On December 29, 1929, the French police identified Le Fétiche as the lesbian brothel "Au Fétiche" in 1W1893-105491 (APP). See also D34U3/ 62428/ 3Ju906 (AP). Colette, *The Pure and the Impure*, trans. Herma Briffault, intro. Judith Thurman (1932; New York: New York Review of Books, 2000). In 1931 Colette's novella was partially published in serial form under the title *Ces plaisirs . . .* (These pleasures). The full text was not published until 1941 when it appeared under the title Colette had originally planned to use, *Le pur et l'impur*.

16 Simone Mathilde Dugardin (Moune) was born on April 1, 1904, in Lille. She died in Creteil on December 4, 1981. See 77W5-430532 (APP).

17 Lulu was born Marie Lucie Franchi on either October 27, 1904, or October 27 or 28, 1905. She died on December 31, 1974. She is also referred to in the police files as either Lucienne, Marie, or Willy. See 77W1428-10738; BA 1688 (APP).

18 The quote about Lulu is from Brassaï, "Sodom and Gomorrah: Le Monocle," *The Secret Paris of the 30s*, trans. Richard Miller (London: Thames & Hudson, 1976), n.p. Brassaï incorrectly refers to Lulu as "Lulu de Montparnasse" (not "de Montmartre") presumably because of her notorious association with Montparnasse's Le Monocle. All other sources refer to her as Lulu de Montmartre. Prévost launched Le Monocle as a cabaret féminin in 1932 after revamping L'Ange Bleu, a cabaret he had opened in the same location in Montparnasse in January 1931. By December 1933 Lulu and many of her staff left Prévost's employ for the Buenos-Aires, located on the Right Bank at 66 rue Pigalle. The Buenos-Aires was also referred to variously as Buenos-Ayres and Buenos Aires and featured a show called Buenos-Aires en Monocles. See D34U3 3127/ 507369 (AP).

19 Lulu operated the Buenos-Aires, Le Pavillon du Mystère, Juan-les-Pins, and La Roulotte in succession over almost forty years. See D33U3 574 (AP). Moune ran Le Fétiche in Montparnasse and Les Claudines, Les Cocottes, and La Sirène in Pigalle, sometimes simultaneously, before opening Chez Moune et Léon in 1939, Chez Moune/Le Fétiche in 1940, Le Fétiche in 1947, Chez Moune Doge in 1950, Chez Moune/Le Fétiche (also in 1950), and, later, Le New Moon. She operated the latter two into the 1980s. See D34U3 3127/ 507369 (AP).

20 Police files consistently note the predominance of women in these establishments. See, for example, file 103119, JC/CAB1 (APP).

21 See "Paris Nitery Baedeker," *Variety*, July 2, 1952. *Variety* covered Paris for US audiences and regularly mentioned "lesbos joints." French city guides like Ange Bastiani's *Les bals secrets de Paris* (which listed Le Monocle in 1973 as a club "for tribades in search of kindred spirits") had existed since the nineteenth century. Bastiani, *Les bals secrets de Paris* (Paris: Solar, 1973), 154.

22 Cultural depictions of sapphic spaces reinforced negative social perceptions. See, for example, the lesbian bars described in Colette, *The Pure and the Impure*, and Lucy's bar in Françoise Mallet-Joris, *The Illusionist*, trans. Herma Briffault, intro. Terry Castle (1952; San Francisco: Cleis Press, 2006), esp. 171–86. See also Suzy Solidor's cabaret in Jean de Limur's 1936 film version of *La garçonne*.

23 The entraîneuse was distinct from the taxi-girl, an English term for young women paid to dance with (mainly male) customers in dance halls and nightclubs. Taxi-girls were common in the United States, England, France, and its colonies. See "Papotages: Taxi-Girls," *Chantecler* (Hanoi), November 5, 1933.

24 Marise Querlin, *Femmes sans hommes: Choses vues* (Paris: Éditions de France, 1931), 45.

25 "Paris Nitery Baedeker."

26 Dan Monnel, "De Pigalle à Montparnasse: Itinéraire d'une garçonne ordinaire des années soixante," part 2, *Lesbia magazine* (November 2003). Dan repeated the sentiment in her interview with me. Dan Monnel, interview by author, June 10, 2018, Lille, France.

27 In 1938, Agnès Capri's cabaret (advertised alternately as Chez Agnès Capri, Le Molière, Le Petit Théâtre de la Nuit, and Le Capricorne and located at 5 rue Molière near the Opéra) inaugurated the tradition of the *cabaret théâtre*. Despite its Right Bank location, Capri's cabaret was known as "the laboratory for the [post-WWII] Left Bank style," presenting a novel mélange of genres and mixing short theatrical sketches, songs, pantomimes, marionettes, and comedy skits with jazz, illusionists, and patter. Schlesser, *Le cabaret "rive gauche,"* 180. On inventing the

cabaret théâtre, see Capri's radio interview, "Agnès Capri," *Radioscopie*, France Inter, July 7, 1975.

28 Chez Jane Stick had a small dance floor. To my knowledge, La Vie Parisienne and Sidonie Baba's cabarets did not. According to the Archives de la police de Paris, Stick was frequently cited during World War II for failing to forbid dancing. Jane Stick (also referred to as "Jeanne" Stick) was the stage name of Emilie Joséphine Jeanne Bréard (also spelled "Briard"), born April 10, 1890, in Marseille. On Stick, see dossiers 77 W 996-309364 and 77 W 3761-372376 (APP).

29 Lesbian bars were historically in working-class neighborhoods. See, for example, the Buffalo bars described by Kennedy and Davis in *Boots of Leather*.

30 During the Vichy regime both Solidor's and Stick's cabarets were considered *établissements du 2e catégorie* (second category establishments) in a ranking of three levels of venues permitted to serve champagne. The designation determined the percentage of profit that could be charged per bottle. See the *Bulletin municipal officiel de la Ville de Paris*, February 6, 1941, 97–98. Thus, for example, in 1943, for champagne that cost between 70 and 109 francs per bottle, a category A cabaret was permitted to charge up to 370 francs, whereas a category B cabaret could charge no more than 310, and category C no more than 260. *Bulletin municipal officiel de la Ville de Paris*, August 9, 1943, 740. By 1943 Solidor's La Vie Parisienne had advanced from category B to category A and was authorized to remain open until 1 a.m. (rather than being required to close at 11 p.m. like most similar establishments at this time). *Bulletin municipal officiel de la Ville de Paris*, August 9, 1943, 740; June 23, 1943, 574. These "improvements" indicate Solidor was esteemed by the Vichy administration—a fact that did not work in her favor after the Liberation.

31 Laurence Senelick, *Cabaret Performance*, vol. 2, *Europe 1920–1940, Sketches, Songs, Monologues, Memoirs* (Baltimore: Johns Hopkins University Press, 1993), xi–xiii. This changed in the postwar era when Left Bank cabarets around Saint-Germain-des-Prés became known as avant-garde bastions of existentialism, bohemianism, and social anarchism. See the documentary *Il est minuit, Paris s'éveille*, dir. Yves Jeuland (2012), released on DVD by the Institut National de l'Audiovisuel in 2014.

32 See Senelick, *Cabaret Performance*, xiii. Martin Pénet illustrates how French *chansons de variétés* testified to the rising visibility of sexual minorities. Pénet, "L'expression homosexuelle dans les chansons françaises de l'entre-deux guerres: Entre dérision et ambiguïté," *Revue d'histoire moderne et contemporaine*, no. 53–54 (October–December 2006): 106–27.

33 On cabaret culture and the "production of intimacy," see Shane Vogel, *The Scene of the Harlem Cabaret: Race, Sexuality, Performance* (Chicago: University of Chicago Press, 2009), 39–73.

34 Senelick, *Cabaret Performance*, xi.

35 "Le Carroll's, Paris," *Variety*, February 24, 1960. See also the uncatalogued publicity pamphlet for La Vie Parisienne, Fonds Solidor.

36 Rolande Aurivel, *Dans l'ombre et au soleil de Lesbos*, with a preface by Elula Perrin (Paris: Éditions Walter Rauschenbusch, 1988), 22.

37 The quote ("Programme de Goût et de Qualité" / "Tasteful, Quality Programming") is from a 1937–38 program for Solidor's La Vie Parisienne. See 8MUS02, Fonds Solidor. At eighty-four, Aurivel admitted to frequenting Solidor's cabaret

but claimed that she and her girlfriend Edith rarely visited cabarets féminins, suggesting that such spaces were considered unsuitable for young women. Aurivel in the documentary *Pour mémoire: Portrait de Rolande Aurivel*, dir. Claudie Lesselier (1988).

38 Cabarets artistiques were generally safer than lesbian bars in the United States, which middle-class women often avoided. On middle-class lesbian avoidance of working-class lesbian bar culture in the United States, see Faderman, *Odd Girls*, 181–86, and Kennedy and Davis, *Boots of Leather*, 134.

39 There were a few outliers, like Frede's short-lived Le Masque (also known as Le Hasard) in the seventeenth arrondissement.

40 The expression riffs on Nadine Cattan and Anne Clerval's "lesbian microterritories" in their "Un droit à la ville? Réseaux virtuels et centralités éphémères des lesbiennes à Paris," *Justice spatiale / Spatial Justice*, no. 3 (2011): 5. Wenjing Yu notes that it was common for some performers—like strippers—to vaunt their talents in successive cabarets (not all of them lesbian) across the course of a single night. See Yu, "Cabarets féminins," 39.

41 The quoted expression is from Cattan and Clerval, "Un droit à la ville?," 15. Given women's vulnerability to male violence in the public sphere, this spatial proximity offered important protections. See Cattan and Clerval, "Un droit à la ville?," 13.

42 See 1W 1032-46033 (APP); 77W 1428-10738 (APP); BA 1688 BRAIME (APP); 1W12-52656 (APP).

43 *Mädchen in Uniform*, directed by Leontine Sagan (now a lesbian cult classic promoted for its antifascist message), recounts a sapphic romance between a schoolgirl and her teacher. In a key scene the young protagonist cross-dresses as the male lead in a school play. The film was remade in 1958 under the direction of Géza von Radványi.

44 Report 196.685 of May 27, 1933, unsigned, in 1W 1032-46033 (APP).

45 1W 1032-46033 (APP).

46 According to *Police magazine*, Lulu's venue was still open in 1938. See Jean Moris, "Le secret des femmes damnées," part 2, *Police magazine*, October 2, 1938. It seems possible that Lulu operated clandestinely in order to avoid regulation.

47 Henri Lefebvre, *The Production of Space*, trans. Donald Nicholson Smith (Oxford: Blackwell, 1991), 320.

48 The term "imagined community" comes from Benedict Anderson, *Imagined Communities: Reflections on the Origins and Spread of Nationalism*, rev. ed. (London: Verso, 2006).

49 See especially Régis Revenin, *Homosexualité et prostitution masculines à Paris, 1870–1918* (Paris: L'Harmattan, 2005); William Peniston, *Pederasts and Others: Urban Culture and Sexual Identity in Nineteenth-Century Paris* (New York: Harrington Park Press, 2004); and Andrew Israel Ross, *Public City, Public Sex: Homosexuality, Prostitution, and Urban Culture in Nineteenth-Century Paris* (Philadelphia: Temple University Press, 2019).

50 See Laure Murat, *La loi du genre: Une histoire culturelle du "troisième sexe"* (Paris: Fayard, 2006), 68, 70–71. Murat further argues that the virtual absence of lesbianism from police registers suggests that lesbian prostitution was not considered widespread enough to warrant attention at that time. Pierre Miquel asserts that "female homosexuality was very rarely present in the vice files" in the first half of the twentieth century. Miquel, *La main courante: Les archives indiscrètes de*

la police parisienne, 1900–1945 (Paris: Éditions Albin Michel, 1997), 162. However, my work demonstrates that female homosexuality was indeed an object of police interest and files to that effect do exist. We have simply been looking in the wrong places.

51 Renamed the Brigade des Moeurs in 1914 when the Brigade Mondaine was detached from the Service des Garnis (which collected the cards filled by clients prior to renting hotel rooms or lodgings) and merged with a new service aimed at repressing drug traffic (Section mixte S), the name was officially changed back to Brigade Mondaine in 1930. It kept this appellation until 1975. On the history of the Brigade Mondaine, see Véronique Willemin, *La mondaine: Histoire et archives de la police des moeurs* (Paris: Éditions Hoëbeke, 2009), esp. 50–93.

52 Ross, *Public City, Public Sex*, 109. Alexandre Parent-Duchâtelet's 1836 sociological study *De la prostitution dans la ville de Paris, considérée sous le rapport de l'hygiène publique, de la morale et de l'administration* (Brussels: Hauman, Cattoir, 1836) linked the two sexual practices.

53 See Nicole Canet, *Maisons closes 1860–1946: Bordels de femmes, bordels d'hommes* (Paris: La Galerie au Bonheur du Jour, 2009), 12. Prostitutes lodged in maisons de tolérance, whereas they simply rented rooms for their work with clients in *maisons de rendez-vous*. Ross, *Public City, Public Sex*, 36–37.

54 Canet, *Maisons closes*, 40.

55 Mel Gordon reports that a bordello known as the Temple de Sappho in the second arrondissement was a "*point d'attraction* for the indigenous lesbian set." However, Gordon's claim is not supported by documentation, and I have found no mention of it in my research. Mel Gordon, *Horizontal Collaboration: The Erotic World of Paris, 1920–1946* (Port Townsend: Feral House, 2015), 102.

56 René Guetta, "A 'La grenouille'—Chez 'Moune et Léon,'" *Marianne: Grand hebdomadaire littéraire illustré*, March 8, 1939.

57 Lulu is identified as the "tenancière d'une maison galante" in BA 1688 BRAIME (APP). The charge of endangerment to national security was motivated by an anonymous letter dated October 26, 1935, signed "a friend," accusing Lulu (who the writer assumes "must not be entirely unknown to [police] services") and her former employee Pierre Chaix (identified as a diplomat from Central Europe who then inexplicably worked as a bouncer in nightclubs around Montmartre and Pigalle) as "a danger for national defense" because of the latter's frequent absences from Paris and ability to speak multiple languages. The missive sparked an inquest into Lulu's record but was later dismissed as inconclusive. Report to the prefect of police, January 27, 1936, 1W 1032-46033 (APP). See also Jean Moris, "Le secret des femmes damnées," part 1, *Police magazine*, September 25, 1938.

58 File 165114, JC/CAB2 (APP). Common criminal backgrounds did not necessarily result in common treatment. For example, Lulu's connections with the Corsican mob who controlled Pigalle at the time appear to have shielded her from a certain amount of police harassment.

59 Azenor in *Instants de vie, portrait d'Hélène Azénor*, dir. Claudie Lesselier (1987).

60 Pimping was punishable by both fines and prison time.

61 Michel Du Coglay, *Chez les mauvais garçons: Choses vues* (Paris: Éditions Raoul Saillard, 1937), 42–43.

62 Choisy, *Un mois chez les filles*, 61–62.

63 File 164141, JC/CAB3 (APP).
64 1W 1893-105491/ art. 69000-78 (APP).
65 1W 1032-46033 (APP).
66 By May 16, 1946, Stick was suspected of treason. See 77W 3761-372376 (APP).
67 77W 996-309364 (APP).
68 77W 996-309364 (APP).
69 The police were not unfamiliar with the address; as discussed earlier, Lulu launched Le Pavillon du Mystère on her property in 1933, and undercover officers attended the opening. Files 1W 1032-46033, 77W 1428-10738, BA 1688 BRAIME, and 1W 12-52656 (APP).
70 "Lulu de Montmartre est arretée," *Ce soir*, June 20, 1939; "Lulu de Montmartre avait voulu faire 'chanter' un client de son cabaret," *Ce soir*, June 20, 1939; "Lulu de Montmartre avait fait chanter un gros entrepreneur," *Le midi socialiste*, June 21, 1939; "La jalousie de Lulu de Montmartre était interessée," *Ce soir*, July 26, 1939; "Lulu de Montmartre," *Le petit parisien*, July 26, 1939; "Ses soeurs Denizot et Lulu de Montmartre devant le tribunal de Versailles," *Ce soir*, July 28, 1939; "Lulu de Montmartre et ses comparses avaient composé une scène de chantage," *La dépêche du Berry*, July 29, 1939; "Lulu de Montmartre le sursis pour un an de prison," *Ce soir*, July 29, 1939; "Un an de prison à Lulu de Montmartre," *Le matin*, February 13, 1939.
71 Monnel, interview.
72 Rue Fontaine was officially renamed rue Pierre-Fontaine in honor of the architect of the same name in 2004.
73 D33U3 485/ 374906/ (AP). Information about both the original location and inception of Le Fétiche is generally incorrect. Most internet sites give 1936 as the year the cabaret opened. Evidence from the Archives de Paris and print sources place the year as 1926. See Choisy, *Un mois chez les filles*, 61–62. The venue relocated multiple times. By April 30, 1938, *Paris-soir* lists the cabaret on 7 rue Fromentin and not, as some (including Schlesser, *Le cabaret "rive gauche,"* 171) claim, on rue Florentin.
74 Leslie Choquette, "Paris-Lesbos: Lesbian Social Space in the Modern City, 1870–1940," *Proceedings of the Annual Meeting of the Western Society for French History* 26 (1999): 125; Choisy, *Un mois chez les filles*, 83.
75 Choisy, *Un mois chez les filles*, 85. Moune managed at least six sapphic venues, which she often relocated to maintain a close proximity with a prior establishment after it was forcibly closed in response to police repression or local complaints.
76 Brassaï, "Sodom and Gomorrah," in *The Secret Paris*, n.p.
77 After Lulu's departure, Le Monocle's first owner, René Louis Prévost, sold the cabaret to Joseph Forello, a thirty-five-year-old Italian immigrant who retained ownership of the establishment until September 1940. D33U3 634 (AP).
78 Frede's partner Miki states that Frede had been advised to try her luck at Le Fétiche, but, according to Denis Cosnard, she ended up at Le Monocle instead. Since Frede discusses her time at Le Monocle in a 1971 television interview on *Dim Dam Dom*, it seems likely that Miki was mistaken. See "Frede," *Dim Dam Dom*, dir. Pierre Philippe, Channel 2, ORTF, broadcast February 21, 1971.
79 On Boby/Bobbie's career, see file 165114, JC/CAB2 (APP). See also "Cabaret

L'actress Bar Caroll's [*sic*] Conquet, Simone dite 'Bobbie,'" *L'intransigeant*, December 16, 1933. On February 16, 1936, an advertisement for Le Monocle in *L'intransigeant* lists the venue as "Chez Boby."

80 "Torrid Three from Gay Paree," *Female Mimics* 1, no. 3 (1963): 55.

81 D33U3 633/ 594923 (AP).

82 19920486/2 (AN).

83 Léa Lootgieter and Pauline Paris, *Les dessous lesbiens de la chanson* (Donnemarie-Dontilly: Éditions IXe, 2019). Edith apparently followed in her mother's footsteps. Frede reports that the older Piaf sang at Le Monocle in the 1930s. See "Frede," *Dim Dam Dom*.

84 Léon Marie bought the venue. By 1934 he incorporated as Favre and Company. Moune is listed as one of the personnel at the Buenos-Aires in an advertisement that appeared in *Paris-soir* on January 13, 1934.

85 *La semaine à Paris*, May 17, 1935.

86 See advertisement in *L'intransigeant*, January 7, 1938.

87 *Paris-soir*, April 30, 1938.

88 *Paris-soir*, May 19, 1938.

89 "Ou aller cette nuit," *Paris-soir*, August 16, 1938.

90 The term *la lorette* was coined to refer to the streetwalkers who promenaded there in the mid-nineteenth century. See Maurice Alhoy, *Physiologie de la Lorette* (Paris: D'Aubert et Cie., 1841), and Alexandre Dupouy and Marc Lemonier, *Histoire(s) du Paris libertin* (Paris: La Musardine, 2003), 235.

91 Frede managed La Silhouette for the owner, Maria Léontine Louise Dezoteau, née Leroux. D34U3 3234/ 713262 (AP). A cabaret of the same name had been operated on the premises since 1933. See 77 W 3175-481955 (APP). See also the advertisement for La Silhouette in *Paris-soir*, May 5, 1939.

92 Monnel, "De Pigalle à Montparnasse," part 2. File 164821, JC/CAB2 (APP). Stick renamed the bar Le Perroquet au Nid, but the old name stuck; the venue, still under Stick's management, was once again referred to as the Entre Nous into the 1970s.

93 *Paris-soir*, April 16, 1939. The surname "Carton" sometimes associated with Moune derives from her married name "Cantin." Moune is listed as the "widow Cantin" in all official papers.

94 Countering stereotypes, here the two feminine women (one identified as the actress Cécile Sorel) and the two masculine women are shown as pairs. René Guetta, "La Sirène," *Marianne: Grand hebdomadaire littéraire illustré*, July 26, 1939.

95 Chez Moune was opened on the site of "Le Madelon 40, an American Bar and Grill," a bar where Moune was either the administrator or artistic director from 1940 to 1943. D33U3 754/ 727408 (AP) and 19920486/2, Archives nationales (hereafter cited as AN).

96 D33U3 979/ 939470 (AP).

97 19920486/2 (AN).

98 In 1949, the cabaret at 2 rue Frochot is also referred to in the press as La Sirène. Undated clipping, 8MUS04, Solidor Pressbooks, Fonds Solidor.

99 Despite owning her home in Argenteuil, Lulu also kept a pied-à-terre in the neighborhood at 12 rue Frochot.

100 D33U3 879/ 1023231 (AP).

101 Calamity Joe also failed and was followed by the Kat's Club, which closed in 2014.

102 Le Carroll's first opened in 1939 as L'Actress American Bar. It was renamed Carroll's (or Carrol's [*sic*]) Actress Bar in 1946 in homage to Madeleine Carroll, the star of Alfred Hitchcock's 1935 thriller, *The 39 Steps*. Carroll owned a home in France and was awarded the Legion of Honor for her work on behalf of the French people during World War II. In 1948 the venue was registered with the city as the Carrols [*sic*] or Carrols' [*sic*] Club. In calling cards and in the press it is also alternately identified as Le Carroll's or Le Carroll's Club. On the club's changing name, see files 103191/983935, 98957/953881, 882Y/980133, and 2476/957646 (AP). See also Denis Cosnard, *Frede* (Paris: Éditions des Équateurs, 2017), 110.

103 JW3260-481879 (APP).

104 "Carroll's Paris," *Variety*, February 22, 1950. Jane Stick became famous in the early 1930s. She toured to Algeria in 1931, performing, according to the local papers, "with a simplicity that many Algerians don't understand, songs that are rather . . . daring." Jicet, "A travers les spectacles," *Les spectacles d'Alger*, January 7, 1931. On the opening of her Parisian cabaret on the rue de Ponthieu, see "Cabarets," *L'intransigeant*, June 11, 1937, and D33U3 863/ 983935 (AP). Le Carroll's was owned by Jacques Sicre and originally managed by Henri de Maeyer. Frede took over management of Le Carroll's in November 1948, after closing her cabaret at square Villaret-de-Joyeuse. See Cosnard, *Frede*, 111.

105 See the advertisement in *La semaine à Paris*, January 22, 1937. My thanks to Hélène Hazéra for bringing Jacqueline Batell, whose real name was Jacqueline Schiffmann, to my attention. Batell's hit songs for Solidor included "Filles de Saint-Malo," "La belle escale," and "Tout comme un homme." Dauberson recorded Batell's "Des fleurs pour mademoiselle," which might be called a hymn to the "sapphic spinster" in 1952.

106 Eartha Kitt performs briefly in this venue in a scene from Luciano Emmer's 1951 film *Parigi è sempre Parigi* (Paris is always Paris), starring Marcello Mastroianni.

107 Miki Leff Papers.

108 File 165114, JC/CAB2 (APP). See also Cosnard, *Frede*, 119. Cosnard identifies Bobbie as "Boby," but he is referring to the same woman.

109 Jacques-Louis Delpal, *Ultra-guide Paris la nuit* (1968; Paris: Gouraud Éditeur, 1969), 76.

110 "Frédé," *Dim Dam Dom*.

111 Dossier of the artist Dany Dauberson, biographical notice, FRBNF40930054, Bibliothèque-musée de l'Opéra (hereafter cited as BMO).

112 Clipping, 8MUS04, Solidor Pressbook 1948, Fonds Solidor.

113 "Dany Dauberson nouvelle Suzy Solidor," *Radar*, March 6, 1949, Solidor Pressbooks, Fonds Solidor.

114 The change of ownership for La Vie Parisienne from Suzy Solidor to Colette Mars and Mireille Moignet is recorded in the files D33U3 816/ 871871 (AP) and D33U3 951/ 871872 (AP). After four years, Mars and Moignet put the venue under management, hiring first Yvonne Englund (in 1950), then (in 1951) a company formed by Odette Laure (stage name of Odette Yvonne Marie Dhommée, another Solidor discovery) and Huguette Marchal before briefly renting the venue out as a Brazilian club. See file D33U3 44408/79178 (AP). Frede and Miki purchased La Vie Parisienne from Mars in 1961 and sold the club in 1970 after Frede fell ill. See also Cosnard, *Frede*, 198–99, 211.

115 Ross, *Public City, Public Sex*, 58.

116 See Revenin, *Homosexualité et prostitution masculines*, 60.

117 La Vie Parisienne was first registered as "Vie pas Chère [Cheap Life] à la Vie Parisienne" in the city archives in 1933. This is the earliest trace of the establishment that I have been able to locate. See D33U3 617/ 571456 (AP).

118 Bady's name (Mme Abel née Line Pens) is listed beneath Solidor's (Mlle Rocher Suzy) on the business record filed with the city of Paris. See D33U3 617/ 571456 (AP).

119 The quotation is from a police report that recounts Bady's biography. See the January 11, 1943, dossier Rocher and Abel, 1W 1762-102-821 (APP). According to the police, Line Bady's real name was Jeanne Abel. Married at twenty-one but childless and soon permanently separated from her spouse, Bady was born Jeanne Ferdinande Pens in Charleroi, Belgium, on July 11, 1897. Due to her criminal activities and same-sex desires, Bady was targeted by the police for surveillance during the war.

120 The filmmaker Michelle Porte, for example, met her life partner at Solidor's cabaret. Michelle Porte, interview by author, May 7. 2013, Paris, France.

121 *Samedi soir*, December 25, 1948, 8MUS04, Solidor Pressbook 1948, Fonds Solidor.

122 Solidor's pressbooks include clippings about each of the female artists she mentored. 8MUS04, Solidor Pressbooks, Fonds Solidor.

123 "Femmes doubles," *Marianne: Grand hebdomadaire littéraire illustré*, April 18, 1934.

124 *La vie parisienne*, January 7, 1933. On April 27, 1933, *L'action française* specified that the cabaret was called "Le Joubertin." See also *L'intransigeant*, April 21, 1933. Duvernon wrote regular columns for the right-leaning, high-circulation Parisian evening newspaper *L'intransigeant*, on occasion even covering her own performances. She was living at the time "on the eighth floor of an elegant house in Passy" with Renée Hamon (or Hamon-Heyman), who later entertained a passionate "friendship" with the writer Colette. H. F. P., "Cocktail-partie chez Solange Duvernon," *Comedia*, June 23, 1932, Recueil: Factice d'art de presse sur Solange Duvernon (BNF). Like Baba, Hamon was a journalist for *L'intransigeant*. It is possible that they met there. Hamon was later dubbed "le petit corsaire" by Colette (with whom she corresponded from about 1937 to Hamon's early death from cancer at age forty-six in 1943). Hamon's second marriage (to Harald Heyman, a man thirty years her senior with whom she lived between 1928 and 1932) appears to have ended when she left him for Baba. Between 1933 and 1936 Hamon made a world tour by bicycle. She is best known today for her exchange of letters with Colette. Colette's replies to Hamon are published. See Colette, *Lettres au petit corsaire* (Paris: Flammarion, 1963).

125 This opening was announced in *La vie parisienne* on July 11, 1936.

126 Michel Georges-Michel, "Au balcon du club, Rachilde chez Sidonie Baba," *Le cri de Paris*, May 19, 1939. On May 18, 1939, *Le populaire de Paris* also reported that Baba was opening "L'Heureuse Galère."

127 77W 620-231867 (APP). See also *La vie parisienne*, January 14, 1943.

128 According to Hexagone Gay, Aux Quatre Mules opened in 1954. "Les années 50," Hexagone Gay, accessed November 18, 2017, http://www.hexagonegay.com/region/paris50.html. See also Roger Cousin, "Baba Sidonie," *Mémoires de guerre* (blog),

April 14, 2011, http://la-loupe.over-blog.net/article-baba-sidonie-71745631.html; "Les années 60," Hexagone Gay, accessed April 15, 2018, http://www.hexagonegay .com/region/paris60.html.

129 Agnès Capri is the stage name of Sophie Rose Fridman, or Fridmann, born March 15, 1907. 77W 3185-482006 (APP).

130 File 135241, JC/HP2 (APP). On October 3, 1940, the Vichy government passed the first Jewish status laws and authorized the internment of foreign Jews. Capri's group took refuge first in Bordeaux, then in Bayonne, Biarritz, and Toulouse, before settling on the Côte d'Azur. With Calmon's assistance and Capri's Jewish identity kept secret, Capri continued to work. Eventually lodging at the Gallia Palace Hotel in Cannes, Capri formed the Théâtre Agnès Capri. On this period, see the private correspondence in the Fonds KOCHNO-1310 (BMO). These letters reveal the powerful influence that Calmon exerted over Capri, an influence their friend Victor Grandpierre called "crazy and dangerous." Letter from Victor Grandpierre to Christian Bérard, May 1, 1942, Nice, Fonds KOCHNO-1310 (BMO). On Capri's tempestuous romantic connection with Calmon, see Agnès Capri, *Sept épées de mélancolie* (Paris: Julliard, 1975), 293.

131 The Agnès Capri opened in 1948. 77 W 4595-505208 (APP).

132 See Karine Jay, "Suzy Solidor (1900–1983): Portrait d'une artiste à la frange d'orée d'art" (master's thesis, Université de Jean Moulin Lyon III, 1994–96), 150; and Marie-Hélène Carbonel, *Suzy Solidor, une vie d'amours* (Gémenos: Éditions Autre Temps, 2007), 173–243.

133 Germaine Ramos, "Colette Mars," *La semaine radiophonique*, no. 35 (September 7, 1947): n.p.

134 "Colette Mars: J'adore l'aventure," *À tout coeur*, no. 224 (January 30, 1951): 8–9.

135 "Colette Mars: J'adore l'aventure," 9.

136 Ramos, "Colette Mars," n.p.

137 In 2017 this was the equivalent of seventy-five thousand euros. On the transfer of La Vie Parisienne from Mars and Moignet to Frede and Miki, see Cosnard, *Frede*, 198–99. See also D33U3 816/ 871871 (AP).

138 Miki's statement clarifies that owning a business did not necessarily equate to owning a lease. This is one of the reasons why some cabarets changed addresses so often.

139 Miki Leff Papers. Mars's police file incorrectly states that she sold La Vie Parisienne to Frede on December 20, 1954. 77W 4202-438177 (APP).

140 "L'Elephant Blanc Belies Tag as Shuttered Paris Café-Terpery Reopens," *Variety*, April 10, 1963.

141 For tabloid coverage, see "La fin terrible de Cécilia, médecin de campagne," *Ici Paris*, April 18–24, 1967. Cécilia was the name of a character that Nicole Berger played on television.

142 Monnel, interview. L'Heure Bleue was owned by Mme Raymonde Delay (divorced) from the 1950s until her death in 1970, after which the license was taken over by Mademoiselle Maryse Nicole Godet. 19920486/32 (AN). Mademoiselle Colette Madeleine Fournier managed the cabaret from 1962 for Madame Delay. 19920486/21 AN.

143 Monnel, "De Pigalle à Montparnasse," part 2, 22.

144 Monnel, "De Pigalle à Montparnasse," part 2, 24.

145 Catherine Gonnard and Jöelle Matos, "Les filles," *Têtu, madame* (July 2000).

146 Denis Cosnard implies that Frede and Miki sold the Frede Carroll's on the rue Sainte-Anne to Emaer on September 1, 1970 (Cosnard, *Frede*, 212). Emaer merely rented the space; in September 1973 Miki was still receiving payments from the Société Frede Carroll's for bookkeeping work, and Miki inherited the business after Frede's death in 1976. Moreover, according to the Hussieres de justice associés Paris, it was Miki (and not Emaer) who sold the company to Ysolde Chrétien on June 8, 1977, for 289,975 francs. Miki Leff Papers.

147 Renaud Vincent, "Les 'nuits blues' parisiennes. Rue Sainte-Anne: La rue aux hommes. Le conseil de Paris saisi d'une plainte," *France soir*, October 25, 1975. The rue Sainte-Anne has changed considerably since the 1970s.

148 Philippe Baverel, "A Paris, la République en marche va s'installer rue Sainte-Anne," *Le parisien*, August 17, 2017.

149 Josy, interviews by author, June 18, 2013, January 2018, Paris, France.

150 Michael Sibalis argues that "the effort to appropriate urban space for sexual activity has been the work of gay men in particular, whereas lesbians have tended to be more discreet and more private in the conduct of their sexual lives." Sibalis, "Paris," 10–11. Feminist scholars emphasize, however, that this outcome issues not from lesbians' lesser desire for "territorial appropriation" nor from differences of affect, but rather from their "doubly dominated" status as both women and sexual minorities in a patriarchal system. Basically, lesbian households make less money, and so lesbians have less commercial power and less choice regarding where they live and work. See Cattan and Clerval, "Un droit à la ville?," 1, 10. In contrast (and although *Becoming Lesbian* also explores how queer women utilized virtual spaces to forge identities and create community), my research demonstrates that women who love women have historically been both interested in and capable of making lasting territorial claims on the public domain.

151 Manuel Castells, *The City and the Grassroots: A Cross-Cultural Theory of Urban Social Movements* (Berkeley: University of California Press, 1983), 140. Stéphane Leroy reiterated Castells's conclusions twenty-plus years later in "Le Paris gay," 582. For an overview of the early scholarship on the relationship between sexuality and geography, see Jon Binnie and Gill Valentine, "Geographies of Sexuality—A Review of Progress," *Progress in Human Geography* 23, no. 2 (1999): 175–87.

152 The cabaret was on the Route nationale 7 between Cannes and Nice. Miki Leff Papers.

153 Capri, *Sept épées*, 281. The description of Trenet comes from Lizzy Davies, "French Singer's Aide Accused over Will," *The Guardian*, August 23, 2008, https://www.theguardian.com/world/2008/aug/24/france.

154 Jennings, *Tomboys and Bachelor Girls*, 107.

155 See Michael Sibalis, "Urban Space and Homosexuality: The Example of the Marais, Paris' 'Gay Ghetto,'" *Urban Studies* 41, no. 9 (August 2004): 1739–58. Stéphane Leroy echoes this trajectory in "Le Paris gay," 590.

156 Sibalis, "Paris," 31.

157 Leroy, "Le Paris gay," 591.

158 Tamagne, "Paris: 'Resting on Its Laurels'?," 242.

159 Tamagne, "Paris: 'Resting on Its Laurels'?," 249, 255. The absence of any discussion of sapphic cabarets—excepting one mention of Suzy Solidor and another

of Le Monocle—from Tamagne's two-volume history of homosexuality in interwar Berlin, London, and Paris is striking. Tamagne, *History of Homosexuality*, 1:68, 273.

160 Henri Lefebvre, *Le droit à la ville* (Paris: Éditions Anthropos, 1968).

161 In Pigalle and Montmartre, cabarets féminins were surrounded by businesses welcoming homosexuals of both sexes. Frede's La Silhouette was next door to Le Fiacre, a cabaret opened by gay male performer O'Dett (alias René Gil) in 1934. It was also around the corner from Liberty's, a legendary cabaret established in 1919 on Place Blanche that featured male and female queer performers including Agnès Capri, Mick Micheyl, and Suzy Solidor after World War II. Liberty's occupied the former Chez Palmyre, the Pigalle restaurant frequented by lesbians during the Belle Époque. The impact of mixed-gender spaces on queer female culture is hard to determine; some venues hosted "women's nights" each week, but otherwise claimed hetero or mainly gay male profiles.

CHAPTER THREE

1 This chapter is a revised version of my article "A Woman Dressed Like a Man: Gender Trouble at the Sapphic Cabaret, Paris 1930–1960," *French Historical Studies* 44, no. 4 (2021): 711–48. Reprinted with permission.

2 "On dit, on dit," *La vie parisienne*, September 24, 1932. *La vie parisienne* was a society paper with a sustained interest in female homosexuality. See Clara Sadoun Édouard, "Presse, mondanité et saphisme décoratif," *Romantisme* 1. no. 159 (2013): 59–71.

3 Anaïs Nin, *Fire: From "A Journal of Love." The Unexpurgated Diary of Anaïs Nin, 1934–1937* (San Diego: Harcourt, 1995), 181–82.

4 Unidentified press clipping in English, dated 1954, Miki Leff Papers.

5 On the importing of the Anglo-American "butch/femme" (or "butch/fem") into the French context, see Christine Lemoine and Ingrid Renard, *Attirances: Lesbiennes fem, lesbiennes butchs* (Paris: Éditions Gaies et Lesbiennes, 2001). Lemoine and Renard employ *fem* in their work to distinguish the term from the French word *femme* meaning "woman" and "wife."

6 On the history of butch/femme identities in the United States, see Elizabeth Lapovsky Kennedy and Madeleine D. Davis, *Boots of Leather, Slippers of Gold: The History of a Lesbian Community* (New York: Routledge, 1993). For Britain, see Rebecca Jennings, *Tomboys and Bachelor Girls: A Lesbian History of Postwar Britain 1945–71* (Manchester: Manchester University Press, 2007). For Germany, see Katie Sutton, *The Masculine Woman in Weimar Germany* (New York: Berghahn Books, 2011). For France, see Carolyn J. Dean, *The Frail Social Body: Pornography, Homosexuality, and Other Fantasies in Interwar France* (Berkeley: University of California Press, 2000).

7 After the opening of sapphic cabarets in the 1930s, overtly masculine women were increasingly depicted in the French mass media. Florence Tamagne contends that such women first became common figures of social satire and political critique after the 1922 publication of Victor Margueritte's *La garçonne*. See Florence Tamagne, "Caricatures homophobes et stéréotypes de genres en France et en Allemagne: La presse satirique de 1900 au milieu des années 30," *Le temps*

des médias 1, no. 1 (2003): 44. Kelly Hankin reviews the extensive literature on the lesbian bar in *The Girls in the Back Room: Looking at the Lesbian Bar* (Minneapolis: University of Minnesota Press, 2002), xii–xiii.

8 According to Carolyn J. Dean, "the lesbian" was not considered difficult to identify in late nineteenth-century France despite being contradictorily explained as "*both* a manly woman and the womanliest woman." However, Dean maintains that by the interwar period, the dissolution of gender boundaries blurred the lines between lesbians and other women, rendering the former less visible—and hence more threatening. Dean, *The Frail Social Body*, 187. In contrast, I claim that the promotion of the butch/femme dyad within the sapphic cabaret in the 1930s helped consolidate lesbian identity and, in so doing, made women who desired women (whether masculine or feminine) more visible to both queer and heterosexual publics.

9 On lesbian cafés, restaurants, and brasseries in fin de siècle Paris, see Leslie Choquette, "Beyond the Myth of Lesbian Montmartre: The Case of Chez Palmyre," *Historical Reflections / Réflexions historiques* 42, no. 2 (Summer 2016): 75–96.

10 The vision of the "invert" holds an ambiguous place in the history of sexuality, serving as a precursor to both modern homosexuality and transgender identity. See Laure Murat, *La loi du genre: Une histoire culturelle du "troisième sexe"* (Paris: Fayard, 2006).

11 Historians situate this transition in different periods. George Chauncey argues that in 1920s America, "the liberalization of gender norms" made it possible to see women in active roles; if a woman could initiate sex, then gender inversion was no longer a convincing explanation for homosexual desire. George Chauncey, "From Sexual Inversion to Homosexuality: Medicine and the Changing Conceptualization of Female Deviance," *Salmagundi*, no. 58/59 (Fall 1982–Winter 1983): 143–44. Régis Revenin places this shift in the 1960s, when he claims that the "hetero-homo" binary became hegemonic. Régis Revenin, *Une histoire des garçons et des filles* (Paris: Vendémiaire, 2015).

12 It is noteworthy that this narrative (which explains homosexuality as a result of either gender inversion or object choice) has contributed to effacing what Emily Skidmore calls the "trans potential" of many historical subjects. See Emily Skidmore, *True Sex: The Lives of Trans Men at the Turn of the Century* (New York: New York University Press, 2017).

13 This is not to say that women did not perform female masculinity of their own volition but to emphasize the role of marketing in promoting such practices in France.

14 Mary-Louise Roberts, *Disruptive Acts: The New Woman in Fin-de-Siècle France* (Chicago: University of Chicago Press, 2002), 177.

15 Lavallière was known for her love affairs with women. See Nicole Albert, *Lesbian Decadence: Representations in Art and Literature of Fin-de-Siècle France*, trans. Nancy Erber and William A. Peniston (2005; New York: Columbia University Press, 2016), 146.

16 Sutton, *The Masculine Woman*, 127.

17 The website Hexagone Gay offers a brief but useful introduction to the history of *travestis* and *transformistes* in France. See "Les années 10," Hexagone Gay, accessed December 31, 2017, http://www.hexagonegay.com/10.html.

18 Vander Clyde was also known as Van der Clyde and Vander Clyde Broadway. Amy

Lyford, "'Le Numéro Barbette': Photography and the Politics of Embodiment in Interwar Paris," in Whitney Chadwick and Tirza True Latimer, eds. *The Modern Woman Revisited: Paris between the Wars*, ed. Whitney Chadwick and Tirza True Latimer (New Brunswick, NJ: Rutgers University Press, 2003), 223–33. Lyford argues that Barbette's performance diffused interwar anxieties about gender roles by turning gender into "a cultural commodity, a spectacle" (225).

19 Clubs where drag was popular included the Dancing Dubois and the Dancing Firnimondi in Toulon; the Alcazar music hall in Marseille; and L'Escale, La Rotonde, and La Tour in Saint-Tropez.

20 La Petite Chaumière later relocated to 11 rue Ravignan. In 1927 Colette's first husband, Henry Gauthier-Villars, known as Willy, observed, "In the Music-Hall, the vogue of men disguised as women has developed significantly." Willy, *The Third Sex*, trans., intro., and notes by Lawrence R. Schehr (Urbana: University of Illinois Press, 2007), 93.

21 John Grand-Carteret, quoted in Nicole Albert, "Travestissement," in *Dictionnaire des cultures gays et lesbiennes*, ed. Didier Eribon (Paris: Larousse, 2003), 476.

22 Numerous press, advertising, and personal sources attest to this. *Fantasio* magazine, for example, describes a Montmartre cabaret féminin populated by women "who dress voluntarily as gentlemen" (October 15, 1924).

23 "Simultaneously a signifier of castration (detachable, artifactual, made to be put on and taken off) and of empowerment," Garber continues, "the monocle when worn by a *woman* emphasizes, indeed parodies, the contingent nature of the power conferred by this instrumental affectation." Marjorie Garber, *Vested Interests: Cross-Dressing and Cultural Anxiety* (New York: Routledge, 1992), 153–54.

24 Laura Doan, *Fashioning Sapphism: The Origins of a Modern English Lesbian Culture* (New York: Columbia University Press, 2001), 108; Garber, *Vested Interests*, 154.

25 Colette, *The Pure and the Impure*, trans. Herma Briffault, intro. by Judith Thurman (New York: New York Review of Books, 2000), 75; Maryse Choisy, "Dames seules," *Le rire* (special edition), May 12, 1932, n.p..

26 Such categories have multiplied prodigiously in recent decades and now include such terms as nonbinary, genderfluid, and agender.

27 See, for example, contemporary medical explanations for what the *Diagnostic and Statistical Manual of Mental Disorders* (*DSM-5*) used to call transgenderism and since May 2013 has identified as "gender dysphoria."

28 Victor Margueritte, *La garçonne* (Paris: Flammarion, 1922). See also Christine Bard, *Les garçonnes: Modes et fantasmes des années folles* (Paris: Flammarion, 1998).

29 To this end, and although it is sometimes difficult to discern, in the images that follow *all* of the masculine women are wearing skirts. Whether this choice was mainly in compliance with the November 7, 1800, French law that forbade women from wearing pants in Paris unless they possessed a police permit is impossible to say. While an exception to the law was made in 1882 for female cyclists and equestrians, as noted in the introduction, the ruling was not abrogr準ated until 2013. Christine Bard, *Une histoire politique du pantalon* (Paris: Éditions du Seuil, 2010).

30 Henry Miller, quoted in Anne Wilkes Tucker, *Brassaï: The Eye of Paris* (Houston: Museum of Fine Arts, 1999), 43.

31 A second version of *Voluptés de Paris* was published in 1935. Unhappy with the

production values, Brassaï disowned both publications. In 1976 he republished the Le Monocle photographs in *Le Paris secret*.

32 The quotes are from Allen Ellenzweig and George Stambolian, *The Homoerotic Photograph: Male Images from Durieu/Delacroix to Mapplethorpe* (New York: Columbia University Press, 1992), 66, 74. See also François Buot, *Gay Paris: Une histoire du Paris interlope entre 1900 et 1940* (Paris: Fayard, 2013), 116; Helmut Gernsheim, quoted in Tucker, *Brassaï*, 39; and Florence Tamagne, *A History of Homosexuality in Europe: Berlin, London, Paris, 1919–1939* (New York: Algora Publishing, 2004), 1:68. Although Frances E. Hutchins's sophisticated analysis reminds us of the constructed nature of these shots (they were posed), her emphasis on "femme" invisibility nevertheless implies that the photographs depict "real" "butch/femme" couples. See Frances E. Hutchins, "The Pleasures of Discovery: Representations of Queer Space by Brassaï and Colette," in *Lesbian Inscriptions in Francophone Society and Culture*, ed. Renate Günther and Wendy Michallat (Manchester: Manchester University Press, 2007), 189–204.

33 Publication rights for this photograph could not be obtained. It can be accessed at multiple sites online. Other women are frequently incorrectly identified as Lulu in Brassaï's photographs. The real Lulu can be seen here in figure 3.1.

34 Eve Pascal discusses the pinky ring as a "distinctive sign" of sapphism in Léa Lootgieter, "Femmes des sixties," *Well Well Well: La revue lesbienne* 1 (2014): 94.

35 Xavier Demange, quoted in Tucker, *Brassaï*, 43.

36 Jack Halberstam, *The Queer Art of Failure* (Durham, NC: Duke University Press, 2011), 101.

37 On Frede's life, see Denis Cosnard, *Frede* (Paris: Éditions des Équateurs, 2017); and Jany Casanova, "Frède [*sic*] Carroll [*sic*] écrit des mémoires fracassants." *La vie parisienne* 103, no. 201 (September 1967). See the Miki Leff Papers, especially thirty-three pages of notes for her memoir written on a yellow legal pad, likely around 2000; Pierre Philippe's 1971 half-hour documentary "Frédé" on *Dim Dam Dom*; and 77W 995-308704 (APP).

38 Suzanne's rechristening as the gender-ambiguous Frede (a diminutive of either the feminine "Frédérique" or the masculine "Frédéric") was not unusual; many entraîneuses either adopted or were given a masculine alias to fit a newly gendered image. Of the thirty-eight entraîneuses (of ninety-two) identified as lesbians in the police files discussed below, more than half were associated with masculine monikers.

39 "Frédé," *Dim Dam Dom*.

40 Jean Moris, "Le secret des femmes damnées," part 1, *Police magazine*, September 25, 1938, 6. Sometimes the mannish entraîneuse also bound her breasts. Kiki K., interview by author, January 18, 2018, Toulouse, France.

41 File 163878, JC/CAB4 (APP), is one of several files that contains photos of an entraîneuse in both masculine and feminine attire.

42 On race and colonialism in interwar Paris, see Tyler Stovall, *Paris Noir: African Americans in the City of Light* (Boston: Houghton Mifflen, 1996). For a gendered perspective, see Jennifer Boittin, *Colonial Metropolis: The Urban Grounds of Anti-Imperialism and Feminism in Interwar Paris* (Omaha: University of Nebraska Press, 2010). On Bricktop and Baker, see T. Denean Sharpley-Whiting, *Bricktop's Paris: African-American Women in Paris between the Two World Wars* (Albany:

State University of New York Press, 2015); see also Jean-Claude Baker and Chris Chase, *Josephine: The Hungry Heart* (New York: Random House, 1993); and Matthew Pratt Guterl, *Josephine Baker and the Rainbow Tribe* (Cambridge, MA: Harvard University Press, 2014). Both Baker and Bricktop purportedly engaged in affairs with other women, including each other.

43 Maryse Choisy, *Un mois chez les filles: Reportage* (Paris: Éditions Montaigne, 1928; repr., Paris: Éditions Stock, 2015), 38.

44 I am thinking of photographs by Albert Harlingue of Le Monocle in the 1930s and by Francis Bay and Willy Rizzo of Le Carroll's Club in the 1950s.

45 While this requires more research, my sources uniformly suggest the persistence of racially gendered hierarchies in these cabarets linking whiteness to masculinity. This differentiates their dynamics considerably from those seen in lesbian bars, cabarets, and theatres in the United States, where many butch lesbians were Black or Brown. See, for example, James F. Wilson, *Bulldaggers, Pansies, and Chocolate Babies: Performance, Race, and Sexuality in the Harlem Renaissance* (Ann Arbor: University of Michigan Press, 2010), especially chapter 5, "'In My Well of Loneliness': Gladys Bentley's Bulldykin' Blues" (154–91). Kennedy and Davis in *Boots of Leather* argue for the precocious emergence of a kind of racial egalitarianism inside lesbian bars that was so powerful that it produced racially mixed working-class lesbian communities in Buffalo, New York, during the 1940s and 1950s. We see nothing of the kind in France at this time.

46 On this process, see Skidmore, *True Sex*, 99.

47 Moris, "Le secret des femmes damnées," part 1, 11.

48 My thanks to Alexandre Dupouy for showing me a matchbook from Chez Moune during our meetings in the summer of 2023. In her master's thesis, Wenjing Yu (whom I introduced to Dupouy) suggests that *garçonnes* may have personalized such matchbooks and given them to favored clients. I am more doubtful about whether they would have had the means to do so. Wenjing Yu, "Cabarets féminins: Histoires d'une visibilité exceptionelle d'espaces lesbiens (1920–1960)" (master's thesis, L'École des hautes études en science sociales, 2022–23), 35–36.

49 Evelyn Waugh, "Labels," *Fortnightly Review* 127 (April 1930): 496. Did Waugh grasp this gendered performance as "homosexual" rather than simply immoral? Its staging within a space known for same-sex transgression suggests that he did.

50 "Who Wears the Pants?," *Variety*, May 14, 1958, 52.

51 See "Torrid Three from Gay Paree," *Female Mimics* 1, no. 3 (1963): 60, 61.

52 Evelyne Rochedereux, interview by author, December 15, 2010, Le Croisic, France.

53 Monique Isselé, interview by author, June 17, 2013, Paris, France.

54 Hélène Azenor, *Histoire d'UNE* (Paris: Les Octaviennes, 1988), 209.

55 Azenor, in *Instants de vie, portrait d'Hélène Azénor*, dir. Claudie Lesselier (1987).

56 She did, however, take her girlfriend to Suzy Solidor's La Vie Parisienne, a space that lacked cross-dressed staff and was less visibly "different." Aurivel, in *Pour mémoire: Portrait de Rolande Aurivel*, dir. Claudie Lesselier (1988).

57 Shari Benstock, *Women of the Left Bank: Paris, 1900–1940* (Austin: University of Texas Press, 1986), 11.

58 Barbara Bell, *Just Take Your Frock Off: A Lesbian Life* (Brighton: Ourstory Books, 1999), 45–46.

59 On fashion as a visible marker of queer subjectivity, see Adam Geczy and Vicki

Karaminas, *Queer Style* (London: Bloomsbury, 2013); and Valerie Steele, ed., *A Queer History of Fashion: From the Closet to the Catwalk* (New York: Fashion Institute of Technology, 2013).

60 Isselé, interview.

61 We must remember that in France women "didn't have the right to wear pants, even in winter." Eve Pascal, quoted in Lootgieter, "Femmes des sixties," 94.

62 Isselé, interview.

63 Mel Gordon, *Horizontal Collaboration: The Erotic World of Paris, 1920–1946* (Port Townsend: Feral House, 2015), 219.

64 Kevin Mumford, *Interzones: Black/White Sex Districts in Chicago and New York in the Early Twentieth Century* (New York: Columbia University Press, 1997), xiv.

65 The files addressed here are from the series JC/CAB 1, 2, 3, and 4, as well as JC/HP 2, at the Archives de la préfecture de police de Paris (APP). The JC series derives from the files of the Brigade Mondaine. My thanks to Isabelle Tarisca and the archivists at the APP for their assistance in accessing these documents.

66 Whereas Régis Revenin informed me (email, December 5, 2017) that he had found only three files on lesbians in the Paris police archives from 1933 to the present when researching his book *Une histoire des garçons et des filles*, searches under the rubric "Cabaret" produced, as this article demonstrates, vastly different results.

67 Since the police archives are far from complete, there is no way of knowing whether similar reports were kept on entraîneuses at other times and then discarded or destroyed. Pierre Miquel identifies key holdings and lacunae in *La main courante: Les archives indiscrètes de la police parisienne, 1900–1945* (Paris: Éditions Albin Michel, 1997), 27–28.

68 There is a distinct difference between the quality of these images: In the former, when registering for employment, the women are often smiling and carefully coiffed and made-up. In the latter, when booked for arrest, the tone is more somber.

69 In 1936 the passage of the Jean Zay law extended compulsory education from thirteen to fourteen. This age was raised to sixteen in 1959.

70 File 166150, JC/CAB3 (APP).

71 File 161282, JC/CAB1 (APP).

72 File 167329, JC/CAB2 (APP).

73 For more on lesbians of color in the postwar years, see chapter 9.

74 The exception was the feminine "Lydie." File 165886, JC/CAB4 (APP).

75 Chez Moune and Le Carroll's Club were more apt to pay wages than Le Monocle, and Le Carroll's Club paid higher wages (600 to 800 francs per shift) than either of the other two venues. The fact that most of the women who were salaried are described in the police files as feminine types who denied being lesbians suggests that it may have been harder to attract feminine than masculine women to work in cabarets féminins.

76 See Jean Fourastié and Jacqueline Fourastié, *Pouvoir d'achat, prix et salaires* (Paris: Gallimard, 1977), 37. This calculation is based on an average hourly wage of between 86 and 116 francs for an eight-hour day in October 1951.

77 Convicted female prisoners were often incarcerated in the women's prison at Fresnes, a place known for same-sex activity. It was also the site where numerous members of the French resistance were held, tortured, and executed during World War II.

78 File 133188, JC/CAB4 (APP).

79 To preserve anonymity, I refer to the women in these files by nickname or (if one isn't specified) by their initials. File 164137, JC/CAB3 (APP).

80 File 165647, JC/CAB3 (APP).

81 File 165641, JC/HP2 (APP).

82 File 163875, JC/CAB4 (APP).

83 File 158811, JC/CAB4 (APP).

84 File 166611, JC/CAB3 (APP).

85 Emphasis mine. Carmen Tessier, "Les potins de la commère," *France soir*, February 7, 1951.

86 File 162533, JC/CAB2 (APP).

87 File 162533, JC/CAB2 (APP).

88 For press coverage, see Recueil: Caroll's [*sic*] Cabaret, 1950–1960, 8-SW-86 (BNF).

89 Frede discussed the incident in "Frédé," *Dim Dam Dom*.

90 "Le Carroll's, Paris," *Variety*, February 24, 1960, 101. See also "Le Carroll's, Paris," *Variety*, October 17, 1956, 65; and "Le Carroll's, Paris," *Variety*, July 20, 1955, 50 ("Femcee chores are well handled by ex-U.S. model Mickey Michaels"). The expression "femcee" is repeated in reference to Miki in *Variety*'s articles on Le Carroll's Paris on July 20, 1955, May 30, 1956, and November 4, 1959, with the latter edition getting her family name right ("Leff") and complimenting her on her "good French" (75).

91 File 166136, JC/CAB3 (APP).

92 File 167378, JC/CAB3 (APP).

93 File 164723, JC/CAB2 (APP).

94 File 124856, JC/CAB3 (APP).

95 File 167329, JC/CAB2 (APP).

96 File 165756, JC/CAB3 (APP).

97 File 158811, JC/CAB4 (APP).

98 File 163870, JC/CAB4 (APP).

99 File 125449, JC/CAB3 (APP).

100 File 164821, JC/CAB2 (APP).

101 By making "sexual commerce into spectacle," the sapphic cabarets thus participated in what Andrew Israel Ross has called "the domestication of street solicitation" that began in the late nineteenth century. See Ross, *Public City, Public Sex: Homosexuality, Prostitution, and Urban Culture in Nineteenth-Century Paris* (Philadelphia: Temple University Press, 2019), 203.

102 1W1893-105491 (APP). The police files also provide no trace of prostitution between female entraîneuses and male and female couples, although both of these practices were commonplace according to my interviewees.

103 Bell, *Just Take Your Frock Off*, 120.

104 Véronique Willemin, *La mondaine: Histoire et archives de la police des moeurs* (Paris: Éditions Hoëbeke, 2009), 84.

105 Monique Isselé, interview by author, January 14, 2018, Paris, France.

106 Marino, interview by author, April 29, 2013, Paris, France.

107 Dan Monnel, "De Pigalle à Montparnasse: Itinéraire d'une garçonne ordinaire des années soixante," part 1, *Lesbia magazine* (October 2003): 23.

108 Marino, interview.

109 Nicole Miquel, interview by author, May 15, 2013, Paris, France.

110 Dan Monnel, "De Pigalle à Montparnasse: Itinéraire d'une garçonne ordinaire des années soixante," part 2, *Lesbia magazine* (November 2003): 22. Dan elaborated on this story in our 2018 interview.

111 Moreover, among those women who did desire women, it is also possible that some may not have identified as female, providing us with examples of trans "before trans." While I disagree with what I argue is an inadequate attention to queer sexuality in her work, on the idea of trans "before trans" in France, see Rachel Mesch, *Before Trans: Three Gender Stories from Nineteenth-Century France* (Stanford: Stanford University Press, 2020).

112 Michael Sibalis, "Homophobia: Vichy France, and the 'Crime of Homosexuality': The Origins of the Ordinance of 6 August 1942," *GLQ: A Journal of Lesbian and Gay Studies* 8, no. 3 (2002): 301–18.

113 De Gaulle, quoted in Julian Jackson, *Living in Arcadia: Homosexuality, Politics and Morality in France from the Liberation to AIDS* (Chicago: University of Chicago Press, 2009), 43. The heterosexual age of majority was raised to fifteen in 1945.

114 My thanks to Laura Doan for this observation.

CHAPTER FOUR

1 Usually directed by Jean Kerchbron, *Cabaret du soir* first aired twice monthly for half an hour at either 9:05 p.m., 9:50 p.m., 10:05 p.m., or 10:30 p.m. From May 1958 to January 1959 it mostly aired monthly. I viewed twenty-four of the twenty-six shows in Inathèque's archive. Half of the September 14, 1957, and all of the December 7, 1957, broadcasts are missing.

It is unclear how Mars and Sandrel met. They may have been introduced on a TV shoot when Sandrel reported on an April 30, 1955, evening news broadcast on the distribution of clothing to needy villagers; Mars was among the celebrities charged with performing this task. Under a year later they began producing their own show.

2 G. N. Aznar, "Notre couverture: Micheline Sandrel," *La semaine radiophonique*, no. 40 (October 5, 1958): 2. Not everyone loved the show. One unhappy couple complained: "At present we [prefer] to go to sleep." "L'opinion des téléspectateurs," *Télévision programme magazine*, no. 128 (April 6–12, 1958): 44.

3 *Cabaret du soir* was shot on a soundstage at the Centre Alfred Lelluch.

4 *Cabaret du soir* resembled American musical variety shows like *The Ed Sullivan Show* (1948–71). However, because it was produced in a cabaret environment rather than on a proscenium theatre, it had a more intimate ambiance.

5 Like *Cabaret du soir*, *Trente-six chandelles*, *Magazine féminin*, and *Lectures pour tous* (all discussed below) aired weekly in the 1950s in Algeria, Belgium, and Germany, among other countries. See general listings in *Télévision programme magazine* for programming schedules.

6 Tamara Chaplin, *Turning On the Mind: French Philosophers on Television* (Chicago: University of Chicago Press, 2007), 31, 41. On the televised variety show's popular roots in the music hall, see Raymond Williams, *Television: Technology and Cultural Form* (Hanover: Wesleyan University Press, 1974), 58–60.

7 Female variety show producers include Aimée Mortimer, Denise Glaser,

Jacqueline Joubert, Michèle Arnaud, Mick Micheyl, Colette Mars, and Micheline Sandrel, among others. The limited scholarship on variety shows focuses almost exclusively on programs produced by men (e.g., Henri Spade, Robert Chazal, Jean Nohain, Guy Lux, and Jean-Christophe Averty—the latter especially known for his creativity). See Laurent Gervereau, "Chercher le lien: Les variétés à la télévision," in *La grande aventure du petit écran: La télévision française 1935–1975*, ed. Jérôme Bourdon et al. (Paris: Musée d'histoire contemporaine-BDIC / INA, 1997), 203–21. Most scholars of French TV (myself included) have focused rather on the state's use of the new technology as an instrument for cultural democracy and educational uplift. See, for example, Jérôme Bourdon, *Histoire de la télévision sous de Gaulle* (Paris: Presses des Mines, 2014) (on politics and television); Chaplin, *Turning On the Mind* (on the televising of philosophy); and Isabelle Veyrat-Masson, *Quand la télévision explore le temps: L'histoire au petit écran, 1953–2000* (Paris: Fayard, 2000) (on the televising of history).

8 Geoff Hare, "Popular Music on French Radio and Television," in *Popular Music in France from Chanson to Techno*, ed. Hugh Dauncey and Steve Cannon (London: Routledge, 2016), 68.

9 I first workshopped this material at the "Arts, féminisms, archives audiovisuelles . . . mise en place des méthodologies" conference at the Foundation Hartung Bergman, Antibes, France, in August 2012. Catherine Gonnard and Elisabeth Lebovici also participated and presented research on these topics. Their work was later published as "Inventer son genre dans le langage de la télévision," *GLAD!*, November 15, 2016, http://www.revue-glad.org/209. My work is indebted to their scholarship and to multiple interviews with Gonnard between 2010 and 2018.

10 Most performers were white, and most performances (like the cabarets that they were modeled on) tended to reinforce racial stereotypes. When nonwhite bodies were present, they were mainly either foreign (African American jazz musicians), spoofed (the occasional blackface), or abject caricatures (the African savage).

11 On "queering television," see Samuel A. Chambers, *The Queer Politics of Television* (London: I.B. Taurus, 2009), especially 18–23. On media as creating "the preconditions of intelligibility" that make queer counterpublics possible, see Michael Warner, *Publics and Counterpublics* (New York: Zone Books, 2005).

12 Nancy Fraser, "Rethinking the Public Sphere: A Contribution to the Critique of Actually Existing Democracy," *Social Text*, no. 25/26 (1990): 79n25.

13 Chambers, *Queer Politics*, 35.

14 On television, the majority of this work focuses on queer fictional characters, generally represented as either tragic, criminal, comic, or titillating. When the genre is nonfiction, the broadcast often targets "the homosexual" as an object of inquiry. For France, see Brigitte Rollet, *Télévisions et homosexualité: 10 ans de fictions françaises 1995–2005* (Paris: L'Harmattan, 2007), and Scott Gunther, *The Elastic Closet: A History of Homosexuality in France, 1942–Present* (London: Palgrave Macmillan, 2009), especially 105–19 on the French cable TV station Pink TV (which began airing in 2004). On this practice in the media more broadly, see Larry Gross, *Up From Invisibility: Lesbians, Gay Men, and the Media in America* (New York: Columbia University Press, 2001). My information is also derived from informal discussions with archivists during more than twenty years of working at Inathèque.

15 I have tried to circumvent this conundrum by searching not only by key term (*homosexual/le*, *lesbienne*, etc.) but also by proper name or by the titles of films,

books, or songs. The catch is that I already have to know what I am looking for in order to find it. My search results are also dependent on archivists who may not know how (or are not authorized) to see (and hence name) that which I seek. As INA archivist Rachel Denoeud notes, this problem exceeds queer populations. Since INA's archivists are not charged to enter information pertaining to sexuality, gender, race, age, ability, or religion into program summaries unless that information is relevant to the broadcast, research that seeks to analyze any minority group on French TV is equally thwarted (Rachel Denoeud, phone conversation with the author, February 9, 2016). For queer TV history, this vexed situation improved slightly in 2013 when INA's professional website established two rubrics for archiving homosexuality: the first focuses on AIDS, the second on gay and lesbian activism. Catherine Gonnard was key in establishing these rubrics and is among the few to have successfully mined the French television archive for queer material. To date, however, there is no rubric for LGBTQ+ culture. Gonnard's history as a militant in the French homosexual and lesbian movements and as an archivist at INA render her uniquely equipped to conduct such research. Her counsel over the last decade has been invaluable. See also Gonnard interviewed by Léa Lootgieter, "La télévision est toujours en décalage avec les mouvements LGBT," Les OUT d'or, accessed July 31, 2019, http://2017.outdor.fr/catherine-gonnard/index.html.

16 This is the story for France, but also for the United States, where as Steven Capsuto reports, the *Washington Post* announced that 1976 was TV's "Year of the Gay." Capsuto also refers to "the near invisibility of [the topic in] the 1950s and 1960s." Steven Capsuto, *Alternate Channels: The Uncensored Story of Gay and Lesbian Images on Radio and Television, 1930s to the Present* (New York: Ballentine Books, 2000), xiii, 5. Ron Becker, in contrast, situates the watershed in the 1990s in the US context, arguing that "throughout its first four decades, [American] television virtually denied the existence of homosexuality." Ron Becker, *Gay TV and Straight America* (New Brunswick, NJ: Rutgers University Press, 2006), 3. The first British broadcast on homosexuality, "Homosexuality and the Law, a Prologue," aired in 1954 and focused, as the title suggests, on the juridical status of mainly male same-sex sexual behavior. Notwithstanding two documentaries in 1964 (on gay men) and 1965 (on lesbians), however, it wasn't until the 1970s that British TV began addressing homosexuality consistently. Terry Sanderson, *Mediawatch: The Treatment of Male and Female Homosexuality in the British Media* (London: Cassell, 1995), 16–17.

17 On England, see "Les libertés individuelles: l'Angleterre," *XXème siècle*, Channel 1, ORTF, broadcast June 9, 1970. On the United States, see "Le rêve américain: 2ème partie: l'âme," *XXème siècle*, Channel 1, ORTF, broadcast May 10, 1971. On Holland and Spain, see "L'église demain? 1ère partie," *XXème siècle*, Channel 1, ORTF, broadcast December 8, 1970.

18 The 1971 French translation of Kate Millett's *Sexual Politics* attracted considerable TV attention and occasioned some of these discussions. See "Kate Millett, et la condition de la femme," *Variances*, Channel 1, ORTF, broadcast July 20, 1971.

19 For television historians and archivists, the problem of source identification gets easier after the emergence of the homosexual rights movements in the 1970s because program participants publicly claim nonnormative sexual identities

(thus fashioning the historically salient categories through which they are subsequently known). See "Portrait d'un psychiatre," *Émission médicale*, Channel 1, ORTF, broadcast October 19, 1970; "Pour ou contre l'éducation sexuelle à l'école," *Procès*, Channel 1, ORTF, broadcast April 25, 1972; "L'homosexualité," *Émission médicale*, Channel 1, ORTF, broadcast November 29, 1973. The first broadcast explicitly focused on female homosexuality, which aired in 1977 on *L'huile sur le feu* and is discussed in chapter 5, below, follows this format.

20 The exception here is Gonnard and Lebovici, whose work covers some of the same ground as mine. Mathieu Cadot maintains, "In the 1960s, homosexuality was completely nonexistent on French television." Mathieu Cadot, "Visibilité, acceptation, hétérocentrisme: Les représentations actuelles de l'homosexualité à la télévision française" (master's thesis, Université Lumière Lyon 2, 2004), 20. See also Isabelle Gavillet, "Constructions sociales, scientifiques et médiatiques d'un lieu commun: L'acceptation croissante de l'homosexualité à la télévision," *MEI (Médiation et information)*, no. 20 (2004): 83–92. Beginning in the 1990s most queer performances were in dramas or sitcoms. Brigitte Rollet notes that between 1995 and 2005 there were only eighteen lesbian characters on French fiction TV, most of whom were "not exactly role models." Brigitte Rollet, "In the Margins and Off-Centre: Lesbian Characters on French Television 1995–2005," in *Lesbian Inscriptions in Francophone Society and Culture*, ed. Renate Günther and Wendy Michallat (Manchester: Manchester University Press, 2007), 82; see also Rollet, *Télévisions et homosexualité*. It was not until 2004 that Pink TV (France's first satellite channel dedicated to queer and "queer friendly" programming) began providing queer network professionals with a production platform for content aimed specifically at French LGBTQ+ audiences. That same year, the global launch of YouTube offered opportunities for amateur videographers—queer and otherwise—to make their own media creations widely available. These developments have saturated cyberspace, offering queer audiences new access to queer generated AV content.

21 Rollet, "In the Margins," 98.

22 On queering the history of homosexuality, see Laura Doan, *Disturbing Practices: History, Sexuality, and Women's Experience of Modern War* (Chicago: University of Chicago Press, 2013). On queering TV, see David Glyn Davis and Gary Needham, eds., *Queer TV: Theories, Histories, Politics* (London: Routledge, 2009). *Queer TV* includes important early essays by Amy Villarejo and Lynne Joyrich, among others. Chambers in *Queer Politics* usefully differentiates between a "queer politics of television," "queer TV," and "gay television" (18–23). See also Gonnard and Lebovici, "Inventer son genre."

23 The Eurovision network originated from the European Broadcasting Union. The entirety of the French nation was networked by 1961. "Le réseau de la télévision française un veritable journal en images," *Télévision programme magazine*, no. 101 (September 29–October 5, 1957): 6–7; Christian Quidet, "L'Eurovision," *Télévision programme magazine*, no. 105 (October 27–November 2, 1957): 39–41. See also "Images d'Afrique: La T.V. au Maroc et en Tunisie," *La semaine radiophonique*, no. 8 (February 2, 1954): 4–5.

24 Quote from Jean d'Arcy, director of television programming at RTF from 1952 to 1959, cited in Chaplin, *Turning On the Mind*, 34.

25 A special state tax known as the *redevance audiovisuelle* helped cover costs.

26 For average numbers of viewers per set, see "180,000 téléspectateurs français ont l'oeil sur Télé-Luxembourg," *Télévision programme magazine*, no. 105 (October 27–November 2, 1957): 46–47. On télé-clubs, see Joffre Dumazedier, *Television and Rural Adult Education: The Télé-Clubs in France*, with assistance by A. Kedros and B. Sylwan (UNESCO, 1956). See also Marie-Françoise Levy, "La création des *télé-clubs*: L'expérience de l'Aisne," in *La télévision dans la République dans les années 50*, ed. Marie-Françoise Levy (Paris: Éditions Complexe, 1999), 107–32; and chapter 1 of Chaplin, *Turning On the Mind*.

27 Chaplin, *Turning On the Mind*, 31–36. See also Hélène Duccini, "Carré blanc et signalétique télévisée en France, 1961–1998," *Le temps des médias*, no. 1 (2003): 70.

28 Removed from the lofty intellectual and cultural aims of the state broadcaster, these postwar shows were a vigorous response to the privations of the war years.

29 This situation is noteworthy when contrasted against the trend in French cinema toward, as Damon R. Young argues, "making sex public" between the early 1950s and the late 1970s. A trenchant example of cinematic sex is the young Brigitte Bardot in Roger Vadim's 1956 film *And God Created Woman* in which Bardot, as Juliet, "performs sexual abandon decoupled from the private sphere" in the penultimate scene where she dances wildly at the Whiskey Club. I would argue that Young's thesis that sex in postwar cinema was "shaped by a tension between an emergent fantasy of the liberal sexual subject and an enduring conception of the 'heterosexual family as *constitutive* of the social'" became similarly valid for television, only later (from the 1970s to the 1990s). Damon R. Young, *Making Sex Public and Other Cinematic Fantasies* (Durham, NC: Duke University Press, 2018), 15.

30 The white rectangle was replaced by a white square in 1964 and was most often used when films were broadcast, since cinema was understood to produce more "troubling" images. Female announcers known as *speakerines* also offered advice to adults about whether upcoming broadcasts were appropriate for young viewers.

31 Noëlle Noblecourt would later claim that she was fired for refusing the advances of Raymond Marcillac, the news director at TF1 in the 1960s. *Les documents du dimanche*, "Sexe, censure et télévision," *Les documents du dimanche*, dir. Daniel Costelle and Isabelle Clarke, France 2, broadcast April 8, 2001.

32 Louvier was publicly explicit about her preference for women. See Nicole Louvier, *Qui qu'en grogne* (Paris: La Table Rond, 1953); Louvier, *Chansons interdites* (Paris: La Table Ronde, 1953); and Louvier, *Les dialogues de la nuit blanche* (Paris: La Jeune Parque, 1967). Louvier was also excoriated in the press for attacking the misogyny of entertainment industry impresarios in her novel *Les marchands* (Paris: La Table Ronde, 1959).

33 Éliane Victor interviewed on "Les femmes aussi," *La belle télévision: Quarante ans de télévision*, dir. Maurice Dugowson, France 3, broadcast August 22, 1990. On women on French TV between 1960 and 1975, see Marie-Françoise Lévy, "Les femmes du temps present à la télévision: La mutation des identités (1960–1975)," in *Les années 68: Le temps de la contestation*, ed. Geneviève Dreyfus-Armand et al. (Paris: Éditions Complexe, 2008), 199–218.

34 The Motion Picture Production Code, known as the Hays Code, was a set of guidelines that were voluntarily adopted in 1930 by the US motion picture industry.

35 Patricia White, *Uninvited: Classical Hollywood Cinema and Lesbian Representability* (Bloomington: Indiana University Press, 1999), 16. This chapter is indebted to White's brilliant analysis of lesbian desire and difference on the silver screen.

36 This latter question is especially crucial if one is arguing as I do that the medium can speak of these matters to audiences beyond the initiated. My claim that early French TV ensured broad access to queer sensibilities thus extends beyond the confines of Gonnard and Lebovici's argument that these broadcasts spoke mainly to marginal—i.e., queer—female audiences. Gonnard and Lebovici, "Inventer son genre."

37 White identifies visual coding, extratextual information, and intertextuality in her work. White, *Uninvited*, 16–17. I insist on linguistic coding as well, especially because of the centrality of song to sapphic cabaret performance. On lesbian intertextuality in literature, see Elaine Marks, "Lesbian Intertextuality," in *Homosexualities and French Literature*, ed. George Stambolian and Elaine Marks (Ithaca, NY: Cornell University Press, 1979), 353–77. For an introduction to intertextuality, see Graham Allen, *Intertextuality* (London: Routledge, 2000). My work on intertextuality is also informed by Judith Mayne's *Cinema and Spectatorship* (New York: Routledge, 1993) and Mary Ann Doane's *The Desire to Desire: The Women's Films of the 1940s* (Bloomington: Indiana University Press, 1987). On intertextuality in media more broadly, see Ulrike H. Meinhof and Jonathan Smith, *Intertextuality and the Media: From Genre to Everyday Life* (Manchester: Manchester University Press, 2000).

38 For Solidor's comment, see "Télé Paris à Deauville," *Télé Paris*, RTF Télévision, broadcast August 23, 1954. Solidor's second cabaret, which opened the same year as this broadcast, was named simply Chez Suzy Solidor.

39 Chez Tonton was run by Gaston Baheux. The famous *transformistes* Charpini and Claude Véga were regulars. Mick Micheyl was among the entertainers who got her start there. A popular cabaret among Germans during the war, it closed in 1956. Interestingly, *tonton* can also imply "police informer" in French.

40 Judith Butler, *Gender Trouble: Feminism and the Subversion of Identity* (New York: Routledge, 1999), 34.

41 Martin Pénet, "L'expression homosexuelle dans les chansons françaises de l'entre-deux guerres: Entre dérision et ambiguïté," *Revue d'histoire moderne et contemporaine*, no. 53–54 (October–December 2006): 108. See also Léa Lootgieter and Pauline Paris, *Les dessous lesbiens de la chanson* (Donnemarie-Dontilly: Éditions IXe), 2019.

42 Lootgieter and Paris decrypt a century of French songs expressing female same-sex desire in *Les dessous lesbiens de la chanson*. Many of these were sung by women discussed in this chapter. Performers purported to be straight also popularized songs with openly homosexual content; Charles Aznavour's "Comme ils disent" became famous for addressing the topic with tolerance in 1972. Juliette Gréco's 1971 interpretation of F. Bottin's "Les pingouins" (with its linguistic reference to *gouines*—slang for lesbian) was equally accepting but more coded.

43 *Cabaret du soir*, RTF Télévision, broadcast January 3, 1959.

44 Thanks to Jane Kuntz for suggestions regarding translating the lyrics.

45 Marie-Hélène Carbonel claims that in addition to having a business relationship, Mars and Solidor were lovers. Carbonel, *Suzy Solidor, une vie d'amours* (Gémenos: Éditions Autre Temps, 2007), 240.

46 These rumors were promoted in the tabloids and the press. For a discussion of the Italian scandal, see Jean Dominique, "Dany Dauberson: Je me lave mes cheveux plusiers fois par jour," *Music-Hall*, no. 4 (1960): 30–31. It was also reported in the German press in *Der Spiegel*, no. 8 (April 4, 1960): 79.

47 For biographical details, see "Dany Dauberson: dossier biographique" (1951), FRBNF40930054 (BMO).

48 White, *Uninvited*, 17.

49 "Claudine à l'école," *Les films du dimanche*, RTF Télévision, broadcast April 11, 1954.

50 Pierre-Jean Vaillard on *Bouquet de joie*, RTF Télévision, broadcast September 24, 1956. The synopsis of this broadcast contains the very first mention of the word *lesbienne* in INA's database.

51 See references to Margueritte's *La garçonne* on *Des goûts et des couleurs*, RTF Télévision, broadcast November 8, 1956; *Cinépanorama*, RTF Télévision, broadcast January 24, 1957; *Trente-six chandelles*, RTF Télévision, broadcast February 4, 1957; *Cabaret du soir*, RTF Télévision,, broadcast September 14, 1957. Catherine Gonnard and Elisabeth Lebovici also discussed these themes in a conference presentation at the University of Lausanne, "Gros plans sur *La garçonne* (1957), une performance de genre," n.d. Notes from that presentation are available at https://www.unil.ch/cin/files/live/sites/cin/files/Colloques/Genre%20et%20m%C3%A9dias%202019/R%C3%A9sum%C3%A9s/GENRE_MEDIAS_Gonnard-Lebovici.pdf, accessed December 15, 2021.

52 I poach "to-be-looked-at-ness" from Laura Mulvey's groundbreaking 1973 article, "Visual Pleasure and Narrative Cinema," republished in *Visual Culture: The Reader*, ed. Jessica Evans and Stuart Hall (London: Sage, 2002), 383.

53 In 1947 at age thirty-one Mars made the cover of *La semaine radiophonique* after charming audiences in Raymond Lamy's film *Miroir* starring Jean Gabin. *La semaine radiophonique*, no. 36 (September 7, 1947). For her work with Gabin in *Miroir*, see also *Mon film*, no. 71 (December 3, 1947). By 1957 Mars had appeared in five more films, often playing cabaret singers or courtesans. Mars's film resumé includes *Aux yeux du souvenir* (1948), dir. Jean Delannoy; *Sombre dimanche* (1948), dir. Jacqueline Audry; *Menace de mort* (1950), dir. Raymond Leboursier; *Les dents longues* (1953), dir. Daniel Gélin; *Leguigon guérisseur* (1954), dir. Maurice Labro; *Cargaison blanche* (1958), dir. Georges Lacombe; *La garçonne* (1957), dir. Jacqueline Audry; *Les sultans* (1966), dir. Jean Delannoy; and *Dernier domicile connu* (1970), dir. José Giovanni.

54 "Colette Mars: J'adore l'aventure," *À tout coeur*, no. 224 (January 30, 1951).

55 "Télé-Paris," *Télé-Paris*, RTF Télévision, broadcast January 20, 1954; reprised on *Cabaret du soir*, RTF Télévision, broadcast January 18, 1958. Released as Colette Mars, *Mon p'tit fichu* (Disques Vogue, 1955), 33½ RPM.

56 Director Jacqueline Audry produced sixteen feature films between 1946 and 1969 and is one of the most important, and most understudied, female directors of her time. She is known for her "women's films." Audry's most audacious

effort was the 1951 lesbian-themed *Olivia*. She also adapted Colette's literary work for the screen. Brigitte Rollet's biography, *Jacqueline Audry: La femme à la camera* (Rennes: Presses Universitaires de Rennes, 2015), avoids speculating about Audry's personal life while depicting her as a feminist filmmaker whose work challenged heteronormative expectations.

57 Debar's androgynous allure later inspired Audry to cast the actress as the lead in her 1959 biopic about the cross-dressing Chevalier d'Éon, *Le secret du chevalier d'Éon*.

58 Gonnard and Lebovici also make this argument in "Gros plans sur *La garçonne* (1957)."

59 On Sandrel's career, see *Télé-59*, April 19–25, 1959.

60 See "Cabaret du soir," *Télévision programme magazine*, no. 98 (September 8–14, 1957).

61 *Cabaret du soir*, RTF Télévision, broadcast February 15, 1958.

62 Solidor's quote is from "Suzy Solidor révèle son étrange destin de femme sans homme," *Confessions*, no. 1 (November 26, 1936). In 1958 Yvonne de Bremond d'Ars was riding on the success of the second of what would become nineteen mystery novels about the antique business, *C'est arrivé en plein Paris, passionate aventure d'antiquaire* (Paris: H. Lefebvre, 1957). Both her novels and her window displays attracted media attention: she appears on French TV and radio more than fifteen times. See, for example, *Lectures pour tous*, RTF Télévision, broadcast February 11, 1959; and "Vitrines du Faubourg Saint Honoré," *JT nuit*, RTF Télévision, broadcast June 13, 1959. In the latter, Micheline Sandrel is the journalist. Mick Micheyl also figures in the broadcast.

63 Esther Newton, "The Mythic Mannish Lesbian," *Signs* 9, no. 4 (Summer 1984): 557–75.

64 One of the earliest representations of (male) homosexuality on French TV was a 1959 comedy sketch known as "Le deux Hortenses" or "Les antiquaires" featuring Jean Poiret and Michel Serrault. See "Jean Poiret et Michel Serrault, 'Les deux Hortenses' ou 'Les antiquaires,'" *La clé des champs*, RTF Télévision, broadcast April 27, 1959. This routine, about a pair of outrageously effeminate antiquarians (one of whom tries to sell his male partner—using terms generally reserved for a piece of costly antique furniture—to a male customer), later formed the basis for Poiret's wildly successful 1973 play (and 1978 film) *La cage aux folles*. Like Bremond d'Ars, both Solidor and Mars ran antique shops in their later years.

65 The Comtesse—identified for TV viewers in another broadcast as Yvonne's "precious collaborator"—is also shown at Yvonne's side on *L'art de vivre*, RTF Télévision, broadcast January 21, 1963, a documentary about Yvonne de Bremond d'Ars shot in the home that the women shared. See also "Vitrines du Faubourg Saint Honoré."

66 Sara Ahmed, *Queer Phenomenology* (Durham, NC: Duke University Press, 2006), 96; emphasis in original. Lillian Faderman describes how so-called Boston marriages between women in the United States at the end of the nineteenth century performed a similar function. Lillian Faderman, *Odd Girls and Twilight Lovers: A History of Lesbian Life in Twentieth-Century America* (New York: Columbia University Press, 1991), esp. 11–37.

67 Gonnard and Lebovici, "Inventer son genre."

68 Gonnard and Lebovici, "Inventer son genre."

69 Each table was designated for a specific group of guests: theatre, film, sports, "regulars," literature, and the table identified as "très parisienne" (very Parisian). "Cabaret du soir," *Télévision programme magazine*, no. 100 (September 22–28, 1957).

70 Ahmed, *Queer Phenomenology*, 81–82.

71 In this they manifest a growing acceptance in postwar France of the idea that, as Sarah Fishman observes, "not all women were necessarily destined for marriage and motherhood." Fishman, *From Vichy to the Sexual Revolution: Gender and Family Life in Postwar France* (New York: Oxford University Press, 2017), xxiii.

72 Gonnard and Lebovici, "Inventer son genre." Gonnard and Lebovici remind us that some queer representations were unkind: when the male duo Charpini and Brancato (popular before the war) appear on the show, the latter performed, in Gonnard and Lebovici's words, "female roles with a good dose of self-deprecating mockery." In another *Cabaret du soir* broadcast, Charpini recalls his father's and Brancato's mother's "troubling" (i.e., homophobic) reaction to the duo's performances. *Cabaret du soir*, RTF Télévision, broadcast June 28, 1958. Citing Leo Strauss's *La persécution et l'art d'écrire* (Paris: Gallimard, 2009), 55, Gonnard and Lebovici argue that although such caricatural routines may amuse a heterosexual public, the laughter they induce can ring hollow for those reflected in the parody performed. See Gonnard and Lebovici, "Inventer son genre."

73 *Cabaret du soir*, RTF Télévision, broadcast January 25, 1949.

74 "Edwige Feuillère, invitée d'honneur du Cabaret du soir," *Télévision programme magazine*, no. 122 (February 23–March 1, 1958): 38.

75 Kiki Kazan, interview by author, January 14, 2011, Toulouse, France.

76 Gonnard and Lebovici, "Inventer son genre."

77 According to Kelly Ricciardi Colvin, one of the ironic results of French women's enfranchisement in 1945 was the deployment of femininity in postwar France in ways that delimited women's political agency. Kelly Ricciardi Colvin, *Gender and French Identity after the Second World War, 1944–1954* (London: Bloomsbury, 2017), 4–5. The resurgence of femininity was reinforced by a national focus on domestic consumption that was likewise reflected in fashion, most obviously by Christian Dior's wasp-waisted ultrafeminine "New Look." On women's roles as domestic consumers and motors for French postwar economic recovery, see Rebecca J. Pulju, *Women and Mass Consumer Society in Postwar France* (Cambridge: Cambridge University Press, 2011).

78 There were exceptions, especially in film (think of Marlene Dietrich in *Morocco* [1930] or Greta Garbo in *Queen Christina* [1933]), but here female masculinity is nonetheless sexualized for heterosexual consumption.

79 Solidor Birthday Photo Albums (1979–1981), Fonds Solidor.

80 Carbonel, *Suzy Solidor*, 310. See also the undated captioned photographs from Haut-de-Cagnes in Solidor's photograph album 13MUS03, Fonds Solidor.

81 The identification between Solidor and Bruant is apparent in portraits of her completed in 1962 by Marie-Madeleine de Rasky and in 1964 by John S. Churchill, both visible in the unpaginated catalogue *Donation Solidor 1973, Ville de Cagnes-sur-mer Château-Musée* (1973; Cagnes-sur-Mer: Imprimerie Zimmerman, 1982).

82 André David, "Chroniques du snobisme," *Marianne: Grand hebdomadaire littéraire illustré*, March 8, 1933, 15.

83 "Voici des mains," *Le monde illustré*, February 4, 1939 (BNF).
84 "Genres," undated press clipping, 8MUS01, Solidor Pressbooks 1937–1938, Fonds Solidor.
85 "Je suis un vieux garcon, dit Suzy Solidor," *Samedi soir*, December 25, 1948.
86 "Odette Laure," *Les joies de la vie*, RTF Télévision, broadcast October 6, 1958. After working for Solidor, Laure managed La Vie Parisienne from 1954 to 1959 for Colette Mars once the latter had purchased the venue.
87 Télé-Luxembourg was established in 1955. Its accessibility in the north of France meant that the number of sets in the region quickly outstripped the national average. See "180,000 téléspectateurs français," 46–47; and "L'état et les stations périphérique," *Télé liberté information*, no. 34 (June–July 1969): 17. Dauberson's Télé-Luxembourg appearance was rebroadcast on French TV in the 1992 special "Le retour des ménestrels," *La chance aux chansons*, France 2, broadcast December 1, 1992. Dauberson's first TV appearance was on *Télé-Paris à Cannes* in 1955. See "Télé-Paris à Cannes," *Télé-Paris*, RTF Télévision, broadcast August 1, 1955.
88 *Combat*, October 22, 1952, 2.
89 This was Dauberson's fourth TV appearance. *Sur un air de cabaret*, RTF Télévision, broadcast December 4, 1956.
90 It is a televised image she'll repeat. See, for example, Dany Dauberson, "Ça te va bien," on *Les jeunes mariés du printemps*, RTF Télévision, broadcast March 16, 1959.
91 "Entretien avec la chanteuse Dany Dauberson," *Dimanche en France*, RTF Télévision, broadcast November 16, 1958.
92 Dany Dauberson on "De New York à Los Angeles," *Ce soir à*, RTF Télévision, broadcast December 3, 1960.
93 Dauberson explained the hairstyle by claiming that a well-known hairdresser had accidentally burned her hair off when he used the wrong product on her. According to this story, she was obliged to cancel her performances and hide out for a month while she waited for her hair to grow back. The tale seems likely to have been an attempt to justify her choice of cut. Dominique, "Dany Dauberson."
94 Serious performances of female masculinity such as this on French television were extremely rare. In contrast, gender-play and cross-dressing were common stock for men, but when men masqueraded as women on musical variety shows, it was invariably to comedic effect.
95 The location (outside Paris) and occupation (sport) apparently rendered pants acceptable. *Au delà de l'écran*, Channel 1, ORTF, broadcast March 21, 1965.
96 *Der Spiegel*, no. 8 (April 4, 1960): 79.
97 *Music-Hall*, no. 4 (1960): 30–31.
98 Micheyl never commented publicly about her personal life, and journalists rarely asked. In a 2010 biography of the singer, Micheyl is quoted referring in guarded terms to actor Jean Marais as among the most important loves of her life—a fact all the more ironic since Marais (although purportedly bisexual) was Jean Cocteau's long-term lover. Claude Secondi, *Mick Micheyl: Des planches à l'acier* (Villeurbanne: Éditions du Mot Passant, 2010), 136–37.
99 "Télé-Paris," *Télé-Paris*, RTF Télévision, broadcast January 1, 1952.
100 "Mick Micheyl," *JT 20H*, RTF Télévision, broadcast May 23, 1964.
101 Pierre Poulain, "Zoom sur Mick Micheyl," *Télé liberté information*, no. 37 (November–December 1969): 9.

102 *Noir et blanc*, March 8, 1963.

103 Secondi, *Mick Micheyl*, 137.

104 "Elle était tout pour moi," *Lesbia*, no. 54 (October 1987): 23. In contrast, Micheyl claimed that her fans were either heartsick young people or invalids. "Après la peinture et la chanson, Mick Micheyl va se consacrer désormais à la mise en scene," *Music-Hall*, no. 43 (September 1958): 32–33.

105 "Elle était tout pour moi," 23.

106 *Télé-Paris*, January 1, 1952.

107 Data from *Discorama*, RTF Télévision, broadcast June 12, 1959.

108 "Défi à Mick Micheyl," *Les coulisses de l'exploit*, Channel 1, ORTF, broadcast April 21, 1965; "Mick Micheyl," *Aujourd'hui Madame*, Channel 1, ORTF, broadcast June 27, 1973; "Le week-end relax au Touquet Paris Plage," *Temps présent*, Channel 1, ORTF, broadcast October 8, 1966; "Mick Micheyl," *JT nuit*, Channel 1, ORTF, broadcast December 14, 1966; "Mick Micheyl à Moscou," *JT nuit*, Channel 1, ORTF, broadcast December 26, 1967; "Les îles," *Entente cordiale*, Channel 1, ORTF, broadcast February 9, 1972; etc.

109 Indeed, according to her friend the celebrity musician known as "Dave" (born Wouter Otto Levenbach in Amsterdam), the one televised scene we have of Mick Micheyl in a kitchen, frying eggs in the company of a black man identified in the archival notice as "her husband," actually depicts Mick in the company of one of her impresario Roland Ribet's male lovers. See "Magazine des femmes: Mick Micheyl and Co," *JT 13H*, Channel 1, ORTF, broadcast June 18, 1973. Dave (Wouter Otto Levenbach), interview by author, Oct.ober 18, 2017, Paris, France. Mick Micheyl promoted the young Dave's career by featuring him on *Ce sacré métier*, Channel 1, ORTF, broadcast January 23, 1969.

110 When interviewed as "Anne Monaco," Kiki stated that her real name was George, but she is also sometimes referred to as Andrée Jourdain. See "Anne Monaco, nouvelle Minstinguette," *À tout coeur*, no. 231 (March 20, 1951): 10–11, 20. Micheyl's comment is from Mick Micheyl, *Dieu est-il bien dans ma peau?* (Lyon: Presses de la Cité, 1984), n.p. In 1957 Mick Micheyl starred as a woman named "Kiki" in Stany Cordier's film *Paris Music-Hall*. It is possible that the moniker was a secret homage to her lover. Micheyl was also the film's coproducer and composer. Charles Aznavour, drag impersonator Claude Véga, and Georgette Anys—the actress and *patronne* of the Bal de la Montagne Sainte-Geneviève discussed in chapter 1—also starred.

111 See "Anne Monaco, nouvelle Mistinguette," 20; and Gilles Schlesser, *Le cabaret "rive gauche": De la Rose Rouge au Bateau ivre: 1946–1974* (Paris: Éditions de l'Archipel, 2006), 183.

112 "Baptême d'une guenon par Anne Monaco," *JT 20H*, RTF Télévision, broadcast November 11, 1953.

113 Dave, interview. Roland Ribet's memoir *L'impresario impertinent* (Paris: Jacques Grancher, 1993) makes no such personal revelations.

114 Entertainment producers also pushed discretion during these years. Dave described to me how industry professionals counseled him to appear in public with other women in order to derail rumors of his homosexuality. Dave, interview.

115 Eve Pascal argues that while Louvier's romantic lyrics were sometimes directed at men (for example, her hit song "Mon petit copain" or "My boyfriend"), "we

all knew that she was talking about a woman." Louvier was one of the few lesbian celebrities who "dared to speak directly to lesbians, even on the radio," according to Pascal. Pascal, quoted in Léa Lootgieter, "Femme des sixties," *Well Well Well: La revue lesbienne* 1 (2014): 94.

116 Gonnard and Lebovici also make this observation in "Inventer son genre."

117 John D'Emilio, "Capitalism and Gay Identity," in *The Lesbian and Gay Studies Reader*, ed. Henry Abelove, Michèle Aina Barale, and David M. Halperin (New York: Routledge, 1993), 467–76.

118 Jeannine Allain, "Chansons interdites de Nicole Louvier," *Arcadie: Revue littéraire et scientifique*, no. 54 (June 1958).

119 Although Louvier later claimed there was nothing "hot" about the song's lyrics ("It was a simply a love song, barely even physical," she states), the version recorded by Swiss singer Lys Assia was censored and denied radio play. See the radio coverage on "Parole de femmes," *Tours de chant*, France Culture, aired March 9, 1988.

120 For radio, see *Rendez-vous en Ile de France*, Inter Variétés, ORTF, aired October 19, 1964; for TV, see, e.g., "Nicole Louvier," *Au delà de l'écran*, RTF Télévision, broadcast March 17, 1963.

121 See, for example, "Le match de Paris présente deux filles et trois garçons qui sont la chanson française 1954," *Paris match*, no. 254 (February 6–13, 1954); and "Nicole Louvier: J'écris des choses qui font rougir," *Music-Hall*, no. 9 (1955): 24, 47.

122 For Louvier's critique of the entertainment industry, see Louvier, *Les marchands*.

123 *Magazine féminin*, RTF Télévision, broadcast February 5, 1959; January 23, 1965; and November 25, 1967.

124 *Magazine féminin*, February 5, 1959. In 1967 Sandrel won the literary prize from *La vie parisienne* for her *Guide de l'amant*. When asked at the awards ceremony whether she preferred a male lover or husband, she coyly responded, "Neither one nor the other. I've accorded the same number of pages to each." "Micheline Sandrel lauréate du Prix littéraire de 'La vie parisienne,'" *La vie parisienne*, no. 199 (July 1967).

125 Georges Perec, *Les choses* (Paris: Julliard, 1965).

126 Gonnard and Lebovici, "Inventer son genre."

127 Virginia Woolf, *A Room of One's Own* (1929; London: Hogarth Press, 1935). Although they analyze a different program, Gonnard and Lebovici come to similar conclusions in "Inventer son genre."

128 "La naissance d'un compositeur de chansons," *Qui l'aime la suivre*, Paris Inter, RTF, aired October 10, 1960, coproduced by Nicole Louvier.

129 See the interview with Louvier rebroadcast on "Parole de femmes," *Boulevard des archives*, France Culture, Radio France, aired March 9, 1998.

130 *Âge tendre et tête de bois*, RTF Télévision, broadcast November 21, 1961. The musical variety show hosted by Albert Raisner aired on RTF and then ORTF between 1961 and 1966.

131 Sylviane Francesconi, interview by author, January 11, 2011, Toulouse, France.

132 "Dan" Monnel, interview by author, June 10, 2018, Lille, France.

133 Cocteau's drawing with the corrected dedication is reproduced on the frontispiece of a tribute to Gribouille. See Gribouille, *Je vais mourir demain*, preface by Françoise Mallet-Joris, intro. by Marie-Thérèse Orain (Saint-Cyr-sur-Loire:

Éditions Christian Pirot, 2001). Details about Gribouille's biography are contained in Orain's lengthy introduction, "Lettre ouverte à Pinpin," 11–33.

134 *École des vedettes*, RTF Télévision, broadcast November 19, 1962.

135 Mallet-Joris, preface to Gribouille, *Je vais mourir*, 7.

136 While in custody she acquired the nickname "Gribouille" after the headstrong protagonist in George Sand's novel *Histoire du véritable Gribouille*. Sand's character is the youngest son of seven children; in part 1 he throws himself into the river for fear of getting wet. In part 2 he throws himself into the fire for fear of being burned.

137 *Un quart d'heure avec* . . . [Suzy Solidor], RDF/RTF, aired April 7, 1948; "Interview de la chanteuse Suzy Solidor: Entre poésie et chansons," *Magazine bleu*, Nice Côte d'Azur, RTF, aired August 16, 1961.

138 Marie-Françoise Orain, interview by author, November 19, 2017, Paris, France.

139 Gribouille, *Je vais mourir demain*.

140 Gonnard and Lebovici, "Inventer son genre."

141 The organization, called Salut Gribouille, placed a notice in *Lesbia magazine* in order to raise money. See "Gribouille," *Lesbia magazine*, no. 174 (September 1998): 5.

142 Two examples of queer broadcasts on French TV book shows are Monique Wittig's interview on the book show *Lectures pour tous* apropos of her recently published novel *L'Opoponax* (Wittig on *Lectures pour tous*, Channel 1, ORTF, broadcast October 7, 1964) and the interview with Simone de Beauvoir's literary protégée Violette Leduc (whose autobiography *La bâtarde* contains explicitly lesbian passages and whose 1966 novella *Thérèse et Isabelle* about adolescent lesbian love inspired a 1968 film of the same name) on the same show later that year (*Lectures pour tous*, Channel 1, ORTF, broadcast November 18, 1964).

143 Heather Love, *Feeling Backward: Loss and the Politics of Queer History* (Cambridge, MA: Harvard University Press, 2007), 12. Drawing on Adorno, Tia DeNora argues that music is a "mediator" of the social, which "helps to structure such things as styles of consciousness . . . or modes of embodiment." Tia DeNora, *Music in Everyday Life* (Cambridge: Cambridge University Press, 2000), 46–47.

144 I discuss this scholarship in chapter 1.

145 David Halperin explores the idea that homosexuality "is not only a sexual practice but also a cultural practice" and "that there is a relation between sexuality and social or aesthetic form" in his book, *How to Be Gay* (Cambridge, MA: Harvard University Press, 2012), 35. Gonnard and Lebovici agree in "Inventer son genre."

146 The quote is from Warner, *Publics and Counterpublics*, 15.

147 Amy Villarejo, *Lesbian Rule: Cultural Criticism and the Value of Desire* (Durham, NC: Duke University Press, 2003), 18.

148 Warner, *Publics and Counterpublics*, 62–63.

149 Warner, *Publics and Counterpublics*, 114.

CHAPTER FIVE

1 The broadcast began airing on the ORTF's newly launched Channel 2 on March 7, 1965. The title *Dim Dam Dom* was shorthand: "Dim" for *dimanche* (Sunday),

"Dam" for *dames*, and "Dom" for *d'Hommes* (men). De Galard was among a group of nineteen women who held producing and directing posts at the RTF/ORTF between 1958 and 1974. Rachel Denoeud, "Femmes de radio et télévision dans les fonds de l'INA," November 14, 2019, https://inatheque.hypotheses.org/15919.

2 *Dim Dam Dom* was known for its surprising pairings: in one hard-hitting episode writer Marguerite Duras interviewed the only female director of a women's prison in France (Paris's La Petite Roquette, where several of the entraîneuses discussed in chapter 3 served time). "Marguerite Duras à la petite Roquette," *Dim Dam Dom*, Channel 2, ORTF, broadcast November 12, 1966.

3 De Galard told journalist Pierre Philippe to shoot preliminary footage for two portraits, one on Agnès Capri and one on Frede. She chose the latter. "Frédé," *Dim Dam Dom*, dir. Pierre Philippe, Channel 2, ORTF, broadcast February 21, 1971. "Frédé" was shot almost entirely at La Grange in Mareil-le-Guyon, the country home to which Frede—already suffering from cancer—had retreated with her partner Miki after putting their business on the rue Sainte-Anne under new management in September 1970.

4 *Dim Dam Dom* briefly addressed female homosexuality in a sequence on writer Violette Leduc ten months earlier. In that broadcast, Leduc divulges the true story behind her novella *Thérèse et Isabelle* (about two young girls who fall in love in boarding school) and refers to her nine-year relationship with a woman (Hermione), but Leduc's writing and relationships with men take center stage. See "Violette Leduc racontée par elle-même," *Dim Dam Dom*, Channel 2, ORTF, broadcast April 6, 1970.

5 "L'homosexualité, ce douloureux problème," *Allô Ménie*, Radio-télévision Luxembourg, aired March 10, 1971, accessed March 20, 2021, https://www.youtube.com/watch?v=SGHRtoi3en0. A transcript is published in "L'homosexualité, ce douloureux problème," *La revue h*, no. 1 (Summer 1996): 52–59. The title of Lionel Bernard's 2000 film, *L'homophobie, ce douloureux problème*, is both an ironic comment on Grégoire's show and a tragic testament to how heinous attitudes toward homosexuality remain today.

6 Michael Sibalis, "Gay Liberation Comes to France: The Front Homosexuel d'Action Révolutionnaire (FHAR)," *French History and Civilization: Papers from the George Rudé Society*, no. 1 (2005), https://h-france.net/rude/wp-content/uploads/2017/08/vol1_Sibalis2.pdf.

7 Quotes are from Sibalis, "Gay Liberation," 266; Jacques Girard, *Le mouvement homosexuel en France, 1945–1980* (Paris: Syros, 1981), 82–83; Julian Jackson, *Living in Arcadia: Homosexuality, Politics and Morality in France from the Liberation to AIDS* (Chicago: University of Chicago Press, 2009), 183–84; and Jean Le Bitoux, Bruno Proth, and Hervé Chevaux, *Citoyen de seconde zone: Trente ans de lutte pour la reconnaissance de l'homosexualité en France (1971–2002)* (Paris: Hachette, 2003), 88.

8 See Denis Quinqueton, "Pourquoi le 10 mars est une date essentielle pour les droits des LGBT+ en France," *Têtu*, March 3, 2021, https://tetu.com/2021/03/10/pourquoi-le-10-mars-est-une-date-essentielle-pour-les-droits-des-lgbt-en-france/.

9 One earlier discussion of lesbianism can be found in a 1967 televised report on

the making of Claude Chabrol's lesbian-themed film *Les biches*. See "Tournage du film 'Les Biches,'" *Côte d'Azur actualités*, Channel 1, ORTF, broadcast November 28, 1967.

10 "Les homosexuels," *Les dossiers de l'écran*, Antenne 2, broadcast January 21, 1975. Figures from Mathias Quéré, *Qui sème le vent récolte la tapette: Une histoire des groups de libération homosexuels en France de 1974–1979* (Clermont-Ferrand: La Source d'Or, 2018), 42.

11 The quote is from Patrice Corriveau, *Judging Homosexuals: A History of Gay Persecution in Quebec and France*, trans. Käthe Roth (Vancouver: University of British Columbia Press, 2011), 155.

12 On French resistance to homosexual marriage and parenthood, see work by sociologist Martine Gross, especially *Parent ou homo, faut-il choisir? Idées reçues sur l'homoparentalité* (Paris: Le Cavalier Bleu, 2013). On AIDS in the French media, see, for example, "Maladies d'amour: Danger," *Aujourd'hui la vie*, Antenne 2, broadcast June 23, 1983; "Inquiétude des hémophiles face aux dons du sang contaminés par le virus du SIDA," *Rennes soir*, Channel 3, broadcast June 27, 1973; "Psychose cancer gay aux USA," *TF1 13 heures le journal*, TF1, broadcast June 27, 1983; "Le virus du SIDA et le vaccin de l'hépatite B," *Émission: Antenne 2 le journal de 20H*, Antenne 2, broadcast June 28, 1983; "Une nouvelle maladie ou le SIDA," *Enquête publique*, Antenne 2, broadcast September 29, 1983; "SIDA, la nouvelle peste," *Vendredi*, FR3, broadcast October 14, 1983.

13 Corriveau, *Judging Homosexuals*, 156.

14 For a definition of *homoparentalité* (homosexual parenting) in France, see Gross, *Parent ou homo*, 9–10.

15 Jérôme Bourdon, *Haute fidélité: Pouvoir et télévision, 1935–1994* (Paris: Éditions du Seuil, 1994), appendix, statistical tables, n.p.

16 "Conférence de presse de M. Georges Pompidou Président de la République," dir. Alexandre Tarta, Channel 1, ORTF, broadcast July 2, 1970.

17 These numbers are based on searches in INA Mediapro (the database constructed for professional commercial—not academic or general—access to the French national television archive) using the terms "homosexual*," "homosexualité," and "lesbian*" in 2016. Because the databases are regularly updated, these numbers change as archiving progresses. They have already increased since I ran these searches. These numbers nevertheless offer us a baseline for analysis.

18 This number underestimates the number of broadcasts dealing with female same-sex desire since it represents *only* broadcasts that include the term "lesbien*" in the database notice and does *not* include broadcasts indexed under terms like "homosexuelle" or "homosexualité féminin," etc.

19 For foreign coverage, see "Les libertés individuelles: L'Angleterre," *XXème siècle*, Channel 1, ORTF, broadcast June 9, 1970; "Manifestation d'homosexuels aux États-Unis," *JT nuit*, Channel 1, ORTF, broadcast June 29, 1970; "L'église, demain? 1ère partie," *XXème siècle*, Channel 1, ORTF, broadcast December 8, 1970.

20 "Portrait d'un psychiatre," *Émission médicale*, Channel 1, ORTF, broadcast October 19, 1970.

21 "L'homosexualité," *Émission médicale*, Channel 1, ORTF, broadcast November 29, 1973. In the early 1970s it was still illegal for two men to dance together in public.

22 "Arcadie: Mouvement homophile de France," *Tribune libre*, FR3, broadcast January 7, 1977.
23 "Les homosexuels," *Les mercredis de l'information*, TF1, broadcast November 16, 1983.
24 "La sexualité racontée par les femmes," *Apostrophes*, Antenne 2, broadcast November 7, 1975.
25 Corriveau, *Judging Homosexuals*, 155.
26 In 2010 a file outlining details of Morissens's trial was located in the unarchived donation of Catherine Gonnard at the Bibliothèque Marguerite Durand in Paris. This donation has since been archived. See also Michel Vincineau, "À propos de l'Affaire Morissens," *Socialisme* (August 1983): 371–75. A published appeal to the French lesbian community can be found in "Comité de soutien à Éliane Morissens," *Les cahiers du GRIF*, no. 6 (1982): 15–16.
27 European Commission of Human Rights, "Application no. 11389/85: Eliane Morissens v/Belgium," *Decisions and Reports*, no. 56 (1988): 127–37.
28 "Les homosexuels," *Antenne 2 le journal de 20H*, Antenne 2, broadcast November 4, 1979.
29 For examples of masking, see "Comité d'Urgence Anti-Répression Homosexuelle," *Tribune libre*, FR3, broadcast April 27, 1983; "Haute Normandie: Le dossier—1er volet—L'homosexualité," *Normandie actualités*, FR3, broadcast June 24, 1983; "Les homosexuels," *Les mercredis de l'information*; "Une bonne mère mais," *Agora*, FR3, broadcast March 28, 1984; "Homosexuels en province," *Français si vous parliez*, FR3 / France 3, broadcast October 13, 1992. Lesbians who marched in early gay pride marches also often wore white masks. Sylvie M., interview by author, June 27, 2013, Marseille, France.
30 The few prewar Parisian sapphic cabarets that remained open (namely Chez Moune and Le Monocle) were increasingly indissociable from the underworld of illicit sex and illegal drugs. Catherine Gonnard and Jöelle Matos, "Les Filles," *Têtu, madame* (July 2000). Perrin purportedly paid the police and mafia to keep this world at bay; in her view, the Kat was the first sapphic club to be visible, legitimate, profitable, and unashamed of promoting female same-sex desire.
31 Perrin nonetheless claimed that men constituted only a tiny portion of the crowd. "Entretien: Elula Perrin," *Le magazine de la discothèque et des disc-jockeys*, no. 8756 (November 1980). See also Gil Cerisay, "Elula Perrin, une lesbienne qui tolère les hommes," *Sexpol*, no. 26 (March 1978): 22–24; and Edmée, "Elula Perrin: 'Les hommes? Ils dérangent le paysage!,'" *Tribune de Genève*, February 1981.
32 Caroline, a pharmacist from Bourges, took the train to Paris several times a year to visit this temple of sapphic desire. "My goal," she confided, "was to find a woman who would take me home, so that I wouldn't have to pay for a hotel." Caroline Godon-Gauthier, interview by author, May 18, 2013, Tours, France.
33 "The New Queen of Lesbos," *Cleo*, August 1982; Elula Perrin, *Les femmes préfèrent les femmes* (Paris: Éditions Ramsay, 1977).
34 See Elula Perrin, *Tant qu'il y aura des femmes* (Paris: Éditions Ramsay, 1978); *Alice au pays des femmes* (Paris: Éditions Ramsay, 1980); *Mousson de femmes* (Paris: Éditions Ramsay, 1985); *Coup de gueule pour l'amour des femmes* (Paris: Éditions Ramsay, 1995); *L'eurasienne* (Paris: Éditions Osmond, 1997); *Va y avoir mistral* (Paris: Double Interligne, 1999); *Bulles et noctambules: Histoire de la nuit*

au féminin (Paris: Double Interligne, 2000); *Revolte des amours mortes* (Paris: Éditions La Cerisaie, 2004); *Un amour, deux femmes* (Paris: Éditions La Cerisaie, 2004); and, with Hélène de Monferrand, *Ne tirez pas sur la violoniste* (Paris: Double Interligne, 1998) and *L'habit ne fait pas la nonne* (Paris: Double Interligne, 1998).

35 An incomplete list of newspapers and magazines in which Elula appeared includes: *Le figaro*, *Le Monde*, *Libération*, *Le quotidien de Paris*, *Nice matin*, *La presse de la Manche*, *La Suisse*, *Les nouvelles littéraires*, *Le nouvel observateur*, *Der Spiegel*, *Sieté Dias*, *Elle*, *Marie-Claire*, *Vogue hommes*, *Ah Nana!*, *Biba*, *TYNAIKA* (the biggest Greek women's magazine), *Gai pied*, *Lesbia*, *Homophonies*, *Têtu*, *madame*, *Arcadie*, *Choisir*, *Désormais*, *Union*, *Sexpol*, *Playboy*, and *Gay Life*.

36 "L'homosexualité féminine," *L'huile sur le feu*, Antenne 2, broadcast July 11, 1977. An abridged transcript of the broadcast can be found in Philippe Bouvard, *L'huile sur le feu* (Paris: Antenne 2 / Éditions Mengès, 1977), 287–305. The broadcast was a follow-up to a special on male homosexuality that had aired three months earlier featuring Amoroso and writer Jean-Louis Bory.

37 In the United States, the first "out" lesbian appeared on TV fifteen years earlier, when a woman called "Terry" was interviewed during coverage of the Daughters of Bilitis convention in Hollywood in 1962. Steven Capsuto, *Alternate Channels: The Uncensored Story of Gay and Lesbian Images on Radio and Television, 1930s to the Present* (New York: Ballentine Books, 2000), 43.

38 Biographical details on Elula Perrin from Perrin, *Women Prefer Women*, trans. Harold J. Salemson (New York: Bantam Books, 1978), and Valérie Léonard, interviews by author, April 27, 2011, January 26, 2013, and February 19, 2014, Paris, France.

39 Catherine Gonnard, interview by author, June 21, 2010, Paris, France.

40 Martine Fougeron and Anne Tremblay, "The Queen of the Katmandou," unidentified press clipping from 1977, Elula Perrin Pressbooks, collection of Valérie Léonard, Paris, France (hereafter cited as EP Pressbooks).

41 Perrin, quoted in *Elula, les hommes on s'en fout*, dirs. Josée Constantin and Catherine Gonnard (Canal+/Le Village, 2000).

42 Catherine Allex, "Hommage à Elula Perrin," *Lesbia magazine*, no. 226 (July–August 2003): 20.

43 Perrin, quoted in Cerisay, "Elula Perrin."

44 Perrin interviewed in *Ah! Nana*, no. 8 (1978?) (EP Pressbooks).

45 Elula Perrin, "J'm'assume," *Le crapouillet* (Spring 1981).

46 Perrin, quoted in Claude Saurraute, "Aimer les femmes," *Le Monde*, July 13, 1977.

47 Perrin, quoted in Suzette Triton (Robichon), "Un livre d'Elula Perrin," *Rouge*, no. 628 (April 18, 1978?) (EP Pressbooks).

48 Perrin, quoted in Saurraute, "Aimer les femmes."

49 Perrin on "Les lesbiennes," *Hot Talk* (no. 13), presented by Brigitte Lahaie, XXL, 1998, excerpted in Constantin and Gonnard, *Elula, les hommes on s'en fout*.

50 Perrin, quoted in Démeron, "Celle qui ose dire," *Marie Claire* (September 1977) (EP Pressbooks).

51 Perrin, quoted in Edmée, "Elula Perrin."

52 Patricia, interviewed in Christiane Jouve, "Le pied à l'étrier," *Lesbia*, no. 20 (September 1984): 24. See also Dominique's critique of *Les femmes préfèrent les femmes*

in "Bouquins," *Quand les femmes s'aiment*, no 2 (November 1978): 21 (EP Pressbooks).

53 Undated letter no. 209 from Colette F., Letters sent to the Groupe de lesbiennes du Centre des femmes de Lyon (1977 and 1981), private archive of Patricia Mercader, Lyon, France (hereafter cited as QLFSA-PM).

54 Perrin, "J'm'assume."

55 Perrin, *Women Prefer Women*, 231.

56 "L'homosexualité," *Aujourd'hui la vie*, Antenne 2, broadcast May 28, 1982.

57 "Amour de femmes," *52 sur la une: Le magazine du grand reportage*, TF1, broadcast July 21, 1993.

58 "Les homosexuels," *Les mercredis de l'information.*

59 Chantal Labat interviewed by Christiane Jouve, "Cocorico, en France, on a même des homos!," *Lesbia*, no. 13 (January 1984): 12, 14.

60 "Je suis une femme qui aime les femmes," *Bas les masques*, Antenne 2, broadcast October 5, 1994.

61 On Marie-Antoinette as lesbian, see Elizabeth Colwill, "Pass as a Woman, Act Like a Man: Marie-Antoinette as Tribade in the Pornography of the French Revolution," in *Homosexuality in Modern France*, ed. Jeffrey Merrick and Bryant T. Ragan (New York: Oxford University Press, 1996), 54–79; Lynn Hunt, "The Many Bodies of Marie-Antoinette: Political Pornography and the Problem of the Feminine in the French Revolution," in *The French Revolution: Recent Debates and New Controversies*, 2nd ed., ed. Gary Kates (New York: Routledge, 2001): 201–18; and Lynn Hunt, *The Family Romance of the French Revolution* (Los Angeles: University of California Press, 1992).

62 In her 1931 *Femmes sans hommes: Choses vues*, journalist Marise Querlin articulates this argument. Querlin asks: "Do the two partners of a lesbian ménage have any traits in common?" and replies "Both have the same aversion to the male and a dislike of maternity." Marise Querlin, *Women without Men*, trans. Malcolm McCraw (New York: Dell Publishing, 1965), 43.

63 Simone de Beauvoir, *The Second Sex*, ed. and trans. H. M. Parshley (New York: Vintage Books, 1989), 436–37.

64 On republican motherhood, see Jane Rendall, *The Origins of Modern Feminism: Women in Britain, France and the United States 1780–1860* (London: Palgrave, 1985), 33–72.

65 Corinne App et al., eds., *40 ans de slogans féministes 1970–2010* (Donnemarie-Dontilly: Éditions IXe, 2011), 47, 49, 39.

66 Doris Varichon, "Mères lesbiennes en procès: Strategies de défense contre les retraites de gardes d'enfants (1976–1982)," in *Lesbiennes, Pédés, arrêtons de raser les murs: Luttes et debats des mouvements lesbiens et homosexuels (1970–1990)*, ed. Hugo Bouvard, Ilana Eloit, and Mathias Quéré (Paris: La Dispute/SNÉDIT, 2023), 101–15.

67 I speak about this group at greater length in chapter 6.

68 While not exclusively homosexual, the GRED (1979–87) was founded by gay men during the Université d'été homosexuelle in Marseille in 1979. GRED produced the review *Le petit gredin* (1981–87) as well as shows on the homosexual radio station Fréquence Gaie, discussed in the next chapter. Gay French men (like writer and pedophile Gabriel Matzneff) who advocated sex with children and adolescents

had been attracting "bad press" since the early 1970s. See Jean Bérard and Nicolas Sallée, "The Age of Consent," trans. Ethan Rundell, *Clio: Women, Gender, History*, no. 42 (2015): 19–123 (esp. 103–6); and Julian Bourg, "Boy Trouble: French Pedophiliac Discourse of the 1970s," in *Between Marx and Coca-Cola: Youth Cultures in Changing European Societies, 1960s–1980*, ed. Axel Schildt and Detlef Siegfried (New York: Berghahn Books, 2006), 287–312. On homosexuality and pedophilia in France, see also Antoine Idier, *Les Alinéas du Placard: L'abrogation du délit d'homosexualité (1977–1982)* (Paris: Éditions Cartouche/TMR, 2013), 43–80. In 1981 the sentencing of Jacques Dugué to six years in prison for child-related sex crimes also caused a media circus.

69 On Evelyne's case, see Varichon, "Mères lesbiennes en procès," 108–15.

70 "Le problème de la garde d'un enfant retirée à sa mère à cause de son homosexualité," *JT FR3 Rhône Alpes*, FR3, broadcast December 11, 1981.

71 Note the banners in "Manifestation de protestation contre les discriminations à l'égard des homosexuels à Lyon," *JT FR3 Rhône Alpes*, FR3, broadcast December 12, 1981.

72 "Manifestation contre le procès d'une mère homosexuelle," *JT FR3 Rhône Alpes*, FR3, broadcast April 24, 1982. Halimi was president of the feminist organization Choisir. She first came to public attention in 1962 when she published (with Simone de Beauvoir) an account of her defense of Algerian activist Djamila Boupacha, a woman unjustly raped and tortured during the Algerian War. Gisèle Halimi and Simone de Beauvoir, *Djamila Boupacha* (Paris: Gallimard, 1962). Halimi went on to win the pivotal "Bobigny trial" in 1972 that led to the legalization of abortion in France in 1975. She then defended two Belgian lesbians raped in a campground outside Marseille in 1974. The trial, held in 1978 in Aix-en-Provence, helped transform rape from a misdemeanor to a capital crime in France. In 1981, Halimi organized the meeting between François Mitterrand and Choisir in which the newly elected president declared his intentions to eradicate discrimination against homosexuals.

73 Antoine Idier, "À Lyon, l'homosexualité en procès," *Bulletin municipal official de Lyon*, December 12, 2011.

74 Quotations and titles from press coverage in this paragraph and the next are from Évelyne Le Garrec's discussion of the case. See Évelyne Le Garrec, *Des femmes qui s'aiment* (Paris: Éditions du Seuil, 1984), 12–14.

75 "Femmes libérées," *Apostrophes*, Antenne 2, broadcast November 9, 1984.

76 "Interview de l'avocat d'un couple d'homosexuelles," *Télé pays de la Loire*, FR3, broadcast February 20, 1982.

77 Catherine (Zoé) Polet, "Lesbos invisible," *Lesbia*, no. 10 (September 1983): 23.

78 "Femmes homosexuelles," *TF1 dernière*, TF1, broadcast April 19, 1983.

79 "Couple homosexuel," *Antenne 2 midi*, Antenne 2, broadcast May 4, 1983.

80 "Couple d'homosexuelles en procès à Nantes," *Télé pays de la Loire*, FR3, October 6, 1983.

81 "Jugement du procès intenté par les homosexuelles Nadia et Annie," *Télé pays de la Loire*, FR3, broadcast December 1, 1983.

82 "Procès homosexuelles contre la sécurité sociale à Nantes," *Soir 3*, FR3, broadcast January 19, 1984.

83 "Nicole et Armelle," *Antenne 2 midi*, Antenne 2, broadcast March 18, 1982.

84 Pascal Ory, *L'entre-deux Mai: Histoire culturelle de la France (Mai 1968–Mai 1981)* (Paris: Éditions du Seuil, 1983), 185; Todd Shepard, *Sex, France & Arab Men, 1962–1979* (Chicago: University of Chicago Press, 2017).

85 Homosexuality was identified as a medical pathology in France until 1981. On the medical status of homosexuality in France, see Malick Briki, *Psychiatrie et homosexualité: Lectures médicales et juridiques de l'homosexualité dans les sociétés occidentales de 1850 à nos jours* (Presses Universitaires de Franche-Comté, 2009).

86 On heteronormative sexual politics and 1968, see Michael Sibalis, "Mai 68: Le Comité d'Action Pédérastique Révolutionnaire occupe la Sorbonne," *Genre, sexualité & société* 10 (Autumn 2013), https://journals.openedition.org/gss/3009; Julian Bourg, "'Your Sexual Revolution Is Not Ours': French Feminist 'Moralism' and the Limits of Desire," in *Gender and Sexuality in 1968: Transformative Politics in the Cultural Imagination*, ed. Lessie Jo Frazier and Deborah Cohen (New York: Palgrave, 2009), 93, 94. On 1968, sexual politics, and sex education, see Tamara Chaplin, "Orgasm without Limits: May '68 and the History of Sex Education in Modern France," in *May '68, Rethinking France's Last Revolution*, ed. Julian Jackson (London: Palgrave, 2011), 376–96.

87 Evelyne Rochedereux, interview by author, December 17, 2010, Le Croisic, France.

88 Antoinette Fouque, *There are Two Sexes: Essays in Feminology*, ed. Sylvina Boissonas, trans. David Macey and Catherine Porter (1995; New York: Columbia University Press, 2015), 27. See also Claire Duchen, *Feminism in France: From May '68 to Mitterrand* (London: Routledge, 1986), 8.

89 Kursheed Wadia, "Women and the Events of May 1968," in *The May 1968 Events in France*, by Keith A. Reader with Kursheed Wadia (New York: St Martin's Press, 1993), 150, 152.

90 Féminism, Masculin, Avenir was renamed Féminisme, Marxisme, Action (Feminism, Marxism, Action) following the exclusion of men from the group.

91 The singular "woman" (Movement for the Liberation of the Woman) was later pluralized.

92 FMA published a piece in *Le nouvel observateur*. Wittig authored an article in *L'idiot internationale*. Frédéric Martel, *The Pink and the Black: Homosexuals in France since 1968*, trans. Jane Marie Todd (Stanford: Stanford University Press, 1999), 34.

93 Christine Delphy, interview by author, January 12, 2011, Paris, France. On Delphy's participation in the MLF, see also the interview with Christine Delphy in director Carole Roussopoulos's film about the MLF, *Debout! Une histoire du mouvement de libération des femmes, 1970–1980* (1999), as well as the films *Je ne suis pas féministe, mais . . .*, dir. Florence Tissot and Sylvie Tissot (2015); and *L'abécédaire de Christine Delphy*, dir. Florence Tissot and Sylvie Tissot (2015). For a personal account of the MLF years from a lesbian perspective, see Marie-Jo Bonnet, *Mon MLF* (Paris: Éditions Albin Michel, 2018).

94 On TV, see "Manifestations femmes place de l'Étoile," *JT 20H*, Channel 1, ORTF, broadcast August 26, 1970. In the press, see, for example, the front page of *L'aurore*, August 27, 1970. The media often identified the women as representing the movement of the liberation of the French woman (in the singular).

95 *Inter actualités de 08H00*, France Inter, aired August 27, 1970.

96 All six (Delphy; novelist Christiane Rochefort; writers Monique Wittig, Cathy

Bernheim, and Anne Zelensky; as well as the American Namascar Shaktini) became prominent figures in the feminist and homosexual rights movements.

97 "A feminist," quoted in Martel, *The Pink and the Black*, 38. Martel then states that according to political scientist Françoise Picq, of 120 women who joined the movement between 1970 and 1972, one-third were heterosexual, one-third bisexual, and one-third homosexual (*The Pink and the Black*, 38). By 1986 the numbers had changed: three-quarters of the same women were now claiming heterosexuality. The rest identified either as homo- or bisexual. See Nadja Ringart, "Quand ce n'était qu'un début," *Crise de la societé, féminisme et changement* (Paris: Tierce, 1991), cited in Martel, *The Pink and the Black*, 385n19.

98 On the Estates General, see "Le féminisme," *Aujourd'hui madame*, Channel 2, ORTF, broadcast September 10, 1971. This was the first of two broadcasts on this show entirely dedicated to the topic (see below).

99 "Bilan des États généraux de la femme," *Vingt quatre heures sur la deux*, Channel 2, ORTF, broadcast November 23, 1970.

100 The term "l'ennemi principal" is drawn from Christine Delphy, *L'ennemi principal 1: Économie politique du patriarcat* (Paris: Éditions Syllepse, 1998) and *L'ennemi principal 2: Penser le genre* (Paris: Éditions Syllepse, 2001). Delphy's dedication to solidarity among women later led her to part ways with radical lesbians who condemned heterosexual feminists for "collaborating" with the enemy.

101 "Kate Millett, et la condition de la femme," *Variances*, Channel 1, ORTF, broadcast July 20, 1971.

102 "Les assises du MLF," *JT 13H*, Channel 1, ORTF, broadcast May 15, 1972. See also Martel, *The Pink and the Black*, 45.

103 "Le féminisme," *Aujourd'hui madame*, Channel 2, ORTF, broadcast May 3, 1972. The first broadcast aired on September 10, 1971.

104 "Le MPLPF," *Sérieux s'abstenir*, Channel 1, ORTF, broadcast June 8, 1972. The sketch ends in an orgy of misogyny when the male underlings plot the demise of their female masters by poisoning the lot.

105 "La grève des femmes," *JT 20H*, Channel 2, ORTF, broadcast June 9, 1974.

106 "Stand MLF à l'Eurofoire de Nancy," *Lorraine soir*, Channel 3, ORTF, broadcast June 13, 1974.

107 "Anne Zelensky à propos de son engagement féministe," *L'equilibre: Cécile ou la raison des femmes*, TF1, ORTF, broadcast October 22, 1975. See also Zelensky's memoir (published under the name Anne Tristan), Anne Tristan and Annie de Pisan, *Histoires du M.L.F.*, preface by Simone de Beauvoir (Paris: Calmann-Lévy, 1977).

108 "Thérèse Clerc, militante du MLAC," *Présence protestante*, TF1, broadcast November 9, 1975.

109 "Histoires du MLF," *TF1 actualités dernière*, TF1, broadcast April 22, 1977. See also Tristan and Pisan, *Histoires du M.L.F.*

110 "Une journée avec Delphine Seyrig," *L'invité du jeudi*, Antenne 2, broadcast April 24, 1980 (INA).

111 On these crises, see the next chapter.

112 Ilana Eloit, "Trouble dans le féminisme: Du 'Nous, les femmes' au 'Nous, les lesbiennes': Genèse du sujet politique lesbien en France (1970–1980)," *20 & 21 Revue d'histoire*, no. 148 (October–December 2020): 129–45.

113 Christine Bard, "Le lesbianism comme construction politique," in *Le siècle des feminisms*, ed. Elaine Gubin et al. (Paris: Éditions de l'Atelier, 2004), 114.

114 Eloit, "Trouble dans le féminisme," 130–31.

115 On French feminism as a barrier to lesbian politics, see the interview with Sam Bourcier (as Marie-Hélène Bourcier) in Christelle Taraud, *Les féminismes en questions: Éléments pour une cartographie* (Paris: Éditions Amsterdam, 2005), 35–59, 45.

116 Eloit, "Trouble dans le féminisme," 130.

117 Brigitte Boucheron makes this argument in "Introduction à une histoire du mouvement lesbien en France," in *Invisibilité, visibilité des lesbiennes*, ed. Actes du Colloque organisé par la Coordination Lesbienne en France à l'Hôtel de Ville de Paris (Montreuil: CLF, 2007), 37–61, as does Eloit in "Trouble dans le féminisme."

118 Letter from Jocelyne to Danièle Cottereau, September 6, 1984, Radio Fréquence Gaie, collection of Danièle Cottereau, Aulnay-sous-Bois, France.

119 Adrienne Rich, "Compulsory Heterosexuality and Lesbian Existence," *Signs* 5, no. 4 (Summer 1980): 631–60.

120 On #BalanceTonPorc, see the book by French journalist Sandra Muller, who coined the hashtag, *#balancetonporc* (Paris: Flammarion, 2018). On the international controversy over Catherine Deneuve's denunciation of the movement, see Jean Elisabeth Pedersen, "Representations of Women in the French Imaginary: Historicizing the Gallic Singularity," *French Politics, Culture, and Society* 38, no. 1 (March 2020): 1–20. On France, femininity, and gender difference, see the now classic (and controversial) work by Mona Ozouf, *Les mots des femmes: Essai sur la singularité française* (Paris: Fayard, 1995).

CHAPTER SIX

1 Danièle Cottereau, interview by author, June 17, 2013, Aulnay-sous-bois, France.

2 Cait McKinney, *Information Activism: A Queer History of Lesbian Media Technologies* (Durham, NC: Duke University Press, 2020), 2.

3 McKinney, *Information Activism*, 2.

4 McKinney, *Information Activism*, 211; emphasis in original.

5 "Bal ce soir à la salle Wagram: Les répondeuses en direct," M.O.D., dated by hand March 23, 1979, Fonds Les Répondeuses, Bibliothèque Marguerite Durand, Paris. Unless otherwise noted, sources for Les Répondeuses are from the Bibliothèque Marguerite Durand (BMD), Paris, in the Fonds Les Répondeuses, Cartons I–III. When I accessed these sources in 2010, they were not yet catalogued. Consequently, they are identified here by date (when possible), not carton, and cited hereafter as Fonds LR/BMD. Cataloguing was completed in 2018.

6 Folder groupes/revues/lieux d'affichage, Fonds LR/BMD.

7 *La gazette*, no. 1 (January 1979): n.p. Folder groupes/revues/lieux d'affichage, Fonds LR/BMD. An earlier issue of *La gazette* (no. 0) was printed in December 1978.

8 Flyer, "La fête des répondeuses, March 23, 1979, Salle Wagram," Folder groupes/revues/lieux d'affichage, Fonds LR/BMD.

9 "La libération des femmes: Un mouvement à suivre . . ." *Aujourd'hui la vie*, Antenne 2, broadcast March 7, 1982.

10 Undated note, handwritten in blue script, Fonds LR/BMD.
11 Call on May 10, 1978, Fonds LR/BMD.
12 Call on May 3, 1978, Fonds LR/BMD.
13 Call on June 1, 1978, Fonds LR/BMD.
14 Call on May 15, 1977, Fonds LR/BMD. The meeting was held May 21 and 22, 1977.
15 On the Saint-Ay meeting, see Centre lyonnais d'études féministes (Collectif), *Chronique d'une passion: Le mouvement de Libération des femmes à Lyon* (Paris: L'Harmattan, 1989), 114.
16 Call on June 1, 1978, Fonds LR/BMD.
17 Tea dance organized by Lieu de Femmes, October 25, 1978; party for liberation from lesbian shame, May 15, 1977; message for lesbian roommates, March 22, 1978; message from the Commission sexualité du groupe lesbiennes de Paris, May 10, 1978; advertisement for *Quand les femmes s'aiment*, May 2, 1981. All in Fonds LR/BMD.
18 Call on March 22, 1978, Fonds LR/BMD.
19 Call on May 1, 1978, Fonds LR/BMD.
20 Call on March 22, 1978, Fonds LR/BMD.
21 Call on April 24, 1978, Fonds LR/BMD.
22 Call on April 25, 1978, Fonds LR/BMD.
23 Call on March 25, 1978, Fonds LR/BMD.
24 Suzette Robichon (who published as Suzette Triton), interview by author, May 13, 2013, Paris, France. At least three lesbian-identified groups preceded this: two in Paris (the Gouines rouges, founded in 1971 and dissolved in 1973, and the Groupe des lesbiennes féministes, founded in 1975), and one in Lyon (the Groupe de lesbiennes du Centre des femmes de Lyon, founded in 1976).
25 Letter, undated, likely 1981, Fonds LR/BMD. The letter is signed in typescript, "un gout doux venu d'ailleurs" ("a sweet taste from elsewhere," with the signature a homophone for the term *goudou* or "lesbian"). Across the bottom in red pen is written, "Merci de faire passer le message suivant, Christiane" (Thanks for passing on the following message, Christiane).
26 Letter from Corine B., October 12, 1981, Fonds LR/BMD.
27 Danielle Ghighi, Élisabeth Motsch, and Marie Khulmann from the MLF's group Révolution! were cofounders. Carabosses was run by a collective of about fifteen women. See the notice "Carabosses" in *Les cahiers du GRIF* 23–24 (1978): 185.
28 Flyer, Agence France-Press, March 9, 1981, Fonds LR/BMD.
29 Call on May 13, 1977, Fonds LR/BMD.
30 Call on March 8, 1978, Fonds LR/BMD.
31 Call, undated, 1977, Fonds LR/BMD.
32 Call on February 16, 1978, Fonds LR/BMD.
33 Call on May 5, 1978, Fonds LR/BMD.
34 Call on March 29, 1978, Fonds LR/BMD.
35 The 3F in "La libération des femmes," *Aujourd'hui la vie*.
36 "Qu'est-ce que les 3 F?," *Lesbia*, no. 2 (January 1983): 19.
37 Tract, "Quand les lesbiennes sortent de leurs trous," G.L.B.N.-Les Baragouineuses, March 1980, Archives recherches cultures lesbiennes, Paris, France.
38 In France these included the lesbian support lines Permanence Lesbiennes and Partages (run by women who worked phones at the homosexual switchboard SOS Gaie in Paris) as well as Fil Rose (out of Angers).

39 “Une journée avec Delphine Seyrig,” *L’invité du jeudi*, Antenne 2, broadcast April 24, 1980.

40 An excerpt from the film is reproduced in “La libération des femmes,” *Aujourd’hui la vie*. Anne Zelensky, Marie-Jo Bonnet, and Cathy Bernheim (all involved with other women) were interviewed; none speak to female homosexuality, despite its centrality to the material under analysis.

41 For example, see “C’est bon à savoir,” *Elle*, March 12, 1981.

42 *La gazette*, no. 0 (December 1978): 1.

43 See “Trois Répondeuses menacées,” *Libération*, December 30, 1981. The paper published a correction on February 1, 1981, in which they stated that Les Répondeuses were not themselves the object of the threats.

44 *La gazette*, no. 0 (December 1978): 1.

45 *La gazette*, no. 0 (December 1978): 2.

46 Ilana Eloit, “‘Le bonheur était dans les pages de ce mensuel’: La naissance de la presse lesbienne et la fabrique d’un espace à soi (1976–1990),” *Le temps des medias* 2, no. 29 (2017): 105; emphasis in the original.

47 The history of the Groupe de lesbiennes du Centre des femmes de Lyon and *Quand les femmes s’aiment* is analyzed in Centre lyonnais d’études féministes (Collectif), *Chronique d’une passion*. See, especially, pp. 106–40 (on the group) and 175–200 (on the journal). My work is indebted to the women who wrote that history, especially Patricia Mercader and Brigitte Lhomond, who spoke with me in Lyon in 2013. Mercader provided access to the Groupe’s archives.

48 Centre lyonnais d’études féministes (Collectif), *Chronique d’une passion*, 175. *QLFSA* was preceded by the *Journal des lesbiennes féministes* (four issues, 1976–77). That publication was less professional, shorter, and more like a newsletter or bulletin.

49 Editorial, *QLFSA* 1 (April 1978): 2.

50 *QLFSA* 1 (April 1978): 24.

51 *QLFSA* 2 (November 1978): 2.

52 After the first issue, printing was outsourced to the leftist workshop the Ateliers d’impression presse nouvelle, but the women continued to handle layout to reduce costs and retain control. On the Ateliers, see “Les A.I.P.N. sont ouverts,” *La liberté d’imprimer: Journal de l’association des amis des ateliers d’impression presse nouvelle*, no. 2 (February 1977).

53 Centre lyonnais d’études féministes (Collectif), *Chronique d’une passion*, 191.

54 *QLFSA* 1 (April 1978): 3.

55 Both Kiki and a woman named Madé drew illustrations for the journal.

56 Nelly Mélo, “Dossier: Presse lesbienne. Europe: *Quand les femmes s’aiment*,” *Amazones d’hier, lesbiennes d’aujourd’hui* 5, no. 3 (March 1988): 166–69.

57 Centre lyonnais d’études féministes (Collectif), *Chronique d’une passion*, 178.

58 Male frontal nudity was forbidden in the French press until 1977. Depictions of an erect penis or sexual intercourse remained censored until the 1980s, but homosexual pornography proliferated in these years in the pages of magazines like *Man*, *Olympe*, and *Nous les hommes*. There was no equivalent pornographic press by women for women.

59 Martine et al., “Pochette surprise,” *QLFSA* 2 (November 1978): 25–26.

60 *QLFSA* 3/4 (March 1979): 27.

61 *QLFSA* 3/4 (March 1979): 17.

62 *QLFSA* 5 (May 1979): 28.
63 *QLFSA* 7 (June 1980): 10–11.
64 Centre lyonnais d'études féministes (Collectif), *Chronique d'une passion*, 189.
65 Chantal Ibre, "Mères lesbiennes," *QLFSA* 2 (November 1978): 8–10.
66 "On reproche aux homos de ne pas faire d'enfants, Quand ils en font, on les leur enlève . . . ," *QLFSA* 6 (March 1980): 11.
67 The Université d'été homosexuelle was a militant mixed-gender conference held in Marseille. It is still active today and is now known as the Universités d'été euroméditerranéennes des homosexualités. The CUARH pushed the Socialist Party to abolish discriminatory laws against homosexual minors after it came to power in 1980. A young Catherine Gonnard honed her activist skills in this organization.
68 On the CUARH, see Antoine Idier, *Les Alinéas du Placard: L'abrogation du délit d'homosexualité (1977–1982)* (Paris: Éditions Cartouche/TMR, 2013), esp. 81–96.
69 *QLFSA* 6 (March 1980): 11.
70 On the trademarking, see the manifesto by the Association mouvement pour les luttes féministes, *Chroniques d'une imposture: Du mouvement de libération des femmes à une marque commerciale* (Paris: Primavera, 1981). On Fouque, see Lisa Greenwald, *Daughters of 1968: Redefining French Feminism and the Women's Liberation Movement* (Lincoln: University of Nebraska Press, 2018). Drawing on Lacanian psychoanalysis, Fouque's Psychépo grounded women's emancipation not in political activism but in an essentialized understanding of a feminine libidinal economy that refused the oedipal resolution in which access to subjectivity requires rejection of the mother.
71 The story of how *Questions féministes* was resurrected under Christine Delphy's leadership as *Nouvelle questions féministes* has been covered elsewhere. For work in English, see especially Stevi Jackson, *Christine Delphy* (London: Sage, 1996), 20–26; Claire Duchen, *Feminism in France: From May '68 to Mitterrand* (London: Routledge, 1986); and Clare Duchen, ed. and trans. *French Connections: Voices from the Women's Movement* (Amherst: University of Massachusetts Press, 1987).
72 Wittig made the claim in a 1978 MLA paper, published in English as "The Straight Mind" in Monique Wittig, *The Straight Mind and Other Essays*, foreword and trans. Louise Turcotte (Boston: Beacon Press, 1992), 32.
73 Although this argument was the fuel that lit the fire, lesbians and feminists in France and beyond had been debating the feasibility of fighting patriarchy while working within a heterosocial/heterosexual system for some time. See Louise Turcotte, foreword to Wittig, *The Straight Mind*, ix.
74 FLR, quoted in Duchen, *French Connections*, 95.
75 Martine Laroche and Michèle Larrouy, eds., *Mouvements de presse: Des années 1970s à nos jours, luttes féministes et lesbiennes* (Paris: Éditions des ARCL, 2009), 88.
76 Posters, tracts, manifestos, and journals produced by the FLR are held at the Archives recherches cultures lesbiennes in Paris. Among the few English translations of the original texts are those published in Duchen, *French Connections*. Marion Page self-published some of the original French materials in 2010 in a collection of texts available for purchase in Paris at the Archives recherches cultures

lesbiennes and the lesbian-feminist bookstore Violette & Co., as well as by mail order from impatiente@orange.fr for the price of fifteen euros, five of which were donated to the ARCL.

77 During the 1980s, for example, radical lesbians were excluded from a number of national meetings, such as the feminist retreat at Caen in 1980. While not excluded from meetings held in Exoudun (Poitiers) and L'Euzière (Gard) the following year, conflicts between radical lesbians and lesbian feminists dominated the proceedings.

78 Catherine Gonnard remembers the only meeting of the FLR she ever attended as "the worst experience of my lesbian life!" Gonnard, interview by author, June 21, 2010, Paris, France.

79 All quotations in this paragraph from *QLFSA* 5 (May 1979): 22–29.

80 *QLFSA* 7 (June 1980): 5.

81 *QLFSA* 7 (June 1980): 8.

82 To date, the Archives recherches cultures lesbiennes located at the Maison des Femmes de Paris at 163 rue de Charenton remains the principal archive dedicated to lesbianism in France. The FLR also produced two short-lived journals (*Espaces* and *Chroniques aiguës et graves*) and networked with radical lesbians in Quebec, Belgium, Great Britain, and Switzerland.

83 Antagonisms from this period continue to fracture lesbian solidarity. The woman responsible for this quotation agreed to its inclusion on condition of anonymity. Interview by author, January 16, 2011. See Tamara Chaplin, "Utopian Gaiety: French Lesbian Activism and the Politics of Pleasure (1974–2016)," in *Making Waves: French Feminisms and their Legacies, 1975–2015*, ed. Margaret Atack et al. (Liverpool: Liverpool University Press, 2019), 115–28.

84 In 1989 several members analyzed these letters in Centre lyonnais d'études féministes (Collectif), *Chronique d'une passion*, 195–200.

85 Five hundred twenty letters are alphabetized by last name and numbered consecutively. Another dozen or so are not. When possible, I use these numbers to identify letters parenthetically in the text; unnumbered letters are identified in endnotes by date, along with the acronym QLFSA-PM to designate Mercader's private collection.

86 Patricia Mercader, interview by author, June 12, 2013, Lyon, France; and Brigitte Lhomond, interview by author, June 11, 2013, Lyon, France. On the politics of lesbian personal ads in *Lesbia*, see Anna Livia, "*Camionneuses s'abstenir*: Lesbian Community Creation through the Personals," in *Language and Sexuality: Contesting Meaning in Theory and Practice*, ed. Katheryn Campbell-Kibler et al. (Stanford: CSLI Publications, 2002), 191–206.

87 On lesbian identity and the power of naming, see Natacha Chetcuti, *Se dire lesbien: Vie de couple, sexualité, représentation de soi* (Paris: Éditions Payot, 2010).

88 Chetcuti, *Se dire lesbien*.

89 Unnumbered letter dated March 16, 1979, QLFSA-PM.

90 *QLFSA* 2 (November 1978): 21.

91 Centre lyonnais d'études féministes (Collectif), *Chronique d'une passion*, 194.

92 "Relations avec A.I.P.N.," letter dated March 25, 1979, QLFSA-PM.

93 On the history of the lesbian press, see Laroche and Larrouy, *Mouvements de presse*.

94 On February 8, 1978, for example, Les Répondeuses received a query about the status of pirate radio, asking if free radio broadcasts would be legalized soon.

95 Radio Mauve was launched by Pascal Navarro and the militant homosexual Guy Hocquenghem in the latter's apartment. Radio Onz-Debrouille replaced Radio Fil Rose after its demise, taking over its equipment and airing until 1981. On the early history of pirate radio in France, see Frank Ténot, *Radios privées, radios pirates* (Paris: Denoël, 1978).

96 *Lesbia*, no. 26 (March 1985): 10.

97 Danièle Cottereau, phone interview by author, December 2, 2023.

98 Frédéric Martel, *The Pink and the Black: Homosexuals in France since 1968*, trans. Jane Marie Todd (Stanford: Stanford University Press, 1999), 163.

99 Mirella Le Petit, "Fréquence Gaie: Le droit à la difference," *Télé-poche*, no. 903 (June 1, 1983).

100 Christiane Jouve, C. Marjollet, and M. Gruzeau, "Les lesbiennes à l'antenne, les homos en stereo," *Lesbia*, no. 4 (March 1983): 9.

101 Geneviève Pastre, interviewed by Catherine Marjollet in "Voyage en Grande Lesbiannie avec Geneviève Pastre," *Lesbia*, no. 7 (June 1983): 3.

102 Jouve, Marjollet, and Gruzeau, "Les lesbiennes à l'antenne," 9.

103 Éric Lamien, "Fréquence gaie," in *Dictionnaire des cultures gays et lesbiennes*, edited by Didier Eribon (Paris: Larousse, 2003), 201. In her memoir, Danièle set the number of daily auditors at between 500,000 and 800,000. Danièle Cottereau, *Amazones du soir, bonsoir!* (Paris: Éditions Le Gueuloir, 2011), 117.

104 Cottereau, interview.

105 "Lesbia infos" and "Le deuxième souffle des émissions roses," *Lesbia*, no. 17 (May 1984): 8, 11, 42. See also Catherine (Zoé) Polet, "Coup de foudre," *Lesbia*, no. 10 (September 1983): 23. The acronym FEE spells the word for "fairy" in French (*fée*). Founded in 1982, FEE, which is dedicated to promoting lesbian and bisexual community and activism in Brittany, was still active in 2023.

106 "Liste des antennes roses," *Lesbia*, no. 4 (April 1983): 10. The list reports that French listeners could also tune in to stations from Belgium (like the broadcast "Antenne Rose" on Radio Air Libre, at 1.3 MHz out of Brussels) and (when in Canada) Montreal.

107 Personal collection of Danièle Cottereau, Aulnay-sous-Bois, France (hereafter cited as FG-DC). "Amazones du soir" appears in the sources as both the plural "Amazones" and the singular "Amazone." Cottereau chose the plural form for her memoirs. For consistency, I follow that use here.

108 Danièle Cottereau, "Amazones du soir, bonsoir! En B.D.," September 23, 1984, FG-DC.

109 Agnès Pascale, Genévìève, Noëlle, Francisca, Mijane, Marie-Christine, Audrée, two Dominiques, another Danielle, Christine, and Laurence also participated in these broadcasts.

110 Cottereau, interview.

111 Letter to Danièle Cottereau, unsigned, undated, FG-DC. The reference is from Marcel Proust's *Swann's Way* and refers to how particular foods can evoke specific memories.

112 Letter from Martine to Danièle Cottereau, June 24, 1983, FG-DC.

113 Letter from Monique to Danièle Cottereau, October 7, 1984, FG-DC.

114 Excerpts from these cassettes can be heard on a radio documentary about Danièle, "Allô Danièle? À la recherche des ondes lesbiennes," France Culture, aired January 17, 2021.
115 Letter from Agnès to Danièle Cottereau, undated, FG-DC.
116 Cottereau, interview.
117 Letter from Jocelyne to Danièle Cottereau, November 8, 1983, FG-DC.
118 An undated, untitled excerpt from this show is recorded on the cassette that Danièle loaned me.
119 Cottereau, interview.
120 Cottereau, interview.
121 Letter from Hélène to Danièle Cottereau, June 16, 1983, FG-DC.
122 Cottereau, interview.
123 Letter from Jocelyne to Danièle Cottereau, quoted in Cottereau, *Amazones, du soir*, 132.
124 Letter from Laurence to Danièle Cottereau, undated, FG-DC.
125 Letter from Valérie to Danièle Cottereau, December 14, 1984, FG-DC.
126 Letter from Dani to Danièle Cottereau, March 31, 1984, FG-DC.
127 Letter from Anne to Danièle Cottereau, quoted in Cottereau, *Amazones, du soir*, 130.
128 Cottereau, quoted on "Allô Danièle?"
129 Cottereau, interview.
130 Barbara Osorovitz, phone conversation with the author, February 11, 2023.
131 Letter from Valérie to Danièle Cottereau, November 21, 1984, FG-DC.
132 Letter from Valérie to Cottereau.
133 Cottereau, *Amazones, du soir*, 124.
134 Letter from Danièle Cottereau to Geneviève Pastre, February 9, 1984, FG-DC. See also Danièle Cottereau, "À propos de Fréquence gaie," *Lesbia*, no. 28 (May 1985): 45.
135 Letter from Valérie to Danièle Cottereau, December 14, 1984, FG-DC.
136 Christiane Jouve, "La nouvelle Fréquence gaie," *Lesbia magazine*, no. 26 (March 1985): 10.
137 Lamien, "Fréquence gaie," 202.
138 "Plateau invité: Didier Varrod," *A2 dernière*, Antenne 2, broadcast July 27, 1982.
139 Cottereau, interview, and Cottereau, *Amazones, du soir*, 118.
140 Cottereau, quoted on "Allô Danièle?"
141 Letter from Jocelyne to Danièle Cottereau, May 18, 1984, FG-DC.
142 Martel, *The Pink and the Black*, 153.
143 McKinney, *Information Activism*, 6; emphasis in the original.
144 Meetings were held in Saint-Ay (May 1977), Exoudun (August 1977), Lyon (1978), Paussac (July 1979), Marcevol (July 1980), and L'Euzière (June 1981). In 1980 a French lesbian delegation participated in the first international conference of lesbians (convoked by the International Lesbian Information Service) in Geneva, Switzerland.
145 Dena Goodman sees letter writing as a highly gendered process wherein "by addressing oneself to another," aristocratic and bourgeois women gained access to themselves. Dena Goodman, *Becoming a Woman in the Age of Letters* (Ithaca, NY: Cornell University Press, 2009), 2. Harry Oosterhuis convincingly claims

that letters sent to the sexologist Richard von Krafft-Ebing shaped the making of a medicalized model of homosexual identity at the end of the nineteenth century. Harry Oosterhuis, *Stepchildren of Nature: Krafft-Ebing, Psychiatry, and the Making of Sexual Identity* (Chicago: University of Chicago Press, 2000).

146 Martha Hanna, "A Republic of Letters: The Epistolary Tradition in France during World War I," *American Historical Review* 108, no. 5 (2003): 1348.

147 Jean d'Arcy was director of programming for the RTF from 1952 to 1959. He was named director of radio and television at the United Nations in 1961. Jean d'Arcy, "Direct Broadcast Satellites and the Right to Communicate," *EBU Review* 118 (1969): 14–18.

148 Lauren Berlant quoted in Judith Coffin, *Sex, Love, and Letters: Writing Simone de Beauvoir* (Ithaca, NY: Cornell University Press, 2020), 18; emphasis in the original.

149 Coffin, *Sex, Love, and Letters*, 19.

150 Chetcuti, *Se dire lesbien*, 19.

151 Judith Coffin, "Sex, Love, and Letters: Writing Simone de Beauvoir, 1949–1963," *American Historical Review* 115, no. 4 (2010): 1064.

152 Nelly Mélo et al., "Lettre du 30 avril 1982, non publiée par *Masques*," in Laroche and Larrouy, *Mouvements de presse*, 55–56.

153 Suzette Robichon, "La presse des lesbiennes; un des moteurs de notre histoire?," in *Mouvement des lesbiennes, lesbiennes en mouvement: Dans le cadre des 40 ans du MLF*, ed. Actes du colloque et des ateliers Chronologie lesbienne (Montreuil: Coordination Lesbienne en France / Éditions Prospero, 2010), 32.

CHAPTER SEVEN

1 This chapter is a revised version of my article "Lesbians Online: Queer Identity and Community Formation on the French Minitel," *Journal of the History of Sexuality* 23, no. 3 (September 2014): 451–72; reprinted with permission.

2 The field of "cyberqueer studies" initially focused on the United States, Britain, and Asia. Nina Wakeford produced foundational work on the topic. See Nina Wakeford, "New Technologies and 'Cyberqueer' Research," in *Handbook of Lesbian and Gay Studies*, ed. Diane Richardson and Steven Seidman (London: Sage, 2002), 115–45; and Nina Wakeford, "Cyberqueer," in *Lesbian and Gay Studies: A Critical Introduction*, ed. Andy Medhurst and Sally R. Munt (London: Cassell, 1997), 20–38. See also Kate O'Riordan and David J. Phillips, eds., *Queer Online: Media, Technology & Sexuality* (New York: Peter Lang, 2007). On English language hegemony in cyberqueer environments, see Jillana B. Enteen, *Virtual English: Queer Internets and Digital Creolization* (New York: Routledge, 2010). For a general history of the Minitel in English, see Julien Mailland and Kevin Drisco, *Minitel: Welcome to the Internet* (Cambridge, MA: MIT Press, 2017).

3 On French gay male Minitel use, see Mattias Duyves, "The Minitel: The Glittering Future of a New Invention," in *Gay Studies from the French Cultures: Voices from France, Belgium, Brazil, Canada, and the Netherlands*, ed. Rommel Mendès-Leite and Pierre-Olivier de Busscher (New York: Haworth, 1993), 193–203. See also Anna Livia, "Public and Clandestine: Gay Men's Pseudonyms on the French Minitel," *Sexualities* 5, no. 2 (May 2002): 201–17.

4 Amy T. Goodloe, "Computer Networks and Services," in *Encyclopedia of Lesbian and Gay Histories and Cultures*, vol. 1, *Lesbian Histories and Cultures: An Encyclopedia*, ed. Bonnie Zimmerman (New York: Garland, 2000), 200.

5 M. Perier, quoted in Frédéric Brunnquell, *Les associations familiales: Combien de divisions, dossier, enquête* (Paris: Dagorno, 1994), 104.

6 Wakeford, "New Technologies," 118.

7 Wakeford, "New Technologies," 118.

8 Duyves, "The Minitel," 197.

9 Jean Le Bitoux, Bruno Proth, and Hervé Chevaux, *Citoyen de seconde zone: Trente ans de lutte pour la reconnaissance de l'homosexualité en France (1971–2002)* (Paris: Hachette, 2003), 316.

10 See Goodloe, "Computer Networks," and Eva Isaksson, "Living with Lesbian Lists," Sapphonet, 1997, accessed July 14, 2013, http://www.sappho.net/lesbian-lists/lll.html. Wakeford in "Cyberqueer" and "New Technologies" also relies on these sources. See also the interview with Goodloe originally broadcast in 1996 on the US television series *Net Café* (focused on the 1990s internet boom), in the episode "Women on the Web," accessed July 14, 2013, https://archive.org/details/nc105_women. The interview with Goodloe begins at 15:50. *Net Café* was a spin-off of the PBS series *Computer Chronicles*.

11 Early online exchanges were rarely saved. Those whose sexual orientations are marginalized are also more likely to destroy evidence of online activity, rendering work on cyberqueer history even more precarious. My work on the lesbian Minitel is only possible because the GTs left a significant paper trail in the archvives of the BMD and the ARCL in Paris, which I was able to supplement through oral interviews with some of the group's main actors. Many of these materials were not yet indexed when I conducted this research. These are cited by archive location and digital image number in my personal database.

12 Isaksson, "Living with Lesbian Lists," and Wakeford, "New Technologies," 120.

13 Wakeford, "New Technologies," 120.

14 Goodloe, "Computer Networks," 201.

15 Isaksson, "Living with Lesbian Lists."

16 Isaksson, "Living with Lesbian Lists."

17 By way of comparison, 27 percent of Danes and 5 percent of Germans had internet connectivity in 1997. Figures from John Tagliabue, "Online Cohabitation: Internet and Minitel; Videotex System in France Proves Unusually Resilient," *New York Times*, June 2, 2001, http://www.nytimes.com/2001/06/02/business/online-cohabitation-internet-minitel-videotex-system-france-proves-unusually.html?pagewanted=all&src=pm. See also Jean-Yves Rincé, *Le Minitel* (Paris: Presses Universitaires de France, 1990); and André Lemos, "The Labyrinth of Minitel," in *Cultures of the Internet: Virtual Spaces, Real Histories, Living Bodies*, ed. Rob Shields (London: Sage, 1996), 33–48. On the importance of computers to French global status, see Simon Nora and Alain Minc, *L'informatisation de la société* (Paris: La Documentation Française, 1978). On postwar French anxiety over American progress in industry, technology, and business, see Jean-Jacques Servan-Schrieber, *Le défi américain* (Paris: Denoël, 1967).

18 See Organization for Economic Co-operation and Development, Directorate for Science, Technology and Industry, and Committee on Information, Computer and Communications Policy, Working Party on the Information Economy, *France's*

Experience with the Minitel: Lessons for Electronic Commerce over the Internet, vol. 6, no. 88 (Paris: OECD, 1998), 11.

19 Nonprofit organizations could be reached at minimal cost by dialing 3614 and were charged uniquely for time spent online. Commercial calls to 3615 were more than twice as expensive because they billed for both time spent online and services rendered. Rincé, *Le Minitel*, 103.

20 For arguments linking the Minitel to homosexuality, see Organization for Economic Co-operation and Development, *France's Experience with the Minitel*, esp. 14–16.

21 Jean Le Bitoux, "Le guêpier des années Gai pied," accessed February 10, 2011, http://www.france.qrd.org/media/gai%20pied/ (link is no longer active); and Le Bitoux, Proth, and Chevaux, *Citoyen de seconde zone*, 256–57.

22 On gay male Minitel use, see Duyves, "The Minitel," and Livia, "Public and Clandestine."

23 Catherine Gonnard, interview by author, June 28, 2010, Paris, France.

24 Docs. 1613–52, Archives recherches cultures lesbiennes, Paris, France (hereafter cited as ARCL).

25 For a list of those present, see Chaplin, "Lesbians Online," 459.

26 Information et coordination par et pour les lesbiennes is not referred to with an acronym in the sources. I have used one here (ICPPL) for clarity.

27 Doc. 1613, ARCL.

28 These goals were later formalized in the GTs' articles of association. See article 2, "Objet," in *Récépissé de Déclaration d'association*, No. 9259. This document was filed in Rennes in the Préfecture d'Ille-et-Vilaine on October 25, 1985. A copy exists at the ARCL.

29 Docs. 1273 and 1274, ARCL.

30 Wakeford, "New Technologies," 119.

31 Given that the average connection time ranged from four to ten minutes, the charges were extremely modest, particularly when compared to costs associated with calls to the message boards of the Minitel Rose on the for-profit line, 3615. See Sertel, communication statistics, June 16, 1986, doc. 1319, ARCL.

32 Docs. 1644–68 and 1877, ARCL.

33 Docs. 1631–754, ARCL.

34 Organization for Economic Co-operation and Development, *France's Experience with the Minitel*, 31.

35 Organization for Economic Co-operation and Development, *France's Experience with the Minitel*, 31.

36 Danièle and Corine of the GTs from Paris, quoted in "Les Goudous Télématiques," *Lesbia*, no. 40 (June 1986): 16–17.

37 Doc. 1192, ARCL.

38 Doc. 1192, ARCL.

39 Doc. 1067, ARCL.

40 Doc. 1106, ARCL.

41 Doc. 1192, ARCL.

42 Doc. 1093, ARCL.

43 Doc. 5376, ARCL.

44 Livia, "Public and Clandestine."

45 *Lesbia*, "Les Goudous Télématiques."

46 Duyves, "The Minitel," 202.

47 Doc. 1446, ARCL.

48 Shelley Correll, "The Ethnography of an Electronic Bar: The Lesbian Café," *Journal of Contemporary Ethnography* 24, no. 3 (October 1995): 270–98, esp. 295–96.

49 See "Goudou chez vous par Minitel," *Lesbia*, no. 35 (January 1986); "Annie et Charlotte au pays du Minitel," *Lesbia*, no. 36 (February 1986); "Coût coût Goudou!," *Lesbia*, no. 37 (March 1986); "Mots doux sur Minitel," *Lesbia*, no. 38 (April 1986); "Minitelles interactives," *Lesbia*, no. 39 (May 1986); and *Lesbia*, "Les Goudous Télématiques."

50 Doc. 1433, ARCL.

51 *Lesbia*, "Annie et Charlotte."

52 *Lesbia*, "Coût coût Goudou!," and "Les Goudous Télématiques."

53 Annie Cariou, interview by author, April 30, 2011, Paris, France.

54 Gonnard, interview.

55 Docs. 1754–815, ARCL.

56 Cariou, interview.

57 Mary Bryson observes that cyberstudies often commit this fault in reverse; they compare male and female subjects to identify the impact of gender difference on technology use but ignore the effects of sexual orientation, race, class, or age. See Mary Bryson, "When Jill Jacks In: Queer Women and the Net," *Feminist Media Studies* 4, no. 3 (2004): 239–54.

58 Doc. 1234, ARCL.

59 Docs. 1685, 1691, and 1693, ARCL.

60 Sexuality was hotly debated throughout lesbian and feminist communities in both North America and Europe at this time. For a general overview of the American context, see Lisa Duggan and Nan D. Hunter, *Sex Wars: Sexual Dissent and Political Culture*, 10th anniversary ed. (London: Routledge, 2006).

61 The CLF's website remains accessible, but the organization was dissolved on November 4, 2017. Other examples of French lesbian cybernetworks include the website of Bagdam Espace Lesbien run by Brigitte Boucheron at http://www.bagdam.org in Toulouse and the Centre Évolutif Lilith at http://celmrs.free.fr/ in Marseille.

CHAPTER EIGHT

1 Parts of this chapter also appear in my chapter "Utopian Gaiety: French Lesbian Activism and the Politics of Pleasure (1974–2016)," in *Making Waves: French Feminisms and Their Legacies, 1975–2015*, ed. Margaret Atack et al. (Liverpool: Liverpool University Press, 2019), 115–28; reprinted with permission.

2 Although the women who organize the Festival du Printemps lesbien regularly threaten that "this year is our last," at the time of publication the festival was still being produced annually. Jacqueline Julien, interview by author, January 22, 2015, Pech-Luna, France.

3 For footage, see *LEZbiennes sinon rien! 1989–2009: 20 ans d'Espace lesbien à Toulouse*, dir. Joséphine Ajdelbaum and Barbara Wolman (2009). The definition for

"Lesbopolis" is adapted from the definition for "metropolis" in Collins Dictionary online, accessed September 16, 2023, https://www.collinsdictionary.com/us/dictionary/english/metropolis.

4 Béatrice Dillies, "La ville rose, terre promise des lesbiennes en France," *La dépêche*, September 4, 2004.

5 Emmanuel Le Roy Ladurie, "Occitania in Historical Perspective," *Review (Fernand Braudel Center)* 1, no. 1 (Summer 1977): 23.

6 Brigitte Boucheron, interview by author, January 5, 2011, Toulouse, France.

7 The expression is from Rosemary Wakeman, *Modernizing the Provincial City: Toulouse, 1945–1975* (Cambridge, MA: Harvard University Press, 1997), 13.

8 See Robert A. Schneider, *Public Life in Toulouse, 1463–1789* (Ithaca, NY: Cornell University Press, 1989); and Ronald Aminzade, *Class, Politics, and Early Industrial Capitalism: A Study of Mid-Nineteenth-Century Toulouse, France* (Albany: State University of New York Press, 1981).

9 Wakeman, *Modernizing the Provincial City*, 26.

10 Wakeman, *Modernizing the Provincial City*, 29.

11 Jacqueline Julien, email to the author, February 1, 2015; emphasis in the original.

12 Jacqueline Julien, "La reine Pergame," in *Le Liseron*, special edition in memory of Thérèse Yakovenko (Poitiers, 1997), 2.

13 Jacques Pauvert also coedited work by Françoise Sagan, Guy Debord, and Régine Deforges (by whom he fathered an illegitimate child). His career helped loosen French censorship and pornography laws. The presence of Pauvert's publications helped establish the bookstore's reputation as a purveyor of politically and socially challenging texts. Éliane Laubus, interview by author, May 20, 2013, Limbre, France.

14 Unpublished interview with Brigitte Boucheron by Natasha Chetcuti, March 10, 2010, shared with the author.

15 Boucheron, interview.

16 Boucheron, interview.

17 Unless otherwise attributed, the quotes that follow are from Jacqueline Julien's unpublished text for Irène Corradin, shared with the author by email, February 8, 2015, and from Jacqueline's early interviews with me.

18 The reference is to Adrienne Rich, "Compulsory Heterosexuality and Lesbian Existence." Although she claims that she "has always been a lesbian," Julien married a man and had a son in her early twenties. Jacqueline Julien, interview by author, January 6, 2011, Toulouse, France.

19 Julien, "La reine Pergame," 1.

20 Julien, interview, January 6, 2011.

21 Laubus, interview, 2013.

22 Julien, "La reine Pergame," 2; and Julien, email to the author, February 1, 2015. Éliane worked at Pergame on the side; her day job was at the lycée.

23 Julien, "La reine Pergame," 3.

24 Éliane Laubus, interview by author, June 19, 2022, Limbre, France.

25 Brigitte Boucheron, under the pseudonym "Manon," quoted in Anna Reymondeaux, "Mouvements lesbiens et gays à Poitiers: 1975–1992. Du Féminisme à la Gay Pride: Naissance des mouvements identitaires" (Master's Thesis, Université de Poitiers, 2008), 23.

26 Boucheron, quoted in Reymondeaux, “Mouvements lesbiens et gays,” 23.
27 Boucheron, unpublished interview by Chetcuti.
28 The only similar venue in Poitiers was La Taverne, a space allocated to student associations after the student revolutions of May ’68 utilized by leftist groups (including feminists) and equipped with printing facilities. La Taverne closed in June 1984 when it lost its funding and was taken over by the National Institute of Statistics and Economic Studies. See Reymondeaux, “Mouvements lesbiens et gays,” 27.
29 Éliane Laubus, under the pseudonym “Fanny,” quoted in Reymondeaux, “Mouvements lesbiens et gays,” 24. Éliane later clarified to me that the “lesbians” she referred to would not have identified as such, choosing, rather, to call themselves homosexuels or feminists. Laubus, interview.
30 On “desiring machines” (*production désirante* in French), see Gilles Deleuze and Félix Guattari, *Anti-Oedipus* (Paris: Éditions de Minuit, 1972). On “lieu de mémoire,” see Pierre Nora, “Between Memory and History: Les Lieux de Mémoire,” in “Memory and Counter-Memory,” special issue, *Representations*, no. 26 (Spring 1989): 7.
31 Éliane Laubus, phone conversation with the author, February 5, 2015.
32 Sonia Ruiz, interview by author, January 7, 2011, Toulouse, France.
33 Ruiz, interview. Such observations were commonplace among early members of the women’s movement.
34 The phrase is (of course) adapted from the title of Virginia Woolf’s *A Room of One’s Own*.
35 Jacqueline Julien, “À Toulouse: Du féminisme lesbien au lesbianisme féministe,” Bagdam Espace Lesbien, accessed February 6, 2015, http://www.bagdam.org /articles/lesbianisme.html.
36 Julien, “À Toulouse.”
37 On the “nest,” see Julien, “À Toulouse”; the “destination of homosexuality” is from Julien, interview, January 6, 2011.
38 Boucheron, interview; Julien, interview, January 6, 2011.
39 Julien, “À Toulouse.”
40 Julien, “À Toulouse.”
41 Jacqueline Julien, “Lesbian Life in Twentieth-Century France,” unpublished talk at University of Illinois at Urbana-Champaign, August 27, 2012.
42 Boucheron, interview.
43 Bagdam newsletter, “Le fonctionnement” (September 1995–October 1996), Bagdam Cafée/Bagdam Espace Lesbien/Le Printemps Lesbien (à Toulouse), collection of Brigitte Boucheron, Toulouse, France (hereafter cited as BBC).
44 Until 1992 most media coverage linking Bagdam Cafée to lesbianism appeared in sources produced by and for lesbians. See, for example, “Bagdam Cafée,” *Lesbia magazine*, no. 75 (September 1989): 10; and “Construire nos espaces: Rencontre avec les animatrices du Bagdam Cafée, novembre 1989,” *Bulletin des archives lesbiennes*, no. 9 (June 1990): 11–12 (BBC).
45 This goal differentiated them from German lesbians, who were often separatists and disinterested in questions of visibility. Barbara Wolman, interview by author, January 8, 2011, Toulouse, France.
46 *InfoSud*, undated clipping (BBC).

47 *Toulouse pratique*, 1990–1991, undated clipping (BBC).
48 *La grande famille*, Canal+, broadcast November 6, 1990 (BBC).
49 Sophie Nogier, photographer for *Lesbia magazine*; Béatrice D. substitute teacher; Sophie-Anne Bled, *Lesbia* journalist and secretary of ACT UP–Paris; and Marie-France Le Dars, the creator of a lesbian Minitel site, also appear.
50 See also Jacqueline Julien, cited in Carole Gaborit, "Actualités: Canal+ de goudous," *Lesbia magazine* (December 1990): 9.
51 Gaborit, "Actualités," 8.
52 "Y a-t-il une culture lesbienne?," *Ça se discute*, hosted by Jean-Luc Delarue, France 2, broadcast January 16, 1996.
53 Boucheron, interview.
54 "La sexualité lesbienne," *Vent Sud*, France 3 Sud Midi Atlantique, broadcast March 20, 1996.
55 Quotes below are from a 2013 DVD copy of the 1992 slideshow *Longitude femme, latitude lesbienne*, produced, directed, and written by Jacqueline Julien and Caroline Godon-Gauthier, provided to me by Jacqueline Julien. Caroline Godon-Gauthier gave me a copy of the original handwritten script.
56 Caroline Godon-Gauthier, interview by author, May 18, 2013, Tours, France.
57 The motto regularly appears under their logo. See, for example, the March 19, 2024, newsletter advertising the 2024 Festival du Printemps lesbien. Email to the author, March 18, 2024.
58 In 2009, about one hundred of these were still functioning. See Sarah Kershaw, "My Sister's Keeper," *New York Times*, January 30, 2009.
59 Sara Warner, *Acts of Gaiety: LGBT Performance and the Politics of Pleasure* (Ann Arbor: University of Michigan Press, 2013).
60 Brigitte Boucheron, "Mail à Ludi sur la mixité," Bagdam Espace Lesbien, May 2008, http://www.bagdam.org/articles/ludi.html; emphases in the original.
61 Boucheron, "Mail à Ludi"; emphases in the original.
62 Ruiz, interview.
63 See the six volumes of *Espace Lesbien: Rencontres et revue d'études lesbiennes*: "Mémoires, langages, sexualités," no. 1 (October 2000); "La grande dissidence et le grand effroi," no. 2 (June 2001); "Le sexe sur le bout de la langue," no. 3 (September 2002); "Fureur et jubilation," no. 4 (April 2004); "Tout sur l'amour," no. 5 (April 2006); "L'Arme du rire," no. 6 (April 2009). All from Boucheron's private collection (BCC).
64 Julien, interview, January 6, 2011.
65 Françoise Flamant, *Women's Lands: Construction d'une utopie, Oregon, USA, 1970–2010* (Donnemarie-Dontilly: Éditions IXe, 2015).
66 Program for Festival du Printemps lesbien (2016), 3 (BBC).
67 See the Human Dignity Trust's report "Map of Countries That Criminalise LGBT People," accessed September 15, 2023, https://www.humandignitytrust.org/lgbt-the-law/map-of-criminalisation/?type_filter_submitted=&type_filter%5B%5D=death_pen applies.
68 Marian Lens, in Ajdelbaum and Wolman, *LEZbiennes sinon rien!*
69 Ruth Levitas, *Utopia as Method: The Imaginary Reconstitution of Society* (Houndmills: Palgrave Macmillan, 2013), 153, 218.
70 Levitas, *Utopia as Method*, 220.

71 Heather Love, *Feeling Backward: Loss and the Politics of Queer History* (Cambridge, MA: Harvard University Press, 2007), 3–4.

72 Love, *Feeling Backward*, 19.

73 Love, *Feeling Backward*, 12.

74 Warner, *Acts of Gaiety*, xi.

75 Warner, *Acts of Gaiety*, xiii. Lisa Duggan defines "homonormativity" as a neoliberal form of sexual politics that "does not contest dominant heteronormative assumptions and institutions, but upholds and sustains them, while promising the possibility of a demobilized gay constituency and a privatized, depoliticized gay culture anchored in domesticity and consumption." Lisa Duggan, *The Twilight of Equality? Neoliberalism, Cultural Politics, and the Attack on Democracy* (Boston: Beacon Press, 2003), 50.

76 José Esteban Muñoz, *Cruising Utopia: The Then and There of Queer Futurity* (New York: New York University Press, 2009), 189. Muñoz disagrees here with Annamarie Jagose's argument in *Lesbian Utopics*. Jagose denied that the "lesbian" is a utopic category and critiqued the kind of "utopic projections" that "claim cultural exteriority" as their "origin or destination." Rather, she argues that "those positions claimed for the category 'lesbian' as outside, and hence marking an escape from, regulation are more properly effects of those regulatory structures since the outside is a phantasmic projection from the inside." Annemarie Jagose, *Lesbian Utopics* (New York: Routledge, 1994), 163.

77 Muñoz, *Cruising Utopia*, 185.

CHAPTER NINE

1 Jacqueline Julien, "L'insoutenable visibilité de l'être," in *Invisibilité, visibilité des lesbiennes*, ed. Actes du Colloque organisé par la Coordination Lesbienne en France à l'Hôtel de Ville de Paris (Montreuil: CLF, 2007), 65.

2 On *parité*, see Joan Wallach Scott, *Parité: Sexual Equality and the Crisis of French Universalism* (Chicago: University of Chicago Press, 2005), and Réjane Sénac, *L'égalité sous conditions: Genre, parité, diversité* (Paris: Presses de Sciences Po, 2015).

3 SOS Homophobie, *Enquête sur la visibilité des lesbiennes et la lesbophobie, 2015*, preface by Natacha Chetcuti-Osorovitz (Merculès: Imprimerie CPI France-Quercy, 2015).

4 SOS Homophobie, *Enquête*, 75.

5 SOS Homophobie, *Enquête*, 73.

6 The survey is reprinted in the appendix to SOS Homophobie, *Enquête*, 76–79.

7 See, for example, Étienne Balibar and Immanuel Wallerstein, *Race, nation, class: Les identités ambiguës* (1988; Paris: La Découverte, 2007).

8 Kimberlé Crenshaw, "Mapping the Margins: Intersectionality, Identity Politics, and Violence against Women of Color," *Stanford Law Review* 43, no. 6 (1991): 1241–99. Crenshaw's article was translated into French in 2005 as Crenshaw and Oristelle Bonis, "Cartographies des marges: Intersectionnalité, politique de l'identité et violences contre les femmes de couleur," *Cahiers du genre* 39, no. 2 (2005): 51–82. See also Kimberlé Crenshaw, "Demarginalizing the Intersection of Race and Sex: A Black Feminist Critique of Antidiscrimination Doctrine,

Feminist Theory and Antiracist Politics," *University of Chicago Legal Forum* (1989), http://chicagounbound.uchicago.edu/uclf/vol1989/iss1/8.

9 On the gender paradox, see Joan Wallach Scott, *Only Paradoxes to Offer: French Feminists and the Rights of Man* (Cambridge, MA: Harvard University Press, 1997).

10 Douce Dibondo, "La Parole à," in *Rapport sur l'homophobie 2019*, ed. SOS Homophobie (Paris: SOS Homophobie, 2019), 147. On the French relationship to race, see Pap Ndiaye, *La condition noire* (Paris: Calmann-Lévy, 2008). On the relationship between race and class in France, see Didier Fassin and Éric Fassin, eds., *De la question sociale à la question raciale? Representer la société française* (Paris: La Découverte, 2006). On the relationship between France, colonialism, and race, see Colette Guillaumin, *L'idéologie raciste: Genèse et langage actuel*, 2nd ed. (Paris: Gallimard, 2002). On the relationship between colonialism, racism, and sexism in France, see Elsa Dorlin, *La matrice de la race: Généaologie sexuelle et coloniale de la nation française* (Paris: La Découverte, 2006).

11 Emilia Roig on Franceinfo, "L'Assemblée nationale supprime à l'unanimité le mot 'race' de la Constitution," updated July 12, 2018, https://www.francetvinfo.fr/societe/droits-des-femmes/l-assemblee-nationale-supprime-a-l-unanimite-le-mot-race-de-la-constitution-et-interdit-la-distinction-de-sexe_2847351.html.

12 On the erasure of homosexuality within racialized communities, see Itay Lotem, "'L'homosexualité? Ça n'existe pas en banlieue': The Indigènes de la République and Gay Marriage, between Intersectionality and Homophobia," *Modern and Contemporary France* 27, no. 2 (2019): 205–21.

13 Todd Shepard, *Sex, France & Arab Men, 1962–1979* (Chicago: University of Chicago Press, 2017), 100.

14 Frantz Fanon, *A Dying Colonialism*, trans. Haakon Chevalier, intro. Adolfo Gilly (New York: Grove Press, 1965), esp. chapter 1, "Algeria Unveiled," 35–63; Joan Wallach Scott, *The Politics of the Veil* (Princeton, NJ: Princeton University Press, 2007).

15 Blasé A. Provitola, "In Visibilities: The *Groupe du 6 novembre* and the Production of Liberal Lesbian Identity in Contemporary France," *Modern and Contemporary France* 27, no. 2 (2019): 227–28. See also Provitola's PhD dissertation, "Sex, Race and the Epistemology of Desire in the Literature and Culture of Contemporary France" (PhD diss., Columbia University, 2019).

16 Paola Bacchetta, "Groupe du 6 novembre: Lesbiennes issues du colonialisme, de l'esclavage et de l'immigration," in *Global Encyclopedia of Lesbian, Gay, Bisexual, Transgender, and Queer History*, ed. Howard Chiang et al. (Farmington Hills, MI: Charles Scribner's Sons, 2019), 624.

17 Paola Bacchetta, "QTPOC Critiques of 'Post-Raciality,' Segregationality, Coloniality, and Capitalism in France," in *Decolonizing Sexualities: Transnational Perspectives, Critical Interventions*, ed. Sandeep Bakshi, Suhraiya Jivraj, and Silvia Posocco (Oxford: Counter Press, 2016), 267.

18 Annie Astier, interview by author, June 16, 2013, Saint-Véran, France.

19 Sylvie P., interview by author, June 7, 2013, Strasbourg, France.

20 Catherine Vautier-Péanne, interview by author, June 18, 2013, Paris, France.

21 Aresky, interview by author, June 25, 2013, Marseille, France.

22 Nicole Bonnin, interview by author, May 21, 2013, Poitiers, France.
23 Bernadette S., interview by author, June 15, 2013, Grenoble, France.
24 Jacqueline Julien, interview by author, January 22, 2015, Pech-Luna, France.
25 Anita F., interview by author, June 26, 2013, Marseille, France.
26 Nicole Miquel, interview by author, May 15, 2013, Paris, France.
27 Kachina, interview by author, June 25, 2013, Marseille, France.
28 Danielle R., interview by author, January 5, 2013, Paris, France.
29 In 2022 conversion therapy was outlawed in France. It was still legal in Switzerland in December of that year.
30 "Être gay en 1984," *Les dossiers de l'écran*, Antenne 2, broadcast September 4, 1984.
31 Raphaël Stainville, "Insecurité: C'était intenable, nous sommes partis," *Le figaro*, August 3, 2010; Marie-Laure Combes and Aurélien Fleurot, "Amiens-Nord, une 'zone de non-droit,'" *Europe 1*, August 15, 2012; "Des 'minis états islamiques' en France," *Radio-télévision Suisse*, September 25, 2014.
32 Filo, interview by author, June 25, 2013, Marseille, France.
33 Paola Bacchetta demonstrates that this vision was bolstered by government-supported organizations like Ni putes, ni soumises (Neither Whores, Nor Virgins) and SOS Racisme. The latter's slogan *Touche pas à mon pote* ("Don't touch my pal" in the masculine form) implicitly figured white French people, "presumably men and boys, in the position of saviors of men and boys of color while erasing women, girls, and folks of all other genders altogether." Bacchetta, "QTPOC Critiques," 268, 275.
34 Mouvement d'information et d'expression des lesbiennes (MIEL), *Être lesbienne aujourd'hui: Le M.I.E.L. enquête* (Paris: MIEL, 1988).
35 MIEL, *Être lesbienne aujourd'hui*, 28.
36 MIEL, *Être lesbienne aujourd'hui*, 29.
37 See Guillaumin, *L'idéologie raciste*, and Guillaumin, *Sexe, race et pratique du pouvoir: L'idée de la nature* (Paris: Côté-Femmes, 1992), a collection of her articles published between 1977 and 1990.
38 The march was held on Saturday, March 30, 1986. The flyer is undated. Fonds Les Goudous Télématiques BMD. This collection was not yet catalogued at the time of consultation.
39 Souad Benani, "Lesbiennes maghrébines: Briser le silence. Sexualité et les beurs au féminin," *Bulletin des Archives recherches cultures lesbiennes*, no. 5 (February 1987). The article was previously published in *Sans frontières* as "La beur génération."
40 Provitola, "In Visibilities," 225.
41 Bacchetta, "Groupe du 6 novembre," 624.
42 Bacchetta, "Groupe du 6 novembre," 623.
43 These included the Groupe de femmes algériennes (Algerian Women's Group) established in Paris in 1978 and the Groupe de femmes marocaines (Moroccan Women's Group) established in Paris in 1980.
44 Bacchetta, "QTPOC Critiques," 269.
45 Groupe du 6 novembre, *Warriors/Guérrières* (Paris: Nomades'Langues, 2001), 8; emphasis in original.

46 Groupe du 6 novembre, quoted in Martine Laroche and Michèle Larrouy, eds., *Mouvements de presse: Des années 1970s à nos jours, luttes féministes et lesbiennes* (Paris: Éditions des ARCL, 2009), 159.
47 H. Kaddour, "The Continuity," in *Warriors/Guérrières*, 34.
48 Quote is from excerpts of *Warriors/Guérrières* published on the website of the Coordination lesbienne en France, accessed March 2, 2023, https://www.coordinationlesbienne.org/spip.php?article141.
49 Other sessions focused on agism, fatphobia, lesbophobia, sexuality, poverty, violence, and radical lesbianism. "Sommaire," Coordination Lesbienne Nationale, spring meeting, Die (Drôme), Pentecôte, May 1999, Dossier CLN (ARCL).
50 Jennifer Gay, "Atelier 'Racisme 2', Mixte," pamphlet, Coordination Lesbienne Nationale, spring meeting, Die (Drôme), Pentecôte, May 1999, 3, Dossier CLN (ARCL).
51 Marie-Hélène Lefebvre, "Racisme: ateliers 2 et 3," pamphlet, Coordination Lesbienne Nationale, spring meeting, Die (Drôme), Pentecôte, May 1999, 4, Dossier CLN (ARCL).
52 Kadri, quoted in Collectif des raciné-e-s, *Plumes de queers racisé-e-s*, February 13, 2019, https://desracinees.files.wordpress.com/2019/02/fanzinedalilacolor.pdf.
53 Christine Bouchara, "Plus que jamais les lesbiennes se font du cinéma," *Lesbia magazine*, no. 188 (December 1999): 31.
54 "Présentation générale," Cineffable, accessed February 28, 2023, https://www.cineffable.fr/fr/c_asso.htm.
55 "Evènements [*sic*] du 11e Festival 1999," Cineffable, accessed March 3, 2023, https://www.cineffable.fr/pages/arch_11debat.htm.
56 See the description of the film published in the 1999 program, accessed online March 23, 2024, https://www.cineffable.fr/festivals/11efestival/Films11/filmsNR.htm#omb.
57 Dalila Kadri (1949–2017) went on to make another film on lesbians of color in France, *Lucioles* (Kali Productions, 2004).
58 See "Evènements [*sic*] du 11e Festival 1999." Quotations in this paragraph from the debate are from this website.
59 Jacqueline Pasquier, interview by author, June 20, 2013, Paris, France.
60 Jacqueline Pasquier, "Au fil du XXIe festival," *Lesbia magazine*, no. 188 (December 1999): 33.
61 "Racisme. Sexisme. Homophobie," *Madivine*, no. 1 (April 2000).
62 Groupe du 6 novembre, "Lesbia magazine persiste et oppose un refus solennel à la publication de la réponse. Halte à l'antiracisme bon teint!," *Madivine*, no. 1 (April 2000): 7.
63 "Statement by Lesbiennes of Color (LOCs, Lesbians of Color) in France against Racism in LGBTQ Communities in Germany," *No Homonationalism* (blog), July 29, 2010, http://nohomonationalism.blogspot.com/2010/07/statement-by-lesbiennes-of-color-locs.html.
64 Collectif des raciné-e-s, *Plumes de queers*.
65 Salima Amari, *Lesbiennes de l'immigration: Construction de soi et relations familiales* (Vulaines sur Seine: Éditions du Croquant, 2018).
66 Amari, *Lesbiennes de l'immigration*, 13.
67 Amari, *Lesbiennes de l'immigration*, 338.

68 fisopulp, "Pulp Gay-Pride 1998," uploaded on April 12, 2007, YouTube vie, 3:24, accessed March 4, 2023, https://www.youtube.com/watch?v=kYgtuU-LvAA.

69 Elisabeth Lebovici, "*Housewife*, la redistribution du sensible," accessed March 4, 2023, https://www.academia.edu/37369835/Housewife_la_redistribution_du_sensible; reprinted in Natacha Chetcuti and Nelly Quemener, "Miroir/Miroirs—Numéro 4," *Plus Gouine La Vie? Politique Des Répresentations* (September 2015).

70 Lebovici, "*Housewife*."

71 Lebovici, "*Housewife*."

72 Fany Corral, quoted in Géraldine Sarratia, "Les clubs mythiques (3/7): Le Pulp, une nouvelle identité lesbienne," *Les inrockuptibles*, July 17, 2011, https://www.lesinrocks.com/actu/les-clubs-mythiques-37-le-pulp-une-nouvelle-identite-lesbienne-39194-17-07-2011/.

73 Didier Lestrade, "Le Pulp: The Politics of Dancing," Red Bull Music Academy Daily, June 1, 2016, https://daily.redbullmusicacademy.com/2016/06/le-pulp-feature.

74 Mimi Cassaro, quoted in Lebovici, "*Housewife*."

75 Lebovici's "*Housewife*" brings this publication to life.

76 Le Dauphin later wrote for *Têtu* and edited the short-lived *Têtu, madame*. She has also appeared on TV talk shows and worked as a photographer and international journalist. Since 1996, artist Dana Wyse has created and written for her fictional business, Jesus Had a Sister Productions, a pharmaceutical company whose mythical products were regularly advertised in *Housewife*. See "About," Dana Wyse, accessed October 21, 2023, https://danawyse.com/about/.

77 "Black Is Beautiful," *Housewife: Le magazine du Pulp*, no. 9 (March 1998.)

78 Lestrade, "Le Pulp."

79 Clémentine Goldszal, "Souvenirs du Pulp, paradis perdu de la culture lesbienne parisienne," *Le Monde*, August 20, 2022, https://www.lemonde.fr/m-le-mag/article/2022/08/20/au-pulp-les-filles-menent-la-danse-des-nuits-parisiennes_6138526_4500055.html.

80 "Décès de la DJ SexToy," *Le nouvel obs*, February 12, 2002, https://www.nouvelobs.com/culture/20020207.OBS2975/deces-de-la-dj-sextoy.html.

81 Laurie Marhoefer, "Queer Fascism and the End of Gay History," *Notches*, June 19, 2018, https://notchesblog.com/2018/06/19/queer-fascism-and-the-end-of-gay-history/.

82 Frank Chaumont, *Homo-Ghetto. Gays et lesbiennes dans les cités: Les clandestins de la République* (Paris: Le Cherche Midi, 2009), 10.

83 Ni putes, ni soumises was founded in 2003 in response to horrific acts of violence—from gang rapes to murder—perpetrated by Arab men against Arab women in the banlieues.

84 Oscar Lopez, "Don't Be Fooled by Marine Le Pen's Gay Pandering—Her Party Is Awful for LGBTQ Equality," *Slate*, May 7, 2017, https://slate.com/human-interest/2017/05/marine-le-pens-gay-pandering-doesnt-excuse-her-national-front-party-on-lgbt-equality.html.

85 Caroline Fourest is a vehement opponent of the radical right but is likewise a vehement proponent of *laïcité*. See, for example, her *Les anti-PaCS, ou, La dernière croisade homophobe* (Paris: Éditions Prochoix, 1999) and *Tirs croisés: La laïcité à l'épreuve des intégismes juif, chrétien et muselman* (Paris: Calmann-Lévy, 2003).

86 Bourcier, quoted in Christelle Taraud, *Les féminismes en questions: Éléments pour une cartographie* (Paris: Éditions Amsterdam, 2005), 47.

CONCLUSION

1 Liliane Robert (also known as Liliane Debernard), interview by author, March 11, 2016, Cannes, France.
2 Jean-Marc Nicolaï, interview by author, March 10, 2016, Haut-de-Cagnes, France.
3 For a brilliant philosophical analysis of this issue, see Miranda Fricker, *Epistemic Injustice: Power and the Ethics of Knowing* (Oxford: Oxford University Press, 2007).
4 Marianne Blidon, "En quête de reconnaissance: La justice spatiale à l'épreuve de l'hétéronormativité," translated by Melanie Mauthner and Claire Hancock as "Seeking Recognition: Spatial Justice versus Heteronormativity," *Justice spatiale / Spatial Justice*, no. 3 (March 2011): 2.

BIBLIOGRAPHY

INTERVIEWS AND PERSONAL COMMUNICATIONS

Isabelle A., interview by author, April 27, 2011, Montreuil, France
Martine A., interview by author, June 27, 2013, Marseille, France
Agnès, interview by author, June 27, 2013, Marseille, France
Stéphanie Arc, interview by author, May 13, 2013, Paris, France
Aresky, interview by author, June 25, 2013, Marseille, France
Annie Astier, interview by author, June 16, 2013, Saint-Véran, France
Brigitte B., interview by author, June 20, 2013, Paris, France
Claude B., interview by author, March 10, 2016, Nice, France
Liliane B., interview by author, May 20, 2013, Limbre, France
Dominique Beauchery, interview by author, June 25, 2013, Paris, France
Marie-Paule Belle, interview by author, October 20, 2017, Paris, France
Anne Beniguel, interviews by author, April 4, 12, 2013, Paris, France
Cathy Bernheim, interview by author, May 14, 2013, Paris, France
Monik Blachon, interview by author, June 16, 2013, Saint-Véran, France
Sylvina Boissonas, interview by author, June 23, 2015, Paris, France
Marie-Jo Bonnet, interview by author, May 15, 2013, Paris, France
Nicole Bonnin, interview by author, May 21, 2013, Poitiers, France
Brigitte Boucheron, interview by author, January 5, 2011, Toulouse, France
Marie-Hélène Carbonel, interview by author, March 10, 2016, Nice, France
Annie Cariou, interview by author, April 30, 2011, Paris, France
Choud, interview by author, June 9, 2013, Lyon, France
Thérèse Clerc, interview by author, June 19, 2013, Montreuil, France
Irène Corradin, interview by author, January 13, 2011, Toulouse, France
Danièle Cottereau, phone interview by author, December 2, 2023; interview by author, June 17, 2013, Aulnay-sous-Bois, France
Marie-Christine Darfeuille, interview by author, June 30, 2013, Espenel, France
Dave (Wouter Otto Levenbach), interview by author, October 18, 2017, Paris, France

Odile Debloos, interview by author, May 11, 2013, Amiens, France
Christine Delphy, interview by author, January 12, 2011, Paris, France
Rachel Denoeud, phone conversation with the author, February 9, 2016
Catherine Deudon, interview by author, May 7, 2013, Paris, France
Marie-Josephe Devillers, interview by author, April 30, 2013, Paris, France
Dominique, interview by author, June 27, 2013, Marseille, France
Evelyne, interview by author, June 25, 2013, Marseille, France
Anita F., interview by author, June 26, 2013, Marseille, France
Catherine Facerias, interview by author, May 23, 2013, Paris, France
Anne-Marie Faure, interview by author, June 15, 2015, Paris, France
Nicole Fernández Ferrer, interview by author, May 6, 2013, Paris, France
Filo, interview by author, June 25, 2013, Marseille, France
Françoise Flamant, interviews by author, December 5, 7, 2010, Paris, France
Isabel Fournier, interview by author, June 14, 2013, Grenoble, France
Sylviane Francesconi, interview by author, January 11, 2011, Toulouse, France
Annette Freudinger, interview by author, June 26, 2013, Marseille, France
Sylvie Gaume, interview by author, June 27, 2013, Marseille, France
Jennifer Gay, interview by author, July 3, 2013, Grâne, France
Raymonde Gérard, interview by author, May 10, 2013, Amiens, France
Marie-Noëlle Gerolami, interview by author, April 29, 2013, Paris, France
Mireille Girouin, interview by author, June 30, 2013, Espenel, France
Caroline Godon-Gauthier, interview by author, May 18, 2013, Tours, France
Grazia Gonik, interview by author, July 5, 2013, Grâne, France
Catherine Gonnard, interviews by author, 2010–2018, Paris, France
Roseau Grange, interview by author, June 22, 2015, Paris, France
Claire Guillaud, interview by author, June 13, 2012, Lyon, France
Patricia Guillaume, interview by author, June 26, 2013, Marseille, France
Marie-Geneviève Havel, interview by author, May 22, 2013, Paris, France
Hélène Hazéra, interview by author, June 13, 2018, Paris, France
Hélène, interview by author, June 27, 2013, Marseille, France
Mathilde Huet, interview by author, June 18, 2013, Paris, France
Françoise Huron, interview by author, May 20, 2013, Poitiers, France
Michèle Idels, interview by author, June 23, 2015, Paris, France
Monique Isselé, interviews by author, June 17, 2013, January 14, 2018, Paris, France
Josy, interviews by author, June 18, 2013, January 2018, Paris, France
Jacqueline Julien, interviews by author, 2011–2023, Toulouse, Pech-Luna, Cassis, and Paris, France; emails to the author, February 1, 8, 2015
Cy Jung, interview by author, May 2, 2013, Paris, France
Kiki K., interviews by author, January 14, 2011, January 18, 2018, Toulouse, France
Kachina, interview by author, June 25, 2013, Marseille, France
Catherine Lara, interview by author, January 17, 2018, Paris, France
Martine Laroche, interview by author, April 22, 2011, Paris, France
Éliane Laubus, interviews by author, May 20, 2013, June 19, 2022, Limbre, France; phone conversation and email with the author, February 5, 2015
Christine Lavigne, interview by author, May 20, 2013, Poitiers, France
Elisabeth Lebovici, interview by author, May 23, 2013, Paris, France

Christine Le Doaré, interview by author, June 19, 2013, Paris, France
Christine Lemoine, interview by author, May 5, 2013, Paris, France
Valérie Léonard, interviews by author, April 27, 2011, January 26, 2013, February 19, 2014, Paris, France
Brigitte Lhomond, interview by author, June 11, 2013, Lyon, France
Sylvie M., interview by author, June 27, 2013, Marseille, France
Marie-Louise, interview by author, June 30, 2013, Espenel, France
Marino, interviews by author, April 29, 2013, June 18, 2013, Paris, France
Catherine Marjollet, interview by author, June 28, 2013, Marseille, France
Marise Martinez, interview by author, June 6, 2013, Strasbourg, France
Sylvie Meinier, interview by author, June 14, 2013, Grenoble, France
Patricia Mercader, interview by author, June 12, 2013, Lyon, France
Nicole Miquel, interview by author, May 15, 2013, Paris, France
Hélène de Monferrand, interview by author, June 20, 2013, Paris, France
"Dan" Monnel, interview by author, June 10, 2018, Lille, France
Catherine Morin-LeSech, interview by author, April 30, 2013, Paris, France
Isabelle Moulins, interview by author, June 26, 2013, Marseille, France
Natalie, interview by author, June 6, 2013, Strasbourg, France
Jean-Marc Nicolaï, interview by author, March 10, 2016, Haut-de-Cagnes, France
Nouria, interview by author, June 25, 2013, Marseille, France
Nicole Olliel, interview by author, June 14, 2013, Grenoble, France
Marie-Françoise Orain, interview by author, November 19, 2017, Paris, France
Barbara Osorovitz, phone conversation with the author, February 11, 2023
Sylvie P., interview by author, June 7, 2013, Strasbourg, France
Marion Page, interviews by author, May 8, 9, 2013, Le Quesnoy, France
Jacqueline Pasquier, interview by author, June 20, 2013, Paris, France
Paula, interview by author, July 5, 2013, Ardèche, France
Michèle Philibert, interview by author, June 25, 2013, Marseille, France
Dominique Poggi, interview by author, June 17, 2015, Paris, France
Michelle Porte, interview by author, May 7, 2013, Paris, France
Isabelle Prieur, interview by author, May 11, 2013, Amiens, France
Danielle R., interview by author, January 5, 2013, Paris, France
Cécile Ramade, interview by author, June 14, 2013, Grenoble, France
Régis Revenin, email to author, December 5, 2017
Liliane Robert, interview by author, March 11, 2016, Cannes, France
Suzette (Triton) Robichon, interview by author, May 13, 2013, Paris, France
Evelyne Rochedereux, interviews by author, December 15, 17, 18, 19, 2010, Le Croisic, France
Andrew Israel Ross, email to author, June 9, 2022
Sonia Ruiz, interview by author, January 7, 2011, Toulouse, France
Bernadette S., interview by author, June 15, 2013, Grenoble, France
Irène Tabellion, interview by author, June 6, 2013, Strasbourg, France
Anne-Marie Thuret, interview by author, December 10, 2011, Le Croisic, France
Catherine Vautier-Péanne, interview by author, June 18, 2013, Paris, France
Marie Vendeville, interview by author, January 10, 2011, Toulouse, France
Mireille Vigne, interview by author, June 13, 2013, Lyon, France
Barbara Wolman, interview by author, January 8, 2011, Toulouse, France

ARCHIVES

Private Archives

Bagdam Cafée/Bagdam Espace Lesbien/Le Printemps Lesbien (à Toulouse), collection of Brigitte Boucheron, Toulouse, France (BBC)
Marilyn "Miki" Leff Papers, collection of Roy Winnick, Princeton, NJ, USA (Miki Leff Papers)
Elula Perrin Pressbooks, collection of Valérie Léonard, Paris, France (EP Pressbooks)
Quand les femmes s'aiment, collection of Patricia Mercader, Lyon, France (QLFSA-PM)
Radio Fréquence Gaie, collection of Danièle Cottereau, Aulnay-sous-Bois, France (FG-DC)

Public Archives

Archives de la préfecture de police de Paris (APP), Paris, France
Archives de la ville de Paris (AP), Paris, France
Archives d'Éros, Paris, France
Archives nationales (AN), Paris, France
Archives recherches cultures lesbiennes (ARCL), Paris, France
Bibliothèque Marguerite Durand (BMD), Paris, France
    Fonds Les Goudous Télématiques (unarchived at time of consultation)
    Fonds Les Répondeuses (Fonds LR/BMD), cartons I–III (unarchived at time of consultation)
Bibliothèque-musée de l'Opéra (BMO), Paris, France
    Fonds KOCHNO-1310
Bibliothèque nationale de France (BNF) site François Mitterrand, Paris, France
    Recueil: Caroll's [*sic*] Cabaret, 1950–1960, 8-SW-86
Centre des archives du féminisme, Angers, France
Centre Louise Labé, Université Lumière Lyon 2, Lyon, France
Human Sexuality Collection, Rare and Manuscript Collections, Cornell University Library, Ithaca, New York
Inathèque de France, Paris, France
Institut national de l'audiovisuel, Bry-sur-Marne, France
Musée Renoir (Château-musée archives), Cagnes-sur-Mer, France
    Fonds Suzy Solidor
        Solidor Birthday Photo Albums (1979–1981)
        Solidor Pressbooks (1937–1948)
Réunion des musées nationaux Grand Palais, Paris, France
University of Illinois Urbana-Champaign University Library

AUDIOVISUAL SOURCES

Except when otherwise noted, all radio and television broadcasts are from the archives of the Institut national de l'audiovisuel (Fonds INA).

Radio

Allô Ménie. "L'homosexualité, ce douloureux problème." Radio-télévision Luxembourg, aired March 10, 1971. Available online at https://www.youtube.com/watch?v=SGHRtoi3en0, accessed March 20, 2021.

Boulevard des archives. "Parole de femmes." France Culture, Radio France, aired March 9, 1998.

France Culture. "Allô Danièle? À la recherche des ondes lesbiennes." Radio France, aired January 17, 2021.

———. "La mémoire de Suzy." Radio France, aired August 15, 1978.

Inter actualités de 08H00. France Inter, aired August 27, 1970.

Magazine bleu. "Interview de la chanteuse Suzy Solidor: Entre poésie et chansons." Nice Côte d'Azur, RTF, aired August 16, 1961.

Un quart d'heure avec . . . "Suzy Solidor." RDF/RTF, aired April 7, 1948.

Qui l'aime la suivre. "La naissance d'un compositeur de chansons." Paris Inter, RTF, aired October 10, 1960.

Radioscopie. "Agnès Capri." France Inter, aired July 7, 1975.

Rendez-vous en Ile de France. Inter Variétés, ORTF, aired October 19, 1964.

Tours de chant. "Parole de femmes." France Culture, Radio France, aired March 9, 1988.

Television

52 sur la une: Le magazine du grand reportage. "Amour de femmes." TF1, broadcast July 21, 1993.

A2 dernière. "Plateau invité: Didier Varrod." Antenne 2, broadcast July 27, 1982.

Âge tendre et tête de bois. RTF Télévision, broadcast November 21, 1961.

Agora. "Une bonne mère mais." FR3, broadcast March 28, 1984.

Antenne 2 le journal de 20H. "Les homosexuels." Antenne 2, broadcast November 4, 1979.

Antenne 2 midi. "Couple homosexuel." Antenne 2, broadcast May 4, 1983.

———. "Nicole et Armelle." Antenne 2, broadcast March 18, 1982.

Apostrophes. "Femmes libérées." Antenne 2, broadcast November 9, 1984.

———. "La sexualité racontée par les femmes." Antenne 2, broadcast November 7, 1975.

L'art de vivre. RTF Télévision, broadcast January 21, 1963.

Au delà de l'écran. Channel 1, ORTF, broadcast March 21, 1965.

———. "Nicole Louvier." RTF Télévision, broadcast March 17, 1963.

Aujourd'hui la vie. "L'homosexualité." Antenne 2, broadcast May 28, 1982.

———. "La libération des femmes: Un mouvement à suivre . . ." Antenne 2, broadcast March 7, 1982.

———. "Maladies d'amour: Danger." Antenne 2, broadcast June 23, 1983.

Aujourd'hui madame. "Le féminisme." Directed by Jacques Gérard Cornu. Channel 2, ORTF, broadcast September 10, 1971.

———. "Le féminisme." Directed by Jacques Gérard Cornu. Channel 2, ORTF, broadcast May 3, 1972.

———. "Mick Micheyl." Channel 1, ORTF, broadcast June 27, 1973.

Bas les masques. "Je suis une femme qui aime les femmes." Directed by Dominique Colonna. Antenne 2, broadcast October 5, 1994.
La belle télévision: Quarant ans de télévision. "Les femmes aussi." Directed by Maurice Dugowson. France 3, broadcast August 22, 1990.
Bouquet de joie. RTF Télévision, broadcast September 24, 1956.
Cabaret du soir. Directed by Jean Kerchbron. RTF Télévision, broadcast May 1958–January 1959.
Ça se discute. "Y a-t-il une culture lesbienne?" Hosted by Jean-Luc Delarue. France 2, broadcast January 16, 1996.
Ce sacré métier. Channel 1, ORTF, broadcast January 23, 1969.
Ce soir à. "De New York à Los Angeles." RTF Télévision, broadcast December 3, 1960.
La chance aux chansons. "Le retour des ménestrels." France 2, broadcast December 1, 1992.
Cinépanorama. RTF Télévision, broadcast January 24, 1957.
La clé des champs. "Jean Poiret et Michel Serrault, 'Les deux Hortenses' ou 'Les antiquaires.'" RTF Télévision, broadcast April 27, 1959.
"Conférence de presse de M. Georges Pompidou Président de la République." Directed by Alexandre Tarta. Channel 1, ORTF, broadcast July 2, 1970.
Côte d'Azur actualités. "Tournage du film 'Les Biches.'" Channel 1, ORTF, broadcast November 28, 1967.
Les coulisses de l'exploit. "Défi à Mick Micheyl." Channel 1, ORTF, broadcast April 21, 1965.
Des goûts et des couleurs. RTF Télévision, broadcast November 8, 1956.
Dimanche en France. "Entretien avec la chanteuse Dany Dauberson." RTF Télévision, broadcast November 16, 1958.
Dim Dam Dom. "Frédé." Directed by Pierre Philippe. Channel 2, ORTF, broadcast February 21, 1971.
———. "Marguerite Duras à la petite Roquette." Channel 2, ORTF, broadcast November 12, 1966.
———. "Violette Leduc racontée par elle-même." Channel 2, ORTF, broadcast April 6, 1970.
Discorama. RTF Télévision, broadcast June 12, 1959.
Les documents du dimanche. "Sexe, censure et télévision." Directed by Daniel Costelle and Isabelle Clarke. France 2, broadcast April 8, 2001.
Les dossiers de l'écran. "Les homosexuels." Antenne 2, broadcast January 21, 1975.
———. "Être gay en 1984." Antenne 2, broadcast September 4, 1984.
École des vedettes. RTF Télévision, broadcast November 19, 1962.
Émission: Antenne 2 le journal de 20H. "Le virus du SIDA et le vaccin de l'hépatite B." Antenne 2, broadcast June 28, 1983.
Émission médicale. "L'homosexualité." Channel 1, ORTF, broadcast November 29, 1973.
———. "Portrait d'un psychiatre." Channel 1, ORTF, broadcast October 19, 1970.
Enquête publique. "Une nouvelle maladie ou le SIDA." Antenne 2, broadcast September 29, 1983.
Entente cordiale. "Les îles." Channel 1, ORTF, broadcast February 9, 1972.

L'equilibre: Cécile ou la raison des femmes. "Anne Zelensky à propos de son engagement féministe." TF1, ORTF, broadcast October 22, 1975.
Les films du dimanche. "Claudine à l'école." RTF Télévision, broadcast April 11, 1954.
Français si vous parliez. "Homosexuels en province." France 3, broadcast October 13, 1992.
La grande famille. Canal+, broadcast November 6, 1990.
L'huile sur le feu. "L'homosexualité féminine." Antenne 2, broadcast July 11, 1977.
L'invité du jeudi. "Une journée avec Delphine Seyrig." Antenne 2, broadcast April 24, 1980.
Les jeunes mariés du printemps. RTF Télévision, broadcast March 16, 1959.
Les joies de la vie. "Odette Laure." RTF Télévision, broadcast October 6, 1958.
JT 13H. "Les assises du MLF." Channel 1, ORTF, broadcast May 15, 1972.
———. "Magazine des femmes: Mick Micheyl and Co." Channel 1, ORTF, broadcast June 18, 1973.
JT 20H. "Baptême d'une guenon par Anne Monaco." RTF Télévision, broadcast November 11, 1953.
———. "La grève des femmes." Channel 2, ORTF, broadcast June 9, 1974.
———. "Manifestations femmes place de l'Étoile." Channel 1, ORTF, broadcast August 26, 1970.
———. "Mick Micheyl." RTF Télévision, broadcast May 23, 1964.
JT FR3 Rhône Alpes. "Manifestation contre le procès d'une mère homosexuelle." FR3, broadcast April 24, 1982.
———. "Manifestation de protestation contre les discriminations à l'égard des homosexuels à Lyon." FR3, broadcast December 12, 1981.
———. "Le problème de la garde d'un enfant retirée à sa mère à cause de son homosexualité." FR3, broadcast December 11, 1981.
JT nuit. "Manifestation d'homosexuels aux États-Unis." Channel 1, ORTF, broadcast June 29, 1970.
———. "Mick Micheyl." Channel 1, ORTF, broadcast December 14, 1966.
———. "Mick Micheyl à Moscou." Channel 1, ORTF, broadcast December 26, 1967.
———. "Vitrines du Faubourg Saint Honoré." RTF Télévision, broadcast June 13, 1959.
Lectures pour tous. RTF Télévision, broadcast February 11, 1959; Channel 1, ORTF, broadcast October 7, 1964; November 18, 1964.
Lorraine soir. "Stand MLF à l'Eurofoire de Nancy." Channel 3, ORTF, broadcast June 13, 1974.
Magazine féminin. RTF Télévision, broadcast February 5, 1959; Channel 1, ORTF, broadcast January 23, 1965; November 25, 1967.
Les mercredis de l'information. "Les homosexuels." TF1, broadcast November 16, 1983.
Net Café. "Women on the Web." Hosted by Jane Wither, Andrew deVries, and Stewart Cheifet. PBS, broadcast 1996. Available online at http://archive.org/details/nc105_women.
Normandie actualités. "Haute Normandie: Le dossier—1er volet—L'homosexualité." FR3, broadcast June 24, 1983.

Présence protestante. “Thérèse Clerc, militante du MLAC.” TF1, broadcast November 9, 1975.
Procès. “Pour ou contre l’éducation sexuelle à l’école.” Channel 1, ORTF, broadcast April 25, 1972.
Rennes soir. “Inquiétude des hémophiles face aux dons du sang contaminés par le virus du SIDA.” Channel 3, broadcast June 27, 1973.
Sérieux s’abstenir. “Le MPLPF.” Directed by Henry Polage. Channel 1, ORTF, broadcast June 8, 1972.
Soir 3. “Procès homosexuelles contre la sécurité sociale à Nantes.” FR3, broadcast January 19, 1984.
Sur un air de cabaret. RTF Télévision, broadcast December 4, 1956.
Suzy Solidor: Un étrange destin. Directed by Alain Gallet. France 3 Ouest, broadcast February 28, 2006.
Télé-Paris. “Télé-Paris.” RTF Télévision, broadcast January 1, 1952.
———. “Télé-Paris.” RTF Télévision, broadcast January 20, 1954.
———. “Télé-Paris à Cannes.” RTF Télévision, broadcast August 1, 1955.
———. “Télé-Paris à Deauville.” RTF Télévision, broadcast August 23, 1954.
Télé pays de la Loire. “Couple d’homosexuelles en procès à Nantes.” FR3, broadcast October 6, 1983.
———. “Interview de l’avocat d’un couple d’homosexuelles.” FR3, broadcast February 20, 1982.
———. “Jugement du procès intenté par les homosexuelles Nadia et Annie.” FR3, broadcast December 1, 1983.
Temps présent. “Le week-end relax au Touquet Paris Plage.” Channel 1, ORTF, broadcast October 8, 1966.
TF1 13 heures le journal. “Psychose cancer gay aux USA.” TF1, broadcast June 27, 1983.
TF1 actualités dernière. “Histoires du MLF.” TF1, broadcast April 22, 1977.
TF1 dernière. “Femmes homosexuelles.” TF1, broadcast April 19, 1983.
Trente-six chandelles. RTF Télévision, broadcast February 4, 1957.
Tribune libre. “Arcadie: Mouvement homophile de France.” FR3, broadcast January 7, 1977.
———. “Comité d’Urgence Anti-Répression Homosexuelle.” FR3, broadcast April 27, 1983.
Variances. “Kate Millett, et la condition de la femme.” Channel 1, ORTF, broadcast July 20, 1971.
Vendredi. “SIDA, la nouvelle peste.” FR3, broadcast October 14, 1983.
Vent Sud. “La sexualité lesbienne.” France 3 Sud Midi Atlantique, broadcast March 20, 1996.
Vingt quatre heures sur la deux. “Bilan des États généraux de la femme.” Channel 2, ORTF, broadcast November 23, 1970.
XXème siècle. “L’église, demain? 1ère partie.” Channel 1, ORTF, broadcast December 8, 1970.
———. “Les libertés individuelles: L’Angleterre.” Channel 1, ORTF, broadcast June 9, 1970.
———. “Le rêve américain: 2ème partie: l’âme.” Channel 1, ORTF, broadcast May 10, 1971.

Films and Videos

Ajdelbaum, Joséphine, and Barbara Wolman, dirs. *LEZbiennes sinon rien! 1989–2009: 20 ans d'Espace lesbien à Toulouse*. 2009; France: V. Ideaux, Bagdam, 2009.

Akerman, Chantal, dir. *Jeanne Dielman, 23 quai du Commerce, 1080 Brussels*. 1975; France: Olympic Films, 1976.

Audry, Jacqueline, dir. *La garçonne*. 1956; France: Élysée Films, Les Films Corona, 1957.

——, dir. *Olivia*. 1951; France: Memnon Films, Filmsonor Marceau, 1951.

——, dir. *Le secret du chevalier d'Éon*. 1959; France: Gray-Film, Paris Élysée Films, Discifilm, 1959.

Bernard, Lionel, dir. *L'homophobie, ce douloureux problème*. 2000; France: Dominant 7, Canal+, 2000.

Constantin, Josée, and Catherine Gonnard, dirs. *Elula, les hommes on s'en fout*. 2000; France: Canal+, Le Village, 2000.

Cordier, Stany, dir. *Paris Music-Hall*. 1957; France: R.C.M. - Réalisations Cinématographiques Musicales, Jeannic Films, Société Technique et Financière de Cinématographie (STFC), 1957.

Dieudonné, Albert, and Jean de Limur, dirs. *La garçonne*. 1936; France: Franco-London Films, Cinéma Production, 1936.

Du Plessy, Armand, dir. *La garçonne*. 1923; France, Belgium: Armand de Plessy, 1923.

Emmer, Luciano, dir. *Parigi è sempre Parigi*. 1951; Italy, France: Fortezza Films, Omnium International, 1951.

Jeuland, Yves, dir. *Il est minuit, Paris s'éveille*. 2012; France: Zadig Productions, Arte France, 2012.

Julien, Jacqueline, and Caroline Godon-Gauthier, dirs. *Longitude femme, latitude lesbienne*. 2013 [1992]; France, 1992.

Lamy, Raymond, dir. *Miroir*. 1947; France: Alcina, Sud-Pacifique Films, Les Films de la Pléiade, Compagnie Parisienne de Location de Films (CPLF), 1947.

Lesselier, Claudie, dir. *Instants de vie, portrait d'Hélène Azénor*. 1987. Available online at the Centre audiovisuel Simone de Beauvoir, https://base.centre-simone-de-beauvoir.com/diaz-instants-de-vie-portrait-d-h%C3%A9l%C3%A8ne-azenor-510-191-0-1.html?ref=d6333a87b12eee1d40d0378645b71897.

——, dir. *Pour mémoire: Portrait de Rolande Aurivel*. 1988. Available online at the Centre audiovisuel Simone de Beauvoir, https://base.centre-simone-de-beauvoir.com/diaz-pour-m%C3%A9moire-portrait-de-rolande-aurivel-510-215-0-1.html?ref=d6333a87b12eee1d40d0378645b71897.

Roussopoulos, Carole, dir. *Debout! Une histoire du mouvement de libération des femmes, 1970–1980*. 1999; Switzerland, France: Carole Roussopoulos, 1999.

Sagan, Leontine, dir. *Mädchen in Uniform*. 1931; Germany: Deutsche Film-Gemeinschaft, Bild und Ton GmbH, 1931.

Tissot, Florence, and Sylvie Tissot, dirs. *L'abécédaire de Christine Delphy*. 2015; France: Les Mots Sont Importants, Catherine Romatowski, 2015.

——, dirs. *Je ne suis pas féministe, mais . . .* 2015; France: Les Mots Sont Importants, Catherine Romatowski, 2015.

Records

Dauberson, Dany. *No. 4*. Pathé, 1956.
Mars, Colette. "La garçonne." *Colette Mars*. Columbia Records, 1957.
———. *Mon p'tit fichu*. Disques Vogue, 1955.
Solidor, Suzy. *Suzy Solidor: Succès et raretès 1933–1939*. Chansophone, 1992.

PERIODICALS AND NEWSPAPERS

General

L'action française
À tout coeur
L'aurore
Ce soir
Chantecler (Hanoi)
Combat
Confessions
Le cri de Paris
Der Spiegel
Fantasio
Le figaro
France soir
La gazette
Gringoire
L'humanité
Ici Paris
L'intransigeant
Libération
Marianne: Grand hebdomadaire littéraire illustré
Le matin
Mon ciné
Le Monde
Mon film
Music-Hall
Le parisien
Paris-soir
Le petit parisien
Police magazine
Le populaire de Paris
Samedi soir
La semaine à Paris
La semaine radiophonique
Les spectacles d'Alger
Télé-59
Télé-poche
Télévision programme magazine
Variety
La vie parisienne

Lesbian, Feminist, LGBTQ+ (Selected)

Ah! Nana (1976–1978)
Amazones d'hier, lesbiennes d'aujourd'hui (1982–1999)
L'antinorm (1972–1974)
Arcadie: Revue littéraire et scientifique (1954–1982)
Bulletin des Archives recherches cultures lesbiennes (ARCL) (1981–1992)
Les cahiers du GRIF (1973–1994)
Chroniques aiguës et graves (1982–1983)
Clit 007 / Clit International (1981–1985, 1985–1986)
Désormais (1979–1980)
Espace Lesbien: Rencontres et revue d'études lesbiennes (2000–2009)
Espaces (1982–1983)
Esprit de CEL: Journal du Centre Évolutif Lilith (1994–2001)
Gai pied / Gai pied hebdo (1979–1992)

La grimoire: Journale lesbienne internationale (1987–1997)
Groupe des lesbiennes féministes (1975–1978)
Homophonies (1980–1986)
Housewife: Le magazine du Pulp (1997–2000)
Lesbia (and *Lesbia magazine*) (1982–2012)
Lesbiennes féministes (1976–1977?)
Lettres à Sappho (1985–1988)
La lune rousse (1977–1982)
Madivine, journal lesbien lyonnais (1983, 2000)
Masques, revue des homosexualités (1979–1985)
Paroles de lesbiennes féministes (1980–1981)
Quand les femmes s'aiment (*QLFSA*) (1978–1980)
Question féministes (1977–1980) / *Nouvelle questions féministes* (1981–2020)
Saphonies (1986–?)
Têtu (1995–2015, 2015–2018, 2018–)
Vlasta, fictions/utopies amazoniennes (1983–1985)
Well Well Well: La revue lesbienne (2014–)

SELECTED WEBSITES

Archives d'Éros, https://www.archivesderos.com/
Archives recherches cultures lesbiennes, http://www.arcl.fr
Bagdam Espace Lesbien, http://www.bagdam.org
Balance ton porc, http://www.balancetonporc.com
Centre Évolutif Lilith, http://celmrs.free.fr
Cineffable, https://www.cineffable.fr
Coordination lesbienne en France (CLF), https://www.coordinationlesbienne.org
Hexagone gay, http://www.hexagonegay.com
Human Dignity Trust, http://www.humandignitytrust.org
Institut national de l'audiovisuel, http://www.institut-national-audiovisuel.fr

PRIMARY SOURCES

Alhoy, Maurice. *Physiologie de la Lorette*. Paris: D'Aubert et Cie., 1841.

Allain, Jeannine. "Chansons interdites de Nicole Louvier." *Arcadie: Revue littéraire et scientifique*, no. 54 (June 1958).

Allex, Catherine. "Hommage à Elula Perrin." *Lesbia magazine*, no. 226 (July–August 2003).

Association mouvement pour les luttes féministes. *Chroniques d'une imposture: Du mouvement de libération des femmes à une marque commerciale*. Paris: Primavera, 1981.

À tout coeur. "Anne Monaco, nouvelle Mistinguette." No. 231 (March 20, 1951).

———. "Colette Mars: J'adore l'aventure." No. 224 (January 30, 1951).

Aurivel, Rolande. *Dans l'ombre et au soleil de Lesbos*. Preface by Elula Perrin. Paris: Éditions Walter Rauschenbusch, 1988.

Azenor, Hélène. *Histoire d'UNE*. Paris: Les Octaviennes, 1988.

Aznar, G. N. "Notre couverture: Micheline Sandrel." *La semaine radiophonique*, no. 40 (October 5, 1958).

Bastia, Jean. *Le quotidien de Montmartre*, no. 29 (March 23, 1930).

Baverel, Philippe. "A Paris, la République en marche va s'installer rue Sainte-Anne." *Le parisien*, August 17, 2017.

Beauvoir, Simone de. *The Second Sex*. Edited and translated by H. M. Parshley. New York: Vintage Books, 1989.

Bec et ongles: Satirique hebdomadaire. "Un gros débat." December 9, 1933.

Bell, Barbara. *Just Take Your Frock Off: A Lesbian Life*. Brighton: Ourstory Books, 1999.

Benani, Souad. "Lesbiennes maghrébines: Briser le silence. Sexualité et les beurs au féminin." *Bulletin des Archives recherches cultures lesbiennes*, no. 5 (February 1987).

Berger, M. H. "Première chanteuse de music-hall 'télévisionée par les PTT.'" *Excelsior*, June 29, 1935.

Blaire, Elaine. "Designing Women: Making Space for Women to Behave Badly in 'Portrait of a Lady on Fire' and 'The Favourite.'" *New York Review of Books*, December 17, 2020.

Bouchara, Christine. "Plus que jamais les lesbiennes se font du cinéma." *Lesbia magazine*, no. 188 (December 1999).

Boucheron, Brigitte. "Introduction à une histoire du mouvement lesbien en France." In *Invisibilité, visibilité des lesbiennes*, edited by Actes du Colloque organisé par la Coordination Lesbienne en France à l'Hôtel de Ville de Paris, 37–61. Montreuil: CLF, 2007.

———. "Mail à Ludi sur la mixité." Bagdam Espace Lesbien, May 2008. http://www.bagdam.org/articles/ludi.html.

Bouvard, Philippe. *L'huile sur le feu*. Paris: Antenne 2 / Éditions Mengès, 1977.

Brassaï. *The Secret Paris of the 30s*. Translated by Richard Miller. London: Thames & Hudson, 1976.

Bremond d'Ars, Yvonne de. *C'est arrivé en plein Paris, passionate aventure d'antiquaire*. Paris: H. Lefebvre, 1957.

Bulletin des archives lesbiennes. "Construire nos espaces: Rencontre avec les animatrices du Bagdam Cafée, novembre 1989." No. 9 (June 1990).

Bulletin municipal officiel de la Ville de Paris. February 6, 1941; August 9, 1943; June 23, 1943.

Les cahiers du GRIF. "Carabosses." Vol. 23–24 (1978): 185.

———. "Comité de soutien à Éliane Morissens." No. 6 (1982): 15–16.

Capri, Agnès. *Sept épées de mélancolie*. Paris: Julliard, 1975.

Casanova, Jany. "Frède [*sic*] Carroll [*sic*] écrit des mémoires fracassants." *La vie parisienne* 103, no. 201 (September 1967).

Cerisay, Gil. "Elula Perrin, une lesbienne qui tolère les hommes." *Sexpol*, no. 26 (March 1978).

Ce soir. "La jalousie de Lulu de Montmartre était interessée." July 26, 1939.

———. "Lulu de Montmartre avait voulu faire 'chanter' un client de son cabaret." June 20, 1939.

———. "Lulu de Montmartre est arretée." June 20, 1939.

———. "Lulu de Montmartre le sursis pour un an de prison." July 29, 1939.

———. "Ses soeurs Denizot et Lulu de Montmartre devant le tribunal de Versailles." July 28, 1939.
Chantecler (Hanoi). "Le bain de Suzy." November 5, 1933.
———. "Papotages: Taxi-Girls." November 5, 1933.
Charles-Étienne. *Le bal des folles*. Paris: Curio, 1930.
———. *Notre-Dame-de-Lesbos*. Paris: Librairie des Lettres, 1919.
Chetcuti, Natasha. Unpublished interview with Brigitte Boucheron. March 10, 2010. Shared with the author.
Chevalier, Julien. *De l'inversion de l'instinct sexuel au point de vue médico-légal*. Lyon: Imprimerie Nouvelle, 1885.
Choisy, Maryse. *L'amour dans les prisons*. Paris: Éditions Montaigne, 1930.
———. "Dames seules." *Le rire* (special edition), May 12, 1932.
———. *Un mois chez les filles: Reportage*. Paris: Éditions Montaigne, 1928. Reprint, Paris: Éditions Stock, 2015.
———. *Un mois chez les hommes*. Paris: Éditions de France, 1929.
Cleo. "The New Queen of Lesbos." August 1982.
Cocteau, Jean. "Suzy Solidor." *Music-Hall*, no. 3 (1955).
Colette. *Lettres au petit corsaire*. Paris: Flammarion, 1963.
———. *The Pure and the Impure*. 1932. Translated by Herma Briffault. Introduction by Judith Thurman. New York: New York Review of Books, 2000.
Collectif des raciné-e-s. *Plumes de queers racisé-e-s*. February 13, 2019. https://desracinees.files.wordpress.com/2019/02/fanzinedalilacolor.pdf.
Combes, Marie-Laure, and Aurélien Fleurot. "Amiens-Nord, une 'zone de non-droit.'" *Europe 1*, August 15, 2012.
Confessions. "Suzy Solidor révèle son étrange destin de femme sans homme." No. 1 (November 26, 1936): 11–14; and no. 1 (December 3, 1936): 21–25.
Cottereau, Danièle. *Amazones du soir, bonsoir!* Paris: Éditions Le Gueuloir, 2011.
———. "À propos de Fréquence gaie." *Lesbia*, no. 28 (May 1985).
David, André. "Chroniques du snobisme." *Marianne: Grand hebdomadaire littéraire illustré*, March 8, 1933.
Davies, Lizzy. "French Singer's Aide Accused over Will." *The Guardian*, August 23, 2008. https://www.theguardian.com/world/2008/aug/24/france.
Debord, Guy. *La société du spectacle*. Paris: Buchet/Chastel, 1967.
Delcourt, Pierre. *Le vol à Paris*. Paris: A. Piaget, 1888.
Deleuze, Gilles, and Félix Guattari. *Anti-Oedipus*. Paris: Éditions de Minuit, 1972.
Delpal, Jacques-Louis. *Ultra-guide Paris la nuit*. 1968; Paris: Gouraud Éditeur, 1969.
Delphy, Christine. *L'ennemi principal 1: Économie politique du patriarcat*. Paris: Éditions Syllepse, 1998.
———. *L'ennemi principal 2: Penser le genre*. Paris: Éditions Syllepse, 2001.
La dépêche du Berry. "Lulu de Montmartre et ses comparses avaient composé une scène de chantage." July 29, 1939.
Dibondo, Douce. "La parole à." In *Rapport sur l'homophobie 2019*, edited by SOS Homophobie, 147–48. Paris: SOS Homophobie, 2019.
Dillies, Béatrice. "La ville rose, terre promise des lesbiennes en France." *La dépêche*, September 4, 2004.
Dominique, Jean. "Dany Dauberson: Je me lave mes cheveux plusiers fois par jour." *Music-Hall*, no. 4 (1960).

Donation Solidor 1973, Ville de Cagnes-sur-mer Château-Musée. 1973; Cagnes-sur-Mer: Imprimerie Zimmerman, 1982.

Drouin, Henri. *Femmes damnées*. Paris: NRF/Gallimard, 1929.

Du Coglay, Michel. *Chez les mauvais garçons: Choses vues*. Paris: Éditions Raoul Saillard, 1937.

Dumazedier, Joffre. *Television and Rural Adult Education: The Télé-Clubs in France*. With assistance by A. Kedros and B. Sylwan. UNESCO, 1956.

Edmée. "Elula Perrin: 'Les hommes? Ils dérangent le paysage!'" *Tribune de Genève*, February 1981.

Elle. "C'est bon à savoir." March 12, 1981.

Ellis, Havelock. *Studies in the Psychology of Sex*. Vol. 2, *Sexual Inversion*. 2nd ed. Philadelphia: F.A. Davis, 1908.

Espace Lesbien: Rencontres et revue d'études lesbiennes. "L'arme du rire." No. 6 (April 2009).

———. "Fureur et jubilation." No. 4 (April 2004).

———. "La grande dissidence et le grand effroi." No. 2 (June 2001).

———. "Mémoires, langages, sexualités." No. 1 (October 2000).

———. "Le sexe sur le bout de la langue." No. 3 (September 2002).

———. "Tout sur l'amour." No. 5 (April 2006).

European Commission of Human Rights. "Application no. 11389/85: Eliane Morissens v/Belgium." *Decisions and Reports*, no. 56 (1988): 127–37.

Fanon, Frantz. *A Dying Colonialism*. Translated by Haakon Chevalier. Introduction by Adolfo Gilly. New York: Grove Press, 1965.

Female Mimics. "Torrid Three from Gay Paree." Vol. 1, no. 3 (1963).

fisopulp. "Pulp Gay-Pride 1998." Uploaded on April 12, 2007. YouTube video, 3:24. https://www.youtube.com/watch?v=kYgtuU-LvAA.

Fouque, Antoinette. *There Are Two Sexes: Essays in Feminology*. Edited by Sylvina Boissonas. Translated by David Macey and Catherine Porter. 1995; New York: Columbia University Press, 2015.

Gaborit, Carole. "Actualités: Canal+ de goudous." *Lesbia magazine* (December 1990).

Gay, Jennifer. "Atelier 'Racisme 2,' Mixte." Pamphlet. Coordination Lesbienne Nationale, spring meeting, Die (Drôme), Pentecôte, May 1999.

Georges-Michel, Michel. "Au balcon du club, Rachilde chez Sidonie Baba." *Le cri de Paris*, May 19, 1939.

Goldszal, Clémentine. "Souvenirs du Pulp, paradis perdu de la culture lesbienne parisienne." *Le Monde*, August 20, 2022. https://www.lemonde.fr/m-le-mag/article/2022/08/20/au-pulp-les-filles-menent-la-danse-des-nuits-parisiennes_6138526_4500055.html.

Gonnard, Catherine, and Elisabeth Lebovici. "Gros plans sur *La garçonne* (1957), une performance de genre." N.d. Notes from this presentation are available at https://www.unil.ch/cin/files/live/sites/cin/files/Colloques/Genre%20et%20m%C3%A9dias%202019/R%C3%A9sum%C3%A9s/GENRE_MEDIAS_Gonnard-Lebovici.pdf, accessed December 15, 2021.

Gonnard, Catherine, and Jöelle Matos. "Les filles." *Têtu, madame* (July 2000).

Gribouille. *Je vais mourir demain*. Preface by Françoise Mallet-Joris. Introduction by Marie-Thérèse Orain. Saint-Cyr-sur-Loire: Éditions Christian Pirot, 2001.

Groupe du 6 novembre. "Lesbia magazine persiste et oppose un refus solennel à la publication de la réponse. Halte à l'antiracisme bon teint!" *Madivine*, no. 1 (April 2006).

——. *Warriors/Guérrières*. Paris: Nomades'Langues, 2001. Available online at https://www.coordinationlesbienne.org/spip.php?article141.

Guetta, René. "A 'La grenouille'—Chez 'Moune et Léon.'" *Marianne: Grand hebdomadaire littéraire illustré*, March 8, 1939.

——. "La Sirène." *Marianne: Grand hebdomadaire littéraire illustré*, July 26, 1939.

Halimi, Gisèle, and Simone de Beauvoir. *Djamila Boupacha*. Paris: Gallimard, 1962.

Hemingway, Ernest. *The Sun Also Rises*. New York: Charles Scribner's Sons, 1926.

H. F. P. "Cocktail-partie chez Solange Duvernon." *Comedia*, June 23, 1932.

L'humanité. "'Yéyette-aux-yeux-doux' préféra Raoul à Chérif." May 25, 1939.

Ibre, Chantal. "Mères lesbiennes." *QLFSA* 2 (November 1978).

Ici Paris. "La fin terrible de Cécilia, médecin de campagne." April 18–24, 1967.

L'intransigeant. "Cabaret l'actress Bar Caroll's [*sic*] Conquet, Simone dite 'Bobbie.'" December 16, 1933.

——. "Cabarets." June 11, 1937.

——. "Le Monocle." February 16, 1936.

Jicet. "A travers les spectacles." *Les spectacles d'Alger*, January 7, 1931.

Jouve, Christiane. "Cocorico, en France, on a même des homos!" *Lesbia*, no. 13 (January 1984).

——. "La nouvelle Fréquence gaie." *Lesbia magazine*, no. 26 (March 1985).

——. "Le pied à l'étrier." *Lesbia*, no. 20 (September 1984).

Jouve, Christiane, C. Marjollet, and M. Gruzeau. "Les lesbiennes à l'antenne, les homos en stereo." *Lesbia*, no. 4 (March 1983).

Julien, Jacqueline. "À Toulouse: Du féminisme lesbien au lesbianisme féministe." Bagdam Espace Lesbien. Accessed February 6, 2015. http://www.bagdam.org/articles/lesbianisme.html.

——. "L'insoutenable visibilité de l'être." In *Invisibilité, visibilité des lesbiennes*, edited by Actes du Colloque organisé par la Coordination Lesbienne en France à l'Hôtel de Ville de Paris, 65–80. Montreuil: CLF, 2007.

——. "Lesbian Life in Twentieth-Century France." Unpublished talk at University of Illinois at Urbana-Champaign, August 27, 2012.

——. "La reine Pergame." In *Le Liseron*, special edition in memory of Thérèse Yakovenko, 1–5. Poitiers, 1997.

Kershaw, Sarah. "My Sister's Keeper." *New York Times*, January 30, 2009.

Lefebvre, Henri. *Le droit à la ville*. Paris: Éditions Anthropos, 1968.

——. *The Production of Space*. Translated by Donald Nicholson Smith. Oxford: Blackwell, 1991.

Lefebvre, Marie-Hélène. "Racisme: ateliers 2 et 3." Pamphlet. Coordination Lesbienne Nationale, spring meeting, Die (Drôme), Pentecôte, May 1999.

Le Garrec, Évelyne. *Des femmes qui s'aiment*. Paris: Éditions du Seuil, 1984.

Le Petit, Mirella. "Fréquence Gaie: Le droit à la difference." *Télé-poche*, no. 903 (June 1, 1983).

Le Pointeur. "Cibles: Suzy Solidor." *La vie parisienne*, February 26, 1938.

Lesbia. "Annie et Charlotte au pays du Minitel." No. 36 (February 1986).

——. "Coût coût Goudou!" No. 37 (March 1986).

———. "Le deuxième souffle des émissions roses." No. 17 (May 1984).
———. "Elle était tout pour moi." No. 54 (October 1987).
———. "Goudou chez vous par Minitel." No. 35 (January 1986).
———. "Les Goudous Télématiques." No. 40 (June 1986).
———. "Lesbia infos." No. 17 (May 1984).
———. "Liste des antennes roses." No. 4 (April 1983).
———. "Minitelles interactives." No. 39 (May 1986).
———. "Mots doux sur Minitel." No. 38 (April 1986).
———. "Qu'est-ce que les 3 F?" No. 2 (January 1983).
Lesbia magazine. "Bagdam Cafée." No. 75 (September 1989).
———. "Gribouille." No. 174 (September 1998).
Lestrade, Didier. "Le Pulp: The Politics of Dancing." Red Bull Music Academy Daily, June 1, 2016. https://daily.redbullmusicacademy.com/2016/06/le-pulp-feature.
Libération. "Trois Répondeuses menacées." December 30, 1981.
La liberté d'imprimer: Journal de l'association des amis des ateliers d'impression presse nouvelle. "Les A.I.P.N. sont ouverts." No. 2 (February 1977).
Louvier, Nicole. *Chansons interdites*. Paris: La Table Ronde, 1953.
———. *Les dialogues de la nuit blanche*. Paris: La Jeune Parque, 1967.
———. *Les marchands*. Paris: La Table Ronde, 1959.
———. *Qui qu'en grogne*. Paris: La Table Ronde, 1953.
Madivine. "Racisme. Sexisme. Homophobie." No. 1 (April 2000).
Le magazine de la discothèque et des disc-jockeys. "Entretien: Elula Perrin." No. 8756 (November 1980).
Mallet-Joris, Françoise. *The Illusionist*. Translated by Herma Briffault. Introduction by Terry Castle. 1952; San Francisco: Cleis Press, 2006.
Margueritte, Victor. *La garçonne*. Paris: Flammarion, 1922.
Marianne: Grand hebdomadaire littéraire illustré. "Femmes doubles." April 18, 1934.
Marjollet, Catherine. "Voyage en Grande Lesbiannie avec Geneviève Pastre." *Lesbia*, no. 7 (June 1983).
Martine, Beatrice, Dominique, Josiane, and Claire. "Pochette surprise." *QLFSA* 2 (November 1978).
Le matin. "Un an de prison à Lulu de Montmartre." February 13, 1939.
Mélo, Nelly. "Dossier: Presse lesbienne. Europe: *Quand les femmes s'aiment*." *Amazones d'hier, lesbiennes d'aujourd'hui* 5, no. 3 (March 1988).
Mélo, Nelly, Suzette Triton (Robichon), Fidélio, Nella Nobili, Edith Zha, Michèle Ouerd, Bernadette Stanwyck, and Odile. "Lettre du 30 avril 1982, non publiée par *Masques*." In *Mouvements de presse: Des années 1970s a nos jours, luttes feminists et lesbiennes*, edited by Martine Laroche and Michèle Larrouy, 55–56. Paris: Éditions des ARCL, 2009.
Micheyl, Mick. *Dieu est-il bien dans ma peau?* Lyon: Presses de la Cité, 1984.
Le midi socialiste. "Lulu de Montmartre avait fait chanter un gros entrepreneur." June 21, 1939.
Le monde illustré. "Voici des mains." February 4, 1939.
Monnel, Dan. "De Pigalle à Montparnasse: Itinéraire d'une garçonne ordinaire des années soixante." Part 1. *Lesbia magazine* (October 2003).
———. "De Pigalle à Montparnasse: Itinéraire d'une garçonne ordinaire des années soixante." Part 2. *Lesbia magazine* (November 2003).

Moris, Jean. "Le secret des femmes damnées." Part 1. *Police magazine*, September 25, 1938.

———. "Le secret des femmes damnées." Part 2. *Police magazine*, October 2, 1938.

Mouvement d'information et d'expression des lesbiennes (MIEL). *Être lesbienne aujourd'hui: Le M.I.E.L. enquête*. Paris: MIEL, 1988.

Music-Hall. "Après la peinture et la chanson, Mick Micheyl va se consacrer désormais à la mise en scene." No. 43 (September 1958).

———. "Nicole Louvier: J'écris des choses qui font rougir." No. 9 (1955).

Nin, Anaïs. *Fire: From "A Journal of Love." The Unexpurgated Diary of Anaïs Nin, 1934–1937*. San Diego: Harcourt, 1995.

No Homonationalism (blog). "Statement by Lesbiennes of Color (LOCs, Lesbians of Color) in France against Racism in LGBTQ Communities in Germany." July 29, 2010. http://nohomonationalism.blogspot.com/2010/07/statement-by-lesbiennes-of-color-locs.html.

Le nouvel obs. "Décès de la DJ SexToy." February 12, 2002. https://www.nouvelobs.com/culture/20020207.OBS2975/deces-de-la-dj-sextoy.html.

Ozouf, Mona. *Les mots des femmes: Essai sur la singularité française*. Paris: Fayard, 1995.

Parent-Duchâtelet, Alexandre. *De la prostitution dans la ville de Paris, considérée sous le rapport de l'hygiène publique, de la morale et de l'administration*. Brussels: Hauman, Cattoir, 1836.

Paris match. "Le match de Paris présente deux filles et trois garçons qui sont la chanson française 1954." No. 254 (February 6–13, 1954).

Paris-soir. "Le fétiche." April 30, 1938.

———. "Ou aller cette nuit." August 16, 1938.

Pasquier, Jacqueline. "Au fil du XXIe festival." *Lesbia magazine*, no. 188 (December 1999).

Perec, Georges. *Les choses*. Paris: Julliard, 1965.

Perrin, Elula. *Alice au pays des femmes*. Paris: Éditions Ramsay, 1980.

———. *Un amour, deux femmes*. Paris: Éditions La Cerisaie, 2004.

———. *Bulles et noctambules: Histoire de la nuit au féminin*. Paris: Double Interligne, 2000.

———. *Coup de gueule pour l'amour des femmes*. Paris: Éditions Ramsay, 1995.

———. *L'eurasienne*. Paris: Éditions Osmond, 1997.

———. *Les femmes préfèrent les femmes*. Paris: Éditions Ramsay, 1977.

———. "J'm'assume." *Le crapouillet* (Spring 1981).

———. *Mousson de femmes*. Paris: Éditions Ramsay, 1985.

———. *Revolte des amours mortes*. Paris: Éditions La Cerisaie, 2004.

———. *Tant qu'il y aura des femmes*. Paris: Éditions Ramsay, 1978.

———. *Va y avoir mistral*. Paris: Double Interligne, 1999.

———. *Women Prefer Women*. Translated by Harold J. Salemson. New York: Bantam Books, 1978.

Perrin, Elula, and Hélène de Monferrand. *L'habit ne fait pas la nonne*. Paris: Double Interligne, 1998.

———. *Ne tirez pas sur la violoniste*. Paris: Double Interligne, 1998.

Le petit parisien. "Lulu de Montmartre." July 26, 1939.

Polet, Catherine (Zoé). "Coup de foudre." *Lesbia*, no. 10 (September 1983).
———. "Lesbos invisible." *Lesbia*, no. 10 (September 1983).
Poulain, Pierre. "Zoom sur Mick Micheyl." *Télé liberté information*, no. 37 (November–December 1969).
Prose, Francine. *Lovers at the Chameleon Club, Paris 1932*. New York: Harper Perennial, 2015.
Querlin, Marise. *Femmes sans hommes: Choses vues*. Paris: Éditions de France, 1931.
———. *Women without Men*. Translated by Malcolm McCraw. New York: Dell Publishing, 1965.
Quidet, Christian. "L'Eurovision." *Télévision programme magazine*, no. 105 (October 27–November 2, 1957).
Radar. "Dany Dauberson nouvelle Suzy Solidor." March 6, 1949.
Radio-télévision suisse. "Des 'minis états islamiques' en France." September 25, 2014.
Raffalovich, Marc-André. *Uranisme et unisexualité: Étude sur différentes manifestations de l'instinct sexuel*. Lyon: A. Storck; Paris: Masson & Cie, 1896.
Ramos, Germaine. "Colette Mars." *La semaine radiophonique*, no. 35 (September 7, 1947).
Régnier, Pierre de. "Noirs et blanches." Paris, ma grand'ville, *Gringoire*, January 12, 1939.
La revue h. "L'homosexualité, ce douloureux problème," No. 1 (Summer 1996): 52–59.
Rey, Étienne. "Propos parisiens." *La vie parisienne*, July 7, 1934–December 29, 1934.
Ribet, Roland. *L'impresario impertinent*. Paris: Jacques Grancher, 1993.
Rich, Adrienne. "Compulsory Heterosexuality and Lesbian Existence." *Signs* 5, no. 4 (Summer 1980): 631–60.
Samedi soir. "Je suis un vieux garcon, dit Suzy Solidor." December 25, 1948.
Sandrel, Micheline. *Le guide de l'amant parfait et du mari passable*. Paris: Éditions de la Pensée Moderne, 1966.
Sarratia, Géraldine. "Les clubs mythiques (3/7): Le Pulp, une nouvelle identité lesbienne." *Les inrockuptibles*, July 17, 2011. https://www.lesinrocks.com/actu/les-clubs-mythiques-37-le-pulp-une-nouvelle-identite-lesbienne-39194-17-07-2011/.
Saurraute, Claude. "Aimer les femmes." *Le Monde*, July 13, 1977.
La semaine radiophonique. "Images d'Afrique: La T.V. au Maroc et en Tunisie." No. 8 (February 2, 1954).
Solidor, Suzy. *Fil d'or*. Paris: Éditions de France, 1940.
———. *Le fortuné de l'Amphitrite*. Paris: Éditions de France, 1941.
———. *Térésine*. Paris: Éditions de France, 1939.
———. *La vie commence au large*. Brussels: Éditions du Sablon, 1944.
SOS Homophobie. *Enquête sur la visibilité des lesbiennes et la lesbophobie, 2015*. Preface by Natacha Chetcuti-Osorovitz. Merculès: Imprimerie CPI France-Quercy, 2015.
Stainville, Raphaël. "Insecurité: C'était intenable, nous sommes partis." *Le figaro*, August 3, 2010.
Télé liberté information. "L'état et les stations périphérique." No. 34 (June–July 1969).
Télévision programme magazine. "180,000 téléspectateurs français ont l'oeil sur Télé-Luxembourg." No. 105 (October 27–November 2, 1957).

———. “Cabaret du soir.” No. 98 (September 8–14, 1957).
———. “Cabaret du soir.” No. 100 (September 22–28, 1957).
———. “Edwige Feuillère, invitée d’honneur du Cabaret du soir.” No. 122 (February 23–March 1, 1958).
———. “L’opinion des téléspectateurs.” No. 128 (April 6–12, 1958).
———. “Le réseau de la télévision française un veritable journal en images.” No. 101 (September 29–October 5, 1957).
Tessier, Carmen. “Les potins de la commère.” *France soir*, February 7, 1951.
Tristan, Anne, and Annie de Pisan. *Histoires du M.L.F.* Preface by Simone de Beauvoir. Paris: Calmann-Lévy, 1977.
Variety. “Carroll’s Paris.” February 22, 1950.
———. “Le Carroll’s, Paris.” July 20, 1955.
———. “Le Carroll’s Paris.” May 30, 1956.
———. “Le Carroll’s, Paris.” October 17, 1956.
———. “Le Carroll’s, Paris.” November 4, 1959.
———. “Le Carroll’s, Paris.” February 24, 1960.
———. “L’Elephant Blanc Belies Tag as Shuttered Paris Café-Terpery Reopens.” April 10, 1963.
———. “Paris Nitery Baedeker.” July 2, 1952.
———. “Who Wears the Pants?” May 14, 1958.
La vie parisienne. “Micheline Sandrel lauréate du Prix littéraire de ‘La vie parisienne.’” No. 199 (July 1967).
———. “On dit, on dit.” September 24, 1932.
Vignaud, Jean. “Les lettres sur les femmes.” *Le petit parisien*, March 31, 1931.
Vincent, Renaud. “Les ‘nuits blues’ parisiennes. Rue Sainte-Anne: La rue aux hommes. Le conseil de Paris saisi d’une plainte.” *France soir*, October 25, 1975.
Vincineau, Michel. “À propos de l’Affaire Morissens,” *Socialisme* (August 1983): 371–75.
Virmaître, Charles. *Paris-Impur*. 2nd ed. Paris: A. Charles Librairie, 1889.
———. *Trottoirs et lupanars*. Paris: Librairie Jouffroy, 1893.
Waugh, Evelyn. “Labels.” *Fortnightly Review* 127 (April 1930): 485–99.
Westphal, Karl Friedrich Otto. “Die conträre Sexualemfindung: Sympton eines neuropathischen (psychopathischen) Zustandes.” *Archiv für Psychiatrie und Nervenkrankheiten*, no. 2 (1869–70): 73–108.
Willy. *The Third Sex*. Translated, introduction, and notes by Lawrence R. Schehr. Urbana: University of Illinois Press, 2007.
Wittig, Monique. *The Straight Mind and Other Essays*. Foreword and translated by Louise Turcotte. Boston: Beacon Press, 1992.
Woolf, Virginia. *A Room of One’s Own*. 1929; London: Hogarth Press, 1935.
Y. F. “Les débuts à l’écran de Suzy Solidor.” *Mon ciné*, January 23, 1936.

SECONDARY SOURCES

Abrams, Lynn. *Oral History Theory*. London: Routledge, 2016.
Adler, Sy, and Johanna Brenner. “Gender and Space: Lesbians and Gay Men in the City.” *International Journal of Urban and Regional Research* 16, no. 1 (1992): 24–34.

Ahmed, Sara. *Queer Phenomenology*. Durham, NC: Duke University Press, 2006.

Albert, Nicole. *Lesbian Decadence: Representations in Art and Literature of Fin-de-Siècle France*. Translated by Nancy Erber and William A. Peniston. 2005; New York: Columbia University Press, 2016.

———. "Travestissement." In *Dictionnaire des cultures gays et lesbiennes*, edited by Didier Eribon, 476–78. Paris: Larousse, 2003.

Allen, Graham. *Intertextuality*. London: Routledge, 2000.

Amari, Salima. *Lesbiennes de l'immigration: Construction de soi et relations familiales*. Vulaines sur Seine: Éditions du Croquant, 2018.

Aminzade, Ronald. *Class, Politics, and Early Industrial Capitalism: A Study of Mid-Nineteenth-Century-Toulouse, France*. Albany: State University of New York Press, 1981.

Anderson, Benedict. *Imagined Communities: Reflections on the Origins and Spread of Nationalism*. Rev. ed. London: Verso, 2006.

App, Corinne, Anne-Marie Faure-Fraisse, Béatrice Fraenkel, and Lydie Rauzier, eds. *40 ans de slogans féministes 1970–2010*. Donnemarie-Dontilly: Éditions IXe, 2011.

Bacchetta, Paola. "Groupe du 6 novembre: Lesbiennes issues du colonialisme, de l'esclavage et de l'immigration." In *Global Encyclopedia of Lesbian, Gay, Bisexual, Transgender, and Queer History*, edited by Howard Chiang et al., 623–25. Farmington Hills, MI: Charles Scribner's Sons, 2019.

———. "QTPOC Critiques of 'Post-Raciality,' Segregationality, Coloniality, and Capitalism in France." In *Decolonizing Sexualities: Transnational Perspectives, Critical Interventions*, edited by Sandeep Bakshi, Suhraiya Jivraj, and Silvia Posocco, 264–81. Oxford: Counter Press, 2016.

Baker, Jean-Claude, and Chris Chase. *Josephine: The Hungry Heart*. New York: Random House, 1993.

Balibar, Étienne, and Immanuel Wallerstein. *Race, nation, classe: Les identités ambiguës*. 1988; Paris: La Découverte, 2007.

Barbedette, Gilles, and Michel Carassou. *Paris Gay 1925*. Paris: Presses de la Renaissance, 1981.

Bard, Christine. "Le droit au pantalon: Du pittoresque au symbolique." *La vie des idées*, March 1, 2013. https://laviedesidees.fr/Le-droit-au-pantalon.html.

———. *Les femmes dans la société française au 20e siècle*. Paris: HER/Armand Colin, 2001.

———. *Les garçonnes: Modes et fantasmes des années folles*. Paris: Flammarion, 1998.

———. *Une histoire politique du pantalon*. Paris: Éditions du Seuil, 2010.

———. "Le lesbianism comme construction politique." In *Le siècle des feminisms*, edited by Elaine Gubin, Catherine Jacques, Florence Rochefort, Brigitte Studer, Françoise Thébaud, and Michelle Zancarini-Fournel, 114. Paris: Éditions de l'Atelier, 2004.

Barney, Natalie Clifford. *Women Lovers, or the Third Woman*. Edited and translated by Chelsea Ray. Madison: University of Wisconsin Press, 2016.

Bastiani, Ange. *Les bals secrets de Paris*. Paris: Solar, 1973.

Becker, Ron. *Gay TV and Straight America*. New Brunswick, NJ: Rutgers University Press, 2006.

Benstock, Shari. *Women of the Left Bank: Paris, 1900–1940*. Austin: University of Texas Press, 1986.

Bérard, Jean, and Nicolas Sallée. "The Age of Consent." Translated by Ethan Rundell. *Clio: Women, Gender, History*, no. 42 (2015): 99–124.

Berenson, Edward, Vincent Duclert, and Christophe Prochasson, eds. *The French Republic: History, Values, Debates*. Ithaca, NY: Cornell University Press, 2011.

Binnie, Jon, and Gill Valentine. "Geographies of Sexuality—A Review of Progress." *Progress in Human Geography* 23, no. 2 (1999): 175–87.

Blanchard, Véronique. *Vagabondes, voleuses, vicieuses: Adolescentes sous contrôle de la Libération à la libération sexuelle*. Paris: Éditions François Bourin, 2019.

Blidon, Marianne. "En quête de reconnaissance: La justice spatiale à l'épreuve de l'hétéronormativité." Translated by Melanie Mauthner and Claire Hancock as "Seeking Recognition: Spatial Justice versus Heteronormativity." *Justice spatiale / Spatial Justice*, no. 3 (March 2011): 1–13.

Boittin, Jennifer. *Colonial Metropolis: The Urban Grounds of Anti-Imperialism and Feminism in Interwar Paris*. Omaha: University of Nebraska Press, 2010.

Bonnet, Marie-Jo. *Mon MLF*. Paris: Éditions Albin Michel, 2018.

———. *Les relations amoureuses entre les femmes XVIe–XXe siècle*. 1995; Paris: Éditions Odile Jacob, 2001.

Borrillo, Daniel, and Éric Fassin, eds. *Au-delà du PaCS: L'expertise familiale à l'épreuve de l'homosexualité*. Paris: Presses Universitaires de France, 2001.

Bourdon, Jérôme. *Haute fidélité: Pouvoir et télévision, 1935–1994*. Paris: Éditions du Seuil, 1994.

———. *Histoire de la télévision sous de Gaulle*. Paris: Presses des Mines, 2014.

Bourg, Julian. "Boy Trouble: French Pedophiliac Discourse of the 1970s." In *Between Marx and Coca-Cola: Youth Cultures in Changing European Societies, 1960s–1980*, edited by Axel Schildt and Detlef Siegfried, 287–312. New York: Berghahn Books, 2006.

———. "'Your Sexual Revolution Is Not Ours': French Feminist 'Moralism' and the Limits of Desire." In *Gender and Sexuality in 1968: Transformative Politics in the Cultural Imagination*, edited by Lessie Jo Frazier and Deborah Cohen, 85–113. New York: Palgrave, 2009.

Bouvard, Hugo, Ilana Eloit, and Mathias Quéré, eds. *Lesbiennes, Pédés, arrêtons de raser les murs: Luttes et debats des mouvements lesbiens et homosexuels (1970–1990)*. Paris: La Dispute/SNÉDIT, 2023.

Boyd, Nan Alamilla. *Wide-Open Town: A History of Queer San Francisco to 1965*. Berkeley: University of California Press, 2003.

Briki, Malick. *Psychiatrie et homosexualité: Lectures médicales et juridiques de l'homosexualité dans les sociétés occidentales de 1850 à nos jours*. Presses Universitaires de Franche-Comté, 2009.

Brunnquell, Frédéric. *Les associations familiales: Combien de divisions, dossier, enquête*. Paris: Dagorno, 1994.

Bryson, Mary. "When Jill Jacks In: Queer Women and the Net." *Feminist Media Studies* 4, no. 3 (2004): 239–54.

Buot, François. *Gay Paris: Une histoire du Paris interlope entre 1900 et 1940*. Paris: Fayard, 2013.

Butler, Judith. *Gender Trouble: Feminism and the Subversion of Identity*. New York: Routledge, 1999.

Cadot, Mathieu. "Visibilité, acceptation, hétérocentrisme: Les représentations actuelles de l'homosexualité à la télévision française." Master's thesis, Université Lumière Lyon 2, 2004.

Canet, Nicole. *Maisons closes 1860–1946: Bordels de femmes, bordels d'hommes*. Paris: La Galerie au Bonheur du Jour, 2009.

Capsuto, Steven. *Alternate Channels: The Uncensored Story of Gay and Lesbian Images on Radio and Television, 1930s to the Present*. New York: Ballentine Books, 2000.

Carbonel, Marie-Hélène. *Suzy Solidor, une vie d'amours*. Gémenos: Éditions Autre Temps, 2007.

Cardon, Patrick. "A Homosexual Militant at the Beginning of the Century: Marc André Raffalovich." In *Gay Studies from the French Cultures: Voices from France, Belgium, Brazil, Canada, and the Netherlands*, edited by Rommel Mendès-Leite and Pierre-Olivier de Busscher, 183–91. New York: Haworth, 1993.

Castells, Manuel. *The City and the Grassroots: A Cross-Cultural Theory of Urban Social Movements*. Berkeley: University of California Press, 1983.

Castle, Terry. *The Apparitional Lesbian: Female Homosexuality and Modern Culture*. New York: Columbia University Press, 1993.

Cattan, Nadine, and Anne Clerval. "Un droit à la ville? Réseaux virtuels et centralités éphémères des lesbiennes à Paris." *Justice spatiale / Spatial Justice*, no. 3 (2011): 1–19.

Centre lyonnais d'études féministes (Collectif). *Chronique d'une passion: Le mouvement de Libération des femmes à Lyon*. Paris: L'Harmattan, 1989.

Chamberland, Line. "Remembering Lesbian Bars: Montreal, 1955–1975." In *Gay Studies from the French Cultures: Voices from France, Belgium, Brazil, Canada, and the Netherlands*, edited by Rommel Mendès-Leite and Pierre-Olivier de Busscher, 231–69. New York: Haworth, 1993.

Chambers, Samuel A. *The Queer Politics of Television*. London: I.B. Tauris, 2009.

Chaperon, Sylvie. *Les origines de la sexologie (1850–1900)*. Paris: Éditions Audibert, 2007.

Chaplin, Tamara. "Lesbians Online: Queer Identity and Community Formation on the French Minitel." *Journal of the History of Sexuality* 23, no. 3 (September 2014): 451–72.

———. "Orgasm without Limits: May '68 and the History of Sex Education in Modern France." In *May '68, Rethinking France's Last Revolution*, edited by Julian Jackson, 376–96. London: Palgrave, 2011.

———. *Turning On the Mind: French Philosophers on Television*. Chicago: University of Chicago Press, 2007.

———. "Utopian Gaiety: French Lesbian Activism and the Politics of Pleasure (1974–2016)." In *Making Waves: French Feminisms and Their Legacies, 1975–2015*, edited by Margaret Atack, Alison S. Fell, Diana Holmes, and Imogen Long, 115–28. Liverpool: Liverpool University Press, 2019.

———. "A Woman Dressed Like a Man: Gender Trouble at the Sapphic Cabaret, Paris 1930–1960." *French Historical Studies* 44, no. 4 (2021): 711–48.

Chaumont, Frank. *Homo-Ghetto. Gays et lesbiennes dans les cités: Les clandestins de la République*. Paris: Le Cherche Midi, 2009.

Chauncey, George. "From Sexual Inversion to Homosexuality: Medicine and the Changing Conceptualization of Female Deviance." *Salmagundi*, no. 58/59 (Fall 1982–Winter 1983): 114–46.

———. *Gay New York: Gender, Urban Culture and the Making of the Gay Male World, 1890–1940*. New York: Basic Books, 1995.

Chenoune, Farid. "Leur bal: Notes sur des photos de Magic-City, bal des tantes de l'entre-deux guerres." *Modes pratiques*, no. 1 (November 2015). https://devisu.inha.fr/modespratiques/117.

Chetcuti, Natacha. *Se dire lesbien: Vie de couple, sexualité, représentation de soi*. Paris: Éditions Payot, 2010.

Choquette, Leslie. "Beyond the Myth of Lesbian Montmartre: The Case of Chez Palmyre." *Historical Reflections / Réflexions historiques* 42, no. 2 (Summer 2016): 75–96.

———. "Gay Paree: The Origins of Lesbian and Gay Commercial Culture in the French Third Republic." *Contemporary French Civilization* 41, no. 1 (2016): 1–24.

———. "Paris-Lesbos: Lesbian Social Space in the Modern City, 1870–1940." *Proceedings of the Annual Meeting of the Western Society for French History* 26 (1999): 122–32.

Coffin, Judith. *Sex, Love, and Letters: Writing Simone de Beauvoir*. Ithaca, NY: Cornell University Press, 2020.

———. "Sex, Love, and Letters: Writing Simone de Beauvoir, 1949–1963." *American Historical Review* 115, no. 4 (2010): 1061–88.

Colvin, Kelly Ricciardi. *Gender and French Identity after the Second World War, 1944–1954*. London: Bloomsbury, 2017.

Colwill, Elizabeth. "Pass as a Woman, Act Like a Man: Marie-Antoinette as Tribade in the Pornography of the French Revolution." In *Homosexuality in Modern France*, edited by Jeffrey Merrick and Bryant T. Ragan, 54–79. New York: Oxford University Press, 1996.

Copley, Antony R. H. *Sexual Moralities in France, 1780–1980: New Ideas on the Family, Divorce, and Homosexuality*. London: Routledge, 1989.

Correll, Shelley. "The Ethnography of an Electronic Bar: The Lesbian Café." *Journal of Contemporary Ethnography* 24, no. 3 (October 1995): 270–98.

Corriveau, Patrice. *Judging Homosexuals: A History of Gay Persecution in Quebec and France*. Translated by Käthe Roth. Vancouver: University of British Columbia Press, 2011.

Cosnard, Denis. *Frede*. Paris: Éditions des Équateurs, 2017.

Cousin, Roger. "Baba Sidonie." *Mémoires de guerre* (blog), April 14, 2011. http://la-loupe.over-blog.net/article-baba-sidonie-71745631.html.

Crenshaw, Kimberlé. "Demarginalizing the Intersection of Race and Sex: A Black Feminist Critique of Antidiscrimination Doctrine, Feminist Theory and Antiracist Politics." *University of Chicago Legal Forum* (1989). http://chicagounbound.uchicago.edu/uclf/vol1989/iss1/8.

———. "Mapping the Margins: Intersectionality, Identity Politics, and Violence against Women of Color." *Stanford Law Review* 43, no. 6 (1991): 1241–99.

Cryle, Peter. "Foretelling Pathology: The Poetics of Prognosis." *French Cultural Studies* 17, no. 1 (2006): 107–22.

D'Arcy, Jean. "Direct Broadcast Satellites and the Right to Communicate." *EBU Review* 118 (1969).

Davidson, Arnold I. *The Emergence of Sexuality: Historical Epistemology and the Formation of Concepts*. Cambridge, MA: Harvard University Press, 2004.

Davis, David Glyn, and Gary Needham, eds. *Queer TV: Theories, Histories, Politics*. London: Routledge, 2009.

Dean, Carolyn J. *The Frail Social Body: Pornography, Homosexuality, and Other Fantasies in Interwar France*. Berkeley: University of California Press, 2000.

D'Emilio, John. "Capitalism and Gay Identity." In *The Lesbian and Gay Studies Reader*, edited by Henry Abelove, Michèle Aina Barale, and David M. Halperin, 467–76. New York: Routledge, 1993.

Denoeud, Rachel. "Femmes de radio et télévision dans les fonds de l'INA." November 14, 2019. https://inatheque.hypotheses.org/15919.

DeNora, Tia. *Music in Everyday Life*. Cambridge: Cambridge University Press, 2000.

Doan, Laura. *Disturbing Practices: History, Sexuality, and Women's Experience of Modern War*. Chicago: University of Chicago Press, 2013.

———. *Fashioning Sapphism: The Origins of a Modern English Lesbian Culture*. New York: Columbia University Press, 2001.

Doan, Laura, and Jane Garrity, eds. *Sapphic Modernities: Sexuality, Women and National Culture*. New York: Palgrave Macmillan, 2006.

Doane, Mary Ann. *The Desire to Desire: The Women's Films of the 1940s*. Bloomington: Indiana University Press, 1987.

Dorlin, Elsa. *La matrice de la race: Généaologie sexuelle et coloniale de la nation française*. Paris: La Découverte, 2006.

Duccini, Hélène. "Carré blanc et signalétique télévisée en France, 1961–1998." *Le temps des médias*, no. 1 (2003): 65–76.

Duchen, Claire. *Feminism in France: From May '68 to Mitterrand*. London: Routledge, 1986.

———, ed. and trans. *French Connections: Voices from the Women's Movement*. Amherst: University of Massachusetts Press, 1987.

Ducongé, Ada Smith, and James Haskins. *Bricktop*. New York: Atheneum, 1983.

Duggan, Lisa. *The Twilight of Equality? Neoliberalism, Cultural Politics, and the Attack on Democracy*. Boston: Beacon Press, 2003.

Duggan, Lisa, and Nan D. Hunter. *Sex Wars: Sexual Dissent and Political Culture*. 10th anniversary ed. London: Routledge, 2006.

Dupouy, Alexandre, and Marc Lemonier. *Histoire(s) du Paris libertin*. Paris: La Musardine, 2003.

Duthoo, Charlotte. *Les nuits Solidor: Mémoires imaginaires d'une égérie*. Paris: Le Cherche Midi, 2021.

Duyves, Mattias. "The Minitel: The Glittering Future of a New Invention." In *Gay Studies from the French Cultures: Voices from France, Belgium, Brazil, Canada, and the Netherlands*, edited by Rommel Mendès-Leite and Pierre-Olivier de Busscher, 193–203. New York: Haworth, 1993.

Édouard, Clara Sadoun. "Presse, mondanité et saphisme décoratif." *Romantisme* 1, no. 159 (2013): 59–71.

Ellenzweig, Allen, and George Stambolian. *The Homoerotic Photograph: Male Images from Durieu/Delacroix to Mapplethorpe*. New York: Columbia University Press, 1992.

Eloit, Ilana. "'Le bonheur était dans les pages de ce mensuel': La naissance de la presse lesbienne et la fabrique d'un espace à soi (1976–1990)." *Le temps des médias* 2, no. 29 (2017): 93–108.

———. "Lesbian Trouble: Feminism, Heterosexuality, and the French Nation (1970–1981)." PhD diss., London School of Economics, August 2018.

———. "Trouble dans le féminisme: Du 'Nous, les femmes' au 'Nous, les lesbiennes': Genèse du sujet politique lesbien en France (1970–1980)." *20 & 21 Revue d'histoire*, no. 148 (October–December 2020): 129–45.

Enteen, Jillana B. *Virtual English: Queer Internets and Digital Creolization*. New York: Routledge, 2010.

Evans, David. *Sexual Citizenship: The Material Construction of Sexualities*. London: Routledge, 1993.

Faderman, Lillian. *Odd Girls and Twilight Lovers: A History of Lesbian Life in Twentieth-Century America*. New York: Columbia University Press, 1991.

Faderman, Lillian, and Stuart Timmons. *Gay L.A.: A History of Sexual Outlaws, Power Politics and Lipstick Lesbians*. New York: Basic Books, 2006.

Fassin, Didier, and Éric Fassin, eds. *De la question sociale à la question raciale? Representer la société française*. Paris: La Découverte, 2006.

Finn, Michael. "Female Sterilization and Artificial Insemination at the French Fin de Siècle: Facts and Fictions." *Journal of the History of Sexuality* 18, no. 1 (January 2009): 26–43.

Fishman, Sarah. *From Vichy to the Sexual Revolution: Gender and Family Life in Postwar France*. New York: Oxford University Press, 2017.

Flamant, Françoise. *Women's Lands: Construction d'une utopie, Oregon, USA, 1970–2010*. Donnemarie-Dontilly: Éditions IXe, 2015.

Foucault, Michel. *The History of Sexuality*. Vol. 1, *An Introduction*. Translated by Robert Hurley. 1976; New York: Viking, 1988.

Fourastié, Jean, and Jacqueline Fourastié. *Pouvoir d'achat, prix et salaires*. Paris: Gallimard, 1977.

Fourest, Caroline. *Les anti-PaCS, ou, La la dernière croisade homophobe*. Paris: Éditions Prochoix, 1999.

———. *Tirs croisés: La laïcité à l'épreuve des intégismes juif, chrétien et muselman*. Paris: Calmann-Lévy, 2003.

Franceinfo. "L'Assemblée nationale supprime à l'unanimité le mot 'race' de la Constitution." Updated July 12, 2018. https://www.francetvinfo.fr/societe/droits-des-femmes/l-assemblee-nationale-supprime-a-l-unanimite-le-mot-race-de-la-constitution-et-interdit-la-distinction-de-sexe_2847351.html.

Francis, Claude, and Fernande Gontier. *Colette*. Paris: Perrin, 1997.

Fraser, Nancy. "Rethinking the Public Sphere: A Contribution to the Critique of Actually Existing Democracy." *Social Text*, no. 25/26 (1990): 56–80.

Fricker, Miranda. *Epistemic Injustice: Power and the Ethics of Knowing*. Oxford: Oxford University Press, 2007.

Garber, Marjorie. *Vested Interests: Cross-Dressing and Cultural Anxiety*. New York: Routledge, 1992.

Gavillet, Isabelle. "Constructions sociales, scientifiques et médiatiques d'un lieu commun: L'acceptation croissante de l'homosexualité à la télévision." *MEI (Médiation et information)*, no. 20 (2004): 83–92.

Geczy, Adam, and Vicki Karaminas. *Queer Style*. London: Bloomsbury, 2013.

Gervereau, Laurent. "Chercher le lien: Les variétés à la télévision." In *La grande aventure du petit écran: La télévision française 1935–1975*, edited by Jérôme Bourdon et al., 203–21. Paris: Musée d'histoire contemporaine-BDIC / INA, 1997.

Gevisser, Mark. *The Pink Line: The World's Queer Frontiers*. London: Profile Books, 2020.

Ginzberg, Carlo. *The Cheese and the Worms: The Cosmos of a Sixteenth-Century Miller*. Baltimore: Johns Hopkins University Press, 1992.

Girard, Jacques. *Le mouvement homosexuel en France, 1945–1980*. Paris: Syros, 1981.

Gonnard, Catherine, and Elisabeth Lebovici. "Inventer son genre dans le langage de la télévision." *GLAD!*, November 15, 2016. http://www.revue-glad.org/209.

Goodloe, Amy T. "Computer Networks and Services." In *Encyclopedia of Lesbian and Gay Histories and Cultures*, vol. 1, *Lesbian Histories and Cultures: An Encyclopedia*, edited by Bonnie Zimmerman, 200. New York: Garland, 2000.

Goodman, Dena. *Becoming a Woman in the Age of Letters*. Ithaca, NY: Cornell University Press, 2009.

Gordon, Mel. *Horizontal Collaboration: The Erotic World of Paris, 1920–1946*. Port Townsend: Feral House, 2015.

Greenwald, Lisa. *Daughters of 1968: Redefining French Feminism and the Women's Liberation Movement*. Lincoln: University of Nebraska Press, 2018.

Gross, Larry. *Up from Invisibility: Lesbians, Gay Men, and the Media in America*. New York: Columbia University Press, 2001.

Gross, Martine. *Parent ou homo, faut-il choisir? Idées reçues sur l'homoparentalité*. Paris: Le Cavalier Bleu, 2013.

Guillaumin, Colette. *L'idéologie raciste: Genèse et langage actuel*. 2nd ed. Paris: Gallimard, 2002.

———. *Sexe, race et pratique du pouvoir: L'idée de la nature*. Paris: Côté-Femmes, 1992.

Gunther, Scott. *The Elastic Closet: A History of Homosexuality in France, 1942–Present*. London: Palgrave Macmillan, 2009.

Guterl, Matthew Pratt. *Josephine Baker and the Rainbow Tribe*. Cambridge, MA: Harvard University Press, 2014.

Gutterman, Lauren Jae. *Her Neighbor's Wife: A History of Lesbian Desire within Marriage*. Philadelphia: University of Pennsylvania Press, 2020.

Habermas, Jürgen. *The Structural Transformation of the Public Sphere: An Inquiry into a Category of Bourgeois Society*. 1962; Cambridge, MA: MIT Press, 1991.

Halberstam, Jack. *Female Masculinity*. 1998; Durham, NC: Duke University Press, 2019.

———. *The Queer Art of Failure*. Durham, NC: Duke University Press, 2011.

———. *Trans*: A Quick and Quirky Account of Gender Variability*. Oakland: University of California Press, 2018.

Halperin, David. "Forgetting Foucault: Acts, Identities, and the History of Sexuality." *Representations* 63 (1998): 93–120.

——. *How to Be Gay*. Cambridge, MA: Harvard University Press, 2012.

Hankin, Kelly. *The Girls in the Back Room: Looking at the Lesbian Bar*. Minneapolis: University of Minnesota Press, 2002.

Hanna, Martha. "A Republic of Letters: The Epistolary Tradition in France during World War I." *American Historical Review* 108, no. 5 (2003): 1338–61.

Hare, Geoff. "Popular Music on French Radio and Television." In *Popular Music in France from Chanson to Techno*, edited by Hugh Dauncey and Steve Cannon, 57–75. London: Routledge, 2016.

Harvey, David. *Social Justice and the City*. London: Edward Arnold, 1973.

Hekma, Gert. "Amsterdam Gay Bar Culture 1930–1970." Accessed June 23, 2022. https://www.academia.edu/14426607/Amsterdam_Gay_Bar_Culture_1930_1970?email_work_card=title. Originally published in Hungarian in *Budapesti Negyed* 55 (2007): 215–26.

——. "Sexual Citizenship." GLBTQ Archives. Accessed June 11, 2022. http://www.glbtqarchive.com/ssh/sexual_citizenship_S.pdf.

Human Dignity Trust. "Map of Countries That Criminalise LGBT People." Accessed September 15, 2023. https://www.humandignitytrust.org/lgbt-the-law/map-of-criminalisation/?type_filter_submitted=&type_filter%5B%5D=death_pen_applies.

Hunt, Lynn. *The Family Romance of the French Revolution*. Los Angeles: University of California Press, 1992.

——. "The Many Bodies of Marie-Antoinette: Political Pornography and the Problem of the Feminine in the French Revolution." In *The French Revolution: Recent Debates and New Controversies*, 2nd ed., edited by Gary Kates, 201–18. New York: Routledge, 2001.

Hutchins, Frances E. "The Pleasures of Discovery: Representations of Queer Space by Brassaï and Colette." In *Lesbian Inscriptions in Francophone Society and Culture*, edited by Renate Günther and Wendy Michallat, 189–204. Manchester: Manchester University Press, 2007.

Idier, Antoine. *Les Alinéas du Placard: L'abrogation du délit d'homosexualité (1977–1982)*. Paris: Éditions Cartouche/TMR, 2013.

——. "À Lyon, l'homosexualité en procès." *Bulletin municipal official de Lyon*, December 12, 2011.

Isaksson, Eva. "Living with Lesbian Lists." Sappho.net, 1997. Accessed July 14, 2013. http://www.sappho.net/lesbian-lists/lll.html.

Jackson, Jeffrey H. *Paper Bullets: Two Artists Who Risked Their Lives to Defy the Nazis*. Chapel Hill, NC: Algonquin Books, 2020.

Jackson, Julian. *Living in Arcadia: Homosexuality, Politics and Morality in France from the Liberation to AIDS*. Chicago: University of Chicago Press, 2009.

Jackson, Stevi. *Christine Delphy*. London: Sage, 1996.

Jagose, Annemarie. *Lesbian Utopics*. New York: Routledge, 1994.

Jay, Karine. "Suzy Solidor (1900–1983): Portrait d'une artiste à la frange d'orée d'art." Master's thesis, Université de Jean Moulin Lyon III, 1994–96.

Jennings, Jeremy. "Citizenship, Republicanism and Multiculturalism in Contemporary France." *British Journal of Political Science* 30, no. 4 (October 2000): 575–97.

Jennings, Rebecca. *A Lesbian History of Britain: Love and Sex between Women since 1500*. Oxford: Greenwood World Publishing, 2007.

———. *Tomboys and Bachelor Girls: A Lesbian History of Post-war Britain 1945–71*. Manchester: Manchester University Press, 2007.

———. *Unnamed Desires: A Sydney Lesbian History*. Melbourne: Monash University Publishing, 2015.

Johnson, Colin R. *Just Queer Folks: Gender and Sexuality in Rural America*. Philadelphia: Temple University Press, 2013.

Johnston, David K. *The Lavender Scare: The Cold War Persecution of Gays and Lesbians in the Federal Government*. Chicago: University of Chicago Press, 2004.

Kahn, Janet, and Patricia Gozemba. "In and around the Lighthouse: Working-Class Lesbian Bar Culture in the 1950s and 1960s." In *Gendered Domains: Rethinking Public and Private in Women's History*, edited by Dorothy Helly and Susan Reverby, 90–106. Ithaca, NY: Cornell University Press, 1992.

Kennedy, Elizabeth Lapovsky, and Madeleine D. Davis. *Boots of Leather, Slippers of Gold: The History of a Lesbian Community*. New York: Routledge, 1993.

Ladurie, Emmanuel Le Roy. "Occitania in Historical Perspective." *Review (Fernand Braudel Center)* 1, no. 1 (Summer 1977): 20–30.

Lamien, Éric. "Fréquence gaie." In *Dictionnaire des cultures gays et lesbiennes*, edited by Didier Eribon, 201–2. Paris: Larousse, 2003.

Landes, Joan B. *Women and the Public Sphere in the Age of the French Revolution*. Ithaca, NY: Cornell University Press, 1988.

Laroche, Martine, and Michèle Larrouy, eds. *Mouvements de presse: Des années 1970s à nos jours, luttes féministes et lesbiennes*. Paris: Éditions des ARCL, 2009.

Latimer, Tirza True. *Women Together, Women Apart: Portraits of Lesbian Paris*. New Brunswick, NJ: Rutgers University Press, 2005.

Le Bitoux, Jean. "Le guêpier des années Gai pied." Accessed February 10, 2011. http://www.france.qrd.org/media/gai%20pied/. This web page is no longer live.

Le Bitoux, Jean, Bruno Proth, and Hervé Chevaux. *Citoyen de seconde zone: Trente ans de lutte pour la reconnaissance de l'homosexualité en France (1971–2002)*. Paris: Hachette, 2003.

Lebovici, Elisabeth. "*Housewife*, la redistribution du sensible." Accessed March 4, 2023. https://www.academia.edu/37369835/Housewife_la_redistribution_du_sensible.

Leffingwell, Hannah. "'Our Point of Departure Is Feminist': *Féminin Masculin Avenir* and the Intersectional Origins of Women's Liberation in France, 1967–1980." *Gender & History* 34, no. 1 (2022): 263–81.

Lemoine, Christine, and Ingrid Renard. *Attirances: Lesbiennes fems, lesbiennes butchs*. Paris: Éditions Gaies et Lesbiennes, 2001.

Lemos, André. "The Labyrinth of Minitel." In *Cultures of the Internet: Virtual Spaces, Real Histories, Living Bodies*, edited by Rob Shields, 33–48. London: Sage, 1996.

Leroy, Stéphane. "Le Paris gay: Éléments pour une géographie de l'homosexualité." *Annales de Géographie* 114, no. 646 (2005): 579–601.

Lesselier, Claudie. "Aspects de l'expérience lesbienne en France, 1930–1968." DEA thesis, Université Paris 8, 1987.

———. "Formes de résistances et d'expression lesbiennes dans les années 1950 et

1960 en France." In *Homosexualités: Expression/répression*, edited by Louis-Georges Tin and Geneviève Pastre, 105–16. Paris: Éditions Stock, 2000.

———. "'Pourquoi une femme avec une femme?' Écrire l'amour lesbien, 1945–1968." *Amazones d'hier, lesbiennes d'aujourd'hui* 18 (March 1987): 14–32.

———. "Silenced Resistances and Conflictual Identities: Lesbians in France, 1930–1968." *Journal of Homosexuality* 25, no.1/2 (1993): 105–25.

Levitas, Ruth. *Utopia as Method: The Imaginary Reconstitution of Society*. Houndmills: Palgrave Macmillan, 2013.

Levy, Marie-Françoise. "La création des *télé-clubs*: L'expérience de l'Aisne." In *La télévision dans la République dans les années 50*, edited by Marie-Françoise Levy, 107–32. Paris: Éditions Complexe, 1999.

———. "Les femmes du temps present à la télévision: La mutation des identités (1960–1975)." In *Les années 68: Le temps de la contestation*, edited by Geneviève Dreyfus-Armand, Robert Frank, Marie-Françoise Lévy, and Michelle Zancarini-Fournel, 199–218. Paris: Éditions Complexe, 2008.

Lewis, Brian. *Wolfenden's Witnesses: Homosexuality in Postwar Britain*. New York: Palgrave Macmillan, 2016.

Lhomond, Brigitte. "Between Man and Woman: The Character of the Lesbian." *Journal of the History of Homosexuality* 25, no. 1/2 (1993): 63–73.

———. Preface to the republication of *Histoire de la femme* by Dr. Caufeynon. Paris: Côté-Femmes, 1989.

Livia, Anna. "*Camionneuses s'abstenir*: Lesbian Community Creation through the Personals." In *Language and Sexuality: Contesting Meaning in Theory and Practice*, edited by Katheryn Campbell-Kibler, Robert J. Podesva, Sarah J. Roberts, and Andrew Wong, 191–206. Stanford: CSLI Publications, 2002.

———. "Public and Clandestine: Gay Men's Pseudonyms on the French Minitel." *Sexualities* 5, no. 2 (May 2002): 201–17.

Lootgieter, Léa. "Femmes des sixties." *Well Well Well: La revue lesbienne* 1 (2014).

———. "La télévision est toujours en décalage avec les mouvements LGBT." Les OUT d'or. Accessed July 31, 2019. http://2017.outdor.fr/2017/catherine-gonnard/index.html.

Lootgieter, Léa, and Pauline Paris. *Les dessous lesbiens de la chanson*. Donnemarie-Dontilly: Éditions IXe, 2019.

Lopez, Oscar. "Don't Be Fooled by Marine Le Pen's Gay Pandering—Her Party Is Awful for LGBTQ Equality." *Slate*, May 7, 2017. https://slate.com/human-interest/2017/05/marine-le-pens-gay-pandering-doesnt-excuse-her-national-front-party-on-lgbt-equality.html.

Lotem, Itay. "'L'homosexualité? Ça n'existe pas en banlieue': The Indigènes de la République and Gay Marriage, between Intersectionality and Homophobia." *Modern and Contemporary France* 27, no. 2 (2019): 205–21.

Love, Heather. *Feeling Backward: Loss and the Politics of Queer History*. Cambridge, MA: Harvard University Press, 2007.

Lucey, Michael. *Someone: The Pragmatics of Misfit Sexualities, from Colette to Hervé Guibert*. Chicago: University of Chicago Press, 2019.

Lybeck, Marti M. *Desiring Emancipation: New Women and Homosexuality in Germany, 1890–1933*. Albany: State University of New York Press, 2015.

Lyford, Amy. "'Le Numéro Barbette': Photography and the Politics of Embodiment in Interwar Paris." In *The Modern Woman Revisited: Paris between the Wars*, edited by Whitney Chadwick and Tirza True Latimer, 223–33. New Brunswick, NJ: Rutgers University Press, 2003.

Mah, Harold. "Phantasies of the Public Sphere: Rethinking the Habermas of the Historians." *Journal of Modern History* 72 (March 2000): 153–82.

Mailland, Julien, and Kevin Drisco. *Minitel: Welcome to the Internet*. Cambridge, MA: MIT Press, 2017.

Maira, Daniel. "Des tribades et des godemichés: Mollesses viriles dans le *Recueil des dames* de Brantôme." *French Studies* 70, no. 4 (2016): 503–18.

Marhoefer, Laurie. "Queer Fascism and the End of Gay History." *Notches*, June 19, 2018, https://notchesblog.com/2018/06/19/queer-fascism-and-the-end-of-gay-history/.

———. *Sex and the Weimar Republic: German Homosexual Emancipation and the Rise of the Nazis*. Toronto: University of Toronto Press, 2015.

Marks, Elaine. "Lesbian Intertextuality." In *Homosexualities and French Literature*, edited by George Stambolian and Elaine Marks, 353–77. Ithaca, NY: Cornell University Press, 1979.

Martel, Frédéric. *The Pink and the Black: Homosexuals in France since 1968*. Translated by Jane Marie Todd. Stanford: Stanford University Press, 1999.

Mayne, Judith. *Cinema and Spectatorship*. New York: Routledge, 1993.

McCaffrey, Enda. *The Gay Republic: Sexuality, Citizenship and Subversion in France*. Burlington, VT: Ashgate, 2005.

McKinney, Cait. *Information Activism: A Queer History of Lesbian Media Technologies*. Durham, NC: Duke University Press, 2020.

McLaren, Angus. *The Trials of Masculinity: Policing Sexual Boundaries, 1870–1930*. Chicago: University of Chicago Press, 1997.

McLellan, Diana. *The Girls: Sappho Goes to Hollywood*. New York: Griffin, 2000.

Meinhof, Ulrike H., and Jonathan Smith. *Intertextuality and the Media: From Genre to Everyday Life*. Manchester: Manchester University Press, 2000.

Mesch, Rachel. *Before Trans: Three Gender Stories from Nineteenth-Century France*. Stanford: Stanford University Press, 2020.

Millward, Liz. *Making a Scene: Lesbians and Community across Canada, 1964–1984*. Vancouver: University of British Columbia Press, 2015.

Miquel, Pierre. *La main courante: Les archives indiscrètes de la police parisienne, 1900–1945*. Paris: Éditions Albin Michel, 1997.

Morin-Delaurière, Camille. "Étude comparée de Rennes et de Paris: Une autre histoire des relations entre les mouvements féministes et lesbien en France (1970–1980)." *Féminismes et lesbianismes* 33, no. 2 (2020).

Muel-Dreyfus, Francine. *Vichy and the Eternal Feminine: A Contribution to a Political Sociology of Gender*. Durham, NC: Duke University Press, 2001.

Muller, Sandra. *#balancetonporc*. Paris: Flammarion, 2018.

Mulvey, Laura. "Visual Pleasure and Narrative Cinema." Reprinted in *Visual Culture: The Reader*, edited by Jessica Evans and Stuart Hall, 381–89. London: Sage, 2002.

Mumford, Kevin. *Interzones: Black/White Sex Districts in Chicago and New York in the Early Twentieth Century*. New York: Columbia University Press, 1997.

Muñoz, José Esteban. *Cruising Utopia: The Then and There of Queer Futurity*. New York: New York University Press, 2009.

Murat, Laure. *La loi du genre: Une histoire culturelle du "troisième sexe."* Paris: Fayard, 2006.

Najmabadi, Afsaneh. "Beyond the Americas: Are Gender and Sexuality Useful Categories of Analysis?" *Journal of Women's History* 18, no. 1 (Spring 2006): 11–21.

Nathans, Benjamin. "Habermas's 'Public Sphere' in the Era of the French Revolution." *French Historical Studies* 16, no. 3 (Spring 1990): 620–24.

Ndiaye, Pap. *La condition noire*. Paris: Calmann-Lévy, 2008.

Nestle, Joan. *A Restricted Country: Documents of Desire and Resistance*. New York: Firebrand Books, 1987.

Newton, Esther. "The Mythic Mannish Lesbian." *Signs* 9, no. 4 (Summer 1984): 557–75.

Nora, Pierre. "Between Memory and History: Les Lieux de Mémoire." In "Memory and Counter-Memory." Special issue, *Representations*, no. 26 (Spring 1989): 7–24.

Nora, Simon, and Alain Minc. *L'informatisation de la société*. Paris: La Documentation Française, 1978.

Nye, Robert. *Masculinity and Male Codes of Honor in Modern France*. New York: Oxford University Press, 1993.

Oosterhuis, Harry. *Stepchildren of Nature: Krafft-Ebing, Psychiatry, and the Making of Sexual Identity*. Chicago: University of Chicago Press, 2000.

Organization for Economic Co-operation and Development, Directorate for Science, Technology and Industry, and Committee on Information, Computer and Communications Policy, Working Party on the Information Economy. *France's Experience with the Minitel: Lessons for Electronic Commerce over the Internet*. Vol. 6, no. 88. Paris: OECD, 1998.

O'Riordan, Kate, and David J. Phillips, eds. *Queer Online: Media, Technology & Sexuality*. New York: Peter Lang, 2007.

Ory, Pascal. *L'entre-deux Mai: Histoire culturelle de la France (Mai 1968–Mai 1981)*. Paris: Éditions du Seuil, 1983.

Pauly, Anne. "Chez Moune: Chic lesbien et lutte des classes." Red Bull Music Academy Daily, September 29, 2016. http://fr.redbullmusicacademy.com/daily/2016/09/chez-moune-chic-lesbien-et-lutte-des-classes. This web page is no longer live.

Pedersen, Jean Elisabeth. "Representations of Women in the French Imaginary: Historicizing the Gallic Singularity." *French Politics, Culture, and Society* 38, no. 1 (March 2020): 1–20.

Pénet, Martin. "L'expression homosexuelle dans les chansons françaises de l'entre-deux guerres: Entre dérision et ambiguïté." *Revue d'histoire moderne et contemporaine*, no. 53–54 (October–December 2006): 106–27.

———. "IV - 1919/1939: Des années vraiment folles par Martin Pénet." *Contribution subjective à une mémoire gaie: Littérature, cinéma, arts, histoire . . .* (blog), published February 7, 2018, by Jean-Yves Alt. http://culture-et-debats.over-blog.com/article-341637.html.

Peniston, William. *Pederasts and Others: Urban Culture and Sexual Identity in Nineteenth-Century Paris*. New York: Harrington Park Press, 2004.

Perreau, Bruno. *Queer Theory: The French Response*. Stanford: Stanford University Press, 2016.

Podmore, Julie A. "Gone 'Underground'? Lesbian Visibility and the Consolidation of Queer Space in Montréal." *Social and Cultural Geography* 7, no. 4 (2006): 595–625.

Podmore, Julie A., and Line Chamberland. "Entering the Urban Frame: Early Lesbian Activism and Public Space in Montréal." *Journal of Lesbian Studies* 19 (2015): 192–211.

Pollard, Miranda. *Reign of Virtue: Mobilizing Gender in Vichy France*. Chicago: University of Chicago Press, 1998.

Portelli, Alessandro. "The Peculiarities of Oral History." *History Workshop Journal* 12, no. 1 (Autumn 1981): 96–107.

Provencher, Denis M. *Queer French: Globalization, Language, and Sexual Citizenship in France*. Hampshire: Ashgate, 2007.

Provitola, Blase A. "In Visibilities: The *Groupe du 6 novembre* and the Production of Liberal Lesbian Identity in Contemporary France." *Modern and Contemporary France* 27, no. 2 (2019): 223–41.

———. "Sex, Race and the Epistemology of Desire in the Literature and Culture of Contemporary France." PhD diss., Columbia University, 2019.

Pulju, Rebecca J. *Women and Mass Consumer Society in Postwar France*. Cambridge: Cambridge University Press, 2011.

Quéré, Mathias. *Qui sème le vent récolte la tapette: Une histoire des groups de libération homosexuels en France de 1974–1979*. Clermont-Ferrand: La Source d'Or, 2018.

Quinqueton, Denis. "Pourquoi le 10 mars est une date essentielle pour les droits des LGBT+ en France." *Têtu*, March 3, 2021. https://tetu.com/2021/03/10/pourquoi-le-10-mars-est-une-date-essentielle-pour-les-droits-des-lgbt-en-france/.

Rendall, Jane. *The Origins of Modern Feminism: Women in Britain, France and the United States 1780–1860*. London: Palgrave, 1985.

Revenin, Régis. *Une histoire des garçons et des filles*. Paris: Vendémiaire, 2015.

———. *Homosexualité et prostitution masculines à Paris, 1870–1918*. Paris: L'Harmattan, 2005.

Reymondeaux, Anna. "Mouvements lesbiens et gays à Poitiers: 1975–1992. Du Féminisme à la Gay Pride: Naissance des mouvements identitaires." Master's thesis, Université de Poitiers, 2008.

Rincé, Jean-Yves. *Le Minitel*. Paris: Presses Universitaires de France, 1990.

Roberts, Mary-Louise. *Civilization without Sexes: Reconstructing Gender in Postwar France, 1917–1927*. Chicago: University of Chicago Press, 1994.

———. *Disruptive Acts: The New Woman in Fin-de-Siècle France*. Chicago: University of Chicago Press, 2002.

Robichon, Suzette. "La presse des lesbiennes; un des moteurs de notre histoire?" In *Mouvement des lesbiennes, lesbiennes en mouvement: Dans le cadre des 40 ans du MLF*, edited by Actes du colloque et des ateliers Chronologie lesbienne, 27–38. Montreuil: Coordination Lesbienne en France / Éditions Prospero, 2010.

Roellig, Ruth Margarete. *Berlins lesbische Frauen*. Leipzig: Gebauer, 1928.

Rollet, Brigitte. "In the Margins and Off-Centre: Lesbian Characters on French Television 1995–2005." In *Lesbian Inscriptions in Francophone Society and Culture*, edited by Renate Günther and Wendy Michallat, 81–102. Manchester: Manchester University Press, 2007.

———. *Jacqueline Audry: La femme à la camera*. Rennes: Presses Universitaires de Rennes, 2015.

———. *Télévisions et homosexualité: 10 ans de fictions françaises 1995–2005*. Paris: L'Harmattan, 2007.

Rose, David C. "Paris Lesbos." *Journal of Lesbian Studies* 13 (2009): 362–72.

Ross, Andrew Israel. *Public City, Public Sex: Homosexuality, Prostitution, and Urban Culture in Nineteenth-Century Paris*. Philadelphia: Temple University Press, 2019.

Rustin, Michael. "Reflections on the Biographical Turn in the Social Sciences." In *The Turn to Biographical Methods in the Social Sciences*, edited by Prue Chamberlayne, Joanna Bornat, and Tom Wengraf, 33–52. London: Routledge, 2000.

Sanderson, Terry. *Mediawatch: The Treatment of Male and Female Homosexuality in the British Media*. London: Cassell, 1995.

Sautman, Francesca Canadé. "Invisible Women: Lesbian Working-Class Culture in France, 1880–1930." In *Homosexuality in Modern France*, edited by Jeffrey Merrick and Bryant T. Ragan Jr., 177–201. New York: Oxford University Press, 1996.

Schlesser, Gilles. *Le cabaret "rive gauche": De la Rose Rouge au Bateau ivre: 1946–1974*. Paris: Éditions de l'Archipel, 2006.

Schneider, Robert A. *Public Life in Toulouse, 1463–1789*. Ithaca, NY: Cornell University Press, 1989.

Schultz, Gretchen. *Sapphic Fathers: Discourses of Same-Sex Desire from Nineteenth-Century France*. Toronto: University of Toronto Press, 2014.

Schwartz, Vanessa. *Spectacular Realities: Early Mass Culture in Fin-de-Siècle Paris*. Berkeley: University of California Press, 1998.

Scott, Joan Wallach. *Only Paradoxes to Offer: French Feminists and the Rights of Man*. Cambridge, MA: Harvard University Press, 1997.

———. *Parité: Sexual Equality and the Crisis of French Universalism*. Chicago: University of Chicago Press, 2005.

———. *The Politics of the Veil*. Princeton, NJ: Princeton University Press, 2007.

Secondi, Claude. *Mick Micheyl: Des planches à l'acier*. Villeurbanne: Éditions du Mot Passant, 2010.

Sedgwick, Eve Kosofsky. *Between Men: English Literature and Male Homosexual Desire*. New York: Columbia University Press, 1985.

Sénac, Réjane. *L'égalité sous conditions: Genre, parité, diversité*. Paris: Presses de Sciences Po, 2015.

Senelick, Laurence. *Cabaret Performance*. Vol. 2, *Europe 1920–1940, Sketches, Songs, Monologues, Memoirs*. Baltimore: Johns Hopkins University Press, 1993.

Servan-Schrieber, Jean-Jacques. *Le défi américain*. Paris: Denoël, 1967.

Sharpley-Whiting, T. Denean. *Bricktop's Paris: African-American Women in Paris between the Two World Wars*. Albany: State University of New York Press, 2015.

Shaw, Jennifer. *Exist Otherwise: The Life and Works of Claude Cahun*. London: Reaktion Books, 2017.

Shepard, Todd. *Sex, France & Arab Men, 1962–1979*. Chicago: University of Chicago Press, 2017.

Sibalis, Michael. "Gay Liberation Comes to France: The Front Homosexuel d'Action Révolutionnaire (FHAR)." *French History and Civilization: Papers from the George Rudé Society*, no. 1 (2005). https://h-france.net/rude/wp-content/uploads/2017/08/vol1_Sibalis2.pdf.

———. "Homophobia, Vichy France, and the 'Crime of Homosexuality': The Origins of the Ordinance of 6 August 1942." *GLQ: A Journal of Lesbian and Gay Studies* 8, no. 3 (2002): 301–18.

———. "Mai 68: Le Comité d'Action Pédérastique Révolutionnaire occupe la Sorbonne." *Genre, sexualité & société* 10 (Autumn 2013). https://journals.openedition.org/gss/3009.

———. "Paris." In *Queer Sites: Gay Urban Histories since 1660*, edited by David Higgs, 10–37. London: Routledge, 1999.

———. "Urban Space and Homosexuality: The Example of the Marais, Paris' 'Gay Ghetto.'" *Urban Studies* 41, no. 9 (August 2004): 1739–58.

———. "La vie homosexuelle en France pendant la Seconde Guerre mondiale." In *Homosexuel.le.s en Europe pendant la Seconde Guerre mondiale*, edited by Régis Schlagdenhauffen, Julie Le Gac, and Farbice Virgili, 131–51. Paris: Nouveau Monde, 2017.

Skidmore, Emily. *True Sex: The Lives of Trans Men at the Turn of the Century*. New York: New York University Press, 2017.

Soja, Edward. *Seeking Spatial Justice*. Minneapolis: University of Minnesota Press, 2010.

Steele, Valerie, ed. *A Queer History of Fashion: From the Closet to the Catwalk*. New York: Fashion Institute of Technology, 2013.

Stein, Marc. *City of Sisterly and Brotherly Loves: Lesbian and Gay Philadelphia, 1945–1972*. Chicago: University of Chicago Press, 2000.

Stovall, Tyler. *Paris Noir: African Americans in the City of Light*. Boston: Houghton Mifflin, 1996.

Surkis, Judith. *Sexing the Citizen: Morality and Masculinity in France, 1870–1920*. Ithaca, NY: Cornell University Press, 2006.

Sutton, Katie. *The Masculine Woman in Weimar Germany*. New York: Berghahn Books, 2011.

Tagliabue, John. "Online Cohabitation: Internet and Minitel; Videotex System in France Proves Unusually Resilient." *New York Times*, June 2, 2001. http://www.nytimes.com/2001/06/02/business/online-cohabitation-internet-minitel-videotex-system-france-proves-unusually.html?pagewanted=all&src=pm.

Tamagne, Florence. "Caricatures homophobes et stéréotypes de genres en France et en Allemagne: La presse satirique de 1900 au milieu des années 30." *Le temps des médias* 1, no. 1 (2003): 42–53.

———. *Histoire de l'homosexualité en Europe: Berlin, Londres, Paris, 1919–1939*. Paris: Éditions du Seuil, 2000.

———. *A History of Homosexuality in Europe: Berlin, London, Paris, 1919–1939*. 2 vols. New York: Algora Publishing, 2004.

———. "Paris: 'Resting on Its Laurels'?" In *Queer Cities, Queer Cultures: Europe since 1945*, edited by Matt Cook and Jennifer Evans, 240–60. London: Bloomsbury, 2014.

Taraud, Christelle. *Les féminismes en questions: Éléments pour une cartographie*. Paris: Éditions Amsterdam, 2005.

Ténot, Frank. *Radios privées, radios pirates*. Paris: Denoël, 1978.

Thompson, Victoria. "Creating Boundaries: Homosexuality and the Changing Social Order in France, 1830–1870." In *Homosexuality in Modern France*, edited by Jeffrey Merrick and Bryant T. Ragan Jr., 102–27. New York: Oxford University Press, 1996.

Thorpe, Roey. "The Changing Face of Lesbian Bars in Detroit, 1938–1965." In *Creating a Place for Ourselves: Lesbian, Gay, and Bisexual Community Histories*, edited by Brett Beemyn, 165–82. New York: Routledge, 1997.

Traub, Valerie. *Thinking Sex with the Early Moderns*. Philadelphia: University of Pennsylvania Press, 2016.

Tucker, Anne Wilkes. *Brassaï: The Eye of Paris*. Houston: Museum of Fine Arts, 1999.

Vacher, Emile. Interview by Mondomix, January 1, 2009. http://blogs.mondomix.com/accordeon.php/2009/01/23/emile-vacher. This web page is no longer live.

Varichon, Doris. "Mères lesbiennes en procès: Strategies de défense contre les retraites de gardes d'enfants (1976–1982)." In *Lesbiennes, Pédés, arrêtons de raser les murs: Luttes et debats des mouvements lesbiens et homosexuels (1970–1990)*, edited by Hugo Bouvard, Ilana Eloit, and Mathias Quéré, 101–15. Paris: La Dispute/SNÉDIT, 2023.

Veyrat-Masson, Isabelle. *Quand la télévision explore le temps: L'histoire au petit écran, 1953–2000*. Paris: Fayard, 2000.

Villarejo, Amy. *Lesbian Rule: Cultural Criticism and the Value of Desire*. Durham, NC: Duke University Press, 2003.

Vogel, Shane. *The Scene of the Harlem Cabaret: Race, Sexuality, Performance*. Chicago: University of Chicago Press, 2009.

Wadia, Kursheed. "Women and the Events of May 1968." In *The May 1968 Events in France*, by Keith A. Reader with Kursheed Wadia, 148–66. New York: St. Martin's Press, 1993.

Wakeford, Nina. "Cyberqueer." In *Lesbian and Gay Studies: A Critical Introduction*, edited by Andy Medhurst and Sally R. Munt. London: Cassell, 1997.

———. "New Technologies and 'Cyberqueer' Research." In *Handbook of Lesbian and Gay Studies*, edited by Diane Richardson and Steven Seidman, 115–45. London: Sage, 2002.

Wakeman, Rosemary. *Modernizing the Provincial City: Toulouse, 1945–1975*. Cambridge, MA: Harvard University Press, 1997.

Warner, Michael. *Publics and Counterpublics*. New York: Zone Books, 2005.

Warner, Sara. *Acts of Gaiety: LGBT Performance and the Politics of Pleasure*. Ann Arbor: University of Michigan Press, 2013.

Watney, Simon. *Policing Desire: Pornography, AIDS, and the Media*. Minneapolis: University of Minnesota Press, 1996.

Weiss, Andrea. *Paris Was a Woman: Portraits from the Left Bank*. San Francisco: Harper San Francisco, 1995.

Whisnant, Clayton J. *Queer Identities and Politics in Germany, A History 1880–1945*. New York: Harrington Park Press, 2016.

White, Patricia. *Uninvited: Classical Hollywood Cinema and Lesbian Representability*. Bloomington: Indiana University Press, 1999.

Willemin, Véronique. *La mondaine: Histoire et archives de la police des moeurs*. Paris: Éditions Hoëbeke, 2009.

Willette, Adolphe. *Feu Pierrot*. Paris: Floury, 1919.

Williams, Raymond. *Television: Technology and Cultural Form*. Hanover: Wesleyan University Press, 1974.

Wilson, Elizabeth. *The Sphinx in the City: Urban Life, the Control of Disorder, and Women*. Berkeley: University of California Press, 1991.

Wilson, James F. *Bulldaggers, Pansies, and Chocolate Babies: Performance, Race, and Sexuality in the Harlem Renaissance*. Ann Arbor: University of Michigan Press, 2010.

Wilson, Michael L. "Suspect Physiognomy: The Male Prostitute in Belle Époque Print Culture." *Proceedings of the Western Society for French History* 34 (2006): 193–204.

Yagil, Limore. *Au nom de l'art, 1933–1945: Exils, solidarités et engagements*. Paris: Fayard, 2015.

Young, Damon R. *Making Sex Public and Other Cinematic Fantasies*. Durham, NC: Duke University Press, 2018.

Yu, Wenjing. "Cabarets féminins: Histoires d'une visibilité exceptionelle d'espaces lesbiens (1920–1960)." Master's thesis, L'École des hautes études en science sociales, 2022–2023.

INDEX

Page numbers in italics refer to figures.